Linux® Timesaving Techniques™ For Dummies

`D0505382`

Favorite Picks

There are a lot of great open-source tools bundled with Linux distributions, and many more available on the Web. Here's a list of quick techniques using our favorite timesaving tools that work great with Linux:

To Save Time	Find More Info Here
Hire a SpamAssassin to clean up your e-mail.	Technique 47
Use Synaptic to keep your programs up-to-date.	Technique 19
Share remote desktops with VNC.	Technique 35
Download desktop eye candy with SuperKaramba.	Technique 14
Read your HTTPMail and skip the ads with hotway.	Technique 46
Build your own system monitors with KDE System Guard.	Technique 41
Test your network security with Nessus.	Technique 37
Harden your system with Bastille.	Technique 60
Install Webmin for help with system administration.	Technique 17
Build a jail with User Mode Linux.	Technique 58

Help! I'm Stuck!

Some Linux programs suck you in and don't let you out. Here are some handy commands you can use to break free:

If You Get Stuck In	Break Out with This Command
The vi editor	Press Esc Esc, type :q, and then press Enter.
	If vi complains you've not saved your work, and you're willing to lose any changes, press Esc Esc, and then type :q! Then press Enter.
The emacs editor	Press Ctrl-X-C.
The bash shell displaying > prompt	Press Ctrl-C.

For Dummies: Bestselling Book Series for Beginners

Linux® Timesaving Techniques™ For Dummies®

Cheat Sheet

Handy bash Commands

Some quick `bash` commands you'll find useful are:

Command	Function	Syntax
cd	Change directory.	cd *newdirectory*
cp	Copy files.	cp *oldfile newfile*
find	Find files.	Check out Technique 12.
grep	Find data within files.	grep *searchpattern filename*
ls	Display directory contents.	ls
ls -l	Display detailed *dir* contents.	ls -l
mkdir	Create a new directory.	mkdir *directoryname*
more	Display the contents of a file.	more *filename*
mount	Mount a CD drive.	mount /dev/cdrom
mv	Move a file.	mv *oldname newname*
pwd	Display your current directory.	pwd
rm	Delete a file.	rm *filename*
su -	Grant superuser privileges.	su -
umount	Unmount a CD drive.	umount /dev/cdrom

Remember: Don't forget to use the `man` and `info` pages. For most of the common Linux commands, you can enter `man` *command-name* or `info` *command-name* at the command line to display a screenful of documentation. Use the spacebar to move down a screen, or navigate through the document with the arrow keys. Press the q key to quit when you're done reviewing the document.

Securing Your System

Keep an eye on security bulletins and mailing lists to stay up-to-date on the latest bugs, viruses, and menaces. Check out the official information at the following Web sites:

- ✔ www.cert.org
- ✔ www.us-cert.gov
- ✔ www.ciac.org/ciac
- ✔ www.mandrakesecure.net
- ✔ www.suse.com/us/private/support/security
- ✔ www.redhat.com/solutions/security/

For security-related techniques, check out:

- ✔ Technique 27: Closing Those Prying Eyes
- ✔ Technique 31: Gaining Privileges
- ✔ Technique 33: Securing Your Connections with SSH
- ✔ Technique 34: Protecting Yourself with a Firewall
- ✔ Technique 37: Evaluating Your Network Security with Nessus
- ✔ Technique 58: Quarantining Suspicious Programs with UML
- ✔ Technique 60: Securing the Fort with Bastille

For Dummies: Bestselling Book Series for Beginners

Linux® Timesaving Techniques™ FOR DUMMIES®

by Susan Douglas and Korry Douglas

WILEY

Wiley Publishing, Inc.

Linux® Timesaving Techniques™ For Dummies®

Published by
Wiley Publishing, Inc.
111 River Street
Hoboken, NJ 07030-5774

Copyright © 2004 by Wiley Publishing, Inc., Indianapolis, Indiana

Published by Wiley Publishing, Inc., Indianapolis, Indiana

Published simultaneously in Canada

For general information on our other products and services or to obtain technical support, please contact our Customer Care Department within the U.S. at 800-762-2974, outside the U.S. at 317-572-3993, or fax 317-572-4002.

Wiley also publishes its books in a variety of electronic formats. Some content that appears in print may not be available in electronic books.

Library of Congress Control Number: 2004101962

ISBN: 0-7645-7173-7

Manufactured in the United States of America

10 9 8 7 6 5 4 3 2 1

1V/SR/QX/QU/IN

WILEY

About the Authors

Susan Douglas is the CEO of Conjectrix, Inc., a software consulting firm specializing in database- and security-related issues. When she's not busy at the computer, Susan is probably throwing pottery, glassblowing, or horseback riding.

Korry Douglas is the Director of Research and Development for Appx Software. When he's not working on computers, he's making elegant sawdust in the woodshop.

Together, they are the coauthors of *Red Hat Linux Fedora Desktop For Dummies* and *PostgreSQL*.

Susan and Korry enjoy life on a farm in rural Virginia where they raise horses and small livestock. They both telecommute, so they have more time to spend with their 200 or so animal friends. If they're not at home, they're out riding roller coasters.

Authors' Acknowledgments

We would like to thank all the staff at Wiley who have supported this project, from start to finish. Without the help and direction of Terri Varveris, organizing this book would have been an impossible task. Becky Huehls's editorial help and guidance have kept this project rolling along on schedule (fairly painlessly, we might add). We also want to extend a big thanks to the technical editors who've kept us honest throughout the course of the book.

Thanks go also to all the supporting staff at Wiley that we've never met. We know you're out there, and we appreciate your efforts and support.

Thank you also to all the programmers and developers that make open-source software such an interesting, productive, and fun environment to work in.

Publisher's Acknowledgments

We're proud of this book; please send us your comments through our online registration form located at www.dummies.com/register/.

Some of the people who helped bring this book to market include the following:

Acquisitions, Editorial, and Media Development

Associate Project Editor: Rebecca Huehls

Acquisitions Editor: Terri Varveris

Senior Copy Editor: Kim Darosett

Technical Editors: Terry Collings, Corey Hynes

Editorial Manager: Leah Cameron

Media Development Manager: Laura VanWinkle

Media Development Supervisor: Richard Graves

Editorial Assistant: Amanda Foxworth

Cartoons: Rich Tennant (www.the5thwave.com)

Composition

Project Coordinator: Barbara Moore

Layout and Graphics: Lauren Goddard, Denny Hager, Stephanie D. Jumper, Michael Kruzil, Lynsey Osborn, Jacque Schneider

Proofreaders: Laura Albert, Vicki Broyles, Brian H. Walls

Indexer: Steve Rath

Publishing and Editorial for Technology Dummies

Richard Swadley, Vice President and Executive Group Publisher

Andy Cummings, Vice President and Publisher

Mary Bednarek, Executive Editorial Director

Mary C. Corder, Editorial Director

Publishing for Consumer Dummies

Diane Graves Steele, Vice President and Publisher

Joyce Pepple, Acquisitions Director

Composition Services

Gerry Fahey, Vice President of Production Services

Contents at a Glance

Table of Contents

Introduction

L inux is open-source software at it's finest. Open-source software is all about taking control of your desktop away from the big corporations and putting it into the hands of the developers working with your best interests at heart. The software is freely available on the Internet for you to download — you can even help develop the projects if you want to get involved. Decisions about what's on your desktop aren't being made based on the profit margins yielded by the software. Instead, the best interests of the user are of primary concern to the developers.

Although open-source software is great, have you ever tried to read the documentation that comes with it? Some of it is very good, but most of it is written for geeks, by geeks, and a good part of it is flat-out missing. Don't blame the developers — they are doing this for free after all. . . .

Our goal in writing this book is to empower you with some of the stronger features of Linux (and some great open-source tools) to solve everyday problems, without the headaches and lost time that go with trying to figure out how to use the tools. Linux provides simple, fast, and powerful solutions to meet the demands of day-to-day computer use and system administration — our goal is to save you time, while making the tools easy to use.

Saving Time with This Book

The *Timesaving Techniques For Dummies* books focus on high-payoff techniques that save you time, either on the spot or somewhere down the road. And these books get to the point in a hurry, with step-by-step instructions to pace you through the tasks you need to do, without any of the fluff you don't want. We've identified more than 60 techniques that Linux users need to know to make the most of their time. In addition, each technique includes figures that make following along a breeze. Decide for yourself how to use this book: Read it cover to cover if you like, or skip right to the technique that interests you the most.

In *Linux Timesaving Techniques For Dummies*, you can find out how to

- **Tame time-consuming tasks:** We're letting you in on more than 60 tips and tricks for your Linux system, so you can spend more time on creating great results and less time on fiddling with a feature so that it works correctly.

- **Take your skills up a notch:** You're already familiar with the basics of using Linux. Now this book takes you to the next level, helping you become a more powerful user.

- **Customize Linux to meet your needs:** Spending some upfront time customizing Linux so that it works faster, more reliably, and more like how you work on a daily basis can save you time (and aggravation) later.

- **Fine-tune your system:** You can fine-tune your Linux system for better performance and usability. Customizing your system to better serve users saves everyone time.

- **Improve your system security:** Building a secure user environment with good user hygiene and regular backups will save everyone time. With adequate security in place, your chances of having to restore your system are minimized.

- **Automate repetitive tasks:** You can automate and schedule repetitive tasks to run while you're away, and save the bandwidth for the times that you need it most.

Foolish Assumptions

We assume very little. We do, however, assume you have a computer that is currently running Fedora, Mandrake, or SuSE Linux (or that you're considering a conversion), and that you more than likely are connected to the Internet.

We assume that you know the needs of your users and the demands of your system. We try to clearly identify what aspects of a technique are best suited to an individual user or a large corporate network, but we assume you know which one you are.

We assume you make backups on a regular basis. If you don't, go immediately to Part IX: Backing Up Means Never Having to Say You're Sorry.

We assume you don't want to get bogged down in a lot of useless details, so we concentrate on getting techniques implemented quickly, without a lot of overhead spent on theory. That's a big timesaver, too.

What's in This Book

This book is organized into parts — groups of techniques about a common subject that will save you time and help you get your system running better. Each technique is written to be independent of the others, so you only need to implement those techniques that are important to you and your users. From time to time, we may send you to another technique to implement a feature that we'll be using in our current technique — we just don't want to waste valuable space repeating ourselves. Each of the parts is about a different facet of a Linux system so you can scan the part title easily, looking for problem-solving techniques that will help you, quick.

Part I: Making the Desktop Work for You

Part I is full of tips and techniques to help you make the most of your time at the desktop. Teaching your system how to recognize file types (so you don't have to specify them every time you open a file), keyboard shortcuts, and customizing your prompt are included among the techniques. We also include a rundown on the KDE protocols and the GNOME virtual file systems — the handy tools that work in a browser window to access other sources (like cameras or CDs). You'll also find techniques about using automagic variables and history files to make the command line simple, easy, and quick.

Part II: Getting the Most from Your File System

This part focuses on moving and sharing data. Using Windows filesharing across a network, finding the files you need when you need them, and some quick downloading techniques are included in this part. This part also includes a technique about using User Mode Linux to create a playpen with a built-in copy of Fedora — handy if you need to jail a server or just want to experiment with program modifications safely.

Part III: Good Housekeeping with Linux

You'll find techniques to help you make the most of the RPM tool (the Red Hat Package Manager) for installations, updates, and queries. Part III also includes a technique introducing you to Synaptic — a handy tool that will keep your software current and up-to-date with just a few clicks of the mouse. We'll also introduce you to task scheduling tools that can help you automate administrative tasks to run without any supervision at all. Everyday timesaving doesn't get much better than Part III.

Part IV: Tweaking the Kernel on Your Linux System

The techniques in Part IV are dedicated to the kernel. We'll show you how to build a new kernel, clean up an old kernel, or find out about the condition of your existing kernel. We'll also introduce you to SE Linux — the new security-enhanced kernel fresh with this release of Fedora.

Part V: Securing Your Workspace

Part V is all about security — we'll introduce you to PAM (Pluggable Authentication Modules), and show you quick ways to encrypt e-mail and files to keep the prying eyes of snoops out of your personal documents. We'll also show you how to safeguard your system by using `sudo` to dole out the superuser privileges to only those users on your system who need them. Your system will be a safer place with the techniques in Part V implemented.

Part VI: Networking Like a Professional

The techniques in Part VI focus on using network features and network analysis tools to your advantage. We'll show you how to set up and use remote desktops from your local system, as well as how to share desktops with remote users. We'll also show you how to take care of your network security by building sturdy but supple firewalls, and how to harden those firewalls with the network security analysis tool, Nessus. We'll also show you how to watch network traffic to see what's traveling across your network to your users.

Part VII: Monitoring Your System

In this part, we'll introduce you to tools that will help you keep an eye on your system resources and control runaway processes. We'll also show you some quick ways to take care of users and their accounts — both new users and old.

Part VIII: Serving Up the Internet and More

In Part VIII, we'll focus on server-related issues. We'll show you the quick way to build and configure an Apache Web server, a Sendmail mail server, and a MySQL database server, as well as how to monitor your servers once they're in place. We'll also show you how to make your new Web site a more secure place with SSL certificates, and the easy way to create your own certificate signing authority. Then we'll delve into e-mail — you'll save a ton of time with our techniques that help you avoid spam with SpamAssassin and retrieve your HTTPMail (that's Hotmail, MSN, and Lycos mail) with `hotway`, avoiding all of the ads and pop-ups that come with most Internet mail accounts.

Part IX: Backing Up Means Never Having to Say You're Sorry

The techniques in this part are all about backing up. Techniques include getting ready to back up your data, choosing a fast but sturdy backup scheme, implementing a good backup routine, and backing up to remote storage. We'll also introduce you to CVS archiving — a great way to keep not only current renditions of projects, but also a living history of a project's growth.

Part X: Programming Tricks

These techniques will help you save time in your programming projects. You'll find a technique that helps you use prewritten, open-source APIs in your own code to help you cover ground quickly. You'll also find a technique that focuses on moving data in and out of your PHP code. We'll also introduce you to a great graphical debugger (DDD) that will save you time when you need to debug your code — that's the last thing you want to spend too much time on.

Part XI: The Scary (Or Fun!) Stuff

This part contains a medley of timesaving techniques that will help you burn CDs, find dangerous programs, create a UML jail, troubleshoot problem programs, and more. We'll introduce you to Bastille, a system-hardening, open-source tool that makes most security schemes look wimpy. We'll also give you the rundown on LIDS — an under-documented but powerful security tool that you can use on your system to create a secure user environment. We'll

throw in an introduction to Zenity — a handy toolkit you can use to add graphical prompts to any user shell scripts you use on your system.

Icons Used in This Book

Each technique in this book has icons pointing to special information, sometimes quite emphatically. Each icon has its own purpose.

When there's a way to save time, either now or in the future, this icon leads the way. Home in on these icons when every second counts.

This icon points to handy hints that will help you work through the steps in each technique or to handy troubleshooting info.

These icons are your trail of breadcrumbs, leading back to information that you'll want to remember.

When you see a Warning icon, there's a chance your data or your system is at risk. You won't see many of these, but when you do, proceed with caution.

Part I

Making the Desktop Work for You

The 5th Wave By Rich Tennant

"The funny thing is he's spent 9 hours organizing his computer desktop."

Technique 1

Finding the Power in KDE Protocols

When you type a typical URL, such as `http://www.google.com/index.html`, into your Web browser, you likely don't think about how you're making use of it. That is, you don't think about `http://` being a *protocol,* `www.google.com` being an *address* that the protocol handler knows how to deal with, and `index.html` identifying a resource at that address.

If you haven't thought about URLs and their individual parts for a while, you may be surprised to find out that KDE adds a number of new protocol handlers, called *KIO slaves,* that know how to serve up data from new and unusual sources, such as CDs and remote systems, through the Konqueror Web browser.

Using the right protocol saves you the time of manually copying resources all over the Web. The protocols are a varied bunch. In this technique, we show you protocols that work with audio CDs or your digital camera, handle remote file management, manage printers and e-mail, and read documentation. Check them out — you can save time in lots of ways.

Discovering Your Protocols

Finding out about KDE protocols is not an easy task. They aren't well documented, and they can be tough to find. Some are universally helpful, whereas others are more specialized (such as the LinPoch project at `linpoch.sourceforge.net`, which lets you interact with Nokia cell phones from KDE applications). Here's how to see what protocols are installed on the following versions of Linux:

- ✓ **Fedora:** Open the KDE Menu and choose System Tools⇨Info Center; then click Protocols.

- ✓ **SuSe:** Open the KDE Menu and choose System⇨Monitor⇨Info Center.

- ✓ **Mandrake:** Open the KDE Menu and choose System⇨Configuration⇨ KDE⇨Information⇨Protocols.

The Available IO Slaves column displays a list of available protocols. For more information about a protocol, click the protocol name, and the documentation is displayed in the right column.

> Some of the protocols are not documented. If you find one that sounds interesting, search the Web to see if someone has written about it.

> Depending on which version of KDE you have and which options are installed, the protocols you find will vary.

Working with CD Audio Tracks Using audiocd:

Linux gives you all sorts of ways to rip the tracks off audio CDs, but we haven't found anything easier than KDE's `audiocd:` protocol. This protocol is a breeze to use:

1. **Insert a music CD into your drive.**

If your CD player program starts, just close it.

2. **Open the Konqueror Web Browser.**

3. **When Konqueror opens, enter** `audiocd:/` **in the Location bar and press Enter.**

If your copy of KDE was compiled with `audiocd:` support, the Web browser displays options for ripping the audio files, as shown in Figure 1-1.

(See the preceding section to find out how to view a list of available protocols.) See Table 1-1 for details on what the options do and how they work.

• **Figure 1-1:** The KDE audiocd: protocol.

> Not all copies of KDE are created equal. The copy of KDE currently distributed with Fedora includes support for copying to `.wav`, `.cda`, and `.ogg` files, but it doesn't include the information to create MP3s. You can get a copy of KDE that has MP3 compiled in at `www.kde.org`.

> Depending on your MP3 player, you may be able to save lots of time loading files. If your player can emulate a hard drive, you can open it with Konqueror and drag your music on and off the player.

TABLE 1-1: RIPPING AUDIO FILES WITH AUDIOCD:

Option	What Is It?	How to Use It
CDA Files	A directory that contains one file for each audio track on the CD (track01.cda, track02.cda,...).	Drag one of these .cda files to your desktop (or to another folder), and audiocd: copies the raw audio track to the new location.
By Track	A directory that contains one file for each audio track (track01.wav, track02.wav,...).	Drag one of these .wav files to your desktop (or to another folder), and audiocd: converts the audio track to WAV format.
Ogg Vorbis	A directory that contains one file for each audio track, in Ogg Vorbis format (such as 16 Burning Down The House.ogg, 14 Once In A Lifetime.ogg,...).	Drag one of these .ogg files to your desktop (or to another folder), and audiocd: converts the audio track to Ogg Vorbis format.

Option	What Is It?	How to Use It
MP3	A directory that contains audio tracks in MP3 format.	Drag an `.mp3` file to your desktop (or to another folder), and `audiocd:` converts the audio track to MP3 format.
By Name	A directory that contains audio tracks (with song names) in WAV format (`16 Burning Down The House.wav`, `14 Once In A Lifetime.wav`,...). This directory is similar to By Track, except that you get to see song titles in the By Name directory (By Track only shows you the track numbers). You won't see a By Name directory if Konqueror can't find your CD in the Web's `cddb` database.	
Album Name	A directory that contains one file for each audio track, in WAV format (identical to By Name except that the directory name is the album name).	

Managing Snapshots with the camera: Protocol

The `camera:` protocol treats your digital camera like it's just another storage device, only this one is full of pictures. `camera:` gives you thumbnail previews of the photos on your camera, so you can easily identify and move your images to where you need them. Just drag the images to your desktop (or to another folder). Double-click an image file to open it with your favorite editor (see Technique 3 to find out how to choose an editor), and you're working in a snap.

 You can also use an image as your desktop wallpaper. Drag the thumbnail to the desktop and choose Set as Wallpaper from the menu that appears.

To use the `camera:` protocol, follow these steps:

1. **Plug in your digital camera and be sure it's turned on.**

2. **Open the Konqueror Web Browser.**

3. **Type** `camera:/` **in the address line and press Enter.**

That's all there is to it (see Figure 1-2).

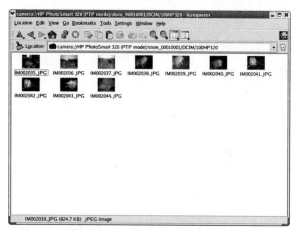

• **Figure 1-2:** The camera: protocol, in action.

From here, finding your way around the inside of your camera is just a matter of exploring.

 When we plug in our HP PhotoSmart 320 digital camera and use the `camera:` protocol, we see the single directory HP PhotoSmart 320 (PTP mode). Underneath the HP PhotoSmart 320 folder, our pictures are in a subdirectory named `store_00010001/DCIM/100HP320`. The directory structure used by your digital camera is likely to be different. Use Konqueror to find your way around the inside of your camera. After you know where your images are stored, you should be able to open those images directly from KDE-friendly applications like KuickShow and KView.

 Don't bother trying to remember a long, complex URL that corresponds to where your pictures are stored. Instead, drag the folder to your desktop and choose Link Here. Then, whenever you want to play with your camera, plug it in and click the shortcut.

One thing to note — your pictures reside only in your camera until you copy them onto your computer. Be sure to store the pictures on your computer before deleting them from your camera. After you copy the pictures you want to keep, it's easy to erase the images from your camera; just delete them or drag them to the trash like any other file.

Remote File Management with fish:

`fish:` is a remote file access protocol. Using `fish:`, you can work with files stored on a remote Linux system as if they were located right on your desktop. To use `fish:`, open a KDE browser (Konqueror is a good choice) and enter `fish://` followed by the host name (or IP address) of the machine you're fishing for.

Under the hood, `fish:` uses SSH (Secure Shell) to do its work, so you must have an SSH server up and running on the remote machine before you can go fishing. `fish:` prompts you for a user name and password on the remote system before allowing you access to files. After you've connected, you can interact with the remote files and directories in the same way you would deal with local files: Drag them to your desktop, drag them to other folders, drag them to the trash, or just edit them in place.

Here are some quick things you can do with the `fish:` protocol:

  ✔ Manage files on another system with the Konqueror file manager/browser. Using `fish:` and Konqueror, you can easily move, copy,

archive, open, and browse remote files the same way you handle files stored on your computer.

  ✔ Open `fish:` folders on two (or more!) systems and copy files or even entire directories from one machine to another by dragging from one window to another.

  ✔ Create a secure link on your local desktop that points to a remote system. When you open the link, `fish:` prompts you for login information so not just anyone can get access via your computer. To create a desktop link, right-click on your desktop and choose Create New⇨File⇨Link to Location (URL). Type in a name for your link and enter a URL in the form `fish://computer-name/directory`, for example `fish://bastille/home/freddie/Desktop`.

  ✔ Edit remote files with KWrite. When you open a remote file (such as `fish://versaille/.bash_profile`), any changes that you make are automatically saved *back* to the remote system.

 The KDE protocols are a part of KDE, not Linux. That means that any KDE-friendly application (Kate, Konqueror, KMail, and so on) can use them, but non-KDE applications won't understand them. You can open a `fish:` URL in just about any KDE application, and the resource appears as if it were on your local system. Note that not all KDE applications are protocol-enabled, which means that they won't understand `fish:` URLs. You'll just have to try out each application.

Getting Help with help:, info:, and man:

KDE protocols give you fast access to help when you need it. KDE sports three documentation protocols: `man:`, `info:`, and `help:`. To use the protocols, open your Konqueror browser, enter the protocol name in the Location line, and press Enter. Konqueror will take you to the top-level index for the protocol you choose:

✔ man: When you browse through the man: protocol, you see a short index that provides access to the ten or so sections of the Linux man pages.

 The man: protocol is a great way to read man pages because the documentation is pleasantly formatted and cross-referenced.

 When you navigate down one level from the main index, the second level leaves a bit to be desired. For some reason (we assume that someone intends to fill in more information later), it says "no idea" in a column to the right of the topic list. Just ignore this and click your topic, and you'll find the information you need.

✔ info: This protocol gives you access to documentation written in the Texinfo format, a format popular with GNU software. Like man:, info: documentation is cross-referenced and displays a browsable menu with links that take you to the documentation you want to read.

✔ help: This protocol lets you read documentation in KDE's documentation format. To find subjects within help:, type help:/, followed by the topic name. (For example, help:/kate takes you to the Kate handbook.) If you need general information about your KDE environment, a good starting point is help:///khelpcenter.

 Just like Web page bookmarks that you can create when surfing the Web, documentation bookmarks are great navigational time-savers. Bookmark your favorite man pages so they're easily accessible the next time you need them! To create a new bookmark, just choose Bookmarks➪Add Bookmark.

Viewing Your Local Network with the smb: Protocol

Use the smb: protocol to quickly browse other machines on your local SMB (Samba and Windows file/printer sharing) network. Enter smb:/ in the

Konqueror address line and press Return to see the SMB workgroups in your local network. Click an SMB workgroup to see all the computers in that workgroup. Click one of the computers, and you see the resources that computer is willing to share. Just drag and drop the data you need or make clickable links to resources — the time you save will amaze you.

 Use smb: to create desktop shortcuts to your network locations. Just start your copy of Konqueror, enter smb:/ in the address line, and press Enter. Choose a workgroup and then a computer within that workgroup. Now drag a share name to your desktop. Next time you need data from that machine, you have it at the click of a button.

Other KDE Protocols

We haven't covered all the KDE protocols in this technique. There are quite a few others you can explore. Check out the ones listed in Table 1-2.

TABLE 1-2: OTHER KDE PROTOCOLS

Protocol	What You Do with It
print:	Manage printers, print jobs, and print queues from your Web browser.
devices:	Find all your storage devices here — hard drives, NFS and Samba file systems, and removable media.
imap: pop3: mailto:	Send, receive, or just play around with your mailbox as if it were a local file system.
webdav:	Modify a remote Web site or collaborate with others over the Web.

 You can find more protocols on the Web. Search for *KIO slave* at your favorite search engine.

KDE protocols versus GNOME VFS

KDE has protocols, and GNOME has the VFS (virtual file system). KDE protocols and GNOME VFS modules do pretty much the same thing: They make data available from unconventional sources. The name *protocol* may seem a bit misleading, but it's called that because the name of the protocol goes in the protocol part of a URL. We think that *virtual file system* is a more straightforward name than *protocol* because a virtual file system basically creates make-believe file systems and lets you use them to quickly access your data.

Both the KDE protocols and the GNOME VFS work from within a Web browser, but the GNOME VFS works best at the command line. We have to admit that we're fond of KDE for its usability and speed. However, sometimes GNOME can be a real timesaver, as you discover in Technique 2.

Technique

2

Getting GNOME Virtual File Systems to Do the Work for You

Linux supports a wide variety of physical file systems. A file system's job is to make sense of the bytes stored on a disk so that other programs don't have to interpret them. A file system module, for example, might look at the bytes in sector 52033 on your hard disk and say, "Hey, that's a directory." File system modules also work in the other direction as well. For example, a program might ask for a listing of the /tmp directory, and the file system knows how to find that data on the disk. A file system module creates order out of the billion or more bytes of chaos on your disk.

GNOME takes the physical file system one step further by introducing the *virtual* file system (or VFS for short). A virtual file system performs the same function as a physical file system except that the underlying data comes from somewhere beyond your disk. A virtual file system gathers data from an unusual source and makes that data appear as a set of directories, subdirectories, and data files. Using a VFS, you can peek into tar, gzip, and RPM archives, treat remote files as if they were local, and even access CD audio tracks as if they were normal data files. GNOME also has some handy preview tools that let you view fonts and desktop themes as if they were normal files.

In this technique, we show you how to save time by using some of the more useful GNOME VFS modules. When you use the VFS, you don't have to waste time finding (and opening) the right program to view a file in an unconventional location — GNOME does the hard work for you. Whether you use the VFS in a browser or at the command line, the time you save and the power you gain will surprise you.

Using GNOME VFS Modules

The GNOME VFS is still evolving, and not all GNOME applications are VFS savvy. We've found that most (if not all) VFS modules work when you use them from the command line, but some fail in strange and quirky ways when you try to use them from a browser. If you can't get a VFS URL to work, try it at the command line (we show you how in a moment). If it works there, the problem is in the browser.

To use a VFS module, simply use the module name as if it were a protocol. For example, to open a font that's installed on your system, you can browse to the URL fonts://Courier. Finding out which VFS modules are installed on your system can be tricky. The VFS modules are listed in a group of files in /etc/gnome-vfs-2.0/modules, but just because you find a module listed there doesn't mean that the

module is actually installed. You also have to check for the library in /usr/lib/ gnome-vfs-2.0/modules/. To save you some time, Table 2-1 lists some of the most commonly included VFS modules.

/proc is a virtual file system that works in either KDE or GNOME and exposes kernel data — see Technique 26 for more information.

 We cover only a few of the VFS modules distributed with Linux, but you can find others on the Web. If you find another module you want to use, you'll likely need to download and compile it. See Technique 14 for help with downloading and compiling programs.

TABLE 2-1: COMMONLY INCLUDED VFS MODULES

Module Name	What It Does
http:	Accesses data stored on a Web server
https:	Accesses data stored on a secure Web server (typically an e-commerce site)
ftp:	Accesses data stored on an FTP server
mailto:	Sends e-mail
bzip2:	Peeks inside bzip2 archives
cdda:	Treats CD audio tracks as if they were normal files
file:	Accesses data stored in a local physical file system
nntp:	Reads newsgroups by using the network news transport protocol
gzip:	Peeks inside gzip archives
dav:	Accesses data stored on a WebDAV server
pipe:	Accesses data sent to a pipe
ssh:	Connects to a remote SSH server
tar:	Peeks inside uncompressed tar archives
fonts:	Accesses font information
burn:	Burns CDs from within a browser
themes:	Accesses desktop themes installed on your system

Stacking VFS Modules

GNOME VFS URLs can be stacked together. For example, if you have an uncompressed tar file located on a remote system, you can stack a tar URL on top of an `http://` URL to get to the data stored inside. Suppose that you have an uncompressed tar archive named `/tmp/pics.tar` that contains an image named `freddie.jpg` and you want to view that picture with GNOME's Eye Of Gnome viewer.

Sure, you could un-tar the archive and tell the viewer to open the JPG photo (reminding yourself to clean up all the temporary files after you finish). But you can save yourself time and trouble by making VFS worry about those details. Rather than extracting the image to a temporary location, you can use a VFS URL like this:

```
$ eog file:///tmp/pics.tar#tar:/freddie.jpg
```

Here's how the pieces of the command fit together. First, the `eog` part is the name of the command that you're running (Eye Of Gnome). Next, you see a typical URL (`file:///tmp/pics.tar`) that uses the `file:` protocol to open `/tmp/pics.tar`. Next comes the magical part: `#tar:/freddie.jpg`. That tells GNOME to treat everything that precedes `#tar:` as a tar archive and to access the `freddie.jpg` member within.

What happens if the picture that you want to view is stored in a *compressed* tar archive? Simple, just put another VFS component (`gzip`) on the stack, like this:

```
$ eog file:///tmp/pics.tgz#gzip:#tar:/
  freddie.jpg
```

If the `pics.tgz` file lives on a remote Web server, you can combine the `http:` protocol with `gzip:` and `tar:` like this:

```
$ eog http://myserver.example.com/pics.
  tgz#gzip:#tar:/freddie.jpg
```

 Most of the VFS documentation that you find tells you that you can stack VFS URLs with the following syntax: `url#url/suburl`. For example, if you have a tar archive named `/tmp/foo.tar` that contains a file named `bar.txt`, the GNOME VFS documentation tells you that you can access the `bar.txt` file with the URL `file:///tmp/foo.tar#tar/bar.txt`. You can't — the documentation is *wrong*. Instead, you have to use `file:///tmp/foo.tar#tar:/bar.txt`. Notice the extra `:` between `tar` and `/bar.txt`. Without that colon, the `#tar/bar.txt` component acts like a named anchor in an HTML document, not like a VFS module.

Working with Packages: rpm and rpms

The `rpm:` VFS module lets you peek inside an RPM installer file. You can use the `rpm:` VFS to extract select files from an RPM package without having to install the whole thing. `rpm:` also lets you extract metadata (such as the name of the package vendor, the target distribution, and copyright) from a package.

The `rpm:` module creates a virtual file system that represents the contents of the RPM file. If you list the directory of an `rpm:` URL, you see the name of each file that would be installed by that RPM. You also see a number of virtual files that expose the extra data stored inside the RPM. Here's an example:

```
[freddie@bastille] cd /mnt/cdrom/
  Fedora/RPMS
[freddie@bastille] gnomevfs-ls file:
  gnome-applets-2.4.1-1.i386.rpm#rpm:
-r--r--r-- 1 root root 941    Oct   3 2003
  HEADER
-r-xr-xr-x 1 root root 39     Oct   3 2003
  INSTALL
-r-xr-xr-x 1 root root 39     Oct   3 2003
  UPGRADE
```

```
dr-xr-xr-x 3 root root 0      Oct  3 2003
   INFO
-r--r--r-- 1 root root 0      Oct  3 2003
   INFO/NAME-VERSION-RELEASE
-r--r--r-- 1 root root 0      Oct  3 2003
   INFO/GROUP
-r--r--r-- 1 root root 0      Oct  3 2003
   INFO/BUILDHOST
-r--r--r-- 1 root root 0      Oct  3 2003
   INFO/SOURCERPM
-r--r--r-- 1 root root 0      Oct  3 2003
   INFO/DISTRIBUTION
-r--r--r-- 1 root root 0      Oct  3 2003
   INFO/VENDOR
-r--r--r-- 1 root root 0      Oct  3 2003
   INFO/DESCRIPTION
-r--r--r-- 1 root root 0      Oct  3 2003
   INFO/SUMMARY
dr-xr-xr-x 1 root root 0      Oct  3 2003
   INFO/SCRIPTS
-r--r--r-- 1 root root 0      Oct  3 2003
   INFO/SCRIPTS/POSTIN
-r--r--r-- 1 root root 0      Oct  3 2003
   INFO/SCRIPTS/ALL
-r--r--r-- 1 root root 0      Oct  3 2003
   INFO/PACKAGER
-r--r--r-- 1 root root 0      Oct  3 2003
   INFO/URL
-r--r--r-- 1 root root 0      Oct  3 2003
   INFO/SERIAL
-r--r--r-- 1 root root 0      Oct  3 2003
   INFO/COPYRIGHT
-r--r--r-- 1 root root 0      Oct  3 2003
   INFO/LICENSE
-r--r--r-- 1 root root 0      Oct  3 2003
   INFO/BUILDTIME
-r--r--r-- 1 root root 0      Oct  3 2003
   INFO/RPMVERSION
-r--r--r-- 1 root root 0      Oct  3 2003
   INFO/OS
-r--r--r-- 1 root root 0      Oct  3 2003
   INFO/SIZE
-r--r--r-- 1 root root 0      Oct  3 2003
   INFO/REQUIRENAME
-r--r--r-- 1 root root 0      Oct  3 2003
   INFO/OBSOLETES
-r--r--r-- 1 root root 0      Oct  3 2003
   INFO/PROVIDES
-r--r--r-- 1 root root 0      Oct  3 2003
   INFO/CHANGELOG
-rw-r--r-- 1 root root 63419 Oct  3 10:28
   /etc/gconf/schemas/battstat.schemas
```

```
-rw-r--r-- 1 root root 8364  Oct  3 10:28
   /etc/gconf/schemas/cdplayer.schemas
-rw-r--r-- 1 root root 21092 Oct  3 10:27
   /etc/gconf/schemas/charpick.schemas
...
```

The first 28 files listed are virtual files, and the rest are real files that would be installed on your system if you installed this particular package.

You can extract a single file from an archive by using gnomevfs-cat, for example:

```
[freddie@bastille] gnomevfs-cat
   file:gnome-applets-
   2.4.1-1.i386.rpm#rpm:HEADER
Name        : gnome-applets
   Relocations: (not relocateable)
Version     : 2.4.1
   Vendor: Red Hat, Inc.
Release     : 1
   Build Date: Fri Oct  3 10:29:07 2003
Install Date: (not installed)
   Build Host: daffy.perf.redhat.com
Group       : User Interface/Desktops
   Source RPM: gnome-applets-
   2.4.1-1.src.rpm
Size        : 11210002
   License: GPL
Signature   : DSA/SHA1, Tue Oct 28
   19:10:23 2003, Key ID b44269d04f2a6fd2
Packager    : Red Hat, Inc.
   <http://bugzilla.redhat.com/bugzilla>
URL         : http://www.gnome.org/
Summary     : Small applications for the
   Gnome panel.
Description :
Gnome (GNU Network Object Model
   Environment) is a user-friendly set of
applications and desktop tools to be used
   in conjunction with a window
manager for the X Window System. The
   gnome-applets package provides
small utilities for the Gnome panel.
```

Notice that you can access both virtual and real files within the RPM.

The rpms: module (note the *s* on the end) lets you treat the database of installed software as a virtual file system. In other words, when you view the content of an `rpms:` URL, you see a list of the packages (sorted by category) installed on your system.

 You can also use the `deb:` module to play with Debian Package Manager packages.

Putting VFS to Work at the Command Line

The GNOME VFS system includes a few VFS-friendly programs that you can use at the command line (or within shell scripts):

- ✔ `gnomevfs-cat`: This program is equivalent to the normal Linux `cat` command: It writes the contents of a file to standard output. Unlike the simple `cat` command, `gnomevfs-cat` can deal with VFS URLs. `gnomevfs-cat` deals with all of the normal hassle of downloading, unpacking, and cleaning up temporary files when you're finished. For example:

  ```
  $ gnomevfs-cat http://myserver.example.
    com/index.html > index.html
  ```

- ✔ `gnomevfs-copy`: This handy file copy utility is powerful. When you run this program, you can specify a URL for the source, the destination, or both. Just like `gnomevfs-cat`, `gnomevfs-copy` handles the dirty work — it downloads (or uploads!) files for you, inserts new content into existing archives, or extracts content from an archive without all the prep-work and cleanup. For example, here's how to copy a file from a remote Web site to your local system:

  ```
  $ gnomevfs-copy http://myserver.example.
    com/foo.txt file:///tmp/foo.txt
  ```

- ✔ `gnomevfs-info`: This program displays tidbits of information about a given URL. You can see the modification time, file size, and MIME type. (See Technique 3 for more information about MIME types.)

- ✔ `gnomevfs-ls`: This program lists the contents of a directory accessed through a VFS URL. `gnomevfs-ls` is great when you want to browse

through an archive (or an RPM package) stored at a Web site, but you don't want to download the file first. For example, to list the contents of an RPM file, use the following command:

```
$ gnomevfs-ls http://myserver.example.
  com/foor.rpm#rpm:
```

- ✔ `gnomevfs-mkdir`: Use this program to create a directory with a VFS URL. You'll probably find this program most useful when you need to create a directory on a remote system (using the `http:`, `smb:`, or `ftp:` protocols).

Burning CDs with a VFS

One of the handiest VFS modules is `burn:///`, which lets you burn CDs and DVDs from within the Nautilus browser. If you have a CD or DVD burner, browse to `burn:///`, and Nautilus shows you an empty folder. From there, to burn a CD you just drag a file to the folder, insert a blank CD into your drive, and click Write to CD (on the toolbar). Don't forget that you can drag a remote file directly into the `burn:///` folder — just open a second Nautilus window and browse to the server that holds the file you want.

Skinning Your Desktop with VFS

The `themes:` VFS gives you quick access to the desktop themes installed on your system. Browse to `themes:///`, and Nautilus shows you all the themes installed on your system. If you find a theme that you like, just double-click the preview, and you've changed your desktop theme.

Another handy VFS is `fonts:`. The `fonts:` VFS exposes all the fonts installed on your system. Browse to `fonts:///` to see thumbnail samples of all the fonts available on your system (along with the font names).

 If you see a font that you want to use as your desktop font, right-click the icon and choose Set as Application Font from the drop-down menu.

Technique 3

Streamlining Your Work with File Associations

Save Time By

✔ Understanding how MIME classifies data and how your files are affected

✔ Tweaking file associations in KDE

✔ Creating MIME types quickly with GNOME

Click a JPEG file, and KDE opens the image in KuickShow. Click an HTML desktop file, and GNOME opens that file in Mozilla. How does Linux know which program to use? It consults a MIME — not those folks on street corners wearing striped shirts and tons of makeup, but a registry of data types that associates a file type with a specific application.

The default associations are a fine place to start, but after you develop your own preferences about which applications you want to use for certain file types, the defaults can begin to get in your way. You'll save time (and effort) in the long run if you tweak these MIME types to establish quick links between your data files and your favorite applications. For example, if you edit a lot of graphics files but have several graphics editors, you most likely have a favorite. Instead of opening and navigating through your favorite program every time you have to open a graphics file, give your favorite editor the highest priority. Double-click the data icons, and you've opened not only your data, but also your favorite program!

In this technique, we show you how to create new MIME data types and associate your applications with the data types that you use frequently. The technique is a little different depending on which desktop environment (KDE or GNOME) you use, but either way, it's quick and easy.

Classifying Data with MIME

Before you start tweaking your file associations, it's helpful to know the basics about how MIME works with your files. Originally, MIME (Multipurpose Internet Mail Extensions) was designed for e-mail clients to categorize e-mail attachments. Nowadays, it's used in many other programs as well, such as Web browsers, graphics utilities, and productivity tools. The MIME registry performs two distinct functions, but the line between those functions is pretty blurry:

✔ MIME looks at a chunk of data (usually a data file) and categorizes it based on the file extension or based on patterns in the data.

✔ The MIME registry connects applications and data by associating an application with each data type.

Thus, opening a file with MIME is a two-step process: MIME categorizes the data, and then it finds an application that knows how to deal with that kind of data.

Typically, a program that knows how to process a given file type automatically creates MIME associations for that type, but that's not always the case:

✔ If you open a file that doesn't have a MIME association, Linux prompts you to select a program to use. You have to do the grunt work of setting the association yourself.

✔ You may find that you have more than one application that knows how to process a given file type. For example, text/html is often associated with both Konqueror and Mozilla. If a MIME type is associated with more than one application, Linux chooses the application with the highest priority when you open that file type. You can tell Linux which application to use by giving the program you prefer the highest priority in the MIME registry.

 Web pages make great desktop links. After you associate HTML files with your favorite browser, add the links you use most frequently to your desktop. Double-click a link, and it opens in your favorite browser.

When you begin customizing your file associations, you'll find that MIME data types are arranged in a tree-structured hierarchy. At the bottom of the tree, you find the data type definitions themselves. Upper levels in the tree group similar data types. For example, text/html describes the html data type within the text group. MIME can determine a file's data type in two ways:

✔ **By extension:** When you open a file such as backup.tar, MIME searches for the extension (.tar) in its database of known file types. If it finds a match, MIME classifies the file by extension (in this case application/x-tar).

✔ **By content:** Several extensions can map to the same MIME data type; for example, .htm and .html are both classified as text/html. If you

open a file whose extension is not recognized, MIME peeks inside the file and tries to recognize a pattern. For example, all JPEG picture files include the string JFIF near the beginning of the file; PNG pictures include the string PNG near the beginning of the file; and Real Player audio streams begin with four bytes whose values are 0x2e7261fd.

Creating KDE File Associations

Most applications that create data of a given type automatically associate with that type, but occasionally you need to adjust those associations. For example, say that you frequently work with buttons on Web sites, so you always design new buttons as JPEG files in Icon Editor. You can save yourself the time of poking around in the interface by simply changing your default JPEG editor from KuickShow to Icon Editor.

You can use file associations to open a new text file in your favorite editor in a snap with the KDE desktop. Just right-click on the desktop, choose Create New, and then choose Text File from the list of data type options. Enter a name for the new file and click OK, and KDE adds the icon to the desktop. Now, a simple double-click opens the new file in the editor you set with file associations.

With MIME, you can associate any number of applications with a single MIME type, and KDE uses the application with the highest priority to open data of that type. It's easy to change the default program that opens your data in KDE:

1. **In Fedora or SuSE, open the KDE menu and click Control Center.**

If you're using Mandrake, open the KDE Menu and choose System⇨Configuration⇨Configure Your Desktop.

2. **On the left side of the Control Center, click KDE Components and then click File Associations.**

The File Associations – Control Center dialog (shown in Figure 3-1) appears, displaying the pre-defined MIME types in the Known Types area.

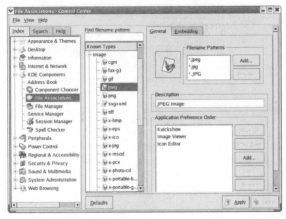

• **Figure 3-1: The File Associations - Control Center dialog.**

3. **In the Known Types area, expand the relevant group to show a list of known image types.**

   For our example, we click the Image group.

4. **Click the file type whose association you want to set or change.**

   We click jpeg. The right side of the dialog displays the current file associations.

5. **In the Application Preference Order box, if you don't see the application that you want to associate with the file type, click the Add button and use the file chooser to find the program that you want.**

6. **In the Application Preference Order box, select the application you want to make the first priority, and then click the Move Up button until the application appears at the top of the list.**

   In our example, we select Icon Editor and then click the Move Up button to move Icon Editor to the top of the list.

7. **When you're finished, click Apply to save your work and close the dialog.**

   Now, when you open the file type (such as a .jpg, or .JPG file), KDE opens the file with the application you selected (Icon Editor, for example).

With the same dialog that you just used to change the application preference order, you can also do the following:

✔ To associate a new file extension with the selected MIME type, click the Add button in the Filename Patterns box. If you need to add a different spelling of a filename extension (which you probably won't have to do often), this is the place to do it.

✔ Choose the icon to the left of the Filename Patterns box to change the icon for this type. Control Center displays a palette of alternate icons that you can choose from — just click the one you like.

 Changing the icon to something you can remember lets you instantly recognize file types in your browser or on your desktop.

 Well-behaved KDE applications (such as Kate, the KDE programmer's editor) know how to deal with MIME file associations. If you open a file whose data type isn't included in Kate's MIME associations, KDE opens the program you've assigned to that file type in your MIME registry.

Creating New MIME Types with GNOME

The GNOME MIME mapping system is a bit more complex than KDE's. GNOME lets you define an icon for each MIME type, a default action (such as print, view, or edit), and a list of applications that know how to deal with that type. MIME defines a two-level hierarchy for data type; for example text/html describes the html type in the text group. GNOME introduces a new layer that collects related groups in categories. This practice is handy in theory, but it makes it a little harder to find the MIME type you're looking for.

This next example sets your JPEG editor to xview — an oldy but a goody that needs special treatment.

xview isn't included in the Default Action list, so you need to add it as a custom program. To associate a new application with an existing MIME type:

1. **Open the GNOME menu and choose Preferences.**

2. **Click File Types and Programs.**

The File Types and Programs dialog, shown in Figure 3-2, appears.

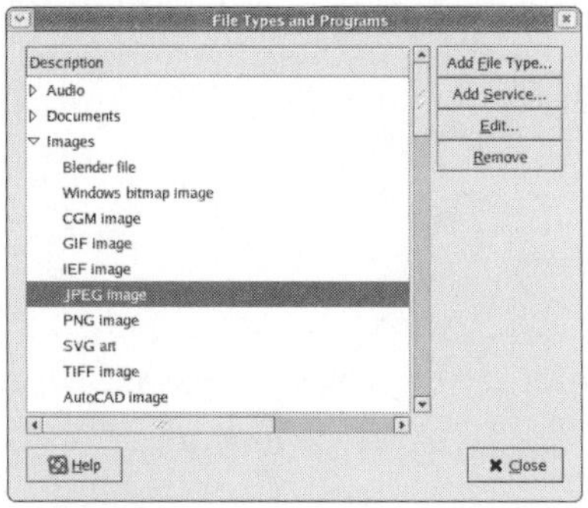

• **Figure 3-2: The File Types and Programs dialog in GNOME.**

 If you're using SuSE, open the GNOME menu and choose Desktop Preferences⯈Advanced⯈ File Types and Programs.

3. **Click the arrow next to the category you want to change, and you'll see the list of MIME types in that category.**

In our case, we chose Images.

 If you ever need to add a new MIME type (one that doesn't already appear in the list of known types), open the File Types and Programs dialog, click the Add File Type button, and follow the on-screen prompts.

4. **Click the MIME type you want to change and then click the Edit button.**

Because we want to assocate xview with JPEG photos, we clicked JPEG Image.

The Edit File Type dialog opens, as shown in Figure 3-3.

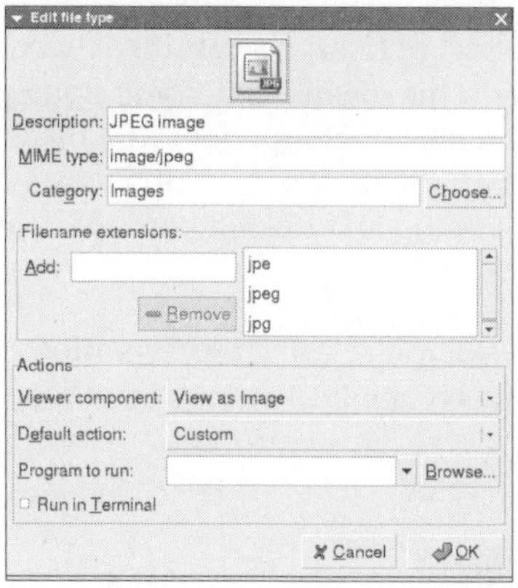

• **Figure 3-3: The Edit File Type dialog in GNOME.**

5. **Select Custom from the Default Action drop-down list.**

6. **Click the Browse button (to the right of the Program to Run box), and find the application that you want to associate with this type.**

The xview program is located in /usr/bin/X11, so we pointed the file chooser to that directory, highlighted xview, and clicked OK.

xview is now your default JPEG editor, and it has been added to the Default Action list. Now if you ever switch to a different default editor again, you can easily go back to xview because it's on the list.

7. **If you want to associate an icon with the newly defined file type, click the No Icon button and select an icon from the icon palette. Click OK when you're finished.**

After you choose the icon, your new icon is displayed at the top of the Edit File Type dialog.

 By changing the icon to something more memorable, you can quickly recognize file types in your browser or on your desktop.

8. **Click OK and then click Close to save your work.**

You may have noticed that the Edit File Type dialog has a drop-down list labeled Viewer Component. Most GNOME-savvy applications can display certain file types *in-line*. This means that if you open a file that has a built-in viewer component, the file is displayed within your application — you don't have to stop what you're doing and open a new application just to see your data.

For example, if you're using the Evolution e-mail client (a GNOME-savvy application) and you receive a JPEG image as an attachment, Evolution allows you to view the image without firing up an external application — the image displays in-line.

When you're modifying MIME types, the Viewer Component drop-down list is disabled unless GNOME has a component that can handle your file. In some cases, GNOME can display your file type with a number of different components; choose the one you prefer from the Viewer Component drop-down list.

Technique 4: Prompting Yourself with a Custom Prompt

Save Time By

- Keeping useful information handy
- Colorizing your prompt to convey useful information
- Saving your prompt preferences
- Warning yourself when you hold potentially dangerous privileges

Your prompt is your connection to the Linux world when you're working in the shell. If you haven't already modified it, your prompt displays your machine name and current directory. But why settle for less information than you could really use?

Customize your prompt to keep information that you need in plain sight when you're working at the command line. You can add information such as the time, date, number of users, and more. In addition to displaying system information, your prompt can change colors. If you use multiple terminal windows connected to multiple machines, use a different-colored prompt on each machine to give you a quick clue about your location, all without taking up screen space.

The prompt also reflects your status as a superuser (or as a mere mortal). Keep an eye on your privilege level to prevent damage from the accidental use of privileges. We've included code in this technique to make the prompt change color when you hold elevated (and thus potentially dangerous) privileges.

In this technique, we show you how to manipulate your prompt to display the information that lets you get the job done quickly. Information is power, and power definitely saves time.

 Long prompts can take up a lot of screen real estate and also consume a lot of space on the printed page. In this technique, we show you complete prompts that enable you to see useful info quickly and easily. However, you don't want to work with these prompts all the time. In other techniques, we shorten the prompt to $ or # to save space.

Making Basic Prompt Transformations

In the bash shell, the prompt is controlled by a set of environment variables, the most important of which is $PS1. Change $PS1, and you change your prompt. The $PS1 variable is displayed when bash is waiting for a command from you. The $PS2 variable is also worth mentioning — it's displayed when bash needs more input to complete a current task.

If $PS1 contains a simple text string (such as "Hi, I'm the prompt"), that string is displayed whenever a command completes and the shell is waiting for the next command. Modifying the prompt is easy: Just enter strings that you want to test and hit Enter, and the results are displayed instantly. Saving your changes takes a bit of maneuvering, but we cover that in the next section. Here's a quick example of how to change the prompt:

```
[freddie@bastille] PS1="Hi, I'm the
   prompt "
Hi, I'm the prompt
```

Notice how the prompt changed from [freddie@bastille] to "Hi, I'm the prompt".

Adding Dynamically Updated Data to Your Prompt

Static prompts, such as the example in the preceding section, are kind of boring, so bash lets you include special character sequences (we'll call them *macros*) that represent changing data. Each macro starts with a backslash and is followed by a single character that tells bash which chunk of data you want to display. For example, if you want to display the current date and time whenever the prompt is displayed, use the \d (date) and \t (time) macros like this:

```
[freddie@bastille] PS1="\d \t "
Thu Dec 18 03:37:48
```

You can mix dynamic macros and static text in the same prompt. To enclose the date and time in brackets, just include the brackets in $PS1:

```
[freddie@bastille] PS1="[\d \t] "
[Thu Dec 18 03:37:50 ]
```

 It's usually a good idea to end each prompt with static text (a character like], -, or >) and a space to make the prompt easier to read.

If you press Enter a few times with this prompt, you see that the macros in $PS1 are evaluated each time the prompt is displayed:

```
[freddie@bastille] PS1="[\d \t] "
[Thu Dec 18 03:37:51 ]
[Thu Dec 18 03:37:51 ]
[Thu Dec 18 03:37:58 ]
[Thu Dec 18 03:38:01 ]
```

You can include as many macros as you want, in any order that you want, in $PS1. For example, to display the current date and time, your user name, your host name, and the current working directory (in that order), try this:

```
[freddie@bastille] PS1="[\d \t \u@\h:\w] "
[Thu Dec 18 03:40:20
   freddie@bastille:/home/freddie]
```

Spacing is important. Be sure to leave some white space between macros to make the info easier to read. Table 4-1 lists some of the most useful macros that you can include in a bash prompt.

TABLE 4-1: HANDY MACROS FOR YOUR PROMPT

Macro	What It Does/Displays	Timesaving Bonus Info
\a	Speaker beep	To keep users on their toes, code the $PS2 variable to beep when the user needs to input additional information. Just enter $PS2="\a >", and the computer beeps when it needs attention!
\d	Weekday (Sun–Sat), month name, and date ("Thu Dec 18", for example)	Handy when you're pulling all-nighters and you need to know when Saturday morning rolls around.

Macro	What It Does/Displays	Timesaving Bonus Info
\D{}	Date and/or time in a format of your choosing	The \D macro must be followed by a format string enclosed in braces. bash interprets the format string by using the same rules as the strftime library function (see man strftime for more details). If the format string is empty, the braces are still required, but bash chooses a display format appropriate to your locale.
\e	Escape character; used for complex strings	Escape characters introduce complex, unfriendly terminal command sequences. We show you a better way later in this technique.
\h	Host name up to the first . (dot)	If you work on a number of different hosts from the same workstation, \h can help you remember which one you're currently connected to.
\H	Entire host name	Similar to \h, but takes up too much screen real estate for our taste.
\n	Newline	Use a new line to create a multiline prompt.
\s	Shell name — such as bash or csh	We've never found a particularly good use for this one because we always stick to bash.
\t	Current time in 24-hour (HH:MM:SS) format	
\T	Current time in 12-hour (HH:MM:SS) format	
\@	Current time in 12-hour (am/pm) format	Is it 5:00 yet?
\A	Current time in 24-hour (HH:MM) format	
\u	Current user name	Include \u if you need to do work on someone else's behalf (in other words, if you're an administrator). That way you won't forget who you are and send flaming e-mail using someone else's name!
\W	Trailing component of your current working directory	This is probably the most useful macro you could include in a custom prompt — sort of a "You Are Here" sign.
\w	Entire current working directory	Similar to \W, but takes up a lot of room on your command line.
\\	Backslash character	
\!	History number	Every command that you execute is stored in a history log, and you can refer to a specific command in the log by its history number. Include the \! macro in your prompt, and you'll see the history number assigned to each command. (We talk more about history processing in Technique 9.)
\$	If the effective UID is 0, a #; otherwise a $	The \$ macro displays a pound sign (#) if you hold superuser privileges or a dollar sign ($) if you don't. You can use the \$ macro to help you remember when you have enough privileges to seriously damage your system, but we show you a better way in the section "Seeing a Red Alert When You Have Superuser Privileges," later in this technique.

Colorizing Your Prompt

Changing the color of your prompt may not save you tons of time, but it can make the prompt more readable and convey extra information without taking up screen real estate.

What kind of information can you encode with colorized prompts? Just about anything. Turn your prompt green when you're logged into one host and blue when you're logged into another. Display your prompt in green when the system load is low, yellow as it increases, and red when you're running into resource bottlenecks. Or, just change the color of your prompt to a fixed color so that it stands out on the screen.

You can colorize your prompt two ways. The most common (but not the most timesaving) way is to include special "escape" characters (characters that your terminal window understands, but humans don't) in your prompt. For example, the following string turns your prompt blue:

```
[freddie@bastille] PS1="\[\033[0;34m\]
   [\u@\h]\[\033[0m\] "
[freddie@bastille]
```

Of course, because this is a black-and-white book, you can't see the color here, but if you try this example, you'll see that the prompt turns blue. This method works, but it has two drawbacks. First, the syntax is hard to read (and hard to get right in the first place). Second, this method works only if your terminal emulator supports ANSI escape sequences — many terminal emulators (and many terminals) don't. Fortunately, you can fix both problems at once by using tput.

When changing the color of your prompt, using tput makes your prompts portable. That is, if you move to another terminal emulator, you don't have to change prompts. tput also

knows the right escape sequences, so you don't have to spend time looking them up.

The blue prompt in the preceding example looks like this when you use tput:

```
[freddie@bastille] BLUE=$(tput setaf 4)
[freddie@bastille] BLACK=$(tput setaf 0)
[freddie@bastille] PS1="\[$BLUE\]\u@\h]\
   [$BLACK\] "
[freddie@bastille]
```

The first line uses tput to find the character sequence that changes the foreground color to blue. The second line finds the character sequence that changes the foreground color to black. Notice that you don't need to know the magic escape sequences; tput keeps a database of terminal descriptions and consults that database to find the sequence that corresponds to the terminal (or terminal emulator) you're using. The third line patches the $BLUE and $BLACK sequences into the $PS1 prompt string.

The $PS1 string, however, is still more complicated than it needs to be — it's got a few extra \[and \] sequences. Those extra characters are required so that bash knows which prompt characters take up screen real estate and which ones don't (the invisible characters must appear between a \[and \] pair).

When you use tput, you can clean up extra characters a bit more by including those extra characters in the $BLUE and $BLACK variables:

```
[freddie@bastille] BLUE="\[$(tput setaf
   4)\]"
[freddie@bastille] BLACK="\[$(tput setaf
   0)\]"
[freddie@bastille] PS1="$BLUE\u@\h]$BLACK "
[freddie@bastille]
```

tput can do much more than just change the foreground color of the prompt. Table 4-2 shows a few of the more useful tput sequences. (For a complete list, see man tput and man terminfo.)

TABLE 4-2: SOME USEFUL TPUT SEQUENCES

Sequence	What You Use It For
tput sgr0	Reset all formatting.
tput bold	Display text in bold font.
tput rev	Display inverse-colored text (white on black instead of black on white, for example).
tput smul	Start underlining text.
tput rmul	Stop underlining text.
tput setaf	Set foreground color.
tput setab	Set background color.

These are your choices for foreground and background colors:

    0 Black

    1 Red

    2 Green

    3 Yellow

    4 Blue

    5 Magenta

    6 Cyan

    7 White

Just find the color you want to use and stick it at the end of the tput setaf or tput setab command.

You can combine the different text effects to produce colored and underlined prompts, boldface inverse fonts, and any combination of your terminal supports. For example, you can display an underlined blue prompt:

```
[freddie@bastille] BLUE="\[$(tput setaf
  4)\]"
[freddie@bastille] ULINE="\[$(tput smul)\]"
[freddie@bastille] RESET="\[$(tput sgr0)\]"
[freddie@bastille] PS1="$BLUE$ULINE[\
  u@\h]$RESET "
[freddie@bastille]
```

Notice that we used tput sgr0 to restore the text back to its normal state (default color, no underline, no bold). That's usually a good idea when you use tput to customize your prompt. Otherwise, whatever you type in after the colorized prompt will be colorized as well.

Seeing a Red Alert When You Have Superuser Privileges

We mention earlier in this technique that we can show you a better way to remind yourself that you hold dangerous superuser privileges. The typical way to distinguish between superuser status and mere-mortal status is to change one character in your prompt (usually the last character) from $ to #. But that's a pretty small change and can easily go unnoticed. Superuser privileges are *dangerous:* one mistake, and you're looking at hours of cleanup.

Here's a way to make your privilege level jump out at you: When you hold superuser privileges, your prompt is displayed in red, and when you don't, your prompt is displayed in blue. The following steps explain how to make this change:

1. **Open a terminal window and give yourself superuser privileges with the** su **command.**

```
$ su
Password:
# su
```

2. **Open the** /etc/bashrc **file in your favorite editor.**

```
# kedit /etc/bashrc
```

If you prefer GNOME, you can use gedit instead:

```
# gedit /etc/bashrc
```

> If you're using SuSE, modify the /etc/bash.bashrc.local file. If the file doesn't already exist, it is automatically created when you save your changes.

3. **Add the following code to the end the file:**

```
function setprompt
{
  local BLUE="\[$(tput setaf 4)\]"
  local RED="\[$(tput setaf 1)\]"
  local RESET="\[$(tput sgr0)\]"

  # If `id -u` returns 0, you have
  # superuser privileges

  if [ `id -u` = 0 ]
   then
     PS1="$RED[\u@\h:\W]$RESET "
   else
     PS1="$BLUE[\u@\h:\W]$RESET "
   fi
}

setprompt
```

4. **Save your work and close the editor; you're finished!**

We want to note a couple of interesting points about this sample code:

✔ First, you must add this function to the /etc/bashrc file, not your own personal ~/.bashrc file. Why? Because you want to modify the prompt not only for yourself, but also for the superuser. (Remember, /etc/bashrc is executed for all users, and ~/.bashrc is executed only when *you* log in.)

✔ Second, notice that we created a shell function and put most of the code inside that function. By declaring the $BLUE, $RED, and $RESET variables as local, they're destroyed as soon as the function (setprompt) ends. If you don't wrap the variables inside a function, you'll find them in your list of environment variables and probably wonder where they came from. We give some more words of shell-scripting wisdom in Techniques 8 and 10.

Saving Your Work

When you find a prompt that you'd like to keep, you want to store the $PS1 variable somewhere so that your prompt returns the next time you log in. The safest place to set $PS1 is in your ~/.bashrc login script. (This script is executed every time you start a new shell.) To save your fancy new prompt:

1. **Start your favorite editor (**kate, kedit, **or the GNOME Text Editor will do).**

2. **Open the file** /home/*user-name*/.bashrc.

Make sure you type in your Linux user name instead of *user-name* and make sure you include the period before the word bashrc. Your .bashrc file will probably look something like this:

```
# .bashrc

# User specific aliases and functions

# Source global definitions
if [ -f /etc/bashrc ]; then
      . /etc/bashrc
fi
```

3. **Add the following code to the end of the file:**

```
# Customize the prompt
BLUE="\[$(tput setaf 4)\]"
ULINE="\[$(tput smul)\]"
RESET="\[$(tput sgr0)\]"
PS1="$BLUE$ULINE[\u@\h]$RESET "
```

4. **Now save your changes and close the editor.**

If you want to change the default prompt for newly created user accounts, give yourself superuser privileges and modify the /etc/skel/.bashrc file. /etc/skel/.bashrc is copied to a user's home directory when his or her user account is created.

Your ~/.bashrc script is executed whenever you log in. If another user logs in, the .bashrc script in that user's home directory is executed. If you want to customize the prompt for all users (not just for new users), store your changes in /etc/bashrc.

Technique 8 spells out the rules for deciding which login script you want to modify — see that technique for all the details.

If you're intrigued by the idea of customizing your bash prompt and want more information, browse around the bashprompt project Web site at

> www.gilesorr.com/bashprompt/howto/
> book1.html

This site offers some great examples and background information.

Technique 5

Getting There Quick with Dynamic Shortcuts

Save Time By

- ✔ Using shortcuts to complete filenames
- ✔ Using environment variables to filter results
- ✔ Customizing name completion for remote logins

Graphical applications look nice, but it's hard to beat the command line for pure speed and raw power. Using bash is an obvious choice when you need to do something fast, but unless you're the perfect typist, keyboard errors can slow you down — especially if you type faster backwards (that is, with the Delete key) or if you're working in a case-sensitive environment like Linux.

With a few shortcut keystrokes, bash will complete your command line for you — we call that feature a *dynamic shortcut*. Not having to retype incorrectly entered commands or filenames can save you hours in no time. With dynamic shortcuts, you make fewer keystrokes . . . and fewer keystrokes mean fewer *wrong* keystrokes. In this technique, we show you how to use shortcuts at the command line to save time and keystrokes and to avoid typing errors.

Completing Names Automatically

bash knows how to complete filenames, command names, user names, and host names on your behalf. Try the following steps:

1. **Open a terminal window. You can find one in the GNOME or KDE Menu under System Tools (or System, if your version of GNOME or KDE doesn't have a System Tools menu choice).**

2. **Type the first few letters of the command, variable, or whatever you're looking for and press the Tab key twice.**

   For example, if you type host, a list of commands that start with the letters *host* appears. See Table 5-1 for more details on autocompleting variables, user names, and so on.

3. **If you need to narrow down your options further, type the next few letters of the command and press the Tab key again.**

   To tell bash how to complete the hostname command, you'd type n. If you have more than one command that begins with the letters *hostn,* bash shows you a list of those commands. Just type enough letters to

TABLE 5-1: GETTING THE ITEM YOU WANT WITH AUTOCOMPLETE

If the Partial Text Begins With . . .	bash Looks For . . .	Example
$	A matching environment variable	If you type `cd $HO` and then press Tab, bash translates that to `cd $HOME`.
~ (tilde)	A matching user name	Typing `cd ~fre` and pressing Tab translates to `cd ~freddie/`.
@	A matching host name	`mail freddie@bas` followed by a tab translates to `freddie@bastille`.
No special symbol	A command name completion and, finally, a filename	Type `more /etc/pass` and then press Tab, and bash completes your command as `more /etc/passwd`.

make the choice unambiguous, and bash will complete the command name.

4. After bash completes the command name, press Enter, and the command is executed.

If, at any time, you press the Tab key and nothing happens (or you just hear a beep), bash either found no completions or a bunch of completions. (In this context, *bunch* is a technical term that means some number greater than one.) If you press Tab a second time, you see a list of all possible completions (if any exist).

Using the Escape Key to Your Advantage

The Tab key completes environment variables, user names, host names, command names, and filenames. You can fine-tune bash completions with the Esc key. Use the Esc key in combination with other keys to limit the type of completion that bash attempts, or to view or insert several completions at once. Table 5-2 has all the details.

 The Esc-key options are very powerful, but we've never bothered to memorize them all. Your number-one timesaving friend is the Tab key. We use it all day long.

bash can complete any filename pattern, not just a prefix. If you have a few tarballs (that is, files whose

names end in `.tgz`) in your current directory, add all of them to the command line like this:

```
[freddie@bastille] ls -l *.tgz <Esc-*>
```

When you press Esc-*, bash replaces the `*.tgz` part with the names of all files matching that pattern.

Environment variables that affect filename completion

Set the following environment variables to screen out files you don't want to include in the completion list:

✔ FIGNORE: This is a colon-separated list of file suffixes to ignore during filename completion. For example, compilers often produce filenames that end in `.o`. If you want the filename completion mechanism to ignore those files, set FIGNORE to `.o`, like this:

```
$ export FIGNORE=.o
```

✔ HOSTFILE: Use this environment variable to tell the completion mechanism which hosts to consider when completing a host name. If you don't set HOSTFILE, bash searches the `/etc/hosts` file. You can use HOSTFILE to limit host name completion to only those hosts that you use frequently. If you've created a file named `~/myhosts` that contains the names of the hosts that you frequent, set HOSTFILE like this:

```
$ export HOSTFILE=~/myhosts
```

If you want your environment variables in place every time you log in, see Technique 8, in which we show you how to modify your login and logout scripts.

TABLE 5-2: USING ESCAPE FOR COMPLETIONS

What to Press	What It Does	Timesaving Bonus Info
Esc-?	Displays all possible completions — command names, filenames, and user names — and presents them in table form for you to read through and complete the command.	Esc-? works very much like the Tab key except that it doesn't actually complete a word; it just shows you the possible completions. If you want to see a (very long) list of all the commands in your search path, press Esc-? in a blank command line.
Esc-*	Inserts all possible completions into your command.	This is helpful if you have few possible completions.
Esc-/	Completes the filename to the left of the cursor.	Esc-/ attempts filename completion only. That's handy when you *know* you want a filename — you won't get a host name or user name by accident.
Esc-~	Completes the user name to the left of the cursor.	Complete user names only — don't try the other completion types.
Esc-$	Completes the variable name to the left of the cursor.	Complete variable names only — don't try the other completion types.
Esc-@	Completes the host name to the left of the cursor.	Complete host names only — don't try the other completion types. This option is useful when you need to type a host name, but you don't have a @ in the command, for example, `ssh bastille`.
Esc-!	Completes the command name to the left of the cursor.	Complete command names only — don't try the other completion types.

Customizing Completion for Maximum Speed

Suppose that you take care of a network of computers and you find yourself logging into remote hosts by using `ssh`. To `ssh` to host `bastille`, you might type in `ssh b` and then press Tab thinking that bash will fill in the rest of the host name (`bastille`) for you. bash doesn't know that `ssh` is always followed by a host name, so instead of doing what you want, bash goes through its normal search routine trying to find a matching filename. To tell bash to complete hostnames for `ssh`, use the following command:

```
[freddie@bastille] complete -A hostname ssh
```

The `-A hostname` part tells bash that you want to complete host names (from the `/etc/hosts` file or from `$HOSTFILE` if defined). The `ssh` part tells bash which command you want to customize. You can customize several (probably related) commands at the same time, for example:

```
[freddie@bastille] complete -A hostname ssh
    sftp rsh ping
```

This command tells bash to complete host names for `ssh`, `sftp`, `rsh`, and `ping`. Of course, you can tell bash to use other completion types, too:

```
[freddie@bastille] complete -A username
    usermod passwd
```

This command tells bash to complete user names after the `usermod` and `passwd` commands. The most useful completion actions are listed in Table 5-3.

TABLE 5-3: USEFUL COMPLETION ACTIONS

Use This Action	To Do This
-A command	Complete command names (useful for the `which` command).
-A directory	Complete directory names (perfect for `cd`).
-A file	Complete filenames.
-A hostname	Complete host names.
-A user	Complete user names.

 bash supports many completion actions in addition to the ones listed in Table 5-3. See `man bash` for more options.

You can also customize completion for a command by creating filters. If you use OpenOffice.org frequently, you may want to customize completion for OOWriter and OOCalc:

```
[freddie@bastille] complete -G "*.sxw"
    oowriter
[freddie@bastille] complete -G "*.sxc"
    oocalc
```

Now when you type `oowriter` and press Tab, bash only completes filenames that end in `.sxw` (the OOWriter file format). The second command tells bash to complete OOCalc spreadsheets when you run `oocalc`.

 Don't forget to save your customizations to one of the bash startup files. See Technique 8 if you're not sure which file to use.

Technique 6

Using cd Shortcuts for Rapid Transit

Save Time By

- ✔ Using bash (rather than a graphical interface) for file management
- ✔ Getting around your disk quickly
- ✔ Defining search paths to take you places fast
- ✔ Remembering where you've been with pushd and popd

You can use Linux for ages without venturing near the terminal window. With all the graphical programs available, you can do virtually anything without ever having to go near the command line. The downside of heavy dependence on a graphical interface is that you lose speed — few graphical programs provide good looks and high power in the same package.

Getting around quickly is a matter of knowing the fastest route, whether you're using the command line or a browser. bash (the program in charge of the command line) knows this, and helps out with a bunch of handy ways to jump to the locations you need when you use the command line.

Backtracking at the command line can be a timesaver, too. In this technique, we show you how to use pushd and popd to make a retraceable path. You'll be moving back and forth through your directories in no time.

We also introduce you to a handy environment variable — CDPATH — that you can use to make directory changes quickly without searching for the correct pathnames. The CDPATH variable makes the command line friendlier and faster.

Can't find your way out of a paper bag? After reading this technique, you'll know not only where you are, but also where you've been and the quickest way to get where you're going!

Using cd and ls to Navigate through bash

The cd command is the mode of travel through the terminal window. With cd, you can go anywhere fast:

- ✔ To return to your home directory, type cd and press Enter.
- ✔ To go to a specific directory, type cd, a space, and the directory name; then press Enter.

✔ To go to a specific directory (with less typing), type cd, a space, and the first few characters of the directory name, and then press Tab to automatically complete the rest of the directory name. (See Technique 5 for more details.)

✔ To go to a subdirectory, type cd, a space, and the subdirectory name; then press Enter.

✔ To go to the parent directory of the directory you're in, type cd .. and press Enter.

✔ To return to the directory you were just in, type cd - and press Enter.

 Use the up-arrow key (↑) to recall complex directory changes from your history file. Just press the up- and down-arrow keys to scroll through the list of commands until you find the one you need.

To find out where you are, use the pwd command. Enter pwd at the command line and press Enter, and bash displays your current directory.

To find the contents of your directory at the command line, use the ls command. These are the basic options:

✔ ls -l gives you expanded information about the items in your directory.

✔ ls -a shows all files — even the hidden ones.

✔ ls -t sorts by date changed. (This is handy if you forget what you've worked on but know when you worked on it. For example, you're trying to remember what you did on Monday.)

✔ ls -R shows the entire tree listings for directories within your current directory.

You can also combine the ls flags. For example, ls -la gives you an expanded listing of all the files in your directory.

With those two basic commands (cd and ls), you can navigate through your file system. Now read on to find out how to pick up some speed.

Setting Your CDPATH Variables to Find Directories Fast

The CDPATH variable contains a list of directory names that bash searches through when you cd to a directory without providing a complete path.

 The directories in your CDPATH should be the directories that contain your most commonly visited subdirectories. The big timesaver comes after you've set your CDPATH: Instead of typing a complex directory name with layers of subdirectories, you simply cd to the endpoint.

CDPATH should contain a series of directory names, each separated by a colon. Save your CDPATH variable to your startup file — ~/.bashrc — so you don't have to type it every time you log in. The following steps explain how to set up CDPATH in GNOME and KDE.

 Files whose names start with a . don't show up on normal directory listings. They're there; you just can't see them when you do an ls.

To set your CDPATH variable, follow these steps:

1. **At the command line:**

If you're using GNOME, enter gedit ~/.bashrc and press Enter.

If you're using KDE, enter kate ~/.bashrc and press Enter.

gedit or kate opens, displaying the contents of your .bashrc file. If you don't have a .bashrc file, the editor creates one for you.

2. **Type the following command:**

```
export CDPATH=/home/freddie/work:/etc/
    sysconfig
```

Substitute your most commonly used pathnames into the preceding string. You can have as many directories as you need — just remember to separate each of them with a colon (:).

3. **Click Save and then close the editor.**

The next time you log in, bash will search through all the directories included in CDPATH whenever you use the cd command.

You've just set the search path for your user account. If you want to define cd paths for other users, see Technique 8.

 If your .bashrc file already has stuff in it, make room at the top of the file and add CDPATH. This way, if .bashrc includes other programs, it's sure to execute the CDPATH command before moving on to the other programs.

When you're finished, your .bashrc file will look something like this:

```
# .bashrc

export
    CDPATH=/home/freddir/work:/etc/sysconfig

# Source global definitions
if [ -f /etc/bashrc ]; then
        . /etc/bashrc
fi
```

 Be careful with CDPATH if you run a lot of shell scripts (such as configure). Most shell scripts assume that CDPATH is *not* defined and get terribly confused if it is.

It's important to remember that CDPATH is a *search path*. That means that cd starts searching in the first directory you list in CDPATH, and it stops searching as soon as it finds the first candidate. If two (or more) of the directories in CDPATH have identically named subdirectories, cd will ignore all but the first (unless you cd to a fully-qualified directory name).

Remembering Where You've Been with pushd and popd

The pushd and popd commands work together to leave a virtual trail of breadcrumbs so that you can

find your way back $HOME again (sorry, we usually try to avoid nerdy puns). You can backtrack quickly without having to remember where you've been.

pushd works exactly like cd except that it records your current directory on a stack of directory names. popd removes the most recent entry in the list and cds to that directory for you. pushd puts a directory on top of the stack, and popd takes a directory back off again — in either case, you're always working at the top of the stack.

Here's how to use the two commands to retrace your steps:

1. **Use pushd to move to a directory (just as you would a cd command):**

```
$ pushd /usr/local/src
```

2. **Then pushd to another directory:**

```
$ pushd /tmp
```

After each pushd, your current location is added to the front of a directory list displayed above your prompt. We discuss how this list is useful in the next section.

3. **Enter popd and press Enter.**

You return to /usr/local/src.

 pushd remembers multiple moves, so you can popd back as far as you need to.

Manipulating Your Stack with dirs

Each time you pushd or popd, as explained in the preceding section, bash automatically executes the dirs command to display the directory stack above your prompt. Consider it bonus information from bash — you may not ask for it, but it's there, and useful.

You can use the dirs command by itself to make quick changes to the stack. The basic dirs command tells you what is on your stack. Use the `dirs` options to manipulate the directory stack to your liking:

✔ `dirs -c` clears the stack. This is handy if your stack is getting too long, or if you want to erase evidence of where you've been.

✔ `dirs -l` takes the abbreviations out of your stack. By default, bash abbreviates your home directory to ~.

✔ `dirs -p` shows you the directories you've visited in a line-by-line format. This is a quick way to clearly see where you've been.

Technique 7

Typing Less and Doing More with Handy Automagic Variables

Save Time By

- ✔ Using your process ID to create unique filenames
- ✔ Using command output to build complex commands
- ✔ Scripting tasks to check for privileges
- ✔ Creating search paths for commands and using shortcuts
- ✔ Creating custom variables

Working at the prompt can be a huge timesaver — no graphics programs to load, no images to refresh, no mouse to chase. What could be better? Well, less typing for starters. It would also be nice if you didn't have to remember things like process IDs or the complete pathnames of seldom-used commands.

Luckily for you (and us), bash can help. bash uses environment variables to keep information handy. Some environment variables you define yourself; others (we like to call them "automagic variables") are defined by bash. You can use environment variables at the command line or within shell scripts. In this technique, we show you a few of the more useful bash variables and how to save time by using variables instead of manually typing everything in. Here's a quick preview of automagic variables' possibilities:

- ✔ The $$ variable holds the process ID of the bash shell. You can use $$ to create unique filenames that won't clash with other users. If you want to browse through a long directory listing, just redirect the output from ls into a temporary file named /tmp/$$ and then open that file (/tmp/$$) with your favorite editor. When you're finished with it, just delete the temporary file with the command rm /tmp/$$.

- ✔ Shell scripting everyday tasks can save you a lot of time and keystrokes. Tasks such as mounting and unmounting CD drives are well suited to scripting, but your scripts should include some verification of user privileges. Use $UID and $EUID to screen your script users to decide if they should be allowed to run that script.

- ✔ When you need to run a program or shell script, bash needs to know not only the name of the program but also the location. With $PATH, you can create search paths for bash so that you need to enter only the name to run the program. In this technique, we tell you how.

- ✔ Another automagic variable creates command-line arguments out of program results. Save time and space by moving data without having to create files. Just use $( ) for command substitution, as described later in this technique.

Show Me the $$: Giving Temporary Files Unique Names

The `$$` variable contains the unique process ID of the shell you're running. To see the value of `$$`, just type in `echo $$`. You can use this ID to generate unique names for temporary files.

 If you have multiple users who create temporary files, setting a naming standard will save time (and confusion). Tell all your users to use `$$` to create the names for their temporary files. Because each process ID is unique, each filename will be unique. If you're careful to remove temporary files when you're done with them, you'll avoid lots of confusion in the long run.

Garbage stacks up: Data directories can grow and grow when you're not looking (nature abhors a vacuum, and so does your disk drive). If you're browsing through a directory that won't fit on one screen, you can pipe the output to `more` like this:

```
$ ls-l | more
```

A better way to browse through a huge directory listing is to make a searchable catalog of the files in that directory, which makes it a lot easier to find the files you're looking for. To create and edit a file containing the contents of a directory, follow these steps:

1. **Navigate to the directory you want to list.**

2. **Enter** `ls -l > /tmp/$$` **and press Enter.**

The file `/tmp/$$` now contains a listing of the files in your current directory. Of course, because `$$` contains your process ID, you've actually created a file with a name like `/tmp/5542` (or whatever your process ID happens to be).

 The `>` directs the output of a command to the file listed to the right of `>`. This technique works with basically any commands that create output.

3. **Enter** `gedit /tmp/$$` **(if you're using GNOME) or alternately** `kate /tmp/$$` **(if you're using KDE).**

Your new file opens, ready for you to use.

We should point out that using `$$` in a filename simply generates a *name* that's likely to be unique — it doesn't actually create a *temporary* file. You still have to delete the file when you're finished with it.

Streamlining Archive Searches

When you need to find a missing file, searching through tarballs and zip files (with obscure names) that have accumulated in your download directory can take eons. You can save time by exposing the archives' contents in the easiest and fastest possible way. Here's how you do it for different file types:

- ✔ **Tarballs:** To find out what's in a tarball without unpacking it, you can easily capture the archive catalog in a temporary file (and then browse the catalog with your favorite editor). To do so, use the following command:

  ```
  $ tar -ztvf tarballname.tgz > /tmp/$$
  ```

  This command displays the filenames from a tarball and captures the output to a temporary file that you can browse at your leisure.

- ✔ **RPM package:** If you want to know which files are included in an RPM package, you can generate a list of the filenames with this command:

  ```
  $ rpm -qpl rpmfilename.rpm > /tmp/$$
  ```

- ✔ **Zip file:** Zip files also tend to pile up. To peek inside a Zip archive, enter the following command:

  ```
  $ unzip -l zipfilename > /tmp/$$
  ```

After you have the archive contents in full view, just check your temporary file for the contents you need. Cruising through your archives to find missing files is easy and fast.

If you have a lot of archives to go through (they do accumulate), work with two windows — one terminal window and a browser window open to your temporary directory. You can open the file with a quick double-click and drag it to the trash when you're done.

If you're a GNOME aficionado, you can use the File Roller tool to peek inside most archives instead of creating a temporary file to hold the catalog. Just open Nautilus, jump to the directory that holds the archive, and click the filename.

Turning the Output of a Command into a Variable with $( )

bash has another trick up its sleeve that can save you a lot of time — it's called *command substitution*. Command substitution turns the output from a command into a variable. Command substitution is a big help with simple results, such as sending e-mail to all the users in a particular group. Command substitution is indispensable for complex jobs like changing the ownership of all the files extracted from an archive.

Command substitution is so named because it substitutes the output from a command into the command line. To use command substitution, just surround a command with parentheses and put a dollar sign in front of it, like this:

```
$ file $(which bzgrep)
/usr/bin/bzgrep: a /bin/sh script
```

When bash sees the contruct $(*command*), it executes the *command* and builds a new command line based on the output generate by *command*. The command file $(which bzgrep) is equivalent to:

```
$ which bzgrep
scribble down the result (/usr/bin/bzgrep)
$ file whatever you scribbled down
```

Here's another example that shows command substitution in action:

1. **Set up the variable and the command:**

```
$ NOW=$(date)
```

The value of $NOW is set to the output of the date command.

2. **To display the value of $NOW, use the echo command:**

```
$ echo $NOW
Fri Dec 26 13:02:01 EST 2003
```

Of course, you can shorten that whole sequence to echo $(date).

Make command substitution a habit — it certainly is for us. Command substitution not only saves typing but also reduces the chance of error.

Here's a good example of how command substitution can reduce typing errors. When you unpack a tarball, files are often scattered all over your system. If you need to change ownership of all those files, your options are to track down and chown those files one at a time, or to build a command with the output generated by another command. Personally, we're more likely to leave a file out of the list than bash is. The following command converts the output of the tar command into a list of filenames for chown to act on:

```
$ chown freddie $(tar -ztvf
   tarballname.tgz)
```

You've used tar to create list of the files that you're interested in and then feed that list to chown as a set of command-line arguments.

tar isn't the only command that can generate a list of names. In this next example, we use grep to generate a list of user names.

The /etc/group file contains one row for each *group* you've defined on your system. Each row contains a group name, a password, a group number, and then a comma-separated list of the users within that group. A typical group file will look something like this:

```
...
support:x:500:george,fred,barney
operators:x:501:elroy
acctg:X:502:wilma,betty,judy,jane
...
```

You can use grep to pull a specific row out of the group file, like this:

```
$ grep support /etc/group
support:x:500:george,fred,barney
```

To extract the user names from a row, use the cut command to pick out a specific "column." Because /etc/group uses a colon to separate columns, you can extract the user names with the following command:

```
$ grep support /etc/group | cut -d ':' -f 4
george,fred,barney
```

The -d ':' part tells cut to use the colon character as a field separator, and the -f 4 part picks out the fourth field.

Now you can use command substitution to feed that list of user names to the mail program (maybe sending a message to everyone in the Accounting, or acctg, department):

```
$ mail $(grep acctg /etc/group | cut -d
  ':' -f 4)
Subject: Downtime

The accounting system will be down this
  weekend
  -- Freddie
.
CC:
$
```

Use variables to hold groups of files or user names when you need to issue a command that affects the whole group.

If you want to see a preview of your command after substitution but before execution, press Esc-Ctrl-E. If the preview looks good, press Enter to execute the command.

Using $UID and $EUID in Shell Scripts

When you create a user account, Linux assigns a numeric user ID to that user. bash stores the user ID in the $UID variable; your effective user ID is kept in the $EUID variable. (Your real user ID is always the same, but your effective user ID changes if you impersonate another user with the su command.) For example, user freddie might be logged on with a $UID of 500, but if freddie uses su to gain superuser privileges, his $EUID changes from 500 to 0.

A superuser's $EUID is always 0. This is a quick and easy way to verify user privileges when you're writing shell scripts.

You can use $EUID inside a shell script to determine whether the user running the script holds extra privileges. For example, it's easy to write a shell script that mounts the CD drive for users who have enough privileges.

If you're using Fedora or Mandrake, follow these steps:

1. **Open your terminal window and enter the following command:**

```
$ gedit /usr/local/bin/mount-cd
```

This command opens the gedit editor and creates a file called mount-cd in the /usr/local/bin directory.

2. **Type in the following text:**

```
#!/bin/bash

if [[ $EUID -eq 0 ]]
  then
    mount /dev/cdrom /mnt/cdrom
  else
      echo "Sorry, you must be a
superuser"
      echo "to mount a CD"
fi
```

3. **Save the file and close gedit.**

4. **At the command line in the terminal window, type this command:**

```
chmod a+x /usr/local/bin/mount-cd
```

This command makes the file executable for everyone on your system.

If your system is running SuSE Linux, follow these steps to create a shell script that mounts the CD drive for users with an effective user ID of 0:

1. **Open your terminal window and enter the following command:**

```
$ gedit /usr/local/bin/mount-cd
```

This command opens the gedit editor and creates a file called mount-cd in the /usr/local/bin directory.

2. **Type in the following text:**

```
#!/bin/bash

if [[ $EUID -eq 0 ]]
  then
   mount /dev/cdrom /media/cdrom
  else
      echo "Sorry, you must be a
superuser"
      echo "to mount a CD"
fi
```

3. **Save the file and close** gedit.

4. **At the command line in the terminal window, type this command:**

```
chmod a+x /usr/local/bin/mount-cd
```

This command makes the file executable for everyone on your system.

Now if users want to mount a CD by using the program you just created, all they need to do is enter mount-cd at the command line. Any user can run this script, but only those users whose $EUIDs are 0 (the superusers) can actually mount a CD.

Getting Quick Access to Programs with $PATH

Shell scripts can be big timesavers, but only if you don't have to search for them. Populating your $PATH environment variable with the directories that contain your most commonly used scripts (and other programs) will save you tons of time (and aggravation) because you can start programs with just a program name rather than a complete pathname.

The $PATH variable is a colon-separated list of directory names that bash searches through to find your program names. Each user has his or her own $PATH variable.

It's a good idea to keep dangerous commands in a directory that's not on the average user's search path (that is, the user's $PATH variable). If you don't, a naive user might accidentally run a damaging program when he doesn't mean to. Keeping dangerous programs out of the normal search path won't stop a malicious user, but it can save you from accidental damage.

 The superuser's $PATH should *never* include a period (.). The '.' directory means "the current directory." As you cd from directory to directory, '.' changes with you. If '.' is in the superuser's search path, a malicious user could drop a Trojan horse into a directory that the superuser is likely to visit. For example, if a malcontent knows that the superuser spends time in the /tmp directory, he could create a Trojan horse with an innocuous-looking name like /tmp/ls.

If the superuser cd's to /tmp and runs the ls command, he may be in danger. If '.' appears early in the search path (earlier than /bin/ls), the superuser will run the Trojan horse instead of the real ls — and he'll be giving the Trojan superuser privileges too! Some high-security sites are even more paranoid — they make sure that the superuser has an empty $PATH, forcing him to type the complete pathname to every command.

To set the `$PATH` environment variable for a user, follow these steps:

1. **At the command line, enter** `gedit ~user/.bashrc` **and press Enter.**

2. **When the editor opens, add the following line to the end of the file:**

   `PATH=$PATH:/foo/bar/baz`

   Substitute your directory name for */foo/bar/baz.*

   The command you just entered appends the directory to the user's current search path.

3. **Click the Save icon and close the editor.**

Now, when this user enters a program name, bash searches through all the directories listed in `$PATH`.

 You can add as many directories to the user's path as you'd like, but remember that as you hand out easy access to commands, you could invite accidents.

Customizing Variables for Rapid Transit

All the environment variables you've seen so far are *automagic* variables — bash defines them for you, and they can change value over time. You can also create *custom* variables to make your life easier. For example, we spend a lot of time in the directory `/usr/local/src` (that's where open-source source code typically lives). In our system-wide login script (`/etc/bashrc`), we define an environment variable named `$SRC` that equates to `/usr/local/src`. That makes it easy to navigate to our workplace — just `cd $SRC` and we're there.

Of course, you can use environment variables to do things other than just `cd`: You can copy files (`cp $SRC/foo.c $DST/`), create archives (`tar -zcvf $SRC/mycode.tgz $SRC/kde/`), or just about anything

else. Unfortunately, most graphical programs don't know how to deal with environment variables, but they can sure save you time at the command line.

Just think of the pathnames you use over and over every day, and you'll see why custom environment variables can be a great timesaver.

The following shell script defines a few custom variables you can use to get somewhere quickly:

```
# File name: setvars.bash
#    Define a few shortcuts
#
export SRC=/usr/local/src        # cd
    $SRC will take me to /usr/local/src
export DESK=~/Desktop            # cd
    $DESK will take me to my desktop
export ACCTG=/opt/data/accounting  # cd
    $ACCTG will take me to my bookkeeping
    data
echo "Your custom variables are ready for
use"
```

To use the code:

1. **Open your favorite editor and create the file** `~/setvars.bash.`

   `$ gedit ~/setvars.bash`

2. **Type in the variables that you want to define (be sure to put the word** `export` **in front of each one).**

   ```
   export SRC=/usr/local/src
   export DESK=~/Desktop
   export ACCTG=/opt/data/accounting
   ```

   Note: Be sure that you don't have any spaces before or after the =; otherwise, bash will complain when you try to run your script.

3. **Save your work and close the editor.**

At the command line, adjust the permissions for the file you've just created, making it executable:

```
$ chmod a+x setvars.bash
```

Now, to execute your program and have your custom variables ready for use, just put a period (.) and a space at the beginning of the command line, like this:

```
$ . setvars.bash
Your custom variables are ready for use
$ echo $SRC
/usr/local/src
$
```

When you run a shell script that defines environment variables (like this one does), you have to put a . at the beginning of the command line. The . character is also known as the *source command*. In fact, you can type source setvars.bash instead of using ., but that's more typing. If you don't source (or '.')

the script, bash will start a new shell session, run your script, and immediately terminate the new shell session.

Why is immediate termination a problem? Because the environment variables are defined in the sub-shell (that new shell session) instead of *your* shell session. When the sub-shell ends, your fancy new variables disappear! The source command tells bash to execute a script within the current shell instead of firing up a new shell.

 After you create the pathname shortcut, you can move to your source code directory by typing cd $SRC and pressing Enter. You're at your location in a snap!

Technique 8

Logging In, Logging Out

Every time you log in, Linux launches a chain of startup programs and shell scripts that prepare your desktop and command line environment. You can customize your command line login scripts to your liking — for example, set color preferences and language preferences and set up the information that will be included in your prompt.

You can also arrange for KDE to automatically start programs for you when you log in. Not having to find all the programs you need to start your day is a great timesaver. Calendars, terminal windows, word processors, and even Tux Racer can be there waiting for you after your first cup of coffee.

Linux defines four sets of login/logout scripts. In this technique, we show you how to decide which scripts you need to change to customize your work environment when you log in or log out:

✔ System-wide gdm login/logout scripts

✔ System-wide shell login scripts

✔ Per-user shell login/logout scripts

✔ Skeleton (or prototype) shell login/logout scripts

This technique is all about saving time by having your work environment ready for you when you need it. Finding the right script to modify at login or logout is the key to success.

Finding the Right Shell Script

When you want to customize some aspect of your desktop (or command line) environment, finding just the right script can be tricky. Some scripts are shared by all users; others are personal scripts that execute for only a given user. If you're using a desktop environment like KDE or GNOME, your choices are even more complex. The following sections explain how to find the right script, when to run your code, and finally how to automatically arrange your desktop just the way you like it, each time you log in.

Choosing your victims

Start out by deciding how intrusive you want your change to be. That is, do you want to change everyone's settings or just your own?

What files you change depends on which of the following settings you're changing:

✔ **Personal settings:** If you change your personal login/logout scripts, you won't interfere with other users. For example, if you want to change your own bash prompt (see Technique 4), modify ~/.bashrc. Personal settings are stored in your home directory.

✔ **New user prototypes:** Change the prototype scripts to provide a starting point for new users (users whose accounts are created *after* you change the prototypes). For example, modify /etc/skel/.bashrc (the prototype .bashrc script) to suggest a default prompt for new users. When you create a new user account, the scripts found in /etc/skel are copied to the new user's home directory. Prototype scripts are stored in /etc/skel.

✔ **System-wide settings:** If you change system-wide scripts, you affect every user on your system. If you want to customize the bash prompt for all users, modify /etc/bashrc (the system-wide bashrc script). System-wide settings are stored in /etc or in a subdirectory of /etc.

 If you want to modify shared, system-wide scripts, you must hold superuser privileges. However, you don't need extra privileges to modify your own scripts.

Timing is everything

Next, determine *when* your code needs to run. Here the choices start to get complex. You can modify scripts that execute when you log in, scripts that execute when you start each new shell, and scripts that execute when you log out.

Here's the sequence of scripts that Linux runs when you log in to a new GNOME or KDE session managed by gdm (the GNOME display manger):

1. /etc/X11/gdm/PostLogin/Default (system wide)

2. /etc/X11/gdm/PreSession/Default (system wide)

3. /etx/X11/xdm/Xsession (system wide)

 The first three scripts run with superuser privileges even if you log in as a non-privileged user. Be careful what you do, or you may introduce vulnerabilities.

4. /etc/profile (system wide)

5. /etc/profile.d/*.sh (system wide)

6. ~/.bash_profile (personal)

7. ~/.bashrc (personal)

8. ~/etc/bashrc (system wide)

On SuSE systems, the first two scripts are found in /etc/opt/gnome/gdm instead of /etc/X11/gdm.

If you're running SuSE Linux or Mandrake Linux, you're probably using the KDE display manager (kdm) instead of GNOME's display manager (gdm), and the login/logout scripts will be different. We recommend using gdm even if you're a KDE user (gdm can create KDE desktops just like kdm can create GNOME desktops). See the sections on switching display managers in SuSE Linux and switching display managers in Mandrake Linux in Technique 35 for more information.

You'll rarely want to modify any of the first three scripts (in fact, we have *never* modified them), but it's common to modify /etc/profile. If you're uncomfortable modifying /etc/profile, just add a new script to /etc/profile.d/, and bash (actually /etc/profile) will happily invoke it for you.

Saving your customizations in a separate script (`/etc/profile.d/myscript.sh`) allows you to more easily debug and maintain the script in the future — your script won't be tangled up in all the "stuff" already in `/etc/profile`. Make sure that the name of any script that you save in `/etc/profile.d/` ends in `.sh`.

Every time you start a new bash shell (by opening a new terminal window or running a shell script), bash executes these scripts:

1. `~/.bashrc` (personal)

2. `/etc/bashrc` (system wide)

Notice that `~/.bashrc` runs *every time* you start a new shell. Don't put any time-consuming tasks in `~/.bashrc`, or you'll spend a lot of time waiting for each shell session to complete its startup code. `~/.bashrc` is a great place to define environment variables (see Technique 7), aliases, and shell functions (see Technique 10).

When you log in to your computer without creating a new GNOME or KDE session (by `ssh`ing from another computer for example), bash executes these scripts:

1. `/etc/profile` (system wide)

2. `/etc/profile.d/*.sh` (system wide)

3. `~/.bash_profile` (personal)

4. `~/.bashrc` (personal)

5. `/etc/bashrc` (system wide)

In case you didn't catch it, there's a pattern here. Each time you log in to your computer (whether you start a new GNOME or KDE session or `ssh` from another computer), bash runs the profile scripts (`/etc/profile`, `/etc/profile.sh/*.sh`, and `~/.bash_profile`). Every time you start a new shell, bash runs the `rc` scripts (`~/.bashrc` and `/etc/.bashrc`). To save yourself some time, be sure to put long-running tasks (such as file indexing or mail checking) in a profile script and not in an `rc` script.

When you log out of a command line `ssh` session, bash executes just one file:

`~/.bash_logout` (personal)

The `~/.bash_logout` script is a good place to invoke cleanup-related tasks. For example, if you have a habit of creating temporary files, delete them in `~/.bash_logout`. You may also want to encrypt sensitive files when you log out (and decrypt them when you log in) — see Technique 28 for more information about encrypting and decrypting files.

When you log out of a KDE or GNOME session, `gdm` (the GNOME display manager) executes just one file:

`/etc/X11/gdm/PostSession/Default`

On SuSE systems, the PostSession/Default script is stored in `/etc/opt/gnome/gdm` instead of `/etc/X11/gdm`.

Cleaning up made easy

Notice that the normal `~/.bash_logout` script is never executed if you use KDE or GNOME — all the cleanup code that's stored in `~/.bash_logout` is ignored. That's a bit inconvenient because you have to maintain two different logout scripts: one that executes when you log out from a command line session and one that executes when you log out from a graphical session.

You *could* try to fix this dual-script problem by creating a new script (with a name of your choosing) and invoking that script from `~/.bash_logout` and `/etc/X11/gdm/PostSession/Default`. That solution would work, but now you're maintaining *three* scripts instead of one!

Here's a better solution to the dual-logout-script problem: Simply modify `/etc/X11/gdm/PostSession/Default` so that it invokes `~/.bash_logout` for you. That way, you (and every other user on your system) can keep cleanup code in `~/.bash_logout` that runs whether you exit a command line session or a graphical session.

Follow these steps to run ~/.bash_logout every time you log out of your computer:

1. **Open a terminal window, give yourself super-user privileges, and move into the PostSession directory:**

```
$ su
Password:
# cd /etc/X11/gdm/PostSession
```

If you're running SuSE Linux, cd to /etc/opt/gnome/gdm instead.

2. **Rename the original PostSession/Default script:**

```
# mv Default Default.dist
```

3. **Use a text editor to create a new file that includes the following code:**

```
#!/bin/bash
if [ -x $HOME/.bash_logout ]
then
  su -c "$HOME/.bash_logout" $USER
fi

SCRIPTDIR=$(dirname $0)

exec $SCRIPTDIR/Default.dist
```

4. **Save your work to** /etc/X11/gdm/PostSession/Default **and close the editor.**

If you're a SuSE user, save your work to /etc/opt/gnome/gdm/PostSession/Default instead.

After making this change, your ~/.bash_logout script will run whether you're using a KDE session, a GNOME session, or a command line ssh session.

Changing prototype scripts

Have you ever wondered how ~/.bash_profile, ~/.bashrc, and ~/.bash_logout got into your home directory to begin with? When you create a new user account, you don't have to write the login and logout scripts yourself, but they must come from somewhere, right? Right! Each time you create a new user account,

Linux copies the *prototype* scripts from a directory named /etc/skel (that's skel as in *skeleton*).

If you try to look at the /etc/skel directory with a normal ls command, it looks empty, but it's not. All the files in /etc/skel have names that start with a period (.), meaning that they are hidden from the ls command. If you really want to see what's in /etc/skel, use ls -a instead (that -a option tells ls to display hidden files as well as normal files). You'll see (at least) three files:

- ✔ **/etc/skel/.bash_profile:** Copied to ~/.bash_profile

- ✔ **/etc/skel/.bashrc:** Copied to ~/.bashrc

- ✔ **/etc/skel/.bash_logout:** Copied to ~/.bash_logout

/etc/skel/.bash_profile may be missing if you're running SuSE Linux. If you want to change a login (or logout) script inherited by new users, change the script in /etc/skel. That way, when you create a new user account, Linux copies the modified script into the spankin' new home directory.

Now you know how the Linux login and logout scripts work. Whenever you feel a need to modify a login (or logout) script, be sure to ask yourself *whom* you want to affect and *when* your code needs to run.

Customizing Your Autostart File

If you're like us, each time you log in to your graphical desktop (KDE or GNOME), you launch a few handy programs: xmms to play some music, Evolution to read e-mail, and Mozilla to surf the Web. Wouldn't it be nice if Linux started those programs automatically, every time you logged in to your desktop?

Meet Autostart. Autostart is the KDE way to have your desktop ready for you every time you log in — no extra keystrokes or mouse clicks are required. KDE autostarts the programs you need and has them waiting for you on your desktop.

Autostart and the login scripts described earlier are somewhat related: They both prepare your environment for you. Login scripts set up your command line environment. Autostart sets up your graphical environment the way you like it.

Autostart is easy to set up and change. Just open a few browser windows and surf and drag, and with a few clicks, Autostart is up and running. To remove something from the Autostart menu, just drag the icon to the Trash.

To arrange your desktop with Autostart, follow these steps:

1. **Double-click the Start Here icon on the desktop to open Konqueror.**

2. **Surf to the Autostart directory:**

   ```
   /home/username/.kde/Autostart
   ```

    If you can't see your .kde directory, you can find it by choosing View⇨Show Hidden Files.

3. **Double-click the Start Here icon again to open another Konqueror window.**

   Now the fun starts!

4. **In the second Konqueror window, start surfing for the programs you want to see on your desktop.**

   Start in the Applications directory, where you'll find your tools (and games) in the appropriate folders.

5. **When you find a program that you want on your desktop at login, grab the icon and drag it to the Autostart folder.**

   When you drop it, a little dialog opens.

6. **In the dialog, choose Link Here.**

   The icon now appears in the Autostart folder.

7. **Repeat Steps 5 and 6 to add additional icons if you want.**

   That's all there is to it. When you reboot, your tools are there waiting for you!

To remove startup programs, open the Autostart folder again and drag the icons you don't want to the Trash. You're just throwing away links, so the originals are still there if you need them.

Technique 9

Making History (Work for You)

Save Time By

- ✔ Using history to recall previous commands
- ✔ Including the history command number in your bash prompt
- ✔ Filtering your history file to prevent accidents
- ✔ Reusing complex command lines

Like any typical Linux user, you likely have a small core of commands, directories, and files that you work with. The bash shell keeps track of every command that you type in the history list — including those commands that you use most frequently. You can take a peek at your history list in a file named ~/.bash_history, where, by default, bash stores the most recent 1,000 commands.

If you know how to move in and out of the history list with ease, history can save you a lot of keystrokes. With Linux, you can use the history list to recall previous commands, modify them if you need to, and execute them again without all that typing (and all those typing mistakes).

In this technique, we show you how to use the history file to save time at the command line. Less typing = fewer mistakes. Fewer mistakes = more commands that work the first time. More commands that work the first time = more time left for other things that you'd rather be doing.

Navigating the History List

To see the history list, type history and press Enter. With the history list ready and waiting for you, you can move through it in all sorts of ways. This section explains the different ways to get to the command you need — quickly. Table 9-1 gives you an overview of your options and when it's best to use them.

Scrolling

You can scroll through the list by using the up- and down-arrow keys:

- ✔ **Up arrow:** Recalls commands starting with the most recent and moving towards the oldest. For example, press the up arrow once to see the previous command and press it again to see the command before that.

TABLE 9-1: NAVIGATING HISTORY QUICKLY

Navigation Method	When It's Useful
Scrolling	Scroll through your history when you know that the command you're looking for is close by. If you have to scroll through more than five or six commands to find the one you want, use a different method.
Recalling by command number	If you include the history command number in your bash prompt (see Technique 4), you can recall a specific command *by number*. That works great if you can see 20 or more commands on your screen at once.
Searching	If the command you're looking for is *not* close by (you've executed a number of commands since the one you want to recall), press Ctrl-R to search for commands that contain a specific pattern. We show you how in "Searching through history."

✔ **Down arrow:** Moves in the opposite direction — it starts at the current command and moves towards the most recent. (You can't use the down-arrow key until you've used the up-arrow key. The down arrow won't anticipate your next move and make up a command for you . . . we wish it did.)

After you find the command that you want, change it if you need to and then press Enter.

Summoning a command by number

Each command is assigned a number when it's placed in the history list. (The first command is command 1, and the numbers increase from there.) When you type `history` and press Enter to see the history list, you also see that a number precedes each command:

```
$ history
53   ssh louvre
54   ssh versailles
55   pwd
56   ls -l
57   rm *.tmp
58   mail franklin
59   history
```

You can use the command number to recall a specific command. Just type an exclamation point (!) and follow it with the number of the command that you want to recall. For example, to recall the `ssh` command in freddie's history, you would enter the following:

```
$ !54
ssh versailles
[freddie@versailles]
```

If you want to use command numbers to refer to your history list, we recommend including the command number in your bash prompt; just include `\!` in `$PS1`. See Technique 4 for more information.

Searching through history

You can also ask bash to search through the history list on your behalf. Press Ctrl-R to start an incremental search. As you type each character, bash recalls the most recent command that includes the characters you've entered. For example, given the command history for `freddie`, an incremental search for `ssh` would go like this:

1. **Press Ctrl-R.**

The prompt changes from `[freddie@bastille]` to `(reverse-i-search)''`:

2. **Type** `s` **(the first character in** `ssh`**).**

bash finds the most recent command that includes an `s` (which is `history`), and the prompt changes to

`(reverse-I-search)'s': hi`s`tory`

3. **Type** `s` **again (the second letter in** `ssh`**).**

bash finds the most recent command that includes `ss` (which is `ssh -A versailles`), and the prompt changes to

`(reverse-I-search)'ss': `s`sh -A versailles`

4. If you want the most recent ssh command (ssh versailles), **just press Enter. If you want an earlier** ssh **command (**ssh louvre**), press Ctrl-R to tell bash to keep looking.**

It's easy to make mistakes while you're getting familiar with the history command. You can save a lot of time if you ask bash to show you each command *after* expansion but *before* the command is executed. The histverify shell option does the trick; just add shopt -s histverify to your ~/.bashrc file.

When you're comfortable with the history feature, you may want to turn off histverify. You can still press Esc and then Ctrl-E to preview your command line after expansion.

Customizing the History List

bash gives you a lot of control over the history list. To customize the history list for how you work, you can modify the defaults and filter out commands that just get in your way.

Adjusting key default settings

Here are the defaults that you'll likely want to modify:

✔ To adjust the number of commands that bash remembers, use $HISTSIZE.

✔ To set the number of commands that bash remembers from session to session, use $HISTFILESIZE.

✔ To change the location of the saved history file from the default (~/.bashrc), modify the $HISTFILE environment variable.

See the previous technique (Technique 8) to find out how to make your preferences permanent so they take effect every time you log in.

Filtering the history list

You can also filter out certain commands from the history list. After you've used the history feature awhile, you'll probably notice that some commands really don't belong in the history list. Here are a few examples:

✔ It's redundant to maintain the history command itself in the history list.

✔ It's unnecessary to record exit commands. (The exit command will log you out of the shell.)

✔ It's a little dangerous to keep rm commands (or other data-destroying commands) in your history list because you might recall them by accident.

You filter out those nasty (or just plain annoying) commands with the $HISTIGNORE variable. Set $HISTIGNORE to a colon-separated list of patterns to exclude from the history list. To filter out the commands we just mentioned, use this:

```
$ export HISTIGNORE="history:exit:rm *"
```

You may also want to filter out repeated commands. To do so, include the magic character & in $HISTIGNORE:

```
$ export HISTIGNORE="&:history:exit:rm *"
```

Occasionally, you'll type in a command that you know you don't want stored in the history list (maybe you're restoring files from an archive and you don't want to risk doing it again later by accident). To exclude from the history list any command that starts with a space or tab, add the pattern [\t]* to $HISTIGNORE (be sure to include the space between [and \):

```
$ export HISTIGNORE=
   "[ \t]*:&:history:exit:rm *"
```

Now, whenever you type in a command that you want to exclude from the history list, just put a space (or a tab) at the beginning of the command line.

Executing Commands Quickly with History Variables

$HOME is the name of your home directory, $PWD is the name of your current working directory, and so on. The history command adds a few more variables to the mix. The history variables let you treat a previous command, or part of a previous command, as a variable. Master the use of these automagic variables, and you'll save time by not having to spot and fix typing mistakes.

 For a quick refresher course in automagic variables, check out Technique 7. It tells you about the predefined variables that bash makes available for your use.

 Most variable names in bash start with a $ character, but the history variable names all start with !.

The !! variable contains the text of the last command. If you type !! at the command line, bash reexecutes your last command:

```
$ ps
  PID TTY          TIME CMD
 5562 pts/4    00:00:00 bash
12442 pts/4    00:00:00 ps
$ !!
  PID TTY          TIME CMD
 5562 pts/4    00:00:00 bash
12464 pts/4    00:00:00 ps
```

 Of course, if you all you want to do is reexecute the previous command, you'd probably just press the up-arrow key and then Enter rather than use !!. The real timesaving advantage of !! is that it contains the *text* of the

previous command, which you can use to create new commands. If you have a complex command that you use frequently, you can save that command into a file with a meaningful name and save yourself the effort of re-creating the command the next time you need it.

Here's an example of how you can use !! to create new commands. You can use the tar command to move a directory structure, but the syntax of the command is a bit hairy:

```
$ tar -cf - * | (cd $DST ; tar -xf - )
```

After you've executed that command, use !! to recall the command and save it to a file:

```
$ echo "!!" > $HOME/bin/movedir
$ chmod u+x $HOME/bin/movedir
```

The next time you want to move a directory, just type movedir and press Enter.

Here are some other handy tricks you can do with automagic variables:

✔ **Dial up a command number quickly.** In Technique 4, we show you how to include the history command number in your bash prompt. Here's the payoff. You can refer to a command by its command number with !*n*. If you display the history command number in your prompt, you can easily recall complex commands by number.

```
[1028]# w -hsf
franklin   :0      2:23m Chromium
georgette  pts/1   0:02m mailx
freddie    pts/2   0:0s  w -hsf
[1029]# killall Chromium
[1030]# !1028
franklin   :0      0:01m bash
georgette  pts/1   0:02m mailx
freddie    pts/2   0:0s  w -hsf
```

✔ **See your command before you execute it.** The Esc, Ctrl-E trick works with history variables, too. To see your command after variable expansion but before execution, just press Esc followed by Ctrl-E:

```
[1031]# !1029 (now press Esc Ctrl-E)
[1031]# killall Chromium
```

✔ **Peel off parts of commands with word designators.** You can also refer to *parts* of a previous command by adding a *word designator* to the end of the history variable. The most useful word designators are $ to refer to the last argument in a command, and * to refer to all arguments. For example, to create a new directory and then move there, use this:

```
$ mkdir /usr/local/src/coolcode
$ cd !!$
$ pwd
/usr/local/src/coolcode
```

Table 9-2 shows the complete list of history variables. Remember that you can include a word designator after the variable name to refer to part of a command.

TABLE 9-2: HISTORY VARIABLES

Variable	Meaning
!!	Previous command
!n	Command number n
!-n	Current command number minus n commands (!-1 is the previous command, !-2 is the command before that, and so on)
!$text$	Most recent command that starts with $text$
!?$text$	Most recent command that includes $text$

Speaking the lingo

Seasoned propeller-heads pronounce ! as "bang," not "exclamation point." So, !! is pronounced "bang bang." The * character is pronounced "splat." You can, of course, combine these to come up with witty phrases like "bang bang splat." If you enter a room where people are using language like this, back away slowly. . . .

Technique 10

Keeping Your Life Simple with Aliases and Functions

Save Time By

✔ Using the predefined aliases that come with bash

✔ Making aliases for common commands

✔ Correcting your spelling with aliases

✔ Using functions to automate downloading and installing

An *alias* is a command line shortcut. Creating an alias means that you spend less time typing. You can create aliases that give meaningful names to obscure commands; provide extra safety when you're doing something dangerous; create an abbreviation for a long, complex command; or just correct typing mistakes.

A *function* is a series of commands designed to perform a task. Functions can work with aliases to make it easy to automate tedious and time-consuming tasks. A function can be one or two lines long, or can grow into extremely complex programs that involve user interaction and error checking. In this technique, we include functions that make it easy to monitor your system with a few quick keystrokes and automate the complex task of exploring and unzipping archives.

In this technique, we've included some of our favorite aliases and functions. Without them, we'd be correcting our spelling all day long. Use them or create your own from our examples to save keystrokes and time at the command line.

Viewing Your Aliases

Viewing your aliases is simple. bash is often configured with a few predefined aliases, so you can test this command even if you haven't created any user-defined aliases yet. To view the aliases in your shell, just type alias and press Enter:

```
$ alias
alias l.='ls -d .* --color=tty'
alias ll='ls -l --color=tty'
alias ls='ls --color=tty'
alias vi='vim'
```

You may see a few more (or less) depending on which Linux packages you've installed. The first three aliases in the preceding list provide shortcuts for common variations of the ls command, which you can see in Table 10-1.

TABLE 10-1: THE LS SHORTCUTS

Type	bash Expands To	To Do This
l.	`ls -d .* --color=tty`	List directory names and hidden files (files whose names start with a . [period]) and colorize the on-screen output
ll	`ls -l --color=tty`	Display a detailed directory listing (in color)
ls	`ls --color=tty`	Display the content of a directory in short format (in color)

The fourth predefined alias is there for old UNIX users who are accustomed to using the `vi` editor. Linux doesn't include `vi` anymore, but it does include a much-improved replacement called `vim`. That old habit of typing in `vi` now starts the new program, `vim`.

These are just a few of the timesaving aliases that you may find in your shell. Read on to find out how to create a few aliases yourself.

Creating Simple Timesaving Aliases

Creating a new alias is easy. Here's an example that creates an alias to fix our most common typing error:

```
$ alias pdw=pwd
```

Now, whenever we want to know our current working directory and we accidentally type in `pdw`, bash helps out by translating the typo into the correct `pwd` command.

bash expands an alias only if it's the first word in the command line. Some of our favorite aliases fix spelling mistakes, create shortcuts, and help us out when we're forgetful.

These are some common spelling corrections you might want to include in your alias list:

```
alias pdw=pwd
alias mroe=more
alias fiel=file
```

You may want to add an alias that translates old familiar commands into Linux form:

```
alias dir="ls -l"
```

Navigational aliases are handy, too:

```
alias up="cd .."
```

You can create aliases for commonly used (but cumbersome) commands, such as unpacking tarballs:

```
alias unpack="tar -zxvf "
```

To display a list of programs that have open network connections (for example, Web browsers or streaming audio), create this alias:

```
alias netcon="netstat -p | grep -v'^unix'"
```

Create an alias that protects you against accidents. For example, the `rm` command (remove file) usually does its work without any more input from you. But, if you include a `-i` on the command line, `rm` asks you to confirm each file that it wants to delete. That can be a lifesaver if you ever type `rm * .tgz` instead of `rm *.tgz`. (The extra space after the * in the first command tells `rm` to delete everything in your directory — which is probably not what you wanted.)

```
alias rm="rm -i"
alias cp="cp -i"
alias mv="mv -i"
```

Turning dangerous commands into safe commands can save you a lot of time. Most users would agree that restoring from a backup is not an enjoyable way to spend an afternoon.

To save your aliases, use your favorite editor to add them to the ~/.bashrc file. This way, each time you log in, your aliases are there when you need them. To add system-wide aliases, check out Technique 8.

Using Aliases for Complex Commands

You can also create aliases that execute complex commands. For example, the following alias converts all GIF files in the current directory into PNG form:

```
alias cnv='for fi in *.gif; do giftopnm
  $fi | pnmtopng > ${fi%%.gif}.png; done'
```

Aliases make it easy to create customized commands that are preconfigured with the arguments and options that you most frequently use. The find command is a great candidate for an alias or two because it's such a complex command (see Technique 12). Here are two aliases that do the heavy lifting for you:

```
alias f='find . -name'
alias fi='find . -iname'
```

After defining these aliases, you can search for a file (by name) like this:

```
$ f myfile.sh
./tmp/myfile.sh
```

Or, use the second alias to search for a filename without regard to letter case:

```
$ fi myfile.sh
./tmp/myfile.sh
./work/MyFile.sh
```

Viewing your alias

When bash sees an alias name at the beginning of the command line, it replaces the alias name with the body of the alias. Normally, the substitution happens behind the scenes, and you can't see it. If you want to see the substitution before you press the Enter key, just press Esc-E. For example, if you type fi myfile.sh and then press Esc-E, bash replaces your command line with find . -name myfile.sh.

Anything that could legally follow the alias body can follow the alias name. This means that you can include additional options on the command line when you use an alias. For example:

```
$ f myfile.sh -ls
819 8 -rw-rw-r-- 1 freddie freddie 5104
   Feb 26 06:57 ./tmp/myfile.sh
```

bash aliases have one weakness: You can't move command line arguments to other parts of the command. For example, consider this alias:

```
alias gf="find . -type f -print0 | xargs
  -0 -e grep -n -e "
```

The gf alias combines find and grep to search for specific text in all the files in a directory tree. You can use the alias like this:

```
$ gf Martini
./recipes/drinks.txt:200: the perfect
   Martini
./spystories/bond.html:22: I prefer my
   Martinis shaken, not stirred
```

The gf alias works great as long as you want to search *every* file in a directory tree, but what if you want to search through .txt files and ignore .html files? You can't do that with an alias because the -name qualifier has to go in the middle of the command line; it can't be at the end. Instead, you need a function, which we explain how to create in the next section.

Automating Tedious Tasks with Functions

A bash function is like an alias on steroids. A function has none of the restrictions of an alias. You can execute many commands within a bash function, and you can pass arguments to a function and use those arguments wherever you need them.

Filtering file searches by file type

Here's another version of gf, this time written as a function instead of an alias:

```
function gfn ()
{
  find . -name "$2" -print0 | xargs -0 -e
  grep -n -e $1
}
```

This function, which we've called gfn to distinguish it from the gf alias, expects two arguments. The first argument is a filename pattern, such as "*.c", that specifies which files you want to search. The second argument to gfn is the text that you want to search for. If you want to search through all the files in your current directory, just use the pattern "*" (the double quotes are important). Now you can search for text in .txt files like this:

```
$ gfn Martini "*.txt"
./recipes/drinks.txt:200: the perfect
  Martini
```

 The $1 variable holds the first command line argument (Martini), and $2 holds the second ("*.txt"). With a function, you can use the command line arguments wherever you need them. (With an alias, the arguments get tacked onto the end of the command line.)

Automatic downloading

In its most basic form, a function is a name that you give to a sequence of one or more commands. Functions are perfect for automating tasks that you find yourself doing over and over again. If you often download, configure, and build software from the Web, you can save time by creating a simple function to automate that task:

```
function loadcode ()
{
  wget -q -O - $1 | tar -zxvf -

  cd $(basename $1 .tar.gz)

  ./configure

  make
}
```

The loadcode function expects a single argument, the URL for a tarball that you want to download and install. To use this function, open your favorite editor, type the text for the loadcode function as shown, and save your changes to ~/.funcs.sh (which is just a random filename we're using for this example). Now, use the source command to install loadcode into your shell:

```
$ source ~/funcs.sh
```

Next, find a package that you want to install and then run the loadcode function like this:

```
$ loadcode
  ftp://ftp.gnu.org/gnu/barcode/barcode-
  0.98.tar.gz
barcode-0.98/
barcode-0.98/CVS/
barcode-0.98/ChangeLog
barcode-0.98/COPYING
barcode-0.98/Makefile.in
barcode-0.98/INSTALL
barcode-0.98/barcode.h
...
```

The loadcode function has four commands inside it. The first command uses wget to download the tarball and feeds the download to tar for unpacking. When you unpack a tarball like barcode-0.98.tar.gz, the content is stored in a subdirectory named barcode-0.98; the second command moves into that directory. The last two commands do the GNU-install two-step: `configure` (in this case, with all the default options) and `make`. When `loadcode` completes, just give yourself superuser privileges and do a `make install`.

`loadcode` is just a name that you've given to a sequence of commands. The commands execute one after the other, and if something goes wrong, the script just keeps going. You can improve this function by adding a bit of error checking:

```
function loadcode ()
{
    if ( wget -q -O - $1 | tar -zxvf - )
    then
      cd $(basename $1 .tar.gz) || return 1
      ./configure && make
    else
      echo "Can't download $1"
    fi
}
```

Now if something goes wrong, `loadcode` fails instead of continuing on its merry (and misleading) way. The new version of `loadcode` shows three ways to check for error conditions:

- ✔ The first command is now wrapped inside an `if` statement. If the `wget` or `tar` commands fail (that is, if they exit with a result code of 0), `loadcode` jumps to the `else` clause and displays a friendly error message. If the `wget` and `tar` commands succeed, `loadcode` jumps into the `then` clause.

- ✔ The `cd` command can fail if the tarball that you're unpacking doesn't follow the usual naming convention. To catch that sort of problem, `loadcode` uses the `||` (logical or) operator to exit if the `cd` command fails. You can read that command as "either `cd` successfully or return 1."

- ✔ The `configure` command can also fail if you don't have all the prerequisites for the package you're installing. In this case, `loadcode` uses the `&&` operator to catch a configuration failure. You can read that command as "`configure` and, if that succeeds, `make`."

Monitoring Your System in a Snap

So far, you've seen functions and aliases designed to work with the command line, but you can also spawn graphical programs from the command line. Here is an alias that spawns a new `xterm` window that displays the output of the `top` command (sort of a build-it-yourself system monitor):

```
alias xtop="xterm -e top &"
```

After defining this alias, just type `xtop` to open a new window that runs the `top` command (see Figure 10-1).

If you want to run a program that has a more complex command line, just define a function. For example, the following function opens a new window that displays the last few lines of a file and continues to display new text as it's added to the file:

```
function xtail ()
{
  xterm -e "tail -f $1" &
}
```

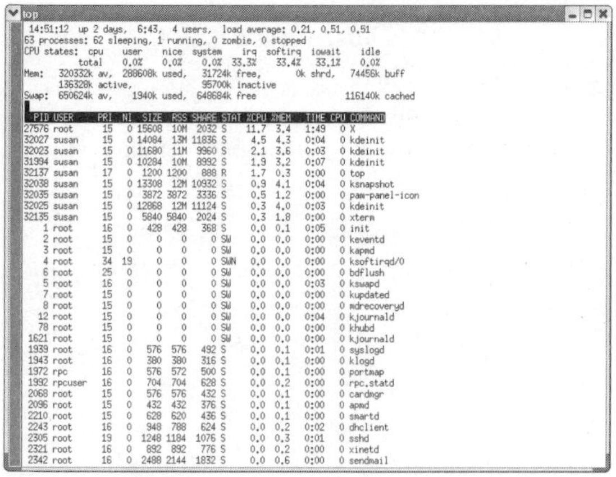

• **Figure 10-1: Running** top **in its own window.**

If you have superuser privileges, you can use xtail to watch the system log file:

```
# xtail /var/log/messages
```

Un-tarring the Easy Way

You can also save time by creating self-adjusting functions that adapt to command line arguments.

You know that the tar command (at least the GNU version of tar) can handle uncompressed, gzip-compressed, and bzip2-compressed archives. It's easy to create a wrapper function that invokes tar with the right set of flags based on the archive that you give it. The tarls function (see Listing 10-1) uses the file command to determine whether the given archive is compressed and, if so, which compression method was used. tarls is much longer than the other functions in this technique, so we've included two timesaving features in this listing:

✔ **Local variables that hold intermediate results:** You *could* rewrite this function without the local variables, but it would be much more time-consuming to maintain.

✔ **Comments that help future maintainers understand our rationale:** bash syntax can get awfully cryptic, and you'll save yourself a lot of time in the future by commenting your code now.

LISTING 10-1: CHOOSING THE RIGHT PROGRAM BASED ON FILE TYPE

```
function tarls ()
{
  # Figure what type of file we are working with.

  local filetype       # Output from the file command
  local tartype        # $filetype without filename
  local compresstype   # First word from $tartype
  local tarflags       # Flags given to the tar command

  # Given an argument like:
  #   icons.tgz
  # filetype will contain
  #   icons.tgz: gzip compressed data

  filetype=$(file "$1" )

  # Now strip the leading filename
  # from $filetype, leaving
  #   gzip compressed data
```

```
tartype=${filetype#$1:}

# Finally, grab the first word
# from $tartype, leaving
#    gzip

compresstype=$(echo $tartype | cut -d ' ' -f 1 )

case $compresstype in
    gzip)  tarflags=-ztvf;;
    bzip2) tarflags=-jtvf;;
    POSIX) tarflags=-tvf;;
    *)     echo "Unknown archive type"; return 1;;
esac;

tar $tarflags $1
}
```

Part II

Getting the Most from Your File System

The 5th Wave   By Rich Tennant

"So far he's called up a cobra, 2 pythons, and a bunch of skinks, but still not the file we're looking for."

Technique 11

Sharing Files and Printers in a Windows World

Most networks sport an assortment of computers. A few Linux machines, a couple of Windows machines, and a Mac or two are combined to create a network that is fast, versatile, and user friendly. We're not trying to suggest that Linux isn't the best thing since sliced bread, but in reality, a complete conversion to a Linux-only network isn't always possible. Sometimes, the Penguin just has to learn how to get along with Windows.

The need to share data across a network is nothing new, but with more networks being made up of assorted machines, the open-source software movement has grown to include a lot of excellent (and might we add, free) software that knows how to deal with data sharing — programs that let you share data and hardware across your network painlessly and fast.

In this technique, we show you how to share data and printers across your network. Saving time, saving money . . . all in all, creating a friendlier world.

What Is Samba?

Most people think of the Brazilian dance when they hear the word *samba*. We prefer to think of the triplochiton scleroxylon (commonly known as the Samba tree), a west African tree having axillary cymose panicles. We have no idea what a cymose panicle is, axillary or otherwise.

In the Linux world, Samba is a suite of resource-sharing utilities included in most Linux distributions. You use Samba to share Linux file systems, directories, files, and printers with other hosts on your network. Samba is designed specifically to work with the Microsoft Windows file-sharing and printer-sharing features. Two hosts are involved in every Samba connection: The server makes a resource available to clients, and the client accesses the resource shared by a server. A Linux host can act as a client, as a server, or as both.

Under the hood, Samba clients interact with Samba servers by using a protocol called SMB (Server Message Block). SMB is also known as CIFS (Common Internet File System). A server can expose two kinds of resources: printers and shares. A *share* is a directory (and all the subdirectories underneath it). A printer is, well, a printer.

Samba has been around awhile, and it's very stable. You can use Samba to share resources even if you don't have any Windows computers in your network.

 Samba lets you *expose* resources to the rest of the world. We specifically chose the word *expose* to remind you that Samba can share secrets that you may not want to share. It's easy to make Samba reasonably secure, but it's also easy to make Samba insecure. See Technique 37 for some helpful tips about hardening your system against malicious (or accidental) abuse.

Getting Up and Running with Samba

Before you can use Samba to share printers, directory trees, or both, you have to do a little upfront work. The following sections help you check your installation and then enable Samba.

Checking whether Samba is installed

The first step in preparing to use Samba is making sure that you have all the parts installed. Samba is typically distributed in five separate packages, but the exact details vary by distribution:

- ✔ `samba-client` contains the software required to act as a Samba client.

- ✔ `samba` contains the software required to act as a Samba server.

- ✔ `samba-common` contains files required by both `samba` and `samba-client`.

- ✔ `samba-doc` contains the documentation for Samba.

- ✔ `samba-swat` is a browser-based configuration utility for Samba.

 If you want your computer to act as a Samba server (that is, if you want to expose data or printers located on your computer), you must install the `samba` (or `samba-server`) package. However, we recommend installing all the packages because it makes life a lot easier. If you install all four packages, your computer can act as a Samba client or a Samba server, and you'll have a nice configuration tool as well.

To find out if Samba is already installed on your Fedora host, open a terminal window and type in the following command:

```
$ rpm -q samba samba-client samba-common
  samba-swat samba-doc
```

SuSE aficionados should use the command:

```
$ rpm -q samba samba-client samba-doc
```

If you are running Mandrake Linux, type in:

```
$ rpm -q samba-server samba-client samba-
  common samba-swat samba-doc
```

If `rpm` reports that any packages are not installed, dig out your OS install media and install them.

Enabling Samba

Samba runs as a service process, hanging around in the background waiting for client requests. After you have Samba installed, you have to enable it to start the Samba server. If you're running Fedora, follow these steps to enable the Samba service:

1. **Open the GNOME or KDE main menu.**

2. **Choose System Settings⇨Server Settings⇨ Services.**

3. **Enter the superuser password if requested.**

4. **Scroll through the list on the left until you see the SWAT check box.**

5. **Select the SWAT box.**

That tells Linux to automatically start the SWAT service whenever you boot your machine. (See the next section for more on SWAT.)

6. **Scroll back up until you see the SMB service.**

7. **Select the SMB box next to SMB.**

This tells Linux to automatically start the SMB service whenever you boot your machine.

8. **Click Start (in the toolbar), and a window appears telling you that the SMB service has started. Click OK to close the window.**

9. **Click Save to save your changes.**

10. **Press Ctrl-Q to quit (or just close the dialog).**

If you're using Mandrake, start the services at the command line with the commands:

```
# /sbin/service smb start
# /sbin/service swat start
```

If you're using SuSE, you can start the services at the command line with the commands:

```
# /etc/init.d/smb start
# /etc/init.d/swat start
```

Now it's time for a little configuration work. Don't worry, configuring Samba is as easy as swatting flies.

Sharing Linux Resources with Other Computers (SMB Clients)

After you install and start Samba, as described in the previous section, you can start configuring all the computers so that they can share resources, which is what this section is all about.

Samba is controlled primarily by the `/etc/samba/smb.conf` configuration file. If you were to peek at that file immediately after you install Samba (which we don't recommend), you may find it a tad bit intimidating: It's nearly 300 lines long and has all sorts of options and parameters that you typically don't need.

Fortunately, Samba has a graphical configuration tool called SWAT that makes it much easier to manage Samba. SWAT runs a mini-HTTP server on your host (listening for connection requests on port 901) and manages the Samba configuration file (`/etc/samba/smb.conf`) and the Samba password file (`/etc/samba/smbpasswd`) for you.

The first time you run SWAT, it installs a new configuration file that exposes any printers installed on your Linux host along with the users' home directories. You still have to adjust the workgroup name (if necessary) and create Samba user accounts. Then you can share the resources on your Linux computer with other Windows and Linux computers on your network. The following sections contain all the details.

Adjusting the workgroup name and creating user accounts

Before a remote computer can access the data that you expose on your Linux host, the remote computer must prove its identity to Samba. Computers *authenticate* themselves by sending a workgroup name, a user name, and a password to your Samba server. Of course, you have to tell Samba which workgroup names and user names are valid and assign a password to each user account.

To adjust the workgroup name and create user accounts, follow these steps:

1. **Open your Konqueror browser.**

To open Konqueror, double-click Start Here on your desktop.

2. **To connect to SWAT, enter** `http://localhost:901` **in the Location field and press Enter.**

A dialog appears prompting you for a user name and password. You must log in as `root` and provide the superuser password. If you don't, SWAT allows you to log in, but you won't be able to do anything except read the documentation.

3. **Click Globals.**

4. **Scroll down to the Workgroup box.**

The default value for Workgroup is MYGROUP. If you already have a Windows workgroup, enter the workgroup's name here. If not, choose a name (MYGROUP is a reasonable choice) and type it into the Workgroup box.

5. **Click Commit Changes to write your changes to the** `/etc/smb.conf` **file.**

6. **Click Password.**

The password management page appears. This page lets you create new Samba users, delete them, and enable and disable their accounts. Use the top part of the page to manage the Samba server. The bottom part of the page (labeled Client/Server Password Management) lets you change passwords on *other* (client) hosts.

7. **Type your user name into the User Name field and enter a password into the New Password and Re-type New Password fields.**

SMB clients must provide the user name and password that you enter here before they can access the resources that you export (we'll show you how to share specific resources a little later in this technique).

8. **Click Add New User.**

9. **Click Enable User.**

That's it! If everything went well, Samba is up and running, and you can access your Linux home directory (~) from an SMB client. To verify that everything's working, follow these steps:

1. **Open a terminal window.**

2. **Type** `smbclient //localhost/$USER` **and press Enter.**

If you see a message like `Connection to localhost failed`, the Samba server is configured, but not actually running. In this case, log back into SWAT (with your Web browser), click Status, and then click Restart All.

3. **Type in the password that you assigned to your Samba account and press Enter.**

You're greeted with a new prompt (`smb: \>`) that indicates you're running the `smbclient` program, connected to your home directory. You can type `ls` to see a directory listing, `cd` to move to a subdirectory, and `help` for a complete command list. Type `exit` when you're finished.

The `smbclient` program is useful in a pinch (we use it just to make sure everything is configured properly), but you really want to mount your new share on another computer, which we cover next.

Giving a Windows machine access to your home directory

If your other computer is a Linux machine, sit tight, and we'll show you how to mount an SMB share in a few moments. If your other machine is a Windows host, follow these directions to mount the new share:

1. **On your Windows desktop, right-click My Computer or Network Neighborhood and choose Map Network Drive from the pop-up menu.**

2. **Type your host name and share name into the Folder field.**

Windows expects SMB share names to start with two backslashes, then the host name (or IP address) of the SMB server, a single backslash, and the share name. For example, if your Linux host is named `bastille` and you want to mount the home directory of user `franklin`, you would enter the folder name `\\bastille\franklin`.

3. Click Finish.

4. If prompted, enter your Samba user name and password and click OK.

After a short delay, a window appears (on your Windows desktop) displaying the contents of your Linux home directory. You can drag and drop files, copy them, print them, or create new ones. Just remember: The Samba-hosted files you see on your Windows computer are actually stored on your Linux computer.

Sharing Linux files and directories with other computers

The standard configuration that SWAT chooses exposes home directories (and all printers). SWAT makes it easy to create new SMB shares for other directories (even other devices) on your Linux computer. To share your CD drive with others, follow these steps:

1. To connect to SWAT, open your Web browser and jump to `http://localhost:901`.

2. Log in as user `root` when prompted.

3. Click Shares.

The share manager page appears.

4. Type `CD-Drive` into the field next to the Create Share button.

You can choose any name you like for the share name, but don't get *too* fancy. In particular, don't include a forward slash or a backward slash in your share name — SWAT will let you do it, but you won't be able to mount that share from another computer.

5. Click Create Share.

The share parameter page appears.

6. Enter a descriptive name (such as *Shared CD Drive*) in the Comment field.

7. Type `/mnt/cdrom` in the Path field (if you're running SuSE Linux, type `/media/cdrom` instead).

8. Click Commit Changes (near the top of the page).

Now you should be able to remotely access your CD drive from another computer. Note that you still have to mount the CD (`mount /dev/cdrom`) from your Linux host before others can see it. See the section, "Plugging In to Remote Data with Linux Programs Quickly" later in this technique for more details.

Hooking Everyone Up to the Printer

Samba can expose printers as easily as it shares files and directories. In fact, Samba automatically shares your Linux printers with anyone in your SMB workgroup. You can also access (from Linux) printers that are connected to Windows computers. In this section, we show you how to manage Samba printer shares.

Sharing Linux printers with SWAT

If you have any printers connected to your Linux computer (and you've configured them), Samba automatically shares them with other computers in your workgroup; you don't have to expose them yourself. Samba discovers the printers on your computer by reading the `/etc/printcap` file. Normally, you don't edit the `printcap` file yourself; you let a KDE or GNOME helper do that for you.

If you have a printer that you *don't* want to share, you can use SWAT to hide it from other computers:

1. To connect to SWAT, open your Web browser and jump to `http://localhost:901`.

2. Log in as user `root` when prompted.

3. Click Printers.

The printer manager page appears.

4. Click Choose Printer.

The printer parameters page appears.

5. Scroll to the bottom of the page and change Available to No.

6. Click Commit Changes.

Using a Windows printer from Linux

Using a remote printer makes life much easier when you're working on a network. Sharing resources saves a small company not only dollars, but also lots of time in potential maintenance. Sharing a printer means that if Freddie's printer breaks, he can use Roberta's printer and still get his work done on time without shuffling disks, data, or cables.

If you're accessing Windows-hosted resources from a Linux host, you don't need to install the Samba server — just the client. Now, with a few quick clicks, you'll have access to a network printer. Follow these steps:

1. Click the printer icon on your taskbar.

The GNOME Print Manager window opens (see Figure 11-1).

2. If you have no printers loaded, you're asked if you want to run the configuration tool. Click OK.

• **Figure 11-1: The GNOME Print Manager.**

3. You're prompted for the superuser password. Enter the password and click OK.

4. Click New.

After a short delay, the Add a New Print Queue dialog opens, as shown in Figure 11-2.

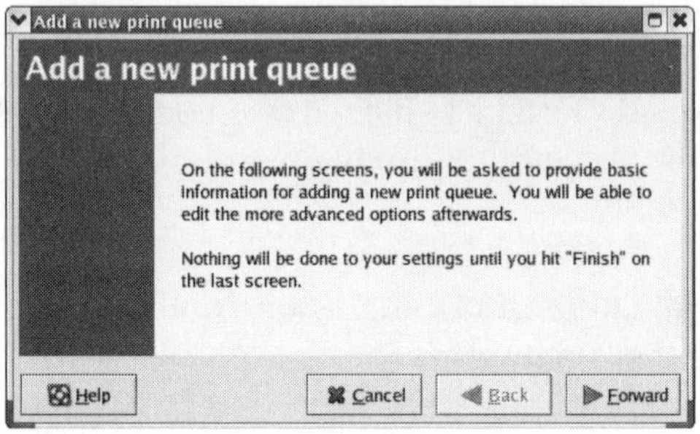

• **Figure 11-2: The Add a New Print Queue dialog.**

5. Click Forward.

6. When the next dialog opens, type in a name and a description for your printer. Click Forward again.

7. In the next dialog (see Figure 11-3), select the SMB queue type and highlight the network share that you want to use.

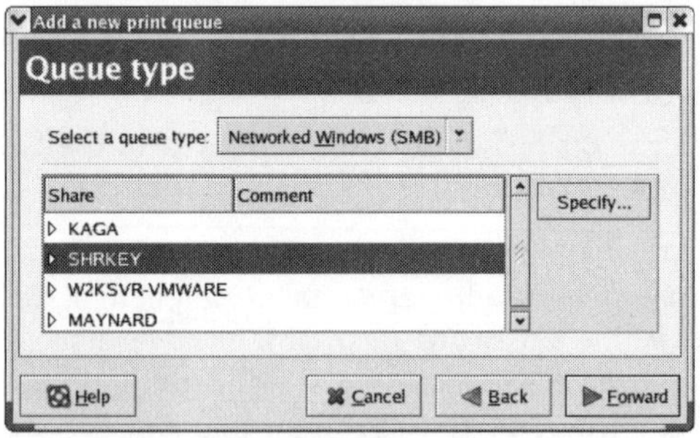

• **Figure 11-3: Select the SMB queue type and highlight the network share.**

8. Click Forward.

The Authentication dialog opens, as shown in Figure 11-4.

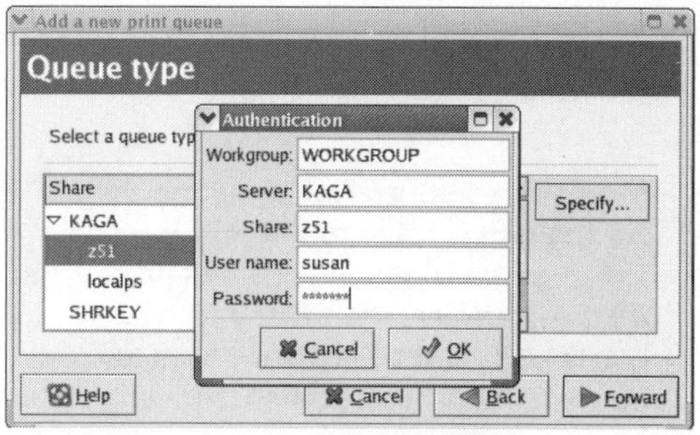

• **Figure 11-4: The Authentication dialog.**

9. Enter the user name and password you use to log into the Windows computer and click OK.

10. In the next dialog that opens, use the list box (initially labeled Generic) to choose your printer type and model.

11. Click Finish, and print a test page to verify that the printer is properly configured.

To print on the remote printer, just click the printer button usually found on the toolbar, or navigate through the File menu. The Print dialog opens to let you adjust the properties of your print job (see Figure 11-5).

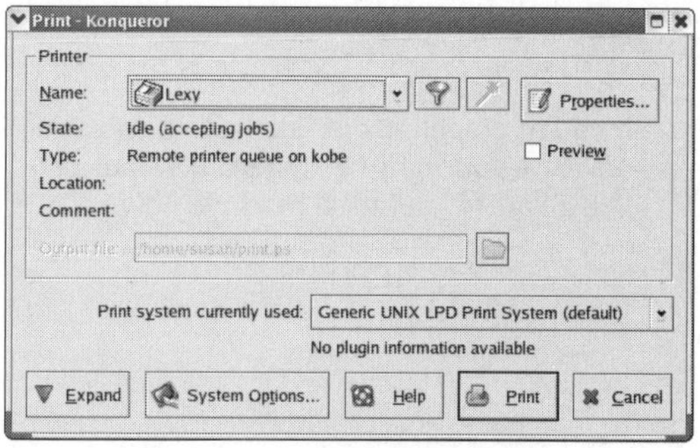

• **Figure 11-5: The Print setup dialog.**

Plugging In to Remote Data with Linux Programs Quickly

Mounting a remote directory on your local system is a great way to use your favorite Linux programs with

Windows data (or data stored on another Linux computer). Just add a quick line or two to the `/etc/fstab` file, and Linux mounts a network share with just one command.

In a typical Linux system, you have to hold superuser privileges to mount a file system. That's very secure, but not very convenient. If you want a non-privileged user to be able to mount his or her own home directory, you need to give some extra privileges to the SMB mount program (see Technique 27 for more information about file permissions and privileges):

1. At the command line, give yourself superuser privileges.

2. Change permissions for `smbmnt`:

```
chmod u+s /usr/bin/smbmnt
```

3. Change ownership for `smbmnt`:

```
Chown root /usr/bin/smbmnt
```

 Granting privileges to programs (instead of to users) can create security risks should some hacker discover a flaw in the `smbmnt` program. Be sure to check out Technique 57 to decide whether privileged programs are right for you.

Now, if you add a line or two to your `/etc/fstab` file, mounting a remote SMB share is a snap. To edit the file, follow these steps:

1. Open a terminal window and give yourself superuser privileges with the `su` command.

2. Type `kwrite /etc/fstab` and press Enter.

A KWrite window opens, with `/etc/fstab` displayed.

3. Add a line at the end of the file that reads like this:

```
//bastille/freddie  /mnt/bastille \
   smbfs   noauto,user   0    0
```

You need to customize the entry in this step as follows:

▶ The first field, `//bastille/freddie`, describes the device to be mounted. This is the computer name, followed by the remote directory name.

▶ The second field, `/mnt/bastille`, defines the mount point. This is the directory on your computer where the content of the remote directory will appear. The mount point can be anywhere in your directory tree that you would like your share to be, but you need to create the directory and set the privileges before you mount it.

▶ The third field is the file system type: `smbfs`. Many file system types work with Linux, but `smbfs` is the choice for what you're doing.

▶ The fourth field, `noauto,user`, describes the options to invoke for this mount. Set the `noauto` option to tell Linux not to mount this file system at boot time (you never want to auto-mount a network share), and set the `user` option to permit a nonprivileged user to mount the share.

▶ The fifth field works with the backup command. You don't want to be backing up this share remotely, so set it to `0`.

▶ The sixth field indicates whether the file system of the share should be checked at boot time. Again, pass on this option and set it to `0`.

4. **Save the file and close KWrite.**

You're ready to mount a share!

Need more information about the `fstab` file? For the fastest route to this info, type `man fstab` at the command line and press Enter. All the documentation is at your fingertips. Use the up- and down-arrow keys to scroll through the documentation, and when you're finished, press q to quit.

Need the documentation in a nicer format? Double-click the Start Here icon on your desktop and enter `man:/` in the Location line. You might need to search a bit for the documentation, but it's more readable and includes hyperlinks to other information related to your topic. Oh, and `fstab` is documented in Section 5.

Now, to mount the new share, just use the `mount` command at the command line:

```
$ mount //bastille/freddie
```

Access your new share just like it's a part of your local machine. You can work on it with all your favorite Linux programs or copy files back and forth effortlessly.

If you're graphically inclined, use Konqueror to navigate your new file system. It works just like a part of your local machine now.

Technique 12

Finding What You Need

Save Time By

- ✔ Locating files by name
- ✔ Finding files by their qualifications and attributes
- ✔ Finding out who's hogging the disk space
- ✔ Executing simple commands with `find` and `exec`
- ✔ Building complex commands with `find` and `xargs`

We've all been there — you create a new file, and then you forget where you put it and what you called it. How do you find it again? Fortunately Linux has a few options for finding lost data fast.

In this technique, we introduce you to the `find` command. `find` can search through your file system looking for files based upon a diverse set of qualifications that you can combine to create complex searches. With `find`, you can search for your file based on information like the modification date, the file size, ownership, and other file attributes. `find` also works with the `xargs` command to build complex commands based on search results. We also show you how to use the `locate` command to search through a system-maintained catalog of files and how to update that catalog to be sure it contains current entries.

We've also included a `diskusage` utility that you can use in conjunction with `find` to play "find the disk hog." If you need to free up resources, this is a quick way to find out who's using all the space.

This technique is all about finding files fast, with whatever information you have on hand. You know what you need to find. You might not remember it's name, but we'll help you find it anyway.

Finding Files with locate

Every night, an automatically scheduled program waltzes across your disk drive(s) and records all the filenames it can find in a database. The `locate` command searches through that database to find files with a particular name.

 If you find your installation of Linux is missing the `locate` command, you can add it by installing the appropriate RPM package: for SuSE, install `findutils-locate-version.rpm`; for Mandrake, install `slocate-version.rpm`; for Fedora, install `slocate-version.rpm`.

You can use `locate` to find data files, directories, or programs. For example, if you can't remember where the `ifconfig` program is located, just type `locate ifconfig` and press Enter. You instantly see a list of all the files on your system whose names include `ifconfig`:

```
$ locate ifconfig
/usr/share/man/man8/ifconfig.8.gz
/usr/share/man/de/man8/ifconfig.8.gz
/usr/share/man/fr/man8/ifconfig.8.gz
/usr/share/man/pt/man8/ifconfig.8.gz
/sbin/ifconfig
```

That's pretty close but not exactly what you were looking for. Save some time by using a regular expression (also known as a filename pattern) to narrow down the results:

```
$ locate -r "/ifconfig$"
/sbin/ifconfig
```

The `-r` flag tells `locate` to expect a regular expression. In this case, you want a list of all filenames where `/ifconfig` appears at the end of the name. (`$` means end of name; see `man -S 7 regex` for a complete list of valid regular expressions.)

 The `locate` command runs quickly because it searches through a database rather than the complete file system. It's a great tool for simple filename searches.

Like anything that's simple and easy, the `locate` command has a few drawbacks:

✔ The database becomes outdated quickly if you add, delete, or rename many files during the day. If you have superuser privileges, you can update the database yourself. Use the same command that the nightly update job executes:

/etc/cron.daily/slocate.cron.

✔ The database is incomplete because the nightly database update excludes several directories (`/tmp`, `/var/tmp`, `/usr/tmp`, `/afs`, and `/net`) and remote file systems.

If you don't have superuser privileges, or your search requirements are more complex than the simple filename matching that `locate` provides, you need to use the `find` command, which is discussed next.

Finding Files with find

The `find` command is one of the most complex and useful commands that you'll find in Linux. `find` searches through a file system looking for files that fit a pattern (which you define) and then performs an action on those files. The most frequently used `find` command searches for a file with a specific name, starting in the current directory:

```
$ find . -name drinks.txt -print ./recipes/
  drinks.txt
```

When you use the `find` command, you have to provide three pieces of information:

✔ **Location:** Where to start searching. Typically, you specify . to start searching in the current directory or / to start searching at the root of your file system tree. If you list multiple directory names, `find` searches in all those directory trees.

✔ **Qualifications:** Which files should be included in the result. In the example, freddie is looking for a file named `drinks.txt`. See the next section for details on handy qualifiers.

✔ **Actions:** What you want `find` to do when it locates a qualifying file. In the example, `-print` simply echoes the relative pathname of the file. See "Acting on What You Find," later in this chapter, for details on putting actions to good use.

Qualifying Your Search with the find Command

find gives you a wide variety of qualifiers, and this section delves into the more timesaving ones. For details on using qualifiers with find, see the preceding section.

Doing updated filename searches

Two of the most frequently used qualifiers are -name and -iname, both of which must be followed by a filename pattern:

- ✔ -name tells find to operate on any files that match the given pattern.

- ✔ -iname does the same except that it ignores case differences.

You can use the normal shell wildcards with -name and -iname. For example, -name "*.c" matches any filenames that end with .c. If you include wildcards, you must surround the filename pattern with quotes to prevent the shell from expanding them before find gets a chance to see it.

The -name and -iname qualifiers make find very similar to the locate command. locate searches through a database of filenames, whereas find searches through the file system. find gives you more up-to-date results but takes much longer to perform a thorough search.

Adding time-based qualifications

You can also search for files based on time of last access, content-modification time, or attribute-modification time. The content-modification time of a file is updated whenever you write to that file. The attribute-modification time of a file is updated whenever you make a change to the file's attributes (by changing ownership or permissions, for example).

Table 12-1 lists qualifications that select files based on their timestamps.

TABLE 12-1: QUALIFICATIONS THAT SEARCH FOR TIMESTAMPS

Qualification	What It Finds
-atime n	True if the file was last accessed n days ago
-amin n	True if the file was last accessed n minutes ago
-ctime n	True if the file's attributes were last changed n days ago
-cmin n	True if the file's attributes were last changed n minutes ago
-mtime n	True if the file's contents were last changed n days ago
-mmin n	True if the file's contents were last changed n minutes ago

To find files in your home directory (and all subdirectories) that were last changed a week ago, use this command:

```
$ find ~ -mtime 7 -print
```

If you run this command, you may be surprised by the results. -mtime 7 *does not* show you all the files modified in the previous seven days; it shows the files modified *exactly* seven days ago. To locate files modified in the previous seven days (yesterday, or the day before, or the day before that, . . .), specify -mtime -7 (note the minus sign in front of the 7), as follows:

```
$ find ~ -mtime -7 -print
```

You can read that command as "find files where the date of last modification is less than seven days ago." Now suppose you change the command to this:

```
$ find ~ -mtime +7 -print
```

You see a list of files whose dates of last modification are greater than seven days ago. You can find files modified within a range of dates by using both the + and - signs. For example, to find all files modified four or five days ago, use this command:

```
$ find ~ find . -mtime +3 -mtime -6 -print
```

Read this command as "modified more than three days ago but less than six days ago."

You can use the -atime qualifier to find unused (or at least not recently used) user files on your system:

```
$ find / -atime +90 -print
```

Filtering by file size

The find command also lets you filter files based on their size. The -size *n* qualifier selects any files whose size is *n*.

The + and - tricks that you can use for time qualifications work with -size qualifications, too: -size +n selects all files larger than *n,* and -size -n selects all files smaller than *n*. When you use -size *n*, you can specify *n* in terms of bytes, kilobytes, or 512-byte blocks:

- ✔ To specify a byte count, follow -size *n* with a c.

- ✔ To specify a number of kilobytes (1024 bytes), follow -size *n* with the letter k.

- ✔ The default unit is 512-byte blocks, but you can make your intention explicit with a suffix of b.

As find examines each file, it rounds the file's size up to the nearest unit (kilobyte or block) and *then* applies the qualifier. For example, -size 2k selects files between 1025 and 2048 bytes long.

Table 12-2 shows a few examples using the -size qualifier.

TABLE 12-2: EXAMPLES USING THE -SIZE QUALIFIER

Command	Result
-size 2048c	Files exactly 2048 bytes long
-size +2048c	Files 2049 bytes or larger
-size -2048c	Files smaller than 2048 bytes
-size 2k	Files between 1024 and 2048 bytes long
-size +2k	Files larger than 2048 bytes
-size -2k	Files smaller than 1025 bytes
-size +1k -size -3k	Files larger than 1024 bytes and smaller than 2049 bytes

The rounding that find performs can be confusing, so we've written a short shell function that translates a value like 2M (megabytes) or 3G (gigabytes) into the equivalent number of bytes. Listing 12-1 shows the unit function.

LISTING 12-1: THE UNIT FUNCTION

```
function unit ()
{
    # Extract the last character from
    # the first (and only) parameter.
    #
    # Given a value like 5M, the suffix
    # is the character 'M'

    suffix=${1: -1: 1}

    # Remove the suffix from the argument
    # and we should be left with number
    # units ('5' if we were given 5M)

    count=${1%%$suffix}

    case $suffix in
      K|k) echo $(expr $count \* 1024)c;;
      M|m) echo $(expr $count \*
      1048576)c;;
      G|g) echo $(expr $count \*
      1073741824)c;;
        *) echo $1"c"
    esac;
}
```

Use the `unit` function to make `find` behave a bit more predictably. For example, the following command

```
$ find ~ -size +$(unit 2M) -print
```

translates into

```
$ find ~ -size +2097152c -print
```

Press Esc-E to view the translated command line before you press Enter. (Notice that `unit` included the `c` suffix, which forces `find` to turn off its funky rounding trick.) The `unit` function translates kilobytes (`K` or `k`), megabytes (`M` or `m`), and gigabytes (`G` or `g`).

Joining qualifications with AND and OR operators

By joining qualifications, you can get more mileage out of the `find` command.

To quickly find large files that haven't been used in a while, combine `-size` and `-atime`.

For example, use the following command to search for files 5 megabytes or larger that haven't been used in the last 30 days:

```
$ find ~ -size +$(unit 5M) -atime +30
  -print
```

By default, `find` joins multiple qualifiers together with the AND operator. Given two qualifiers — `-size +$(unit 5M)` **and** `-atime +30` — a file qualifies only if it meets both criteria.

You can also join qualifiers with the OR operator. To find all files that are either empty or haven't been used in a while (or both), stick an `-or` between the qualifiers, like this:

```
$ find ~ -size 0 -or -atime +30 -print
```

With the `-or` operator, a file must meet either (or both) of the qualifiers to be selected. You can also use `-not` to reverse a qualifier (for example, `-not -size 0`) and `-and` to explicitly *and* qualifiers together. Use quoted parentheses to build complex expressions. For example, the following command finds large files (larger than 5M) that have not been accessed in the previous 30 days and adds empty files to the list as well:

```
find / "(" -size +$(unit 5M) -and -atime
  +30 ")" -or -empty -ls
```

The `-empty` qualifier is a synonym for `-size 0`.

Perusing commonly used qualifications

Table 12-3 shows the most commonly used qualifiers.

TABLE 12-3: COMMONLY USED QUALIFIERS

Qualifier	Result
`-name` *pattern*	Select files that match the given filename pattern.
`-iname` *pattern*	Select files that match the given filename pattern, ignoring differences in letter case.
`-regex` *expression*	Select files that match the given pathname regular expression (similar to `-name` except that `-regex` matches the entire path where `-name` matches only the filename).
`-iregex` *expression*	Select files that match the given pathname regular expression, ignoring differences in letter case (similar to `-iname` except that `-iregex` matches the entire path where `-name` matches only the filename).
`-atime [+|-]`*n* `-ctime [+|-]`*n* `-mtime [+|-]`*n*	Select files that have been accessed (`-atime`), attribute-changed (`-ctime`), or content-changed (`-mtime`) *n* days ago. If *n* is preceded by a +, select files last accessed more than *n* days ago. If *n* is preceded by a -, select files last accessed within that previous *n* days.

(continued)

TABLE 12-3 *(continued)*

Qualifier	Result

`-amin [+|-]n`
 `-cmin [+|-]n`
 `-mmin [+|-]n`
	Same as above except that *n* specifies minutes instead of days.

`-daytime`	Measure `-atime`, `-ctime`, `-mtime`, `-amin`, `-cmin`, and `-mmin` from the beginning of the current day rather than exactly 24 hours ago.
`-size [+|-] n`	Select files *n* bytes long. If *n* is preceded by a +, select files larger than *n*. If *n* is preceded by a -, select files smaller than *n*.
`-empty`	Select empty files and directories.
`-type filetype`	Select files of the given *filetype*. *filetype* may be b to select block devices, c to select character devices, d to select directories, p to select named pipes, f to select regular files, l to select symbolic links, or s to select sockets.
`-user username` `-group groupname`	Select files owned by the given *username* or *groupname*.
`-nouser` `-ngroup`	Select orphan files (that is, files owned by users or groups that no longer exist on your system).
`-perm [+|-]` *permissions*	Select files based on their permissions. The most useful values for *permissions* are `-perm +ug+s`; this matches any files that are setuid or setgid and could be used to impersonate other users (see Technique 57 for more information).
`-xdev`	Select files only on the given file system. Use this option to avoid searching other disk drives and remote file systems.

Acting on What You Find

As we mention earlier in "Finding Files with find," actions tell find what to do when it finds a qualifying file. The -print command that you've been tacking on the end of each find command displays the name of each qualifying file, but find can do a whole lot more than that. The following sections give you the timesaving highlights.

Cracking open a file's info with -ls

You can use the -ls action to see more details about each selected file:

```
$ find ~ -size +$(unit 5M) -print
/home/freddie/bigdatafile
/home/freddie/tmp/deleteme
```

```
$ find ~ -size +$(unit 5M) -ls
35525 8204 -rw-rw-r-- 1 freddie freddie
   8388608 Dec 20 09:52
   /home/freddie/bigdatafile
44201 6156 -rw-rw-r-- 1 freddie freddie
   6291457 Dec 20 09:52
   /home/freddie/tmp/deleteme
```

-ls gives you far more details than are provided by -print. -ls displays the following columns (from left to right):

- ✔ The file's *inode* number (a number that uniquely identifies each file within its file system)

- ✔ The number of 1K blocks consumed by the file

- ✔ The file's type and permissions

- ✔ The number of hard links to the file

- ✔ The file's owner

- ✔ The file's size (in bytes)

✔ The date and time of the most recent modification

✔ The file's name

Displaying specific info with -printf

In most cases, the -ls action gives you more information than you really need. You can use the -printf action to view only those nuggets of knowledge that you want. To use -printf, you have to follow the action with directives that specify the information you want to display. For example, take a look at the following command:

```
find ~ -size +(unit 5M) -printf %p %s %u
```

This command displays the file's complete pathname (%p), size in bytes (%s), and owner (%u), like this:

```
$ find ~ -size +$(unit 5M) -printf %p %s %u
/home/freddie/bigdatafile 8388608 freddie
/home/freddie/tmp/deleteme 6291457 freddie
```

-printf offers a wide variety of directives (see man find for a complete list), but we show you only a few of the more useful ones in Table 12-4.

TABLE 12-4: COMMON PRINTF DIRECTIVES

Directive	Meaning
-%p	Complete pathname of the selected file
-%f	Same as %p with the leading directory names stripped off
%h	Same as %p with the filename stripped off the end
%u	Name of the user who owns the selected file
%U	Numeric user ID of the user who owns the selected file
%s	Size of file (in bytes)

Checking disk usage by user

The -printf action is extremely useful when you want to feed the results from a find command into another program. With -printf, you can customize the output from a find command to fit the needs of the program that you're running. Listing 12-2 shows a shell script that summarizes disk usage by user.

LISTING 12-2: DISK USAGE

```
#!/bin/bash
# Filename: diskusage

# Create three arrays, each indexed by
    numeric user ID
#   $sizes[] will accumulate the disk
    space consumed by each user
#   $uids[] will store the numeric
    user ID for each user
#   $users[] will store the user name
    for each user

# The caller will send us lines of the
    form
#     numeric-user-id filesize username

while read uid filesize user
do
    # Find the current amount of space
    used by this $uid
    size=${sizes[$uid]:-0}

    # Add the space consumed by this
    file and store it back
    # in $sized[$uid]
    let sizes[$uid]=$filesize+$size

    # Store the numeric user ID and
    user name too
    uids[$uid]=$uid
    users[$uid]=$user
done

# We've now accumulated all of the disk
    space usage
# for the caller, display the results

for uid in ${uids[*]}
do
    printf "%15d\t%s\n" ${sizes[$uid]}
    ${users[$uid]}
done
```

To use the `diskusage` script, follow these steps:

1. **Open your favorite editor and type in the text shown in Listing 12-2.**

2. **Save your script to a file named** `diskusage` **in a directory that's included in your search path.**

   `/usr/local/bin` is usually a good place.

3. **Use** `chmod` **to make the file executable:**

   `chmod a+x /usr/local/bin/diskusage`

To use `diskusage`, use the `find` command to locate the files that you're interested in and use `-printf` to create the output required by `diskusage`:

```
$ find /home -type f -printf "%U %s %u\n"
  | diskusage
 211128211      franklin
    602579      1001
4525391478      root
8756011463      freddie
```

Whenever `find` locates a qualifying file, it feeds the owner ID, file size, and owner name to `diskusage`. `diskusage` adds up the disk space consumed by each user and prints the results when `find` stops feeding it. The nice thing about this combination is that you can select files so many ways with `find`, and no matter which qualifiers you choose, `diskusage` happily sums things up for you. For example, you can change the previous command to see disk space, by user, that hasn't been accessed within the last 30 days:

```
$ find /home -type f -atime +30 -printf
  "%U %s %u\n" | diskusage
   128211      franklin
   602579      1001
4000324962      root
 22315532      freddie
```

If you compare these results with the previous results, you'll see that although freddie is a disk hog, he's at least using the data that he's storing. User 1001, on the other hand, hasn't even logged in during the last month.

 When `diskusage` displays a numeric user ID instead of a user name, the user account has probably been deleted. This is a quick and easy way to find abandoned files and recycle disk space.

Executing commands with find

It's time to switch gears and look at a very powerful (and occasionally dangerous) feature of `find`: the `-exec` action.

You've seen that the `-print`, `-ls`, and `-printf` actions display information about selected files. The `-exec` action executes a program of your choosing with the files that `find` has selected. Suppose that you're a system administrator and one of your coworkers has recently left the company. Your task is to find all the files owned by that user (call him `ted`) and give them to user `franklin`. The `-user` qualifier will locate the files that you're interested in, and `-exec` will execute a command (in this case, `chown`) on each of those files:

```
$ find / -user ted -exec chown franklin
  '{}' ';'
```

This command may look a bit cryptic to you (it sure looks cryptic to us). `find` executes the `-exec` action once for each selected file. When `find` executes the command, it replaces {} with the name of the selected file. You must include a quoted semicolon at the end of the command (';'). You can probably imagine all sorts of uses for the `-exec` action — removing old files, moving certain files to other locations, fixing permissions, and so on.

 Never, never, never use the `-exec` action without first viewing the list of qualified files with `-ls` or `-print`. Never. Make sure that you know exactly which files will be acted upon.

To avoid running `find` twice (once to see which files are selected and again to execute the required commands), use the `-ok` action instead of `-exec`. When you use `-ok`, `find` asks if you want to execute each command. If you answer `y` (or `Y`, or `yes`, or `Yes`, . . .), `find` executes the command. If you answer anything else, `find` moves on to the next file.

When you select a large number of files, executing the `-exec` (or `-ok`) action on each file, one at a time, can be painfully slow. Many Linux commands can process multiple files in a single pass, and you can use `find` to produce the argument list for those commands.

Building Complex Commands with xargs

The `xargs` command builds long command lines for you. `xargs` reads filenames from the output of another command (like `find`) and builds commands by using those filenames. For example, look at the following command:

```
$ echo /tmp/icons.tar | xargs tar -tvf
```

`xargs` reads the filename from the `echo` command and constructs the new command:

```
$ tar -tvf /tmp/icons.tar
```

`xargs` isn't particularly useful when you need to process a single filename, but `find` usually produces a whole mess of filenames. To use `find` and `xargs` together, craft a `find` command that locates the files that you're interested in and use the action `-print0` to echo the selected filenames. Pipe the output of the `find` command to `xargs` like this:

```
$ find /home -user ted -print0 | xargs -0
  -e grep -n "secret password"
```

When you execute this command, find lists the names of all files owned by user `ted` and feeds that list to `xargs`, and `xargs` then constructs (and executes) a `grep` command for you. `xargs` tries to group many files into a single command. If you find the three files /home/ted/secrets, /home/ted/mail, and /home/ted/work, for example, `xargs` executes the command:

```
grep "secret password" /home/ted/secrets
  /home/ted/mail /home/ted/work
```

rather than three separate commands.

Technique 13

Moving Made Easy with Archives

Archiving data makes it easy to move multiple files with the same effort that it takes to move a single file. An archive is a file that *contains* other files. You can build an archive out of just about anything: text files, programs, pictures, audio files, and even other archives. Archives are easy to build, and you can compress an archive to help speed up data transfers. For example, a *tarball* is nothing more than an archive built with the `tar` command.

Using good tools to create archives saves time. In this technique, we introduce you to File Roller, a handy feature that's included with GNOME. With File Roller, you can not only create an archive, but also inspect an archive's contents before unpacking it. You can save time by choosing just the portions of archives that you need to unpack.

The `tar` command creates archives at the command line and works well with the RPM query commands and the `find` command. We show you how to use `tar` in powerful combinations to build complex, custom archives.

The `split` command can split large files or archives into bite-sized pieces for transferring. If a connection drops midtransfer, you can resend only the portion of the file that didn't make it. We also show you how to use checksums to make sure that your entire file got to its destination.

Every day is moving day on a computer, and doing a good job packing makes moving easier. Good labels on neat packages make it easier to find things when you need to unpack them again. In this technique, we show you tools and tricks that make moving easier.

Creating Archives with File Roller

You can e-mail multiple files just as easily as a single file when you bundle the files together in an archive. Creating compressed archives for e-mail attachments saves time and bandwidth for both the sender and the receiver.

If you're running the GNOME desktop, File Roller is probably installed automatically. If you need to add File Roller, you'll find it (in most Linux distributions) in an RPM package called `file-roller-version.rpm`. See Technique 17 for help installing RPM packages.

GNOME's File Roller is the easy way to browse and choose the files to include in an archive. To make a tarball using File Roller, follow these steps:

1. **Open the Main Menu and choose Run Command.**

   The Run Command dialog, shown in Figure 13-1, opens.

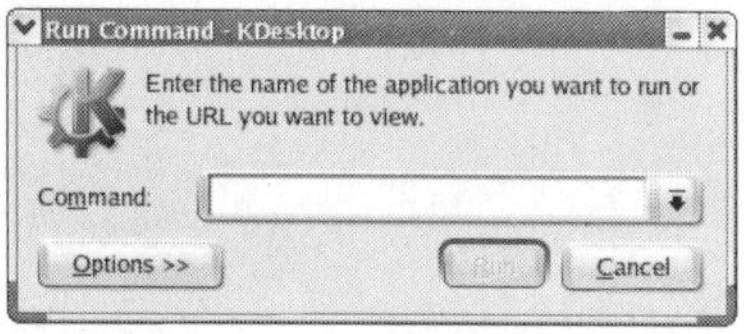

• **Figure 13-1: The Run Command dialog.**

KDE and GNOME auto-launch File Roller if you've configured your MIME database. (See Technique 3 for more information on MIME.)

2. **Enter `file-roller` in the Command field and click Run.**

   The File Roller window opens ready to build a tarball (see Figure 13-2).

3. **Click New on the toolbar to open the New Archive file chooser (see Figure 13-3).**

4. **In the Archive Type drop-down list, select the type you want to create.**

   In this case, choose the Tar Compressed with gzip option.

5. **Enter your tarball name in the Selection field and click OK.**

   Now it's time to add files to your archive.

6. **Click Add (on the toolbar) to open the file chooser window. Use the file chooser to browse directories for the files that you want to include and then add them to the tarball.**

   Double-click a selection to add it to the archive. To add additional files to an archive, click Add on the toolbar, and double-click the next file to be included.

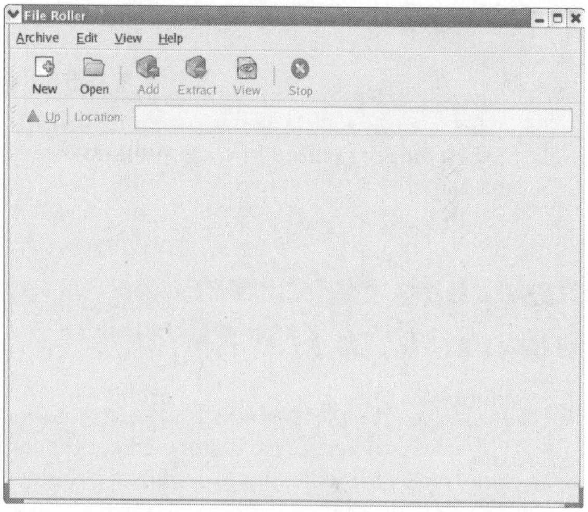

• **Figure 13-2: The File Roller window.**

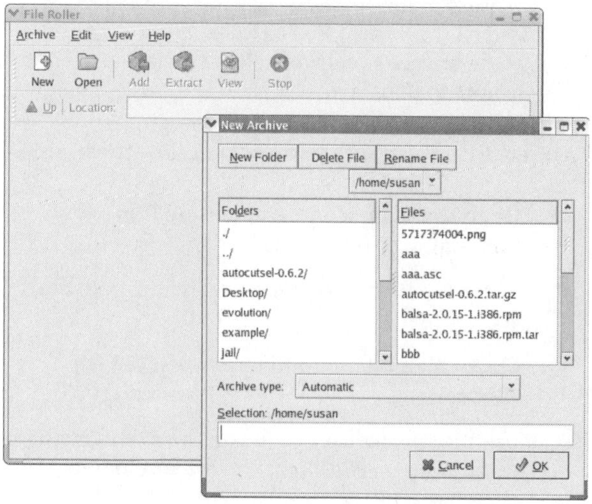

• **Figure 13-3: The New Archive file chooser.**

You can include a tarball in an archive, but it won't get any smaller. One serving of compression per file, please.

7. **When you're finished adding files to the archive, close the File Roller window.**

The archive is waiting for you in the directory you created it in, which is usually your home directory. Just attach the archive to your e-mail and send it off.

 Use File Roller to create archives to send via SSH or FTP. Multiple files are easier to manage when they're bundled, and compressing the data makes it travel faster.

Inspecting and Extracting Archives with File Roller

File Roller makes it easy to inspect and extract files from archives. With just a few quick clicks, you can see the contents of the files included in an archive or extract the portion of the archive you need.

 The File Roller is especially handy if you share data via e-mail. Use File Roller to check out the archive's contents before you take the time to unpack it.

To open an archive with File Roller, follow these steps:

1. **Open the Main Menu and choose Run Command.**

2. **Enter** file-roller **in the Command field and click Run.**

3. **Click Open on the toolbar to open the file chooser.**

4. **Use the file chooser to locate the archive you want to open. Highlight the archive name and click OK.**

The contents of the archive appear in the File Roller window.

After you open an archive, you can extract a file (or files) from it by following these steps:

1. **Highlight the file(s) in the list and click Extract.**

The Extract dialog opens, as shown in Figure 13-4.

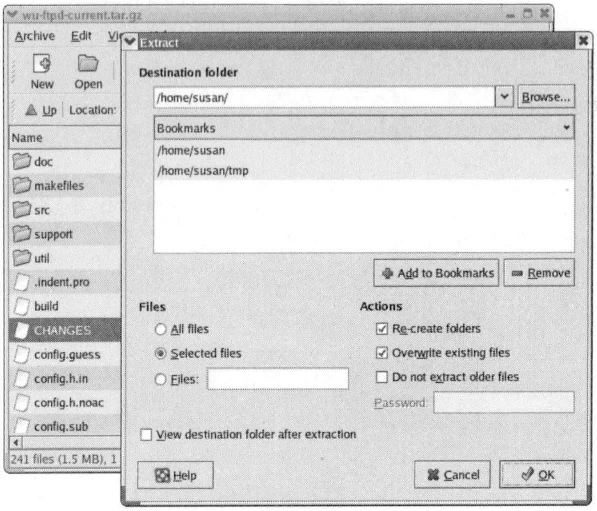

• **Figure 13-4:** The Extract dialog.

2. **In the Destination Folder field, type the name of the folder where you want to save the extracted files, or from the Bookmarks list, choose a bookmark to use for the destination.**

 Add often-used directories — such as ~/tmp — to the Bookmarks list. Later, when you need one of these directories, just double-click the directory to select it as the destination folder.

3. **If you highlighted more than one file before you clicked Extract in Step 1, choose from the following options in the Files area:**

   ▶ **All Files:** Unpack the entire archive.

   ▶ **Selected Files:** Extract the files highlighted on the previous screen (hold down Shift to select multiple files).

   ▶ **Files:** Specify files by name, or groups by using wildcards (such as *.png or *.txt).

4. **Check the Re-create Folders box to restore the folder structure.**

We've never encountered a case where we *didn't* want to re-create folders. If you don't select the Re-create Folders check box, all the subdirectories and their contents end up in your current directory. Cleaning up the unpacked pile of structureless files wastes time.

5. **Check the Overwrite Existing Files box to replace any file with a duplicate name in your folder.**

6. **Check the Do Not Extract Older Files box to preserve the most recent copy of the file.**

If the copy on your computer is more current than the archived copy, the older file is not extracted. This option works only if the Overwrite Existing Files option is checked.

7. **Check the View Destination Folder After Extraction box to open a file manager window with your newly unpacked archive.**

8. **When you're ready, click OK to unpack the file(s).**

If the destination folder doesn't already exist, File Roller asks if you want to create it.

Inspect suspicious-looking files that are included in a tarball before unpacking it. To do so, right-click the filename and choose View File from the drop-down menu to display the file's contents. If the file looks questionable, don't open it!

Adding Functionality to tar with Complex Commands

The File Roller enables you to quickly and easily build or unpack archives, but sometimes using the command line with the `tar` command is the way to go. The following sections explain how combining

the `tar` command with other functions can give you extra power when you need it.

Building archives from the command line

You can build simple archives (containing one file or many) with the `tar` command. Here is a basic `tar` command to create a gzip-compressed archive:

```
$ tar -zcvf archivename filestoarchive
```

If you want to archive multiple files, just list them at the end of the command line (separate the names with a space character).

Compressing an archive increases the time it takes to create the archive. If you don't need to transfer the file over the Web or if the data is already compressed (such as RPMs), skip the `-z` or `-j` options when you create the archive.

`tar` has a lot of powerful options, the most useful of which are listed in Table 13-1.

TABLE 13-1: USEFUL TAR OPTIONS

Option	What It Does
`-z`	Compress to (or uncompress from) gzip form.
`-j`	Compress to (or uncompress from) bzip2 form.
`-c`	Create an archive.
`-x`	Extract from an archive.
`-t`	Display a list of the files in the archive.
`-v`	Verbose — tell me what you're doing.
`-f file`	Write to (or read from) the archive *file*.

Enter `man tar` at the command line for a complete listing of `tar` options and flags.

The GNU man pages are handy, but they can be a bit overwhelming at times. Take a deep breath and remember that you can close the page at any time by entering `q`.

Archiving complex search results

Use the pipe character (|) to combine programs like `find` and `rpm` with the `tar` command to create archives that contain the results of complex searches.

Using `tar` with `find` can seem complex, but it is very useful. One example of a combined command is as follows:

```
$ find / -user freddie | tar -zcvf
    fredfiles -T -
```

This command finds all the files owned by the user Freddie and sends the output (the list of filenames) to the `tar` command. The `-T -` portion of the command instructs `tar` to read the list of filenames from its standard input (which, in this case, is the output of the `find` command) rather than from the command line.

For more in-depth information about using the `find` command, see Technique 12.

Backing up an installed package

Use `tar` with `rpm` to create a backup of an installed package. To back up an installed copy of the `webmin` package, use this command:

```
$ rpm -ql webmin | tar -cvf webminbackup
    -T -
```

 For more information about using `rpm` queries, see Technique 16.

Uprooting Entire Directory Trees with scp

Sometimes, you need to move more than a single file — you need to move an entire directory tree (a directory and all the files and subdirectories underneath it). When that's the case, use `scp` to get the job done quickly and easily. For example:

✔ If you carry your work to and from the office on a laptop, use the `scp` to copy files from your laptop to your home computer (and back again).

✔ You can also use the `scp -r` command to quickly move a user from one machine to another.

✔ If you're upgrading to a new system, `scp -r` is an easy way to quickly transfer your work with no disruptions.

 `scp` was designed to copy files from one computer to another. You can also use `scp` to copy a file from one place to another *within* your computer, just like you would use `cp`. We find `scp` to be much more intuitive when it comes to copying directory trees.

To move a directory tree with `scp`, open your terminal window and enter this command:

```
$ scp -r user@host:source user@host:
    destination
```

That's all there is to it. The `-r` flag tells `scp` to copy *source* and everything underneath it.

Table 13-2 highlights two options worthy of mention.

TABLE 13-2: WORTHWHILE SCP OPTIONS

Option	What It Does
`-C`	Compresses the data stream for faster transfers.
`-l limit`	Throttles file transfers to no more than *limit*K bits per second. (Use this option if you're sharing a network connection and you don't want to hog all the bandwidth).

Getting familiar with `scp` (and its secure shell cousin, `ssh`) is definitely worth the time. `scp` is a fast, secure, and easy way to move files and archives from one location to another. `scp` and `ssh` share many command-line options because `scp` is built from `ssh`. For more information about `ssh`, see Technique 33.

Splitting Big Files into Manageable Chunks

While you're working across the Web or across a network, the inevitable happens: You lose the network connection mid-upload. You have to go all the way back to the beginning and start the transfer over.

ISPs are known to place limits on the size of incoming files. E-mails with oversized attachments are returned undelivered and unseen by the recipients. How can you get around that?

To transfer a large file to a user with limited access (or over a questionable connection), use the `split` command. `split` doesn't actually speed up the transfer, but it does speed up the recovery if a connection drops.

`split` breaks a file (any file — archives, pictures, data . . . you name it) into segments that you can reassemble on the other end.

> To reassemble the split file *accurately,* all the pieces must be included. split can't tell if they're all there or not — it just re-assembles what it has. If great-aunt Gertrude's nose looks a bit off, you may have lost a segment.

Use the following command to break a file into 1-megabyte segments for transfer:

```
$ split --bytes=1m filetosplit
  segmentprefix
```

`split` appends the `segmentprefix` with a unique suffix. When it's finished, you still have the original file, but you also have a set of 1 megabyte segments. If you started with a 2.5 megabyte file, you end up with three segments: The first two contain 1 megabyte each, and the third file contains the leftovers.

It's a good idea to calculate an MD5 checksum on the original file to compare it to the reassembled result. Save the number generated by the following command — you'll need it later:

```
$ md5sum filetosplit
```

> *md5* stands for message digest #5. It's a cryptographic program that's good at detecting differences between files. It's kind of like a fingerprint for a file.

> Send the checksum with the attachments or save them to compare to the checksum of the reassembled file. If the checksums match, you can be sure that the entire file was received and reassembled.

It's easy to move all the segments securely with one `scp` command:

```
$ scp segmentprefix.* user@host:directory
```

> To rebuild the file after the upload, use `ssh` to log in to the remote machine, and use `cd` to move to the directory containing the segments.

To reassemble the segments, enter this command:

```
$ cat segmentprefix.* > filename
```

`cat` rebuilds the file into its original structure.

After the file is rebuilt, run a new MD5 checksum and compare it to the fingerprint of the original file. The two fingerprints should be identical.

```
$ md5sum originalfilename
```

> If you've sent the `split` file to a friend running Windows, the `type` command will concatenate `split` files on Windows.

Technique 14

Downloading and Uploading Files in a Snap

The Internet is pervasive. Few days go by when we aren't researching *something* on the Web. When you use the Internet, you're constantly moving data. Using the right tools to upload and download files can make a huge difference in the time it takes you to get the job done.

In this technique, we walk you through downloading and compiling a software tarball. You can find tarballs all over the Web, with great, time-saving software just waiting to be downloaded. The example we show you is for another timesaver — SuperKaramba — that just happens to be fun, too.

When it comes to moving data around, don't overlook the command line. Using wget to create mirrors of Web sites you visit frequently is a great way to save time — you don't have to wait for page downloads, and you can take the entire site with you when you travel. You can even schedule wget to perform mirror updates at night, when the network traffic is low. Now that's a timesaver.

wget also has a few other tricks up its sleeve for downloading. It can play spider, cruising the Web sites in your bookmarks or links files checking to see if all the links still work. wget doesn't give up on downloads if a connection drops. It's a persistent agent and will try again to complete a download.

We also show you how to use curl to manage file uploads. Unlike ftp, curl manages uploads with just one entry at the command line. You can schedule your uploads, just like your downloads, to happen without your help.

Building Software from Downloaded tarballs

Free software packages are all over the Web. Many packages are available in RPM format, but some of the really good stuff only comes wrapped up in a tarball that you have to compile yourself.

No problem — you can deal with tarballs. First, we give you the basic steps and then we explain how to use those steps for SuperKaramba.

Compiling a tarball: The basic steps

The basic steps don't vary much for most software you find on the Web:

1. **Download the tarball.**

2. **Unpack the tarball (see Technique 13 for more information).**

3. **Use** `configure` **to determine the software needs.**

4. **Use the** `make` **command to run the compiler.**

5. **Run** `make install` **to run the install script for the package.**

If there are any variations in the procedure or any software prerequisites, the download page should include instructions specific to the package.

Downloading and compiling SuperKaramba

SuperKaramba is a tool that builds custom desktop features. In this section, we present the basic steps for downloading and compiling SuperKaramba as a fun and useful example of how you apply the basic steps to an actual program.

With SuperKaramba, anyone (not just the propeller-heads) can create desktop accessories fast. Use SuperKaramba to display information you've read over the Internet, create custom toolbars, or create virtual pets (Chia-Penguins perhaps?). You can download some pretty cool, ready-to-run SuperKaramba resources, too!

If you're running SuSE, you're in luck — SuperKaramba is already included with the KDE desktop in a standard installation. If you're running SuSE, just open the main menu and choose System⇨Desktop Applet⇨ karamba.

If you're running Mandrake, you'll find SuperKaramba is included with the standard distribution, but you need to install it. You may want to download and compile your own version anyway, to check out the most recent features as they develop.

To build SuperKaramba, follow these steps:

1. **Open your browser and surf to**
   `netdragon.sourceforge.net`

2. **Click the Download SuperKaramba link at the bottom of the page.**

3. **Scroll down to the Official Releases and click the link for SuperKaramba source code.**

Why use a tarball when an RPM package is available? Well, if the RPM package that you find isn't from an official source, the integrity of the software may be questionable. Although it is possible for someone to introduce a Trojan horse into source code (just like a prebuilt version), it doesn't happen often. RPM packages are platform specific, and the platform you need may not be available.

4. **Click the link for the most recent release:**
   ```
   $ superkaramba-0.33.tar.gz
   ```

5. **The download page instructs you to choose a mirror site near you. Click the link for the site nearest you and then save the file to your desktop.**

6. **Open a terminal window and move to your** `Desktop` **directory:**
   ```
   $ cd ~/Desktop
   ```

7. **Unpack the tarball with the following command:**
   ```
   $ tar -zxvf superkaramba-0.33.tar.gz
   ```

8. **Move into the** `superkaramba-0.33` **directory:**
   ```
   $ cd superkaramba-0.33
   ```

9. **Enter the following command:**

```
$ ./configure --prefix=$(kde-config
  -prefix)
```

configure determines the correct set of tools and compiler options to customize the software for your computer.

 The `--prefix=$(kde-config -prefix)` portion of the command is unique to KDE. Use configure --help to get more configuration options for KDE and non-KDE programs.

If configure complains about any problems, now is the time to correct them. configure does remarkably well at describing the cause of any problem it encounters. If you see an error message that just doesn't seem to make sense, type the text of the message in to Google and you're likely to find a solution waiting for you somewhere out there on the Web.

10. **Enter this command:**

```
$ make
```

make runs the compiler for you. The compiler is translating the source code into a program one bit at a time. The make program coordinates the build — think of it as the job site foreman.

11. **Give yourself superuser privileges:**

```
$ su
```

Enter the superuser password when prompted.

12. **Enter this command:**

```
# make install
```

make install runs the install script for the package. Depending on the package you're installing, the install script includes activities like copying documentation into place, setting up user accounts, and so on.

13. **Turn in your superuser privileges with the** exit **command.**

After SuperKaramba is installed, you can use it to decorate your desktop. See the sidebar, "Installing a SuperKaramba theme" for details.

Installing a SuperKaramba theme

After you install SuperKaramba, we suggest grabbing a theme or two to see how easy this program makes changing your desktop. SuperKaramba themes are different from other desktop themes. They're active desktop decorations — little accessories for your desktop that actually function.

One desktop applet that we really like is Liquid Weather++. You could go to KDE-look.org and spend hours looking through the pages of Karamba themes — do that later. To find Liquid Weather++ quickly, go to www.google.com and search for *Liquid Weather Karamba,* and follow the link.

To download and unpack Liquid Weather++, follow these steps:

1. **Open your favorite browser and surf to the download site for Liquid Weather++.**

2. **Click the download link and save the tarball to your desktop.**

Notice that this tarball is different; it ends with the .bz2 file extension. Different flavors of tarballs exist — gzips and bzips. Gzips and bzips are basically the same, but bzips generally offer better compression and download speed. You can unzip either kind with Linux.

3. **Open your terminal window and move to the** Desktop **directory.**

```
$ cd Desktop
```

4. **Create a** themes **directory with this command:**

```
$ mkdir themes
```

5. **Move to the** themes **directory:**

```
$ cd themes
```

6. **Unpack the tarball with this command:**

```
$ tar -jxvf ../tarball
```

This extracts the tarball into the themes directory.

To start SuperKaramba, open the Main Menu and choose Run Command. Enter superkaramba in the Command field and click Run. The SuperKaramba window opens, as shown in the following figure.

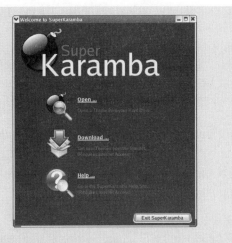

To run Liquid Weather, click Open on the SuperKaramba menu page. Browse to `~/Desktop/themes/liquid_weather_plus` and choose `liquid_weather.theme` from the files listed. Double-click the icon to open a weather report on your desktop (see the following figure).

To customize Liquid Weather, right-click on the weather screen and choose Configure Theme⇨Enter Your Location's Code. Enter your zip code (or weather code if you're in Britain) and choose OK, and the weather forecast is updated to your region.

Versatile Downloading with wget

`wget` uses the HTTP, HTTPS, and FTP protocols from the command line to retrieve files or Web sites. `wget` is handy if you have a slow or undependable Internet connection. If a connection drops partway through a download, `wget` keeps trying. If the server allows it, `wget` will continue the download where it left off.

`wget` has a lot of options that combine to make it a versatile download tool. You can use it in the following ways:

- ✔ For recursive Web site downloads
- ✔ For updating Web site mirrors
- ✔ As a spider to verify links
- ✔ For executing scheduled downloads
- ✔ As a persistent agent to download large files

 `wget` works quietly in the background with no further input from you. You can schedule `wget` (with Task Scheduler) to start downloads when network use is at its lowest so that you don't interfere with other users. For more information about scheduling tasks with Task Scheduler, check out Technique 20.

Mirroring sites with wget

You might wonder why anyone would mirror a Web site. Many generous people who support the open source movement help provide the world with extra information and closer, quicker downloads by setting up servers and creating sites that mirror and distribute open source software and information.

You can also use site mirrors for quicker access to sites that you use often. Not only do you have quicker access to the site, but you can also take it with you anywhere you go — even without a Web connection.

Download an entire Web site recursively with the following command:

```
$ wget -r -k http://www.website.com
```

The `-r` in this command stands for *recursive* (meaning that `wget` copies the directory you name and all the files and subdirectories underneath it) — by default, `wget` copies five levels of subdirectories to your local system. The `-k` (or `--convert-links` if you want to type it out) redirects the links on those five levels to refer back to your local system. If you leave out the -k option, the documents that you download will still point back to the original Web site.

If you find yourself setting up a site mirror, either for internal use or for the world, you'll want to keep it up-to-date. Schedule a job (with Task Scheduler) to run every night:

```
$ wget -r --mirror -k
    http://www.website.com
```

The --mirror option checks your copy of the site against the version published on the Web, and downloads only those files that have changed.

Verifying your bookmarks with wget

If you're anything like us, your bookmark collection is, well, a mess. Bookmarks accumulate over time and pages that you may have been interested in a few months (or years) ago might not be there any more. It's a good idea to weed out obsolete links now and then just to keep your bookmark collection under control. Use wget to check all the links on your bookmarks or links page, with one easy command. To make wget impersonate a spider and investigate links, use this command:

```
$ wget --spider --force-html -i
    bookmarks.html
```

wget visits each link, and reports successful or unsuccessful connections for each entry in your bookmarks page.

 Forget where you left your bookmarks? Use the command locate -i bookmark to generate a list of all the files with the word *bookmark* in their name.

Downloading files with wget

To use wget to download a file from an FTP server, enter the following command:

```
$ wget ftp://www.sitename.com/filename
```

If the download is interrupted, resume the download with this command:

```
$ wget -c ftp://www.sitename.com/filename
```

The -c option instructs wget to resume the download where it left off.

Downloading and unpacking in one quick step

You can redirect the output of a wget download to a tar command to download and unpack in one easy step:

```
$ wget -O - http://tarball | tar -zxvf -
```

The -O option redirects the output to the tar command. tar then unpacks it to a subdirectory in your current directory.

wget's optional flags

Dozens of flags work with wget — we've noted a few in Table 14-1. For a complete list, type man wget at the command line.

TABLE 14-1: HANDY WGET OPTIONS

Option	What It Does
-b	Goes to background after starting.
-q	Turns off the output of wget.
-v	Displays long debugging messages.
-nv	Displays errors or basic info only.
-t count	Tries count times before giving up.
-nc	Doesn't overwrite files.

One other option worthy of mention is --limit-rate=bandwidth. Use this flag to limit the download speed so you don't steal all the bandwidth away from other users on your system.

```
$ wget --limit-rate=20k
```

The preceding command limits the download rate to 20 kilobytes per second — a very generous gesture if you're sharing a network link.

 If you use a proxy server to connect to the Internet, wget can use it, too. wget uses the $http_proxy environment variable to find your proxy server. Enter the command

```
$ export http_proxy proxyaddress:port
```

at the command line to set the environment variable. Add this environment variable to your bash startup script to run the command each time you log in.

Downloading and Uploading with curl

curl (a client for URL) works with the HTTP and FTP protocols to download or upload files. curl is an easy way to upload files when you're maintaining a Web site, or to keep files synchronized with the work of remote employees.

 curl is a powerful download tool, too. For more information about the features of curl, type man curl at the command line.

When you upload with ftp, you have to drive the entire process. You have to enter passwords, type in the put commands one at a time, and disconnect when you're finished. Unlike ftp, curl can do its job without additional user input. You can also schedule curl to do large uploads when the network is quietest — you'll get the best throughput and provide the least aggravation to other users.

To upload a file with curl, enter this command:

```
$ curl -T uploadfile
    ftp://ftp.sitename.com/filename
```

Replace *uploadfile* with your local filename and substitute the ftp sitename information into the command, and the file is on its way. That's all there is to it.

 Set up an ftp server where remote employees' can save their work. Schedule a nightly job on the remote employees' machines to keep up-to-date with their important files — and they won't have to babysit the upload!

If you create an ftp server to hold your employees' nightly updates, you'll want that server to be secure. To use curl to upload a file to a secure site, use the following command:

```
$ curl -T uploadfile -u user:passwd
    ftp://ftp.sitename.com/filename
```

curl gives you the option to update single files, multiple files, or entire systems with a single command. When you combine the powerful uploads that you can get with curl with the scheduling features of Task Scheduler, you'll find lots of ways to save time!

 Visit the CURL Web site at curl.haxx.se for a complete overview of the curl project.

The basics of URL syntax

Have you ever wondered what that string of characters you type into your Web browser is made of?

A simple address like http://www.wiley.com tells the browser to use the http protocol to connect to a host named wiley.com.

A more complex address like http://www.wiley.com/newbooks.html tells your browser to open the newbooks.html resource at the host wiley.com.

An ftp URL often contains a user name and password for the ftp server. The address ftp://freddie:FuNkY@bastille/mixers.html tells ftp that the user freddie, with a password of FuNkY, wants to log into bastille to access the resource mixers.html.

Technique 15

Building a Playpen with User Mode Linux

Save Time By

✓ Creating a virtual work environment with User Mode Linux

✓ Using ADIOS to set up a Fedora VM

✓ Using graphical interfaces to your advantage in server management

✓ Making permanent changes to your virtual machine

Sometimes, you could really use a second computer — someplace safe and secure to hold a server or to try out some new software. Are you interested in trying the latest features in the Linux kernel, but you're stuck with version 2.4 for a while? User Mode Linux (UML) is what you're looking for.

User Mode Linux is a virtual machine (VM) — which is just like a regular computer, but it's built entirely of software. The physical computer that contains the VM is called the *host*. The host and the virtual machine can share resources such as files, disk drives, and network interfaces.

With UML, you can even simulate hardware that you don't have. If you have a single Linux computer, you can run two or three UML sessions to simulate a local area network. You can try out new kernels while safeguarding your real work on a familiar kernel. You can also use UML to create *jails* for hack-vulnerable programs (such as Apache or DNS servers). A jail is an environment that confines a dangerous program by limiting access to important files and devices that the program doesn't need (and more importantly, shouldn't damage).

In this technique, we show you how to install a UML system based on the Fedora Core distribution. This technique is one you can really build on. After you've installed a virtual machine, you can jump ahead to Technique 24 to find out how to build a new kernel and try it out in a safe environment before you install it, or you can skip ahead to Technique 58 to create a UML jail.

Choosing the ADIOS Version of User Mode Linux

You can download, compile, and install UML by hand, but we know a much quicker way thanks to the nice folks at the Queensland University of Technology in Brisbane, Australia. They have put together a package named ADIOS that makes it easy to install UML, loaded with a Fedora distribution, onto your Linux system. Download and install ADIOS, and you'll have a complete Fedora Core server that you can use for tons of other things.

Every Linux computer needs two major components: a kernel and a root file system. The same is true for UML — you need a UML kernel and a root file system. The root file system contains the configuration files, data files, and programs that run inside the VM. A UML kernel is a full Linux kernel compiled to run on Linux rather than a real CPU. When the VM needs access to a piece of hardware, it asks the host to do the dirty work. The ADIOS root file system is built from Fedora Core (release 1, Yarrow at the time we write this). It includes a version 2.4 kernel and a basic set of Fedora RPM packages. ADIOS offers some nice features that make it stand apart from other UML packages:

- ✔ **A minimal set of packages is already installed.** Each ADIOS root file system comes with a minimal set of RPM packages (just enough to get up and running). That means that your VMs are as small as is practical and are not bloated with software that could introduce vulnerabilities.

- ✔ **RPM is already up and running.** You can use the Red Hat package manager to install new packages into the virtual machine or to remove things you don't need. Just start the VM, mount your install media, and use the normal RPM commands to install new packages.

- ✔ **ADIOS automatically configures network interfaces.** Each ADIOS VM comes with a virtual Ethernet interface configured to talk to your host's TCP/IP network. That means that you can log into the VM from your host, transfer files, mount host drives, and even run a Web browser — all from the safety of your VM.

- ✔ **ADIOS can create an X desktop for you.** When you run `startx` within the VM, a new window appears on your desktop. Inside that window, you see the VM's desktop.

- ✔ **Root privileges are not required.** After you've installed ADIOS, you can relinquish your superuser privileges. UML lets you create new VMs

without requiring superuser privileges, which makes your system less vulnerable to typo-related accidents.

- ✔ **The Linux Intrusion Detection System is included.** Two of the four ADIOS VM's include LIDS (Linux Intrusion Detection System). LIDS protects your VM in a number of ways, but most importantly, it takes away most of the privileges from the superuser account. When you're running under LIDS, a hacker who somehow gains superuser privileges cannot destroy your system. We tell you more about LIDS in Technique 58.

- ✔ **SELinux is included.** SELinux (security-enhanced Linux) is a hardened version of Linux developed by the U.S. National Security Agency. Like LIDS, SELinux closes vulnerabilities and limits the superuser's power. SELinux is more difficult to use than LIDS.

Setting Up ADIOS

Now that we've convinced you to use ADIOS, you need to set it up. To do so takes three steps: First, you download ADIOS, then you burn it to CD, and finally, you install it. ADIOS makes it easy to install UML and the Fedora file system.

Downloading ADIOS

To download ADIOS, open a Web browser and navigate to the address `dc.qut.edu.au/adios/iso/uml/`. Right-click `uml-fedora1-1.00.iso` and choose Save Link Target As. Highlight your `Desktop` directory, click Open, and then click Save.

The version specified in the name of the ISO file is the operating system *inside* the VM. In other words, when you install this ISO disc image, you're installing Fedora Linux in the UML VM.

The ADIOS package is 121 megabytes long, so when you download it, this would be a good time to get a cup of coffee, go to a meeting, and so on. A better idea might be to schedule this download to happen at night when the network load is low — see Technique 20 for help.

Because this is such a big package to download, you should verify that the bits that you received are really the same bits that the server sent you (in other words, make sure that the file didn't get corrupted in transit). When the download completes, use your command line to compute the MD5 checksum and compare it to the corresponding checksum from the Web site. Type the following command and then press Enter:

```
$ md5sum ~/Desktop/uml-fedora1-1.00.iso
```

(If you didn't save the download to your `Desktop` directory, substitute the correct pathname.) The command line displays the checksum:

```
bf8237afa555e99ec31b7e1aaff5856e
```

If your checksum matches the one on the Web site, your download succeeded.

 It's important to check your sum against the one on the Web site (instead of the one you see in this book) in case the package has been changed.

If the checksums don't match, delete your local copy and download the package again.

Burning ADIOS to CD

ADIOS is distributed as an ISO disc image. If you have a CD burner, copy the ISO image to your CD (see Technique 56 for details). If not, mount the disc image by using the Linux loopback device:

1. Open a terminal window and use the `su` command to give yourself superuser privileges:

```
$ su
Password:
```

2. Create a mount point for the loopback driver:

```
# mkdir /mnt/loop
```

3. Mount the disc image over the loopback mount point:

```
# mount -o loop ~username/Desktop/
    uml-fedora-1.00.iso /mnt/loop
```

The content of the ADIOS disc image appears in the `/mnt/loop` directory. (In other words, if you `cd` to `/mnt/loop`, you see the file system *inside* the `uml-fedora-1.00.iso` disc image.) If you've burned ADIOS onto a CD and mounted the CD, ADIOS appears in `/mnt/cdrom`.

Installing ADIOS

To install ADIOS, follow these steps:

1. Make sure you have complete superuser privileges by using the `su-` command:

```
$ su -
Password:
#
```

2. Move to the mount point (either `/mnt/loop` or `/mnt/cdrom`):

```
# cd /mnt/loop
```

3. Run the INSTALL program:

```
# ./INSTALL
```

The installer program takes a few moments to copy the root file system to your computer and then asks you a few questions.

4. ADIOS asks whether you want to install Mozilla Firebird. Answer *y* here to run Firebird within the UML VMs.

5. When prompted, type *y* to install the IceWM window manager.

This is a lightweight desktop environment, which takes up a lot less room (and CPU) than GNOME or KDE.

6. **When prompted, enter** y **to install Xnest on your host.**

Xnest lets you view the VM's graphical desktop within a window on *your* desktop.

7. **If prompted, answer** y **to add** iptables **rules to modify your network firewall so that you can talk to the VM from your local network.**

If you're using KDE, the installer creates a new submenu (named User Mode Linux) on your KDE main menu. To start UML, open the KDE main menu and choose User Mode Linux⇨LIDS Off.

 At installation, UML adds four options to your menu. LIDS and SELinux are *hardening* systems that make your computer less vulnerable to attacks from nasty people. We tell you more about UML jails in Technique 58 and more about LIDS in Technique 61. For now, use UML LIDS Off — it will behave just like a standard installation of Fedora.

A console window appears, showing a typical Linux boot sequence; that's your new virtual machine (see Figure 15-1).

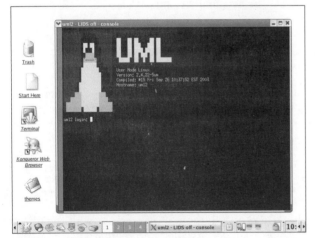

• **Figure 15-1: The UML login screen.**

When your UML VM has finished booting, login as user root (the initial password is 12qwaszx).

 To shut down your virtual machine, enter halt at the command line.

Finding Your Way around UML

When you first start up a VM, the *host* file system is mounted on /mnt/host. This means that the VM can access every file and directory on your host. Go ahead — take a look:

```
[root@uml1/] ls /mnt/host
bin     etc      jail          misc   proc   tmp
boot    home     lib           mnt    root   usr
dev     initrd   lost+found    opt    sbin   var
```

Here are some more important things you'll likely want to do from the VM:

✔ **Use the resources of the host computer:** Preface the resource pathname with /mnt/host. For example, to access the CD drive, enter the following command:

```
$ cd /mnt/host/mnt/cdrom
```

 Before you can use a host file system from within the VM, you have to mount the file system from the host. For example, if you want to use the CD drive from within the VM, you must mount /dev/cdrom in the host. Then use the /mnt/host prefix to access the peripheral devices.

✔ **Find the programs on your host:** ADIOS has configured the $PATH environment variable to match the $PATH in your host (adjusting it to find commands first within the VM and then on the host). If $PATH is set to /bin:/usr/bin on the host, UML changes that to /mnt/host/bin:/mnt/host/usr/bin. This means that all the programs you use on the host are available within the VM (although configuration files may not be in the right place).

✔ **Get the IP address:** Your new VM has a virtual Ethernet adapter. You can find the IP address with the `ifconfig` command:

```
# /sbin/ifconfig eth0 | grep inet
inet addr: 192.168.201.1
     Bcast:192.168.201.255
     Mask: 255.255.255.0
```

Typically, the first VM you create has an IP address of 192.168.201.1, the second VM has an IP address of 192.168.202.1, and so on. You can `ping` the VM from your host or `ping` the host from your VM. You can also `ssh` from one to the other.

Connecting to the Internet from an ADIOS VM

If you want your VM to be able to access the rest of the Internet, you need to turn on NAT (Network Address Translation). NAT enables you to share a physical network interface among multiple computers (in this case, one physical computer and a few virtual computers). Here's how to turn on NAT in Fedora or Mandrake Linux:

1. **From the host computer (not from the VM), open your terminal window and give yourself superuser privileges with the `su` command.**

2. **Enter the following command:**

```
# kate /etc/sysconfig/iptables
```

The Kate text editor opens, with the `iptables` file ready to edit.

3. **Add the following code to the end of the file:**

```
*nat
:POSTROUTING ACCEPT [0:0]
:OUTPUT ACCEPT [0:0]
:PREROUTING ACCEPT [0:0]
COMMIT
```

4. **Save your work and close the editor.**

5. **Execute the following command to restart your firewall with the new rules you just put in place:**

```
# /sbin/service iptables restart
```

 If you're using SuSE, check out Technique 34 for information about enabling NAT within your firewall.

Now you should be able to access the Internet (and your local network) from within the VM.

Using a GUI with UML

IceWM is a minimal desktop environment — it doesn't come with a ton of bells and whistles, but it's also not a big resource hog.

While you're configuring your VM, the GUI can be a great help. But after you're up and running, you'll probably use the command line for most of your work. Having a GUI that's a bit sparse really isn't a problem — you won't be here for that long.

To run IceWM, open a virtual machine and enter `startx` at the command line. A new window opens, displaying the IceWM window manager.

Click the IceWM button in the upper-left corner to open the drop-down menu. The other buttons on the taskbar control your workspaces within IceWM, open an Xterm window, or start the Mozilla browser.

Installing Software into UML

The ADIOS distribution of UML comes with the RPM package manager installed and ready to use, making software installation quick and easy. In fact, you don't have to copy an RPM package into the VM before you install it; just mount the host drive that contains the package and nab the file by using the /mnt/host prefix.

As an example, we walk you through an installation of Webmin. Webmin is a handy tool for managing servers from within a Web browser. Webmin takes care of just about every system administration task you can think of, making it a great addtion to UML. In the next section, we show you how to install Webmin into the VM prototype so all your VMs have quick and easy access to Webmin.

If you need to set up a server that makes resources available to the outside world (such as a Web server or an e-mail server), build the server inside a VM. If troublemakers do get in, you can limit their access to the rest of your system. We show you how in Technique 58.

To install Webmin in a UML Virtual Machine, follow these steps:

1. **On your *host* machine, open a Web browser and browse to** www.webmin.com**. Click the RPM download link in the upper-right corner.**

You jump to the download server page.

You can surf from inside UML and download directly into your virtual machine, but it's faster to download to your host machine and access the result via /mnt/host.

2. **Click the Download link for the location that's closest to you. When the Download Manager opens, click the Save button to save the file.**

3. **From within the VM,** cd **to the directory that contains the RPM package that you just saved:**

```
$ cd /mnt/host/home/user
```

Don't forget to include /mnt/host in your path because you saved the package on the host.

4. **Unpack the RPM package with the following command:**

```
$ rpm -Uhv webmin-1.121-1.noarch.rpm
```

If you downloaded a new version, substitute its name in the command.

5. **Press Enter, and the whirring begins.**

Webmin creates a mini–Web server *inside* your VM. You can use Webmin from your *host* machine to set up the servers you install in the VM. Just open a browser on your host machine and jump to

```
192.168.201.1:10000
```

Log in as root and enter your password, and you can quickly manage your virtual servers from the comfort of your host's browser!

Merging Changes to Your Prototype

If you run many VMs at the same time, each new VM starts out with its own copy of the original ADIOS root file system (we call that the *prototype* file system because new VMs are created from that file system). This means that software you install in one VM won't show up in the other VMs.

Occasionally, you may want to install a tool in *every* virtual machine on your host. To make a permanent change to your prototype file system, change one of the VMs and then *merge* the changes back into what then becomes your new prototype UML virtual machine.

Merging changes can be a timesaver if you need to set up multiple VMs with similar attributes (for example, you want to use Webmin to manage all your servers). Make your changes to one machine and commit those changes to the prototype. New VMs will reflect the changes.

To merge your changes back into the prototype file system, follow these steps:

1. **Open a copy of UML and make the changes you want reflected in all your VMs.**

2. **Shut down the VM by using the** `halt` **command.**

3. **Open a terminal window and enter the following command:**

   ```
   $ uml_moo -d /tmp/root_fs1
   ```

4. **Press Enter.**

   That's it — all the changes you've made to the virtual machine are merged into the prototype UML. Next time you start a new VM, your changes will be waiting for you.

 Your original root file system is never modified by changes you make to an open VM unless you merge the changes back into the prototype. All your modifications are recorded in a separate file.

Peeking into the virtual file cabinet

When you start a new UML VM, a few new files appear in the `/tmp/uml` directory. If you casually browse through `/tmp/uml`, you may be alarmed to see some huge files. If you've started a single VM, you'll see a file named `/tmp/uml/root_fs1`. That's the root file system for your VM. Use the `ls -l` command to see this file, and you'll discover it's over 500 megabytes long! Start a second VM and another 500 megabyte file appears for the second root file system. Don't worry, the apparent file size is *very* misleading.

UML uses a brilliant strategy known as copy-on-write, or COW. When you start a VM, UML mounts the original root file system (`/opt/uml/root_fs`) in read-only mode, but it also creates a second file (`/tmp/uml/root_fs1`). When your VM modifies a file within its root file system, the changes are written to the `/tmp/uml/root_fs1` file, not to the original file. If you really mess up something in your VM (or if an intruder has made his or her way into your VM), COW makes it easy to revert to a fresh copy of Linux — just remove the COW file (`root_fs1`) from `/tmp/uml`. The next time you start the VM, UML creates a fresh new COW file for you.

Part III

Good Housekeeping with Linux

The 5th Wave   By Rich Tennant

"One of the first things you want to do before doing system maintenance is fog the users to keep them calm during the procedure."

16 Technique

Red-lining RPM Queries

Save Time By

- Using rpm to locate files
- Creating a catalog of your install media
- Finding package dependencies
- Querying remote packages before bringing them home

RPM (the Red Hat Package Manager) is typically used to install software, but behind the scenes, RPM maintains a database of useful information. Every RPM package includes a mini-database that contains basic information about the package itself. When you install an RPM package, the mini-database is added to the master database of installed packages. The rpm command can peek inside the RPM databases to tell you about software that you've already installed or packages that you may want to try out.

An RPM package typically contains a collection of programs, data files, and documentation. A package can also contain scripts that execute when you install, remove, upgrade, or verify the package. Each package also contains a package *digest* that contains information about the package itself. The digest can tell you a lot about the package: who built the package, when they built it, and what the package is supposed to do. The digest also lists prerequisites for the package (that is, you must install package *A* before you install package *B*).

An RPM package also contains two components critical to ensuring that you're installing software from a trusted source. When an RPM package is created, the person creating the package signs the package with a digital signature. You can use the digital signature to determine whether the package has been modified since it was signed (a mismatched signature tells you that the package has been tampered with). Every file installed by a package is fingerprinted at the time the package is created; you can come back at a later date and verify the fingerprint of the installed version to make sure that the file has not been tampered with since installation. We show you how to verify digital signatures and fingerprints in Technique 18.

In this technique, we show you how to use the rpm command to query RPM databases in useful and interesting ways. We also show you how to save time by creating a complete catalog of your installation media for handy reference.

Querying RPM Packages for Content

If you've ever used RPM from the command line, you know about the -i (install) and -U (upgrade) options, but you may not be familiar with RPM's query features. When you run a query against an RPM database, you have to tell rpm which database you want to view. If you want to peek inside a package file (typically a file whose name ends in .rpm), include --package *filename* on the command line (or -p *filename* for short); otherwise, rpm will display information from the master database of packages that you've already installed.

Table 16-1 shows some of the most useful rpm query options. To use each of the commands, just open a terminal window and type in the command — no special privileges are required.

You can run each of the commands shown in Table 16-1 against multiple packages (or package files) at once. Just list the names that you're interested in at the end of the command like this:

```
$ rpm -q kdebase gnome-desktop
kdebase-3.1.4.2
ghome-desktop-2.4.0-1
```

When you view a package's digest, rpm tells you which *group* the package belongs to, for example:

```
$ rpm -qi kdebase
Name        : kdebase
Version     : 3.1.4
Release     : 2
Install Date: Tue 28 Oct 2003 03:11:28
Group       : User Interface/Desktops
```

The kdebase package is part of the group User Interface/Desktops. You can use the group name to select the packages that you're interested in. To find all the games installed on your system (or at least those games installed with RPM), use this command:

```
$ rpm -qg "Amusements/Games"
tuxracer-0.61-23
chromium-0.9.12-24
```

To display a list of all the RPM group names on your system, type in the following command:

```
$ rpm -qa --qf "%{GROUP}\n" | sort -u
```

In addition to the queries shown in Table 16-1, here are a few combinations that we find particularly handy:

TABLE 16-1: SOME HANDY RPM QUERY OPTIONS

To Do This	Use This Query for Installed Packages	Use This Query for RPM Package Files
Display the package version number	rpm -q *package-name*	rpm -qp *filename*.rpm
Display the package digest (a summary of the package content)	rpm -qi *package-name*	rpm -qpi *filename*.rpm
Display the prerequisites for the package	pm -qR *package-name* r	rpm -qpR *filename*.rpm
Display the list of files installed by the package	rpm -ql *package-name*	rpm -qpl *filename*.rpm
Display only documentation files installed by the package	rpm -qd *package-name*	rpm -qpd *filename*.rpm
Display only configuration files installed by the package	rpm -qc *package-name*	rpm -qpc *filename*.rpm

✔ `rpm -qf filename`

This query displays the name of the package that *owns* the given file. Use this query when you run into a file and you don't know where it came from. You have to include the complete pathname of the file that you're interested in, not just the filename.

✔ `rpm -qa --last | head -n 10`

This query displays the names (and install dates) of the ten most-recently-installed packages.

✔ `rpm -qa | grep -i name`

Use this query to locate an installed package when you don't know the exact spelling of the package name. (The `-i` option tells `grep` to do a case-insensitive search.)

Digesting Information

Every RPM package includes a digest. Here's a rundown of the information included in a typical digest (not all packages include every item that we list here):

✔ **Package name:** A package whose name includes *devel* is meant for developers. A package whose name starts with *lib* doesn't do anything all by itself; it adds features to other packages. lib-packages are typically prerequisites for other packages.

✔ **Version number**

✔ **RPM build date**

✔ **Author or vendor's name**

✔ **Project Web site:** The project Web site is a great place to look for more documentation, add-ons, and ways to commune with other users.

✔ **Product license type**

✔ **Product description**

✔ **Name of the source RPM:** Most packages are built from a *source* RPM. The source RPM contains the source code for the package.

✔ **RPM size**

Some open-source software packages are distributed for noncommercial use only. Check the information digest to be sure that you're not violating the license.

Creating a Package Index

When you download a distribution from the Web site, you typically download a set of disc images. The standard Fedora distribution takes four CDs (unless you want the source code, too — in which case, it takes eight). The Fedora distribution contains lots of files . . . 300,682 according to our latest distribution. What if you need to know which disk just two or three of them are on?

Fortunately, Linux makes that information readily available and easy to store. With just a few easy steps, you can create a complete catalog that contains a list of the CD contents. After you make the index, you can open it with a text editor (like Kate) and search for what you need.

Creating (and saving) a package index will save you time whenever you need to install a new package: You won't have to search through all the CDs for the one you need.

To create a package index for the Fedora distribution, follow these steps:

1. **Open a terminal window and give yourself superuser privileges:**

```
$ su
Password:
$
```

2. **Insert and mount the first install disc:**

```
# mount /dev/cdrom /mnt/cdrom
```

3. **Move to the RPMS directory:**

```
# cd /mnt/cdrom/Fedora/RPMS
```

4. **Enter the following command:**

```
# for name in*.rpm
```

This command starts a *for loop:* The bash shell executes each command in the loop a number of times. The variable `$name` holds the name of the next package file each time through the loop. When you press Enter, the shell displays a different prompt to tell you that you're in the middle of a complex command.

5. **Next to the new prompt, enter the next line of code and press Enter:**

```
> do
```

6. **On the next line, enter this command:**

```
> rpm -qpi $name >> ~/DiscOne
```

This command displays the digest from the package file (`$name`) and appends the output to the file `~/DiscOne`.

7. **Then enter this:**

```
> rpm -qpl $name >> ~/DiscOne
```

This appends the name of each file in the package to the end of `~/DiscOne`.

8. **Enter** done **and press Enter.**

If you have more than one install disc, repeat this sequence for each disc (but change the name of the output file to `~/DiscTwo`, `~/DiscThree`, and so on).

 The procedure to create a package index is similar for the SuSE or Mandrake Linux distributions. Just substitute the appropriate file and directory names.

This sequence of commands takes a while to complete, but when it's done, you have a file in your home directory that you can use over and over. To find the files you need, just open the package list with the editor of your choice, and search.

Querying for Prerequisites

Before installing an RPM package, it's handy to know what other packages you'll need to install at the same time. The prerequisites can vary from needing a specific version of the Linux kernel, to needing some pretty exotic libraries.

 To save yourself time and grief, query your RPM package for its dependencies before you install it. If you need a library file that hasn't been seen in recent history, or 20 or 30 other obscure files, it might be quicker to find a piece of software that's not so needy.

To query an RPM package for its dependencies, use the following command:

```
$ rpm -qpR name.rpm
```

Run the command on Webmin, and the result looks something like this:

```
$ rpm -qpR webmin-1.121-1.noarch.rpm
/bin/sh
/usr/bin/perl
```

You can see that Webmin needs a bash shell and `perl` to install and run properly. These are easy requirements — you can find these two common packages on most distribution discs!

Don't Put That in Your Drive; You Don't Know Where That's Been!

Everywhere on the Web you see them . . . RPMs just waiting to be grabbed. But how do you know what's in them? Should you really be downloading things to your safe and secure system without at least looking at them first?

You can use `rpm` with a remote FTP site to query for the contents of a remote package. After you see the contents, you can decide if it's something worth bringing home.

 Just remember, if someone really wants to be malicious and change filenames and mask creation information, he or she can. `chroot` jails can be a big help in isolating programs you want to try but don't trust completely (see Technique 58 for more information).

Usually, downloads from the Web come from an FTP or HTTP server. To perform a remote query on an FTP server, use this command:

```
$ rpm -ql ftp://ftp.example.com/path.rpm
```

To perform a remote query on an HTTP server, enter the following command:

```
$ rpm -ql http://www.example.com/path.rpm
```

These queries are straightforward. If you need to, you can include user names and passwords, just like you would in a normal URL. See Technique 14 for more information about downloading from Web servers or FTP servers.

In Technique 18, we show you how to verify a package's digital signature *before* you install it. We also show you to find out whether the files installed by a given package have been changed since you installed them — a great way to watch for tampering fingers wandering around on your computer.

Technique 17

Installing Made Easy with RPM

Throughout the book, we tell you to see Technique 17 for help installing RPM packages (that is, software packages installed with the `rpm` command). Here's where we share how this handy trick is done. This is a good technique to bookmark because you'll be using it a lot.

RPM (the Red Hat Package Manager) works great at the command line or with a graphical interface. The command line gives you raw speed and power, but it's not as friendly as a browser-based interface. Fortunately, you get to choose the method that you prefer.

RPM also makes quick work of uninstalling programs — no more lost disk space or time wasted trying to chase down all the program files. With one command, you can erase programs that are no longer used or don't live up to their initial promises.

In this technique, we show you how to use RPM to install new software at lightning speeds. Other package managers are available, but RPM is the standard method for installing software on Linux systems. We don't want to give you the impression that RPM is the only way to install, but for speed and simplicity, RPM is a good choice.

Dissecting an RPM Package

An RPM package is a collection of files and (usually) a few scripts that run whenever you install or remove the package. You can peek inside an RPM package with the command `rpm -qpl package-name` (we show you some other handy RPM queries in Technique 16).

The name of an RPM package tells you a lot about what's inside it. For example, most Linux distributions include two related packages named `kdeedu-3.1.4-1.i386.rpm` and `kdeedu-devel-3.1.4-1.i386.rpm`. The naming convention for RPM packages is `name-version-platform.rpm`. In the first package, the *name* of the package is `kdeedu`, the *version* is `3.1.4.1`, and the *platform* is `i386`. The second package is named `kdeedu-devel` and shares the same version number and platform. Here's how you use each part of the package name:

✔ **Name:** This part is how you refer to the package after it's been installed. For example, if you install the `kdeedu-3.1.4-1.i386.rpm` package file and later want to remove it, you specify only the `kdeedu` part of the package name.

✔ **Version:** This number is used to compare two versions of the same package — the higher the version number, the newer the package.

✔ **Platform:** This part tells you which CPU the package was built for. An i386 (Intel 80386) package will run on all Intel 80386, 80486, and Pentium CPUs (and compatible CPUs like the Athlon). An i686 package will run on Pentium CPUs but may not work on older Intel CPUs. You'll also run across PPC (PowerPC Macintoshes and IBM RISC computers) packages; you can't use these unless you have a Power PC CPU. You may also see packages built for the `noarch` platform. `noarch` packages are not CPU-dependent. A `noarch` package is typically a program written in a portable language, such as Java or Python, or it may simply be a collection of text files.

The `kdeedu` and `kdeedu-devel` packages are related. The `kdeedu` package installs the programs and documentation you need to *run* KDE Education programs; `kdeedu-devel` installs the files that you would need if you wanted to *develop* (that is, alter and rebuild) the KDE Education programs. The `-devel` on the end of the package name is your clue that an RPM package is meant for developers rather than users.

Not all package names follow the conventions that we've described, but the vast majority do.

Using RPM at the Command Line

Using RPM at the command line to install a program is an easy and straightforward process. As an example, we explain how to download and install Webmin in this section. Webmin is a great tool that we refer to in several other techniques.

Use Webmin to manage your system administration chores. It's a browser-based tool that can help you manage users, create disk partitions, restore from backup, and more. Check it out.

If you aren't sure about the pedigree of the package that you're installing, see Technique 18 to find out how to trace the lineage of packages that come from dubious sources. Technique 18 explains how to use digital signatures to ensure that a package hasn't been tampered with. A digital signature also ensures that a package comes from the person who claims to have created it in the first place.

To download and install Webmin, follow these steps:

1. **Open your Web browser and surf to**

`www.webmin.com`

2. **In the upper-right corner of the screen is a link labeled RPM. Click the link to open a download page.**

3. **Click a Download site near you.**

The Download Manager window opens.

4. **Click Save to start the download and then go make a quick cup of coffee....**

5. **Open your terminal window and navigate to the directory holding your new download.**

The directory name is displayed in the status bar of the Download Manager.

6. **Give yourself superuser privileges with the `su` command.**

7. **Type in the following command:**

`rpm -Uhv webmin-1.121-1.noarch.rpm`

The easiest way to enter a long filename like this is to type the first few letters and then press Tab. (See Technique 5 for details.)

8. **Press Enter.**

After a short delay, `rpm` informs you that Webmin is installed.

When you install Webmin, you see a message like this: `You can now login to http://localhost:10000/`. That's the URL of the mini–Web server that Webmin installed on your system. Jump to that URL in your favorite browser, and you're connected to Webmin. Check it out!

If you try to install a package that requires other packages, `rpm` tells you about it. Check the notes on the download page. If the developer is friendly, he or she will tell you what you need and where to find it. See Technique 18 to learn about a tool (Synaptic) that helps resolve interpackage dependencies automatically.

Removing RPMs

RPM packages are just as easy to get rid of as they are to install. To remove a program installed with RPM, open your terminal window, give yourself superuser privileges, and issue the following command:

```
rpm --erase package_name
```

To find the package name to erase, look at the file that you used to install the package. The package name precedes the version number in the name of the package file.

If you're having trouble finding the package name for the software you want to remove, see Technique 16. In that technique, you find a whole mess of RPM queries that you can use to track down packages and the stuff that they install.

Flagging Down RPM

To put it mildly, the `rpm` command has a *ton* of options. Some of the most useful flags are listed in Table 17-1.

TABLE 17-1: HANDY RPM FLAGS

Flag	What It Does
-i	Installs a new package, but displays an error message if an older version is already installed
-U	Installs a new package, upgrading an older version if found
-e	Uninstalls a package
-h	Displays a progress bar while it's working
-v	Gives a bit more feedback while it's working

Our favorite combination is `-Uhv`. That installs (or upgrades) a package, displays a progress bar, and displays an informative message if something goes wrong.

Type `rpm --help | more` at the command line for a quick view of all the flags and options.

Getting Graphic with RPM

Web-wide, open-source software is often distributed in RPM form. We refer you to a lot of RPMs in this book, but you'll no doubt be surfing and finding more timesavers daily.

Fedora, Mandrake, and SuSE each come with their own tools for managing RPM packages included on the distribution media. In the sections that follow, you'll find step-by-step directions on how to use each distribution's package management tool.

Quick installations from distribution media with Fedora's Package Manager

Adding packages from the Fedora distribution media (CD or DVD) is easy. To install a package from your Fedora disc, follow these steps:

1. **Put the DVD or CD in the drive and wait for the disc to mount. Depending on your current user privileges, you may be prompted for a password.**

The Add or Remove Packages window opens, as shown in Figure 17-1.

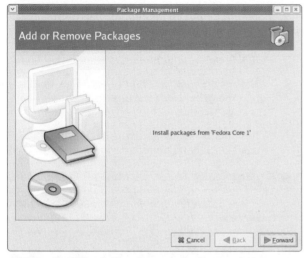

• **Figure 17-1: The Add or Remove Packages window.**

2. **Click Forward.**

Fedora searches your system to see which packages are already installed. Then the Add or Remove Packages detail window opens, displaying the current status of your system packages, as shown in Figure 17-2.

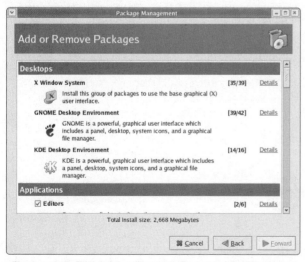

• **Figure 17-2: The Add or Remove Packages detail window.**

3. **To change the packages that are currently on your system, either check (to install) or uncheck (to remove) the box next to a package.**

To the right of the checked package names is a fraction that represents the number of programs installed and how many programs are available in that package.

The packages with unchecked boxes to the left of their names aren't installed, but contain programs that you can install. To view the contents of a package, click Details to the right of the package listing, and a dialog opens, showing the detailed contents of the package you've chosen (see Figure 17-3).

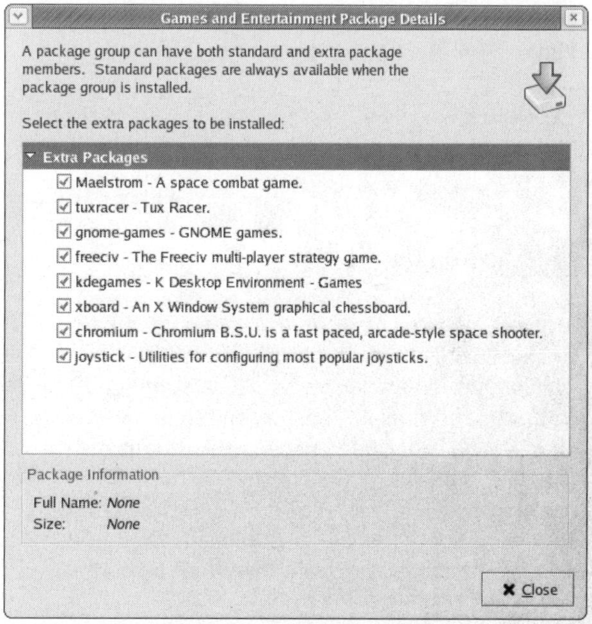

• **Figure 17-3: The Package Details dialog.**

The changes you make to the check boxes represent the status of your system packages after the update is complete.

4. **After you've identified the packages you want to install (or remove), click Forward.**

A list of changes is displayed, as shown in Figure 17-4.

Package Management

Package Installation Overview

23 packages are queued for installation

This will take 210,032 Kilobytes of diskspace.

Packages to be Installed

arts-devel-8:1.1.4-3.i386	1,124 Kilobytes
cdparanoia-devel-0:.alpha9.8-18.i386	140 Kilobytes
cups-devel-1:1.1.19-13.i386	364 Kilobytes
kdbg-1:1.2.9-1.i386	1,096 Kilobytes
kdebase-devel-6:3.1.4-6.i386	320 Kilobytes
kdegraphics-devel-7:3.1.4-1.i386	92 Kilobytes
kdelibs-devel-6:3.1.4-4.i386	94,532 Kilobytes
kdenetwork-devel-7:3.1.4-1.i386	372 Kilobytes
kdepim-6:3.1.4-1.i386	8,816 Kilobytes
kdepim-devel-6:3.1.4-1.i386	180 Kilobytes
kdesdk-0:3.1.4-1.i386	8,096 Kilobytes
kdesdk-devel-0:3.1.4-1.i386	128 Kilobytes

[✖ Cancel] [◀ Back] [▶ Forward]

• Figure 17-4: The Package Installation Overview dialog.

5. **Click Forward.**

Fedora goes to work, upgrading your system. If everything goes well, you see a screen telling you the package update is complete.

6. **Click Finish.**

One of the nice features of the Add or Remove Packages tool is that it automatically resolves inter-package dependencies for you (the command line rpm command doesn't). One of the not-so-nice features of Add or Remove Packages is that it only works with packages distributed on the Fedora distribution discs. In Technique 19, we show you how to automatically resolve interpackage dependencies, even for packages that you download from the Web.

 You can also start Fedora's Package Manager from the Main Menu. Open the Main Menu and choose System Settings⇨Add/Remove Applications.

Using SuSE's package manager to your advantage

The SuSE Linux distribution comes with a powerful package manager called YaST (Yet another Setup Tool). YaST makes adding software a snap. Follow these steps to install an RPM package from the SuSE distribution media with YaST:

1. **Open the Main Menu and choose System⇨YaST.**

Enter your root password if prompted.

2. **Click Install and Remove Software.**

3. **Use the arrow to the right of the Filter field to open the drop-down list box and choose Package Groups.**

The window displays a list of the available and installed RPM packages, as shown in Figure 17-5.

• Figure 17-5: The YaST package manager.

The package manager window features four panels:

✔ The upper-left panel displays package groups. Use the tree control to browse through the groups and subgroups. When you highlight a group in the tree control, the panel in the upper right displays the packages within that group.

 The filter selector enables you to change the views in the upper-left panel: You can choose from selections, package groups, search, and installation summary.

✔ Use the Package Summary panel in the upper-right corner of the window to view a list of packages.

To the left of the package name is a check box. This is not an ordinary check box: Each time you click the check box, it displays a new icon. A check mark in the box means that the package will be installed. A trash can means it will be removed. The (slightly cryptic) update symbol will check for package updates.

✔ The lower-right corner of the screen displays a tab-controlled dialog with information about the currently highlighted RPM package. Choose from the tab controls to view information about the package and its dependencies.

✔ The lower-left corner of the screen contains a handy bar graph, displaying your current disk usage.

To add a new RPM package, follow these steps:

1. **Select the check box to the left of the package name in the Package Summary panel.**

Want to install a package quick, just to test the technique? May we recommend tuxracer. It's lots of good clean fun. You'll find it in the Games category.

2. **Click the Check Dependencies button.**

A dialog opens, verifying that all package dependencies are okay.

3. **Click the OK button.**

4. **Click the Accept button in the lower-right corner of the screen.**

A screen opens, displaying the installation progress. YaST takes it from here, adding your new software and updating the system.

Using Rpmdrake to install from media

The Rpmdrake package installer included with Mandrake makes it easy to install RPM packages from the distribution media. Just follow these steps:

1. **Open the main menu and choose System⇨ Configuration⇨Packaging⇨Install Software.**

2. **Enter your root password if prompted.**

The Rpmdrake package installer opens (see Figure 17-6).

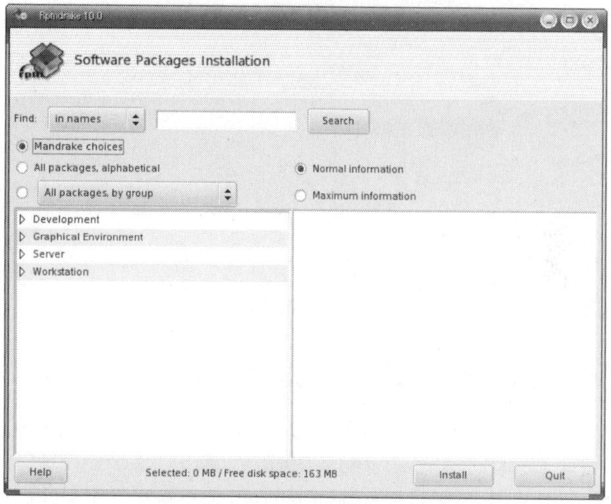

• **Figure 17-6:** The Rpmdrake package installer.

3. **Click the All Packages Alphabetical option button to display a list of the packages on your installation media.**

Highlight a package name in the list to see detailed information about the package in the right panel.

4. **Click the check box next to the name of the package you want to install (see Figure 17-7).**

If other packages need to be installed to satisfy the package's dependencies, a dialog opens, asking you to verify their installation.

5. **Click the Install button to add the new package.**

Rpmdrake takes it from there, installing the new RPM package on your system.

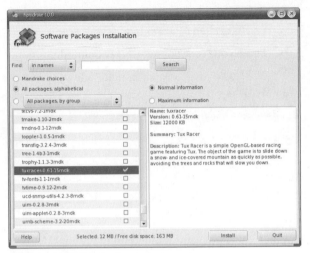

• **Figure 17-7:** The YaST package manager.

Installing from your Konqueror browser

With the Konqueror (KDE) browser, you can install RPM packages with just a couple of clicks from the comfort of your browser window. You can use the Konqueror browser to install RPM packages down-loaded from the Web, or from disk.

If you're using Fedora, follow these steps:

1. **Open your Konqueror browser and navigate to the directory holding the** `.rpm` **file.**

2. **Double-click the package filename.**

In a snap, the Package Manager walks you through the installation.

Follow these steps if you're running SuSE:

1. **Open the Konqueror browser and surf to the file's location.**

2. **Click the package's icon to view a description of the package's content.**

 Change to the Files tab to see a list of the files included in the RPM package.

3. **Click the Install Package with YaST button.**

Enter the superuser password if prompted.

YaST takes it from there, and installs your package!

If you're a Mandrake user, follow these steps:

1. **Open the Konqueror browser and move to the directory containing the RPM package.**

2. **Right-click on the package's icon, and choose Software Installer from the pop-up menu.**

3. **Enter your root password if prompted and click OK.**

A message dialog opens, asking if you would like to install the software package on your computer or just save the file.

 If you need additional files to satisfy the dependencies of the package, you'll be prompted to accept their installation as well.

4. **Click the Install It button.**

A progress bar opens, and the package is installed. That's all there is to it!

 Be sure you're getting RPM packages from a reputable source. A not-so-friendly but crafty programmer with an axe to grind could poten-tially infect an RPM package with a virus and do mega-harm to your system. Technique 18 shows you how to verify that a package comes from the person who claims to have built it. Be sure to perform backups on a regular basis if you're doing a lot of downloading (see Techniques 49 and 50 for more information about backing up your system).

Technique 18

Getting Comfortable with RPM

Save Time By

- Updating rather than installing your software
- Verifying your system integrity
- Keeping an eye on file ownership
- Determining whether a package has been tampered with

In Techniques 16 and 17, we show you the fast (and powerful) installation and query features of RPM (the Red Hat Package Manager). In this technique, we introduce you to some of the eclectic (but handy) features that often go by the wayside — verify and update.

RPM just might be your system's best friend. After all, it knows more about your system than anyone. RPM maintains a database of information about the packages installed on your system. By comparing that database to the current state of your system, RPM can tell you if a package has been altered after you installed it. The `--verify` feature can help you detect intruders, users trying to do things they shouldn't be doing, or configuration problems just waiting to ruin your weekend.

RPM can also verify the digital signature (and integrity) of a package before you install it to see if the package has been tampered with. You can save yourself hours of misery by keeping your system safe from potential Trojan horses. If the key signature doesn't match, you don't install it.

In this technique, we walk you through some RPM features that you may not be familiar with. Some of these features are great timesavers — you just need to know about them.

Saving Time with --upgrade

When you add a new package to your system, you can use `rpm --install` to install or `rpm --upgrade` to upgrade. We recommend going the upgrade route rather than the install route. `rpm --install` fails if an older version of the package is already installed, but `rpm --upgrade` upgrades an existing package *or* installs a new one, whichever is appropriate.

 To use any of the RPM features that modify the `rpm` database — including installing and updating — you need to hold superuser privileges. If the `rpm` command displays a cryptic message (such as `cannot get exclusive lock` or `cannot open Packages index`), check your privileges.

When you use `--install`, `rpm` first looks at your system to see if the package is already installed. If it is, `rpm` complains about file conflicts. (And if you look *very* closely, you also see a message that states the package is already installed — a message that's kind of hard to see among all the other complaints.)

When you use `--upgrade`, `rpm` checks to see if the package is installed and, if so, compares the installed package to the version you're trying to install. If you're installing a more recent version, `rpm` upgrades to the more recent version. If you're trying to install an older version, it tells you that your currently installed software is more recent than the copy you're trying to upgrade to, and quits. If the package is not currently installed on your system, `rpm` installs it.

Here's our favorite command line for installing new software:

```
# rpm --upgrade -vh filename.rpm
```

You can use this command to do initial installs *or* to upgrade versions. bash doesn't care which because it knows that your intention is to get the most recent copy of the program on your system as quickly as possible.

 An easy timesaver is to use the shortcut version of the upgrade command to install RPM packages, `# rpm -Uvh filename.rpm`.

All the command line options that work with `--install` also work with `--upgrade`. Check out the man page (`man rpm`) for a complete list.

Verifying Your System

When you install a package, RPM records detailed information about the package content in a database. The database includes information such as expected file size, expected owner, and expected permissions. RPM also stores an MD5 checksum (effectively a fingerprint that uniquely identifies the file content; see the sidebar, "What's this MD5 stuff anyway?") for each file in each package. At your request, RPM compares the information stored in the database with the installed version of a given package.

When you run the command `rpm --verify package-name`, `rpm` searches through the list of files owned by that package and compares the file as it exists on your hard drive with the information stored in the database. For each file, `-verify` compares the file's size, permissions, group and owner, modification time, and MD5 checksum. RPM verifies that packages you've installed are still in good form and haven't been tampered with.

You can verify a single package, a group of packages, or all the packages installed on your computer. If your packages are clean, `rpm --verify` completes without printing any messages. If `rpm --verify` finds a file that's out of whack, it displays a cryptic looking string of characters that tells you what's wrong. The failure codes are listed in Table 18-1.

TABLE 18-1: RPM --VERIFY FAILURE CODES

Code	Meaning
S	The file's size differs from the expected value.
M	The file's permissions differ from the expected values.
5	The MD5 checksum has changed — this one is important because it means someone has tampered with a file *after* you installed it.
D	This file is a device-interface file, and the major or minor device numbers differ from the expected values.
L	This file is a symbolic link but is pointing to the wrong place.
U	The file's ownership has changed — watch this one. A change in ownership can alert you to an intruder who's trying to gain extra privileges or to modify files he (or she) shouldn't modify.
G	The file's group ownership has changed.
T	The modification time has changed.

We've purposefully damaged one of the files on our computer just to see what `--verify` reports:

```
$ rpm --verify coreutils
S.5....T d /usr/share/man/man1/yes.1.gz
```

The failure codes tell us that the file has changed size (`S`), its MD5 checksum is wrong (`5`), and the modification time doesn't match the value stored in the RPM database (`T`).

Check out any inconsistencies that `--verify` uncovers because they could indicate intruders or other problems waiting to bite you:

- ✔ The MD5 checksum value is like a fingerprint of the data within a file. If the number changes, the content has changed.

- ✔ If the user ownership changes, users might be getting in and giving themselves privileges they shouldn't have.

- ✔ Likewise, a change in group ownership could indicate an intruder.

- ✔ If the MD5 checksum has changed, but the modification time has *not* changed, an intruder may be trying to cover his or her tracks.

To verify a single package, include the package name on the command line, like this:

```
$ rpm --verify bash
```

You can also verify all the packages within a group:

```
$ rpm --verify --group "Amusements/Games"
```

To verify all the packages installed on your computer, use the following command:

```
$ rpm --verify --all
```

Verifying your entire system takes quite some time, but when you're done, you'll have a very thorough understanding of the state of your system.

 The `--verify` command can take awhile to complete. Start the command and let it run while you're in a meeting or when you go home at night.

What's this MD5 stuff anyway?

MD5 is a *message-digest* algorithm (in fact, MD5 is a rather uninspired acronym for message digest number 5). A message digest is like a fingerprint that belongs to a chunk of data. Two different chunks of data are highly unlikely to have the same fingerprint (that is, the same MD5 checksum). MD5 is *cryptographically strong*, meaning that it would take an incredibly fast computer (or an astonishingly brilliant mathematician) to come up with another chunk of data with the same fingerprint.

A digest algorithm generates two different digest values for two different files. A good digest program pays attention not only to the characters in the file, but also to the *ordering* of the characters in the file (so *ab* generates a different checksum than *ba*).

When an RPM package is first created, RPM computes the MD5 checksum of each file in the package. When you install the package, the MD5 checksums are copied into the RPM database. When you verify a package, RPM recomputes the checksum of each file in the package (it reads through the whole file and computes the checksum again from scratch) and compares that checksum to the value stored in the database. If the checksums are different, the file has been modified.

Reading the Tamper-Proof Seal

When you get a new RPM package, whether from a Web site or on a disc, you really have no guarantee that it hasn't been tampered with — that is, unless you use RPM to verify its digital signature.

Just like the tamper-proof seal on a bottle of aspirin, the digital signature is there to protect you from potential headaches. After all, you would never use medicine from a bottle with a broken seal. A digital signature ensures that a package was created by the person (or organization) claiming to have produced the package.

When you install Linux from a CD or DVD, the disc should include a public key from the packager. Every package included in your Linux distribution is (or at least can be) signed with the packager's private key. You can use RPM (and the public key) to verify each package. When you download a package, look through the project's Web site to see if it makes a public key available. If you find one, use it. (If you can't find a public key, e-mail the maintainers asking them to sign their packages.)

In this section, we use the Fedora install DVD as an example of how to import a public key and then use that key to check the signature of a package — we assume most of you have installation media. Not all vendors include keys on their software, but it's a really good idea to run an integrity check if they do.

To verify the integrity of your Fedora disc, follow these steps:

1. **Open a terminal window and give yourself superuser privileges.**

2. **Insert and mount either the DVD or the first CD of the Fedora distribution, and move to the** cdrom **directory.**

    $ cd /mnt/cdrom

3. **Type the following command and press Enter:**

    $ rpm --import RPM-GPG-KEY

The --import command installs the public key (RPM-GPG-KEY) into your RPM database. After it's there, RPM will use the public key to verify any package you install that's been signed with the corresponding private key. See Technique 28 for more information about how digital signatures, public keys, and private keys all fit together.

 Depending on your distribution, one key or many keys may exist. If multiple keys exist, install them all before checking the package's signature. The easy way to do this is to use rpm --import RPM-GPG*.

4. **Move to the directory of the package you want to verify and press Enter. For our example, enter**

    $ cd /mnt/cdrom/Fedora/RPMS

5. **Enter the following command:**

    $ rpm --checksig bash

6. **Press Tab to autocomplete the package name and then press Enter.**

rpm displays a message that looks something like this:

    bash-2.05b-31.i386.rpm: (sha1) dsa sha1
        md5 gpg OK

From this message, you know that your bash package is OK. If the result set returns a NOT OK or MISSING KEYS, you should at least question the integrity of the package. Some system administrators won't install software that doesn't come with proper digital signatures to avoid any potential problems.

 Some open-source software that has integrity doesn't have keys. We wish it did because the software is good, reputable, and worthy of downloading.

In our example, the key was distributed on the disc with the software. Often, the keys are available at the project's Web site, as a separate download. If you have trouble finding the key, consider e-mailing the site administrator.

Technique 19

Keeping Up-to-Date with apt and Synaptic

Keeping your software up-to-date is important. A new release of your favorite software will likely include new features, fixes for old bugs, and most importantly, fixes for security vulnerabilities. Open-source software evolves astonishingly fast. Given that most, if not all, of the software on your Linux computer is of the open-source variety, keeping current can be quite a chore. Although you could keep a list of your software packages and check the sites regularly for more recent versions, we know a better way.

apt (Advanced Package Tool) is a handy tool that can save you *tons* of time. apt by itself is good; apt coupled with Synaptic is even better. Synaptic is an attractive, friendly wrapper around the apt command line tool. Synaptic knows how to check your installed RPM packages against the most recent versions, download any updates, and automatically resolve package dependencies.

If you've installed many packages with RPM, you know what dependencies are: When you install a new software package, that package may require (or *depend on*) other packages. If you use RPM by itself, you have to satisfy a package's dependencies before you can install the package (that is, you have to install all the other software required by the package that you really want to install). Technique 17 explains how to use RPM from the command line. Quite often, a dependency has dependencies of its own. The chain of dependencies can get very long, very fast. With Synaptic, the frustration and time lost tracking down and installing all the program dependencies are gone — Synaptic handles the process for you.

In this technique, we introduce you to Synaptic. Installing and updating your software has never been so quick or easy.

Setting Up Synaptic and apt in a Snap

apt is a wrapper around the command line tool, rpm. Synaptic is a graphical wrapper around apt. You already have rpm (it's a fundamental Fedora component), but you need to install `apt` and Synaptic before you can use the three tools together to make quick work of package management.

If you're using SuSE, use Google to search for the most recent versions of the `apt` and `synaptic` RPM packages. You'll need two packages — the `apt` package and the `synaptic` package.

To download and install `apt` with Fedora, follow these steps:

1. **Open your favorite browser and surf to**

`apt.freshrpms.net`

2. **Click the link to Fedora Linux 1 (rpm 4.2.x).**

This moves you to the Index of `/pub/freshrpms/ fedora/linux/1/apt`.

3. **Click the link to download the most recent RPM package. Right now, that is**

`apt-0.5.15cnc3-0-1.fr.i386.rpm`

The Download Manager opens (assuming that your browser offers a download manager).

4. **Save the RPM package to your desktop.**

5. **Close the Download Manager and minimize the Web browser (you'll be using it again in a minute).**

6. **Click the RPM Package icon on the desktop.**

7. **If you're not already logged in as the superuser, a query window opens, prompting you for the `root` password. Enter the password and click OK.**

The RPM graphical installer opens, telling you that the system is being prepared for package installation.

8. **When the preparations are complete, click Continue.**

The `apt` package installs.

Now, download the RPM package for Synaptic:

1. **Reopen your browser and surf to**

`dag.wieers.com/packages/synaptic`

2. **Click the download link for**

`synaptic-0.45-0.rhfc1.dag.i386.rpm`

3. **Save the package to your desktop.**

4. **Close the Download Manager and the browser window, and return to the desktop.**

5. **Click the desktop icon for the Synaptic RPM package.**

The graphical installer begins. Again, you may be prompted for the `root` password.

Now that you have `apt` and Synaptic installed, you're ready to update your system.

Keeping Up-to-Date with apt and Synaptic: The Basics

Using `apt` with Synaptic is a quick and easy way to keep your system software up-to-date. To run Synaptic and do a package update, follow these steps:

1. **Open a terminal window and give yourself superuser privileges with the `su` command.**

2. **Type the following command and press Enter:**

`# synaptic`

Synaptic starts and, after a short delay, displays the packages currently installed on your computer (see Figure 19-1). The package list is sorted by category and displayed in a tree-type control panel in the middle of the screen. Click the little arrow to the left of a category to view the packages within that category.

When Synaptic starts, it displays all the packages available at the default repository (you can add more repositories later).

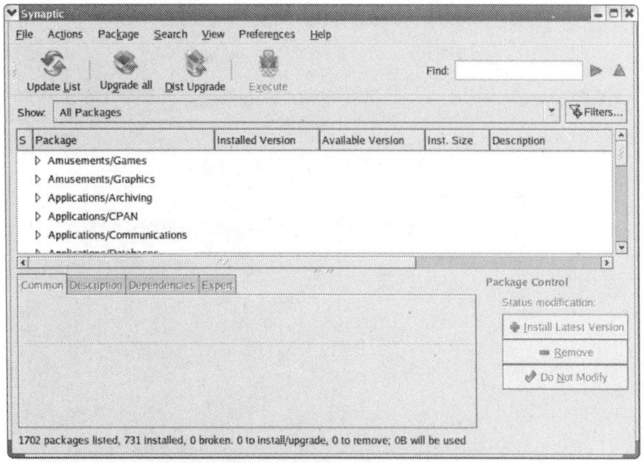

• **Figure 19-1:** The Synaptic startup screen.

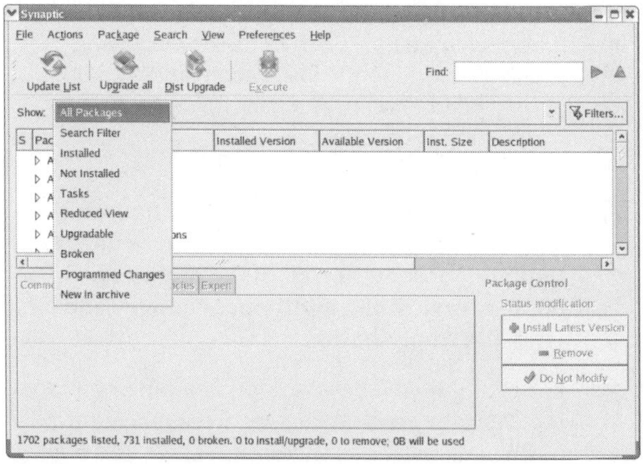

• **Figure 19-2:** The package display options.

3. To filter the choices in the Package list, choose one of the following options from the Show drop-down list (shown in Figure 19-2):

▶ **Installed Packages:** Show only the packages that are currently installed on your computer.

▶ **Not Installed Packages:** Show packages that are in the repository but not currently installed on your computer.

▶ **Tasks:** Show groups of related but otherwise independent packages (such as a complete office or personal productivity suite).

▶ **Upgradable (sic):** Show currently installed packages for which newer versions are available.

▶ **Broken:** Show packages that are currently installed but have unsatisfied dependencies.

▶ **Programmed Changes:** Show packages selected for installation, upgrade, removal, or repair.

▶ **New in Archive:** Show packages that have just been added to the archive list on your computer.

 One of the most useful features is the Upgrad*(e)*able filter. Select Upgradable from the Show drop-down list and then click a tree control to see the outdated packages in that category (see Figure 19-3).

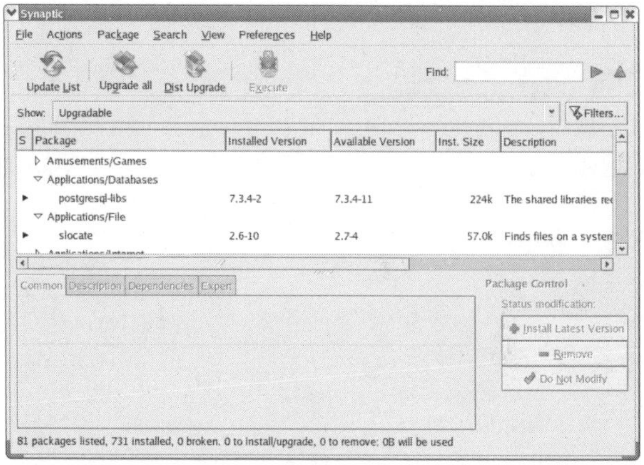

• **Figure 19-3:** Outdated packages.

4. When you find a package that needs to be updated, click the package name to highlight it.

5. Click the Upgrade button (in the lower-right corner of the screen).

Sometimes a package might be changed to include another package in its installation. If this is the case, you need to authorize `apt` to remove the old package before it can update to the new version.

In some cases, the package that needs to be removed isn't included in the new package, but it's blocking the installation anyway. You may need to reinstall a package after the updating is complete.

6. **Depending on the package you're updating, a dialog *may* appear that shows other changes that you must authorize. If the dialog does appear, review the additional changes and click the Apply button.**

   For example, the new version of a package may have new dependencies that were not required by the currently installed release. Or, you may have to upgrade other packages at the same time.

   The packages to be upgraded are highlighted in the list, as shown in Figure 19-4.

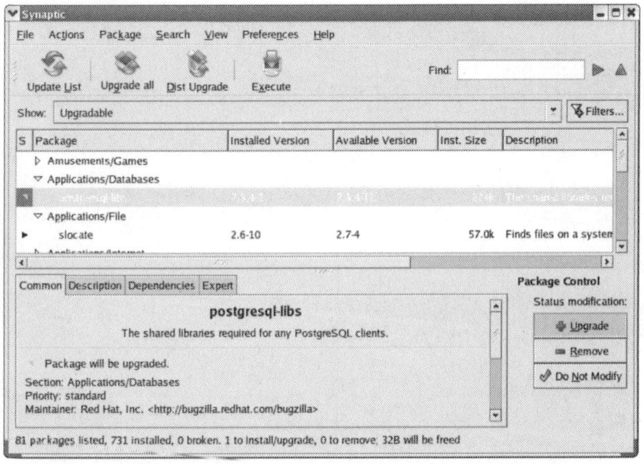

• **Figure 19-4:** Highlighted packages are ready to upgrade.

7. **To carry out the upgrade (and any related changes), click the Execute button (on the toolbar).**

   The Summary dialog opens (see Figure 19-5).

8. **Click the Proceed button in the Summary dialog to continue.**

   The new versions are downloaded, and the upgrade begins — pretty simple.

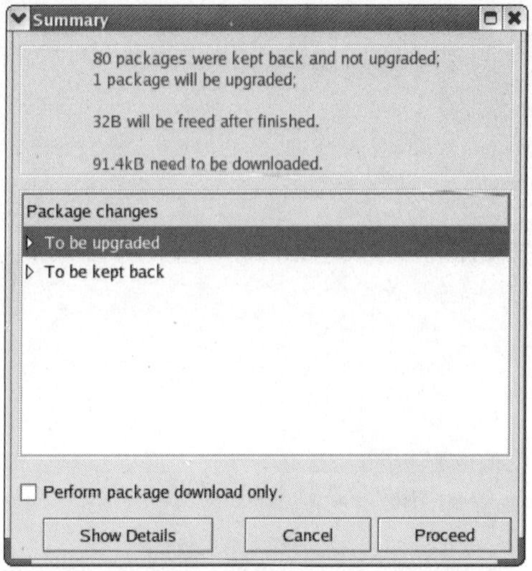

• **Figure 19-5:** The Summary dialog.

Upgrading Your Entire Computer

Synaptic can install and upgrade individual packages, but its real power lies in its ability to upgrade your entire system with just a few quick clicks of the mouse. Synaptic offers two system-update modes:

✔ **Dist Upgrade:** If you want to upgrade to the most recent versions of all the packages currently installed on your system, click the Dist Upgrade (Distribution Upgrade) button on the toolbar. Dist Upgrade updates all the packages on your computer and adds any new software needed to satisfy program dependencies.

✔ **Upgrade All:** If you're short on disk space, use the Upgrade All button to upgrade only those packages that can be freshened *without* installing extra software required by new dependencies.

Handy Hints about Synaptic

Synaptic can install *new* packages too. With so many packages available, the choices can seem overwhelming. Fortunately, Synaptic has a few tools that can help you narrow down the package list to a more manageable size. You can also find out a lot about a package *before* you download and install it on your computer.

Changing repositories

Synaptic works its magic by connecting to software repositories scattered around the Internet. Synaptic comes preconfigured with the information required to connect to a number of repositories, and it's ready to use the repository that's right for a Fedora distribution. Most repositories organize packages into *types* and *sections*. The two most frequently seen types are rpm (installable packages) and rpm-src (source code for package): Unless you want to build your software from source code, stick with the rpm type. Sections are more diverse. At any given repository, you may see sections such as testing, stable, and updates. The section name gives you some idea of how safe the packages are within that section. Stay away from the testing section unless you're in an adventurous mood.

By default, Synaptic enables only the "safe" sections. You may need to make changes to the repository list if a package that you want to install (or upgrade) can't be found in the preconfigured sections. When you enable a section, the Packages list shows new packages distributed from that section (hopefully, the Packages list contains the package you're looking for).

To enable a new section, follow these steps:

1. **In Synaptic, choose Preferences⇨Repositories.**

A dialog appears, showing the repositories that Synaptic currently knows about.

2. **Enable a section by checking the box in the Enabled column to the left of the repository URL.**

 It's safest to choose from the repositories that offer packages for your specific Linux distribution. However, the other repositories include some great packages that might be worth checking out when you have some time to spare.

3. **Click OK to close the repository list, and then click Update List to retrieve a list of available packages.**

This process takes a minute or two, depending on your Web connection speed. Synaptic displays a pop-up as it retrieves index files.

Now when you open a package category, each package is color-coded:

▶ The **white** ones are currently installed.

▶ The **beige** ones have just been added to the list of known packages.

▶ The **red** ones are broken packages (installed packages with unsatisfied dependencies).

▶ The **mint** ones are the packages you've selected to install.

 You can set your own color choices by choosing Preferences⇨Preferences.

Viewing package details

Synaptic's main package list can be a bit overwhelming because it displays so *many* packages. To narrow your choices a bit, use the Show drop-down list to filter out packages in different ways. Our favorite filter is Not Installed — that filter shows all of the packages just waiting to fill up your hard drive (see Figure 19-6).

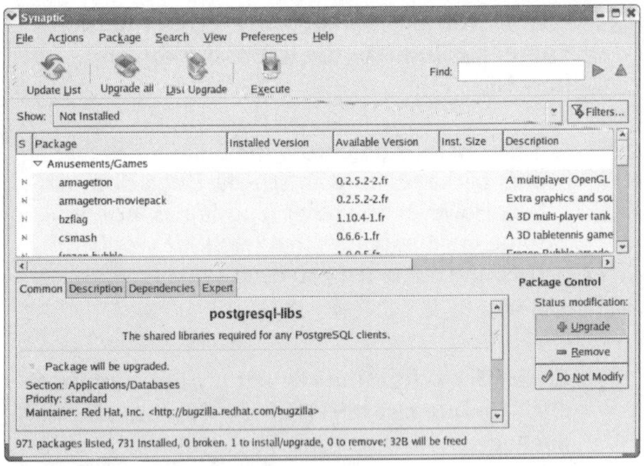

• **Figure 19-6:** Tons of free software.

With so much free software to choose from, it's a good idea to check out the package details before you download.

When you highlight a package, the frame at the bottom of the screen displays information about that package. You can navigate this information by clicking the following tabs:

✔ **Common:** Contains a short summary of the package — what section the program belongs to and who maintains the software.

✔ **Description:** Shows a more detailed description of the package.

✔ **Dependencies:** Shows a list of the *other* packages required by the one you've selected. Any dependencies shown in red are not currently installed, but that's okay; Synaptic automatically resolves dependencies for you.

✔ **Expert:** Offers options for the adventurous — usually alternative versions (which might be untested).

Read through the package information carefully to decide if an alternative package is right for you.

Installing new packages with Synaptic

When you find a package that you want to install, follow these steps:

1. **Highlight the package name and click Install Latest Version.**

If you want to install more packages, highlight each one and click Install Latest Version.

2. **When you've finished selecting packages, click Execute, and the installation begins.**

Depending on the packages you're installing, a dialog *may* appear that shows other changes that you must authorize. If the dialog does appear, review the additional changes and click the Apply button.

For example, the new package may have required other packages or updates to currently-installed packages.

3. **Click the Proceed button in the Summary dialog to continue.**

The new packages are downloaded, and the installation begins — pretty simple.

> Technique 58 shows you how to set up a UML jail. Resolving dependencies within a jail can be a time-consuming chore. Use apt and Synaptic to resolve the dependencies for you.

Importing the Keys to the Repository

Sometimes Synaptic prefers that you have the public keys that were used to sign each package before it allows you to install new software. It's a good idea to install the keys so they're ready when you need them.

Each repository has its own set of keys, and you have to hunt around the repository Web site to find them. To download and install the keys to the primary Fedora repository, follow these steps:

1. **Open your favorite browser and surf to** freshrpms.net/packages.

2. **Right-click the GPG Key Used to Sign All Packages link. Save the file to the desktop.**

3. **Open a terminal window and give yourself superuser privileges with the** su **command.**

4. **Use the following command to import the keys to the repository:**

```
# rpm --import /home/susan/Desktop/RPM-
GPG-KEY.txt
```

The keys to the repository are added to your RPM key ring, where Synaptic can find them if it needs them.

Setting Up Automatic Services

Save Time By

✔ Setting up automatic tasks with Task Scheduler

✔ Editing existing tasks

✔ Creating an environment for your automated tasks

Administrative tasks — such as backing up, updating data files, and updating Web site mirrors — are easy to automate. You can save tons of time by creating automatic tasks that do your job without any help from you. To help you automate these tasks, you have two handy tools at your disposal: Task Scheduler and the Services Configuration Tool.

Task Scheduler is a graphical interface that schedules programs to run automatically with the program cron. Setting up jobs to run when network demands are low can save time (and user frustration from the bogged-down network). Task Scheduler has a nice interface and offers a quick way to set up cron jobs.

In this technique, we'll show you how to automate your work with Task Scheduler.

Letting Task Scheduler Work for You

Task Scheduler is a graphical interface for cron (the Linux scheduling tool). With Task Scheduler, you can set up recurrent downloads, backups, or other system maintenance jobs to run at night (or when your network load is the lightest).

Task Scheduler is part of the kdeadmin package (if you're using KDE, make sure you've installed the kdeadmin package or you won't find Task Scheduler in the KDE Menu). The Mandrake 10.0 Community Edition distribution does not include the kdeadmin package (although later editions may) — if you can't find kdeadmin in your distribution, you'll have to download and install it from the Web.

GNOME doesn't have an *official* task scheduler yet, but if you Google for GNOME and Task Scheduler, you should find a few options.

Before Task Scheduler will work, you need to start the `crond` daemon. To start `crond`, follow these steps:

1. **Open a terminal window and give yourself superuser privileges with the** `su` **command.**

2. **Type in the following command and press Enter.**

If you're a Fedora or Mandrake user, use this command:

`# /sbin/service crond start`

SuSE users should use this command:

`# /etc/init.d/cron start`

Scheduling a new task

After you've started the `crond` daemon, you're ready to set up automated tasks:

1. **To start Task Scheduler, open the Main Menu and choose System Tools⇨Task Scheduler.**

The Task Scheduler window opens, showing a summary of the scheduled tasks and their environment variables (see Figure 20-1).

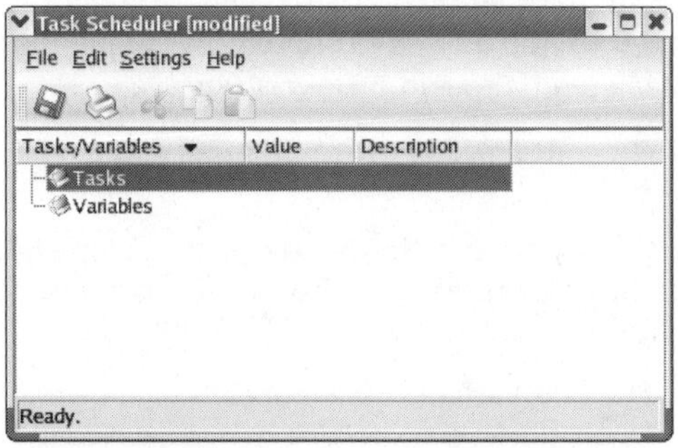

• **Figure 20-1: The Task Scheduler window.**

If you're logged in as `root`, you see everyone's scheduled tasks. If not, you're privileged to see your own tasks only.

2. **To add a new task, right-click the Tasks folder and choose New.**

The Edit Task window opens (see Figure 20-2).

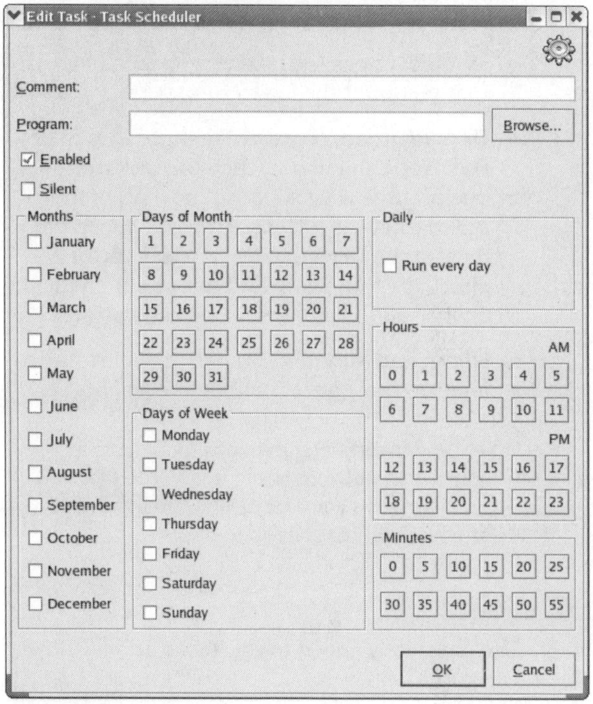

• **Figure 20-2: The Edit Task window.**

3. **To create a new task, fill in the following fields:**

▶ **Comment:** Enter a descriptive name.

▶ **Program:** Enter the command you want to run.

It's a good idea to use the complete pathname for a command, not just the command name. That way, changes to your environment (your `$PATH` variable in particular) won't affect scheduled tasks. For example, enter `/usr/bin/wget -r --mirror -k http://www.website.com` to update a Web site nightly. If you don't know the complete pathname, use the Browse button to find your program. Most of the commands are in `/bin`, `/usr/bin` or `/usr/local/bin`.

► **Enabled:** Check this box to make the task active. If the box isn't checked, the task won't run.

► **Silent:** Check this box to turn off the logging features.

► **Months:** Check the box next to each month that you want the job to run.

► **Days of Month, Days of Week, or Run Every Day:** You can choose when the task runs in one of three ways. Choose the days of the month that the job executes, or choose the days of the week that the job executes, or check the Run Every Day box to automatically choose all the months, days, and dates.

► **Hours and Minutes:** Choose the hours and minutes that the task should begin.

Set up network-intensive jobs to execute at night when network traffic is low. The jobs will run faster, and you'll be saving the bandwidth for when you really need it.

4. **Click OK.**

The new job is added to the Tasks list, as shown in Figure 20-3.

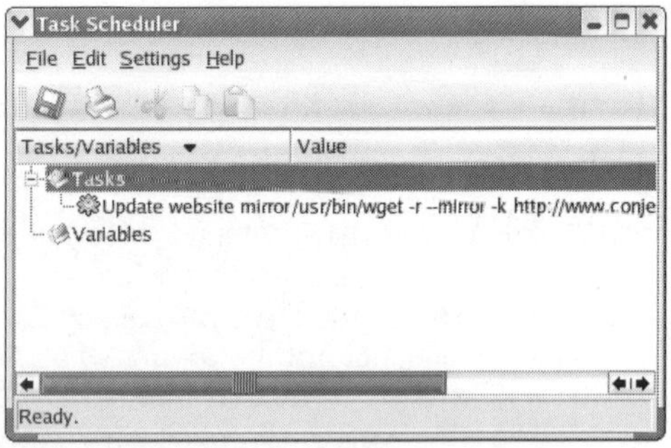

• **Figure 20-3:** The new task is added to the list.

5. **If you're done using Task Scheduler, click Save. Or if you haven't defined the environment variables, see "Adding environment variables," later in this technique, to do so.**

It's hard to predict the environment in which your scheduled tasks will run. Use full path-names and define the environment variables that you need. That also makes you more immune to changes in the system configuration.

If you're scheduling a complex task (one that involves running multiple commands), write yourself a shell script and schedule the script instead of a complex command line. It's much easier to debug a script than a complex command line that resides somewhere in the Task Scheduler's database. Technique 10 has some handy information about creating shell scripts.

Editing a task

If you need to go back and edit a task, open the Main Menu and choose System Tools⇨Task Scheduler. In Task Scheduler, right-click the task (refer to Figure 20-3) and choose Modify from the pop-up menu. When you're done, click Save so that the scheduler remembers the new settings.

Adding environment variables

Task Scheduler works in its own environment, so you need to add any environment variables that your task needs to run properly (such as $PATH).

To add or edit a variable, follow these steps:

1. **Choose System Tools⇨Task Scheduler, right-click Variables, and choose New from the pop-up menu.**

The Edit Variable dialog opens, as shown in Figure 20-4.

2. **To add a new variable, fill in the fields on the dialog:**

► **Variable:** Enter the variable name, or choose from the most common variables in the drop-down list.

If you don't define the HOME, MAILTO, and SHELL variables, they default to your normal values. Change these variables if you want to override the defaults.

The PATH variable holds the search path that cron uses to locate your programs.

▶ **Value:** Enter the variable's value.

▶ **Comment:** Enter a description of the variable.

▶ **Enable:** Check this box to make the variable active. If the box is not checked, the variable doesn't take effect.

3. **Click OK when you've completed this dialog.**

Your new variable is added.

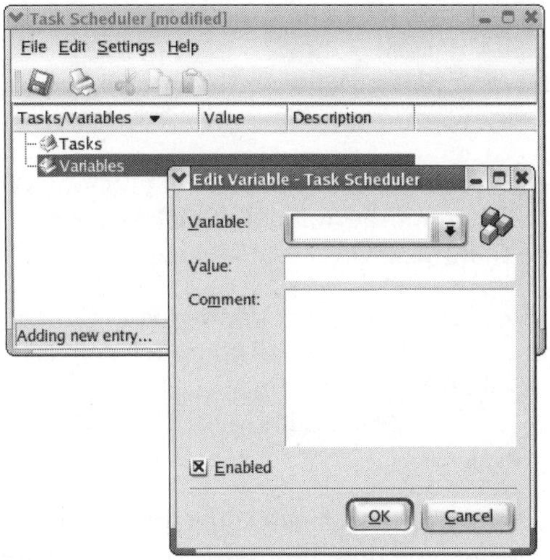

• **Figure 20-4: The Edit Variable dialog.**

4. **When you're finished using Task Scheduler, click the Save icon to save your changes and then close the window.**

Your newly scheduled programs will run without any help from you!

If you use a proxy server to access the net, wget can use the http_proxy variable to speed up data transfers. Create the variable quickly with Task Scheduler, as shown in Figure 20-5.

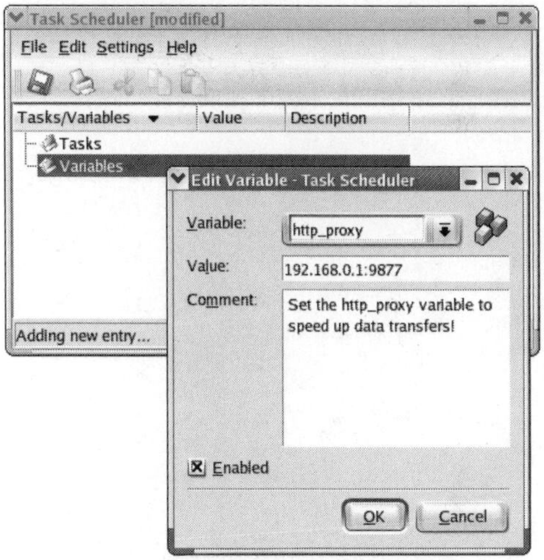

• **Figure 20-5: Setting the http_proxy variable.**

Making Your Inner System Administrator Happy (And Productive)

A s system administrator, you want to be sure that system resources are available when needed. Doling out resources to users that need them and keeping track of the overall system performance are important. Fortunately, tools exist that make it really quick and easy.

Imposing disk quotas is a quick and easy way to control precious system resources. Define user quotas to limit the amount of disk space each user can consume so you're sure that those who need it can get it.

Disk quotas are self-governing. After you've set up the quota (and a grace period), Linux ensures that users can't use up all your disk space. If you need to know whether you've budgeted too little space for some users, a quick glance at the disk quota report tells you how well users are staying within their quotas.

The Linux system accounting package is a small collection of tools that give you quick access to information about how your system is being used. You can quickly determine which users are spending the most time logged in and what resources they're using. You can also spot programs that shouldn't be used at all.

In this technique, we show you how to control your system usage. You're not being a control freak — you're just ensuring that your users have what they need to get their jobs done.

Reining In Resources with Disk Quotas

If you're the administrator of a multiuser system, you've probably encountered *disk hogs* — users who download every game or graphic they can find, keep a copy of every e-mail they've ever received, and keep multiple copies of work in progress. Such users can cause major disk clogs — especially if your resources are limited.

Use the `diskquota` tool to stop resource problems before they start. Placing limits on the storage space or the number of files a user can have on a system will make your users more conscientious about not keeping unneeded files around.

 If users exceed their allotted disk space, they receive a warning, and Linux starts a grace-period countdown. At the end of the grace period, these users are not allowed any additional disk space until they clean up their act.

Installing the quota RPM package

Before you can create and allocate disk quotas, you must install the `quota` RPM package included with most Linux distributions. To install `quota` on your system, follow these steps:

1. Open a terminal window and give yourself superuser privileges with the `su` command.

2. Mount your distribution disc in the CD drive.

3. Use the `cd` command to move to the directory containing the quota RPM package.

4. Install the `quota` package with the following command:

```
# rpm -Uhv quota-version.rpm
```

That's all there is to it. The `quota` package is installed and ready to use.

 If you don't have the distribution disc, but need the package, just Google for it. Downloads of the `quota` RPM package abound on the Web.

Enabling file system quotas

You can create disk quotas for any file system on your computer, but you have to change the `mount` options first. To enable quotas for a particular file system, follow these steps:

1. Open a terminal window and give yourself superuser privileges with the `su -` command.

 Don't forget the hyphen when you type in the `su -` command. The hyphen sets up your search path (`$PATH`) so you can find the superuser's tools.

2. Open the `/etc/fstab` file in your favorite editor (which in our case is `kedit`):

```
# kedit /etc/fstab
```

`kedit` opens, as shown in Figure 21-1.

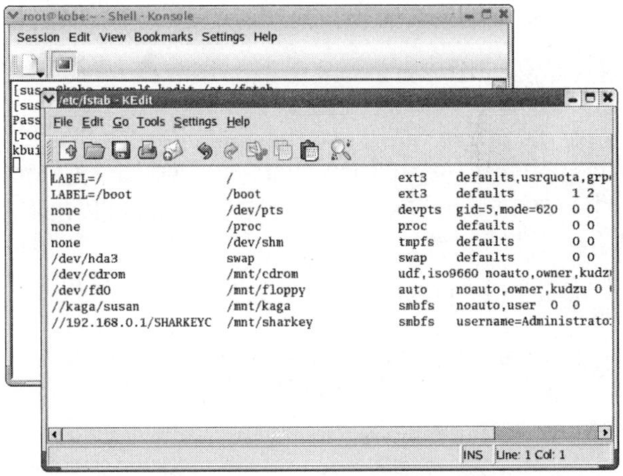

• **Figure 21-1: The** `/etc/fstab` **file opened with** `kedit`**.**

3. Find the file system that you want to modify.

4. Add the `usrquota` and `grpquota` options to the fourth column.

Finding the correct column in a typical `fstab` file can be tricky. The first column contains the device name, the second column specifies the mount point, the third column determines the file system type, and the fourth column contains a comma-separated list of options (typically, `defaults`):

```
LABEL=/  /  ext3
   defaults,usrquota,grpquota  1  1
```

The preceding code shows the changes needed to add quotas for the root file system.

5. Save your changes and close the editor.

Now, remount the file system that you modified to enable the new options. The easiest way to remount an active file system is to reboot.

 What's the quickest way to reboot fast? Just type `reboot` at the command line and press Enter.

Getting your files together

Now it's time to create the quota control files: `aquota.user` and `aquota.group`. These files record the quotas that you assign to each user (or group) on that file system as well as the amount of space currently in use. You'll find the quota control files in the root directory of each quota-enabled file system. When you create the control files, Linux computes the current disk usage to create a starting point for you.

To create the quota control files, follow these steps:

1. **Open a terminal window and give yourself superuser privileges with the `su -` command.**

2. **Type the following command and press Enter:**

`# quotacheck -acugm`

The flags in this command tell `quotacheck` to create (c) a new control file for users (u) and groups (g) in all currently mounted file systems (a).

3. **Type the following command and press Enter:**

`# quotacheck -avugm`

Running the `quotacheck` command again without the create (c) flag populates the control files with the current usage information. The current usage reflects the blocks and files allocated to users (u) and groups (g) on all quota-enabled file systems (a). By default, `quotacheck` won't compute disk usage on mounted file systems. (If you've enabled quotas for the root file system [/], you can't unmount that drive.) The `-m` flag forces `quotacheck` to inspect file systems that can't be remounted in read-only mode.

That's it! The quota files are created, populated, and ready to use.

 Remember that systems vary. The preceding steps work great on our system (and should work well on most simple configurations), but if you need more information about command options that might suit your specific hardware configuration, check out the official documentation. Just enter `info quotacheck` at the command line for fast access to the online documentation.

Setting quotas

At this point, the quota tools have been installed, and the control files are in place (which we explain how to do in preceding sections). Now it's time to impose quotas. Here, we explain how to set quotas for a user name or group and how to set the grace period for users who have met their quotas and need to clean up their files.

 The default editor for `quota` is `vi`, a powerful but unfriendly editor. When you first set quotas, we recommend fixing up the `quota` editor a bit. Our editor of choice is `kedit` or `kate`. See the following steps to find out how.

To set quotas for a user, follow these steps:

1. **Open a terminal window and give yourself superuser privileges with the `su -` command.**

2. **To change the default editor for `quota`, enter the following command:**

`# export EDITOR=$(which kedit)`

 If you prefer another editor, just substitute it for `kedit` in the preceding command.

3. **To edit the control files and define quotas, enter the following command:**

`# edquota username`

`edquota` creates a temporary file that contains the current quota settings for *username* and then opens that file in the editor that you specified, as shown in Figure 21-2.

```
/tmp//EdP_a0YHmWz - KEdit                                    _ □ x
File  Edit  Go  Tools  Settings  Help

 Disk quotas for user duncan (uid 501):
   Filesystem              blocks     soft     hard    inodes     soft     hard
   /dev/hda2                   44    14000    16000        13       50       65

                                                   INS   Line: 4 Col: 1
```

• **Figure 21-2: The disk quota file.**

The quota file that you see contains one line for each quota-enabled file system (the file system name is in the first column). `edquota` lets you control disk usage in 1024-byte blocks. You can also control the total number of files that a given user can create on a file system. (The quota tools all refer to *inode* quotas — inode is essentially a synonym for file.)

The numbers listed under *blocks* and *inodes* show disk space (and file count) currently used by the given user. A Linux quota is defined by three values:

✔ **Soft limit:** This controls the maximum amount of space that you *should* use.

✔ **Hard limit:** This controls the maximum amount of space that you *can* use.

✔ **Grace period:** When you exceed the soft limit, Linux warns you and gives you a grace period. During the grace period, you can continue to accumulate more disk space (up to the hard limit). If, at the end of the grace period, you're still over the soft limit, the soft limit becomes a hard limit.

For example, suppose your soft limit is 2GB, your hard limit is 2.5GB, and the grace period is one week. As soon as your disk usage exceeds 2GB, Linux displays a warning. You can exceed your soft limit for

one week (but you can never go above 2.5GB). After the grace period, you can't create any new files (or write more data to existing files) until you clean up enough stuff to fall back to the 2GB soft limit. You can exceed the soft limit (for a week), but you can't exceed the hard limit.

Deciding how many blocks or inodes a user needs is a matter of system resources. If users need access only to e-mail, they obviously need fewer files (and less disk space) than users doing development work. If you have plenty of room, you can allocate larger pieces of the total pie.

You can also assign quotas to a group of users. To assign group quotas, follow these steps:

1. **Give yourself superuser privileges with the** `su -` **command.**

2. **To edit the control files and define the group quota, use the following command:**

   `# edquota -g groupname`

   The `-g` indicates that the following name is the name of a group.

3. **Edit the quotas as desired (following the same basic rules we discuss earlier in this section), and then save the file and close the editor.**

Linux is far kinder than many people would be. If you exceed a soft limit, your files are still there (Linux doesn't delete the extra data). You just don't get any more space until you trim down a bit.

To set the grace period, enter the following command:

   `# edquota -t`

The editor opens, displaying the current settings for the block and inode grace periods, as shown in Figure 21-3.

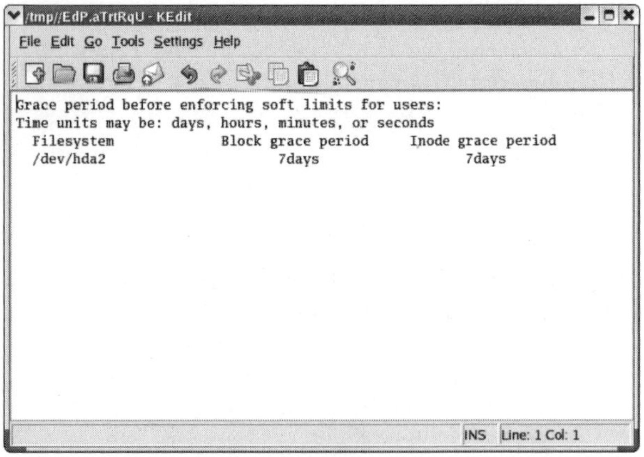

```
▼ /tmp//EdP.aTrtRqU - KEdit                          _ □ ✕
File  Edit  Go  Tools  Settings  Help

⎸ ⬚ 🖫 🖨 ✐  ↺ ⬀ ⬀ 🗋 🗏 🗎 ✂

Grace period before enforcing soft limits for users:
Time units may be: days, hours, minutes, or seconds
  Filesystem              Block grace period    Inode grace period
  /dev/hda2               7days                 7days




                                          INS   Line: 1 Col: 1
```

• **Figure 21-3: The grace period file.**

Change the grace period if you want — you can specify a number of days, hours, minutes, or seconds. Be sure to give yourself a reasonable amount of time to clean things up (at least a day). Save the file and close the editor when you're finished.

Reviewing your quotas

To generate a complete listing of the quota definitions and the current system usage, type in this command:

```
# repquota -vugs /home
```

repquota generates a quota report listing the space used by all users (-u) and groups (-g) on the /home file system. The -v option tells repquota to produce a more detailed (or verbose) report that displays quota definitions that are not currently in use. By default, repquota displays quota information in terms of 1024-byte blocks; the -s flag tells repquota to print the totals in more readable terms (megs instead of blocks). The last argument in the command indicates the file system — in this case, the /home file system. To display quota information for all file systems, use the -a flag instead (repquota -avugs).

The listing shows user quotas first and then group quotas, as shown in Figure 21-4.

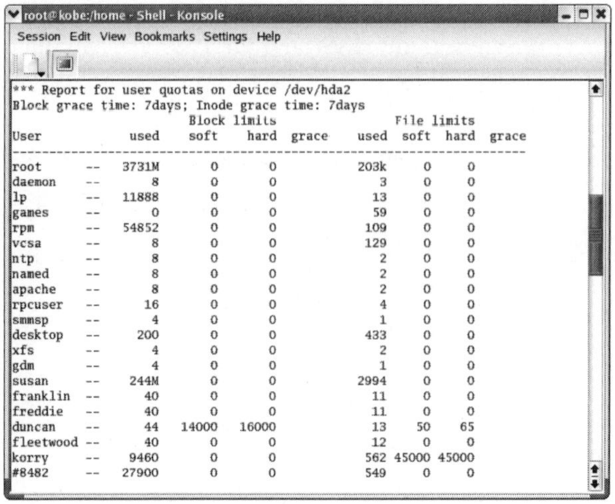

```
▼ root@ kobe:/home - Shell - Konsole                          _ □ ✕
Session  Edit  View  Bookmarks  Settings  Help

⎙  ⬛

*** Report for user quotas on device /dev/hda2
Block grace time: 7days; Inode grace time: 7days
                           Block limits              File limits
User           used      soft   hard  grace    used   soft   hard  grace
---------------------------------------------------------------------------
root       --  3731M       0      0            203k      0      0
daemon     --      8       0      0               3      0      0
lp         --  11888       0      0              13      0      0
games      --      0       0      0              59      0      0
rpm        --  54852       0      0             109      0      0
vcsa       --      8       0      0             129      0      0
ntp        --      8       0      0               2      0      0
named      --      8       0      0               2      0      0
apache     --      8       0      0               2      0      0
rpcuser    --     16       0      0               4      0      0
smmsp      --      4       0      0               1      0      0
desktop    --    200       0      0             433      0      0
xfs        --      4       0      0               2      0      0
gdm        --      4       0      0               1      0      0
susan      --   244M       0      0            2994      0      0
franklin   --     40       0      0              11      0      0
freddie    --     40       0      0              11      0      0
duncan     --     44   14000  16000              13     50     65
fleetwood  --     40       0      0              12      0      0
korry      --   9460       0      0             562  45000  45000
#8482      --  27900       0      0             549      0      0
```

• **Figure 21-4: The user quota report.**

Worthy of note are the grace columns. If a quota has been exceeded, the amount of time left in the grace period is displayed. If the grace period has expired, none appears in the column.

Using System Accounting to Keep Track of Users

Linux gives you a number of command-line tools that can help you keep track of the resources used by a given user (not just disk space, but CPU time, connect time, and memory usage as well). After you've installed the tools, with a few quick keystrokes you can determine which users spend the most time at their keyboards.

Setting up system accounting

To install the psacct package on Fedora or Mandrake, or the equivalent, acct on SuSE, follow these steps:

1. Open a terminal window and give yourself superuser privileges with the su command.

2. Insert and mount your distribution disc.

3. Use the cd **command to move to the directory containing the RPM packages.**

4. Type the following command and press Enter:

```
# rpm -Uhv psacct-version.rpm
```

On SuSE, install the acct package with the command:

```
#rpm -Uhv acct-version.rpm
```

The installation process creates a new background daemon.

To start the psacct service (or acct, if you're running SuSE), follow these steps:

1. Open a terminal window and give yourself superuser privileges with the su **command.**

2. Start the service:

If you're running Fedora, the command is

```
# /sbin/service psacct start
```

If you're running Mandrake, use the command:

```
# /sbin/service psacct start
```

If you're a SuSE user, start the service with the command:

```
# /etc/init.d/acct start
```

Now you're up and running. Linux keeps track of resource usage in the /var/run/utmp and /var/log/wtmp files.

 The wtmp file can grow quickly. It's a good idea to clean it up every now and then.

Looking up user login hours

Of all the information you can call up in a flash, summaries of user login hours are among the most useful. Use the ac command to find out how long (in hours) your users have been logged in. To generate a list of login hours, itemized by user, enter the following command:

```
$ ac -p
```

The result will look something like this:

```
[freddie@bastille freddie]$ ac -p
    freddie   7.03
    duncan    2.02
    franklin  6.54
    root      1.02
    total    16.61
```

To generate a list of total login hours on a daily basis, use the -d flag:

```
$ ac -d
```

The result is a daily list of connect-time hours:

```
[freddie@bastille freddie]$ ac -d
Feb 1total   0.33
Feb 2total  12.54
Todaytotal   1.01
```

One thing to note — the daily total is for everyone logged in.

 This is a quick way to find out total system man hours if you need to answer to accounting about department costs or want to request more resources in a budget meeting.

The two flags we've listed are probably the most useful, but other flags work with the ac command as well. Check out the man page for more ideas — man ac.

Checking out command and program usage

Another useful command that comes courtesy of system accounting is the sa command. Use the sa command to find out which programs are being used on your system. To use the sa command, first you need to give yourself superuser privileges with the su - command. Then to generate a report of command usage, enter the following command:

```
# sa
```

The report shows the command usage for the system, as shown in Figure 21-5.

```
root@kobe;/home - Shell - Konsole                                    _ □ ×
Session  Edit  View  Bookmarks  Settings  Help

[root@kobe home]# sa
  10460  147431.51re    315.03cp     0avio    3420k  ***other*
     56    5393.08re    198.06cp     0avio    2792k  kdeinit*
    296   50793.93re     83.26cp     0avio    5850k  kdeinit*
      9    2124.80re     12.76cp     0avio   19205k  mozilla-bin
      8      37.14re      3.15cp     0avio    1203k  tar
      8    1135.04re      1.75cp     0avio    6378k  ksnapshot
      9    1222.85re      1.66cp     0avio    6792k  nautilus
      4    1222.40re      1.41cp     0avio    7014k  rhn-applet-gui
   2753     242.27re      1.33cp     0avio    8370k  uml_linux_lids*
    706       5.66re      1.07cp     0avio     748k  modprobe
      4    1222.53re      0.74cp     0avio    5630k  gnome-panel
      9       1.11re      0.69cp     0avio    1656k  rpmq
      4    1221.07re      0.64cp     0avio    4566k  mixer_applet2
      4    1222.80re      0.62cp     0avio    3463k  metacity
      7      15.00re      0.52cp     0avio    9074k  gdmgreeter
     35      36.77re      0.47cp     0avio    1131k  wc
      9    1257.86re      0.38cp     0avio    3313k  gconfd-2
     29       6.50re      0.34cp     0avio    1324k  gpg
      5      18.68re      0.32cp     0avio    5747k  python
    279       0.40re      0.28cp     0avio     692k  sed
      4    1221.02re      0.28cp     0avio    4784k  wnck-applet
     71       0.46re      0.27cp     0avio    2065k  cc1
     22    1628.34re      0.26cp     0avio    1632k  sshd*
      2       6.92re      0.25cp     0avio   10788k  superkaramba
      2       8.09re      0.25cp     0avio    3608k  emacs
```

• **Figure 21-5: The result set from the** sa **command.**

The columns in the result set (from left to right) contain the following information:

- ✔ Total number of invocations
- ✔ Total elapsed time
- ✔ Combined system and user time in seconds
- ✔ Average number of I/O operations (not currently used in some versions of Linux)
- ✔ Memory usage in 1K blocks
- ✔ Command name

The sa command generates a list showing a subset of all commands. (Commands executed only once and commands with unprintable characters are grouped into an entry labeled ***other*.) To see a complete list, use this command:

```
# sa --list-all-names
```

To summarize the list by user, use this command:

```
# sa -m
```

For a quick overview of system usage that includes statistics by percentage of resource used, use the following command:

```
#sa -c
```

Combine the sa command with the grep command to show usage of a specific program:

```
# sa | grep program
```

The preceding command returns a report including statistics only on the command named.

 Keeping an eye on command usage can tell you what people are up to. You can find out if a lot of cping is going on that shouldn't be.

These are just some of the options of the sa command. For a complete list, check out the man page — man sa.

22

Spring Cleaning Essentials

Save Time By

✔ Customizing your runlevels

✔ Disabling unused services to close extra, open ports

✔ Removing unused services with the Service Configuration Tool

✔ Cleaning up after ex-users

Cleaning up is an essential part of running a secure and efficient system. You can use resources most efficiently if your system doesn't have an abundance of unused services hanging around in the background, tying up CPU time. Unnecessary services are also an invitation to hackers. Can hackers exploit an open port you've forgotten about? In this technique, we explain the best ways to avoid these pitfalls by

✔ **Tidying up the runlevel you work in most often:** Linux runlevels are collections of services that define your system's capabilities. Each runlevel has a purpose. You can choose from the predefined runlevels or customize runlevels for your use. Shutting down the extra services in the runlevel you're using saves CPU time and system resources.

✔ **Shutting down unused services:** When you leave an unattended service running, listening for a client's request, it can accept a request from either an approved user or a hacker. Shutting down the services that don't need to be running is a good way to tighten system security. That's because when you shut down services, you close off the extra open ports you're not using — and hackers can't use them either.

✔ **Getting rid of old users' stuff:** Old files are another waste of resources — why take up good disk space for outdated data? When users move on and you clean up, be sure to remove all their old files; otherwise, you're just wasting space by storing data that's unlikely to be used again.

The following sections are about cleaning house. By doing so, you'll keep your work environment neat, secure, and productive; and everyone will save time!

Running Down the Runlevels

You can save time and make better use of your system resources by running at the minimum runlevel you need. A *runlevel* is a collection of services. You can customize the services available at each runlevel to make the most of your system resources.

Runlevel basics

Most Linux distributions define the following runlevels:

0 Halt

1 Single-user mode

2 User-definable — nongraphical

3 Multiuser command line environment

4 User-definable — nongraphical

5 Multiuser graphical environment

6 Reboot

The different runlevels are used for different reasons. If you need the system all to yourself for repairs or system maintenance, booting into runlevel 1 guarantees that you're the only user on the system. However, you have to work from a terminal window because runlevel 1 doesn't support a graphical interface.

If you need to save on the system load and your users don't need a graphical interface, you can boot your system into runlevel 3. If your application software doesn't need graphics capabilities, your users will recognize the boost in speed they get from running at the lower runlevel.

For all the bells and whistles of a graphical environment, boot your system into runlevel 5. It's definitely the most comfortable user environment. You can use the command line if you want, but the graphical options are also available. (Runlevel 5 is the default runlevel for Fedora, Mandrake, and SuSE systems.)

Customizing runlevels in Fedora

Customizing a runlevel is easy in Fedora or SuSE Linux, but it's a little trickier in Mandrake. In this section, we show you how to use Fedora's runlevel editor. If you're a SuSE or Mandrake user, skip ahead to the appropriate section.

To turn Fedora services on or off or to edit the services included in your runlevel, follow these steps:

Before you make any changes to your configuration, be sure that you have a working emergency repair disk. If you don't, you might lock yourself out of your computer without giving yourself a way back in. See Technique 24 for details on making a boot disk.

1. **From the Main Menu, choose System Settings⟹Server Settings⟹Services.**

You're prompted for the superuser password.

2. **Enter the superuser password and click OK.**

The Service Configuration window opens, as shown in Figure 22-1. Use the Service Configuration Tool to edit the services that are enabled for your runlevel or to create a new runlevel.

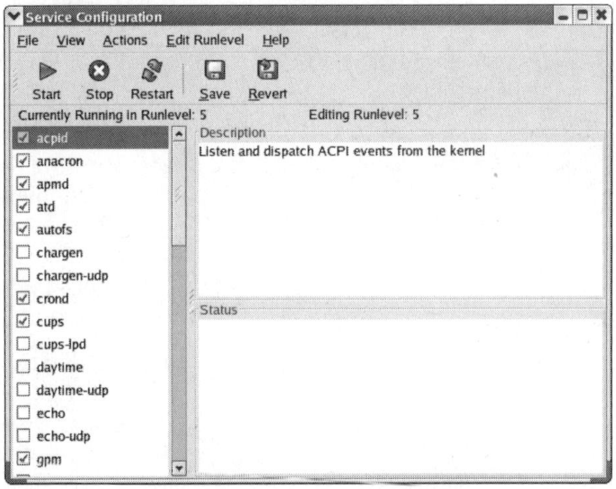

• **Figure 22-1:** The Service Configuration window.

3. **To modify a runlevel other than the default (5), choose Edit Runlevel on the menu bar and select the runlevel you want to customize.**

Runlevels 2 and 4 are user-definable — Fedora set them aside just for you. Be aware that they're not graphical, so you'll be working at the command line. If you're managing a Web server, database server, or e-mail server, configure runlevel 4 to run only the services you need — you can still switch to runlevel 5 (and a graphical desktop) when you need to manage your system.

 Defining a runlevel with only the services you need to run on your system gives you a leaner, meaner machine. Your users will thank you for the extra speed.

4. **Look at the Editing Runlevel indicator above the description frame to make sure the runlevel displayed is correct. (You don't want to accidentally edit the wrong runlevel.)**

5. **To edit the runlevel services, scroll through the list and disable the services your users don't need or enable services that would be handy.**

You can enable or disable a service by checking or unchecking the check box to the left of the service. If the box is checked, the service is on.

 You can get a quick description of the service by highlighting the service name and looking at the description box. Most of the descriptions are pretty informative.

6. **After you've changed the services for your new custom runlevel, click the Save icon on the toolbar.**

You now have a leaner, meaner runlevel to work in.

Customizing runlevels in SuSE

SuSE Linux supports runlevels 1 through 6, but you can't modify runlevel 4 without resorting to a command-line interface. SuSE also adds a few new runlevels: Runlevel B corresponds to the boot process, and runlevel S is another single-user runlevel (just like runlevel 1, but you can customize the services to create two distinct single-user runlevels).

 We strongly recommend that you don't change any of the services in runlevel B (boot) or runlevel 0 (halt), or your system may become inoperable.

 If you need to customize runlevel 4 for some reason, see the man page for the `chkconfig` command.

To turn SuSE services on or off, or edit the services included in each runlevel, follow these steps:

 Before you make any changes to your configuration, be sure that you have a working emergency repair disk. A working boot disk will give you a way back into your system if you accidentally lock yourself out. See Technique 24 for details on making a boot disk.

1. **From the main menu, choose System⇨YaST.**

You're prompted for the superuser password.

2. **Enter the superuser password and click OK.**

3. **When the YaST Control Center appears, click System (in the left-hand pane).**

4. **Click Runlevel Editor, and then click Expert Mode.**

The Runlevel Editor displays the services installed on your computer, as shown in Figure 22-2.

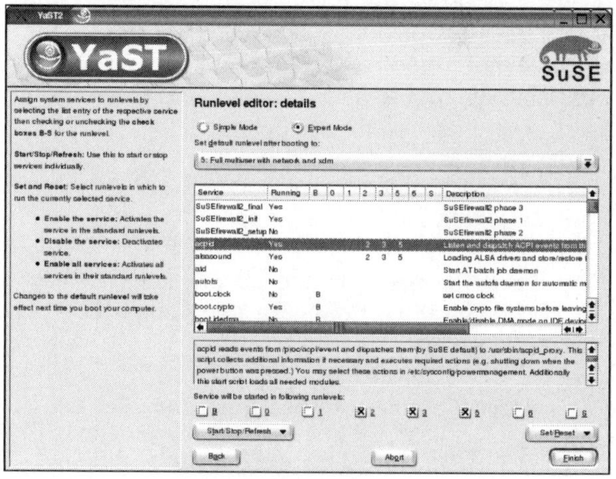

• **Figure 22-2: SuSE's Runlevel Editor.**

5. **To start or stop a service, highlight the service and click the Start/Stop/Refresh button (near the bottom of the window).**

The column labeled Running displays Yes if a given service is currently running or No if the service is not running.

The columns labeled B, 0, 1, 2, 3, 5, 6, and S indicate whether the service is enabled or disabled for that runlevel.

6. **To enable or disable a service, check (enable) or clear (disable) the check box next to the runlevel you want to change.**

   The check boxes are displayed below the list of services (refer to Figure 22-2).

7. **When you're done customizing the runlevels, click Finish.**

8. **When prompted, click Yes to save your changes and close the YaST Control Center.**

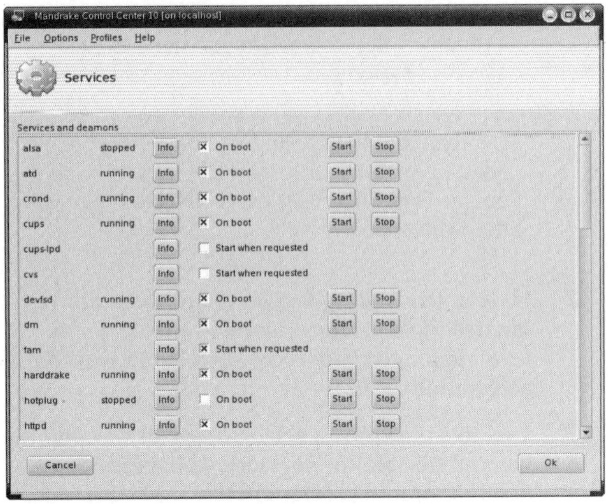

Customizing runlevels in Mandrake

Mandrake Linux offers a runlevel editor that's a bit different. The graphical runlevel editors in Fedora and SuSE Linux let you customize the set of services enabled for each runlevel. Mandrake's graphical editor lets you enable or disable services for *all* runlevels. In other words, if you disable a service using Mandrake's editor, you've disabled that service for all runlevels. You *can* customize individual runlevels, but you have to resort to the command line to do it. See the next section for the details.

To enable or disable services using the Mandrake Control Center, follow these steps:

1. **From the Main Menu, choose System⇨ Configuration⇨Configure Your Computer.**

   You're prompted for the superuser password.

2. **Enter the superuser password and click OK.**

3. **When the Mandrake Control Center appears, click System.**

4. **Click Services.**

   The Services editor displays the services installed on your computer, as shown in Figure 22-3.

• **Figure 22-3:** The Mandrake Services editor.

The name of each service is listed down the left-hand side.

5. **If you're not sure what a particular service does, click the Info button to see a short description.**

6. **To start or stop a service, click the Start or Stop button on that row.**

7. **To enable a service, check the box next to the words On Boot or Start When Requested. To disable a service, clear the check box.**

   Remember, you're enabling (or disabling) the service for *multiple* run levels, not just the current runlevel.

   The services labeled Start When Requested are network servers that start when a client tries to connect to those services. If you disable a network service, the client will typically display a message such as `Connection Refused`. The services labeled On Boot are background processes that run all the time.

8. **When you're finished, click OK to save your changes or Cancel to discard your changes, and then close the Mandrake Control Center.**

Your changes will take effect the next time you boot your computer.

Customizing runlevels at the command line

We mention earlier that Mandrake users must resort to the command line to customize individual runlevels; this section describes how.

The graphical runlevel editors are friendly and easy to use, but sometimes it's faster to hit the command line. Regardless of whether you're using Mandrake, Fedora, or SuSE Linux, you can use the chkconfig command to adjust the services available at a particular runlevel. You can also use chkconfig to view your service configuration. You must have superuser privileges to use the chkconfig command.

To view the configuration for a service, use the command: chkconfig --list *service-name*. For example, to view the runlevels for your Web server (httpd), type in

```
# chkconfig --list httpd
httpd: 0:off 1:off 2:off 3:on 4:on 5:on
  6:off
```

If you leave off the service name, chkconfig will display *all* services.

To enable a service for a given runlevel, use the command: chkconfig --level *runlevel service-name* on. For example, to enable your Web server at runlevel 2, type in

```
# chkconfig --level 2 httpd on
```

To disable a service for a given runlevel, use the command: chkconfig --level *runlevel service-name* off. If you want to disable your Web server at level 5, type the command

```
# chkconfig --level 5 httpd off
```

Switching to a new runlevel

To change into your new runlevel, follow these steps:

1. **Open a terminal window and give yourself superuser privileges with the** su - **command.**

2. **Enter the following command:**

```
# telinit runlevel
```

For example, to switch to runlevel 2, use this:

```
# telinit 2
```

Your system reboots and presents you with a command line to log in.

 Any runlevels lower than 5 aren't graphical.

If you don't like the new runlevel, use the telinit command to return to the previous runlevel and then fine-tune the service settings to better suit your needs.

Disabling Unused Services

Most services leave open ports that can be exploited by hackers. Shutting off the services that you don't use regularly is a good way to close ports that hackers could use to gain access to your system.

 If you use a service infrequently, just turn it off. It is still available when you need it — you can turn it on with a few clicks of the mouse, and off again when you're done. If you never use a service, you're better off removing it altogether. See the next section for details on removing services.

If you find a service that you don't think you'll need, we recommend disabling it for a while before you remove it, just in case you change your mind later. Here are some services that you might want to disable:

 You may not see all of these services on your computer (depending on the software packages you've installed), or you may see a few that we haven't listed here.

✔ acpid: This service controls what happens when you press the power button on your computer. The configuration file for this service is empty by default, so acpid doesn't actually do anything. (See info acpid for more information.)

✔ `apmd`: This service monitors the battery level on laptop computers. If you're not using a laptop, you probably don't need `apmd`.

✔ `atd`: This service runs jobs that you've scheduled with the `at` command. If you don't use the `at` command, disable this service.

✔ `autofs`: This service automatically mounts file systems when you first use them. If you're not using automount file systems (and unless you've configured them yourself, you're not), turn off this service. `autofs` and the related `automount` system are frequently targeted by hackers.

✔ `chargen`: This silly little network service simply generates a stream of characters whenever a client connects. You can safely live without this service.

✔ `chargen-udp`: `chargen`'s cousin, this service sends a stream of characters to a UDP-connected client. If you disable `chargen`, disable `chargen-udp` as well.

✔ `cups`: This service is the Common UNIX Printing System. If you're not printing anything, you don't need `cups`. (You can always turn it back on later if you need it.)

✔ `cups-lpd`: This service provides an `lp`-style interface to `cups`. (`lp` is an older printer protocol.) If you aren't sharing printers with other UNIX systems (systems that use the `lp` protocol), disable this service.

✔ `daytime`: This network service tells a client computer what time it is (at least, what time your computer thinks it is; if you're like us, your VCR always thinks it's 12:00 and so do your computers). `daytime` is rarely used — you can safely disable this service.

✔ `daytime-upd`: This service is the same as `daytime`, except it works with UDP clients instead of TCP clients. Because this protocol is rarely used, you can safely disable this service.

✔ `echo`: This is another silly network service that echoes client input back to the client. (It's interesting to note that this service and the `chargen` service were both proposed by the same person

in 1972.) Unless you're developing network software, you can safely disable this service.

✔ `echo-upd`: This service is the same as `echo`, except it services UDP clients instead of TCP clients. Unless you're developing network software, you can safely disable this service.

✔ `irda`: If you have a laptop, it most likely has an infrared port built in. If you don't use it (or you don't have one), disable `irda`.

✔ `irqbalance`: This service balances the workload on a multi-CPU computer. If you have only a single CPU, disable `irqbalance`.

✔ `isdn`: This service manages ISDN network connections. If you don't have an ISDN connection, you don't need this service.

✔ `ktalk`: This is the KDE `talk` server service. If you don't chat with other users on your computer, disable `ktalk`.

✔ `lisa`: `lisa` discovers SMB (Samba) computers on your local network, giving you a Linux equivalent to the Windows network neighborhood. If you don't have any SMB servers (that is, Samba or Windows servers), you can do without `lisa`.

✔ `nfs`: The NFS server service provides NFS file sharing to other NFS computers. NFS is a frequent target for hackers, so if you don't use NFS sharing, disable NFS (and the `nfslock` service).

✔ `nfslock`: This service provides file locking for the `nfs` service. If you've disabled `nfs`, disable `nfslock` too.

✔ `ntpd`: This service synchronizes the date/time clock on your computer with network time servers. Enable this protocol if you want to standardize your computer's clock with the rest of the world, or disable it if you're happy setting the clock yourself.

✔ `rawdevices`: This service is used by high-performance database servers to access your hard disk without going through the normal file system route. If you're not using a program that needs raw disk access, disable `rawdevices`.

✔ rsync: rsync is a package that speeds up file transfers by sending only the differences between two versions of the same file. Disable this service if you aren't running an rsync server.

✔ saslauthd: SASL is an authentication protocol used by mail servers (and other network servers). If you know you don't need it, disable it; if you're not sure, leave it alone.

✔ sendmail: The sendmail service moves e-mail from your machine to other machines (that is, it delivers the e-mail that you send). If you aren't sending e-mail from your Linux computer or you're using a different mail server, you can safely disable sendmail.

✔ services: This service provides a listing of all the network services that your computer provides to other clients. Disable this service unless you know that you need it.

✔ smb: If your computer acts as a Samba server (see Technique 11), you need the smb service. If not, you can safely disable this service.

✔ snmp: This service is the Simple Network Management Protocol (SNMP) daemon. It services network management requests. If you're unsure whether you need this, disable it for now (SNMP has been the target of some hack attacks).

✔ snmptrapd: This is another component of SNMP. If you disabled snmp, you can disable snmptrapd too.

✔ swat: SWAT is a mini–Web server that you use to configure the Samba server. If you aren't running a Samba server, disable swat.

✔ time: This service is similar to the daytime service. It sends the current date and time (in seconds, since midnight January 1, 1900) to any client that connects to it. You can safely disable this service.

✔ time-udp: This service is the same as time, except it serves UDP clients instead of TCP clients. You can safely disable this service as well.

✔ winbindd: This service pulls user account information from Windows servers, letting you use your Windows user name and password on a Linux computer. If you aren't intimately sharing authentication information with a Windows server, disable winbindd.

Removing Unneeded Services

Having extra, unused services on your system can be a security risk. You may have a service disabled at the moment, but a hacker or Trojan horse can turn it on and exploit its open ports.

 If you find an obscure service that you'll never use, remove it so it's not available for exploitation by a hacker or a Trojan horse.

Removing the services you don't need is a good way to secure your system.

 Don't worry about removing the services you aren't using now. Services are easy to reinstall if you find you need them.

If you're a Fedora user, you can use the same Services Configuration Tool that you use to start or disable services (or configure a custom runlevel) to completely remove services.

To remove a service, Fedora users follow these steps:

1. **Open the Main Menu and choose System Settings⟿Server Settings⟿Services.**

You're prompted to enter the root password.

2. **Type in the root password and click OK.**

The Service Configuration window opens.

3. **Highlight the service you want to remove and choose Actions⟿Delete Service from the menu bar (see Figure 22-4).**

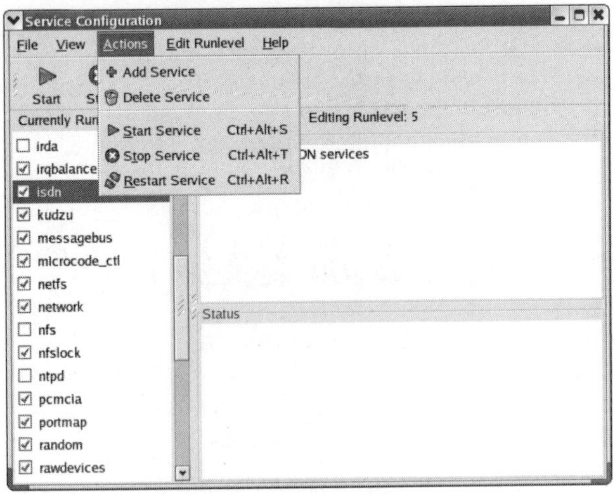

• **Figure 22-4:** The Actions drop-down menu.

A pop-up window appears asking you to verify that you want to remove the service.

4. **Click Yes to remove the service, and in a snap, the service is gone!**

If you're a SuSE or Mandrake user, you can remove a service from the command line by following this procedure:

1. **Open a terminal window and give yourself superuser privileges with the su command.**

2. **Type in the following command and press Enter:**

   `# /sbin/chkconfig --del service-name`

You can also use the chkconfig command on Fedora systems if you don't want to take the time to start the Services Configuration Tool.

 When you delete a service with the Services Configuration Tool, the underlying programs remain on your system; you've deleted only the startup and shutdown scripts for the service. If you want to completely remove the service and its underlying programs and data files, erase the package with the rpm command (see Technique 17).

Removing Old Users and Their Files

When users leave, the clutter they may be leaving behind can tie up valuable system resources. Why store all of their old files, which aren't important anymore, when you can use the disk space for fresh data?

After you've made sure that you've saved any of the ex-users' important documents, you can remove all traces of these users and their files with a few mouse clicks. Removing (and adding) user accounts is easy, and each distribution provides a graphical tool that allows you to manage users without resorting to a command line.

In this section, we show you how to remove user accounts with the Fedora User Manager. If you're a Mandrake user, use the Mandrake User Management tool (found in the main menu at System⇨ Configuration⇨Other⇨User Administration). If SuSE is your favorite flavor, use the User and Group Administration tool in YaST (System⇨YaST⇨ Security and User.

 A quick follow-up with kfind will find any files that former users might have stashed on your system, but that are off the beaten path.

 Before removing a user's account, make note of his or her user ID. You'll need it to clean up after deleting the account.

To remove an old user account, follow these steps:

1. **Open the Main Menu and choose System Settings⇨Users and Groups.**

   You're prompted for the root password.

2. **Enter the root password and click OK.**

   The Fedora User Manager opens, as shown in Figure 22-5.

3. **To delete a user, highlight the user's name in the list and click the Delete button (on the toolbar).**

You're asked to verify that you want to remove the user, as shown in Figure 22-6.

4. **Check the Delete User's Home Directory box if you want to remove the user's old belongings.**

Be sure that you don't need any of the user's old belongings. This is a good time to refer to Technique 50 and back up the user's home directory before deleting it.

5. **Click Yes to remove the user's identity and home directory.**

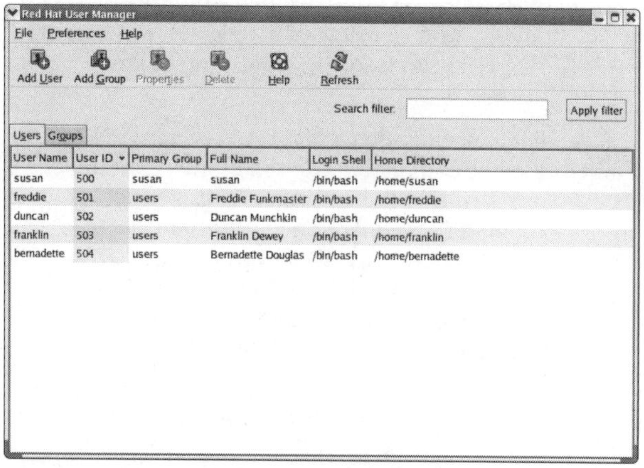

• Figure 22-5: The Fedora User Manager.

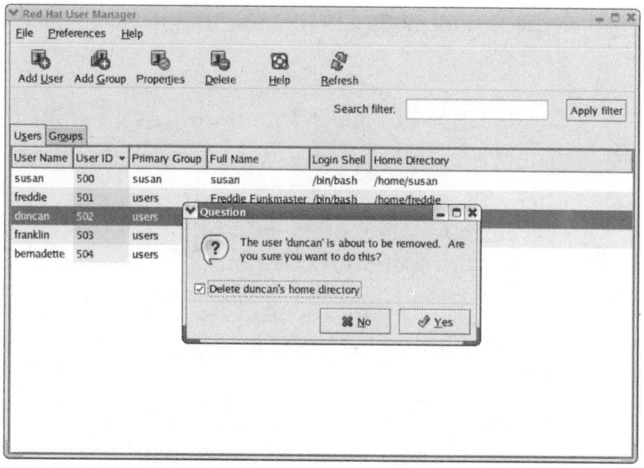

• Figure 22-6: Verify that you want to remove the user's account.

After the user is removed from the user list, and his or her home directory is gone, you can use `kfind` to search for any orphaned files that the user may have left in other directories. To search for other files, follow these steps:

1. **Open the Main Menu and choose Run Command.**

2. **Enter `kfind` in the Command field and click Run.**

The KFind window opens (see Figure 22-7) to the Name/Location tab. The Name field should contain a *. Enter a / in the Look In field.

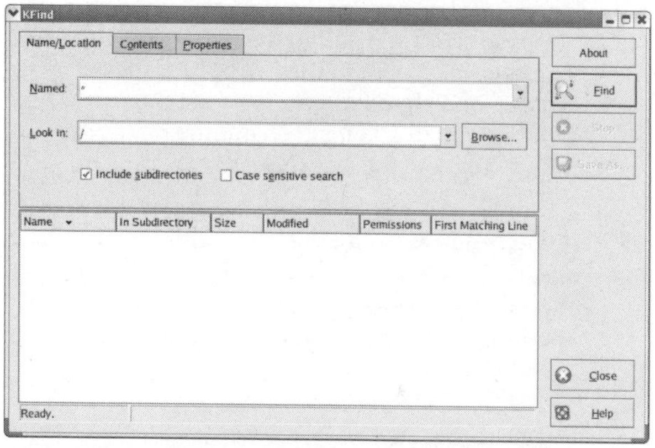

• Figure 22-7: The KFind window.

3. **Click the Properties tab, and enter the user ID of your ex-user in the Files Owned by User field.**

4. **Click the Find button, and the search begins.**

When the search is complete, the frame at the bottom of the window displays all the now-orphaned files previously owned by the ex-user.

5. **Right-click the filename to open a pop-up menu, displaying the filename at the top, followed by your file management choices:**

▶ Copy

▶ Delete

▶ Open Directory

▶ Open With

▶ Open

▶ Properties

You can delete old system files that contain configuration information and preferences for your ex-user without much concern for interfering with other users, but most other files should be investigated more closely.

6. **To delete an old file, choose Delete from the pop-up menu.**

You're asked to confirm the deletion. Click Yes to delete the file.

 You can select multiple files by holding down the Shift key and highlighting the files with a mouse click (or by using the arrow keys to select multiple files). Then right-click the file group and choose Delete from the pop-up menu. You're asked to confirm the deletion. Click Yes, and the files disappear quickly!

7. **If you see files in the list that may contain work or data important to others, right-click and choose Properties from the pop-up menu to open the Properties dialog (see Figure 22-8).**

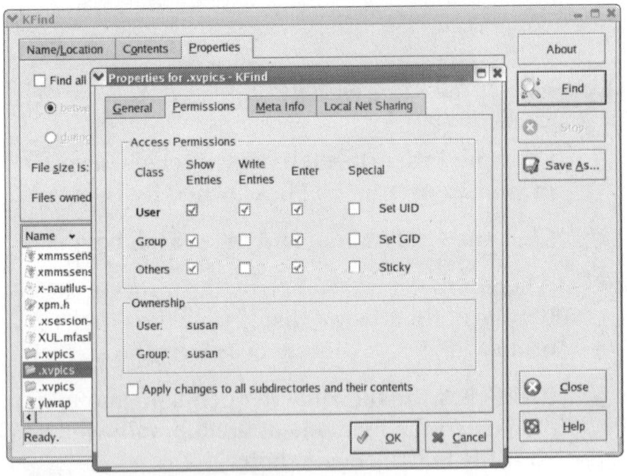

• **Figure 22-8:** The Properties dialog.

8. **Click the Permissions tab to view the file ownership information, and note the name of the group that owns the file.**

It might be prudent to consult with the other members of that group before deleting the file.

9. **If the list includes files that you can't recognize by filename or location, you can**

▶ **Open the file and manually inspect the contents.** Depending on how prolific the ex-user was, this might be the best option to start with. However, if the user left you with hundreds of files, you'll probably want to use the other option.

▶ **Narrow the inspection a bit by deleting the things that aren't important.** Right-click the filename and choose Open from the pop-up menu. You're treated to a view of the file, in the default viewer for that type of file.

If you see a listing with `/proc/processID` in the In Subdirectory column of the result table, it means that the ex-user still has a process running somewhere on your system. Make a note of the process ID so you can use KDE System Guard to kill off the process. (See Technique 41 for complete details; see the following steps for the short version.)

To kill off abandoned processes, follow these steps:

1. **Open a terminal window and gain superuser privileges with the** su **command.**

2. **Type the following command and press Enter:**

```
# ksysguard
```

The KDE System Guard window opens, as shown in Figure 22-9.

3. **Click the Process Table tab to move to a list of currently running processes, and look for the process ID in the PID column.**

4. **When you've found the process ID, highlight the entry for that process and click the Kill button.**

A dialog opens asking if you really want to kill the selected process (see Figure 22-10).

5. **Click Kill to confirm your choice.**

The process is terminated.

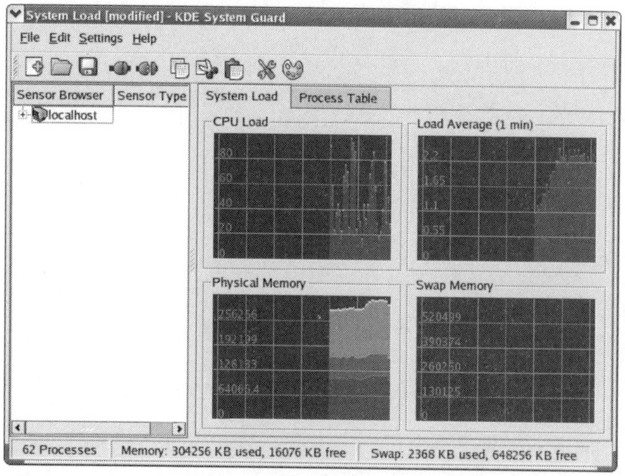

• **Figure 22-9: The KDE System Guard window.**

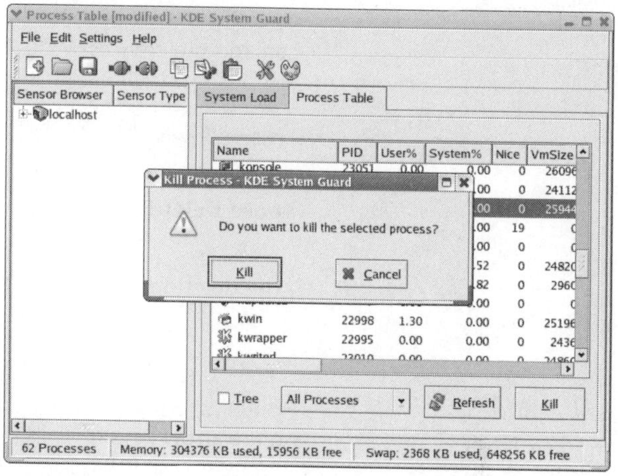

• **Figure 22-10: Confirm the process termination.**

With a little vigilance, you'll avoid the piles of files that ex-users can amass on your system and save the resources for the users that need them.

Part IV

Tweaking the Kernel on Your Linux System

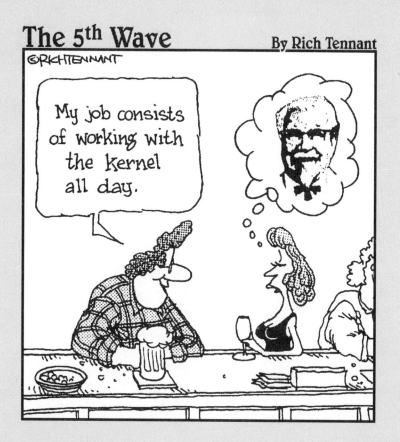

The 5th Wave   By Rich Tennant

@RICHTENNANT

My job consists of working with the kernel all day.

Technique 23

Taking Good Care of Your Kernel

Save Time By

✔ Manipulating your kernel on the fly

✔ Using your boot time parameters to custom-tailor your kernel

The kernel is the software core of your computer. Kernel modules make up the software interface between your system hardware and the system software. On a fresh Linux installation, over 900 kernel modules are ready to load into your kernel. The actual number may vary depending on the specific hardware that Linux finds when it sets up housekeeping, but on our Fedora system, 968 modules exist.

You can also download and install new kernel modules. You can find many open-source modules bouncing around the Web that do everything from silencing annoying beeps to enabling wireless network cards. The beauty of the system is the flexibility that kernel modules provide the computer industry. Every time a new piece of hardware is invented, you don't have to modify and rebuild the Linux kernel — you just add a new module.

Manipulating kernel modules is quick and simple, thanks to a series of commands that work at the command line to update your kernel without a complete rebuild. You can also find-tune your kernel by using the boot time parameters. Boot time parameters are the kernel options that are enforced every time you boot your system.

Not all features are modules, and you may want your kernel to be configured so that some features can't be changed. If that is the case, a complete kernel rebuild is called for (see Technique 24 for information about building a kernel from scratch). If you can get by with a simple patch to the kernel, this is the technique for you. In this technique, we introduce you to the commands that let you customize your kernel — quickly and easily.

Adding and Removing Kernel Modules

Linux contains some handy commands you can use to manipulate your kernel while it's running. The kernel module tools make it easy to experiment with kernel changes without making any lasting or permanent changes.

These commands don't make permanent changes to your kernel; the changes last only until you reboot. To automatically implement a change at boot time, you need to add the change to a startup script. For the quickest way to make a change to your system startup script, check out Technique 26, where we show you a couple of easy-to-follow examples in the section about closing down security gaps with /proc.

To use the kernel tools, you need to open a terminal window and give yourself superuser privileges with the su - command. Be sure to include the hyphen, which ensures that the module tools are on your $PATH search path.

Learning about modules

You can find out what kernel modules are on your system by entering the following command:

```
# ls -R /lib/modules/$(uname -r)
```

If you don't have the kernel module that you need to control a device or configure a piece of hardware, do a Google search for the kernel module you need. Lots of modules are available on the Web.

The modinfo command displays all sorts of information about a kernel module, as shown in Listing 23-1.

LISTING 23-1: VIEWING MODULE INFORMATION WITH MODINFO

```
# modinfo iforce
filename:    /lib/modules/
    2.4.22-1.2115.nptl/kernel/
    drivers/char/joystick/iforce.o
description: "USB/RS232 I-Force
    joysticks and wheels driver"
author:      "Vojtech Pavlik
    <vojtech@suse.cz>, Johann Deneux
    <deneux@ifrance.com>"
license:     "GPL"
```

Installing a module with insmod

The insmod command installs a module into a running kernel (or at least tries to). The typical command syntax is

```
# insmod modulename
```

Taking care of dependencies automatically with modprobe and depmod

We said that insmod tries to install a module, but it's not always successful. Some modules *depend on* other modules. For example, if you want to load the Iforce joystick driver, you must first load the generic serial joystick driver and USB driver. If you try to load a module with unsatisfied symbols, you see error messages like this:

```
unresolved symbol serio_close_R393d70c3
unresolved symbol serio_open_R17abfb2f
unresolved symbol serio_unregister_device
unresolved symbol serio_register_device
```

Deciphering these messages can be nearly impossible.

Fortunately, modprobe solves dependency problems for you. The modprobe command works with the information computed by depmod to automatically load any dependent modules.

depmod computes the interdependencies among kernel modules and writes the results to /lib/modules/$(uname -r)/modules.dep. The modprobe command reads dependency information from that file. depmod runs each time you boot your system so the dependency database is always up-to-date, unless you build or install a new module. To rebuild the dependency database, use the following command:

```
# depmod -a
```

As we mention earlier, modprobe uses the information gathered by depmod to automatically load any modules dependent on the one you want to use. The syntax for modprobe is essentially the same as the syntax for insmod:

```
# modprobe modulename
```

If any of the dependencies *can't* be resolved, modprobe gives up and undoes any of the work it's already done.

Loading a module for a slightly different kernel with insmod and modprobe

Because modprobe automatically resolves any dependencies for you, why would you ever want to use insmod? Every kernel module is compiled for a specific kernel version. Occasionally, you run into a module that's compiled for the wrong kernel, but you're pretty sure it will work with your version. (For example, you may find a great sound card driver compiled for kernel version 2.4.22-1.2115.nptl, and you're running 2.4.22-1.2116.nptl.) If you try to modprobe a module with the wrong version, modprobe won't do it. You can force insmod to load the module (even though it's been built for the wrong version) by including the --force option on the command line:

```
# insmod --force iforce
```

But, insmod will still complain about unresolved dependencies. Don't give up — you can still use

modprobe to do the hard work for you. Just use the -n and -v options:

```
# modprobe -n -v iforce
insmod input.o
insmod usbcore.o
insmod serio.o
insmod iforce.o
```

When you use the -n and -v options, modprobe shows you the insmod commands that you need in order to load dependent modules in the correct order (but it doesn't actually execute those commands). Now you can execute those commands yourself; just be sure to include the --force option when you load the mismatched module:

```
# modprobe -n -v iforce
insmod input.o
insmod usbcore.o
insmod serio.o
insmod iforce.o

# insmod input.o
# insmod usbcore.o
# insmod serio.o
# insmod --force iforce.o
```

The lsmod command displays a list of the modules that are currently loaded on your system (see Figure 23-1).

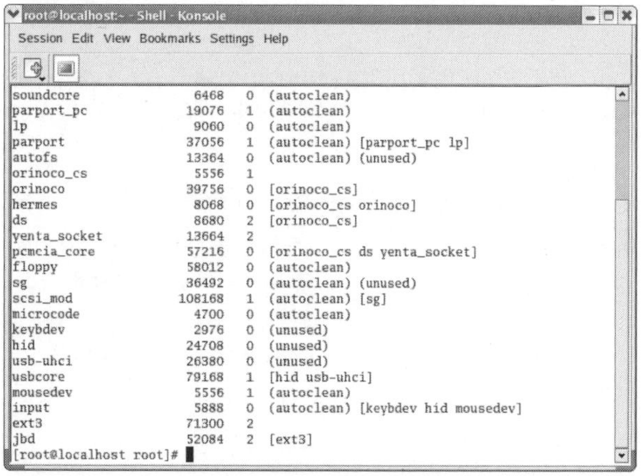

• **Figure 23-1: Currently loaded kernel modules.**

Removing modules with rmmod

The `rmmod` command removes a loadable module from the kernel. You can't remove a module if it's in use (`lsmod` will tell you whether or not the module is being used). To remove a module, use the following command:

```
# rmmod modulename
```

When you delete a module, it's still on your computer; it's just not loaded into the kernel.

Manipulating Boot Time Parameters

The Linux kernel is a program just like any other program (well, maybe that's a bit of oversimplification): It has a command line, and you can specify options and parameters to the kernel when you boot your system.

Each time you boot your system, the boot loader pauses for a moment at the boot selection screen — you usually hit Enter (or just wait for the built-in timer to expire) when you see the selection screen, and your computer happily boots the Linux kernel using the default boot parameters. Linux can do a lot more.

If you're running Fedora Linux, press the A key while the boot selection screen is displayed to modify the

kernel arguments (note, you have only a few seconds before the boot loader starts your kernel). If you're running Mandrake or SuSE Linux, press the Esc key (while the boot selection screen is displayed) to reach the Linux boot prompt.

 If you have multiple kernels or multiple operating systems installed on your system, they're displayed on the boot loader selection screen.

The Linux kernel supports a huge variety of options and parameters, but you only need to know about a few of them.

 To find a complete (though slightly unattractive) list of boot time parameters, install the `kernel-doc` RPM package, which is included with most Linux distributions. You find the list in `/usr/src/linux-$(uname -r)/Documentation/kernel-parameters.txt`. Just open the file with your favorite editor.

The default command line for Fedora is as follows:

```
grub append> ro root=LABEL=/ rhgb
```

If you're running Mandrake or SuSE Linux, the default command line will differ slightly.

Table 23-1 lists various parameters that you may want to use to alter the default command line. You can change the kernel command line to modify the way your Linux kernel boots, or to change the way the Linux kernel runs after it's done booting.

TABLE 23-1: FEDORA BOOT-LINE PARAMETERS

To Do This	Make This Change to the Default Linux Command Line	Timesaving Bonus Info
View detailed boot messages (Fedora only).	Remove the `rhgb` (Red Hat Graphical Boot) from the end of the command line.	Removing `rhgb` saves a little bit of boot time, and you have a better starting point if you have to investigate a boot problem.

To Do This	Make This Change to the Default Linux Command Line	Timesaving Bonus Info
View detailed boot messages (SuSE or Mandrake).	Remove `splash=silent` from the command line.	Enabling detailed boot messages can help you pinpoint the cause of a boot problem.
Make a menu of screen size options appear when you boot.	Add the `vga=ask` option to the end of the command line. For example: `grub append> ro root= LABEL=/ rhgb vga=ask`	Choose a larger screen resolution to fit more text on the screen. If you like a certain text size, you can make the change permanent by changing the `menu.lst` file in the `/boot/grub` directory. To do so, open the file with your favorite text editor and append your changes to the line starting with the word `kernel`. Save the file when you're finished, and next time you boot, the changes take effect. Be careful when you change this file because it's easy to make your system hard to boot.
Include more details in the boot process as the system boots.	Add the word `debug` to the command line. For example: `grub append> ro root= LABEL=/ rhgb debug`	If you're having problems booting, this is a quick way to find the problem.
If you don't use any USB devices, you can turn off the USB device modules.	Add the `no usb` command. For example: `grub append> ro root= LABEL=/ rhgb no usb`	You may gain a bit of CPU performance. ***Warning:*** Make sure you don't depend on USB devices (like mice) before you disable this module.
Turn off power-management control features.	Add the `acpi=off` command to the GRUB command line. For example: `grub append> ro root= LABEL=/ rhgb acpi=off`	You may want to do this if your laptop powers off intermittently or has battery problems (even when it's plugged in).
Boot into a runlevel other than the default.	Add the runlevel (1–5) to the end of the command line. For example: `grub append> ro root= LABEL=/ 5`	Server machines typically don't need a graphical environment most of the time (why run X Windows on a mail or Web server?). Specify the runlevel on the command line if you need to do system maintenance work and want a friendly desktop environment. See Technique 22 for more information about runlevels.
Boot into single-user mode without a password.	Add an `S` to the end of the command line. For example: `grub append> ro root= LABEL=/ rhgb S`	This is incredibly handy if you forget the `root` password. When you're at the command line, you can change the `root` password with the command `sh-2.05b# passwd`. Enter a new password and confirm the new password when prompted. When you're finished, type the command `sh-2.05b# reboot` to reboot the system so you can log in with your newly assigned password. ***Warning:*** *Anyone* can use the `S` option. Be sure you know who has physical access to your computer because with this tidbit of knowledge, anyone can bypass the `root` password.

(continued)

TABLE 23-1 *(continued)*

To Do This	Make This Change to the Default Linux Command Line	Timesaving Bonus Info
Boot into emergency repair mode.	Add the word emergency to the end of the command line. For example: `grub append> ro root=LABEL=/ emergency`	Boot into emergency mode if you discover a problem that prevents you from booting into single-user (or multi-user) mode. When you boot into emergency mode, Linux does not run any of the normal startup scripts — you're dumped at a command line, and you're ready to fix whatever it is that's gone wrong.

Technique 24

Creating a Custom Kernel

Save Time By

- Building a custom kernel that suits your needs
- Adding the kernel source code and dependencies in one easy step with the Package Manager
- Adding device drivers or new file systems to your kernel

Fedora is a collection of applications, daemons, and drivers with a Linux kernel at the core. The kernel deals with hardware and provides basic functions such as creating processes, managing privileges, and managing file systems.

In most cases, you don't need to build your own kernel — plenty of well-configured kernels are available for use. You may need features that aren't currently supported by the kernel included in the most recent Fedora release. You may want to

- Add support for unusual hardware — USB scanners, cameras, joysticks, and sound cards.

- Use additional encryption features that aren't part of the standard Fedora kernel.

- Explore alternative file systems.

- Omit drivers for devices you may never have.

- Omit amateur radio support — unless you're really into amateur radio.

Many kernel features are included in the form of *modules* — chunks of code that are not loaded until you actually use the features. Modules don't take up a lot of space if you don't use them, but removing the unused modules will save you time when you're rebuilding the kernel. You can also gain some security by omitting modules that you don't need.

In this technique, we show you how to build a kernel customized for your needs, based on a safe and sound prototype, and with all the drivers that you need to get your work done quickly.

Reconfiguring Your Kernel — Ready, Set, Go!

The kernel that's included with the Fedora release is a well-functioning and stable piece of software — versatile, dependable, and sturdy. But what if it doesn't include the functionality you need?

No problem — you can just rebuild it. Stick with us, and we'll show you how to make it bigger, better, and stronger . . . whatever you need.

The process of rebuilding your kernel involves several steps, and each step is covered in the following sections. Here's an overview of the process:

1. Make a boot disk.

2. Find the source code.

3. Configure the new kernel.

4. Customize the kernel.

5. And, finally, build the kernel.

Peeling onions

The Linux operating system is like an onion. If you peel away the outer layers (the KDE desktop, the bash shell, and so on), you find a layer of operating system libraries. The libraries provide commonly used functions that enable applications to find things like the current date, the IP address of a given host, and so on.

Underneath the library layer is a set of system calls, which are functions that perform low-level operations like changing your user ID, allocating more memory, and opening a file.

At the core of the onion, you find the kernel. The kernel uses device drivers to manage system hardware. The kernel also schedules disk I/O and CPU usage, responds to external signals, creates and tears down processes, and performs other low-level operations. But the kernel itself is layered, too. The Linux kernel has a portable layer that runs on any computer. At the very center of the onion is a hardware-dependent layer that is customized for each CPU (Intel x86, PowerPC, StrongARM, and so on).

Step 1: Making an Emergency Plan, or Boot Disk

Before building a custom kernel, you need to make a boot disk. A boot disk gives you a way back into your system in a kernel emergency. If you're running Mandrake or SuSE Linux, you can also create a rescue disk. A rescue disk is similar to a boot disk, but it also contains diagnostics that can tell you a little more about your computer if you run into boot problems. The process of creating a boot (or rescue) disk varies by distribution.

To make a boot disk on a Fedora or Mandrake computer, follow these steps:

1. **Insert a floppy disk in your drive, open the terminal window, and give yourself superuser privileges.**

2. **Type the following command:**

```
# /sbin/mkbootdisk `uname -r`
```

After some whirring and clicking, your floppy is bootable.

3. **To test the floppy (a good idea), shut down completely and restart.**

To make a rescue disk on a Mandrake system, follow this procedure:

1. **Insert a floppy disk in your drive, open the terminal window, and give yourself superuser privileges.**

2. **Type the following command and press Enter:**

```
# /sbin/mkrescue
```

3. **To test the floppy (a good idea), shut down completely and restart.**

If you're running SuSE Linux, use the YaST control center to create a boot disk or a rescue disk (or both):

1. **Open the main menu and choose System⇨YaST.**

2. When the YaST control center appears, click System (in the left-hand pane).

3. Click Create a Boot, Rescue, or Module Floppy.

4. Follow the on-screen instructions to create a boot floppy, rescue floppy, and module floppy.

 You may need to boot into your computer's BIOS setup mode to change the boot sequence to test the floppy. How you enter setup varies with your machine, but instructions are typically displayed on-screen at boot time.

You can also use the first install disc of your distribution's CD (or DVD) collection to boot into rescue mode.

To boot into rescue mode on a Mandrake system, follow these steps:

1. Place the first install disc in the CD/DVD drive.

2. Power up your system.

3. When you see the `Press <F1> for more options` prompt, press F1.

A screen full of help text appears, followed by the boot prompt (`boot:`).

4. Type `rescue` and press Enter.

Booting into rescue mode on a SuSE system is similar:

1. Place the first install disc in the CD/DVD drive.

2. Power up your system.

3. When the boot menu appears, use the down arrow key to highlight Rescue System and press Enter.

4. When prompted, choose your preferred language from the menu and press Enter.

To boot into rescue mode on a Fedora computer:

1. Place the first install disc in the CD/DVD drive.

2. Power up your system.

3. When the `boot:` prompt appears, type in the following command and press Enter:

```
boot: linux rescue
```

(Don't type the word `boot:`, that's the boot prompt — just type in `linux rescue` and press Enter.)

4. When prompted, choose your preferred language from the menu and press Enter.

5. Choose your keyboard type from the menu and press Enter.

6. At this point, Fedora asks if you want to start the network devices in your computer. Choose Yes or No (use the left- and right-arrow keys to select the option that you want) and press Enter to continue.

Fedora will try to find the root file system on your hard drive and mount that file system so that you can carry out any repairs that you need to make. If you want to poke around a little without endangering anything on your hard drive, tell Fedora to mount the root file system in read-only mode.

7. Choose the mount mode you prefer (choose Continue to mount your root file system in read/write mode, Read-Only to safeguard your file systems, or Skip to tell Fedora not to mount your root file system).

If Fedora locates and mounts your root file system, you can find it in the directory `/mnt/sysimage`. If you look in that directory, you'll see subdirectories such as `/mnt/sysimage/bin`, `/mnt/sysimage/boot`, `/mnt/sysimage/dev`, and so on. Those subdirectories correspond to the `/bin`, `/boot`, and `/dev` directories on your computer's root file system.

Regardless of which distribution you're using, after you've booted into rescue mode, you eventually end up at a command line. From there, you can mount your root file system (and any other file systems that you may need), make any repairs that you need, and reboot.

Step 2: Finding the Source Code

To rebuild the kernel, you first need to be sure that the source code for the kernel is on your system. Fedora distributes the kernel source in the form of an RPM package. You could use the Red Hat Package Manager to install the kernel source package by hand, but you'd also need to install a number of dependencies. Here's an easier way:

 Reusing the kernel that is included with the latest distribution saves time. It's a lot faster to alter a kernel you already have handy than to go through the work of downloading, customizing, and building a whole new kernel from scratch.

1. **Open the Main Menu and choose System Settings⇨Add/Remove Applications.**

2. **Enter the** `root` **password when prompted.**

The Package Manager checks the system for installed packages and opens the Add or Remove Packages window, showing both the installed and available packages.

3. **Scroll down the list and check the box next to Kernel Development.**

4. **Click the Update button.**

The System Preparation dialog opens.

5. **Click the Continue button.**

If prompted, insert the required disc and click OK.

When the installation is complete, a confirmation window is displayed.

 The Add/Remove Applications tool may get confused if you're installing software from a DVD instead of a CD. If the disc you're using gives you trouble, just insert it and let the autorun procedure start. Then follow the setup wizard to install additional packages.

Step 3: Configuring a New Kernel

After making a boot disk and installing your source code, it's time to configure a new kernel.

To build a custom kernel, follow these steps:

1. **Open a terminal window and give yourself superuser privileges with the** `su` **command.**

2. **Type the following command and press Enter:**

`# cd /usr/src/linux-2.4`

If you're using a kernel version newer than 2.4, `cd` to that directory instead.

3. **Type the following command and press Enter:**

`# make mrproper`

This command cleans up any remnants of previous builds that might confuse your new build.

4. **Identify the type of processor in your computer:**

`# uname -p`

The command displays the processor type that you're currently using (we assume i686 in the examples that follow).

5. **Copy the configuration file that matches your processor type into your current directory:**

`# cp configs/kernel-2.4.22-i686.config`
`  .config`

By using a predefined configuration file, your new kernel starts out in a well-defined and functional state.

6. **Type the following command and press Enter:**

`# make oldconfig`

This step runs for a while and displays a ton of messages. Just ignore the messages and grab some caffeine.

Step 4: Customizing the Kernel

When you're done with the preceding steps, you're ready for the fun part: customization. Here's how it works:

1. **Enter the following command:**

```
# make menuconfig
```

The Linux Kernel Configuration window opens, as shown in Figure 24-1.

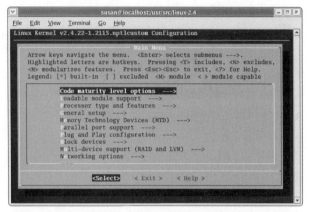

• **Figure 24-1: The Linux Kernel Configuration window.**

> 💣 If you run into some documentation that suggests `make xconfig` rather than `make menuconfig`, ignore it. `xconfig` has a nice user interface, but in the 2.4 kernel series, it has a serious flaw that will cause you all sorts of grief.

2. **The `menuconfig` window (refer to Figure 24-1) displays a list of feature groups. Use the arrow keys to move up and down through the list and press Enter to select the highlighted group.**

The left- and right-arrow keys move you through the `<Select>`, `<Exit>`, and `<Help>` choices at the bottom of the window. To return to the previous screen, choose `<Exit>`.

When you select a feature group and press Enter, you see the list of features within that group (see Figure 24-2). To the left of each feature, you see an indicator that shows the state of the feature (see Table 24-1).

• **Figure 24-2: The File Systems submenu.**

TABLE 24-1: MENUCONFIG INDICATORS

Indicator	Description
[ ]	The feature is not selected and won't be included in the new kernel. You can build the feature as a loadable module.
[*]	The feature will be included (and can only be compiled) in the new kernel.
< >	The feature is *not* selected and won't be compiled as a loadable module.
<M>	The feature will become a loadable kernel module.

> ✊ Indented lines show separate components of a feature. You can't enable a component without the parent feature.

The `<Help>` button displays a help screen that describes the highlighted feature. Most features are well documented and include links to more information, as shown in Figure 24-3.

> 🎯 Finding features in the Kernel Configuration menu is like digging around in an old attic. You'll find features for technologies that are long since retired or so obscure that the average human will likely never know anyone who needs them. Still, if you do need them, they're here — just look around.

```
susan@kobe:/usr/src/linux-2.4 - Shell - Konsole        _ □ ×
Session  Edit  View  Bookmarks  Settings  Help


 Linux Kernel v2.4.22-1.2115.nptlcustom20040126 Configuration
 ┌──────────────────── Quota support ─────────────────────┐
 │ CONFIG_QUOTA:                                           │
 │                                                         │
 │ support (you can download sources from                  │
 │ <http://www.sf.net/projects/linuxquota/>). For further  │
 │ details, read the Quota mini-HOWTO, available from      │
 │                                                         │
 │                                                         │
 │                                                         │
 │                                         (100%)──┐       │
 │                   < Exit >                              │
 └─────────────────────────────────────────────────────────┘
```

• **Figure 24-3: The Configuration help screen.**

3. **Make any changes that you want.**

A couple of useful features to point out are alternate file systems and USB support for otherwise unsupported devices (such as cameras or USB scanners).

 If you have a single CPU in your machine, (which is likely), you should choose to disable SMP support in your new kernel. This feature is included on the Processor Type and Features menu and is labeled Symmetric Multiprocessing Support. Click the button next to the n before continuing.

4. **When you've chosen the options you want to include in your new kernel, choose <Exit> and save your work.**

Step 5: Building the Kernel

Now it's time to start building the kernel. (*Note:* Some of these steps will run for quite some time, so you better grab a donut.) Follow these steps:

1. **At the command line, enter the following command and press Enter:**

make dep

The make dep command computes dependencies for the features that have changed.

2. **Enter the following command and press Enter:**

make clean

This command cleans up old unwanted files to prepare for the build.

3. **Choose a name for your new kernel (typically, just add the current date to the end of the name). Use your favorite editor to change the EXTRAVERSION variable in the Makefile file. To use kate (a KDE-friendly editor), type in the following command and press Enter:**

kate Makefile

4. **Add the date to the end of the EXTRAVERSION variable (after the word custom).**

EXTRAVERSION=-1.2115.nptlcustom012504

Save the file and close the editor.

5. **At the command line, type the following command and press Enter:**

make bzImage

This step takes quite a while, possibly a few hours, because you're compiling most of the kernel source code here.

6. **Type the following command and press Enter:**

make modules

This compiles the source code for the kernel modules that you selected. This step also takes some time.

 You did make a boot disk and test it, right? If not, stop what you're doing, go back to "Step 1: Making an Emergency Plan, or Boot Disk," earlier in this technique, and follow the steps there.

7. **Type the following command and press Enter:**

make modules_install

This step installs the new kernel modules. Don't worry — you're not replacing your current kernel; you're just adding another choice.

8. **Type the following command and press Enter:**

```
# make install
```

This step copies the new kernel into place and adds the kernel to your boot menu.

9. **To use the new kernel, reboot and highlight the new kernel in the list of choices. Then press Enter.**

Your system boots with the newly built kernel.

 Building kernels can be a tricky business. If you experience trouble at boot time (kernel panic!), reboot into your old kernel, and try building the new kernel again.

 Write down error messages! You can Google for them later to see if other Linux users have had similar problems and published work-arounds on the Web.

Coping with the SELinux Security System

Technique 25

Save Time By

- ✔ Exploring the principles of SELinux
- ✔ Understanding SELinux terminology
- ✔ Disabling or disarming SELinux
- ✔ Finding out about your security policy

Fedora Core 2 includes a new enhancement to the Linux kernel: SELinux. Other distributions will incorporate SELinux in later releases. You may not have to worry about it now, but this technique will come in handy later. The SE in SELinux stands for Security Enhanced. The driving force behind SELinux has been the National Security Agency (NSA), which developed SELinux and donated the code to the open-source community.

The SELinux package is a collection of kernel modifications, program modifications, and configuration files that all work together to *harden* your computer against abuse. Old Linux kernels (pre-SELinux) grant *all* privileges to a special user named root (actually, privileges are granted to the user whose numeric user ID is zero, and by convention that user is named root). Any process whose user ID is zero is granted *all* privileges. A process running as user ID zero is called a superuser. If you log in to Linux as user root, you can do anything you want. If you log in as a non-privileged user and then use the su command to become a superuser, you can do anything you want. If you break into a Linux computer and somehow manage to change your user ID to zero, you can do anything you want. SELinux changes that.

Under Linux, access rules are based on the user ID, group ID, and file permissions. With SELinux, access rules are determined by the policy file, and the rules are subject to change.

In this technique, we introduce you to SELinux. It's a relatively new addition to the security force patrolling Fedora. It's got some room to grow, but it shows a lot of promise as a timesaving way to super-harden your system.

Understanding the Principles of SELinux

When you enable SELinux, the kernel grants privileges based on three factors: the security context of your process, the security context of the object that you're trying to access, and a database of access rules called a policy. The important feature that SELinux brings to Linux is *mandatory access control* (MAC). A standard Linux kernel exercises *discretionary access control* (DAC). In a DAC system, a user can grant to any other user access to things that he owns, at his own discretion. DAC sounds friendly, but if you're trying to run a secure organization, you don't want us mere users granting extra privileges to our friends. In a MAC system, ownership and access are governed by a complex and customizable set of rules controlled by the organization.

The normal Linux security mechanism (access modes and user/group IDs) and the SELinux mechanism work together. Before a process can access an object, the process must satisfy *both* mechanisms. If your user ID has write permissions to a given file, it doesn't necessarily mean that SELinux will give its blessing, too — it all depends on the policy.

SELinux introduces a few new terms to the Linux lexicon, and it helps to have a good understanding of those terms before going much further.

Everything is an object

An *object* is something that you can protect and something that you can access. The Fedora Core 2 security policy defines a number of objects: A file is an object, a file system is an object, a network socket is an object, and a device is an object. In all, the FC2 policy defines 12 top-level objects:

- Files (and directories)
- File systems
- File descriptors (a handle to an open file)
- Sockets
- Network nodes
- Network interfaces (eth0, ppp0, and so on)
- Processes
- IPC mechanisms (shared memory, semaphores, and message queues)

- The SELinux security server
- The system log (syslog)
- Kernel capabilities (kill, reboot, set time, and so on)
- Passwords

The policy also defines a number of fine-grained specializations, such as a program file versus a configuration file versus a data file.

Identifying subjects in SELinux

A *subject* is something that can act on an object (think back to your elementary school grammar classes, ugh). A process is a subject. Indirectly, a user is considered a subject, too, because a new process inherits its security context from the user. A program can also play a part in determining the security context of a process, so a program is often considered a subject as well.

Every subject and every object have an associated *security context* (or *context* for short). When a subject wants to access an object, the kernel compares the subject context, the object context, and the type of access requested against a set of rules called the *policy* to decide whether to grant or deny the requested access.

Understanding the security context

A security context is made up of three components: an *identity*, a *role*, and a *type*. You can see the context assigned to your login session with the command id -Z:

```
$ id -Z
user_u:user_r:user_t
```

In this example, the identity is user_u, the role is user_r, and the type is user_t. If you're logged in as user root, you see a different context:

```
# id -Z
root:staff_r:staff_t
```

The FC2 policy doesn't create an identity for every user: Nonprivileged users share the `user_u` identity.

By convention, role names end with `_r`, and type names end with `_t`. A type that belongs to a process is also known as a *domain*. A role is a name given to a group of process types. Every user is assigned a role, and the role determines which process types (or domains) the user is authorized to use.

To see the security context assigned to a file (or directory), use `ls -Z` (we've trimmed a few columns to fit it on the page):

```
# ls -Z /var
system_u:object_r:acct_data_t     account
system_u:object_r:var_t           cache
system_u:object_r:var_t           db
system_u:object_r:var_t           empty
system_u:object_r:xserver_log_t   gdm
system_u:object_r:var_lib_t       lib
system_u:object_r:var_t           local
system_u:object_r:var_lock_t      lock
system_u:object_r:var_log_t       log
...                               ...
```

Notice that in this example, the identity assigned to each file is `system_u`: That's a generic identity just like `user_u`. `user_u` is shared by nonprivileged subjects, and `system_u` is assigned to almost every file object. Most files share the same identity (`system_u`) and role (`object_r`). The type classifies each file according to its security needs.

When you run a program whose type ends with `exec_t`, that program causes a transition from your current domain into a new domain. For example, take a peek at the program that you use to change your password (`/usr/bin/passwd`). The `passwd` program lets you modify files that are normally protected against nonprivileged users: When you change your password, the new password is (typically) stored in `/etc/shadow` — a write-protected file. If you look at the context assigned to `/usr/bin/passwd`, you see this:

```
$ ls --scontext /usr/bin/passwd
system_u:object_r:passwd_exec_t
   /usr/bin/passwd
```

Notice that the type name ends with `_exec_t`; that's your clue that this is a "domain transitioning" program. When you run `/usr/bin/passwd`, your context changes from `user_u:user_r:user_t` to `user_u:user_r:passwd_t`, giving you just enough privileges to modify `/etc/shadow` and `/etc/passwd`. If this sounds suspiciously similar to a `setuid root` program, it is. The important difference is that a domain transition gives you only the privileges required to act on the protected objects that you need, but a `setuid root` program gives you *all* privileges.

Given the number of subjects, objects, and access types on a typical Linux system, SELinux security rules are far more complex than the old system.

Disabling or Disarming SELinux

The SELinux kernel can operate in *enforcing* mode (the default) or in *permissive* mode:

✔ When you run in enforcing mode, the kernel enforces the security policy that you've installed.

✔ When you run in permissive mode, the kernel consults the security policy, but instead of preventing you from doing something that the policy prohibits, the kernel simply logs the violation.

 Running in permissive mode will tell you what kind of problems you're likely to encounter when you switch over to enforcing mode. Policy violations appear at the Linux console and in the system log file (`/var/log/dmesg`).

By default, Fedora Core 2 boots into enforcing mode. If you want to switch over to permissive mode after your computer has booted, use the following command:

```
# echo "0" > /etc/selinux/enforce
```

(You need superuser privileges to write to the `/etc/selinux/enforce`.) To switch back to enforcing mode, use this command:

```
# echo "1" > /etc/selinux/enforce
```

If you want Fedora to run in permissive mode each time you boot, give yourself superuser privileges and type in the following command:

```
# echo "SELINUX=permissive" > /etc/
  sysconfig/selinux
```

If you prefer to run in enforcing mode after each boot, use this command:

```
# echo "SELINUX=enforcing" > /etc/
  sysconfig/selinux
```

If you're sure that you'll never want to use SELinux on your computer, you can completely disable the kernel extensions with the following command:

```
# echo "SELINUX=disabled" > /etc/
  sysconfig/selinux
```

 The difference between permissive and disabled modes is that in permissive mode, the kernel logs policy violations and labels new files with the appropriate security context. If you disable SELinux completely, new files and directories are created without a security context, and if you ever want to turn SELinux back on, you'll have to *relabel* your computer (that is, reapply security contexts). Relabeling can be a lot of work — we recommend running in permissive mode instead of disabling SELinux.

Playing the Right Role

One of the consequences of SELinux is that mere-mortal users can't access objects that they may have been able to access before. For example, if your security context is `user_u:user_r:user_t` and you

run the `ps` (process status) command, you can't see privileged processes.

It's very important to use the correct role when you do system administration work. Some commands work in the `staff_r` role but produce the wrong results. For example, if you create a new user account while you're logged in to the `sysadm_r` role, the home directory for the new account is created with the right context:

```
# id -Z
root:sysadm_r:sysadm_t
# useradd franklin
# ls -Z /home/franklin
root:object_r:user_home_dir_t
```

However, if you create a new account from `root`'s default role (`staff_r`), the home directory is labeled incorrectly:

```
# id -Z
root:staff_r:sysadm_t
# useradd franklin
# ls -Z /home/franklin
root:object_r:home_root_t
```

You may be wondering why the identity component of each context is `root` instead of `franklin`. The answer is a bit confusing. `franklin` is a generic user; that is, `franklin` appears in the Linux user database, but not in the SELinux policy. That means that `franklin` is *not* an identity and therefore can't be assigned as the identity for his home directory. Generic users share a common identity: `user_u`.

To create a new Linux user with a corresponding identity, use `seuseradd` instead of `useradd`:

```
# newrole -r sysadm_r
# seuseradd -r -m trixie
loading new policy...
```

We've thrown another new command at you in this example: `newrole`. `newrole` starts a new shell with a different security context. Your identity stays the same, but your role changes to the one you requested. See `man newrole` for more details.

Finding Out about Your SELinux Policy

At the time we're writing this, Fedora Core 2 provides few utilities that you can use to manage SELinux policies. That will change as software vendors and open-source developers learn more about SELinux. For now, you can use the utilities provided by the `setools` and `setools-gui` RPM packages (included in the Fedora Core 2 distribution) to find out more about the default policy installed on your system. See Technique 17 for more information about installing RPM packages.

The `seinfo` command can show you a wealth of information about your policy. For example, to see a list of all identities, give yourself superuser privileges and then type in the following command:

```
# seinfo --users
Users: 5
    system_u
    user_u
    root
    freddie
    trixie
```

To see the list of roles defined for your system, use this command:

```
# seinfo --roles
Roles: 5
    object_r
    system_r
    sysadm_r
    user_r
    staff_r
```

To see the roles that each identity is allowed to assume, add the `--expand` option, like this:

```
# seinfo --users --expand
Users: 5
    system_u
        system_r
    user_u
        user_r
```

```
    root
        staff_r
        sysadm_r
        system_r
    freddie
        staff_r
        user_r
    trixie
        staff_r
```

To see the domains that a given role is allowed to assume, use `--roles=`*name* `--expand`:

```
# seinfo --roles=sysadm_r --expand
    sysadm_r
        null_device_t
        zero_device_t
        devtty_t
        local_login_t
        remote_login_t
```

Every object class defines a list of permissions, but it's probably easier to think of a permission as an action. For example, you can mount, unmount, and remount an object belonging to the `filesystem` class. To see the permissions (actions) defined for a given class, use this command:

```
# seinfo --classes=filesystem --expand
    filesystem
        mount
        remount
        unmount
        getattr
        relabelfrom
        relabelto
        transition
        associate
        quotamod
        quotaget
```

Use the following command to see the list of types:

```
# seinfo --types
Types: 291
    device_t
    null_device_t
    zero_device_t
    console_device_t
    memory_device_t
```

```
random_device_t
urandom_device_t
devtty_t
...
```

To see the attributes of a given type, use this command:

```
# seinfo --types=bin_t
   bin_t
      file_type
      sysadmfile
```

By convention, an object of type `bin_t` is a file (it has the attribute `file_type`), and it's a system administration file (`sysadmfile`).

26 Technique

Finding Out about Your System with /proc

Save Time By

✓ Using /proc to examine the processes currently running on your system

✓ Exploring your system resources and devices with /proc

✓ Tightening security with /proc

✓ Getting your kernel to recognize native Windows programs

The /proc file system is a virtual file system full of files representing the current state of your Linux kernel. The files in /proc don't really exist on disk; rather, they're collections of data that can be viewed and navigated just like real files. If you look at the modification time for the files in /proc, you'll see that the date is always current. That's accurate because the content of each file is being created on demand as you view it.

You can discover a lot about your system by viewing the contents of the files in /proc. Every process running on your system has a directory in /proc. Each process directory is full of subdirectories and files that contain tidbits of data about the process. Because the information is broken down into small pieces, you can search quickly for just what you need to know about a process.

The /proc file system also contains information about system resources — such as memory usage, CPU usage, and system statistics. The files are constantly being updated, so the information you get from /proc is always current. /proc also maintains information files about all the devices on your network. You can use this information to help debug troublesome new devices.

Using the /proc file system to manipulate the state of the kernel is a real timesaver. Instead of using complex arguments to adjust your kernel, the /proc file system gives you easy access to many of the kernel's variables. You can tighten security with just a few variable settings, and improve on an existing firewall in no time.

In this technique, we introduce you to /proc, and show you some subtle but effective (and quick) changes you can make to the kernel that will make your system safer and save you a few keystrokes in the long run.

Exploring the Process-Related Entries in /proc

Every process running on your system has its own directory in the /proc file system. You can use the files in the process directory to identify the processes running on your system. You can discover who's running the process, what command line arguments started the process, and what files that process currently has open.

The directory name for each process is taken from the process ID. For example, the directory that contains information about process 1 (the `init` process) is named `/proc/1`. To view the process directory, follow these steps:

1. **Open the Konqueror Web browser.**

2. **Type** `file:/proc` **in the Location field and press Enter.**

Press the F9 key to close Konqueror's navigation panel and buy more screen real estate for the directories and files in `/proc`.

You're treated to a view of the contents of the `/proc` directory, as shown in Figure 26-1.

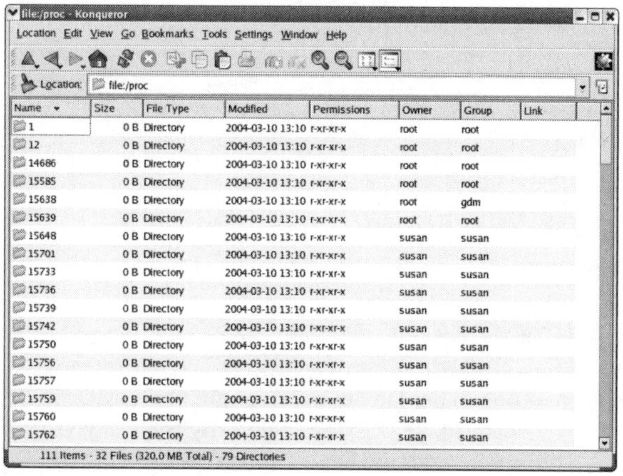

• **Figure 26-1: Viewing** `/proc` **in Konqueror.**

3. **For the best view of the** `/proc` **directory, choose View➪View Mode➪Detailed List View.**

The directories with numerical names contain information about the processes currently running on your system (the directory name corresponds to the process number).

4. **Double-click a process directory to view the directory contents (see Figure 26-2).**

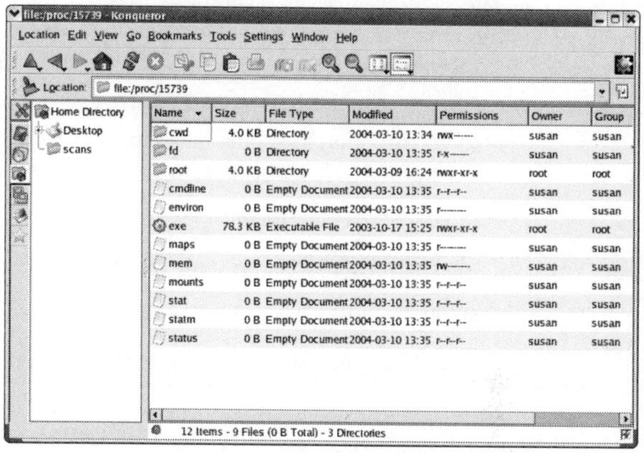

• **Figure 26-2: The contents of a process directory.**

Table 26-1 lists the files and directories where you can find some interesting information about a process.

5. **To view the contents of any file in the process directory, right-click the filename and choose Open With from the pop-up menu.**

6. **Enter** `kedit` **in the Open With field and click OK.**

`kedit` opens, displaying the file contents, as shown in Figure 26-3.

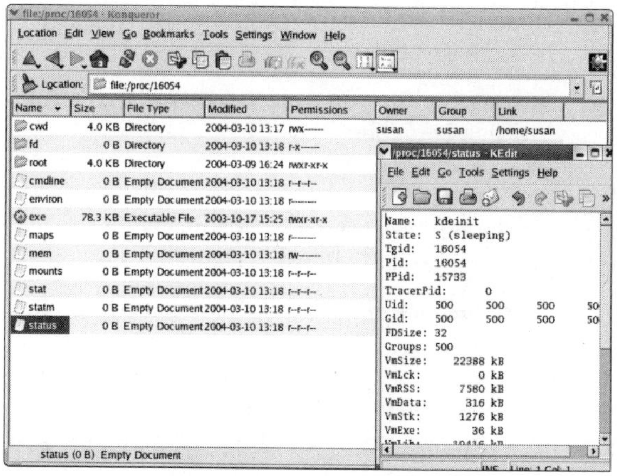

• **Figure 26-3: Exposing the status file with** `kedit`.

TABLE 26-1: PROCESS-RELATED DIRECTORIES IN THE /PROC FILE SYSTEM

Directory	What You Find
cwd	The cwd directory is a symbolic link to the current working directory of the process (the directory named in the Link column). If you're running a bash shell and your current working directory is /tmp, /proc/$$/cwd is a symbolic link to /tmp ($$ is a shell variable that contains your process ID).
fd	The fd directory contains one entry for each open file. Like cwd, the files in the fd subdirectory are symbolic links to the open files. File descriptor 0 is connected to the standard input stream for the process, descriptor 1 is connected to the standard output stream, and descriptor 2 is connected to the standard error stream.
cmdline	Open the cmdline file with kedit to view the command line arguments that started the process.
environ	Open the environ file to view the environment variables used by the process.
mounts	Open the mounts file to view a list of currently mounted devices in use by the process.
status	The status file keeps running statistics about the current process.

7. **When you're done exploring the file contents, close the editor window.**

If you check the Remember Application Association for This Type of File box when you open a file with kedit, you can just double-click to open future files with the editor.

If you prefer working at the command line (or you don't have a graphical interface handy), you can use the more command to display the contents of files within the process directory:

1. **Open a terminal window and move into the process directory.**

2. **Display the file you want to read with the following command:**

```
$ more filename
```

The contents of the file are displayed in the terminal window, as shown in Figure 26-4.

3. **Press the spacebar to see the next page of data.**

Whether you get information with kedit or at the command line, you can find lots of handy information about the processes on your system with /proc.

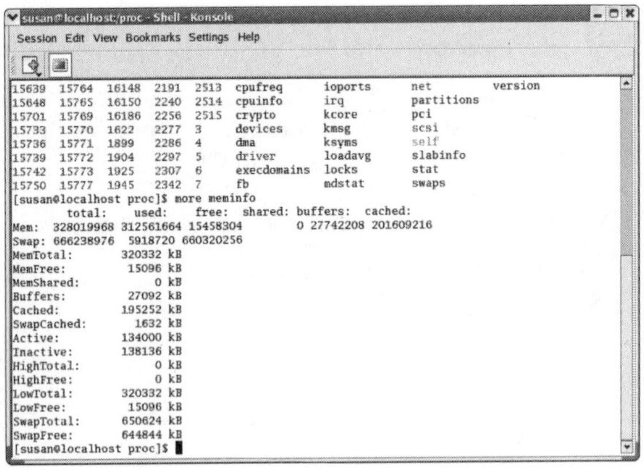

• **Figure 26-4:** Exposing the status file with more.

If you go to /proc/self, you'll find it contains a symbolic link to the process you're running. Look in the Link column for the process ID. Be aware that /proc/self is pretty shifty. If you use a command like ls to look at the /proc/self directory and then look at it again with another tool, it changes. /proc/self magically points to whichever process opens it.

Surveying Your System from /proc

Files that contain configuration information for devices connected to your computer are scattered throughout the `/proc` file system. The `/proc` file system also contains files full of information about system resources. To find the device or system resource information on your system, you may need to do some exploring, but we show you some good places to start.

A few of the files in `/proc` that relate directly to hardware and system resources are worth mentioning:

✔ `/proc/bus/usb`: This file contains information about USB (Universal Serial Bus) devices currently plugged into your system. In this file, you find a rundown of the mice, cameras, and serial storage devices currently connected to your computer, as shown in Figure 26-5.

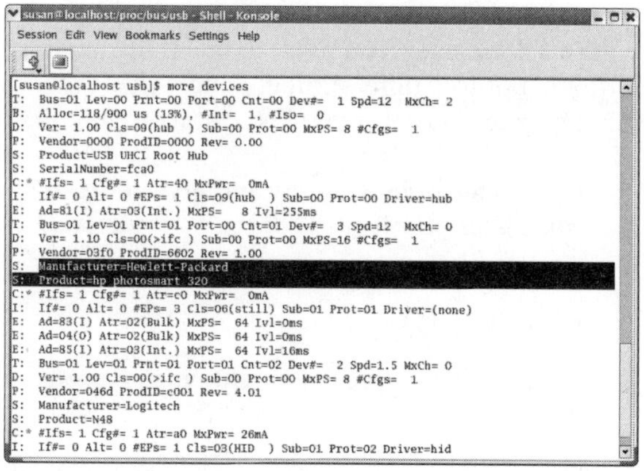

• **Figure 26-5:** Viewing the currently connected USB devices.

If you're having trouble getting a camera or scanner to work, look here first to be sure that the device is properly connected and identified.

✔ `/proc/scsi/scsi`: This file contains information about any SCSI devices currently attached to your system. Check it out if you're having trouble getting a SCSI device to work.

If you're having device driver problems and decide to appeal to a newsgroup for help, include the information you find in the `/proc` file corresponding to the device. The `/proc` file might contain information that helps a newsgroup member determine the cause of your problem.

✔ `/proc/cpuinfo`: This file contains a collection of information about the system's CPU. This is the place to look for all the really geeky details about your CPU.

✔ `/proc/crypto`: The `/proc/crypto` file contains information about the current encryption algorithms and digital signature tools installed on your system.

✔ `/proc/meminfo`: This file contains a wealth of information about your system's memory resources, as shown in Figure 26-6.

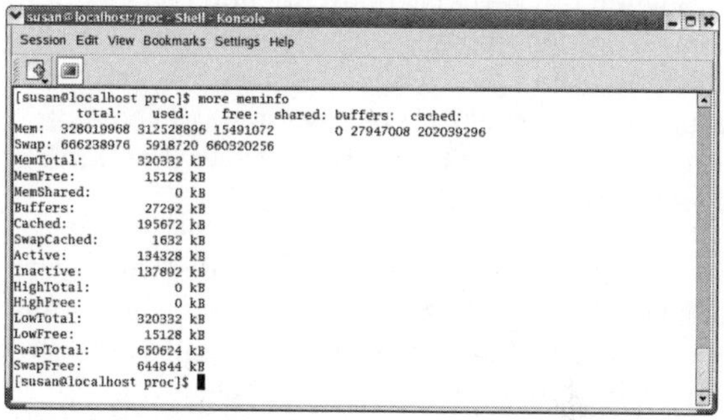

• **Figure 26-6:** Checking out the status of the system's memory.

If your system performance is bad, check out the `/proc/meminfo` file to find out if you're running short on memory.

✔ `/proc/filesystems`: This file contains information about the file system types that can be mounted on your system. Check out `/proc/filesystems` to find out what kind of drives you can mount on your system. If `ntfs` isn't in the list, you can't mount Windows drives on your Linux machine.

✔ `/proc/uptime`: You trivia buffs out there will enjoy this one. This first number in this file is the length of time the system has been running (in seconds), and the second number is the number of seconds that the system has been idle.

Divide the number of seconds idle by the uptime, and you'll find out the percentage of time that your system is running without being used. If you have extra CPU time to share, get in touch with setiathome.ssl.berkeley.edu to share the wealth.

Closing Down Security Gaps with /proc

With just a few quick changes to the files in /proc, you can make a good firewall even better. The Linux kernel includes a number of variables that affect system security. The variables receive their default settings when the kernel is built, but you can customize them to tighten up your security even more. With a little help from /proc, you don't need to completely rebuild your kernel to take advantage of some of these optional benefits; you can tweak the running kernel with the variables in /proc.

Any changes you make in the /proc files will revert back to the stored kernel configuration when you reboot your system. To make the changes take effect every time you reboot, you can create a startup script (or modify an existing one) to apply the changes automatically.

By making changes to the kernel variables, you can close security gaps that are commonly left open in most kernels. The changes in our example won't keep out every hacker or shut down all denial-of-service requests, but they're a good place to start.

If you are running Fedora or Mandrake, you can change the settings of the kernel variables at startup, by following these steps:

1. Open a terminal window and give yourself superuser privileges with the su command.

2. Move to the /etc/rc.d directory:

```
# cd /etc/rc.d
```

3. Open the rc.local file with your favorite editor (we're using kedit):

```
# kedit rc.local
```

4. Add the following lines of code to the end of the rc.local file:

```
echo 1 > /proc/sys/net/ipv4/icmp_echo_
  ignore_broadcasts
echo 1 > /proc/sys/net/ipv4/conf/*/log_
  martians
echo 0 > /proc/sys/net/ipv4/conf/*/
  accept_redirects
```

5. Save the changes and close the editor.

6. Reboot your system to make the changes take effect.

If you're a SuSE user, you need to make the same additions, but to a different file. Follow these steps to change your kernel variables at startup:

1. Open a terminal window and give yourself superuser privileges with the su command.

2. Move to the /etc/init.d directory:

```
# cd /etc/init.d
```

3. Open the boot.local file with your favorite editor (we're using kedit):

```
# kedit boot.local
```

4. Add the following lines of code to the end of the boot.local file:

```
echo 1 > /proc/sys/net/ipv4/icmp_echo_
  ignore_broadcasts
echo 1 > /proc/sys/net/ipv4/conf/*/log_
  martians
echo 0 > /proc/sys/net/ipv4/conf/*/
  accept_redirects
```

5. Save the changes and close the editor.

6. Reboot your system to make the changes take effect.

The three variables we've changed tighten your network security a bit. They are as follows:

✔ `icmp_echo_ignore_broadcasts`: Enabling this variable tells your system to ignore broadcast pings, which can help spare you from denial-of-service attacks.

✔ `log_martians`: Enable this variable to tell the kernel to send a message to the system log when an illegally addressed packet is received. After setting this variable, monitor the `syslog` files (see Technique 41) to find out if you're receiving nasty packets.

✔ `accept_redirects`: Disable this variable to help prevent man-in-the-middle attacks. Turning off `accept_redirects` tells your system to prevent outgoing packets from being redirected. Hackers can't grab your outbound packets looking for sensitive information (such as passwords or credit card numbers).

You can change many variables to affect the state of your kernel. Some of the variables work like on/off switches. To turn on a variable (or enable the variable), echo a 1 to it in the startup script. To turn a variable off (or disable the variable), echo a 0 to it in the startup script. Variables that control time settings or cache sizes are manipulated with integer values.

 You can find many good resources on the Web that list kernel variables and what they control. Google for `/proc/sys variables`, and you'll get dozens of hits that will help you find good settings for your system.

Popping the Cork: Speeding Up WINE with /proc

If you use WINE in your daily life and want a quicker way to start your programs, using the files in `/proc` can help.

 If you're not familiar with WINE (the program, not the beverage), it's a package that lets you run Windows programs on Linux machines. The abbreviation WINE stands for *Wine Is Not*

an Emulator. WINE doesn't emulate Windows machines, but it runs their programs in a Linux environment.

Normally, to start a program with WINE, you need to preface the command with `wine`. With a simple change to the startup file, you can run a Windows program simply by typing its name, just like the Linux programs on your system.

To simplify the startup of your Windows programs in Fedora or Mandrake, follow these steps:

1. **Open a terminal window and give yourself superuser privileges with the `su` command.**

2. **Move to the `/etc/rc.d` directory:**

```
# cd /etc/rc.d
```

3. **Open the `rc.local` file with your favorite editor:**

```
# kedit rc.local
```

4. **Add the following commands to the end of the file:**

```
modprobe binfmt_misc
echo ':Wine:M::MZ::/usr/local/bin/
    wine:' > /proc/sys/fs/binfmt_misc/
    register
```

5. **Save your work and exit the editor.**

6. **Reboot your system to make the changes take effect.**

If you're a SuSE user, you can add similar code to your boot script. To simplify the startup of your Windows programs in SuSE, follow these steps:

1. **Open a terminal window and give yourself superuser privileges with the `su` command.**

2. **Move to the `/etc/init.d` directory:**

```
# cd /etc/init.d
```

3. **Open the `boot.local` file with your favorite editor:**

```
# kedit boot.local
```

4. **Add the following commands to the end of the file:**

```
modprobe binfmt_misc
echo ':Wine:M::MZ::/usr/local/bin/
  wine:' > /proc/sys/fs/binfmt_misc/
  register
```

5. **Save your work and exit the editor.**

6. **Reboot your system to make the changes take effect.**

The preceding steps change the boot script that is executed at boot time. The two lines shown in Step 4 tell Linux to automatically recognize Microsoft Windows programs and execute them with wine. For example, to play Minesweeper, you can simply type the command ./winmine.exe.

When you make this change, you don't have to remember to type wine before entering the program name. This also makes it easier to include Windows programs on menus and shortcuts.

Part V

Securing Your Workspace

The 5th Wave   By Rich Tennant

"A centralized security management system sounds fine, but then what would we do with the dogs?"

27 Technique

Closing Those Prying Eyes

K eeping private documents out of the hands of snoops is easy with well-assigned permissions and good system administration practices.

In this technique, we explain how to use file permissions to limit access to sensitive documents and dangerous programs on a Linux machine. You can set the permissions either at the command line or with a graphical interface. If you have access to a graphical environment (either Konqueror or Nautilus will work), it's definitely the friendlier way to go.

Reading and Understanding File Permissions

Knowing how to read and use file permissions is important for maintaining privacy in your file system. Limiting a user's access is simple when you understand the permissions.

Every file and directory in a Linux computer is owned by one specific user and one specific group. When you try to access a file, you're classified into one of three categories:

- ✔ **Owner:** You're the owner if your effective user ID is the same as the file's owner.

- ✔ **Group member:** You're a member of the group if your effective group ID is the same as the file's group.

- ✔ **Other:** You're an "other" if you're not the owner and not a member of the group.

After you've been categorized, Linux looks at the permissions assigned to your category. For example, if you're accessing a file owned by user freddie and you're logged in as user freddie, Linux examines the *owner* permissions for that file (because you are the owner). If you're not logged in as user freddie but you are a member of the group that owns the file,

Linux examines the *group* permissions for the file. If you're not the owner and you're not a member of the file's group, Linux examines the *other* permissions.

Next, Linux compares the permissions (owner permissions, group permissions, or other permissions) with the type of access you're attempting. If you are the file's owner and are trying to read the file, Linux checks the read bit in the owner permissions. If you're trying to modify the file, Linux checks the write bit on the owner permissions.

You can control three types of access for each user category:

- **Read permissions** grant (or deny) the right to read a file or to list the contents of a directory.

- **Write permissions** control the right to change the contents of the file or directory.

- **Execute permissions** control the right to run a program or script. If you're accessing a directory, the execute permissions control whether you can access the files within the directory.

To display the permissions for an entire directory, enter ls -l at the command line. The -l flag forces ls to display permissions (and the file's owner and group) along with the name of each file (see Figure 27-1).

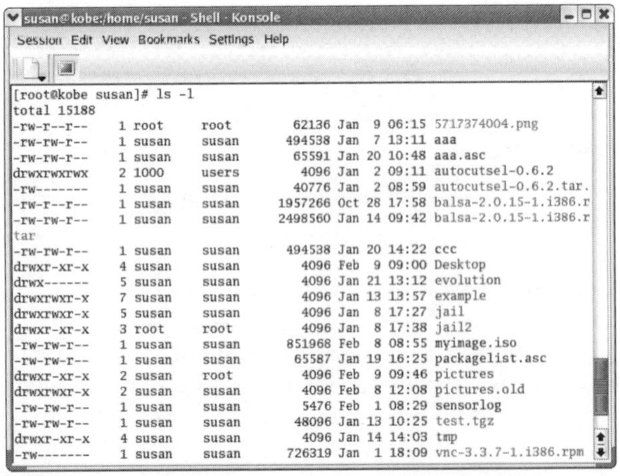

• **Figure 27-1:** The long form of directory contents.

The listing shows seven groups of information. From right to left, they are as follows:

- File permissions
- Link count
- Name of the user that owns the file
- Name of the group that owns the file
- File size (in bytes)
- Date and time the file was last modified
- File (or directory) name

The file permissions are displayed as an odd collection of ten characters, with dashes replacing the privileges that are denied to that user category.

For the sake of dissection, we've chosen the following listing as an example:

```
drwxr-x--- 4 freddie acctg 65595 Jan 20
  14:14 tables
```

The first letter in the permissions column doesn't have anything to do with permissions. Instead, it tells you what kind of file you're dealing with. The most common entries are d for directory or - for file. In our example, the d at the beginning of the listing indicates that it is a directory.

The next three-letter grouping tells you the access permissions for the file's owner (user freddie, in this example). The letters rwx stand for read, write, and execute. freddie has full permissions to this directory.

The next three-letter grouping tells you the group privileges. In our example, r-x stands for read and execute. The acctg group isn't allowed to change files in the directory.

The last three-letter group tells you the file permissions for any other user (not the owner and not a member of the file's group). In our example, the `---` means that anyone who isn't a member of the `acctg` group or isn't the file owner is denied all access to the file.

Controlling Permissions at the Command Line

If you have access to a desktop environment, maintaining permissions is easy and quick with a browser. If you need to set permissions over an SSH connection or for a dedicated server (without a desktop environment), you can use the command line to change ownership and file permissions. See Table 27-1 for details on changing ownership permissions.

Use the `chmod` command to change the permissions for users, groups, or others. Table 27-2 explains how. The `chmod` command also works with the + (plus) and - (minus) signs to turn permissions on and off. Substitute the plus or minus sign for the equal sign in the command, and the permissions listed in the argument are turned on or off. A plus sign turns the listed permission on, and a minus sign turns it off.

For example, the following command turns on read permissions for the user without changing any of the other permissions:

```
$ chmod u+r filename
```

This command turns off write permissions for a group:

```
$chmod g-w filename
```

This command turns off all permissions for non-group users:

```
$ chmod o-rwx filename
```

You can see a pattern starting to form.

If you need to, you can use the command line to set privileges, but there is a friendlier way, as described in the next section.

 If you really want to test the spin in your propeller, you can set the permissions with octal numbers. The process is a little cryptic, but if you're inclined to try it, check out the `info chmod` page and follow the links to Note File Permissions⇨Numeric Modes.

TABLE 27-1: CHANGING OWNERSHIP PERMISSIONS

To Do This	Use This Command
Change ownership of a file or directory at the command line.	`$ chown username filename`
Change ownership of a directory and all the directories below it (that is, just add the `-R` recursive flag).	`$ chown -R username directoryname`
Change the group ownership of a file.	`$ chgrp groupname filename`
Change the group ownership of a directory and all the directories below it.	`$ chgrp -R groupname directoryname`

TABLE 27-2: CHANGING FILE PERMISSIONS

To Do This	Use This Command
Change the user (owner) permissions to include read, write, and execute.	`$ chmod u=rwx filename`
Exclude a permission from the user. You do this by excluding it from the command. For example, to assign read and execute privileges only, use `rx`.	`$ chmod u=rx filename` (***Note:*** `w` is excluded)
Set permissions for a group. Note that you substitute a `g` into the command.	`$ chmod g=rwx filename`
Set permissions for users who aren't group members or an owner.	`$ chmod o=rwx filename`
Deny privileges to nongroup members who aren't owners.	`$ chmod o= filename`

Changing File Permissions from a Desktop

Sometimes the command line is your only choice, but if you have access to a graphical interface, there's a friendlier way to manage file permissions: the Konqueror browser.

 Nautilus offers the same functionality to GNOME users. Double-click the Start Here icon on the desktop and surf along.

To view and modify file permissions with the Konqueror browser, follow these steps:

1. **Click the Start Here or Home icon on your KDE desktop or taskbar.**

2. **When Konqueror opens, locate the file you want to modify.**

 You can navigate to the file you want to modify in one quick step by entering `file:/pathname` in the Location field to step directly into the directory that contains your file.

3. **After you've located the file you want to work with, right-click the file and choose Properties from the pop-up menu.**

The Properties dialog opens, as shown in Figure 27-2.

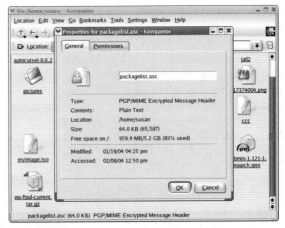

• **Figure 27-2: The Properties dialog.**

4. **Click the Permissions tab.**

The Permissions dialog opens showing the current permissions for the file (see Figure 27-3). The permissions dialog is easy to interpret and change.

 If the check boxes and fields displayed on the window are disabled, you don't have enough privileges to edit the permissions for that file. If you need superuser privileges to change permissions for a file or directory, open a terminal window and use the `su` command to gain superuser privileges. Then type `konqueror` in the command line and press Enter to start a copy of the browser with your newly enhanced privileges.

• **Figure 27-3:** The Permissions dialog.

5. To change read, write, or execute privileges for the file or directory, simply check the boxes next to User, Group, or Others.

If a box is checked, the user (or group) has that permission. If the box is empty, that permission is denied.

> Before you modify the check boxes in the Special column, make sure that you know what you're doing; read the sidebar, "What makes a check box Special?" for details.

6. To change ownership, enter the new user or group owner in the appropriate field.

> Nautilus users: Use the drop-down list boxes to choose from existing users and groups when you change the ownership of a file or directory.

7. After you make the necessary changes to the Permissions dialog, click OK to save your changes and close the dialog.

What makes a check box Special?

Under the column header labeled Special, you see check boxes next to the labels Set UID, Set GID, and Sticky. These check boxes merit special consideration.

✔ **Set UID:** When a Set UID bit is turned on for a program, your EUID (effective user ID) becomes the same as the program's owner when you run the program. You also gain all the privileges of the program's owner. In other words, if user `freddie` runs a Set UID program owned by user `root`, `freddie` has superuser privileges while that program is running.

Set UID affects programs only; it's really not important for data files and directories. If you find a Set UID program, read the WARNING!

Warning: Set UID programs are potentially dangerous. Users can gain extra privileges by using files that grant them superuser privileges. See Technique 57 for information about preventing security breaches uncovered by the `setuid` and `setgid` bits.

✔ **Set GID:** The Set GID bit works similarly to Set UID — anyone running the program gains all the privileges of the group.

When the Set GID box is checked for a *directory*, the files in that directory belong to that group regardless of who puts the files in the directory.

✔ **Sticky:** Checking the Sticky box affects directories only. If this box is checked, you can't remove (or rename) a file in that directory unless you're the file owner.

28 Technique

Using Encryption for Extra Security

Save Time By

✔ Using kgpg in your desktop environment

✔ Using gpg at the command line

✔ Encrypting and signing e-mail with Evolution

✔ Adding Enigmail security to Mozilla

This technique is all about privacy. Keeping private data private can save you a lot of headaches. Public-key cryptography provides a quick and easy way to safeguard e-mail messages and sensitive files. Public-key cryptography involves two *big* numbers: a public key and a private key. When you create a key pair, you keep the private key to yourself and share the public key with anyone you wish. The numbers in a key pair are related in a fiendishly clever way: Data that you encrypt with the public key can be decrypted only with the private key, and data encrypted with the private key can be decrypted only with the public key (private decrypts public, public decrypts private).

If you encrypt a message with your friend's public key, only your friend can decrypt it (because your friend has never shared his private key with anyone, even with you). Encrypt a message with your *private* key and send it to your friend: If he uses your public key to decrypt the message (and the result looks meaningful), he'll know the message came from you. (Nobody else could have sent the message because it's encrypted with your private key, and no one else knows your private key.) You can combine these techniques to encrypt *and* sign a message.

In this technique, we show you how to use gpg (the GNU Privacy Guard) at the command line for those cases where you need security but don't have access to a desktop environment. You can use gpg to encrypt, decrypt, and sign e-mail messages. gpg can also encrypt documents that you don't intend to share with others, so snoops won't be able to read anything you need to keep private. Encrypt the original document, delete the unencrypted version, and only you can decrypt it again to read it.

kgpg (KGpg) is a graphical interface for gpg that runs in the KDE Desktop environment. It's a great tool that packs lots of functionality into a user-friendly package. In this technique, we show you how to download, install, and use kgpg. We also show you how to create a gpg key pair (from the command line and with kgpg). After you've created a key pair, you can distribute your public key to your friends, or you can upload the public key to a server — a number of public-key registries are available on the Web.

In this technique, we also show you ways to keep your e-mail private. Encrypting e-mail adds a new level of security, enabling you to prevent Peeping Toms from reading your e-mail as it travels across the Internet. Add a digital signature to your e-mail messages for extra protection. If your message is tampered with, the recipient knows (because the signature is invalid).

Encryption Made Easy with kgpg and the KDE Desktop

If you're working in a desktop environment, a graphical package such as kgpg makes gpg encryption much faster and easier to use. You still may need to return to the command line if you're encrypting an entire directory tree, but for most of your everyday needs, a graphical tool works great.

kgpg is a user interface that works with the KDE Desktop to make using and managing gpg keys easy and fast. With kgpg, you can encrypt and decrypt files on your desktop in seconds.

- ✔ To get started, you need to create a pair of keys (a public key and a private key). See the section titled "Creating keys with kgpg," later in this technique, for details.

- ✔ To send encrypted e-mail (or e-mail that contains a digital signature), you have to publish your public key. See the section titled "Sharing your key with the world," later in this technique, for more information.

- ✔ To read an encrypted e-mail message (or other secure document), you need to import a public key first. See the section titled "Importing a public key from a public-key server," later in this technique, to understand the process.

- ✔ To encrypt documents that need to be secure, see the section, "Encrypting documents on your home system."

 kgpg is part of the kdeutils package in KDE Versions 3.2 and later. If you're using an older version of KDE, search the Web for a kgpg RPM package that matches your version.

Creating keys with kgpg

gpg keys (both public and private) are stored in a *key ring* (which is a set of files in your ~/.gnupg directory). The first time you run kgpg, it offers to create a new gpg key pair (unless you've already created a key pair with another tool). Here's what you need to do to create a key pair:

1. **Open KGpg:**

   To open kgpg on Fedora Linux, open the Main Menu and choose Accessories⇨More Accessories⇨KGpg.

   If you're using SuSE, open the Main Menu and choose System⇨Security⇨KGpg.

   On Mandrake, find kgpg by opening the Main Menu and choosing System⇨Other⇨KGpg.

2. **In the dialog that appears, click Yes.**

   The Key Generation dialog opens, as shown in Figure 28-1.

3. **Enter your name, e-mail address, and a comment and then click OK.**

    Enter your first name for the real name, your last name for the comment, and your real e-mail address. When you publish your public key on a public-key server, it appears as name(comment)e-mail@addr.com, so everyone can tell with a glance who owns the public key.

   The passphrase dialog appears, as shown in Figure 28-2.

4. **Enter a passphrase in the Password field and then reenter it in the Verify field. Click OK to continue.**

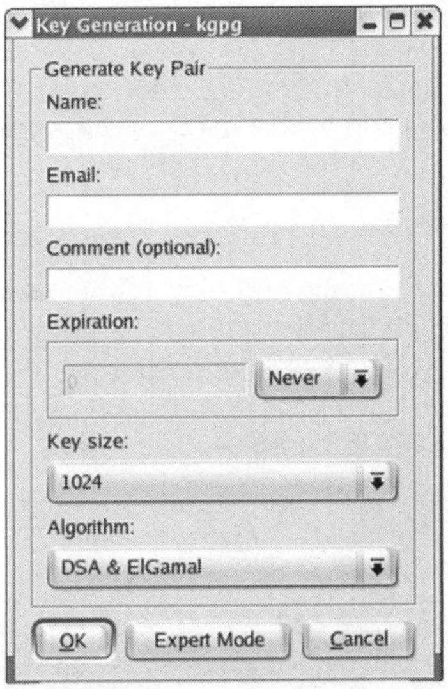

• Figure 28-1: The Key Generation dialog.

It's important to keep your private key private. If gpg simply stored your private key in plain text, anyone with access to your home directory could use your private key. Instead, gpg protects your key ring with a passphrase. You must provide the passphrase whenever you want to encrypt, decrypt, and sign documents. Don't give out your passphrase, or others will be able to decrypt documents encrypted with your key.

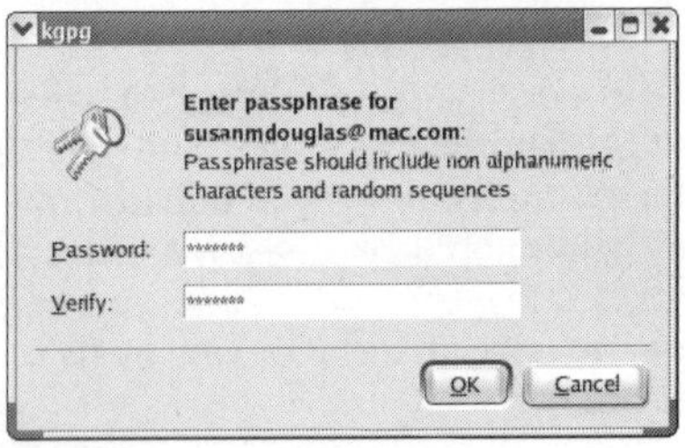

• Figure 28-2: The passphrase dialog.

After you click OK in Step 4, the Tip of the Day window opens. Look carefully, and you'll notice that an icon has been added to the taskbar. The icon looks like a padlock covering a sheet of paper, as shown in the lower-right corner of Figure 28-3. This means your key has been created.

After you've created a key pair, the taskbar icon becomes your interface to kgpg. Click the taskbar icon and choose Open Key Manager from the menu. The Key Management window opens, showing the key you've just created (see Figure 28-4).

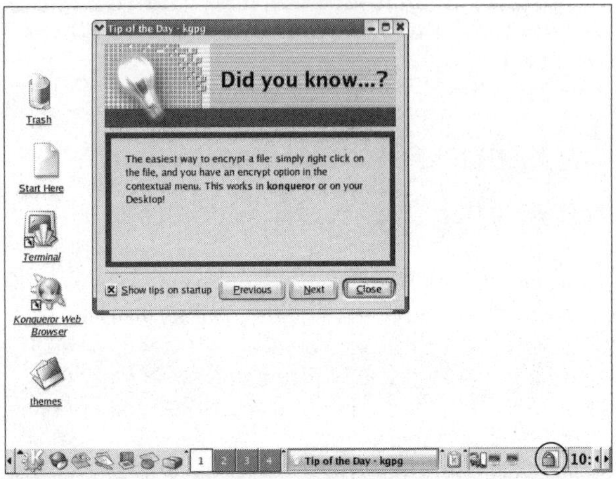

• Figure 28-3: The kgpg icon is now included on the taskbar.

From the Key Management window, you can export your key (to a file, to the clipboard, or to an e-mail message), get key information, sign your key, make changes to your keys, import other keys, generate new key pairs, and more.

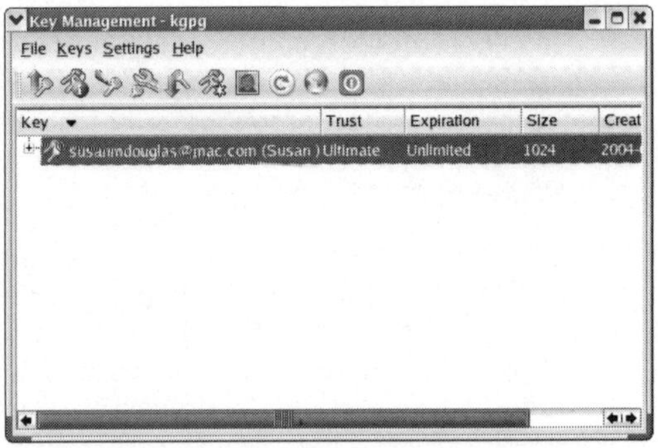

• Figure 28-4: The Key Management window.

Sharing your key with the world

After you have an encryption key pair, you need to publish the public part. Other people can encrypt private messages with your public key, but you're the only person who can decrypt these messages because you hold the private key. When you send an e-mail, sign the message with your private key and the recipient can use your public key to verify that the message really came from you. How do you distribute your public key? Use a public-key server.

A public-key server is a directory that lists people and their public keys. kgpg knows how to export your public key to a key server and how to import keys from a key server. kgpg is preconfigured to talk to two public-key servers, but you can add more servers if you want to.

To publish your public key, follow these steps:

1. **Click the** kgpg **taskbar icon (which looks like a padlock; refer to Figure 28-3) and choose Open Key Manager from the menu.**

   The Key Management window opens (refer to Figure 28-4).

2. **Choose File⇨Key Server Dialog (or click the toolbar icon that looks like a globe).**

   The Key Server Operation dialog appears.

3. **Select the Export tab.**

   The dialog displays two drop-down lists, as shown in Figure 28-5.

4. **Use the Key Server drop-down list to choose the server that you want to distribute your key.**

5. **Use the Key to Be Exported list to select the public key that you want to export.**

6. **After you've chosen the server and key to be exported, click Export.**

Now that you've published yourself, your friends can find your public key on the server that you chose. (Many servers share their public keys with other servers, so after you've published your public key, it appears on other servers as well.) With your public key, someone can send encrypted e-mail to you, and no one else can read the e-mail.

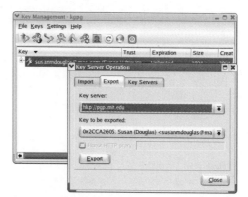

• **Figure 28-5: The Export tab of the Key Server Operation dialog.**

Importing a public key from a public-key server

You can also use kgpg to locate and import keys from a public-key server. Here's how to find and import keys:

1. **Click the** kgpg **taskbar icon (which looks like a padlock) and choose Open Key Manager from the menu.**

   The Key Management window opens.

2. **Choose File⇨Key Server Dialog (or click the toolbar icon that looks like a globe).**

   The Key Server Operation dialog appears.

3. **Select the Import tab.**

4. **Choose a public-key server from the top list box and enter the name or e-mail address of the person you'd like to contact in the second field.**

   You can choose any of the public-key servers listed; they all talk to each other and share the same database of public keys.

5. **Click the Search button to continue.**

   The Search Result dialog appears, as shown in Figure 28-6.

 Common names are likely to yield many results. Search by e-mail address to narrow the field a bit.

• **Figure 28-6: The Search Result dialog.**

6. When you find the key you're looking for, click the key and then click Import to import that key.

After you've imported a public key into your key ring, you can encrypt e-mail (and other documents) with that key. The only person who can decrypt that e-mail is the person who holds the matching private key.

Encrypting and decrypting documents with drag-and-drop ease

kpgp is well-integrated with the rest of KDE, making it quick and easy to encrypt and decrypt files.

 Keep private information private by encrypting your personal files. After encrypting a file, delete the unencrypted version. Decrypt the file again when you need it. Only those entrusted with your passphrase can read your private documents.

To encrypt a document, follow these steps:

1. Open Konqueror and browse to the directory that contains the file you want to encrypt.

2. Right-click the file icon and choose Encrypt File from the menu.

The Encryption dialog opens, as shown in Figure 28-7.

3. Highlight the key you want to use and then click Encrypt.

kgpg encrypts the file with your public key; that way, only someone with the matching private key (that would be you) can decrypt the file.

The newly encrypted file appears in the same directory as the original: The encrypted version has .asc tacked on to the end of the filename. kgpg doesn't delete the original version.

• **Figure 28-7: The Encryption dialog.**

4. If you want to keep the content private, be sure to delete the unencrypted version.

To decrypt an encrypted file, follow these steps:

1. Click the encrypted file in your Konqueror browser.

Konqueror asks for the passphrase to unlock your private key.

2. Enter the proper passphrase.

kgpg decrypts the file and saves it in the same directory as the encrypted version (the name of the encrypted version ends with the extension .asc; the decrypted version does not). The newly decrypted file appears in your browser window.

3. To view a decrypted file in a simple text browser (without saving it), drag the file icon onto the kgpg icon in the taskbar, and choose Show Decrypted File from the menu.

 If you drag an unencrypted document to the trash to delete it, it's still there (and still exposed) until you empty the trash. To really delete an item, right-click the item and choose Delete. If you *do* drag things into the trash, don't forget to take out the garbage by right-clicking the can and choosing Empty Trash Bin!

 kgpg **is well integrated with the Konqueror browser. Click an encrypted file, and it decrypts. Right-click a document and choose Encrypt File from the menu to encrypt a file.**

Encrypting Documents with gpg at the Command Line

Encrypting documents with gpg is an easy and quick way to keep information out of the hands of people who shouldn't have it. If you're using SSH or working on a system without a desktop environment, you can use gpg encryption from the command line to keep your private files private.

Sharing a secret file

To encrypt a private document for your friend's eyes only, you need his public key. When you've received his public key (by e-mail or on disk), save it to a directory. To import a public key into your key ring, open your terminal window, move to the directory containing the public key, and use the following command:

```
$ gpg --import keyname.gpg
```

Now you can encrypt your file with your friend's key by using the following command:

```
$ gpg --encrypt --armor -r keyname
    filename
```

Share the file as you normally would — you can send it by e-mail or hand your friend a CD. Unless someone has your friend's private key, that person won't be able to read the document.

To open the file, your friend uses his private key with the following command:

```
$ gpg --decrypt filename
```

Creating a key pair and receiving encrypted documents

To receive encrypted documents, your friend needs *your* public key. Follow these steps to generate a public/private key pair with gpg at the command line:

1. **Open a terminal window and enter the following command:**

```
$ gpg --gen-key
```

A slightly awkward, but functional menu opens, prompting you to select the kind of key you want.

2. **Type 1 and press Enter.**

You're prompted to enter the key size.

3. **Type 1024 and press Enter.**

gpg asks for an expiration date.

4. **Type 0 to create a nonexpiring key and press Enter.**

gpg notifies you that the key does not expire and asks you to verify that you want to generate a permanent key.

5. **Type y and press Enter.**

6. gpg **asks for your real name. Type it in and press Enter.**

This is used to identify your key in your friend's key ring.

7. **When gpg prompts you for a comment, type one in if you wish.**

The comment is optional. Remember, if you enter one, the public will see it.

8. gpg **prompts you for your e-mail address. Type your e-mail address and press Enter.**

gpg displays your name, comment, and e-mail address.

9. **Verify that the information is correct (or select the appropriate item to change). When the information is correct, enter O (the letter, not the number) to verify that the information is okay and then press Enter.**

You're prompted for a passphrase.

10. **Type a passphrase and press Enter.**

You're asked to repeat the passphrase.

11. **Type the passphrase again and press Enter.**

That's all there is to it — you've created a key.

To exchange your key with others so that you can send and receive encrypted files, you need to do a little more upfront work:

1. **Write your public key to a file by using the following command:**

```
$ gpg --armor --export e-mailaddress >
    filename
```

The `--armor` option tells `gpg` to write your public key in an e-mail–friendly form by using only printable characters.

2. **Send the key file to your friends or post it on your Web site.**

3. **Your friends need to import your public key with the key file (using the `gpg --import` command as described at the beginning of this section) before they can decrypt your messages.**

Now people can send you encrypted files that only you can read with your private key.

If you need to encrypt or decrypt messages on a Windows computer, check out "A Practical Introduction to GPG in Windows" at `www.gnupg.org/(en)/ documentation/guides.html`.

To open a message encrypted with your public key, use the following command:

```
$ gpg --decrypt filename
```

 `gpg` is a powerful encryption program, but it's not completely foolproof. We've only scratched the surface here. Good key management makes a big difference in how well `gpg` can protect your private bits. Many encryption options and security features are available with `gpg`. For more information about encrypting with `gpg`, visit `www.gnupg.org`.

Encrypting documents on your home system

You can use the same key pair that you created to exchange with others (see the preceding section) to encrypt documents for your own use. Encrypt the document and delete the unencrypted version, and only those users that know your passphrase can decrypt and read the document.

Follow these steps to encrypt a document:

1. **Open your terminal window and move into the directory containing the file to be encrypted.**

2. **Enter the following command:**

```
$ gpg --encrypt --armor -r keyname
    filename
```

Substitute the real name you used to create the key pair for `keyname` and the name of the file you want to encrypt into `filename`.

You're prompted for the passphrase you entered when you created your key pair.

3. **Enter the passphrase and press Enter.**

The new, encrypted file appears in your directory as `filename.asc`.

You can now delete the unencrypted document with this command:

```
$ rm filename
```

When you need to use your document again, follow these steps:

1. **Open your terminal window and move to the directory containing the encrypted file.**

2. **Enter the following command:**

```
$ gpg --decrypt filename.asc > newfile
```

You're prompted to enter your passphrase.

3. **Enter your passphrase and press Enter.**

The file is decrypted and written to the filename specified in the command as `newfile`.

That's all there is to it. Encryption is a quick, easy way to keep personal documents private — only people with your passphrase can read encrypted files. If you do a good job keeping that passphrase private, no one other than you can access the files you want to keep to yourself.

Encrypting E-Mail for Added Security

Public-key cryptography can help secure your e-mail in two ways:

- When you send e-mail, encrypt the message with the *recipient's public key* to ensure that only the recipient can read it.

- Sign the message with *your private key,* and the recipient can verify that the message really came from you by validating the signature against your *public* key.

Encrypting an e-mail document ensures that anyone watching the bits fly by on the Web won't be reading your sensitive information. The only person who can read the encrypted message is the person holding the private key.

A *digital signature* seals an e-mail document. If the document is changed in any way, the signature will be disturbed, and the recipient will know about it. When you sign a document, you sign it with your private key. The recipient then uses your public key to verify that the digital signature is authentic and hasn't been tampered with.

The Mozilla e-mail client and Evolution e-mail client both support public-key encryption. The built-in support makes it easy (and quick) to send and receive encrypted e-mail and to apply and verify digital signatures.

Encrypting with Ximian Evolution

If you're already using Evolution to manage your e-mail, adding a bit of security to your outgoing and

incoming letters is a snap. If you've followed the steps in the section titled "Creating keys with kgpg" at the beginning of this technique, Evolution knows how to find your gpg key ring, and can use the keys on it to encrypt and decrypt e-mail with a simple click and a passphrase.

 If you're not already using Evolution, the setup wizard will set you up in a few simple steps. Answer the questions, and you'll be up and running in no time!

To send an encrypted e-mail with Evolution, follow these steps:

1. Open Evolution:

If you're using Fedora, open the main menu and choose Internet⇨Evolution Email to start the Evolution e-mail client.

If you're a Mandrake user, open the main menu and choose Internet⇨Main⇨Evolution.

On SuSE, open the main menu and choose Internet⇨E-Mail⇨Ximian Evolution.

2. Click New to create a new e-mail.

3. Type the recipient's address and your message.

4. Click Security (on the menu bar), and choose GPG Encrypt to encrypt the message and GPG Sign if you want to sign the message.

 Sending an encrypted e-mail encrypts it with the recipient's public key. You have to have the public key in your key ring; if it's not in your key ring, you get an error message.

5. Click Send.

The Enter Password dialog appears, waiting for your gpg passphrase (see Figure 28-8).

6. Enter your passphrase and click OK.

That's all there is to it. The encrypted and signed e-mail is sent on its way.

Opening an encrypted document with Evolution is just as easy as sending one:

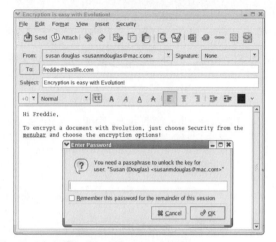

• **Figure 28-8:** The Enter Password dialog.

1. **When an encrypted e-mail arrives in your mailbox, click the message.**

A dialog appears, prompting you for your gpg passphrase.

2. **Enter your passphrase.**

Evolution now has access to your key ring until you close the session.

The message automatically decrypts and opens.

3. **If the message was signed, click the lock icon next to the signature to verify the signature.**

Evolution tells you whether or not the signature is good.

Setting up Mozilla e-mail for encryption

Mozilla e-mail can send encrypted e-mail just as easily as Evolution, but before it's ready to deal with encryption, you need to download and install a plug-in. (Plug-ins are snippets of code that enhance the features offered by a program.)

Follow these steps to download and install the Enigmail plug-in:

1. **Open your terminal window and give yourself superuser privileges with the following command:**

```
$ su
```

2. **Enter your superuser password when prompted.**

3. **Type** mozilla **in the command line and press Enter.**

 You need superuser privileges to install the plug-in, so opening the browser with those privileges transfers the privileges to the browser.

4. **Navigate to** enigmail.mozdev.org.

5. **Click the Download link in the Resources list near the top of the page.**

6. **Scroll down and choose your download from the versions listed under Standard Download.**

Choose the download that most closely matches the version of Mozilla that you're using.

 To find your Mozilla version, choose Help⇨ About Mozilla.

7. **Click the Install button for the Linux version that matches your computer.**

 If can't find an installer for Fedora, Red Hat 9 is close enough.

A dialog appears, stating that a Web site is requesting permission to install.

8. **Click the Install button.**

After some whirring and clicking, the browser informs you that Enigmail installation has completed successfully.

9. **Restart Mozilla at the command line (still with superuser privileges) to complete the installation.**

Now it's time to configure Enigmail:

1. **Open the Edit menu and choose Preferences.**

The Preferences dialog appears.

2. **Choose Privacy & Security⇨Enigmail.**

The Enigmail Preferences dialog appears, as shown in Figure 28-9.

3. **Check the Use From E-Mail Address for Signing to Determine GPG Key box.**

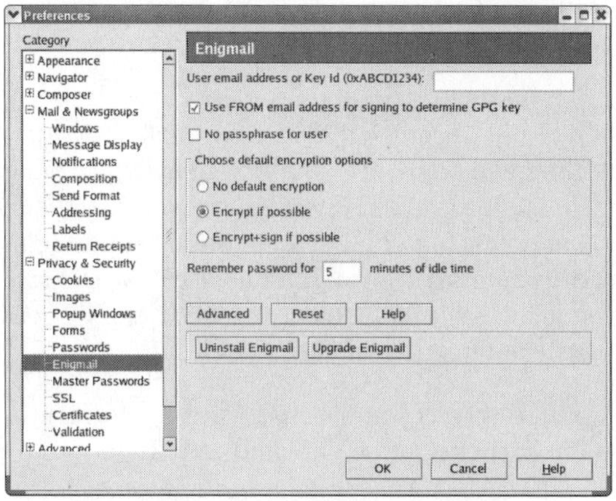

• **Figure 28-9: The Enigmail Preferences dialog.**

4. **Select a default encryption type.**

Your options are No Default Encryption, Encrypt if Possible, or Encrypt + Sign if Possible.

5. **Click OK to save your preferences.**

The Enigmail plug-in is installed and configured. You're now ready to send encrypted e-mail with Mozilla!

Sending and receiving encrypted messages with Mozilla mail

To send an encrypted and signed message with Mozilla and Enigmail, follow these steps:

1. **Open Mozilla's Window menu and choose Mail and Newsgroups.**

The Mozilla mail client appears

2. **Click the Compose icon (on the toolbar).**

A new message window opens.

3. **Compose an e-mail message as you normally would.**

4. **When your message is complete, choose Enigmail from the menu bar.**

The encryption options appear in the Enigmail menu, as shown in Figure 28-10.

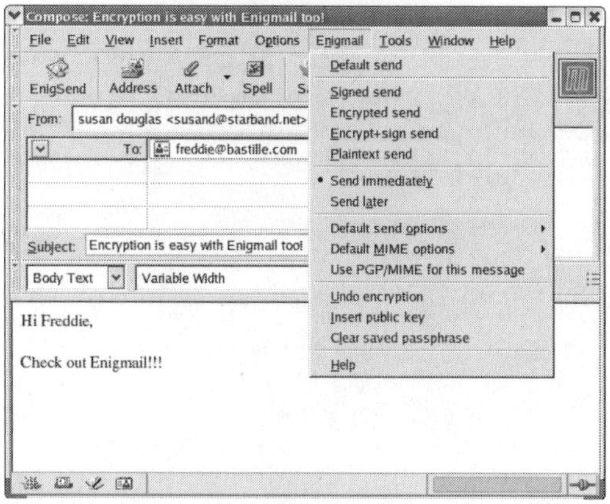

• **Figure 28-10: The Compose/Enigmail menu options.**

5. **Choose a message type from the drop-down menu. Choose either Encrypted Send or Encrypt + Sign Send.**

If you sign an e-mail, the recipient needs your public key to verify the signature.

6. **Enter your passphrase when prompted and click OK.**

Your message is on its way!

When an encrypted e-mail arrives in your inbox, Enigmail automatically decrypts it and verifies the signature. The signature status is shown in the message header, right above the subject line.

If a message does not automatically decrypt, you may need to select Automatically Decrypt/ Verify Messages from the Enigmail menu.

Technique 29

Securing a Large Network with Custom Authentication

If you have more than a handful of computers in your local network, you know the routine: Each time you connect to a different system, you have to type in your user name and password. Chances are, you use the same password to log in to most servers, but you haven't gotten around to synchronizing all your passwords (or maybe you don't *want* to use the same password everywhere, just in case someone discovers it). Keeping your passwords straight is a hassle and a good way to waste time.

In this technique, we introduce you to some simple (but powerful) tools that can make network-wide authentication safe and easy by

✔ **Streamlining password setup and maintenance:** If you're the administrator of a large network, using cross-platform authentication can save you time. With only one password file to maintain, you save time not only in setup but also in maintenance — the fewer files you maintain, the less chance you'll make a mistake while updating information.

✔ **Creating a secure, network-wide login system that's more user friendly:** When you're finished with this technique, you'll have a login system that requires only one login and one password to access any authorized server on your network.

To build a better login, all you need are PAM and Kerberos. First, we show you how to use PAM authentication to access the user database on a Windows machine to authenticate Linux users. Sacrilegious? Not if you already have a Windows domain and you're slowly adding Linux computers.

Kerberos — a secure, single-login, network-wide authentication service — adds security to the mix. When you login to a *kerberized* network, you give your user name and password to the Key Distribution Center (KDC), and in return, you receive a ticket that you can give to other kerberized servers. A Kerberos ticket is like a passport. The KDC verifies your identity and then gives you a set of credentials that you can hand to other servers: If the server trusts the KDC, it accepts your credentials.

By using PAM with Kerberos, you get automagic ticket handling. With one login, you have access to all the kerberized servers on your network.

If you're adding Linux systems to an existing Windows network, connect PAM to your domain controller to centralize your user database. If you're setting a (mostly) Linux network, consider using Kerberos to give secure, single-login access to your users.

At the time we're writing this, Mandrake Linux is not shipped with the software required to handle cross-platform authentication. SuSE Linux *does* ship with the required software, but the necessary configuration tools in SuSE's YaST control center don't seem to work. The methods that we describe in this technique will only work with Fedora Linux.

Using Cross-Platform Authentication with Linux and Windows

If you already have a medium-sized or large network of Windows computers, you're probably using a Windows domain to manage security. A Windows domain is a network of computers that uses a single database to hold user information (user names, user IDs, passwords, and the like). A single machine, called the *primary domain controller,* stores all user information and provides authentication services to the rest of the computers in the domain. A Windows domain often contains backup domain controllers to lighten the load on the primary controller (and to provide authentication should the primary controller fail).

Don't confuse a Windows domain with a DNS domain name. A Windows domain is a network of computers that consolidates all user information in a single database. A DNS domain name is a name that you give to a network of computers.

PAM (the basic authentication framework on Fedora computers) can rely on a Windows domain to authenticate users. If you keep your authentication information on a Windows machine, a simple addition to your PAM configuration lets you share your Windows authentication files with your Linux systems.

Keeping your network user database up-to-date and secure is a lot quicker if you have only one file to maintain. You need to update the user information in only one database, and PAM allows all the Linux machines on your network to use that database for authentication. This streamlined setup also increases network security, because you aren't storing password files all over your network.

Prepping for cross-platform authentication

You need three pieces of information to set up PAM/Windows authentication — get these from your Windows administrator (if that's you, odds are you know these tidbits of trivia):

- ✔ **Your Windows domain name:** Your domain name is the name assigned to your network of trust. It's often the same as the name of your physical network.

- ✔ **The primary domain controller's name:** This is the computer on your network that holds the primary authentication database.

- ✔ **A backup domain controller's name:** This machine keeps a backup of the authentication database. This is important because if the machine holding your primary authentication database goes down, you still want your users to have access to the other machines on the network.

To set up cross-platform authentication, you also need to have the `pam_smb-1.1.7-2.i386.rpm` package installed.

Check to see if the RPM package is installed with the following command:

```
# rpm -q pam_smb
```

If the program isn't installed, you need to add it. Conveniently, it's included with the Fedora distribution. Insert and mount your Fedora media and enter this command:

```
# rpm -Uhv /mnt/cdrom/Fedora/RPMS/pam_smb-
   1.1.7-2.i386.rpm
```

Now you're ready to follow the steps in the next section, where you actually set up authentication.

Setting up cross-platform authentication

With the `pam_smb` package in place, you're ready to set up cross-platform authentication:

1. **Open the Main Menu and choose System Settings⇨Authentication.**

    A dialog may appear, prompting you for the `root` password.

2. **Type the `root` password (if prompted) and press Enter.**

    The Authentication Configuration window opens.

3. **Choose the Authentication tab to view authentication options, as shown in Figure 29-1.**

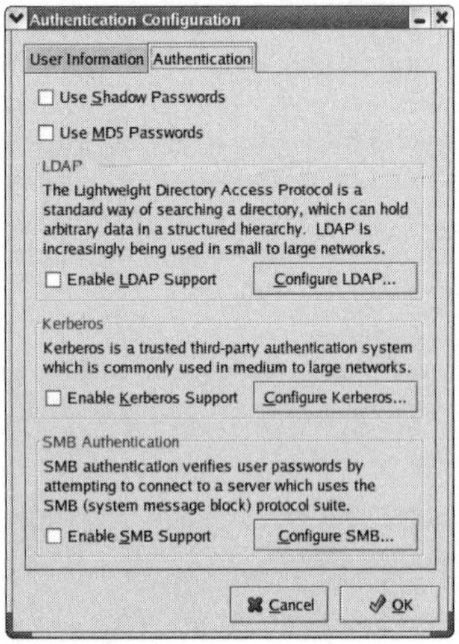

• **Figure 29-1: The Authentication tab.**

4. **Check the Enable SMB Support box and then click the Configure SMB button.**

    The SMB Settings dialog opens, as shown in Figure 29-2.

• **Figure 29-2: The SMB Settings dialog.**

5. **Enter the workgroup (domain) name in the Workgroup field.**

6. **Enter the name of the primary domain controller in the Domain Controllers field, followed by a comma and the backup domain controller's name.**

    Don't add any spaces between the names and the comma.

7. **Click the OK button to close the dialog.**

8. **Click the OK button on the Authentication Configuration window to close that window.**

Now, whenever you log in to your Linux computer, Fedora asks the domain controller to validate your password. If the primary domain controller fails to respond in a reasonable period of time, Fedora contacts the backup domain controller. You still need a user account on your Linux computer (your Linux user ID, home directory, and login shell information are stored in Linux), but the password comes from Windows.

After you follow the preceding steps, there's one more trick to setting up cross-platform authentication: When you create a user account on the Linux machine, leave the password blank. If you want to change the password you use to log in to Linux, change your Windows password.

Using PAM and Kerberos to Serve Up Authentication

If your local network doesn't include a Windows domain controller, PAM can still streamline authentication and increase your network security using Kerberos. Kerberos is a security protocol that uses a trusted third party to verify authentication information. With PAM and Kerberos working together, you get a single, secure network-wide login system, which can save a lot of time.

 This technique is best suited to large networks. You should have a domain in place and a DNS server up and running to take advantage of the benefits of using Kerberos with PAM for authentication.

With this setup, Kerberos makes the login more secure, and PAM makes ticket management automatic. Users first access a kerberized server, where they must prove their identity to the Key Distribution Center (KDC). Only after the verification can users obtain a ticket that represents their fully authenticated identity.

After users log in, they can log in to any machine running Kerberos authentication or use a kerberized server on a remote machine without manually obtaining a ticket for the session. That means you (or your users) log in once and can access any kerberized server on your network without proving your identity again for that login session.

 Kerberos tickets expire over time, so at the end of an eight-hour day, the ticket can't be reused by an intruder.

The process of setting up Kerberos to work with PAM has several phases. Here's an overview of what you need to do:

1. Synchronize the system times.

2. Test the DNS.

3. Set up a KDC.

4. Set up PAM for automagic ticket management.

5. Add users to the KDC.

The following sections explain each step in more detail.

Establishing synchronized system times

For extra security, Kerberos tickets are time sensitive. Just like a real passport, your Kerberos ticket expires after some period of time (you have to prove your identity to the KDC every once in a while to prevent a nefarious hacker from using an old passport that you've left sitting around somewhere).

The time-sensitive nature of Kerberos tickets means that all your kerberized servers (and the KDC) must agree on the current date and time. If the time varies by just five minutes between a Kerberos client machine and the KDC, Kerberos will deny an otherwise valid ticket. To ensure a consistent time, start the NTP daemon and enable the Network Time Protocol on *all* the computers on your network. (The following steps show you how in just a few quick steps.)

The Network Time Protocol (NTP) visits a server located on the Internet and retrieves time updates. It synchronizes the clock on the local machine with the clock on the time server. Setting up the NTP daemon on all the machines on your network to synchronize their clocks with the same time server ensures a consistent time for Kerberos.

Before you enable the Network Time Protocol, you need to start the NTP daemon:

1. **Open the Main menu and choose System Settings⇨Server Settings⇨Services**

   A dialog opens, prompting you for the `root` password.

2. **Enter your `root` password and click OK.**

   The Service Configuration window opens, as shown in Figure 29-3.

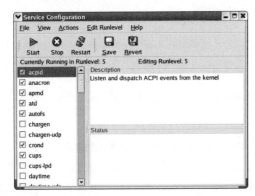

• **Figure 29-3: The Service Configuration window.**

3. Use the scroll bar in the left frame to scroll through the list of services until you find the entry for ntpd.

4. Check the box next to the ntpd entry and click the Start button (on the toolbar).

An Information dialog opens, telling you that the ntpd started successfully.

5. Click OK to close the dialog.

6. Click the Save button to save the changes to your services.

7. Close the Service Configuration window.

Now that the ntpd daemon is running, you're ready to enable the Network Time Protocol. To synchronize your systems time, follow these steps:

1. Open the Main Menu and choose System Settings⇨Date & Time.

A dialog opens, prompting you for the root password.

2. Enter the root password and click OK.

The Date/Time Properties window opens, as shown in Figure 29-4.

3. Check the Enable Network Time Protocol box.

The Server drop-down list becomes activated.

4. Use the Server drop-down list to choose a network time server, or add the name of your own network time server.

• **Figure 29-4: The Date/Time Properties window.**

 The kind people at Red Hat provide two time servers for public use. We recommend using the same server to synchronize all the machines on your network.

Alternatively, if your entire network doesn't have Internet access, you can set up a time server on one of your own computers and synchronize to it, but it's a bit of work. For more information about establishing your own time server, visit www.ntp.org.

5. Click OK.

A confirmation screen verifies that the update is taking place, as shown in Figure 29-5. After some thought, your machine updates the time settings to synchronize with the server. When the update completes, the Date/Time Properties window closes.

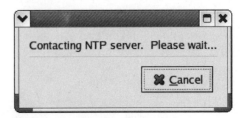

• **Figure 29-5: Confirmation of contact.**

If you configure all your machines to synchronize to the same server, time won't interfere with your Kerberos logins.

Testing your domain name server (DNS)

Kerberos makes extensive use of the DNS server. Before you set up Kerberos, it's a good idea to be sure that all your computers are on a first name basis.

Every computer on your network can talk to any other computer just by knowing its IP address, but with Kerberos, your computers must know each other by name. The easiest way to verify that DNS is working is with a series of pings:

- ✔ Ping the Key Distribution Center by name from each potential client.

- ✔ Ping each client machine by name from the Key Distribution Center.

- ✔ Each potential client should ping any other potential client (by name) that it will access.

Just in case you're not familiar with pinging, a *ping* is like a handshake across the network. To ping a machine, open the terminal window and enter the following command:

```
$ ping machinename
```

Your machine sends a note to the other machine telling it to send back a packet of data. If the DNS service is working properly, you start getting a stream of replies that looks something like this:

```
$ ping bastille
PING bastille (192.168.0.28): 56 data
  bytes
64 bytes from 192.168.0.28: icmp_seq=0
  ttl=64 time=34.893 ms
64 bytes from 192.168.0.28: icmp_seq=1
  ttl=64 time=2.918 ms
--- bastille ping statistics ---
2 packets transmitted, 2 packets received,
  0% packet loss
round-trip min/avg/max = 2.918/18.905/
  34.893 ms
```

Use the Ctrl-C combination to stop pinging.

Setting up a Key Distribution Center

Kerberos can make authentication on a large network quick and easy. The centerpiece to Kerberos authentication is the trusted third party — the Key Distribution Center (KDC). All the other machines on your network look to the KDC for authentication services.

Time is crucial to using Kerberos successfully — the KDC and all the other Kerberos client and server machines must agree on the current time. Be sure that the NTP (Network Time Protocol) is up and running on all your computers. See the earlier section, "Establishing synchronized system times," for details. You should also test your DNS, which we also explain earlier in "Testing your domain name server (DNS)."

Here's how to set up a Key Distribution Center:

1. **Log in to the computer that you want to use as the KDC.**

   You can do this at the console, or by using SSH to log in over the network.

2. **Open a terminal window and give yourself superuser privileges with the su command.**

3. **Insert and mount the Fedora distribution disc.**

4. **Move to the directory containing the RPM packages (/mnt/cdrom/Fedora/RPMS) and use the following commands to install the Kerberos packages:**

   ```
   # rpm -Uhv krb5-libs-1.3.1-6.i386.rpm
   # rpm -Uhv krb5-server-1.3-1.6.i386.rpm
   # rpm -Uhv krb5-workstation-
     1.3-1.6.i386.rpm
   ```

5. **To begin creating a script that will automatically update a few of the configuration files that the KDC needs to operate, open your favorite editor and create a file named /tmp/fixrealm:**

   ```
   # kedit /tmp/fixrealm
   ```

You can make all these changes manually, but to save a bit of time, we've added a quick script to update the configuration files. This tool works only if your DNS server is running and you have a domain in place.

6. **Add the following code to** `/tmp/fixrealm`:

```
#!/bin/bash

OLDDOMAIN=example.com
OLDREALM=EXAMPLE.COM
OLDKDC=kerberos.example.com

NEWDOMAIN=$(dnsdomainname)
NEWREALM=$(echo $NEWDOMAIN | tr
  "[:lower:]" "[:upper:]")
NEWKDC=$(hostname)

function fixup()
{
  cp $1 $1.orig

  echo "Fixing $1 (original saved in
  $1.orig)"

  sed s/$OLDREALM/$NEWREALM/ $1.orig |
  sed s/$OLDDOMAIN/$NEWDOMAIN/ |
  sed s/$OLDKDC/$NEWKDC/ > $1
}

fixup /etc/krb5.conf
fixup /var/kerberos/krb5kdc/kdc.conf
fixup /var/kerberos/krb5kdc/kadm5.acl
```

7. **Save the file and close the editor.**

 Double-check your typing before you save the code. (We managed to wipe out our Kerberos configuration files with just a few typos.)

8. **Make the script executable with the following command:**

```
# chmod a+x /tmp/fixrealm
```

9. **Run the script with the following command:**

```
# /tmp/fixrealm
```

The script saves a copy of the originals and updates the working configuration files by using default values it finds on your network. `fixrealm` shows you its progress as it works.

10. **Create the KDC database with the following command:**

```
# kdb5_util create -s
```

You're prompted for the KDC database masterkey.

11. **Type a password and press Enter.**

You're prompted for the KDC database master-key again to verify the entry.

12. **Retype the password and press Enter.**

 Don't forget this password. It's important!

13. **Add your own user name to the KDC database with the following command:**

```
# kadmin.local -q "addprinc username"
```

14. **Enter the password that you want to use when you log in.**

15. **Reenter your password when prompted.**

The creation of your user account is verified by Kerberos.

Now, you need to start the KDC with the Service Configuration tool. To start the KDC services, follow these steps:

1. **Open the Main Menu and choose System Settings⇨Server Settings⇨Services.**

A dialog opens prompting you for the `root` password.

2. **Enter the `root` password and click OK.**

3. **Use the scroll bar to find the following services:**

▶ krb524

▶ krb5kdc

▶ kadmin

4. **One service at a time, check the box next to the service and click the Start icon.**

You must click the Start icon after checking each box. If you check all three and then click Start, Fedora starts only the last service you checked.

As each service starts, a dialog opens confirming that the service started successfully. Click OK (in the pop-up) and start the next service.

5. **When all three services have been started, click the Save button (in the toolbar) and close the Service Configuration window.**

Your KDC should be up and running and ready to distribute tickets. Don't forget that you need to add each user (or program) that requests authentication to the KDC database.

Jump ahead to the section "Adding users to the Key Distribution Center" for details about adding principals to the KDC database.

Setting up automatic ticket management with Kerberos and PAM

After you've synched your clocks, tested your DNS, and established the Key Distribution Center (KDC) on your network (all explained in earlier sections), you're ready to configure your workstation so that PAM manages your Kerberos login session tickets. To set up Kerberos authentication, you need two pieces of information:

✔ The workgroup name of the computers that trust authentication from your KDC (the Kerberos realm)

✔ The name of the computer that is acting as your KDC

Follow these steps to enable Kerberos authentication:

1. **Open the Main Menu and choose System Settings⇨Authentication.**

A dialog opens, prompting you for the `root` password.

2. **Enter the `root` password and click OK.**

The Authentication Configuration window opens.

3. **Click the Authentication tab.**

4. **Check the Enable Kerberos Support box.**

5. **Click Configure Kerberos.**

The Kerberos Settings dialog opens, as shown in Figure 29-6.

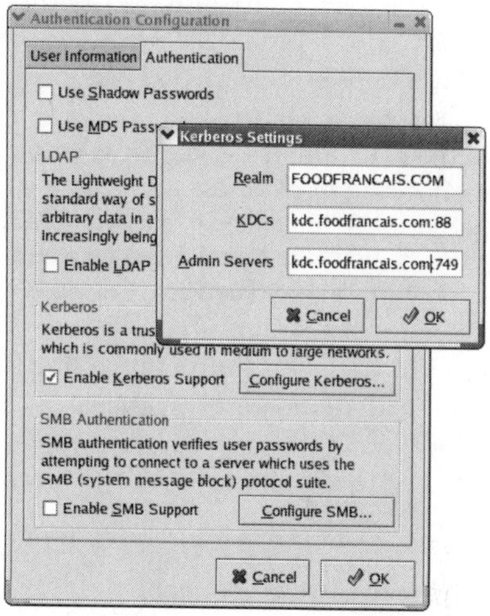

• **Figure 29-6: The Kerberos Settings dialog.**

Fill in the dialog with the information about your Kerberos realm.

6. **Enter the Realm name in the Realm field.**

7. **Enter the KDC name in the KDCs field, followed by a colon and the port number 88.**

`computername:88`

8. **Enter the KDC name in the Admin Servers field, followed by a colon and the port number 749.**

`computername:749`

9. **Click OK to close the dialog and save the settings.**

10. **Click OK to close the Authentication Configuration window.**

Now, each time you log in to your workstation, PAM automatically obtains a Kerberos ticket for you. The Kerberos infrastructure quietly passes that ticket from server to server as you move around your network — the ticket proves that you are who you claim to be.

Adding users to the Key Distribution Center

The KDC doesn't hand out any session tickets unless it recognizes the user. Users must verify their identities to the KDC with a password. Only when they're recognized are they issued a ticket.

 To the KDC, the user is known as a *principal*. A principal can be a host, a user, or a program. A principal is anyone who trusts the KDC. If a program needs to honor tickets across the network, it must be defined as a principal.

After you follow the steps in the preceding four sections, you're ready to add a principal to the KDC:

1. **Log in to the KDC (as user `root`):**

   ```
   # ssh root@kdcname
   ```

2. **Enter the following command:**

   ```
   # kadmin.local -q "addprinc username"
   ```

3. **When prompted, enter the login password for the new principal.**

4. **When prompted, reenter the password.**

   The creation of the new principal is confirmed with a message.

5. **Repeat Steps 2 through 4 to create more principals (users) and then log out of the KDC when you're finished.**

 At this point, you have two passwords: the old login password and the new Kerberos password. If you give the old password when you log in, PAM doesn't get a chance to do its work, and you *won't* be granted a Kerberos ticket. If you give the new password, PAM obtains a ticket for you.

 If you can successfully log in with the new (Kerberos) password, you know that the Kerberos and PAM setup is working. After you know things are running okay, you can remove the old login password.

To remove the old login, open the terminal window and give yourself superuser privileges with the `su` command. Then execute the following command:

```
# passwd -l username
Locking password for username.
passwd: Success
```

After executing this command, only the new Kerberos password will work for logins.

Customizing Authentication with PAM

Technique 30

Save Time By

- Understanding the PAM configuration files
- Building your own authentication rules
- Searching the Web for PAM modules
- Skipping the root password if you dare

Suppose that you've written the world's spiffiest database program. You install it at a few sites, and your users love it. Now, you sell your database to a bank that uses a smart card to identify each user. You have to modify your database to handle smart card authentication. A few months later, you run into a customer that wants to use a retinal scanner to protect access to his data. Again, you have to modify your database to handle retinal scanners. Next, someone wants to use voice authentication. More changes.

In this technique, we introduce you to PAM, which stands for Pluggable Authentication Modules (or methods). Flexible, well-rounded, and ever-expandable, PAM is a great system resource to get to know. It was designed to hide authentication methods from an application. If you modify your database to interact with PAM, you don't have to change your code just because an administrator wants to try out a fancy new authentication tool. With PAM, you can

- **Create complex login procedures (two or three passwords, challenge/response mechanisms, and so on).**

- **Use high-tech methods like biometric scans to authenticate users.** You obviously need extra hardware to use mechanical authentication methods, but if the data is valuable enough to justify the cost of the protection, PAM can help manage the technology.

- **Avoid entering the root password when you need superuser privileges.** With just a few quick file changes, you'll save time whenever you need to su (as well as when you need to use the Linux configuration tools). We don't recommend using PAM to circumvent root for everyone, but if you're working on a system that doesn't need to have tight security, it can make administrative or system tasks a breeze.

This technique shows you how. If you're interested in setting up a Linux host in a Windows domain network or if you want to use Kerberos to authenticate your users, take a peek at Technique 29 as well.

Understanding Modules and Configuration Files: The Basics of PAM Authentication

PAM (Pluggable Authentication Modules) is the program that is responsible for authenticating users who connect to a Linux system. Most programs packaged with Linux distributions use PAM for authentication, as do many other open-source projects.

PAM gains its flexibility from plug-in modules. PAM itself doesn't do a whole lot, relying instead on modules to do the heavy lifting. Developers write the modules to fulfill a number of diverse tasks. Some modules store passwords on an smb mounted network share, while others are specialized to use hardware devices like smart cards and biometric scanners.

PAM keeps track of the level of security you desire in a set of configuration files. You can change the PAM configuration files to require multiple passwords, limit access based on a user/location relationship, or enable biometric devices. Each configuration file specifies a set of modules that PAM employs to authenticate a user.

 With a little extra hardware and PAM, you can use biometric scans or other high-tech devices to secure super-important data.

We explain the basics of finding a module and customizing its rules in the next section. Then, in "Building Good Rules with PAM," we explain the basic syntax of rules and what your customizing options are. And we help you better understand what's actually in a configuration file in "Dissecting a Configuration File" also later in this technique.

Finding a Module and Customizing Its Rules

Adding your own rules to the PAM configuration files is relatively simple when you understand what the different modules do.

If you use Fedora, you can find documentation about PAM modules in

```
$ /usr/share/doc/pam-0.77/txts
```

If you're a Mandrake user, you find documentation about PAM modules in

```
$ /usr/share/doc/pam-doc-0.77.txts
```

If you use SuSE, look for PAM documentation in

```
$ /usr/share/doc/packages/pam/modules
```

Move into the directory, and use the ls command to see a list of the documents available. Use the more command to display the contents of the documentation:

```
$ more README.pam_nologin
```

Press the spacebar while the document is displayed to see more of the document.

When you've found a PAM module you want to use for program authentication, add a rule to the program configuration file that tells PAM when to invoke the module.

Building Good Rules with PAM

This is the section where we begin to break down what your options are for customizing levels of security in PAM. A PAM-enabled program can rely on a chain of one *or more* rules to authenticate the user. PAM configuration rules can seem a bit overwhelming at first, but they're actually quite simple. The basic format of a configuration rule is this:

```
phase control-level module-pathname
  arguments
```

We explain what you need to know about each part of a rule in the following sections.

Phase

Each configuration file controls four different *phases* of the authentication process: authentication, account management, session management, and password management. Each configuration rule belongs to a specific phase according to the first word in the rule:

- ✔ auth: An auth rule verifies that you are who you claim to be, by password, biometric scanner, smart card, or other authentication means.

- ✔ account: Account rules allow or deny access to a service based on available system resources (a certain number of users may be allowed to log in at one time), user location (root users must be sitting in front of the computer console), and other factors. You can use account rules to help control system resources and privileged access.

- ✔ session: Session rules put in place the session information for the user that is logging in. A typical session rule may mount your home directory when you log in or set up a log file that records your entire login session.

- ✔ password: Password rules change the password or other authentication means that a module uses to identify the user.

PAM modules are diverse, each controlling different aspects of authentication and session management. A given module may service all four phases (authentication, account management, session management, and password management) or only a few. For example, the pam_nologin.so module (which prohibits user logins if the file /etc/nologin exists) works in the auth phase, but doesn't have anything to offer the password phase.

 If you need an authentication module for an unusual security application, search the Web. Modules are out there — just search the Web for *PAM modules*.

Control level

The control level determines what happens if the module fails. For example, if the user fails to provide a proper password but passes a retina scan, you may want to let that user into your system.

Here are the control-level options:

- ✔ sufficient: If a rule is satisfied that is deemed sufficient, you are allowed to continue. A user entering a correct password in a step that is deemed sufficient is allowed either to continue with the login process or to access the program.

- ✔ required: This rule must succeed, or the user is not allowed to run the program.

- ✔ optional: This rule does not need to be satisfied for the user to be allowed to use the program.

- ✔ requisite: If two passwords are used to authenticate identity, using the requisite control type stops authentication when the first password fails.

Module pathname

The third feature in a configuration rule is the pathname to the PAM module that the rule uses. The modules are located in /lib/security.

Arguments

The fourth item in a PAM configuration rule is a set of zero or more arguments that gets passed along to the PAM module when the module is invoked. The arguments vary depending on the module. The simplest of arguments is debug, which causes a module to write debugging information to the system log (which is handy if you're having trouble logging into your system).

Dissecting a Configuration File

Modifying a PAM configuration file isn't difficult, but the format appears pretty cryptic at first. In this section, we show you a typical configuration file and explain what each line does. After you can read a PAM configuration file, you can tailor your own files to more closely match your needs.

Each file in the `/etc/pam.d` directory controls PAM authentication for a single client. A client roughly equates to a program, and the filename is the same as the program name. The `/etc/pam.d/login` file contains all the authentication rules for the `login` program, the `sshd` file contains all the authentication rules for `ssh`, and so on.

 The contents of your PAM configuration files may vary. The following is just an example of one possible configuration for a login file.

To peek into the `login` configuration file, open a terminal window and enter the following command:

```
$ kedit /etc/pamd.d/login
```

The PAM configuration file opens, displaying the authentication rules for the `login` command, as shown in Listing 30-1.

Here's a line-by-line breakdown of the rules in this file:

✔ **Line 1:** The first line in `/etc/pam.d/login` is a comment. You can ignore that line for now, but notice that you can include comments in a

PAM configuration file by prefixing the comments with a `#`.

The next three rules are invoked, in order, during the authentication phase. (They all start with the word `auth`.)

✔ **Line 2:** The first authentication rule invokes the `pam_securetty.so` module. If you track down the documentation for that module (see `/usr/share/doc/pam-0.77/txts/README.pam_securetty`), you see that this module allows privileged (that is, `root`) logins only from specific workstations. The idea behind `securetty` is that you can *physically* secure certain workstations (by placing them behind a locked door) and then allow `root` logins from only those workstations. Because the rule is `required` (see the second column), `pam_securetty.so` must return a positive response before PAM will continue with authentication.

 `pam_securetty.so` makes sure that privileged users (like `root`) cannot log in from remote computers. They have to be sitting at one of the workstations listed in `/etc/securetty`.

✔ **Line 3:** The second `auth` rule requires that the `pam_stack.so` module return a positive response when passed the argument `service=system-auth`. `pam_stack.so` doesn't really do any authentication checks by itself. Instead, it switches over to a common set of rules stored in another configuration file. Keeping commonly used rules in a single file makes it easier to manage PAM configuration. `pam_stack.so` returns a positive response if the rules in the *other* file (in this case, `/etc/pam.d/system-auth`) are satisfied.

Listing 30-1: The PAM Login Configuration File

```
1 - #%PAM-1.0
2 - auth        required    pam_securetty.so
3 - auth        required    pam_stack.so service=system-auth
4 - auth        required    pam_nologin.so
5 - account     required    pam_stack.so service=system-auth
6 - session     required    pam_stack.so service=system-auth
7 - session     optional    pam_console.so
8 - password    required    pam_stack.so service=system-auth
```

Quite a few modules use the `system-auth` configuration file. The `system-auth` file holds common configuration information in one file. Each file that needs the common information just refers to the `system-auth` file instead of duplicating that information.

When the authentication rules found in the `system-auth` file are satisfied, PAM continues to the third authentication rule (also `required`).

✔ **Line 4:** The third auth rule requires a positive result from the `pam_nologin.so` module. The `pam_nologin.so` module checks for the existence of the `/etc/nologin` file. If the `/etc/nologin` file exists, only `root` is allowed to log in.

Create the `/etc/nologin` file to block other users from logging in to the system while you're performing system maintenance. Just be sure to delete the file again when you're done because no other users (other than `root`) are allowed to log in while `/etc/nologin` exists.

When the authentication rules are met, and PAM is satisfied that the user is who he or she claims to be, PAM moves on to the account rules. Authentication rules lay out the procedure users must follow in order to prove that they are who they claim to be. Account rules kick in after the authentication process is completed.

✔ **Line 5:** This is the only account rule in this file. The rule simply defers to the account rules in `/etc/pam.d/system-auth`. You can use account rules to enforce policies that aren't related to authentication but are still important — password aging, disabled accounts, and so on.

The `system-auth` file holds the most commonly used system configuration rules. You can look inside the file with the following command:

```
$ kedit /etc/pam.d/system-auth
```

Looking in the `system-auth` file tells you that the `pam_unix.so` module is being invoked. The `pam_unix.so` module is responsible for password aging and other account-related concerns.

When the account-related issues have been satisfied, the `login` program requests that PAM satisfy any session rules that are required. By looking in the configuration file (lines 6 and 7), you can see two session rules — one required and one optional.

✔ **Line 6:** The required rule is applied first. The required rule defers to the `system-auth` configuration file rules, where the `pam_limits.so` module and the `pam_unix.so` module are required to satisfy requirements before the `login` program can continue. `pam_limits.so` enforces limits imposed by the `/etc/security/limits.conf` file (limits on disk usage, CPU usage, memory usage, and so on). The requirements of the `pam_limits.so` module must be met before login is allowed to continue.

✔ **Line 7:** Optional rules don't need to be satisfied to continue — they're optional. This rule specifies that the `pam_console.so` module may or may not be satisfied before the `login` program continues.

The `pam_console` module changes the file permissions when you log in at the console, and changes them back when you log out. The theory behind `pam_console` is that if you have physical access to the machine, you should have physical access to the peripherals. This is a fairly volatile module, and not one we recommend playing with.

✔ **Line 8:** The password rule is invoked only when the `login` program requests that a password be changed. Then PAM looks in the configuration file, sees that the password rule requires that the `system-auth` password rules be satisfied before the user is allowed to change the password. In our `system-auth` file, the password rule requires that the `pam_cracklib` module be satisfied before the new password is accepted. Notice that password rules aren't actually part of the authentication sequence — they're only used to change the password (or retina scan, or fingerprint, or whatever you have configured).

The `pam_cracklib` module works only with the password rule type. It checks the password against a dictionary to see if the new password entered is guessable. If you set `pam_cracklib` to required, only complex, difficult-to-crack passwords will be accepted.

Skipping a Password with PAM

You can tighten security fast with PAM, but you can also relax security standards to save time in certain cases. On a system that's not holding data that is life-and-death important, and that's not an integral link in a network, you can make PAM skip the request for a `root` password when you need superuser privileges at the command line.

The `pam_wheel.so` module returns a positive result whenever members of the `wheel` group try to authenticate themselves. That means that if you're a member of the group named `wheel`, PAM assumes that you've already authenticated yourself and lets you continue without a password. What's the significance of the name `wheel`? We can't figure it out either.

Think twice before disabling `root` passwords. Never having to slow down to enter a password is a definite timesaver, but it's about the loosest security you can have.

The following example works for Fedora or Mandrake. The same technique will work for SuSE, but because SuSE doesn't use a common configuration file (like `system-auth`), you need to decide for yourself which files you want to modify.

To change the PAM configuration files to allow superuser access without a password, follow these steps:

1. Open your terminal window and give yourself superuser privileges.

2. Enter the following command:

```
# kedit /etc/group file
```

The kedit window opens, displaying the contents of `/etc/group`.

3. Find the line in the file that starts with `wheel`.

4. Add a comma, followed by your username, to the line.

```
wheel:x:10:root,username
```

5. Save the file and exit.

6. Enter the following command:

```
$ kedit /etc/pam.d/system-auth
```

7. If you're using Fedora, find the lines that look like this:

```
# Uncomment the following line to \
   implicitly trust users in the \
   "wheel" group.
#auth sufficient    \
   /lib/security/$ISA/pam_wheel.so \
   trust use_uid
```

If you're using Mandrake, you won't have the last line included in your `system-auth` file.

You'll need to add the following line as the second rule in your `system-auth` file:

```
auth sufficient    \
   /lib/security/$ISA/pam_wheel.so \
   trust use_uid
```

8. If you're using Fedora, remove the # from the beginning of the auth rule.

The result should look like this:

```
# Uncomment the following line to \
   implicitly trust users in the \
   "wheel" group.
auth sufficient    \
   /lib/security/$ISA/pam_wheel.so \
   trust use_uid
```

Now, when you use the `su` command, PAM recognizes that you are a member of the `wheel` group and doesn't ask for the `root` password.

If you decide to allow PAM to skip password prompts and you leave your desktop logged in and unattended, you may be asking for trouble.

Technique 31

Gaining Privileges

Save Time By

- Knowing the power of the superuser
- Gaining extra privileges with the su command
- Limiting privileges with sudo

Every Linux system has a user who thinks he's better than everyone else; a user who wants more privileges than anybody else has; a user who can do things others can't do. We call him the *superuser,* but his real name is *root.*

This technique shows you how to gain and use superuser privileges safely from the comfort of your desk — no phone booths or funny tights required. Limiting the power of the superuser is important if you want to keep your system safe and secure. You'll save a lot of time if you don't have to recover from disasters caused by (accidentally) flexing too many superuser muscles. Sometimes you *need* superuser privileges to do system administrator work like configuration, user management, and privilege management. But we show how to limit your exposure by gaining only the privileges that you need and only when you need them.

Feeling the Power

In most systems, a single user, named *root,* holds superuser privileges. (You can think of user *root* as synonymous with *superuser.*) The superuser can do anything he wants on your system, such as the following operations:

- Modify (or delete) any file.
- Change any password.
- Use any device.
- Create new user accounts.
- Delete old user accounts.
- Lock you out of your system.

Sounds like someone you want to keep out of your system, doesn't it?

Sometimes, you need to do those things because users come and go, passwords are forgotten, and files need changing. Save yourself a lot of time by limiting your powers and minimizing the damage that you can do. Save the power for when you really need it.

Gaining Superuser Privileges

Given all the exciting and hazardous things that a superuser can do, how do you become one? Simple: Just type su at the command prompt. Okay, the process is not quite as simple as that — you also have to know the superuser's password.

Here's a short example. Say that you want to modify the /etc/motd file. (The content of /etc/motd is displayed whenever you log in to your system — *motd* stands for *message of the day*.) Customizing /etc/motd is a quick way to alert your users that something important is happening today. On most systems, /etc/motd can be modified only by the superuser, as described in the following steps:

1. **Log in to your system as a normal (that is, non-superuser) user.**

2. **Type the su command at the prompt:**

```
[freddie@bastille /]$ su
```

su requests the superuser password:

```
Password: <enter the superuser password
    here>
```

3. **Enter the password.**

If you've entered the correct password, the prompt changes from $ to # to remind you that you hold elevated privileges. See the "Do-it-yourself identity checking" sidebar for details on an even better way to see your privileges at the prompt.

```
[root@bastille /]#
```

At this point, su starts a new, highly privileged shell for you.

4. **Overwrite the /etc/motd file as follows:**

```
[root@bastille /]# echo "Bastille will
    be down this evening for an upgrade"
    > /etc/motd
[root@bastille /]#
```

5. **Now here's the most important part: Exit the privileged shell, forfeiting your new privileges:**

```
[root@bastille /]# exit
[freddie@bastille /]$
```

Do-it-yourself identity checking

The bash shell is just trying to be helpful when it changes your prompt from $ to # (and back again), but if you modify your prompt, you can't rely on this cue. For a more definitive hint, the id command is your answer. id prints out your current identity:

```
[freddie@bastille /]$ id
uid=501(freddie) gid=501(freddie)
    groups=501(freddie)
```

Notice that id printed your user ID (and name) and a list of groups to which you belong (in this case, a single group named freddie). Now give yourself superuser privileges and try the id command again:

```
[freddie@bastille /]$ su
Password:
[root@bastille /]# id
uid=0(root) gid=0(root) groups=
    0(root),1(bin), ...
[root@bastille /]# exit
[freddie@bastille /]$ id
uid=501(freddie) gid=501(freddie)
    groups=501(freddie)
```

You see that the su command changes more than just your privileges: It changes your identity as well.

Pretending to Be Other Users

Because su gives you a way to become the superuser, you may be thinking that su stands for *superuser*. In fact, su stands for *substitute user:* You can impersonate *any* user with su (as long as you know the right password).

One reason that you might want to impersonate another user is to gain privileges to a particular piece of software, but you may not need all the privileges of the superuser to accomplish what you need to do. If you give yourself only the privileges that you need instead of giving yourself the power to accidentally destroy your system, you'll save yourself a lot of grief and wasted time.

To see how impersonating a user without gaining all the powers of the superuser works, take MySQL as an example. When you install a MySQL database, you usually create a new user account for the MySQL administrator. The MySQL administrator is not a real person (in most cases), it's just a name for a set of privileges. To fire up your MySQL database, you must *become* the MySQL administrator for a while:

```
[freddie@bastille /]$ su - mysql
[mysql@bastille /]$ id
uid = 301(mysql) gid=301(mysql)
   groups=301(mysql)
[mysql@bastille /]$ mysqld_safe &
[mysql@bastille /]$ exit
```

Notice the hyphen in this command, which tells su to invoke the login scripts for user mysql. When you run su without a hyphen, you're impersonating another user. When you run su *with* a hyphen, you're impersonating another user *and* inheriting the environment variables (and shell aliases and functions) that belong to that user.

The most common problem you run into (if you forget the hyphen) is that your $PATH environment variable is wrong. For example, if you forget the hyphen when you su mysql, it's pretty unlikely that the mysqld_safe command will be in *your* $PATH search path: mysqld_safe is on mysql's search path. In other words, su - is a complete impersonation.

Limiting Privileges with sudo

What's wrong with the su command? Running a shell as the superuser is sort of like hunting squirrels with a bazooka; sure, you can hunt squirrels that way, but it's safer to use a smaller armament. If you're running a shell while you have superuser privileges, it's just too easy to make a typing mistake that deletes important information. (Trust us, we've done that a few too many times.)

One way to avoid shooting yourself in the foot is to use sudo instead of su. From a user's point of view, sudo is very similar to su: Each command starts a new program that holds elevated privileges. su gives you all privileges, but sudo gives you only the privileges granted by an administrator. In other words, sudo gives you a way to grant *partial* privileges to those who need them, without giving them the whole bazooka. Really, you need to su only when you configure sudo.

The whole point of using sudo (instead of su) is to save yourself time by avoiding disasters. If you decide to use su in your normal course of work, be sure to read Techniques 49 and 50 (backup and recovery).

sudo is controlled by a configuration file named /etc/sudoers. The layout of a sudoers file can be a bit confusing at first, but don't be intimidated. Here's a simple /etc/sudoers file:

```
# file: /etc/sudoers
freddie    bastille = /bin/mount
```

The first line is a comment (anything that follows a # is treated as a comment). The second line grants user freddie the right to run the /bin/mount command as long as he's logged into a computer named bastille.

Now if freddie wants to mount a file system, he'll have to ask sudo to do the work for him:

```
[freddie@bastille /]$ sudo mount
   /dev/cdrom /mnt/cdrom
[freddie@bastille /]$
```

When you add entries to the sudoers file, be sure to include the complete pathname to each command. If you don't, dastardly users can simply slip a bogus program (with the same name) into their search path and gain privileges that you don't want them to have.

The first time you edit the /etc/sudoers file, you'll notice that it's already filled in with sample entries. Don't even look at them. They're too confusing. Just add the one or two lines that you need and ignore the samples.

Freddie can now mount CDs, but he can't unmount them. That's easy to fix; just add the umount command to the list of privileges:

```
# file: /etc/sudoers
freddie    bastille = /bin/mount, /bin/
  umount
```

Now freddie can mount and unmount file systems. But what if you want freddie to mount and unmount only CDs, not other file systems? That's easy, too:

```
# file: /etc/sudoers
freddie  bastille = /bin/mount /dev/cdrom,
  /bin/umount /dev/cdrom
```

Save time by including host names in the sudoers file, maintaining a single master copy of the file, and copying it to each machine on your network. That way, you don't have to create a separate sudoers file for each machine. In fact, you can store the sudoers file in CVS

(see Technique 13) to maintain a complete history of all the privileges you've ever granted on your entire network.

Of course, you can also list multiple users in the same sudoers file:

```
# file: /etc/sudoers

freddie      bastille  = /bin/mount
  /dev/cdrom, /bin/umount /dev/cdrom

franklin,tex  versaille = /usr/bin/reboot,
  /sbin/dump, /sbin/restore
```

The third line grants two users (franklin and tex) the right to reboot and the rights to backup and restore, but only on a host named versaille.

You can see the pattern: Each entry starts with a user name (or a list of user names), a host name (or a list of host names), an equals sign, and then a command (or list of commands). Each entry grants a set of privileges to one or more users on one or more hosts.

The man pages for sudo (and sudoers) state that you must use the visudo command to edit the /etc/sudoers file. That's not really true; you can use any editor you like. visudo does some extra error checking whenever you save your file, but we find the error messages to be more confusing than helpful.

32 Technique

Every system administrator walks a thin tightrope. On one hand, you must secure your system against both accidental and intentional damage. On the other hand, you can't tighten security to the point where average users can't get their jobs done. In a traditional Linux (or UNIX) system, privileges are granted to the superuser. If you need a privilege, you impersonate the superuser (with the `su` command). The problem with this approach is that you gain *all* privileges as soon as you know the superuser password. Give yourself enough privileges to mount a CD, and you've also gained enough privileges to delete every file on your computer. sudo (see Technique 31) can help by handing out privileges to specific users and programs. But if you have a medium- to large-sized network, managing sudo privileges can become a time consuming chore.

Assigning privileges with sudo aliases can help make quick work of the task. A sudo alias is an easy way to refer to a group of users, hosts, or commands when handing out privileges that are normally given to the superuser. The elements of the superuser privileges can be assigned individually, so the administrator doesn't have to give out the `root` password. Only the privileges that a user really needs are given out.

With sudo aliases, you can create `User_Alias` groups to assign privileges to groups of users. If the group (or department) gains new users, just add those new users to the `User_Alias`, and they automatically have all the privileges shared by that group. No one gets the superuser password, so you don't need to worry about runaway superuser privileges.

Host aliases allow you to control groups of computers with one set of privilege assignments. You can quickly combine user aliases and host aliases to grant access to machine resources to the users that really need the resources, but still restrict the superuser privileges that might pose a security threat to the system.

In this technique, we show you how to save time by using sudo's aliases to assign privileges to groups. When you become a sudo superuser, you really start to save time. In this technique, we show you how to use sudo aliases to save time assigning privileges. And your system will be a safer place for it.

Installing sudo

To find out if sudo is installed on your computer, look for a file called /etc/sudoers. If it's not there, install sudo from your Linux distribution disc. Open a terminal window and give yourself superuser privileges with the su command. Mount the distribution disk, move into the directory holding the RPM packages, and install sudo with the following command:

```
# rpm -Uhv sudo-version.rpm
```

Adding Up the Aliases

The sudoers file holds sudo configuration information; program permissions and sudo aliases are defined in /etc/sudoers. An *alias* (a sudo alias anyway) is a name that you give to a group of one or more users, hosts, commands, or "run as" names.

 The idea behind an alias is that you can assign (or deny) privileges to the named group rather than to each individual group member, making setup and maintenance much easier. For example, you may have a small group of users who perform system maintenance tasks (such as backup and restore operations). Rather than assigning privileges to each individual operator, create an operator alias (a group that includes all your operators) and assign backup and restore privileges to the alias. That way, if you hire new operators, you simply add them to the operator alias, and they have all the privileges they need. Or, if you switch to a different backup program, you can change the privileges assigned to the operator group rather than to each individual.

By modifying the sudoers file, you can create four kinds of aliases:

- ✔ User_Alias: A User_Alias creates a group of users. A User_Alias definition can contain a combination of groups, individual users, and other user aliases.

- ✔ Runas_Alias: Using a Runas_Alias allows a user to borrow the privileges of another user (typically, root). A Runas_Alias definition can include user names, UIDs, user groups, and other Runas_Aliases.

- ✔ Host_Alias: Use a Host_Alias to manage groups of computers if you manage a large network. Assigning a Host_Alias to a group of Web servers allows you to apply sudo rules to all the systems in the group. A Host_Alias can reference host names, IP addresses, netmasks, or other host aliases.

- ✔ Cmnd_Alias: A command alias groups similar commands (similar in their danger levels). Grouping commands like rm, mkfs, and parted (potentially dangerous commands) and limiting access to them can help decrease the likelihood that you'll be restoring from backup anytime soon. A Cmnd_Alias can refer to command names, directories, and other command aliases.

Adding Aliases to the sudo Configuration File

sudo aliases are defined in the /etc/sudoers file. Adding an alias is quick and simple:

1. **Open the terminal window and give yourself superuser privileges with the su - command.**

2. **Tell the visudo command (which you use in a moment) which editor you want to use (the default editor is vi, and we'd rather not go there).**

   For example, if you want to use kedit, use the following command:
   ```
   # export EDITOR=kedit
   ```

   You can use kate, emacs, or another editor if you prefer.

3. **To edit the /etc/sudoers file, enter the following command:**
   ```
   # visudo
   ```

The `/etc/sudoers` file opens.

The file contains four commented lines, acting as placeholders for alias definitions.

4. Enter the aliases under the appropriate headings.

For example, if you're creating a `Cmnd_Alias`, place it under the comment that says `# Cmnd_Alias specifications`. See the next section, "Defining the Alias," for more information about the format of an alias.

5. When you're finished adding aliases, save the file and exit the editor.

When you save the file edits, you may get an error message in the terminal window:

```
Warning: undeclared Host_Alias 'NAME'
  referenced near line 12
>>>sudoers file: syntax error, line
  11<<<
What now?
```

 The `sudoers` error messages aren't very helpful. Odds are, you made a typing error, so enter an `e` to reopen and edit the file and then check your entry. sudo is particularly fussy about capitalization; the first letter of the alias type and the word alias need to be capitalized.

Defining the Alias

Before you can add an alias, you need to decide what the alias will contain. This takes a bit of thought, but as you think about your users and their roles in the workplace, some logical divisions of privileges will probably emerge.

 Model the sudo aliases against the real-world roles that your users take on and the real-world privileges that the company structure might impose. A management hierarchy might translate into a hierarchy of user aliases and privileges.

Here's the basic format of an alias definition:

```
Alias_Type ALIASNAME = member one, member
  two
```

Note that capitalization is important in the `sudoers` file. Alias names may contain only uppercase letters, numbers, and underscores (and must begin with a letter). The words `User_Alias`, `Runas_Alias`, `Host_Alias`, and `Cmnd_Alias` must all be captalized as shown in this sentence.

Creating a User_Alias

To create a `User_Alias` named `ACCTG` consisting of Freddie, Franklin, and Georgette, add the following code to the `/etc/sudoers` file:

```
User_Alias ACCTG = freddie, franklin,
  georgette
```

To create an alias consisting of the members of another group but excluding a certain member, you can define a group as follows:

```
User_Alias MGMT = ACCTG, ! georgette
```

The `!` excludes Georgette from the `MGMT` group.

 You can use the `!` to exclude the rights to certain privileges from certain users, but don't consider that to be absolute security. Wily users can find their way around a lack of privileges if they really want to.

Creating a Runas_Alias

The command to create a `Runas_Alias` is similar to the command to create a `User_Alias`, but you can also specify members by their user numbers:

```
Runas_Alias OPERATORS = #1, murphy,
  rachel, bernie
```

A single user can belong to many aliases — the user gains the privileges of each group. In a small company, the timesaving benefits might not be immediately obvious, but if you're managing the privileges of dozens of users, aliases can really help speed things up.

Simplifying group managment with a Host_Alias

Use the `Host_Alias` to make management of groups of computers easier. To add a `Host_Alias` named FRANCE consisting of `bastille`, `versaille`, and `louvre`, add the following line to the sudo configuration file:

```
Host_Alias SERVERS = bastille, versaille,
    louvre
```

You can also specify computers by IP addresses:

```
Host_Alias SERVERS = 192.168.0.1,
    192.168.0.36, 192.168.0.22
```

You can use a `Host_Alias` in combination with a `User_Alias` to assign the user group privileged access to a group of computers without giving out the superuser password.

Mounting and unmounting CDs without the superuser password

You might want to allow users to mount and unmount CDs without becoming the superuser. If you don't want to expose the privilege on *all* your computers, create a `Host_Alias` that includes the computers that the users will access. To do so, follow these steps:

1. Add the `Host_Alias` to the Host Alias Specification section of the `sudoers` file:

```
Host_Alias CDROMHOSTS = 192.168.0.1,
    192.168.0.28, 192.168.0.218
```

2. Add a line in the User Privilege Specification section of the `sudoers` file that gives the privileges to everyone:

```
ALL CDROMHOSTS = NOPASSWD: /sbin/umount
    /dev/cdrom, /sbin/mount /dev/cdrom
```

 ALL is a built-in alias that matches all items of that particular kind (all users, all hosts, and so on). Use the expression ALL where you would

put a user name, and it will include all the users. Use the expression ALL where you would use a host name, and it will interpret it to mean all the hosts it knows about.

 Instead of using ALL, you can substitute your own `User_Alias` into the command and limit the users that can mount and unmount CDs.

After you set up users by following the steps in this section, the users need to add `sudo` to the front of the `mount` and `umount` commands when entering them to use their sudo privileges.

Including the `NOPASSWD` flag exempts your users from having to enter their sudo passwords. Passwords offer an extra line of security, but for some things (such as mounting a CD), your users will thank you for not requiring a password.

Managing access to dangerous commands with command aliases

Use command aliases to easily manage privileges for dangerous commands. When a user needs to use a dangerous command, you can ration the access instead of giving out the superuser password and unlimited access to *all* commands. Here are some commands you might consider controlling with sudo:

- `su`
- `rm`
- `mkfs`
- `kill`
- `killall`
- `parted`

 One handy command that other users would find helpful, but that normally requires superuser privileges, is `rpm`. If you read Techniques 17 and 18, you already know how handy `rpm` is when it comes to installing and updating software. And with sudo aliases, you can share the tool without sharing the superuser password.

1. To add a command alias to the sudo configuration file, define the `Cmnd_Alias` with the fully qualified pathname to the command:

```
Cmnd_Alias DANGER = /usr/su, /usr/bin/
    kill, /usr/bin/killall, /bin/rm,
    sbin/mkfs
```

 The location of the commands may vary system to system. Use the fully-qualified pathname when you define your command alias.

2. Add a command alias in the Cmnd Alias Specifications section of the `sudoers` file to create an alias for the RPM command:

```
Cmnd_Alias RPM = /bin/rpm
```

3. Then add a line to the `sudoers` file under the **User Privilege Specification section:**

```
OPERATORS ALL = NOPASSWD: RPM
```

This line grants access to the `rpm` command to all members of the `OPERATORS` `User_Alias` on `ALL` host machines.

 `OPERATORS` **must add** `sudo` **to the front of the** `rpm` **command in order for sudo to grant the required privilege:** `$ sudo rpm -Uhv rpmpackage.rpm`.

Technique

33

Securing Your Connections with SSH

In the good old days, if you wanted to log in to a remote computer, you simply ran telnet. The telnet program would reach across a network and give you a remote command line. When you typed a command into the telnet client, the characters that you typed were sent blissfully over the wire, and the telnet server on the other end would execute the command and send the results back to you. Were we really so young then? With the advent of the Internet, new villains appeared, eager to grab our passwords and credit card numbers as they leapt from ISP to ISP. The problem with telnet is that everything that you type is sent across the network *in the clear*. Anyone watching the bits stream across the network can see your private bits. The solution to this problem is SSH.

SSH, which is an acronym for *secure shell,* encrypts your data as it travels across a network so that passwords, financial data, and private e-mail are never exposed to any hacker who can intercept them. An SSH connection consists of two parts: a server and a client. An SSH server waits patiently on a host computer, listening on a specific port for a client to log in. When an SSH client connects to a server, the two programs begin a lengthy negotiating session that results in a fully encrypted connection.

SSH provides a remote command line. With SSH, you can start graphical programs that run on the server but display their data on your local computer.

SSH also provides port forwarding. With port forwarding, you can tunnel through firewalls to gain access to machines on the other side. Forwarded data is protected traveling back and forth to the protected host, while the server remains secure behind its firewall.

In this technique, we introduce you to the benefits of using an SSH client. SSH provides a secure connection across a local network or over the Internet, through firewalls, and with great speed, and it merges with your desktop environment via a quick link. We show you how to use your SSH client (which comes complimentary with Fedora) to do all of these things.

Using SSH for Top-Speed Connections

The great thing about SSH is that you get all the security benefits, plus access to a GUI environment with speeds that can't be matched by the other desktop sharing tools. SSH can compress the bits traveling over the network connection to improve performance. The speed advantage is really evident if you have a low-bandwidth or high-latency connection.

 Think of *latency* as the distance between your computer and the server that you're connected to. If you're connected to a computer 10 feet away from you, you probably have a low-latency connection. If you need to log in to a computer in a foreign land over a satellite connection, all your data travels from your computer, up to the satellite, back down to earth, and then across the rest of the network: That's a high-latency connection.

Setting Up Public-Key Authentication to Secure SSH

When you log in to a typical personal computer, you provide a password. The password authenticates that you are who you claim to be. Anyone who knows your password can fake out a server. Passwords are typically very short and easy to remember; those two qualities make passwords easy to use, but also make them incredibly insecure.

Public-key authentication is an alternative to password authentication. Public-key authentication is very secure, and SSH also makes it convenient. In public-key authentication, each key has two parts — a public key and a private key. You always keep your private key a secret, but you share your public key. The two keys are mathematically related in a way that only Stephen Hawking can understand. A

message encrypted with the public key can be *decrypted* only with the private key. A message encrypted with the private key can be decrypted only with the public key.

To authenticate a connection by using a public key, the server encrypts a message with your public key and sends the result to your client. The SSH client decrypts the message using your private key and reencrypts it with the server's public key. In this exchange, you've proven you are who you say you are *and* verified that you're connected to the proper server.

 Public-key authentication is perfect for telecommuters and those doing customer support work because it enables you to easily access computers that you will log in to often. Just copy your public key once, and you're ready to go.

The public and private keys are stored in the `~/.ssh` directory. To set up key authentication with SSH, here's an overview of what you need to do:

1. **Generate the key pair.**

2. **Give the SSH server a copy of your public key (but keep your private key to yourself).**

   You can copy the public key to the server by using a file transfer tool such as `scp` (*secure* `cp`).

3. **(Optional) Set up your passphrase so that you don't have to enter it every time you log in.**

 Your public/private key pair is generated from a whole mess of random numbers. It's very unlikely that any two key pairs will be identical. A typical key is *at least* 128 characters long.

 Linux automatically contains everything you need to use public-key authentication, so you don't have to install any extra software. Yay!

Generating the key pair

To generate your public/private key pair, follow these steps:

1. **Open a command line, type the following command, and press Enter:**

```
$ ssh-keygen -t rsa
```

You're prompted to enter a file to save the key in.

2. **Press Enter, and SSH will find a good place for the file.**

You're prompted for a passphrase.

3. **Enter a good password.**

Check out the sidebar "Choosing good passwords," later in this chapter, for some ideas about choosing passwords.

4. **Enter the same passphrase again to verify it. Remember the passphrase; you'll need it later.**

SSH acknowledges that it has created your key pair and displays the filenames where the keys are saved. `ssh-keygen` also issues a key fingerprint, but you can ignore that for now. To use your key pair with SSH, you need to distribute the public key, which we explain how to do in the next section.

Distributing your public key

Before you can use your key pair to log in to an SSH server, you have to copy your public key into your `~/.ssh` directory on the server. The easiest way to get your key to the server is to use the `scp` command.

 Don't share anything but your public key by e-mail. The private key is always kept private, encrypted on your system.

Follow the steps shown in Listing 33-1 to transfer your public key to the remote system. After you enter each command, you're prompted for your password on the remote system.

 In the example, substitute your user name on the remote system for `freddie`, and the name (or IP address) of the remote system for `bastille`.

Passing on your passphrase

If you did all that work to avoid typing in a password, why should you have to enter a pass*phrase* instead? The passphrase unlocks your private key for use when you log in to a remote system. Without a passphrase, your private key would be exposed on your local machine for anyone to see.

 If you do a lot of work on a remote machine, add the passphrase to your startup procedure and create desktop shortcuts to save you time logging in and out. The following steps explain how to arrange for KDE or GNOME to prompt you for the passphrase when you log in to your desktop environment. See "Creating Shortcuts to Your Favorite SSH Locations" for information about creating desktop shortcuts.

 If you're in an environment where security is crucial, never walk away from your computer without first logging out. A troublemaker who walks up to your unattended computer can impersonate you if you're logged in. If you follow the steps described in this section, anyone with physical access to your computer can also use your private key while you're logged in.

LISTING 33-1: HANDING OUT YOUR PUBLIC KEY

```
$ ssh freddie@bastille "mkdir .ssh"
Password:
$ ssh freddie@bastille "cat >> .ssh/authorized_keys2" < .ssh/id_rsa.pub
Password:
$ ssh freddie@bastille "chmod 700 .ssh .ssh/authorized_keys2"
Password:
$
```

To eliminate the need to enter your passphrase every time you log in to a remote system, you have to talk KDE (or GNOME) into asking you for the passphrase when you first log in to your local desktop. After the key is unlocked, it's ready for use (and reuse) until you log out of your local desktop.

If you use KDE, the easiest way to set this up is with Konqueror. Here's how:

1. **Open your Konqueror browser and surf to the following directory:**

`~/.kde/Autostart`

2. **Right-click on the browser and choose Create New⇨Link to Application from the pop-up menu.**

3. **Name your link (Passphrase) and click the Execute tab.**

4. **In the Command field, enter the following command:**

`/usr/bin/ssh-add`

5. **Click OK.**

A new Autostart icon appears in the Konqueror window. The next time you log in to KDE, you'll be prompted for your passphrase.

If you're a fan of GNOME, follow along to edit your Autostart folder:

1. **Open the Main Menu and choose Preferences⇨More Preferences⇨Sessions.**

2. **Click the Sessions icon to open the Sessions dialog.**

3. **Click the Startup Programs tab and then click Add.**

The Add Startup Program dialog appears.

4. **Type `/usr/bin/ssh-add` in the Startup Command field and click OK.**

Logging In with SSH and Key Authentication

When you log in to an SSH server using public-key authentication, you're greeted with a remote command line. The commands that you enter are executed by the SSH server until you log out. If you want to use graphical environments, you can access those, too. We give you the details in the following sections.

Starting from the command line

To use your key authentication to log in to a machine with SSH, follow these steps:

1. **At the command line, type `ssh bastille` and press Enter.**

You're prompted for your passphrase (the one you entered when you generated your key set).

2. **Enter the passphrase.**

You're logged in!

A few quick words about fingerprints

The first time you log in with SSH, your local system adds the server's public key to its list of known computers and issues a warning similar to the following:

```
The authenticity of host `192.168.0.135'
  can't be established.
RSA key fingerprint is
b4:2y:88:23:98:33:g1:03:ec:7b:d8:2b:b8:83:
  y3:f8.
Are you sure you want to continue
  connecting (yes/no)?
```

Type `yes` and press Enter to continue.

In the future, if the server's public key changes, SSH will warn you.

 Some nasty people intercept transmissions and redirect logins to steal password information that will enable them to get into places they don't belong. If the system fingerprints don't match, SSH will warn you and you'll know you have a potential man-in-the-middle attack. If that happens, ask the remote system administrator to read you his or her server's fingerprint over the phone.

Getting graphic

You can also run graphical programs from your remote machine on your local desktop. The SSH server forwards X Windows traffic over the SSH connection automatically. Here are a few examples to illustrate how this works:

✔ To see what time it is on the remote system, type the command xclock &. The clock displays the time on your local desktop, but it also displays the time on the server (you can't tell the difference if you're in the same time zone).

✔ To see the files on the server, type konqueror & and press Enter. The Konqueror browser starts running *on the server,* but the display appears on your local desktop.

Creating Shortcuts to Your Favorite SSH Locations

SSH is handy at the command line, but you can also launch SSH sessions from a desktop link. And, if you're a KDE aficionado, you can use the fish: protocol to create a link to a remote file or folder.

To add a desktop link that opens a terminal window connected to an SSH server, follow these steps:

1. **Right-click on your desktop and choose Create New⇨Link to Application.**

A dialog opens.

2. **Type a name for the link and click the Execute tab.**

3. **In the Command field, enter the following command:**

gnome-terminal -x ssh bastille

4. **Click OK.**

Double-click the new link, and you're logged in and working. If you've configured your desktop as we describe earlier in "Passing on your passphrase," you don't need to stop and enter passwords along the way.

> With your remote terminal, you can open any graphical application on your Linux host. At the command line, enter the name of the program — kedit, kate, konqueror . . . the list is endless.

You can open as many windows on your local desktop as your connection will support. These windows work like local windows in all respects, with the exception of drag and drop. Instead of drag and drop, we recommend using scp at the command line. See the next section for details.

If you're using KDE as your desktop environment, you can create a link to a remote file or directory. Double-click a link to a remote directory, and KDE will open the directory with the Konqueror browser. After you double-click a link to a remote file, KDE opens the file using the right application (based on the file's MIME type). Follow these steps to create a new link to a remote directory:

1. **Right-click on the desktop and choose Create New⇨Link to Location (URL) from the pop-up menu.**

2. **Enter the following command in the Enter Link to Location (URL) field and click OK:**

fish://bastille/home

Substitute your remote machine's name or IP address for bastille.

> fish: is a KDE protocol that provides remote file management over an SSH connection. See Technique 1 for more information.

When the dialog closes, a link on the server's /home directory appears on your desktop.

3. **To connect to the remote machine, just double-click the icon.**

A Konqueror browser window opens, showing the /home directory.

Copying Files with scp

scp is similar to the cp command: It copies a file from a source to a destination. The difference between scp and cp is that scp can deal with files stored on remote hosts. scp uses the SSH protocol to encrypt the file being transferred and can take advantage of SSH's compression feature to save you time. You can use scp to completely replace cp. To copy a file from one directory to another (on your local machine), use the following command:

```
$ scp /tmp/drink-recipes.txt /home/
```

If you want to copy a file from an SSH server or to an SSH server, include the remote host name on the command line, like this:

```
$ scp louvre:/pics/monalisa.jpg /tmp/
$ scp /tmp/monalisa.jpg orsay:/pics/
```

 If you see a name that includes a colon, it most likely refers to a remote computer.

The first command copies /pics/monalisa.jpg from host louvre to the /tmp directory on your local computer. The second command copies the picture from your local computer to host orsay. If you haven't copied your public key to louvre or orsay, you're asked for a password.

You can also use scp to copy from one remote machine to another remote machine:

```
$ scp louvre:/pics/monalisa.jpg
  orsay:/pics
```

Enable compression with the -C option:

```
$ scp -C /tmp/monalisa.jpg orsay:/pics/
```

If you don't specify a fully qualified pathname, scp assumes that you want to copy into (or from) your home directory on the remote computer. For example, the command

```
$ scp -C louvre:paintings.list orsay:
```

copies a file from your home directory on louvre to your home directory on orsay.

You can include wildcards in an scp command, but you have to quote them if you want the wildcards to be expanded by the computer on the other end of the connection. For example, to copy all the .jpg files in your home directory on louvre to your local machine, use the following command:

```
$ scp -C "louvre:*.jpg" /tmp/
```

If you forget the quotes, the bash shell expands the wildcard before scp ever gets a chance to see it.

 You can use scp to copy an entire directory tree with the -r option.

Secure (And Fast) Port Forwarding with SSH

No Web site should be without a good firewall because too many villains are out there waiting to attack your computer. Firewalls keep the bad guys out, but they can sure make life tough for those of us wearing the white hats. Fortunately for the good guys, SSH can slip you past a firewall in no time.

Port forwarding lets you securely connect to a specific port on a remote computer without being blocked by a firewall. Neither the remote machine nor your local system can even tell that a firewall is there.

Port forwarding with SSH can solve a lot of problems for you, such as the following:

- ✔ Some software packages require access to specific port numbers.

- ✔ You can reach software on the other side of a firewall.

- ✔ Your data is traveling in encrypted form and can't be seen by villains.

- ✔ Your data is compressed and zips through the network much faster.

Port forwarding is kind of a strange process. The basic idea is that you connect to a port on your local computer, and SSH takes all the data that you send to that port and forwards it to another port on another computer. SSH also sends data back in the other direction for a complete connection.

Here's an example. PostgreSQL database servers typically listen for clients on TCP port 5432. When you run a PostgreSQL client application, the client connects to the server on that port. The client and server exchange SQL queries and results over the connection and disconnect when they're finished. A PostgreSQL client can connect to a server on the same computer (using local port 5432) or a server running on a remote computer (using the remote host name and port 5432).

You can introduce SSH into this mix to solve three different problems:

- ✔ If a firewall is present between the client and the server, SSH can carry the data across the firewall for you.

- ✔ If you have a slow connection to the server, SSH can compress the data stream to improve performance.

- ✔ If you're transmitting sensitive data across an insecure network, SSH will encrypt the data stream for you.

To set up port forwarding between a PostgreSQL client running on your local computer and a PostgreSQL server running on louvre, simply use SSH to log into louvre and include a bit of command line magic:

```
$ ssh -L 5432:louvre:5432 louvre
```

To break that command down a bit, the ssh command connects to the SSH server running on host louvre. The cryptic-looking bit in the middle of the command (-L 5432:louvre:5432) forwards data from port 5432 on your local computer to port 5432 on louvre. Now when you start up a PostgreSQL client, you connect to *local* port 5432, even though the PostgreSQL server is running on a different computer:

```
$ psql -h localhost -p 5432
Welcome to psql, the PostgreSQL
   interactive terminal
freddie=#
```

If you have a firewall between yourself and louvre, you can ask SSH to forward data across the firewall to a third computer. For example, if bastille is acting as a firewall (meaning that you can't directly connect to any machines *behind* bastille), this command arranges for SSH to carry PostgreSQL data across the firewall and deliver it to louvre:

```
$ ssh -L 5432:louvre:5432 bastille
```

Notice that with this command, you're logging into bastille, but SSH is forwarding the data to louvre. SSH can forward data to any machine that bastille can talk to. When SSH forwards data for you, the data stream is automatically encrypted. If you want to compress the data as well, just add a -C to the command line.

Choosing good passwords

Choose your passwords carefully. A good password should include both upper- and lowercase letters, numbers, and punctuation if allowed. The system will set a limit on the length of your password, but generally speaking, the longer the password the better. It's a bad idea to honor pets, children, and spouses in your password unless you've taken care to obscure the name with other characters like Fr3ddi3*! — and even then it's not a great idea. It's also a bad idea to use your license plate number — that should be obvious, but you'd be surprised how many people do it.

Be sure to choose a password that is obscure, but memorable. Writing it down leaves the password susceptible to the prying eyes of anyone who gets access to your workspace. One common mnemonic is to use the first letter of each word in a phrase you won't forget. Throw in some punctuation, or change case now and then, and you have a memorable password that's also hard to guess. All King Edward's Horses Can Master Big Fences! translates to AkehCmBf!, which is pretty unguessable.

Part VI

Networking Like a Professional

The 5th Wave   By Rich Tennant

©RICHTENNANT

"If it works, it works. I've just never seen network cabling connected with Chinese handcuffs before!"

Protecting Yourself with a Firewall

A good firewall is important to any network because it's your first line of defense against intruders. Obviously, if your system has no contact with the outside world (either via the Web or by modem), you don't need a firewall. If your system *does* have contact with the Web, you should consider screening what comes through your network interfaces.

Network information travels in *packets* — groups of data that are encased in layers of envelopes. Each layer of the packet contains a different kind of information about the data within the packet. The outermost layer contains information about the hardware that the packet is coming from. The next layer within contains the IP address for the source and the destination. Inside that envelope is the TCP information — the port numbers and sequence numbers of both the source and destination machines. At the heart of the packet is the packet payload — the real data that you're interested in.

A good firewall can filter the incoming or outgoing packets based on the information contained in any of the envelope layers. Because the envelopes are nested within one another, if you toss the outer envelope, the inner envelopes go with it, and the data never reaches your application.

In this technique, we show you ways to set up a firewall that's tight enough to protect your system, but loose enough to allow useful data in and out. You'll save time with a safer system that gives everyone the access they need to get their jobs done.

Finding Your Firewall

Starting with kernel version 2.4, most Linux distributions include a sophisticated packet filtering package called netfilter. You can use netfilter to build firewalls, perform network address translation (NAT), perform port translation, and alter network packets as they traverse your system. netfilter is part of the Linux kernel — you can configure netfilter with the `iptables` command. Notice that we said that you *can* configure netfilter with the `iptables` command, not that you *should*. Creating a firewall by typing in a bunch of `iptables` commands is something best left to the propeller heads.

Instead, you should use a firewall builder. A firewall builder is a tool that (usually) asks you a series of questions about how you use your computer and then runs a sequence of `iptables` commands on your behalf. A good firewall builder will store your choices in a set of one or more configuration files and then arrange for the corresponding `iptables` commands to execute each time you boot your computer.

You can find a variety of firewall builders on the Web. Some are designed to create a simple firewall as quickly as possible; others are less friendly, but give you more control over the security of your system. SuSE, Mandrake, and Fedora each come with a firewall builder (and they're all different).

Setting up a simple firewall in Mandrake Linux

In keeping with Mandrake's reputation for simplicity, `drakfirewall` (the Mandrake firewall builder) makes it very easy to configure a simple firewall. To run the Mandrake firewall builder, follow these steps:

1. **Open the main menu and choose System↪ Configuration↪Configure your computer.**

The Mandrake Control Center opens.

2. **Choose Security↪Firewall.**

The `drakfirewall` configuration editor opens, as shown in Figure 34-1.

3. **Use the check boxes to configure your firewall.**

Start out by clearing each check box — that will lock your system down so that outsiders can't get through your firewall. Then, check each

service that you want to provide to the outside world. For example, if you want to log in to your computer from another system, select the SSH Server check box. If you're running an Apache Web server, select the Web Server check box.

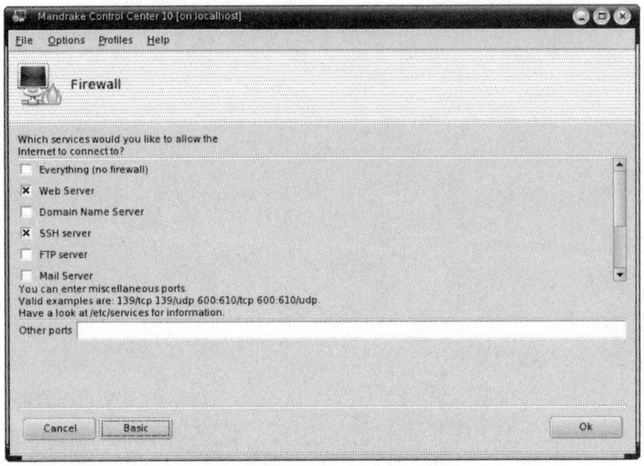

• **Figure 34-1: The Mandrake Firewall Builder.**

If you need to temporarily disable your firewall, select the Everything (No Firewall) check box — `drakfirewall` is kind enough to remember your original settings so that you can restore your firewall again later.

4. **When you're finished, click OK to save your changes.**

When you save your changes, `drakfirewall` saves your choices to a set of configuration files in the `/etc/shorewall` directory and executes a sequence of `iptables` commands that configures netfilter according to your preferences.

Mandrake Linux actually uses *two* firewall builders, one layered atop the other. `drakfirewall` (the tool we just described) is a very high-level firewall builder — it's very simple, but not very flexible. Under the hood, `drakfirewall` drives another firewall builder called Shorewall. You can find more information about Shorewall at `www.shorewall.net`.

Setting up a simple firewall in Fedora Linux

When you installed Fedora, you ran a program called `system-config-security`. You might not have even noticed it — it's part of the installation script, and goes by with just a quick question or two. At installation time, it created a firewall and firewall rules for you. You may have chosen *not* to install a firewall at that time; if that's the case, you have no firewall rules in place.

If you chose not to install a firewall when you installed Fedora, you can change your mind later. The same configuration tool that runs during the install procedure will create (or remove) simple firewall rules. To run Fedora's firewall builder, follow these steps:

1. **Open the Main Menu and choose System Settings⇨Security Level.**

You're prompted for the `root` password.

2. **Enter the `root` password and click OK.**

 If you have a terminal window open and superuser privileges, you can start the configuration tool by entering `system-config-securitylevel` at the command line.

The Security Level Configuration dialog opens. This dialog is similar to the firewall information window you saw at installation time.

3. **From the Security Level drop-down list, select Enable Firewall.**

 If you *disable* the firewall, any custom rules you've created are lost.

4. **To create the most robust firewall possible, enable the firewall with no trusted services or trusted devices.**

That is, deselect all the check boxes, as shown in Figure 34-2.

 The best way to build a robust firewall is to disallow *all* traffic, and then relax the restrictions to allow data to flow. It's easier to recognize your friends one at a time.

• **Figure 34-2:** A very secure firewall.

 If you have multiple network cards listed in the Trusted Devices frame, you can trust devices that connect to your own network, but don't trust the devices that connect to the outside world. That way, the devices within your network can access the machine via SSH or Telnet, but the outside world can't get in.

5. **Click the OK button to continue.**

A pop-up opens, warning you that if you continue, you'll change the existing firewall configuration.

6. **Click Yes to continue.**

Setting up a simple firewall in SuSE Linux

The crew at SuSE have put a lot of work into their firewall builder (called SuSE Firewall2), making it powerful *and* easy to use. Like the Mandrake and Fedora firewall builders, SuSE Firewall2 stores your preferences in a configuration file (`/etc/sysconfig/SUSEfirewall2`) and executes a series of `iptables` commands when you apply your changes.

To run the SuSE firewall builder, follow these steps:

1. Open the main menu and choose System⇨YaST.

The YaST Control Center appears.

2. Click Security and Users (in the left-hand pane), and then click Firewall.

The SuSE Firewall2 window appears, as shown in Figure 34-3.

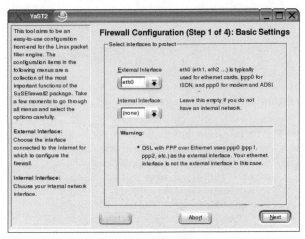

• **Figure 34-3: The SuSE firewall builder (Step 1).**

3. Choose your external interface from the drop-down list.

The external interface is the network interface connected to the outside world (the Internet).

4. If your computer has two network adapters, SuSE assumes the second interface is connected to a local (internal) network — choose the internal interface from the drop-down list.

5. Click Next to move to the next step.

The Services list appears, as shown in Figure 34-4.

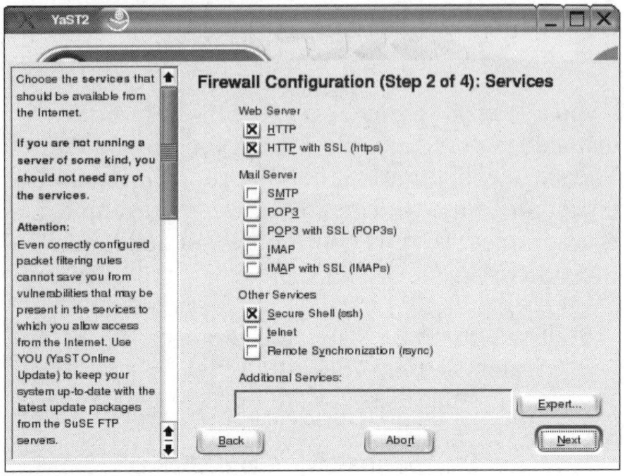

• **Figure 34-4: The SuSE firewall builder (Step 2).**

6. Use the check boxes to configure your firewall.

Start out by clearing each check box — that will lock your system down so that outsiders can't get through your firewall. Then, select each service that you want to provide to the outside world. For example, if you want to log in to your computer from another system, select the Secure Shell (ssh) check box. If you're running an Apache Web server, select the HTTP check box and the HTTP with SSL (https) check box.

If you need to allow other services through your firewall, click the Expert button and list the service names (or port numbers) in the text box provided.

7. Click Next to move to the next step.

The Features dialog appears (see Figure 34-5).

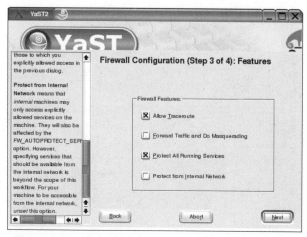

• **Figure 34-5: The SuSE firewall builder (Step 3).**

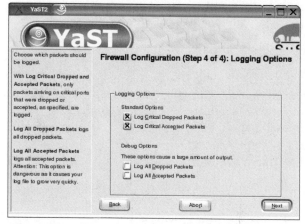

• **Figure 34-6: The SuSE firewall builder (Step 4).**

8. **Select the features that you want, or simply accept the default values.**

We recommend that you select the Allow Traceroute and the Protect All Running Services check boxes. If you're sharing your external interface with other machines (in other words, if your computer is acting as a gateway for an internal network), you should also select the Forward Traffic and Do Masquerading check box.

The text box on the left side of the window explains each option in more detail.

9. **Click Next to move to the last step.**

The Logging Options window appears, as shown in Figure 34-6.

10. **Select the logging and debugging options that you want.**

We recommend accepting the default values. After your firewall has been in place for a while and you're satisfied that it is working properly, you can disable all firewall logging to conserve disk space.

11. **Click Next, and then click Continue to save your changes and (re)start the firewall.**

When you save your changes, SuSE Firewall2 executes a whole slew of `iptables` commands to tell netfilter about your choices.

Editing the Rules with Webmin

After you've configured your firewall with a friendly firewall builder, you may want to fine-tune netfilter to better fit your needs. If you're running Mandrake or Fedora Linux, the graphical firewall builders don't give you many options. SuSE Firewall2 is a bit more powerful, but it was really designed to be simple, not flexible. Relax, you don't have to hit the command line.

The quickest and easiest way to tweak your firewall rules is with a system administration tool called Webmin. With Webmin, you can perform tasks such as configuring servers, managing users and groups, arranging backups, and scheduling cron jobs, all from within your favorite browser. If you prefer, you can use Webmin to do many of the tasks that are handled by Mandrake, SuSE, and Fedora administration tools. Many third-party modules are also available to expand on Webmin's basic capabilities.

We really like Webmin. Go to www.webmin.com when you have some free time, and check it out. Getting familiar with Webmin can be a real timesaver.

Technique 17 gives detailed instructions about downloading and installing Webmin. If you haven't already installed Webmin, see Technique 17 for more information.

Starting a Webmin session

With Webmin installed, start a Webmin session:

1. **Open a browser and go to** http://localhost:10000.

   Webmin opens, displaying a login window, as shown in Figure 34-7.

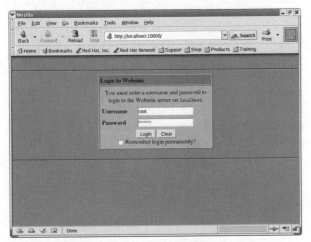

• **Figure 34-7: The Webmin login window.**

2. **Enter** root **in the Username field, and the root password in the Password field. Click Login to continue.**

 Unless you trust everyone who has access to your desktop, we don't recommend clicking the Remember Login Permanently box. Webmin allows access to some sensitive parts of your system.

The opening window of Webmin is displayed, as shown in Figure 34-8. From this window, move from page to page by clicking the round buttons (labeled System, Servers, Networking, and so on) across the top. Each page provides tools to manage different aspects of your system.

• **Figure 34-8: The Webmin main window.**

Reading the rules with Webmin

You can see and manage your firewall rules from the Networking tools page in Webmin. Just click Linux Firewall.

If you're running Fedora Linux, Webmin knows how to read the firewall rules created by Fedora's firewall builder — any changes you make through Webmin will appear the next time you run system-configure-securitylevel.

If you're running Mandrake Linux, Webmin will offer to convert your Shorewall configuration files to the more standard Webmin format (if you choose to convert, any changes you make through Webmin will be discarded when you switch back to the Shorewall configurator). If you prefer to keep Shorewall in place, you can use Webmin's Shorewall Firewall module instead of the Linux Firewall module.

The SuSE firewall builder stores its configuration information in a format that Webmin's Linux Firewall module can't directly read — to use the Linux Firewall module on a SuSE computer, click Module Config (near the top of the page) and select Directly Edit firewall rules instead of savefile. Webmin will interrogate the running kernel to discover the firewall rules you have in place. After you've made any necessary changes, use the `iptables-save` command (at the command-line) to create a savefile — see `man iptables-save` for more information.

In this section, we show you how to read (and modify) firewall rules as they appear in Webmin's Linux Firewall module. We use a firewall generated by Fedora's `system-config-securitylevel` as an example.

When you start the Linux Firewall module, the rules you established with the `system-config-security level` tool (see the section, "Setting up a simple firewall in Fedora Linux," earlier in this technique) are shown in Figure 34-9.

The first rule set on the page displays the rules applied to incoming packets. If you've chosen the default setup for the firewall, the only rule in the set is to always run the chain `RH-Firewall-1-INPUT` (which we describe in a moment). You can add new rules to this chain with the Add Rule button or remove all the rules from the rule set with the Clear All Rules button.

The second rule set decides the fate of forwarded packets (packets routed *through* your computer). Again, the only action defined by default is to run the chain `RH-Firewall-1-INPUT`.

The third rule set displayed on the screen applies to outgoing packets. With the default firewall, no rules are applied to the outgoing packets — only incoming packets.

Near the bottom of the page, you see the rules that make up the `RH-Firewall-1-INPUT` chain, as shown in Figure 34-10. This chain is referred to by the

Incoming and Forwarded actions (at the top of the page). The rules in the `RH-Firewall-1-INPUT` chain control the flow of packets through the firewall.

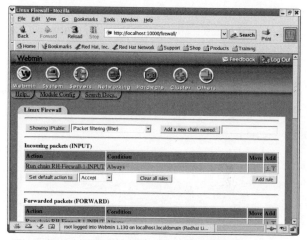

• **Figure 34-9: Webmin displays the firewall rules.**

The Condition column lists the constraints that are placed on incoming packets, and the Action column dictates the actions taken when the conditions are met. When a network packet arrives at your computer, the firewall processes the packet using the rules in the `RH-Firewall-1-INPUT` chain.

Take a peek at the chain shown in Figure 34-10. The first rule states that a packet arriving at interface `lo0` (which is the internal loopback interface that lets your computer talk to itself) should be accepted. As soon as a packet is accepted by the firewall, the rest of the rules are ignored.

If the packet isn't arriving on inteface `lo0`, it's coming from some other interface (like your Ethernet card) and the firewall moves on to the second rule. If the packet is an ICMP message, the firewall accepts it (ICMP is a low-level network management protocol that's reasonably safe). The third and fourth rules accept packets belonging to protocols 50 and 51 (those are "next-generation" IPv6 network packets). The fifth rule states that incoming packets that are part of a previously established connection are okay.

If a packet doesn't satisfy any of the first five conditions, the firewall applies the final rule, which rejects all packets.

The default firewall rules are very secure — they allow just enough traffic to get through that your outbound network connections (like a Web browser) will still work.

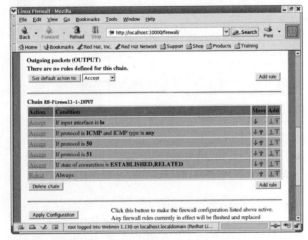

• **Figure 34-10:** The chain of rules.

When a packet enters your network interface, Fedora gives the packet to each rule in the chain, in the sequence listed. Every inbound packet is evaluated according to the Condition listed in the first rule; if the packet satisfies the condition, Fedora takes the action specified in the Action column:

✔ **Do Nothing:** Does nothing with the packet but continues testing with the chain

✔ **Accept:** Accepts the packet into the network, ignoring the remaining rules

✔ **Drop:** Destroys the packet with no relayed message to the other end of the connection

✔ **Reject:** Rejects the packet, but notifies the other end of the connection

✔ **Userspace:** Exports data to a userspace program that's not part of the kernel (you can write your own filters by using Userspace rules)

✔ **Exit Chain:** Exits the chain and returns to previous chain

✔ **Run Chain:** Moves to another chain of rules

If a packet doesn't meet the first condition, it's tested against the next condition. If the packet meets that condition, it is subjected to the specified action or tested against the next rule in line. This testing continues until the packet is either accepted or rejected. By default, the last rule in the chain rejects any packets that are not accepted by earlier rules.

After you understand how the rules are set up in Webmin, you can feel free to change them. The next section explains how.

Changing the rules

Given that the default firewall rules are very secure, you may need to relax them a little to better suit your needs. For example, if you host a Web server on your computer, you may want to allow inbound traffic on TCP port 80 (the port typically used by Web browsers). If you're hosting a Web server for internal use only (that is, you want other computers on your local network to access your server, but nobody else), you can allow inbound traffic on TCP port 80, but only if the packet originates on a nearby address.

Editing existing rules

You can change the actions taken for a condition by following these steps:

1. **Start a Webmin session (see the earlier section, "Starting a Webmin session"), click the Networking button, and then click Linux Firewall.**

2. **On the Linux Firewall page, scroll down to the Action link in the table and click it.**

The Edit Rule window opens, as shown in Figure 34-11. You can change either the condition or action details for a rule from the Edit Rule window.

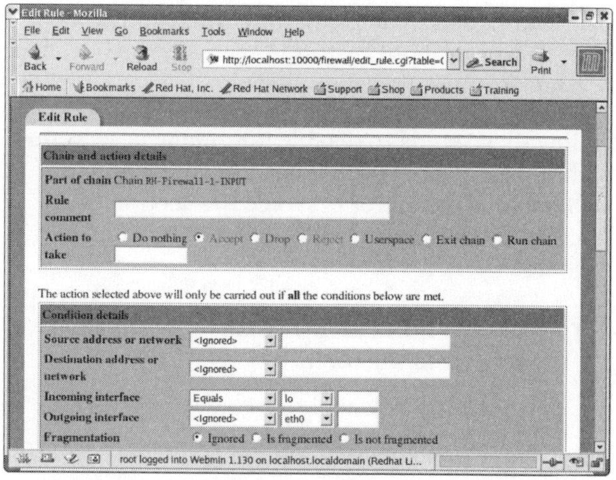

• **Figure 34-11:** The Edit Rule window.

3. To change the action, click the radio button next to the desired action in the Action to Take field.

4. The condition details are a bit more involved, but not hard to change. Under the Condition Details portion of the window, use the drop-down list to enable the filter you want to enforce and then enter the condition parameter in the field to the right of the condition.

For example, to filter packets based on the ICMP network protocol, find the Network Protocol line, change the first list box on that line from Ignored to Equals, and change the second list box to ICMP. (Don't actually do this, it's just an example.)

5. After making any changes to rules in the Edit Rules window, be sure to click the Save button to save the changes.

You go back to the table (refer to Figure 34-10).

6. Click the Apply Configuration button when you return to the chain of rules.

Your new rule is now in effect.

Adding a new rule with Webmin

The rightmost column in the rules table is labeled Add, and it contains a pair of up and down arrows.

To add a new rule *above* an existing rule, click the up arrow. To add a rule *below* it, click the down arrow. Remember, packets travel through the chain from top to bottom, so the order is important.

Use the up and down arrows in the Move column to rearrange the order of the rules within the chain.

You have a really secure firewall in place, but you may need to open up the system for use by others. If you open up a port for a tool like Telnet, you'll be exposing cleartext passwords to anyone who may be spying on your network. Be sure to use secure network programs like SSH — SSH encrypts everything that it sends over your network.

To open up your system for SSH use, follow these steps:

1. Click the down arrow in the Add column of the first rule in the chain of rules table.

The Add Rule window appears, as shown in Figure 34-12.

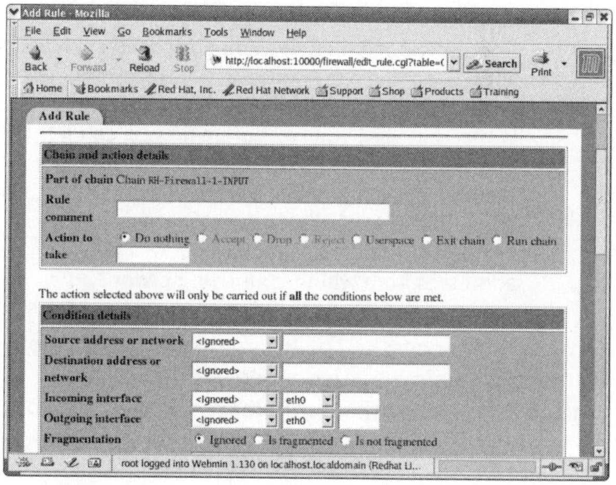

• **Figure 34-12:** The Add Rule window.

2. In the Rule Comment field, enter a comment like this:

```
Accept incoming SSH packets
```

The Rule Comment is there to remind you *why* you created the rule. Be sure to include good comments in your firewall, and you'll save yourself a lot of time later when you need to make another change.

3. Click the Accept radio button.

4. In the Condition Details area, find the Network Protocol line and change the list boxes to Equals and TCP.

5. Find the Destination TCP or UDP Port line and change the list boxes to Equals and 22.

6. Click the Create button at the bottom of the page.

You're returned to the first page where you can see that your new rule has been added to the list.

7. Click Apply Configuration to apply the rule.

You still need to start the sshd daemons, but the firewall will now let an SSH session through. See Technique 33 for useful information about using SSH to share your data without exposing yourself to intruders.

 In some cases, you may want a computer that's already behind a firewall to accept incoming packets only from machines within your network. That way, your corporate firewall can let Internet-originated traffic through, but you can secure *individual* machines more thoroughly. To do this, create a firewall on that machine with a rule that limits inbound packets to addresses from within your own network.

You can limit access to the Internet to protect your system from unfortunate downloads that might bring in viruses or other trouble. You'll save network bandwidth, disk space, and time when you don't have to worry about restoring your system because of someone else's careless download.

Follow these steps to disable Internet access from within your system (you'll have to enable the firewall on your computer first; see the section titled "Finding Your Firewall" at the start of this technique for details):

1. Click the down arrow in the Add column of the first rule in the chain.

The Add Rule window appears.

2. Enter a comment in the Rule Comment field:

```
Close off Internet Access
```

3. Click the Reject radio button.

4. Use the drop-down list boxes to change the Network Protocol condition to Equals and TCP.

5. Change the Source TCP or UDP Port condition to Equals Port 80.

6. Click the Create button at the bottom of the window.

You're returned to the first page where you can see your new rule has been added to the list.

7. Click Apply Configuration to apply the rule.

If you're using a proxy server, you need to disable that port as well. Just add another rule like this one to reject the packets from that port.

Now your system is insulated from incoming packets from the Internet, and disk space and network bandwidth are preserved for in-house use.

Technique

35

Using VNC to Connect to Remote Desktops

Save Time By

✔ Sharing your desktop with VNC

✔ Extending personal invitations to your desktop

✔ Exposing your desktop for others

✔ Using tsclient for remote viewing

✔ Turbo charging cut and paste

✔ Creating desktops on demand with gdm

VNC (an acronym for *virtual network computing*) is a client/server utility that lets you share graphical desktops across a local network or across the Internet. Before VNC server came along, you could use the KDE or GNOME desktop environments only if you were actually sitting in front of the computer. With VNC server, you can create a separate desktop (KDE, GNOME, or whatever environment you prefer) for use from a different computer — located in the next room or in another country.

In this technique, we show you how to set up and use remote viewers and servers. VNC makes it easy. VNC is friendly, intuitive, fast, and free (all in all, some of our favorite software features). You can

✔ Combine the best of different platforms on one monitor.

✔ Share a desktop with another user to get help or collaborate on a project.

✔ Share Linux machines without sharing desktops — each user has his own work environment, complete with privacy. You can even streamline the setup of private remote desktops by creating new VNC desktops on demand.

The time you can save by using other desktops without taking a step is amazing.

Sharing Desktops with VNC

When you run a VNC (virtual network computing) server on your Linux computer, you create a new graphical desktop that you can use from a VNC viewer. Linux is a multi-user operating system: Many users can log into your computer at the same time.

When you run a VNC viewer, you see a remote desktop within a window on your local desktop. If you click the Full Screen option, it feels like you're sitting in front of the VNC server. When you move your mouse, the cursor follows. When you type at the keyboard, the characters are sent to the remote desktop. Open Konqueror on the remote desktop and you can drag files around your remote desktop.

VNC is portable:

✔ You can run the VNC *server* on a Linux computer, a Windows computer, a Macintosh, or on a number of different UNIX distributions.

✔ You can run the VNC *viewer* on a Linux computer, a Windows computer, a variety of UNIX workstations, a Macintosh, or even within a Web browser.

You can run a VNC server on one platform and the VNC viewer on a different platform. For example, if you have a nice big screen on a Windows computer, run a VNC viewer on Windows connected to your Linux VNC server. You may like to keep your e-mail on a Windows-based computer, while using your favorite graphics program on a Mac, but use your Linux desktop for everything else.

With just a few mouse clicks, you can have a window open for each desktop, with each desktop running the programs you like to use on that system. For example, in Figure 35-1, you can see three desktops: in the background you see our workstation (Fedora Core running KDE), in the upper-left you see a Windows desktop, and in the foreground is a remote session waiting for us to log into another Fedora host.

Because each remote desktop appears within its own window on your local desktop, you can work with multiple desktops at the same time.

 Desktop sharing makes it easy to get a second opinion about a problem on your desktop — just let your most technically adept friend log in and help.

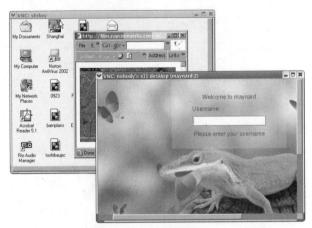

• **Figure 35-1: Multiple remote desktops.**

Inviting Your Friends to Use Your Desktop

If you've installed the KDE Networking package, you can share your desktop with another user (if you *haven't* installed the kdenetwork package, flip back to Technique 17 for a quick refresher). Sharing your desktop is a great way to get help from another user, or to collaborate on a project. When you share your desktop, the other user connects to your desktop using a VNC viewer (such as vncviewer or rdesktop).

To invite another user to share your desktop, follow these steps:

1. **Open the KDE menu.**

2. **If you're running Fedora Linux, choose System Tools⇨More System Tools⇨Desktop Sharing.**

If you're running SuSE Linux, choose System⇨ Remote Access⇨Desktop Sharing.

Mandrake users choose Internet⇨Remote Access⇨Desktop Sharing.

The KDE Desktop Sharing window appears.

3. **Click Create Personal Invitation.**

The Personal Invitation window appears, showing the display information and password that the other user will need to view your desktop.

When you create an invitation, other users have one hour to connect to your desktop using the password displayed on your computer.

4. **Share this information with the other user. You can phone your friend and read him the Host information and Password, or e-mail the information to him.**

When another user connects to your desktop, a window will appear asking if you want to accept the connection. (The window includes the name of the other computer so you can see who's trying to connect.)

5. **If you check the Allow Remote User to Control Keyboard and Mouse box, your friend will be able to take control of your computer from *his* desktop.**

6. **Click Accept Connection.**

The other user will see the contents of your desktop and be able to take control, if you chose to do that.

Serving Up a New Desktop with VNC Server

The KDE Desktop Sharing tool is perfect when you want to let another user see your desktop, but VNC can do much more than that.

When you run a VNC server on your Linux computer, VNC creates a new desktop that you can see only with a VNC viewer. The difference between KDE Desktop Sharing and a VNC server is that, with KDE Desktop Sharing, two or more users are looking at the same desktop at the same time. The VNC server creates a private desktop for the viewer.

 If you need to download VNC server, get the RPM version from `www.realvnc.com`. Check out Technique 17 for information about installing RPM packages.

The first time you run the VNC server, VNC creates a new directory named `~/.vnc`. VNC also creates an `xstartup` file in `~/.vnc`. By default, the VNC server assumes that you want to run the `twm` window manager instead of KDE or GNOME. `twm` is a really old, nasty window manager, which is as powerful and friendly as a thermonuclear fly swatter.

To start your normal desktop environment (KDE or GNOME) in the new VNC desktop instead of `twm`:

```
$ mkdir ~/.vnc
$ cp .Xclients ~/.vnc/xstartup
```

Now open a terminal window, and enter the command:

```
$ vncserver -depth 24
```

 The first time you run `vncserver`, you're prompted to create a password. Remember that password because you'll need it to connect to the new desktop.

`vncserver` displays your new desktop address:

```
New 'kobe:1 (freddie)' desktop is kobe:1
```

That's all there is to it. Your local machine is now ready to serve VNC viewers.

 If you're setting up a Windows host, visit `www.realvnc.com` and download the executables. Using the Setup Wizard, Windows installation is simple and fast, and Windows takes good care of you — right down to putting the icons on the desktop.

 VNC Server and Viewer are out there for OSX, but the Web sites are a bit nomadic in nature right now. Just use your search engine, and you'll find good workable renditions so you can share desktops with your Mac.

We explain a quicker way to create VNC desktops in "Creating New VNC Desktops on Demand" later in this technique. Now you're ready to connect to your server with a VNC viewer.

Using tsclient to View Remote Desktops from Linux

VNC isn't the only desktop sharing protocol that you'll run into (but it's the most portable). If you have access to a Windows Terminal Server (or Windows XP), you can use the RDP (remote desktop protocol) to connect to your Windows desktop. Citrix users can connect to Citrix servers with wfica. You can run VNC server on any Windows computer, but RDP runs much faster if you can use it.

tsclient is a user-friendly interface that can make connections with VNC, RDP, and Citrix ICA desktops. As if that isn't enough, it's included with Fedora and simple to install. You can be connected to a host in minutes with tsclient.

We recommend the tsclient package for all your remote desktop viewing needs. Its graphical interface makes it quick and easy to connect to any remote desktop using the protocols that you've installed. If you've installed the vncviewer RPM package, tsclient gives you a friendly interface to remote VNC desktops. Install rdesktop, and tsclient lets you connect to Windows Terminal Server desktops. tsclient will even build Citrix connections for you if you've installed the Citrix client software on your computer.

Go ahead and install the tsclient and VNC RPM packages (see Technique 17 if you need help with the RPM installer). Install the rdesktop package if you are going to connect to any of the following Windows platforms:

- ✔ Windows NT Terminal Server
- ✔ Windows 2000 Terminal Server

- ✔ Windows XP Professional
- ✔ Windows Server 2003

To run tsclient:

1. **Open the Main Menu.**

2. **Click Run Command (or Run Application if you're a GNOME user).**

The Run Command dialog appears.

3. **Type** tsclient **and click Run.**

When tsclient starts, you see a window like that shown in Figure 35-2.

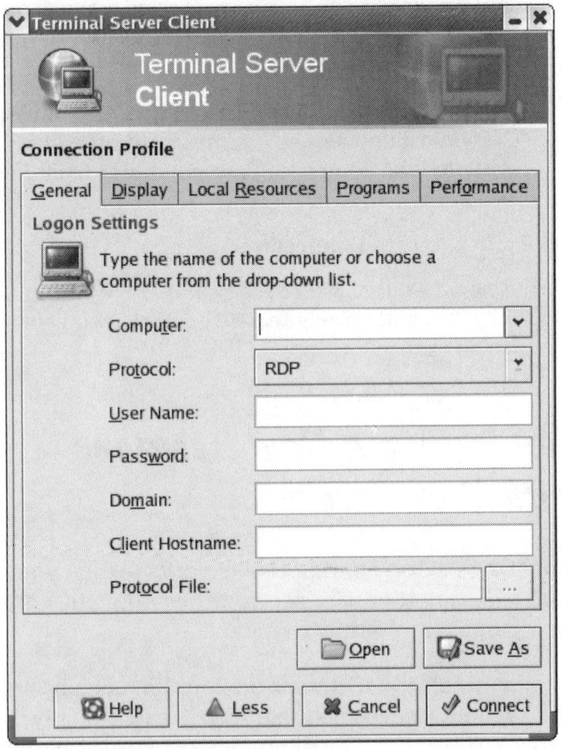

• **Figure 35-2: The tsclient window.**

If you're connecting to a VNC server, read the next section. If you're connecting to an RDP server (a Windows Terminal server, Windows XP, or Citrix server), skip ahead to the section titled "Using tsclient with an RDP server."

Using tsclient with a VNC server

To connect to a VNC desktop:

1. Run `tsclient` **following the steps earlier in this section.**

2. **Choose VNC from the Protocol list box, and type the remote computer name (or IP address) into the Computer field.**

If you are connecting to a Linux- or UNIX-hosted desktop, you may need to include the display number along with the computer name. For example, to connect to desktop 3 on host bastille, you would enter `bastille:3`. If you don't include a desktop number, `tsclient` assumes that you want to connect to desktop 0.

3. **Click More to see all the** `tsclient` **controls and then click the Display tab to choose the initial size for your viewer window and the color depth.**

4. **If you have a fast connection to the server, choose a color depth of 24 bits. If you have a slow dial-up connection, choose a lower color depth.**

 Turn off busy screen savers if you're using VNC viewer, and VNC will run a lot faster. Any little animated graphic can bog down screen repaints when all the bits are getting sent across a network.

The other tabs (Local Resources, Program, and Performance) are not used for VNC connections.

5. **Click Save As to save your connection profile.**

The next time you want to connect to the same desktop, just click Open and choose the connection profile that you've just created.

Make good use of VNC to do customer support by opening a window to your customer's desktop. Diagnosing problems and making fixes over a local network or across the Internet saves travel time, and it leaves you with access to books and tools that you might need.

Using tsclient with an RDP server

After you run `tsclient`, as explained earlier in this section, you're ready to set up `tsclient` so that you can view the remote desktop. Before you can connect to a Windows RDP desktop, you need to be sure your Windows host is ready. Follow the steps for whichever Windows version you're using:

✔ **If the host is running Windows XP Professional:**

1. Open My Computer and double-click Properties.

2. Choose the Remote tab.

3. Check the Allow Users to Connect Remotely box.

✔ **If the host is running a Windows Server Edition:**

1. Choose Start⇨Settings⇨Control Panel⇨ Services.

2. Right-click Terminal Services and click Start.

To connect to an RDP desktop (one of the Windows flavors we mentioned earlier):

1. **Choose RDP (or RDPv5) from the Protocol list-box and type in the name of the computer that you want to connect to.**

When you use the RDP protocol, you have a few more options. (Don't forget to click More to see the full set of `tsclient` controls.)

2. **On the General tab, you can supply a User Name and Password, as well as a Domain name.**

3. **Click the Local Resources tab to redirect sound from the remote desktop to your local computer.**

4. **On the Programs tab you can specify a startup program and directory for the remote desktop.**

If you don't specify a startup program, the remote desktop runs the Explorer shell.

5. Click the Performance tab to optimize the connection. We recommend that you check Enable Bitmap Caching and Do Not Send Motion Events.

 If you see any Windows programs behaving erratically, uncheck Do Not Send Motion Events the next time you connect.

6. Click Save As to create a new profile or Connect to connect to the remote desktop.

 If you're using a remote Windows desktop, anyone who is in the room with the remote computer can see what you're doing — all your mouse movements, typing, and windows are right there for the world to see. Be aware that you might be sharing your e-mail (or embarrassing browsing habits) with someone else when you share desktops!

Making Cut and Paste Commands Work on a Remote Desktop

VNC tries very hard to share clipboard content (cut and paste) between the VNC viewer and the VNC server. You can cut (or copy) from one desktop and paste in the other. VNC tries, but without a little help from a program called autocutsel, the clipboard is pretty unreliable. autocutsel synchronizes the viewer and server clipboards to give you better success and save time in the long run. To install autocutsel:

1. To download the tarball, go to http://lepton.fr/tools/autocutsel, click the download link, and save the tarball to your Desktop directory.

2. Open a terminal window and cd to the directory that contains the downloaded tarball (~/Desktop).

 The complete pathname is visible in the bottom bar of the Download Manager dialog.

3. Extract the tarball with the command:

```
tar -xzvf autocutsel-0.6.2.tar.gz
```

This extracts the contents of the tarball to a new directory called autocutsel-0.6.2.

4. cd to the new directory and type the following command and press Enter:

```
./configure
```

autocutsel clicks and whirs and checks for things it needs.

5. Type make and press Enter.

6. Give yourself superuser privileges with the su command.

7. Type make install and press Enter.

8. Type exit to relinquish your superuser privileges.

Now, to run autocutsel, type autocutsel& at the command line and press Enter.

 See Technique 8 to find out how to add autocutsel to your Startup folder so it starts automatically each time you log in.

autocutsel runs quietly in the background; you won't see any evidence that it's running (except that your clipboard starts working reliably).

 Even without autocutsel, the clipboard (cut and paste) works sometimes. The clipboard isn't too dependable, but it's definitely a time-saver if it works with your programs. If you don't want to take the time to download and install autocutsel, cutting and pasting is still worth a try, but don't waste too much time on this one — it either works or it doesn't.

Creating New VNC Desktops on Demand

In the "Serving Up a New Desktop with VNC Server" section, earlier in this technique, we show you how to manually set up a VNC server. That works well for a quick-and-dirty solution, but to really save time, you can configure the GNOME Display Manager (gdm) to create new desktops on demand. Fedora Linux uses gdm to manage graphical desktops even if you're running KDE. SuSE and Mandrake Linux assume that you want to use the KDE display manager. The technique we describe here works only if you're using the GNOME display manager, so we also show you how to switch from the KDE display manager to gdm. When you hook up gdm and the VNC server, a new desktop is created each time you log in with a VNC viewer. Now that's a timesaver!

> One really great thing about the gdm/VNC combination — lots of users can log in to the same machine and each one gets his own individual desktop. This is a great way to make Linux converts out of your stalwart Windows users.

Switching display managers in SuSE Linux

To switch your SuSE Linux system from kdm (KDE display manager) to gdm (GNOME display manager), follow this procedure:

1. Open the main menu and choose System⇨YaST.

2. If prompted, enter the superuser password and click OK.

3. When the YaST control center appears, choose System, and then choose Editor for /etc/sysconfig Files.

4. When the System Configuration Editor appears, open the Desktop section of the tree control (in the left-hand pane).

5. Open the Display manager section of the tree control and click DISPLAYMANAGER.

Your System Configuration Editor window should look like Figure 35-3.

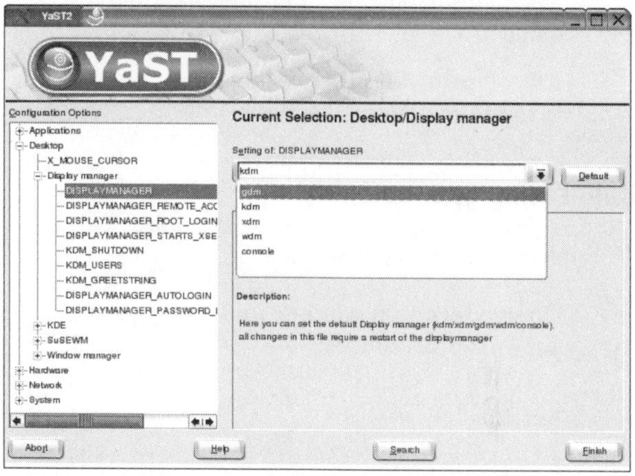

• **Figure 35-3: The System Configuration Editor.**

6. Open the drop-down list labeled Setting of: DISPLAYMANAGER and choose gdm.

7. Click Finish to close the System Configuration Editor, and then close YaST.

8. Reboot your computer.

   When your computer reboots, it runs the GNOME display manager.

Switching display managers in Mandrake Linux

The Mandrake Control Center makes it very easy to switch display managers — just follow these steps:

1. Open the main menu and choose System⇨ Configuration⇨Configure your computer.

2. If prompted, enter the superuser password and click OK.

3. When the Mandrake Control Center appears, click System, and then click Display Manager.

4. Click GDM (GNOME Display Manager), and then click OK.

   At this point, the Display Manager editor asks if you want to restart the dm (display manager) service. Before you click Yes, be sure to close any other applications that you have open on your desktop: When you click Yes, your graphical environment will shutdown and then restart using gdm.

5. After closing all other applications, click Yes to restart the display manager.

Connecting gdm and VNC

To connect gdm and VNC:

1. Open a terminal window and give yourself superuser privileges:

```
$ su
Password:
#
```

2. Start your favorite editor and enter the text shown in Listing 35-1.

You can adjust the "-geometry 1024x768" part if you want a larger or smaller desktop.

3. Save your work in a file named /etc/xinetd.d/vncserver.

4. Open /etc/services and add the following line to the end of the file:

```
vnc 5900/tcp # VNC Server screen :0
```

That defines a TCP protocol named vnc (on port 5900). Whenever xinetd detects a connection attempt on port 5900, it consults /etc/xinetd.d/vncserver to figure out which program to run.

5. Save your work and close the editor.

6. Run the gdm configuration program.

```
# gdmsetup
```

This opens the Login Screen Setup dialog, shown in Figure 35-4.

7. Choose the XDMCP tab, check Enable XDMCP, and then click Close.

8. At the command line, tickle the gdm daemon to make it re-read its configuration file:

```
kill -SIGHUP $(cat /var/run/gdm.pid)
```

• **Figure 35-4: The Login Screen Setup dialog.**

9. Finally, tell xinetd to re-read its configuration files:

```
kill -SIGHUP $(cat /var/run/xinetd.pid)
```

Now you're ready to create new desktops when you need them. When another user wants to connect to your computer (or if you want a new desktop because you're sitting at a different workstation), just log in with a VNC viewer. gdm and VNC will be listening for connections to display 0 (if your computer's name is brussels, you want to connect to brussels:0). When a connection request comes in, VNC creates a new desktop, and you're ready to log in.

LISTING 35-1: /etc/xinetd.d/vncserver

```
service vnc
{
    disable         = no
    socket_type     = stream
    protocol        = tcp
    wait            = no
    user            = nobody
    server          = /usr/bin/Xvnc
    server_args     = -inetd -query
    localhost -once securitytypes=none
    -geometry 1024x768 -depth 24
    log_on_failure  += USERID
}
```

36 Technique

Streamlining Your Network Surveillance

Save Time By

- Checking out file usage with lsof
- Looking for open servers with lsof and grep
- Using the Ethereal Network Analyzer to follow network traffic
- Adding color to Ethereal reports for easy reading

Watching what your users are up to can tell you a lot about the requirements of your network. It can also alert you to practices that are going on that shouldn't be. This technique is all about watching file and network traffic to find out what your users are doing.

You use the lsof command to get a list of all the open files on your system as well as useful information about each file — the file owner, the process that's using it, and more. You can also use the lsof command to find a list of all the files currently in use by a single user — a quick way to see what someone's up to.

When you combine the lsof command with grep, you can query your computer for a list of network services. It's easy to find out what's out there listening for processes — ssh, vnc, webmin, and so on. You can also use the combination of commands to generate a complete list of connections and servers to get a clear picture of the activity on your network.

The Ethereal Network Analyzer tool is included with most standard distributions, and it gives you a cozy place to watch network traffic. You can even colorize and filter network traffic to discover details about the specific information types you're watching for. If too much surfing is going on and clogging network resources, Ethereal helps you to find this out. This tool also tells you who's doing it.

This technique is about being a snoop. Snooping can be a bad thing, or a good thing. Snooping to get people in trouble isn't nice, but snooping for a good cause can be useful. Use this technique wisely, and you can watch for bad guys in your system and network slowdowns that can be averted with a quiet word to a coworker.

Exploring Your Network with lsof

lsof is one of the most powerful tools in the Linux toolbox. lsof displays a list of all the files currently open on your computer. Browsing through the output from lsof gives you a clear picture of who's logged in, what they're running, and what resources they're using. You can also see which background daemons are running and what resources they're using.

Running lsof

To use `lsof`, open a terminal window and give yourself superuser privileges with the `su-` command. Enter the command `lsof` and press Enter.

> You can run `lsof` without giving yourself superuser privileges. However, you can only view processes that you own, and you probably have to use the complete pathname when you invoke `lsof` (`/usr/sbin/lsof`).

> Stretch your terminal window as wide as possible before running `lsof`. Line-wrapping in a narrow window makes the list hard to read.

> If it's not already installed on your system, you can add the `lsof.version.rpm` package from your distribution media. See Technique 17 for helpful hints about installing RPM packages.

The results from the `lsof` command appear, as shown in Figure 36-1.

```
kdeinit   12288  susan  mem    REG    3,2   193584   650566 /usr/lib/libDCOP.so.4.1.0
kdeinit   12288  susan  mem    REG    3,2   104224   651832 /usr/lib/libkdesu.so.4.1.0
kdeinit   12288  susan  mem    REG    3,2  1603424   654558 /usr/lib/libkdecore.so.4.1.0
kdeinit   12288  susan  mem    REG    3,2    14116    52538 /lib/libutil-2.3.2.so
kdeinit   12288  susan  mem    REG    3,2   107716    52535 /lib/ld-2.3.2.so
kdeinit   12288  susan  mem    REG    3,2  1579056   182686 /lib/tls/libc-2.3.2.so
kdeinit   12288  susan  mem    REG    3,2   213212   182687 /lib/tls/libm-2.3.2.so
kdeinit   12288  susan  mem    REG    3,2    16312    52536 /lib/libdl-2.3.2.so
kdeinit   12288  susan  mem    REG    3,2    54520   605277 /usr/X11R6/lib/libXext.so.6.4
kdeinit   12288  susan  mem    REG    3,2    65928   652569 /usr/lib/libz.so.1.2.0.7
kdeinit   12288  susan  mem    REG    3,2    83160   605279 /usr/X11R6/lib/libICE.so.6.3
kdeinit   12288  susan  mem    REG    3,2    32576   605280 /usr/X11R6/lib/libSM.so.6.0
kdeinit   12288  susan  mem    REG    3,2   100040   182688 /lib/tls/libpthread-0.60.so
kdeinit   12288  susan  mem    REG    3,2    90836   603521 /usr/X11R6/lib/libXmu.so.6.2
kdeinit   12288  susan  mem    REG    3,2    53288   181429 /usr/lib/kde3/kio_file.so
kdeinit   12288  susan  mem    REG    3,2    78048    52990 /lib/libresolv-2.3.2.so
kdeinit   12288  susan  mem    REG    3,2  6866224   475502 /usr/lib/qt-3.1/lib/libqt-mt.
so.3.1.2
kdeinit   12288  susan  mem    REG    3,2  2482944   654557 /usr/lib/libkdeui.so.4.1.0
kdeinit   12288  susan  mem    REG    3,2  2791112   654559 /usr/lib/libkio.so.4.1.0
kdeinit   12288  susan  0r     CHR    1,3            67247 /dev/null
kdeinit   12288  susan  1w     FIFO   0,5          6562380 pipe
kdeinit   12288  susan  2w     FIFO   0,5          6562380 pipe
kdeinit   12288  susan  3u     unix 0xc2ccc880     6784967 socket
kdeinit   12288  susan  4r     FIFO   0,5          6779450 pipe
kdeinit   12288  susan  5w     FIFO   0,5          6779450 pipe
```

• **Figure 36-1:** The list of open files.

Interpreting the lsof output

The output from `lsof` contains a wealth of information. Each line represents a file that's currently in use. The columns, from left to right, display the following information:

- Name of the program that's using the file
- Process ID
- User name
- File descriptor or usage type
- File type
- Device where the file is located
- File size
- Inode number
- Complete pathname of the file

The column labeled `FD` displays either a file descriptor number or a usage type.

If you see a number (followed by a letter or two), that's a file descriptor number. The number isn't very useful except in three cases:

- File descriptor number 0 is connected to the standard input stream for the process.
- File descriptor number 1 is connected to the standard output stream.
- File descriptor number 2 is where the program sends error messages.

File descriptors 0, 1, and 2 are usually connected to a terminal device (`/dev/ttynn` or `/dev/ptynn`) for interactive processes. If you see one of those descriptors connected to a file, you know that that stream has been redirected with a > or a <. If a descriptor is connected to a pipe, it's connected to the standard input stream (or standard output stream) of another process with a pipe character |. If an output descriptor (descriptor 1 or 2) is connected to `/dev/null`, output sent to that stream is thrown away. If descriptor 0 is connected to `/dev/null`, that process is reading from an empty file.

The letters following the file descriptor number tell you how the process is using the file:

- r means that the file is opened for read-only access.

- w means that the file is opened for write-only access.

- u means that the file is opened for read and write access.

You may see other letters following the file descriptor number — see the man lsof page for full details.

If you don't see a number in the FD column, lsof is showing you the usage type for that file:

- cwd: This file (actually a directory) is the current working directory for the process.

- rtd: This directory is the root directory for the process. (It's almost always /, except when the process is running in a chroot jail.)

- mem: This is a memory-mapped file (usually a shared object library).

- txt: This is the full pathname of the program.

Again, you may see other usage types, and man lsof will give you a complete list.

Reading file types

The file type column (fifth from the left, labeled TYPE) tells you what kind of file you're looking at. Linux is known for treating just about anything as if it were a file, so you'll see a variety of file types. A typical lsof report shows the following file types:

- REG: A plain old disk file

- DIR: A directory

- FIFO: A named pipe (a connection between two or more processes)

- CHR: A character-type device (such as a serial port or terminal)

- BLK: A block-type device (such as a raw disk drive or CD)

- unix: A UNIX-domain socket (an interprocess communication link)

- IPv4: An IPv4 network connection

- IPv6: An IPv6 network connection

Discovering Network Connections

When you're viewing network information with lsof, the last two file types in the preceding list — IPv4 and IPv6 — are the ones that you're interested in. IPv4 and IPv6 files are active network connections or network service providers (v4 and v6 refer to the network address type).

When lsof finds a network connection, rather than show you a filename, it displays the IP address of the network interface on your computer, the local port number, the IP address of the remote side of the connection, and the connection state.

Here's an example:

```
bastille:38517->louvre (ESTABLISHED)
```

bastille is the name of the local network interface, 38517 is the TCP port assigned to this session, louvre is the name of the computer at the other end of the connection, and (ESTABLISHED) tells you that the network link is up and running.

 The local interface name is useful when you have more than one network card in your computer.

Connections listed as (ESTABLISHED) show you active network connections (such as an ssh session or a Web browser connection). If you see a connection listed as (LISTEN), you're looking at a network server. For example, if you see

```
*.ssh (LISTEN)
```

you're viewing the sshd server. (In this case, the left-most column should tell you that the sshd program is servicing this network port.)

In addition to simply looking for network connections, you can do some other handy things to check out those connections:

✔ **List all listening servers:** You can combine the lsof command with grep to discover the network servers running on your system. The command

```
# lsof | grep LISTEN
```

generates a list of services that are listening on your system — Web servers, ssh daemons, VNC servers, and so on (see Figure 36-2).

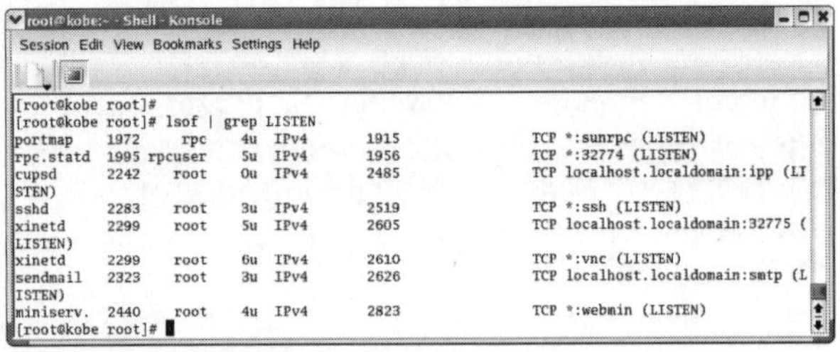

• **Figure 36-2: The list of open services.**

If you find that lsof is running very slowly, add -n to the command line. The -n flag tells lsof to turn off host name resolution. You'll see IP addresses rather than host names, but you'll see them much more quickly.

✔ **Add components next to port names:** If you see a server that displays a port number rather than a service name, you can save yourself time by adding a new entry to the /etc/services file:

1. Track down the program that's serving up the anonymous port.

2. Open /etc/services with kate (or your favorite editor):

```
# kate /etc/services
```

3. Add a line at the end of the file with the service name, port number/protocol, and a comment out to the right, as shown in Figure 36-3.

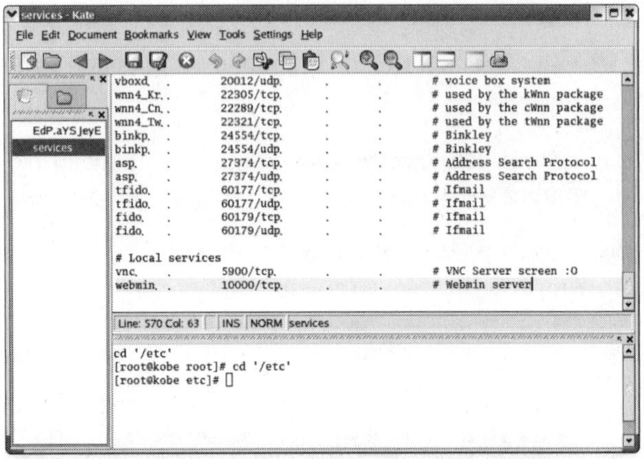

• **Figure 36-3: Adding a friendlier server description.**

4. Save the file and then exit.

The next time you check for open services, you'll see the more recognizable name rather than the port number.

✔ **List all servers and active connections:** If you want to see a list of all the servers *and* active connections on your computer, enter the following command:

```
# lsof -i
```

This command shows you not only the ports that are open and waiting for a connection, but also the ports that are in use.

Other Timesaving lsof Tricks

lsof is a good tool for looking at the network connections on your computer, but it has a few more tricks up its sleeve.

First off, you can limit the files displayed by lsof in a number of ways:

▶ -c *command*: Displays files that are opened by any occurrence of the given *command*. (You can specify a partial *command* name here; for example, -c xm displays files opened by commands whose names start with *xm*.)

▶ -u *username*: Displays files opened by user *username*.

▶ -i TCP@*host*: Displays TCP connections to *host*.

▶ -p *processID*: Displays files opened by the given process.

If you've ever tried to umount a CD that's being used by another user, you know that Linux won't let you. The other user might not even be using the CD; if that user has a terminal window open to the directory, you can't eject the CD until he or she is done. To find out who's hogging the drive, use the following command:

```
# lsof | grep /mnt/cdrom
```

The result set shows you the device user. Hopefully, this user can surrender the drive so others can use it.

Packet Sniffing with the Ethereal Network Analyzer

Normally, your machine doesn't read the network packets that aren't intended for it. The Ethereal Network Analyzer is a *packet sniffer* that watches all the packets that go across your network and lets you open and read the packets you choose.

Starting Ethereal

To open the Ethereal Network Analyzer, follow these steps:

1. **If you're running Fedora Linux, open the Main Menu and choose Internet⇨More Internet Applications⇨Ethereal.**

If you're using SuSE, open the Main Menu and choose Internet⇨Administration.

If you're using Mandrake, open the Main Menu and choose System⇨Monitoring⇨Ethereal.

2. **Enter your password when prompted.**

Ethereal opens, as shown in Figure 36-4.

• **Figure 36-4: The Ethereal main window.**

 The Ethereal Network Analyzer is included with most Linux distributions. If it's not on your menu, it should be on the disc. Just install the RPMs with the following commands:

```
# rpm -Uhv ethereal-version.rpm
# rpm -Uhv ethereal-gnome-version.rpm
```

Capturing packets

To start capturing network packets in Ethereal, follow these steps:

1. **Choose Capture⇨Start.**

The Capture Options setup dialog opens, as shown in Figure 36-5.

2. **In the Interface list box, choose the network interface that you want to watch.**

Typically, you choose eth0.

3. **Check the Update List of Packets in Real Time and Automatic Scrolling in Live Capture boxes.**

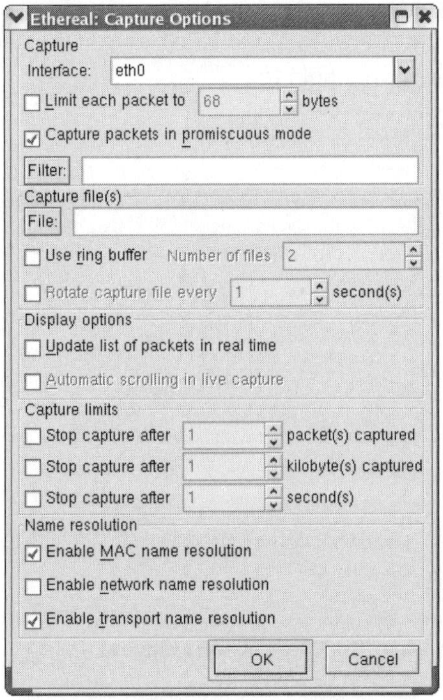

• **Figure 36-5: The Capture Options setup dialog.**

As a rule, checking the Enable Network Name Resolution box really slows things down.

4. **Click OK.**

Ethereal starts sniffing (see Figure 36-6). If you look closely at the Source and Destination columns, you'll see that packets are flowing back and forth between machines.

Use the Start and Stop options in the Capture menu to sample short segments of network usage for a quick scan. Unless you tell Ethereal to save the captured packets, it doesn't create a log file, but the working file can get big fast. If your system has plenty of power, it won't hurt to leave the capture session running, but if you're running on a slow machine, sampling is a good idea.

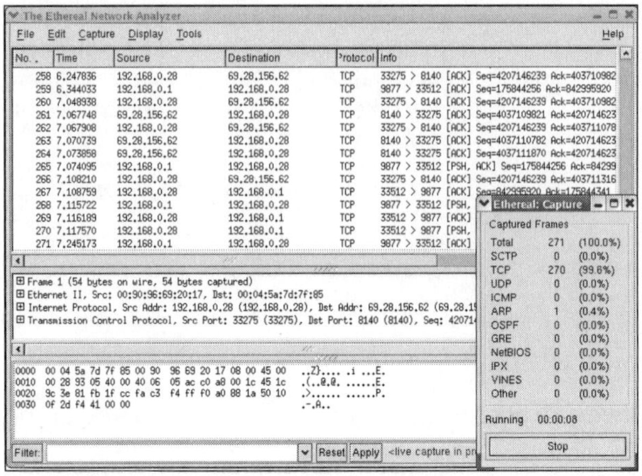

• **Figure 36-6: Ethereal capturing network packets.**

Applying filters to screen packets

To make the traffic easier to follow, apply filters to select only the packets you're interested in. Ethereal filters screen packets by protocol type. You can choose from hundreds of protocols, but many are so obscure that you'll never encounter them.

You can set up an HTTP filter to monitor the Internet traffic between your system and the Web. If excessive surfing is slowing down the network, you can screen all the network packets for the HTTP protocol and find the prime offenders.

To add and apply a filter, follow these steps:

1. **Choose Edit➪Display Filters.**

The Edit Display Filter List dialog opens, as shown in Figure 36-7.

2. **Type** HTTP Packets **in the Filter Name field and type** http **in the Filter String field, and then click New.**

3. **Click Save and then click Close.**

You've created a new filter named HTTP Packets.

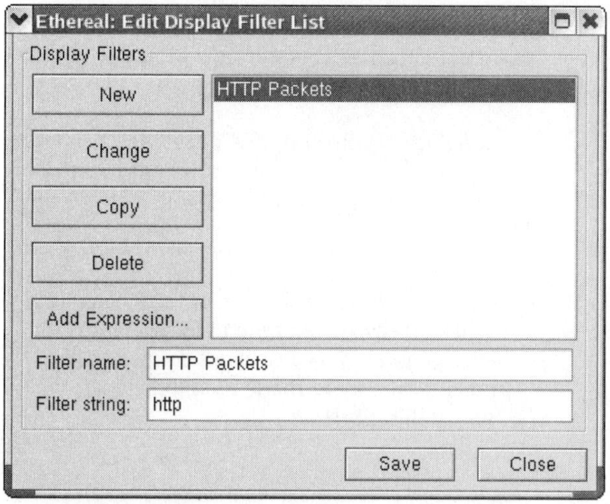

Ethereal: Edit Display Filter List

Display Filters

New

Change

Copy

Delete

Add Expression...

HTTP Packets

Filter name: HTTP Packets

Filter string: http

Save   Close

• **Figure 36-7:** Adding a display filter.

4. To apply the filter, click the Filter button in the lower-left corner of Ethereal's main window.

5. In the Display Filter dialog that appears, highlight the filter name and click OK.

After a short delay, the packet list shows only HTTP packets.

Peeking in packets

When you've found a series of packets that might be interesting, you can take a peek inside. Highlight a packet and choose Tools⊏>Follow TCP Stream. A window opens, displaying the contents of the TCP stream. The dialog displays the chatter between the machines, with each machine responding in a different color.

 Packet data is not meant to be readable by humans. Some protocols contain recognizable text (such as the HTML code that a Web browser uses), but other protocols (like SSH) are encrypted.

Network chatter is sent in a series of wrappers. The outermost layer contains hardware information, and the inner layers hold the meat of the message. The outermost layers are the least human-friendly, and the inner layer is occasionally understandable.

In the middle pane of the Ethereal window, you see a display of the wrappers that make up the packet (refer to Figure 36-6). The wrappers that are higher in the tree control are the machine-friendly wrappers. The lower wrappers are human-friendly.

Expand the lower branches in the tree control to see an interpretation of the packet that's highlighted in the top panel. The bottom window displays the corresponding raw data in the packet.

Color-coding packets coming from your network

The packet listing is much easier to read if you colorize the packets coming from the computers on your network. Follow these steps to add color to the display:

1. Choose Display⊏>Colorize Display.

The Apply Color Filters dialog opens.

2. Click New.

The Edit Color Filter dialog opens.

3. Enter a name in the Name field.

4. In the String field, enter the IP address you want to colorize by using the following form (see Figure 36-8):

```
ip.src == 192.168.0.218
```

5. Click the Foreground Color button and use the color selector to choose the font color. Then click OK.

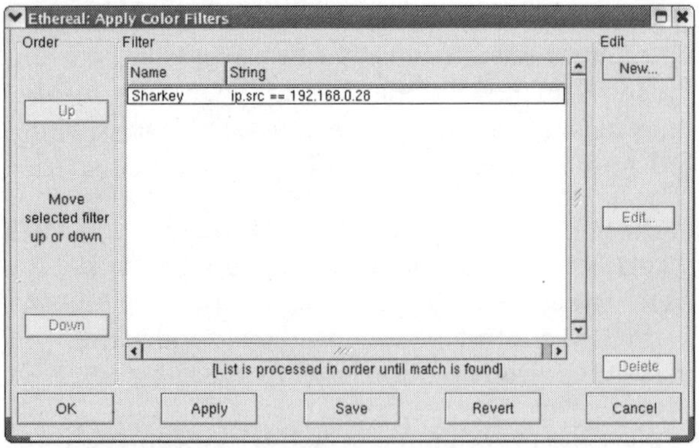

Ethereal: Apply Color Filters

Name	String
Sharkey	ip.src == 192.168.0.28

Order
Up

Move
selected filter
up or down

Down

[List is processed in order until match is found]

Edit
New...

Edit...

Delete

OK   Apply   Save   Revert   Cancel

• **Figure 36-8:** The completed Apply Color Filters dialog.

If you really want conversations to stand out at a glance, choose a background color as well. That can get a bit garish, but it's worth experimenting with.

6. Click OK to close the Color Filter dialog.

7. Click Save and then OK in the Apply Color Filters dialog.

A dialog opens, charting the progress as the filter runs, and in a snap, the display is colorized. The new colors make it easy to tell who's chattering on your network.

Colorize each machine on your local network to make it easy to spot the traffic that's not being generated by a network computer. It's also an easy way to monitor an individual user's traffic.

Technique 37

Evaluating Your Network Security with Nessus

Save Time By

- Using Nessus to evaluate your network security
- Closing any security vulnerabilities you find before a hacker can exploit them

It doesn't matter if you're the administrator of a big network or a small one, a hacker running loose on your system can cause mega-damage (and time loss) in a matter of minutes. Running a tight ship is important. When you set up your network, you're likely to have taken quite a few measures to ensure your network's security, but how do you know you haven't missed something?

A top-notch open-source project called Nessus provides a security scanner that can check your (hopefully) tight ship for leaks — security vulnerabilities that hackers could exploit if they had the chance. If your system freely gives up information about open ports (or more specifically, the services running behind them), hackers can exploit that information easier than they could if they had to make guesses about your system.

Nessus can do a lot more than detect open ports. Here are some other timesaving features Nessus has to offer:

- If the security tests you need aren't included in the distribution, you can write your own customized plug-ins to get the job done.

- Nessus has a friendly graphical user interface with easy-to-read reports, or you can run it from the command line.

- The Nessus project stays up-to-date with recent security issues and provides easy automatic updates of the security test scripts.

- Nessus also supports SSL services, making sure your network is secure while it works on your ports.

- The Nessus plug-ins search for backdoors, denial-of-service vulnerabilities, sturdy firewalls, remote shell accesses, peer-to-peer filesharing, useless services, and tons of other security risks. The database currently has over 2,000 plug-ins.

- Nessus can handle big or small networks with ease, with tailored testing that won't waste a lot of time.

In this technique, we show you how to use Nessus to evaluate your network security. It's a great tool that's easy to use, and the time you save by finding security loopholes before the hackers do will definitely justify the time spent investigating your network security.

Getting Up and Running with Nessus

Setting up Nessus is a matter of a few simple steps. Before you can use Nessus, you need to do the following:

1. **Satisfy its dependencies by installing the other programs that Nessus needs to run.**

2. **Compile and install the Nessus files.**

3. **Create a user identity.**

4. **Create an SSL certificate to ensure that the Nessus transactions are all handled securely on your system.**

Follow along, and you'll be up and running in no time!

Installing programs Nessus needs to run

Nessus has a couple of prerequisites — you need to have GTK (the Gimp Toolkit) installed on your system, as well as the `sharutils` RPM package. If you've installed the GNOME desktop environment, GTK is included. If not, you need to install it.

You can install GTK from your distribution media:

1. **Open a terminal window and gain superuser privileges with the `su` command. Then move to the directory containing the RPM packages.**

2. **Type the following command and press Enter:**

   `# rpm -Uhv gtk2-version.rpm`

   The RPM for GTK installs.

You also need the `sharutils` package, which is included with most Linux distributions.

3. **To install `sharutils`, type the following command and press Enter:**

   `# rpm -Uhv sharutils-version.i386`

   After `sharutils` installs, you've satisfied the dependencies for the Nessus program.

 Using Synaptic to download a Nessus RPM package and install the dependencies is a definite timesaver. Check out Technique 19 for information about Synaptic.

Installing Nessus

Now that the program dependencies have been met, you're ready to download and install Nessus. To download the latest version of Nessus for your system, follow these steps:

1. **Open a Web browser and surf to**

   `www.nessus.org/download.html`

2. **Click the link to the most recent copy of Nessus for UNIX-compatible computers.**

   You're taken to a download page.

3. **On the download page, scroll down to find The Easy and Less Dangerous Way section.**

4. **Click the link to the server nearest to you.**

5. **When the new window opens, click the link for the `nessus-installer.sh` file.**

6. **Save the file to your home directory.**

7. **When the file is done downloading, close the download manager and the browser window.**

You've downloaded the files, and now you need to compile and install Nessus. Fortunately, the kind programmers at Nessus have provided a pretty decent setup tool. To install Nessus, follow these steps:

1. **Open a terminal window and give yourself superuser privileges with the** su **command.**

2. **Move to your home directory, type the following command, and press Enter:**

```
# sh nessus-install.sh
```

The Nessus Installation Script opens, as shown in Figure 37-1.

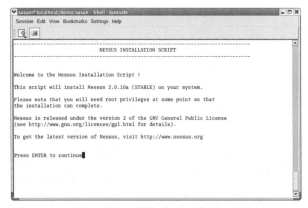

• **Figure 37-1: The Nessus Installation Script window.**

3. **Press Enter to continue.**

The installation script begins extracting the archives and setting up shop.

4. **When prompted, press Enter to accept the default location for the Nessus installation.**

5. **Confirm the installation with another press of the Enter key when prompted.**

Nessus begins compiling the libraries and configuring the sources for your system. You may see a few warnings go by — don't worry about them too much — they're for the authors of the code to watch.

6. **When Nessus prompts you to build libraries, answer** y.

You see a window confirming that the Nessus installation is finished, as shown in Figure 37-2.

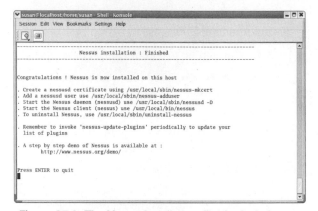

• **Figure 37-2: The Nessus Installation: Finished window.**

You have only a couple more steps to go before you're ready to run Nessus. You still need to add a user and create an SSL certificate for the program.

Adding a user to Nessus

In the wrong hands, Nessus can make life miserable for a system administrator. Although most people use Nessus to scan their own networks, Nessus can be used to discover (and, to a small extent, exploit) vulnerabilities in other computers. To minimize the chances that abuse originates from your computer, Nessus keeps its own user database. Before you can use Nessus, you need to add a user and create a password:

1. **Enter the following command:**

```
# /usr/local/sbin/nessus-adduser
```

The Nessus Add User script starts. The questions are fairly simple and quick.

2. **The script prompts you for a login. Type your user name and press Enter.**

The script prompts you for a means of authentication.

3. **Type** pass **to use password authentication or** cert **to use certificate authentication.**

4. **Press Enter to accept the default (password) and continue.**

You're prompted to enter the login password.

5. **Enter a good password (one that's easy to remember but hard to guess).**

You're prompted to enter a set of rules for the user. Just accept the default (an empty set) and move on to Step 6.

6. **Press Ctrl+D to continue.**

You're asked to confirm the entries for the new user — glance through the summary to make sure everything looks correct.

7. **Press Enter to continue.**

You're done creating a user in Nessus. The last step in the setup process is creating a certificate. See the next section for details.

Generating a certificate

After you add a user for the Nessus security tool, you need to generate an SSL certificate. The Nessus server sends the SSL certificate to your Nessus client so you know that you're connected to the real server and not someone impersonating your server for dastardly purposes. (See Technique 45 for more details on how SSL certificates safeguard your system.) To generate the server certificate, follow these steps:

1. **Still at the command line, start the Nessus certificate generator by typing the following command and pressing Enter:**

```
# /usr/local/sbin/nessus-mkcert
```

The answers to the following questions are used to create the security certificate.

First, you're prompted for the CA certificate lifetime (in days).

2. **Press Enter to accept the default of 1460 days, or enter another length of time.**

You're prompted for the server certificate lifetime.

3. **Press Enter to accept the default.**

4. **Enter an appropriate, two-letter country code and press Enter when you've decided on a location code.**

The default is France.

5. **Enter your state or province and press Enter.**

6. **Enter your city and press Enter.**

7. **Enter your organization name and press Enter.**

The questions are done, and your monitor should be displaying a window confirming that your SSL certificate has been created (see Figure 37-3).

8. **Press Enter to exit the `nessus-mkcert` program and return to the command line.**

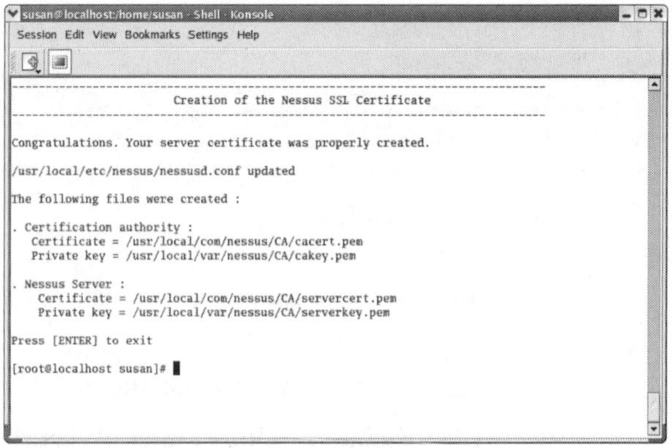

• **Figure 37-3: The new SSL certificate has been created.**

Using Nessus to Scan Your Network

After you download, install, and set up Nessus, add your user account, and create the SSL certificate, you're ready to scan your network for vulnerabilities. The graphical interface makes Nessus quick to use and fairly intuitive. You'll be scanning in no time!

You need to do the setup and installation only the first time you run Nessus. After that, you just start the daemon and the user interface each time you want to scan your system.

Starting the daemon and the interface

Nessus is a client/server program. Before you can scan other machines on your network, you need to start the Nessus daemon. To start the daemon, follow these steps:

1. **Type the following command and press Enter:**

```
# /usr/local/sbin/nessusd -D
```

2. **To start the user interface, type this command and press Enter:**

```
# /usr/local/bin/nessus
```

The Nessus Setup window opens, as shown in Figure 37-4.

• **Figure 37-4: The Nessus Setup window.**

3. **Enter your Nessus login and password in the appropriate fields in the setup window, and then click Log In.**

After validating your password, Nessus opens a dialog, offering you choices about your level of security.

4. **View and approve the certificate to continue.**

Nessus moves you to the Plugins tab of the Nessus Setup window.

A Warning dialog opens, warning you that volatile plug-ins have been disabled (see Figure 37-5).

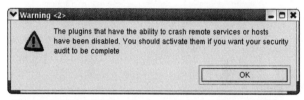

• **Figure 37-5: A fairly ominous-looking warning dialog.**

By default, Nessus disables dangerous plug-ins that may crash the computer you scan. The warning that you see is telling you that your security audit won't be complete without enabling the plug-ins that are a threat to your system.

> If you enable the dangerous plug-ins, you may crash the target system. Are you feeling lucky today?

5. **Click OK to continue.**

On the Plugins tab, you see a list of the plug-ins that are currently installed on your system. They are grouped according to component type in the top frame of the window, as shown in Figure 37-6.

6. **In the Plugin Selection area, highlight one of the types to display a list of the plug-ins that make up that component in the lower part of the window.**

Use the scroll bar to cruise through the list. You can see that the boxes next to the plug-ins that are considered volatile are not checked, as shown in Figure 37-7.

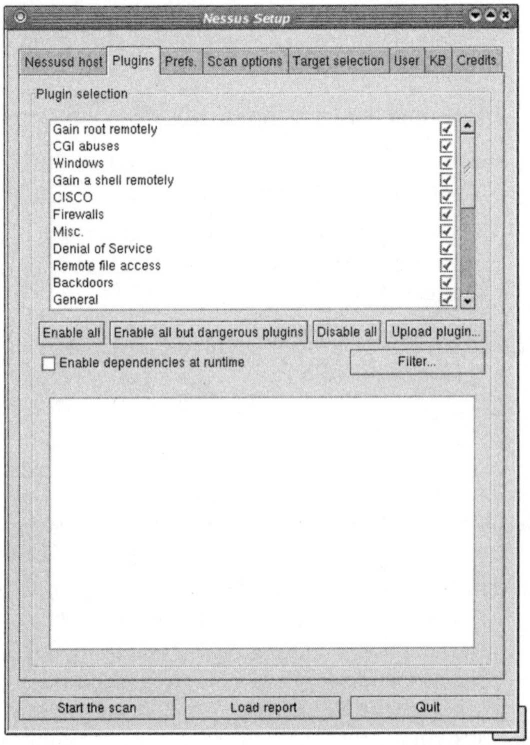

• **Figure 37-6: The Plugins tab of the Nessus Setup window.**

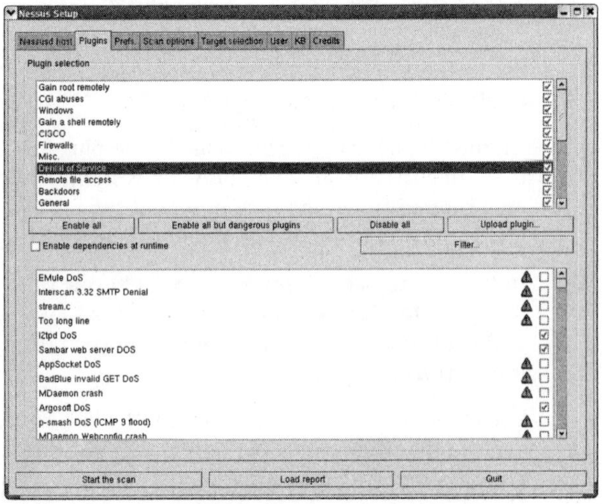

• **Figure 37-7: The Nessus Setup window with volatile plug-ins.**

7. Hover the mouse pointer over the dangerous plug-in's warning icon (the little yellow yield sign with the ! on it) to display a tooltip that tells you what might happen to your system if you invoke this plug-in (see Figure 37-8).

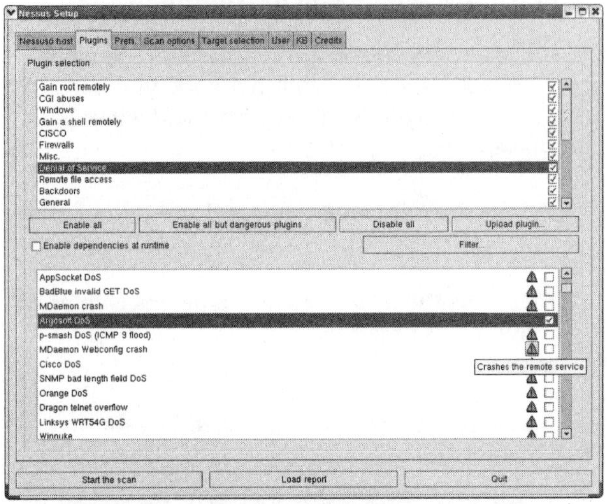

• **Figure 37-8: Check out the warnings.**

8. Click the yield sign to display a more graphic explanation of the problems you may encounter if you enable the plug-in (see the example in Figure 37-9).

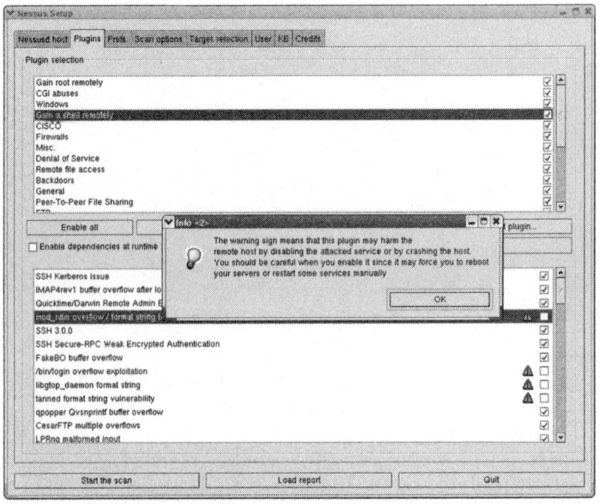

• **Figure 37-9: The complete explanation.**

We don't recommend enabling dangerous plug-ins unless you have a specific security need. Be sure not to probe someone else's machine with a dangerous plug-in enabled because some of the plug-ins can crash the remote machine.

9. **Highlight a plug-in in the list box at the bottom of the window to display a more complete explanation of the specific security threat it's designed to combat (see Figure 37-10).**

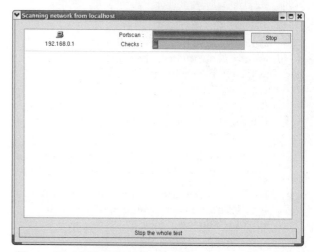

```
▼ /bin/login overflow exploitation                    ⊟ □ ✖

          /bin/login overflow exploitation
   This script is Copyright (C) 2002 Renaud Deraison

            Family : Gain a shell remotely
            Category : destructive_attack
            Nessus Plugin ID : 11136
               CVE : CVE-2001-0797
               Bugtraq ID : 3681
               $Revision: 1.2 $

        What is shown if the attack is successful :

   There is a bug in the remote /bin/login which        ▲
   allows an attacker to gain a shell on this host, without
   even sending a shell code.

   An attacker may use this flaw to log in as any user
   (except root) on the remote host.

   Solution : See http://www.cert.org/advisories/CA-2001-34.html
   Risk factor : High                                   ▼

   ───────────────────────────────────────────────────
                 Set plugin timeout...
   ───────────────────────────────────────────────────
                 Show dependencies
   ───────────────────────────────────────────────────
                      Close
```

• **Figure 37-10: Information about the plug-in.**

10. **Across the middle of the Plugins tab are four buttons, indicating the plug-ins you'd like to apply to your scan. Choose to**

▶ **Enable All:** Enable all the plug-ins currently on your system.

▶ **Enable All but Dangerous Plug-ins:** Don't enable the plug-ins that might cause problems on the target systems.

▶ **Disable All:** Disable all the plug-ins for a minimal scan.

▶ **Upload Plugin:** Upload any plug-ins that you write to the Nessus server.

For a good starting place, click the Enable All but Dangerous Plugins button. That way, you avoid spending time fixing system corruption until you've done some preliminary scans for loose security. Save the risky endeavors for Fridays, before slow weekends, after a good solid backup.

11. **Click the Target Selection tab to select the machine that you want to test. Enter the host name (or IP address) in the Target(s) field and click the Start the Scan button.**

The scan opens another window, where progress bars chart the progress of the scan, as shown in Figure 37-11. When the scan is complete, the original window and a window with the results of the scan appear on your desktop. Now, you need to interpret those results, which we discuss in the next section, "Reading the grim results."

```
▼ Scanning network from localhost                     ⊟ □ ✖

        🖥        Portscan : [████████████]     │ Stop │
     192.168.0.1    Checks : [███        ]




───────────────────────────────────────────────────
                 Stop the whole test
```

• **Figure 37-11: The scan in progress.**

You can enter multiple machines in the Target(s) field by separating the host names (or IP addresses) with a , (comma). Click the Start the Scan button, and a scan of all the systems displays on the desktop.

Reading the grim results

At first glance, the scan report looks pretty good; in fact, it looks empty (see Figure 37-12). Just wait until you start exploring.

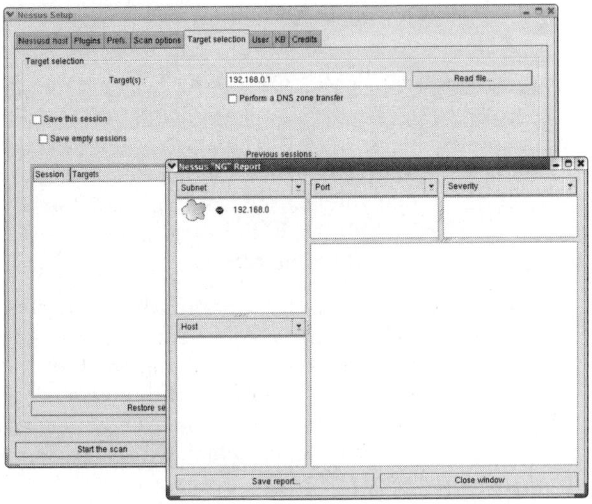

• **Figure 37-12:** The scan results.

The good news is, the reports will tell you what to do about any security breaches Nessus finds. The bad news, well, bear with us. Here's how to delve into the report:

1. **Highlight the subnet for your system in the Subnet frame.**

   The individual machines that you've included in the scan are listed below, in the Host frame.

2. **To see itemized information about what the scan found for each machine, highlight the machine address.**

A list of the ports found open in the scan appears in the Port frame, as shown in Figure 37-13.

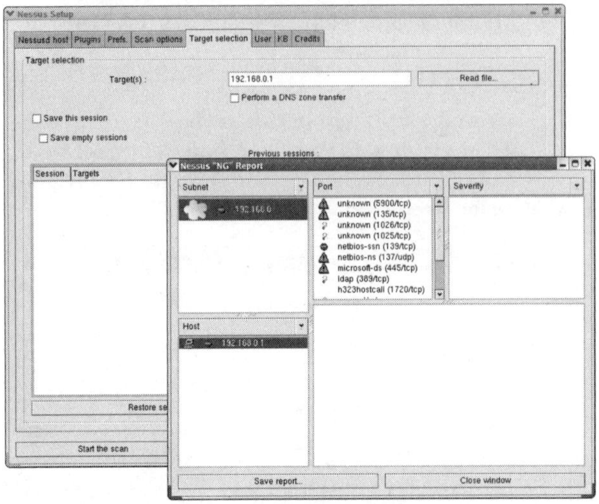

• **Figure 37-13:** The ports that Nessus explored.

The icons to the left of the ports tell you what Nessus found when connecting to those ports. A yellow triangle with a ! in it indicates a port you should be concerned about.

3. **Highlight the port name, and the Security Warning icon displays in the Severity frame, as shown in Figure 37-14. Highlight the security warning to view detailed information about the scan results in the bottom frame of the window.**

   ▶ A red stop sign with a line through it indicates a security hole.

   ▶ A triangle with an exclamation point indicates a security warning.

   ▶ A light bulb indicates a security note (just a bit of trivia you might find interesting).

4. **Highlight one of the ports with an icon next to it to open the details in the Severity frame.**

   You may find that a given port sponsors more than one level of offense.

5. **In the Severity frame, highlight the security level you want to explore to show the scan findings in the frame below (see Figure 37-15).**

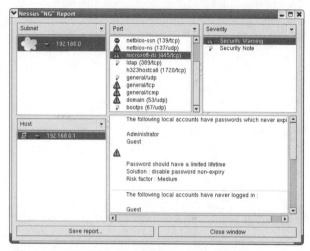

• **Figure 37-14: This port might cause a problem.**

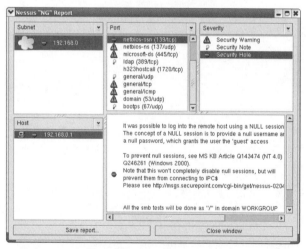

• **Figure 37-15: This is a security hole.**

The really good news is that Nessus doesn't leave you hanging; a solution is included in the lower frame (see Figure 37-16).

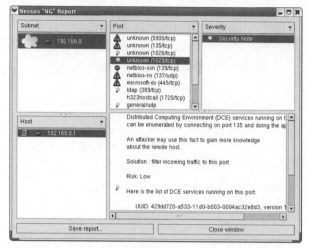

• **Figure 37-16: A security note.**

6. **Click the Security Note icon in the Severity frame to open a list of recommendations about the port. Be sure to scroll down through the report to see the recommendations — they're worth the time and effort.**

7. **It's not a bad idea to save your reports for later use. Just click the Save Report button at the bottom of the report to open the file selection dialog. Specify a location to save the file in, and click OK.**

> Save your reports for later comparisons, and you'll see new problems as they appear.

Keeping Your Plug-ins Up-to-Date

Nessus uses plug-ins to keep its security checks up-to-date. When a new security problem is discovered, it's likely that someone (either at www.nessus.org or in the community of Nessus users) will write a plug-in to handle the vulnerability and publish it for the benefit of other Nessus users. You can update the Nessus plug-ins on your system with one simple command.

To update the Nessus plug-ins, open a command line and give yourself superuser privileges. Then type the following command and press Enter:

```
# /usr/local/sbin/nessus-update-plugins
```

 It's a good idea to update your plug-ins often. Consider setting the update as part of a nightly cron job. Set it up with Task Scheduler as a nightly task, and you'll save time, and the process will be automated.

We've just scratched the surface of what you can do with the Nessus tool; its capabilities go far beyond the reach of this technique. If you're interested in finding out more about Nessus, visit the Web site at www.nessus.org and explore the online documentation. Also check out the man page: $ man nessus.

38 Person-to-Person Networking with IRC

Technique

Save Time By

✓ Networking online with IRC

✓ Customizing your KSirc workspace

There's computer networking, and then there's human networking. You can use IRC channels to network with other Linux users online to help solve problems and get the support you need to solve open-source problems.

IRC stands for Internet Relay Chat. Yes, we're talking about chat rooms — but specifically the chat rooms targeted to open-source and Linux users. Find the right channel though, and you can find quick access to a user or developer who may be able to help solve a problem.

 IRC networking can put you in touch with experts and amateurs who use (and often write) the open-source projects that you use. Sometimes, when the documentation fails you, going online for the answers is the quickest way to find a solution for your problem.

In this technique, we introduce you to KSirc, which is one of the IRC tools included with the KDE distribution. We also show you the way to some productive, helpful chat rooms. Networking with the professionals online can be a great timesaver in a pinch.

Finding the Answers You Seek in a Linux Chat Room

We've tried to provide the quickest, most dependable ways we know to implement system solutions to meet your needs. Unfortunately, system configurations vary, and your needs sometimes extend beyond the borders of what would be considered typical. In those cases, looking through online IRC channels for someone who's encountered a similar situation can help you find a quick solution to your problem.

Most standard Linux distributions come with several IRC clients, and literally dozens of IRC clients are out there. One friendly and usable client is KSirc. KSirc is included in a standard installation of the KDE desktop on both Fedora and SuSE Linux systems.

To use KSirc with Mandrake, you'll first need to install the `kdenetwork-ksirc-version.rpm` package. It's included with the distribution — see Technique 17 for information about installing RPM packages.

Follow these steps to use the KSirc IRC client:

1. On Fedora, open the Main Menu and choose Internet⇨More Internet Applications⇨KSirc.

On SuSE or Mandrake, open the Main Menu and choose Internet⇨Chat⇨Ksirc.

The KSirc Server Control dialog opens, as shown in Figure 38-1.

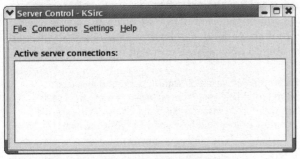

• **Figure 38-1: The KSirc Server Control dialog.**

With no connections, the server control is kind of a sad and worthless place. Establishing some connections is the first step to finding other Linux users.

2. Choose Connections⇨New Server from the menu bar.

The Connect to Server dialog opens, as shown in Figure 38-2.

3. Use the arrow to the right of the Group field to open a drop-down list box of available servers. Scroll down and choose Freenode from the list. Then click the Connect button.

The KSirc connection window opens displaying information about the connection (see Figure 38-3).

• **Figure 38-2: The Connect to Server dialog.**

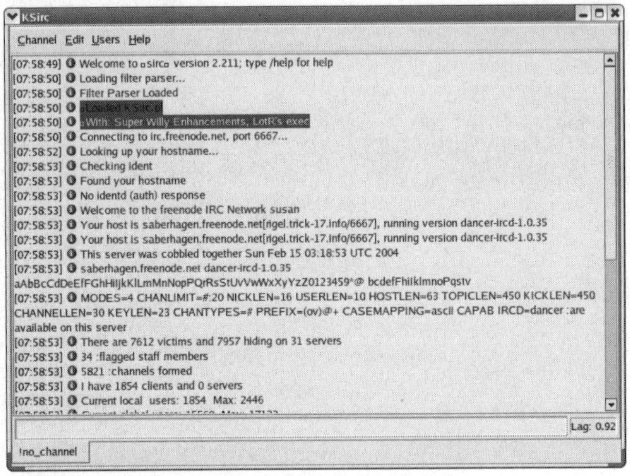

• **Figure 38-3: The KSirc connection window.**

4. Choose Channel⇨New from the menu bar. In the unlabeled field near the bottom of the KSirc window, enter the following command:

```
/list
```

The list of currently active channels begins to scroll by. Literally hundreds of channels are open at any given time, so the list can take a minute or two to load (see Figure 38-4).

Use the scroll bar to view the entire list. The listing shows the current time, the *#name* of the channel, the number of users currently in attendance, and a note about the channel's subject matter.

5. To join the active channel discussing Fedora, enter the following command:

```
/join #Fedora
```

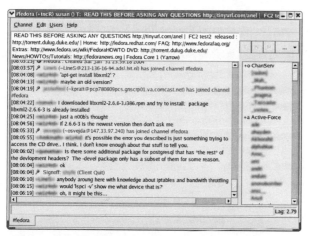

• **Figure 38-4:** The currently open channels.

The Fedora channel is displayed, as shown in Figure 38-5.

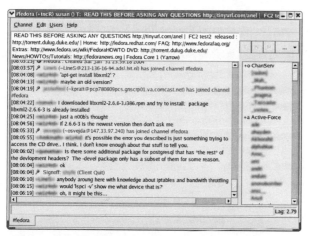

• **Figure 38-5:** The current activity on the Fedora IRC channel.

To join any of the channels displayed in the list of open channels, enter the command /join *#channelname*. If you're interested in SuSE or Mandrake specific channels, skip ahead to the sections titled "Looking for Answers in the SuSE Chat Room" or "Finding Fellow Mandrake Users in the Mandrake Chat Room."

Chatting in the Fedora Chat Room

You're almost ready to start chatting. Before joining the Fedora conversation, you should read the etiquette directives at `tinyurl.com/anel`. It's also a good idea to lurk for a while to check out the flavor of the conversation before jumping in with your questions and/or answers.

 Hackers can be brutal if provoked. Be polite in IRC channels and observe etiquette, even if you're chatting with someone who goes by the nickname of *pigfilth*.

When you're ready to ask a question (or respond to one), follow these steps:

1. **Type into the unlabeled field (near the bottom of the window) and press Enter when you're finished.**

Your question appears in the scrolling region, prefixed with your nickname.

Some IRC servers require you to register before you can talk (but you can usually listen without registering). If you run into such a server, follow the directions that it sends your way.

 You can monitor multiple channels at one time. As you open each channel, a new tab control is added to the bottom of the KSirc window (see Figure 38-6).

2. **When you're done participating in a discussion, you can leave a channel by opening the Channel menu and choosing Close.**

The tab control closes, leaving your remaining channels intact. If you have only one channel running, KSirc closes.

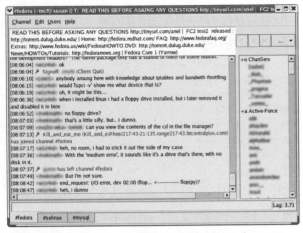

• **Figure 38-6:** You can monitor multiple channels at one time.

Looking for Answers in the SuSE Chat Room

If SuSE Linux is more your style, you'll find lots of help on the Freenode IRC server. Join the SuSE chat-room by entering the command /join #suse in the unlabeled field at the bottom of the KSirc window. The SuSE channel opens, displaying the current conversation in the large window on the left, with the active participants in the panel on the right.

After lurking for a while, you may want to join the conversation. Just enter your comments or inquiries in the field at the bottom of the screen and press Enter. In a flash, you're participating in the chat.

When you're ready to leave the chat room, just choose Channel⇨Close. That's all there is to it!

Finding Fellow Mandrake Users in the Mandrake Chat Room

You should check out the rules of conversation for the Mandrake chat room at http://mandrake.brain.org before joining the conversation in the Mandrake

chat room on the Freenode IRC server. When you are comfortable with the rules of conduct, just enter /join #mandrake in the KSirc chat field and press Enter. The screen promptly presents the current conversation in the Mandrake chat room and the list of users currently in attendance.

When you're finished chatting, just choose Channel⇨ Close.

Customizing KSirc — Who Do You Want to Be Today?

You can customize your KSirc environment to suit your tastes and work habits in a flash with the KSirc Configuration dialog.

To customize KSirc, start a KSirc session and choose Settings⇨Configure KSirc. The Configure KSirc dialog opens, as shown in Figure 38-7.

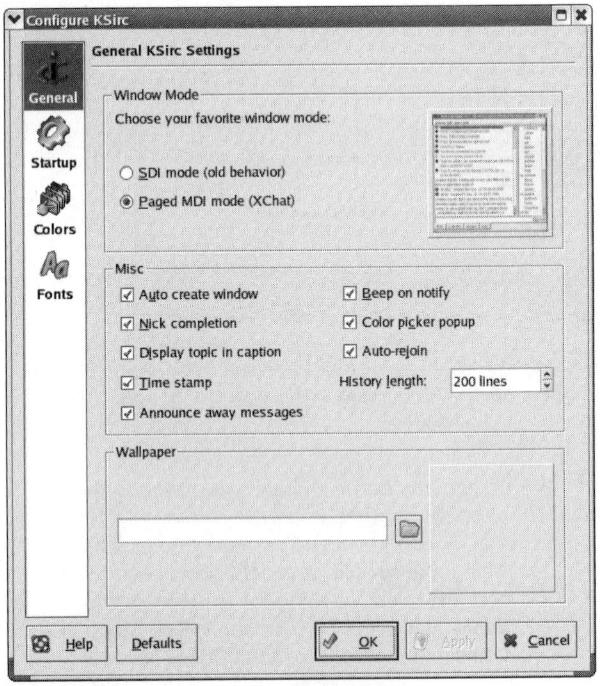

• **Figure 38-7:** The Configure KSirc dialog.

The buttons on the left panel control the four configuration menus:

- **General:** Use the General menu to set options that affect the general look and feel of the session, from the session information included in the display to the wallpaper.

- **Startup:** Use the Startup menu to create a nickname (or an alternative nickname if Funkmaster is already logged in).

- **Colors:** Use the Colors menu to set your color preferences for your IRC session.

- **Fonts:** Use the Fonts menu to set the font type and size for your IRC session.

After you've set your preferences, click OK to save your changes and close the Configure KSirc dialog. The next time you start a KSirc session, your preferences are in place!

Part VII

Monitoring Your System

The 5th Wave   By Rich Tennant

"It appears a server in Atlanta is about to go down, there's a printer backup in Baltimore and an accountant in Chicago is about to make level 3 of the game, 'Tomb Pirate'."

Technique 39

Controlling Troublesome Processes at the Command Line

Save Time By

- Using the tools in `procps` to control processes at the command line
- Using `ps`, `pstree`, and `pgrep` to retrieve process details
- Killing off unwanted processes at the command line
- Setting program priorities at the command line with `renice`

Every now and then a troublesome process gets loose on your system, hogging resources, slowing down the network, and refusing to die. Controlling the troublemakers is a snap, thanks to Linux. With Linux, you have some great command line tools, all bundled up in one little RPM package called `procps` (pronounced "proc ps").

`ps`, `pstree`, and `pgrep` are the stud finders in the toolbox that help you find the troublemaking processes. With `ps`, `pstree`, and `pgrep`, you can identify the process, the user, and the terminal being used. You can also get a good idea of what system resources the process is using to decide if the process should be terminated.

`kill`, `killall`, and `xkill` are the hammers in the toolbox. How big of a hammer you need depends on the scope of the process or processes you're trying to stop, and the precision you need to kill them off. Choose from the three commands to remove any unwanted processes that you've identified.

You can use the `renice` command to level the playing field by assigning the troublemaking process a *nice* value. The processes with lower nice values have to surrender system resources to processes with higher priorities.

In this technique, we introduce you to some handy command line tools that make process management a breeze. With these tools in your toolbox, you can build a better system fast, even if you don't have a graphical environment to help you along the way.

Processing Processes with procps

The tools packaged in the `procps` RPM package are a handy but diverse bunch. They can retrieve information about processes or users, kill off unwanted processes, and watch the activities on your system. `procps` is an all-purpose toolkit designed to provide power at the command line to make process management quick and easy.

Getting familiar with `procps` is a good investment of time. After you know the tools, you'll turn to them again and again.

The `procps` package contains several tools that you can use to monitor and control processes:

- ✔ `ps`
- ✔ `sysctl`
- ✔ `free`
- ✔ `pgrep`
- ✔ `pkill`
- ✔ `top`
- ✔ `w`
- ✔ `watch`

Chances are, `procps` is already installed on your system. If not, you can find the RPM package on the Linux distribution discs.

On Fedora or Mandrake, open a terminal window, and with superuser privileges, mount the disc and install the package with the following command:

```
# rpm -Uhv procps-version.rpm
```

If you're a SuSE user, open a terminal window, and with superuser privileges, mount the disc and install the RPM package with the command:

```
# rpm -Uhv ps-version.rpm
```

See Technique 17 for more information about installing software with `rpm`.

Keeping Track of Process Status with ps, pstree, and pgrep

Before you can control a troublesome process on your system, it helps to have good, solid information

about that process. Knowing the identity of the user, the process ID, and the terminal that is controlling the process is valuable when you need to track down a process and its origins. Statistical information about the process (such as memory usage and CPU time) is also helpful when you need to catch troublemaking programs that might be causing performance problems. `procps` provides several good tools that can help you get that information in the form that helps you most.

Using ps to filter process status information

Most Linux users have at least a passing familiarity with the `ps` command. `ps` stands for *process status,* and it displays just that: the status of a process.

If you just type `ps` without any extra arguments or options, you see a quick synopsis of the programs running within your terminal window:

```
  PID TTY          TIME CMD
10181 pts/7     00:00:00 bash
10521 pts/7     00:00:00 ps
```

This information is organized in four columns:

- ✔ `PID`: The first column shows the process ID, which is a unique number assigned to each process when it starts running.

- ✔ `TTY`: The second column displays your `tty` device name. In this example, `pts/7` means that you're logged into *pseudo-terminal* number 7. (When you open a new terminal window, you create a new pseudo-terminal.)

- ✔ `TIME`: The third column shows the amount of CPU time used by each process.

- ✔ `CMD`: The last column shows the name of the program running within each process.

Note that you don't have to live with the default columns. You can change the way the output looks. See "Viewing ps output the way you want to see it" later in this technique.

The ps command was inherited from UNIX. That's an oversimplification because many flavors of UNIX have existed (HP/UX, AIX, BSD, Digital UNIX, SCO UNIX, and so on). Linux uses the standard GNU version of ps. As a result, the ps command supports a wide variety of command line options. Save yourself some time and learn the portable (that is, long-format) command line options. For example, use ps --pid 1 instead of the equivalent ps -p 1. The long-form options require a bit more typing, but they're much easier to remember.

If you want to see *all* the processes running on your system, add -A to the end of the command line, like this:

```
$ ps -A
  PID TTY        TIME CMD
    1 ?      00:00:04 init
    2 ?      00:00:00 keventd
    3 ?      00:00:00 kapmd
    4 ?      00:00:00 ksoftirqd/0
    6 ?      00:00:00 bdflush
 .... ........ ........ ...........
 5039 tty1   00:00:00 mingetty
 5040 tty2   00:00:00 mingetty
 ... ........ ........ ...........
```

Notice that the TTY column displays a ? for many processes. Those processes are *noninteractive,* and they're generally server-type processes like Apache, xinetd, or MySQL. To see only the interactive processes (processes associated with a terminal or terminal window), use -a instead of -A.

You can also choose processes based on the process characteristics shown in Table 39-1.

TABLE 39-1: PS PROCESS SELECTION OPTIONS

Option	Description
-C command	Displays processes running command
-G group --group group	Displays processes that have the effective group ID group (group can be a group name or a numeric group ID)

Option	Description
-U user --user user	Displays processes that have the effective user ID user (user can be a user name or a numeric user ID)
-g group --Group group	Displays processes that have the real group ID group (group can be a group name or a numeric group ID)
-u user --User user	Displays processes that have the real user ID user (user can be a user name or a numeric user ID)
-p process-ID --pid process-ID	Displays processes that have the process ID process-ID
-t tty-name --tty tty-name	Displays processes running at terminal tty-name

If you list more than one process selector, ps displays all processes that meet *any* of the constraints. For example, to see all processes with an effective or real user ID of freddie, use the following command:

```
$ ps --user freddie --User freddie
```

If you want to select multiple processes based on the same characteristic (but different values), just list each value, separating the values with commas. These two commands are equivalent:

```
$ ps -C bash -C zsh
$ ps -C bash,zsh
```

Viewing ps output the way you want to see it

You can also change the columns listed by the ps command. To specify an output format, use the following option:

```
-o column[,column]...
```

ps lets you choose an output format from 126 different columns! Some of the more useful columns are shown in Table 39-2.

TABLE 39-2: PS COLUMN SPECIFIERS

Column Name	Description
%cpu	Percentage of CPU time used by process
%mem	Percentage of memory used by process
Comm	Command name
Args	Command line arguments
Command	Command name plus command line argument
egroup	Effective group name
egid	Effective group ID (numeric)
rgroup	Real group name
rgid	Real group ID (numeric)
euser	Effective user name
euid	Effective user ID (numeric)
ruser	Real user name
ruid	Real user ID (numeric)
Pid	Process ID
Stat	Process state (running, sleeping, waiting for I/O, and so on)
Cputime	Cumulative CPU time
Tty	Terminal name

Don't worry about memorizing the list of column specifiers; use the command ps L (that's L, not -L) to display the complete list.

Normally, ps displays process information in process ID order. You can choose your own ordering with --sort *column*. For example, to list processes in increasing order by command name, use the following command:

```
$ ps --sort cmd
```

You can use any of the column specifiers displayed by ps L. If you want to sort first by command name and then by process ID, use this command:

```
$ ps --sort cmd,pid
```

If you put a minus sign in front of a sort specifier, you reverse the ordering. For example, the command

```
$ ps --sort cmd,-pid
```

sorts processes first by command name (in ascending, or A–Z, order) and then by process ID in descending (999999–1) order.

ps comes preloaded with a few predefined output formats that display the information you're most likely to need. The default output format shows the process ID, tty, CPU time, and user name. The -l (or *long*) format displays a ton of information about the state of the process (priority, state, process size, and so on). The u option (note: u, not -u) displays user-oriented information (percentage of CPU time, percentage of available memory, and such).

If you experiment with ps, you'll probably find that you frequently use a few output options in combination. Use the alias command (part of the bash shell) to create new commands that correspond to the options that you prefer. For example, to create a new command named psu that displays user-oriented process information, use the following command:

```
$ alias psu="ps -o
    pid,euser,ruser,%cpu,%mem,command"
```

Now, when you type the command psu, you see only the columns that you're interested in.

Of course, you can specify other options when you run the psu command:

```
$ psu -C bash
   PID EUSER     RUSER      %CPU %MEM COMMAND
  9318 freddie   freddie     0.0  0.3 bash
  9380 franklin  franklin    0.0  0.2 bash
  9428 root      root        0.0  0.2 bash
```

See Technique 10 to find out how to save bash aliases so they're available every time you log in.

Making parent-child relationships stand out in a ps listing

When you're looking at a long `ps` listing, it's difficult to discern the parent-child relationships among processes. `ps` has two command line options that make that relationship a little easier to see.

The `-H` option indents child processes; each generation is indented a bit more than the previous generation:

```
$ ps -AH
  PID TTY          TIME CMD
    1 ?        00:00:04 init
 4993 ?        00:00:00   atd
 4647 ?        00:00:00   crond
 5022 ?        00:00:00   dbus-daemon-1
 4240 ?        00:00:00   dhclient
 5045 ?        00:00:00   gdm-binary
 5175 ?        00:00:00     gdm-binary
 5176 ?        00:07:43       X
 5197 ?        00:00:00       startkde
 5323 ?        00:00:00         kwrapper
 5256 ?        00:00:00         ssh-agent
 .... .        ........ .........
```

You can see from this example that the `init` process (process ID 1) is that ancestor of all the other processes. Process 5175 is the parent of two children (5176 and 5197) and the grandparent of process 5323 and process 5256.

To see a slightly fancier display, use the `--forest` option instead of `-H`:

```
$ ps -AH --forest
  PID TTY          TIME CMD
    1 ?        00:00:04 init
 4993 ?        00:00:00 atd
 4647 ?        00:00:00 crond
 5022 ?        00:00:00 dbus-daemon-1
 4240 ?        00:00:00 dhclient
 5045 ?        00:00:00 gdm-binary
 5175 ?        00:00:00  \_ gdm-binary
 5176 ?        00:07:48      \_ X
 5197 ?        00:00:00      \_ startkde
 5256 ?        00:00:00          \_ ssh-agent
 5323 ?        00:00:00          \_ kwrapper
 .... .        ........ .... .........
```

Personally, we find the `--forest` option a tad confusing; we prefer the `pstree` command instead. See the next section for details on `pstree`.

Climbing the family tree with pstree

`pstree` is similar to the `ps` command, but it has far fewer options. When you run `pstree`, you see a graph of processes running on your system, similar to that shown in Figure 39-1.

```
[root@localhost susan]# pstree
init─┬─apmd
     ├─atd
     ├─bdflush
     ├─cardmgr
     ├─crond
     ├─cupsd
     ├─dhclient
     ├─gconfd-2
     ├─gdm-binary───gdm-binary─┬─X
     │                         └─startkde─┬─kwrapper
     │                                    └─ssh-agent
     ├─gpm
     ├─httpd───8*[httpd]
     ├─kapmd
     ├─kdeinit─┬─artsd
     │         ├─autorun
     │         ├─eggcups
     │         ├─2*[kdeinit]
     │         ├─kdeinit───bash───su───bash───pstree
     │         ├─ksnapshot
     │         ├─pam-panel-icon───pam_timestamp_c
     │         └─rhn-applet-gui
     └─10*[kdeinit]
```

• **Figure 39-1: Output from the `pstree` command.**

You can see that `pstree` makes the process tree easy to see. By default, `pstree` compresses the process tree by removing duplicate branches from the display. You can see all the processes running on your system by including the `-c`, `-a`, or `-p` option:

- `-c` simply disables compression.

- `-a` tells `pstree` to display the command line arguments for each process, as shown in Figure 39-2.

- `-p` forces `pstree` to add process IDs to the graph, as shown in Figure 39-3.

You can use the `-p` and `-a` options in the same report. The command `$ pstree -pa` includes in the output the command line arguments for the process as well as the process ID.

```
susan@localhost:/home/susan - Shell - Konsole                          _ □ ×
Session  Edit  View  Bookmarks  Settings  Help

[root@localhost susan]# pstree -a
init
  ├─apmd -p 10 -w 5 -W -P /etc/sysconfig/apm-scripts/apmscript
  ├─atd
  ├─(bdflush)
  ├─cardmgr
  ├─crond
  ├─cupsd
  ├─dhclient -1 -q -lf /var/lib/dhcp/dhclient-eth0.leases -pf /var/run/dhclien
  ├─gconfd-2 14
  ├─gdm-binary -nodaemon
  │   └─gdm-binary -nodaemon
  │       ├─X :0 -audit 0 -auth /var/gdm/:0.Xauth vt7
  │       └─startkde /usr/bin/startkde
  │           ├─kwrapper ksmserver
  │           └─ssh-agent startkde
  ├─gpm -m /dev/mouse -t imps2
  ├─httpd
  │   ├─httpd
  │   ├─httpd
  │   ├─httpd
  │   ├─httpd
  │   ├─httpd
```

• **Figure 39-2:** `pstree -a` **displays command line arguments.**

```
susan@localhost:/home/susan - Shell - Konsole                          _ □ ×
Session  Edit  View  Bookmarks  Settings  Help

[root@localhost susan]# pstree -p
init(1)─┬─apmd(2026)
        ├─atd(2415)
        ├─bdflush(6)
        ├─cardmgr(2000)
        ├─crond(2318)
        ├─cupsd(2202)
        ├─dhclient(2179)
        ├─gconfd-2(4592)
        ├─gdm-binary(2460)───gdm-binary(4424)─┬─X(4425)
        │                                      └─startkde(4454)─┬─kwrapper(4572)
        │                                                       └─ssh-agent(4507)
        ├─gpm(2296)
        ├─httpd(5182)─┬─httpd(5185)
        │             ├─httpd(5186)
        │             ├─httpd(5187)
        │             ├─httpd(5188)
        │             ├─httpd(5189)
        │             ├─httpd(5190)
        │             ├─httpd(5191)
        │             └─httpd(5192)
        ├─kapmd(3)
        └─kdeinit(4537)─┬─artsd(4557)
                        └─autorun(4582)
```

• **Figure 39-3:** `pstree -p` **displays process IDs.**

`pstree` has a few more options that you might find useful:

- ✔ `-h` highlights your current process and all ancestors (see Figure 39-4), making it easy to find yourself in a complex listing.

- ✔ `-u` shows the user name associated with each process. (Actually, `-u` displays the user name only when it changes from parent to child.)

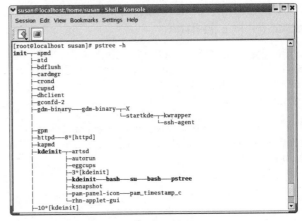

```
susan@localhost:/home/susan - Shell - Konsole                          _ □ ×
Session  Edit  View  Bookmarks  Settings  Help

[root@localhost susan]# pstree -h
init─┬─apmd
     ├─atd
     ├─bdflush
     ├─cardmgr
     ├─crond
     ├─cupsd
     ├─dhclient
     ├─gconfd-2
     ├─gdm-binary───gdm-binary─┬─X
     │                         └─startkde─┬─kwrapper
     │                                    └─ssh-agent
     ├─gpm
     ├─httpd───8*[httpd]
     ├─kapmd
     ├─kdeinit─┬─artsd
     │         ├─autorun
     │         ├─eggcups
     │         ├─3*[kdeinit]
     │         ├─kdeinit───bash───su───bash───pstree
     │         ├─ksnapshot
     │         ├─pam-panel-icon───pam_timestamp_c
     │         └─rhn-applet-gui
     └─10*[kdeinit]
```

• **Figure 39-4:** `pstree` **highlight mode.**

If you want to see the descendents of a specific process, include the process ID at the end of the command, like this:

```
$ pstree 5296
```

To see the processes for a particular user, include the user name at the end of the command line:

```
$ pstree freddie
```

Finding processes with pgrep

`ps` and `pstree` are useful tools when you want to see the big picture, but it can be tough to find the process you're looking for in a long list. That's where `pgrep` comes in. `pgrep` lets you search for specific processes based on a number of process characteristics.

To search for processes running a particular program, run `pgrep` *pattern*. For example, here's how to search for all processes running `mozilla`:

```
$ pgrep mozilla
5385
5391
5393
5395
5400
```

Hmmm . . . that output is a bit terse. Use the -l option to display the program name as well as the process ID:

```
$ pgrep -l mozilla
5385 run-mozilla.sh
5391 mozilla-bin
5393 mozilla-bin
5395 mozilla-bin
5400 mozilla-bin
```

pgrep matches program names based on regular expressions (that is, wildcards), so it displays processes whose names *include* mozilla. For a complete rundown on the regular expression syntax understood by psgrep, see the man page for regex (info regex). If you want an exact match (not a regular expression match), use the -x option. By default, pgrep matches the *pattern* that you provide against the program name for each process. To match the *pattern* anywhere in the command line (not just in the program name), include -f on the command line:

```
$ pgrep -fl mozilla
5385 /usr/ local/mozilla/run-mozilla.sh
5391 /usr/local/mozilla/mozilla-bin
5393 /usr/local/mozilla/mozilla-bin
5395 /usr/local/mozilla/mozilla-bin
5400 /usr/local/mozilla/mozilla-bin
9388 more run-mozilla.sh
```

Notice process 9388: The program running there is more, but because the command line arguments include mozilla, pgrep displays it.

pgrep can also find processes based on the criteria shown in Table 39-3.

TABLE 39-3: PGREP OPTIONS THAT LOOK FOR MATCHING DATA

Option	Description
-P *pid*	Selects processes whose parent is process *pid*
-g *process-group*	Selects processes belonging to process group *process-group*

Option	Description
-s *session-ID*	Selects processes belonging to the login session *session-ID*
-u *user*	Selects processes whose effective user IDs match *user* (*user* can be a user name or a numeric user ID)
-U *user*	Selects processes whose real user IDs match *user* (*user* can be a user name or a numeric user ID)
-G *group*	Selects processes whose effective groups match *group* (*group* can be a group name or a numeric group ID)
-T *terminal*	Selects processes associated with terminal (or pty) *terminal*

In addition to the matching options described in Table 39-3, you can negate the criteria with the -v option. For example, to find all the processes *not* owned by user root, use this command:

```
$ pgrep -U root -v
```

You can also tell pgrep to display only the most recent process that matches your criteria. To do so, just include -n on the command line like this:

```
$ pgrep -n xmms
```

That's handy if you want to find the most recently invoked copy of a program.

As explained earlier, pgrep displays a list of process IDs by default, but you may want to see more information. To help pgrep overcome its minimalism, you feed the output from pgrep (the list of processes that match your criteria) into another program that knows how to use a process ID. For example, here's how to see detailed information about all the processes owned by user freddie or by user franklin:

```
$ ps -l --pid $(pgrep -U freddie,franklin)
```

The bash shell first executes the command inside the parentheses and then builds a new command that incorporates the output from pgrep. That might sound confusing if you're not familiar with the bash command substitution feature, so it may help to break the command down a bit. Assume that the pgrep command returns three process IDs:

```
$ pgrep -U freddie,franklin
5523
7879
8256
```

bash substitutes the output from pgrep into the ps command like this:

```
$ ps -l --pid 5523 7879 8256
```

You can feed the output from pgrep into *any* program that expects a list of process IDs, such as kill. To kill all processes owned by user freddie, you can combine pgrep and kill like this:

```
$ kill $(pgrep -U freddie)
```

Killing Processes with pkill

An easy way to kill off unwanted processes is pkill. pkill is nearly identical to pgrep (in fact, you can select processes using the same criteria in Table 39-3, which you can find earlier in this technique) except that pkill kills the matching processes instead of displaying matching process IDs. To kill all processes owned by user freddie, use the following command:

```
$ pkill -U freddie
```

pkill (and its cousin, kill) work by sending a signal to the targeted process. By default, pkill sends the SIGTERM signal to *suggest* that the target process terminate itself. If you find a program that's not willing to honor SIGTERM, you can be more forceful by using the -SIGKILL option:

```
$ pkill -SIGKILL -U freddie
```

You can send any signal with pkill. For a complete list of signals (and their meanings), see man 7 signal.

Killing Processes with killall

pkill is a bit aggressive, and if you're not careful, it can kill processes that you don't intend to harm. If you want to kill a collection of processes, exercise some caution and use killall instead.

killall isn't as flexible as pkill when it comes to selecting processes, but it has one very nice feature: interactive mode. killall selects processes based on program name. When you run killall, use the --interactive option (or -i for short) to tell killall to prompt you before it kills each process:

```
$ pgrep -lf more
10512 more mozilla/run-mozilla.sh
10513 more /etc/passwd
$ killall --interactive more
Kill more(10512) ? (y/n) y
Kill more(10513) ? (y/n) n
```

Like pkill, killall sends SIGTERM by default. If you want to send a different signal, use the --signal *signal-name* option:

```
$ killall -i --signal SIGKILL more
Kill more(10512) ? (y/n) y
Kill more(10513) ? (y/n) n
```

Closing Windows with xkill

Once in a while, a window appears on your desktop, and you just don't know where it came from. It might be a pop-up ad from a piece of spyware, an annoying message from a program running in the background, or just a program that forgot to identify itself. If you don't know the name of the program that created the window, you can't kill it with kill, pkill, or killall. You need xkill, which kills off a program when you click the program's window. To see xkill in action:

1. Start up a copy of xmms and tell it to play a media stream (see www.shoutcast.com if you're looking for some good music).

2. Now, open a terminal window and run the following command:

```
$ xkill
Select the window whose client you wish
  to kill with button 1....
```

Notice that the mouse cursor has changed from its familiar arrow to something that looks like a target sight in an F-16.

3. Click anywhere on the xmms window, and the media player is killed.

Be careful with xkill — you can easily kill off the wrong program with a single click. xkill will kill just about any window that you click — even the KDE (or GNOME) taskbar!

Make sure that the window you want to kill is visible. You can't move to a different desktop by clicking the pager (the multiple-desktop control down on your taskbar) because you'll kill the pager instead.

If you change your mind after you start xkill, just right-click anywhere on the screen, and xkill will end without doing any damage.

xkill isn't foolproof. It can't kill *every* program, but we've yet to find one that it can't handle. Of course, you need the right privileges to use xkill. You can kill off processes that you own, but you can't kill processes owned by other users.

If you need to kill a process owned by another user, give yourself superuser privileges (with su) before you run xkill.

Getting Your Processes' Priorities Straight

Linux uses a relatively simple scheme for divvying up available CPU time. CPU time is divided into short segments, and each period is called a *quantum*. As each quantum expires, the kernel chooses a new process to run from the list of processes with the highest priorities. Each process is assigned a priority that can change over time. The base priority assigned to a process is known as its *nice* value.

The name is a little strange and so is the numbering scheme. Nice values range from +20 (lowest priority) to –20 (highest priority), and most processes start with a nice value of 0. Think of it this way: A program with a *high* nice value is being nice to other processes by giving up the CPU when someone else needs it.

To view the nice value of an existing process, use this command:

```
$ ps -l process-id
```

You can lower the priority (that is, increase the nice value) of your own processes by using the renice command. For example, here's how to lower the priority of your bash shell:

```
$ renice +10 $$
6297: old priority 0, new priority 10
```

(The $$ shell variable contains the process ID of your shell.)

If you have superuser privileges, you can increase *or decrease* the nice value of *any* process. You can identify processes by process ID (-p pid), process group (-g process-group), or user name (-u user).

You can also use KDE System Guard to renice programs in a graphical environment. Check out Technique 41 for help using KDE System Guard.

40 Technique

Taking Care of New (And Old) Users

Save Time By

✔ Using the Fedora/ Mandrake user manager to add users and groups

✔ Forcing users to update passwords

✔ Changing passwords with a few clicks

✔ Organizing your users into groups

✔ Using filters to find users fast

Even if you're the only user on your system, you likely already know that you need at least two user accounts: you and your alter ego — the superuser. Your wild side (the superuser) is there when you need it to customize configuration files, install software, and remove old files. Your more sensible identity is for moving with speed and agility, without the danger of accidentally wiping out the contents of your online world with a typing error.

If you manage a system with multiple users, or you manage a network, you've likely set up each user with his or her own identity so you don't have roots running around willy-nilly changing passwords and uninstalling packages.

Whether you manage two user accounts or 200, the graphical user manager that comes with your distribution is the timesaving way to manage them. This tool simplifies account-related tasks, letting you avoid command line interaction. You don't have to remember any commands; just point and click to create and manage users and their information. The process of adding new users and modifying existing ones is fast.

Using *groups* to organize file privileges can save you a ton of time. The graphical user manager makes it easy to create and populate groups with its handy checklist. Fedora Linux and Mandrake Linux (currently) use the same user manager tool. As we describe the Fedora user manager, just remember that everything that we tell you applies to the Mandrake user manager as well.

In this technique, we introduce you to the advantages of your distribution's user manager. You'll save time (and a lot of typing) by using this simple tool to keep your user accounts and groups up-to-date. Every file and program on a Linux computer is owned by a single user and a single group. Every file (and program) also has a set of permissions that determine what the owner can do to the file, what members of the group can do, and what everyone else can do.

To make the system a safer place, assign each user a unique user name and password. When you create a separate account for each user, it has the following effects:

✔ Users can't read each other's e-mail or other private documents.

✔ Users can't alter each other's files.

✔ User can't lock others out of the system by changing a shared password.

✔ Users have separate home directories to keep their work in.

✔ Privileges for programs and data files can be assigned to individuals.

This makes your work as a user administrator much quicker and easier.

Managing Users and Groups with the Fedora/Mandrake User Manager

In this section, we give you a tour of the Fedora/Mandrake user manager. If you're a SuSE user, skip ahead to the section, "Managing Users and Groups with the SuSE User Administrator."

The user manager makes user and group management a snap. With just a few clicks, you can set up new users or temporary accounts, change passwords, and manage groups.

The user manager works from either the KDE Desktop or the GNOME desktop. If you're running Fedora Linux, you can start the user manager by opening the main menu and choosing System Settings⇨Users and Groups. If you're running Mandrake Linux, start the user manager by opening the main menu and choosing System⇨Configuration⇨Other⇨User Administration. In either case, enter the superuser password if you are prompted to do so.

The user manager then opens, as shown in Figure 40-1.

The user manager gives you all the access you need to add and modify groups and users. The easy-to-read user lists and intuitive dialogs make it a quick tool to get up and running with.

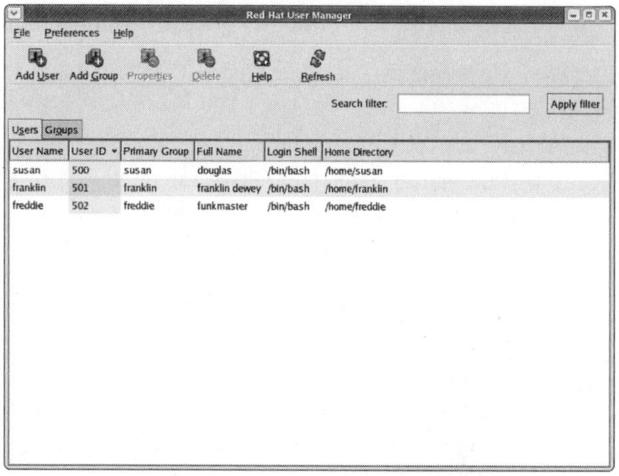

• **Figure 40-1: The Fedora/Mandrake User Manager.**

Adding new users

To add a user, follow these steps:

1. **In the user manager, click the Add User icon on the toolbar.**

   The Create New User dialog opens, as shown in Figure 40-2.

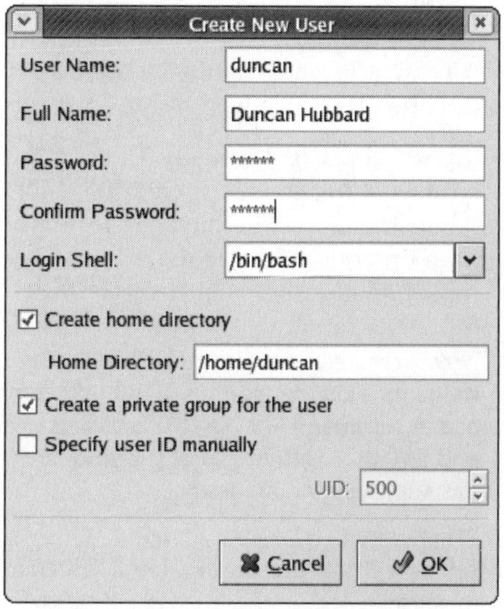

• **Figure 40-2: The Create New User dialog.**

2. **Fill in the fields in the dialog appropriately:**

▶ **User Name:** This is the name that you'll see next to the cursor when you log in to the shell (so make sure it's polite).

▶ **Full Name:** This name is for internal use. If you're managing a large company, you may need to distinguish between your Bobs or Jennifers.

▶ **Password and Confirm Password:** Enter a password and confirm the password in the next field. The password has to be at least six characters long, and it can be any combination of upper- and lowercase letters, numbers, and characters.

▶ **Login Shell:** The option you choose from this drop-down list determines which shell starts when the user opens a terminal window. bash is a good, friendly choice, but if the new user is a real macho-type programmer, he or she might want a more hearty shell like /bin/csh (designed to be friendly to C programmers — need we say more?).

▶ **Create Home Directory:** This defaults to /home/*username* for the user, but you can specify a different directory if you choose.

▶ **Create a Private Group for the User:** Check this box if you want to create a new group.

▶ **Specify User ID Manually:** Check this box if you want to choose the user ID rather than allow the system to manage the numbers. We don't recommend that unless you have a really good reason. Linux knows best.

 Never create a user with a UID of 0. The user manager won't let you do it, but you can do it at the command line. User 0 is always root, and any user with a UID of 0 is also root (and has superuser privileges).

3. **After you fill in the dialog, click OK to add the new user.**

You're finished!

Modifying user accounts

Users come and go — that's the nature of business. If you're responsible for many user accounts, you'll need to change forgotten passwords and delete old accounts. The user manager's graphical interface makes quick work of keeping up with the human resources department.

If you need to delete a user, the process is simple: Just select the user and click Delete on the toolbar.

When you click the Delete button, take note of the Delete User's Home Directory option. Be sure that nothing important is in that directory before you click Yes.

To make changes to a user account, follow these steps:

1. **Double-click a user name in the user manager.**

The User Properties dialog appears, as shown in Figure 40-3. With the User Properties dialog, you can change the user account with just a few clicks.

User Properties
User Data	Account Info	Password Info	Groups
User Name:	freddie
Full Name:	funkmaster
Password:	*****
Confirm Password:	*****
Home Directory:	/home/freddie
Login Shell:	/bin/bash
	Cancel	OK

• **Figure 40-3:** The User Properties dialog.

2. **Adjust different settings on the four tabs, as follows:**

▶ **User Data:** Use this tab to change the user's password, home directory, or login shell.

If a user forgets a password, this is the place to go. The old password is masked, but you can enter a new password for the user in seconds.

▶ **Account Info:** On this tab, check the Local Password Is Locked box to lock the user out of his or her account. Check the Enable Account Expiration option if you want the account to expire on a certain date, and then enter the expiration date.

▶ **Password Info:** Use this tab to control changes to a user's password. You can specify the number of days before a change is allowed, or the number of days before a change is required. You can also set up a warning date, warning the user that his or her password is about to expire, or specify the number of days before the account will be rendered inactive.

Expiring a password limits the amount of time that a hacker can use it. It also takes a fair amount of horsepower to crack a password, so if someone gets an encrypted version of your password file, odds are that the password will have changed by the time that the hacker decrypts it. Good password management is a real timesaver.

▶ **Groups:** Use this tab to specify the groups to which a user belongs. You can also specify the user's primary group here.

3. When you've finished making changes, click OK to save your work.

Adding groups

A *group* is a collection of users. Groups make it easy to manage file permissions. If you have several users that all need to access the same file, create a new group with those users in it.

The user manager makes it a breeze to create and modify groups. To add a group, follow these steps:

1. Open the Main Menu and choose System Settings⇨Users and Groups.

2. Choose the Groups tab.

The currently defined groups are displayed, as shown in Figure 40-4.

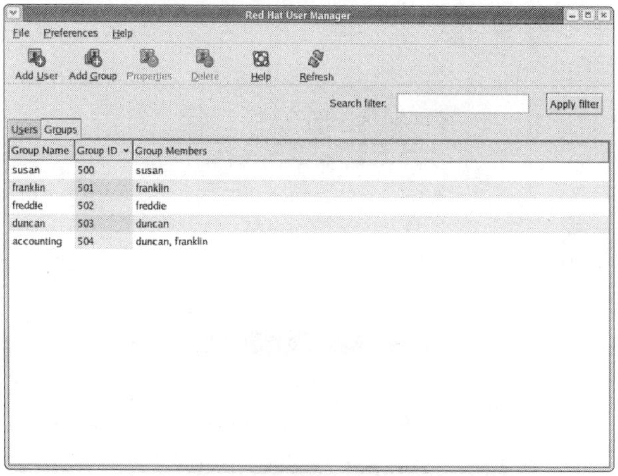

• **Figure 40-4:** The Fedora/Mandrake user manager Groups tab.

3. Click the Add Group button on the toolbar.

The Create New Group dialog appears, as shown in Figure 40-5.

• **Figure 40-5:** The Create New Group dialog.

4. Specify a name in the Group Name field.

5. If you need to specify a group number, you can check the Specify Group ID Manually box, but we recommend accepting the default and letting Linux assign the group number to avoid potential conflict.

6. **Click OK when you're done.**

The group is created. Now, you need to add the members.

7. **Back in the Groups tab of the user manager, double-click the group in the list.**

The Group Properties dialog appears, as shown in Figure 40-6.

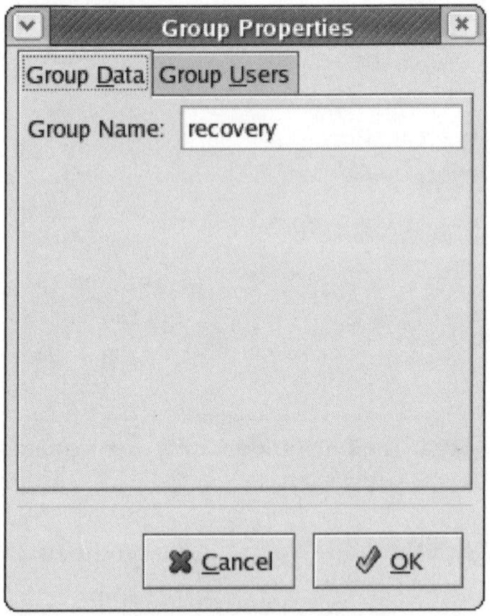

• Figure 40-6: The Group Properties dialog.

8. **To add users to your new group, choose the Group Users tab.**

9. **Check the boxes next to the users that will be members of the group.**

10. **Click OK when you're finished.**

The Groups tab in the user manager is updated to reflect the new group members.

Filtering users and groups

One really handy feature of the Fedora/Mandrake user manager is the Search Filter, located in the upper-right corner of the screen. You can apply the Search Filter to either the Users list or the Groups list.

To use the filter, type in the first few letters of the user name and click Apply Filter. The names are screened to include only those starting with that search string (see Figure 40-7).

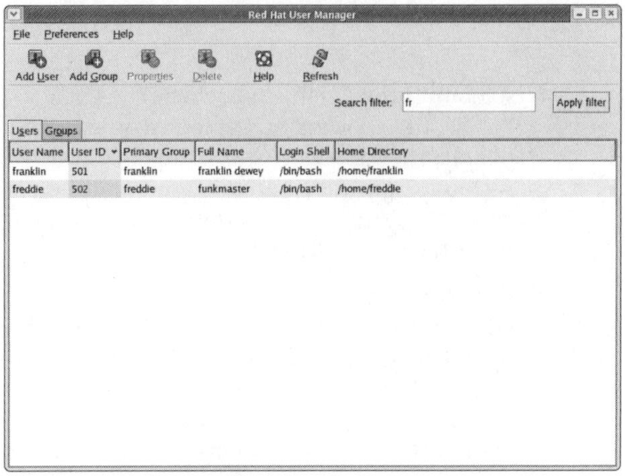

• Figure 40-7: The Users list, filtered for names beginning with *fr*.

To refresh the list to show all users, clear the Search Filter field and click Apply Filter. The list then refreshes, showing all users.

Managing Users and Groups with the SuSE User Administrator

The SuSE user and group administrator is part of the YaST Control Center. SuSE's user and group tools are powerful and friendly — a timesaving combination.

To start the SuSE user administrator, open the main menu and choose System⇨YaST. (Enter the super-user password if prompted). When the YaST control center appears, click Security and Users and then Edit and Create Users.

The user and group administrator opens, as shown in Figure 40-8.

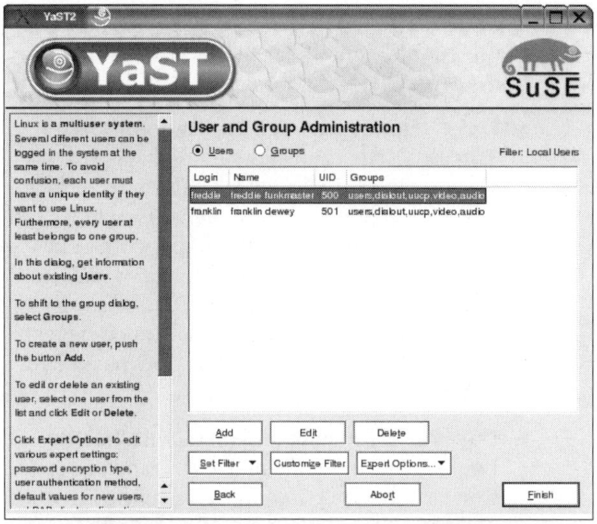

• **Figure 40-8:** The SuSE User and Group Administration dialog.

Adding new users

To add a new user, follow these steps:

1. **In the user administrator, click Add (near the bottom of the window).**

The Add a New Local User dialog opens, as shown in Figure 40-9.

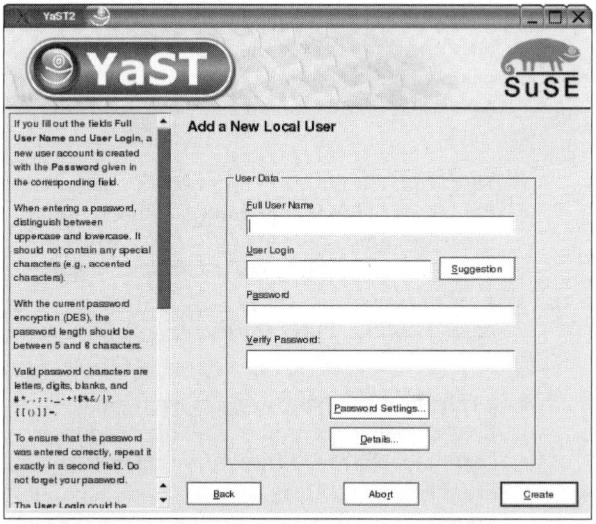

• **Figure 40-9:** The Add a New Local User dialog.

2. **Fill in the fields in the dialog appropriately:**

► **Full User Name:** This name is for internal use. Type in the full name of the new user.

► **User Login:** This is the name of the new user account (in other words, the login name).

► **Password and Verify Password:** Enter a password and verify the password in the next field. The password has to be at least five characters long, and it can be any combination of upper- and lowercase letters, numbers, and characters.

3. **Click Details to open the Add/Edit User Properties dialog, shown in Figure 40-10.**

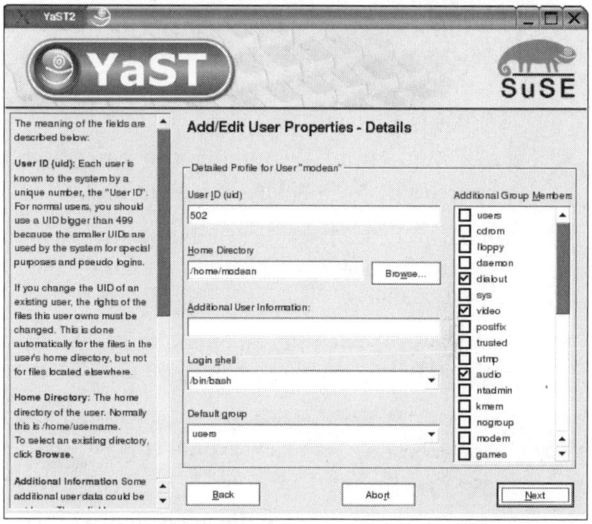

• **Figure 40-10:** The detailed user properties dialog.

4. **Change the fields in the detailed properties dialog to suit your needs:**

► **User ID (uid):** In most cases, you can accept the default user ID chosen by YaST. If, for some reason, you need to choose a different user ID, type in a value between 500 and 6000: YaST will display an error message if the user ID you specify is already in use.

► **Home Directory:** This defaults to /home/ *username*, but you can specify a different directory if you choose.

▶ **Additional User Information:** Enter any extra information that you want to note about this user. The information that you supply here is ignored by most Linux programs, but will be displayed if someone "fingers" this user with the `finger` command (see `man finger` for more information).

▶ **Login Shell:** The option you choose from this drop-down list determines which shell starts when the user opens a terminal window. `bash` is usually a good choice.

▶ **Default Group:** SuSE typically adds new users to the `users` group, but you can choose a different one by selecting the group from the Default Group drop-down list.

▶ **Additional Group Membership:** Use the scrolling list on the right side of the dialog to enroll the user in other groups or to remove the user from other groups.

5. When you're finished with the Add/Edit User Properties dialog, click Next to continue.

Note: If you click Back, YaST silently discards any changes that you made to the Add/Edit User Properties dialog.

6. Click Password Settings to open the Password Settings dialog, shown in Figure 40-11.

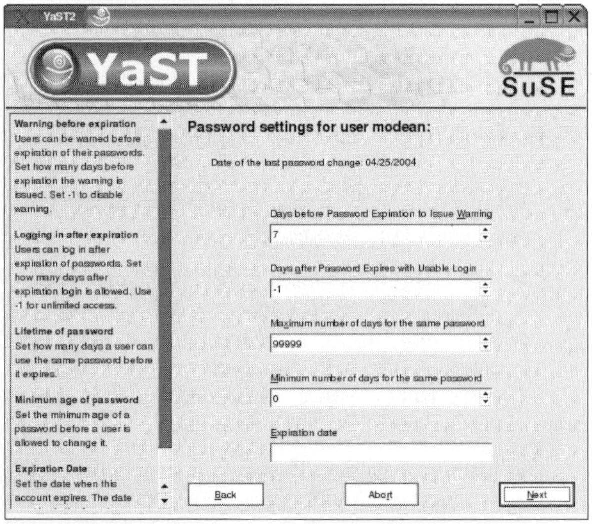

• **Figure 40-11: The Password Settings dialog.**

7. Change the fields in the Password Settings dialog to enable and adjust the password aging options for this user:

▶ **Days Before Password Expiration to Issue Warning:** The typical default value (7) starts warning the user one week before his or her password expires. Each time you log in to Linux, the login program compares the current date to the password expiration date for your account. If your password is about to expire, Linux displays a warning and suggests that you may want to change your password before it expires.

▶ **Days After Password Expires with Usable Login:** This might seem like a strange question at first. If you can log in even though your password has expired, what good is password expiration? When you log in to Linux after your password has expired, you must change your password before you can do any other work. The default value for this field (-1) lets you change your expired password at any time. If you enter some other value in this field, you can only change your expired password within that interval — after that, you'll have to ask the system administrator to reset your password for you.

▶ **Maximum Number of Days for the Same Password:** Enter a value in this field to specify how often the user must change his or her password. If you enter, say, 7 in this field, the user must change his or her password every week.

▶ **Minimum Number of Days for the Same Password:** The default value of 0 means that the user can change his or her password at any time. If, for some reason, you want the user to keep the same password for some period of time, enter the number of days in this field.

▶ **Expiration Date:** If you enter a date in this field, the user account will be disabled after that date. Note that the expiration date is *not* the same thing as password aging. When your password expires, you can change it and continue to use your account. When your account expires, you will no longer be able to log in.

8. **When you're finished with the Password Settings dialog, click Next to continue.**

Note: If you click Back, YaST silently discards any changes that you made to the password settings.

9. **When you're back at the Add a New Local User dialog, click Create to create the account.**

That's it; you've just created a new user account. You now see the User and Group Administration dialog again (refer to Figure 40-8). The user account that you just created will not be active until you click Finish to close the window.

Modifying user accounts

You can also use YaST's User and Group Administration tool to modify and delete user accounts.

If you need to delete a user, the process is simple: Just highlight the user and click Delete. When you delete a user, YaST will ask if you want to delete the user's home directory as well — be sure you've made a backup of any files that may be important before you click Yes.

To modify a user account, highlight the account and click Edit (or just double-click the user name). When you modify an account, you use the same set of dialogs that you used to create the account: Simply change any settings that you want to modify and click Next to save your work.

Adding groups

A *group* is a collection of users. Groups make it easy to manage file permissions. If you have several users who all need to access the same set of files, create a new group with those users in it.

YaST makes it easy to create and modify groups. To add a new group, you use the same User and Group Administration tool that we described previously:

1. **In the User and Group Administrator, click the Groups option button near the top of the dialog.**

2. **Click Add.**

YaST opens the Add a New Local Group dialog, shown in Figure 40-12.

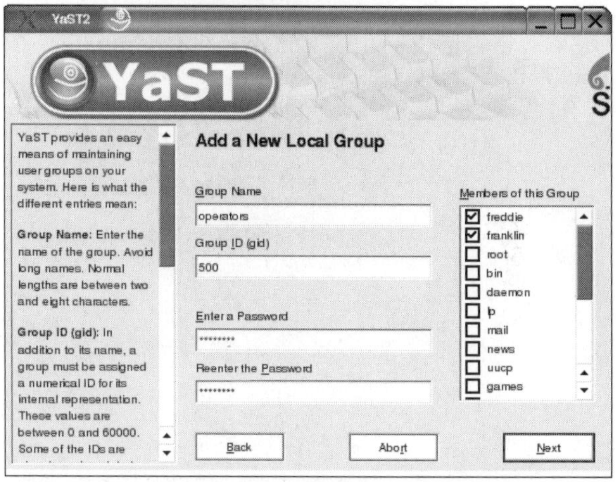

• **Figure 40-12: The Add a New Local Group dialog.**

3. **Type a name for the new group in the Group Name field.**

4. **Enter a Group ID or accept the default gid selected by YaST.**

YaST displays an error message if the group ID you specify is already in use.

5. **If you want Linux to require a password before a user can switch to this group, enter (and confirm) the password.**

In most cases, you can leave the password blank: You must be a member of a group before you can switch to that group, so assigning a group password is usually overkill.

6. **Use the scrolling list at the right side of the dialog to add and remove members of the new group.**

7. **Click Next to save your changes and return to the User and Group Administration dialog.**

Filtering users and groups

The SuSE User and Group Administration tool enables you to filter the users and groups that you see while you're adding and modifying accounts. By default, YaST displays local users. A *local user* is a user whose numeric user ID is in the range 500 through 60,000 (inclusive). A *system user* is a user whose numeric user ID is less than 500 or greater than 60,000. User root is a system account (root's uid is 0). SuSE Linux defines a number of other system accounts such as bin (user bin owns most of the programs in the /bin directory), daemon (used to run many of the background daemons on a typical Linux system), and mail (user mail owns most components of the e-mail processing system).

To switch between local users (or local groups) and system users (or groups), click Set Filter and select the filter you want to use.

Technique

41

Keeping an Eye on Your System

Save Time By

- ✔ Watching the activity in your system logs
- ✔ Customizing your log files
- ✔ Customizing system notifications for better alerts
- ✔ Creating custom resource worksheets with KDE System Guard

Linux log files can provide all sorts of information about your system. In this technique, we show you how to collect and customize that information. We also introduce you to some handy tools that help you monitor your log files and system resources.

The system log viewer is an easy way to review all your log files at once. An easy graphical interface allows you quick click-and-view access to all the logs, in one place. You can also customize the displays to call your attention to problems without having to search through long log files. The filter mechanism built into the system log viewer enables you to quickly and easily find problems related to device failures or programs that just won't start.

The `syslogd` daemon is responsible for deciding what gets written to the log files. The daemon comes preconfigured with a standard set of instructions, but you can customize the rules in the `/etc/syslog.conf` file to make the daemon more sensitive to problems. We show you how in this technique.

KDE System Guard is a great graphical tool that creates custom system and network resource-usage worksheets. You can arrange sensors that display information from your computer *and* other machines on your network to compare system resources in plotted charts and bar graphs. You can also use the process table to manage tasks — kill off runaway programs or change the scheduling priority of processes as they execute. You can also tell at a glance who's running what tasks and who's hogging your resources.

This technique is all about controlling information. Just like a detective, you need sources. The great thing about Linux's information resources is you don't have to pay them off for information. Just keep an eye on them, and they'll tell you what you need to know about the state of your computer.

Keeping an Eye on the System Logs

Log files contain information about the activities on your system. Information about various system processes is recorded into log files. The information in your log files can provide handy clues when things go wrong.

System logs contain a ton of information, but they can be a bit clunky to use. The system log viewer is a great tool to access your information quickly and conveniently, without the clunk.

Graphical system log viewers are included in most Linux distributions, and include handy search features and customizable warnings and alerts. The default log viewers included with Fedora and Mandrake are very similar — we've grouped the instructions for their tools together in the next section, "Viewing and filtering log files with Fedora and Mandrake." The log viewer included with SuSE is a bit more primitive, but it still renders a lot of insight into the activity on your system. You can find instructions for using the SuSE default log viewer later in this technique in the section, "Viewing your log files from SuSE."

Viewing and filtering log files with Fedora and Mandrake

If you're using Fedora or Mandrake, and want to see what's going on in your log files with the System Log viewer, follow these steps:

1. **If you're using Fedora, open the Main Menu and choose System Tools⇨System Logs. On Mandrake, open the Main Menu and choose System Monitoring⇨System Log.**

2. **Enter the superuser password (if prompted to do so).**

   The System Logs window opens. The left panel displays a list of log names.

3. **Select a log file to view details of the log in the window on the right, as shown in Figure 41-1.**

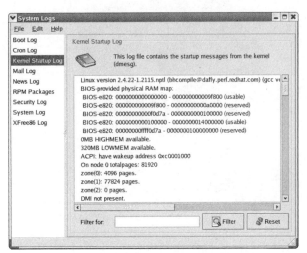

• **Figure 41-1: The Kernel Startup Log file.**

You may have more log files or fewer (and some of the log files may be empty). Use the scroll bars to scan the displayed log file or use the Filter feature to find specific messages.

Follow these steps to use the Filter tool:

1. **Enter the keywords in the Filter For field and click the Filter button.**

   Only those lines that include the keywords are displayed, as shown in Figure 41-2.

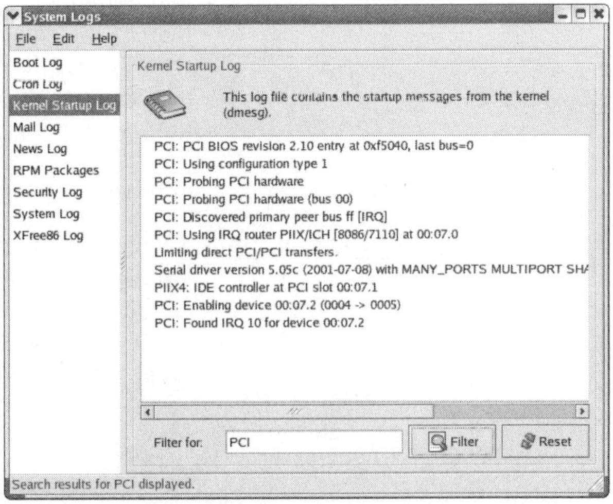

• **Figure 41-2: A filtered result set.**

Unfortunately, the Filter tool is case-sensitive; *error* and *Error* are two different words as far as the viewer is concerned.

2. **To show the complete log file again, click the Reset button.**

Adding and deleting log files from the viewer

The log viewer lets you keep your most commonly viewed log files ready and waiting for you. You can add more log files to the display or remove log files that you're not interested in. The log viewer remembers your preferences from session to session. To customize the set of log files displayed, follow these steps:

1. **Choose Edit⇨Preferences from the log viewer's menu bar.**

The Preferences dialog opens, as shown in Figure 41-3. It has three tabs: Log Files, Alerts, and Warnings.

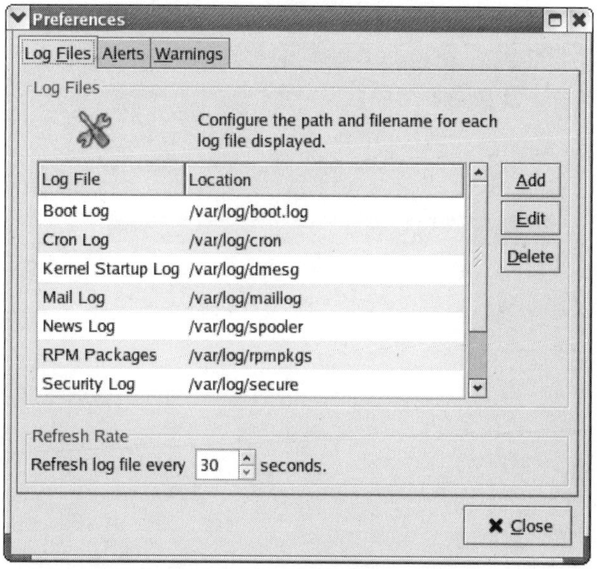

• **Figure 41-3: The Preferences dialog.**

2. **If you want, set the refresh rate on the Log Files tab.**

The refresh rate determines how often the viewer rereads the log files to display new messages. The default refresh rate is every 30 seconds; use the controls next to the field to adjust it.

 Pressing Ctrl-R refreshes the logs immediately from any display in the System Log viewer.

3. **To add a log file, click the Add button on the Log Files tab.**

The New Location dialog appears, as shown in Figure 41-4.

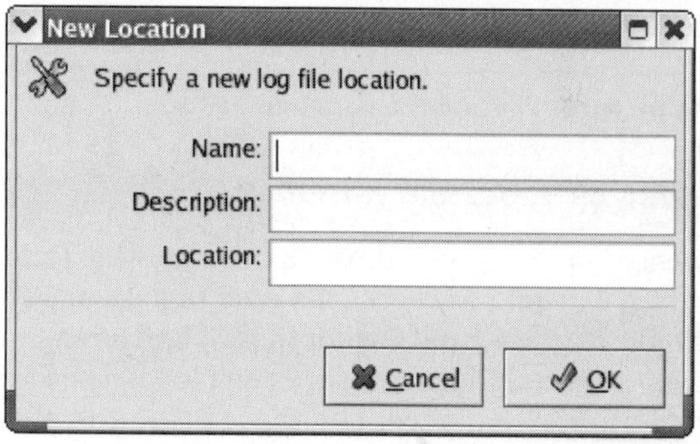

• **Figure 41-4: Add a new log file with the New Location dialog.**

4. **Fill in the dialog and then click OK to add an existing log to the list.**

The System Log viewer is a viewer only; the log file must exist for it to show up in the viewer.

5. **To change the pathname for a log file that's currently in the list, highlight the log's filename and click Edit.**

You'll rarely need to change the pathname for an existing log file unless you've changed the tool that creates the log.

The Log File Locations dialog opens, as shown in Figure 41-5.

6. **Use the Browse button to find the log file (or just type in the name if you know it) and then click OK to save your new location.**

If you want to delete a log file from the viewer's list, select the file and click the Delete button. This doesn't actually delete the log file; it just removes the log file from the list of log files you see in the viewer.

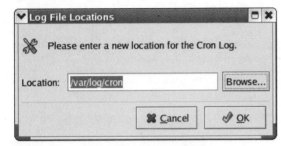

• **Figure 41-5: The Log File Locations editor.**

Setting up alerts and warnings

When you're browsing through a long log file (and log files can get *very* long), it's easy to miss important information amidst all of the trivia. The log viewer can search for keywords in a log file and highlight any entries that contain those keywords. By default, the log viewer will search for words like "fail," "denied," and "error" and display a bright red stop sign when it finds one (the red stop sign is called an *alert*). More innocuous words like "warning" are flagged with a yellow triangle (the yellow triangle is a *warning*). You can adjust the alert and warning keywords to fit your preferences.

To set up alerts, choose File➪Preferences in the log viewer. Then click the Alerts tab to open a dialog with a list of keywords, as shown in Figure 41-6.

Whenever the log viewer sees a message that contains one of the words listed, it displays an alert icon (a red stop sign, with an *x* in it) next to the message. Use the Add and Delete buttons to customize the keyword list.

To set up warnings, choose File➪Preferences in the System Log viewer and then select the Warnings tab. If the log viewer sees a message that contains

any of the words listed on the Warnings tab (see Figure 41-7), it displays a warning icon (a yellow triangle with an ! in it) next to the message.

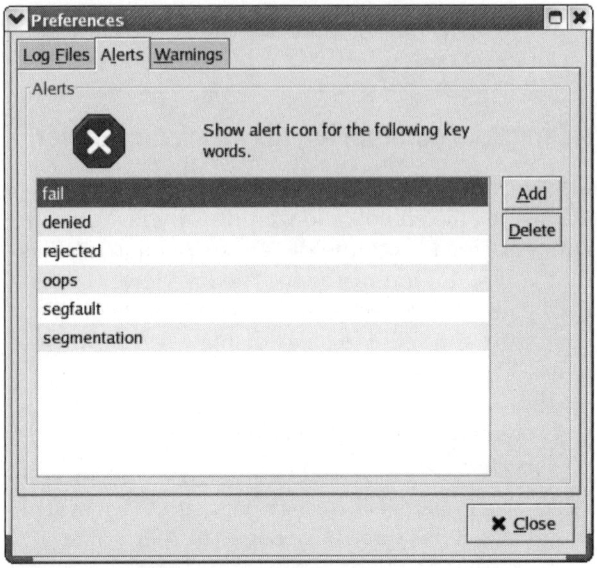

• **Figure 41-6: The Alerts keyword list.**

• **Figure 41-7: The Warnings keyword list.**

Use the Add and Delete buttons to customize the Warnings keyword list. The alert and warning icons make problems easy to spot in a crowded log file.

Viewing your log files from SuSE

The default log viewer included with SuSE (GNOME System Log Viewer) doesn't have as many bells and whistles as the Fedora and Mandrake versions do, but you can still save time while gleaning information from your log files with its help. To monitor your log files from SuSE Linux, follow these steps:

1. **Open the Main Menu and choose System⇨Monitor⇨System Log.**

The GNOME System Log Viewer opens, displaying the contents of the /var/log/messages file (see Figure 41-8).

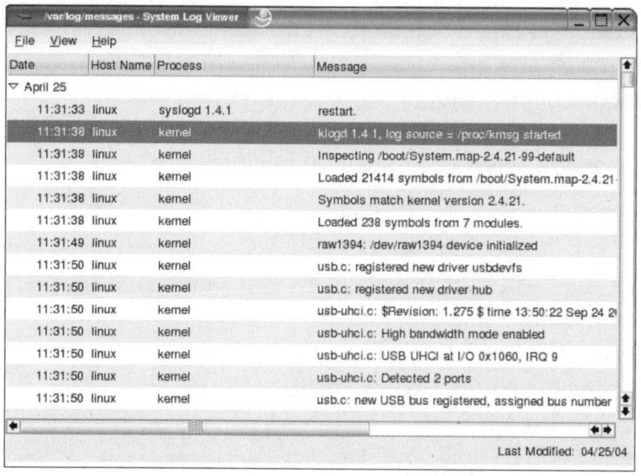

• **Figure 41-8: The GNOME System Log Viewer.**

Use the arrow to the left of the date to open and close the tree control and display the entries for that day.

2. **Double-click an item to open a detailed view of the log entry (see Figure 41-9).**

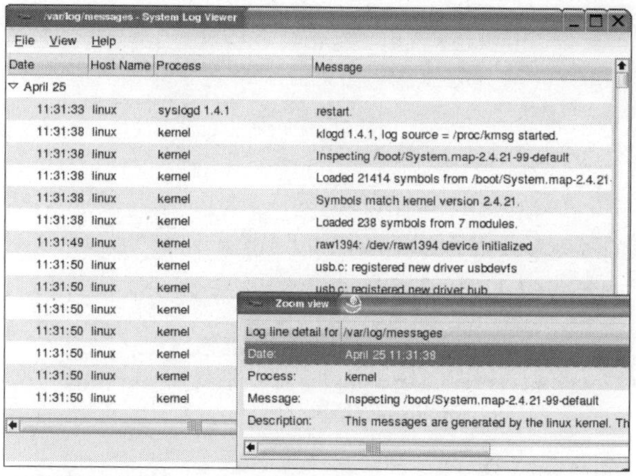

• **Figure 41-9: Details of a log entry.**

Monitoring your log files from SuSE

You can also use the System Log Viewer to monitor the activity in a log file. To monitor the activity in a log file, follow these steps:

1. **Choose File⇨Monitor.**

The Monitor Options dialog opens (see Figure 41-10).

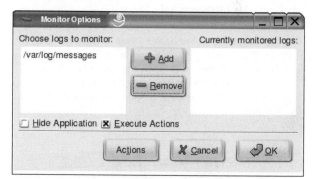

• **Figure 41-10: The Monitor Options dialog.**

2. **Highlight a log file in the left panel and click the Add button.**

The log file is moved to the right panel (see Figure 41-11).

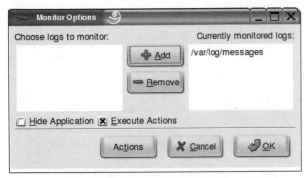

• **Figure 41-11:** Adding a log file to the list of currently monitored logs.

3. **Click the OK button to open a monitor dialog for that log file.**

The Monitoring Logs dialog opens, as shown in Figure 41-12.

• **Figure 41-12:** Current log activity displayed by the Log Monitor.

 Take a quick trip back in time to view the log entries recorded on a prior date by choosing View⇨Calendar to open the Calendar dialog. Log files exist for the dates displayed in bold text — click the date to see the log file for that date.

Customizing Your Log Files

Most log files are recorded by the syslogd daemon. When an application (such as an e-mail relay or a login program) wants to record a log message, it sends the message to syslogd, and syslogd decides what to do with it. Every log message is comprised of three parts:

✔ **Facility:** The facility tells you which subsystem produced the message. Table 41-1 shows some of the facilities recognized by Linux.

✔ **Severity:** The severity (the syslog documentation calls it a *priority*) tells you how important the message is. Table 41-2 lists the severity codes defined by Linux.

✔ **Message text:** The message text tells you about an event detected by the facility.

Most log messages are simply discarded without anyone actually seeing them, but you can customize log handling by adjusting the /etc/syslog.conf configuration file. You can route messages generated by a given facility to a separate log file (for easier viewing) or tell syslogd not to throw out messages that you might want to see.

Each entry in syslog.conf is made up of three parts: a facility code, a severity code, and a target. The facility code and severity code are used to classify incoming messages, and the target tells syslogd what do with matching messages. For example, suppose you have an entry like this:

```
mail.error /var/log/maillog
```

syslogd will route error messages generated by the mail facility to a file named /var/log/maillog. Actually, that entry will route error messages and all messages with a higher severity (crit, alert, and panic) to /var/log/maillog. If you want to route *only* the error messages, put an equal sign in front of the severity, like this:

```
mail.=error /var/log/maillog
```

If you peek at your own syslog.conf file, you'll probably see a few wildcards, too. You can use a * on either side of the dot that separates the facility and severity:

✔ To select all mail messages, regardless of severity (for example), type in an entry like this:

```
mail.* /var/log/maillog
```

✔ To select every critical message, regardless of the facility that produced it, use an entry like this:

```
*.crit /var/log/serious
```

 It's not a good idea to use a wildcard on *both* sides of the period because that would select *all* facilities and *all* severities.

The first two pieces of a `syslog.conf` entry (the facility code and the severity code) decide *which* messages are routed by that entry. The last piece (the target) decides what happens to those messages.

Most `syslog` messages are either discarded or recorded in a log file, but you can also route messages to other destinations. The first character of the target tells `syslogd` whether to send messages to a file, a named pipe, another computer, or a list of users. The following list explains what the different characters accomplish:

✔ `/`: If the first character of the target is a `/`, the target is a filename (or the name of a terminal device).

✔ `@`: If the first character is `@`, the target is a host name (selected messages are routed to the `syslog` daemon on the named computer).

✔ `|`: You can route messages to another program by creating a named pipe and prefixing the name of the pipe with a `|`.

✔ `*`: Route selected messages to a group of one or more users by listing the users (separated by commas), or route messages to all users currently logged in by specifying a target of `*`.

To summarize, here are a few sample `syslog.conf` entries that show you how to specify message targets:

✔ `*.crit /var/log/serious`: Writes critical messages to `/var/log/serious`

✔ `*.crit /dev/console`: Displays critical messages on the console

✔ `*.crit @bastille`: Sends critical messages to the `syslogd` daemon on host `bastille`

✔ `*.crit |/var/log/messages`: Writes critical messages to the named pipe `/var/log/messages`

✔ `*.crit freddie,franklin`: Sends critical messages to users `freddie` and `franklin` (if they're logged in)

✔ `*.crit *`: Sends critical messages to all users

TABLE 41-1: SYSLOG FACILITIES

Facility	Description
Authpriv	Security and authorization messages (you can also spell this facility `Auth`)
Cron	Messages sent by the task schedulers (`cron`, `at`, `anacron`, and so on)
Daemon	Messages sent by daemon processes (also known as services)
FTP	Messages sent by the FTP server
Kern	Messages sent by the Linux kernel
Lpr	Messages sent by the printing subsystem
Mail	Mail-processing messages
News	Usenet news-processing messages
Syslog	Messages sent by the `syslog` facility itself
User	Generic messages not falling into another category
UUCP	UUCP messages (you'll probably never see UUCP messages though)
Local0-Local7	User-definable messages (sort of user-definable anyway)

The severity component indicates the importance of the message. Linux supports the severities shown in Table 41-2.

TABLE 41-2: SYSLOG SEVERITIES

Severity	Description
Panic (or Emerg)	Serious problems — break out the fire extinguisher.
Alert	Something's *about* to go wrong unless you do something to stop it.
Crit	Critical condition encountered (something like "out of disk space" or "out of memory").
Error	An error has occurred.
Warning	Something went wrong, but you can continue to do whatever you were doing.
Notice	Things are okay, but here's something you might like to know.
Info	Things are okay, but you probably won't be interested in this.
Debug	Debug messages intended for propeller-heads.

Keeping an Eye on Resources with KDE System Guard

KDE System Guard is a customizable system monitor capable of monitoring not only your local system, but remote systems as well. The information displays in several easy-to-read formats that make it a snap to see where your performance bottlenecks are. KDE System Guard includes a task manager that tells you with a quick glance who's using system resources. It also gives you easy click-and-kill access to runaway processes.

 If you're using GNOME, KDE System Guard isn't available. Instead, GNOME includes a much simpler tool called System Monitor. To run System Monitor, open the Main Menu and choose System Tools➪System Monitor.

Finding and killing runaway processes

KDE System Guard makes managing processes easy. Here's how to get started:

1. To start KDE System Guard in Fedora, open the Main Menu and choose System Tools➪More System Tools➪KDE System Guard.

If you're using Mandrake, open the Main Menu and choose System➪Monitoring➪KDE System Guard.

From SuSE, open the Main Menu and choose System➪Monitor➪KDE System Guard.

The KDE System Guard window appears, as shown in Figure 41-13.

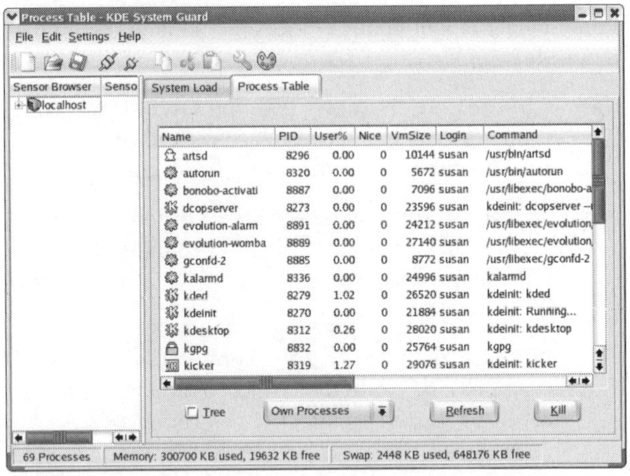

• **Figure 41-13: The KDE System Guard main window.**

2. Click the Process Table tab see a list of the processes running on your system and some of their more important properties.

By default, you see all processes currently running on your system, but you can limit the processes with the drop-down list box at the bottom of the screen (see Figure 41-14).

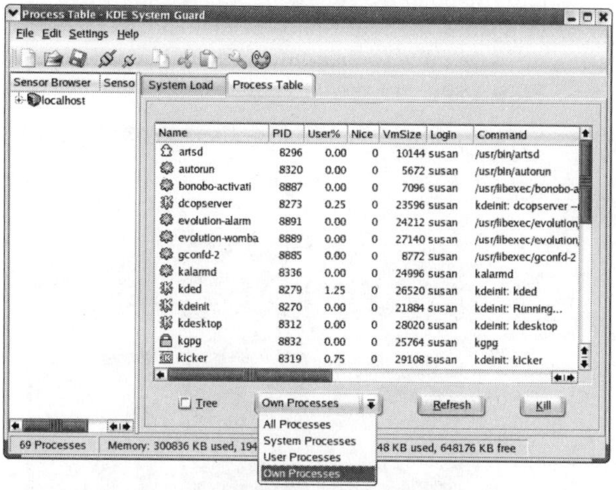

• **Figure 41-14: The process selection drop-down list box.**

3. **Choose one of the four options in the drop-down list box to limit the view:**

   ▶ **All Processes** shows all processes currently running on the system.

   ▶ **System Processes** shows all processes that are currently running that are owned by `root` — processes like services and watchdog programs.

   ▶ **User Processes** shows all processes that are owned by any user on the system.

   ▶ **Own Processes** shows the processes that are owned by the user logged in and running KDE System Guard.

4. **Click the Refresh button to update the selected worksheet.**

   By default, the worksheet updates every two seconds, but you can change the update interval by choosing Edit⇨Work Sheet Properties from the menu bar. The Worksheet Properties dialog opens (see Figure 41-15). To change the update interval, just use the spin control or type in a new number, and then click OK.

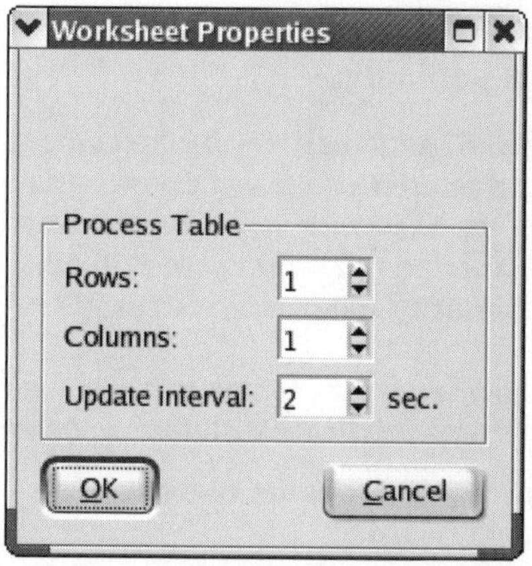

• **Figure 41-15: The Worksheet Properties dialog.**

5. **If you see a runaway process, highlight the process name in the list and click Kill to stop the process.**

   A confirmation dialog appears so you can change your mind (see Figure 41-16).

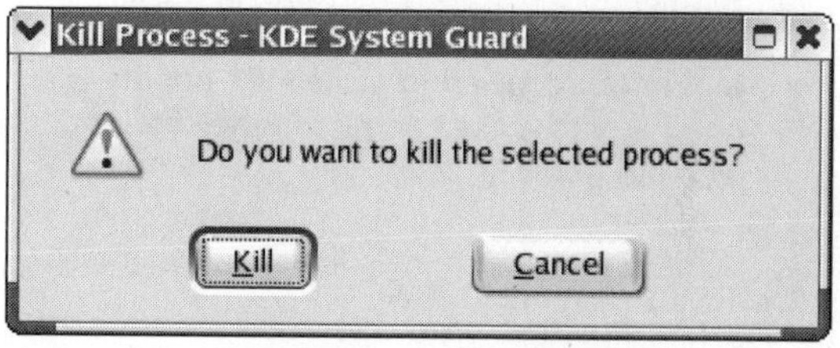

• **Figure 41-16: Confirmation of a process kill.**

6. **Click the Kill button in the warning dialog to stop the process.**

   In a second or two, the process table updates, and you'll see that the victim process is gone.

7. **Back in the Process Table tab, check the Tree box to display the parent-child relationships among processes.**

 If you have multiple copies of the same program running, use the tree format to tell the child processes apart.

Prioritizing processes to smooth a network bottleneck

You can make users play nice by "renicing" the processes that aren't quite as important as others. (Each process has a *nice* value that controls its priority in relation to other processes.) To change a program's priority, follow these steps:

1. **Open a terminal window and give yourself superuser privileges with the** su **command.**

2. **Type** ksysguard **at the command line to open System Guard.**

3. **Right-click on a process name in the list, and choose Renice Process from the pop-up menu.**

4. **Use the bar control to raise or lower the process priority and click OK to confirm the change.**

> In a system with cramped resources, lowering process priorities can give you a short-term solution to a performance bind. In the long-run, you'll probably want to upgrade your system because lowering someone's priority is a good way to make enemies (if they figure out who did it).

Watching your system load

KDE System Guard comes with a built-in worksheet that displays the current system load in an easy-to-understand format. With a quick look, you can see a graph showing CPU Load, Physical Memory, Load Average, and Swap Memory. To use the System Load tool, follow these steps:

1. **In the KDE System Guard window, choose the System Load tab to open the system monitors, shown in Figure 41-17.**

2. **You can add sensors to this display by choosing Edit⇨Work Sheet Properties.**

Each sensor monitors some aspect of your system. For example, the Battery Charge sensor

measures the amount of juice left in your battery (assuming that you're running Linux on a laptop) and the Load Average sensors measure the overall system load for that past minute, five minutes, or 15 minutes (depending on which Load Average sensor you choose).

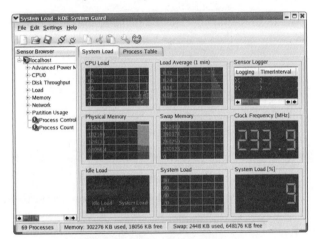

• **Figure 41-17: The System Load worksheet.**

3. **In the Worksheet Properties dialog that appears, add rows or columns to create empty slots in the worksheet for the sensors (see Figure 41-18). Then click OK to close the dialog.**

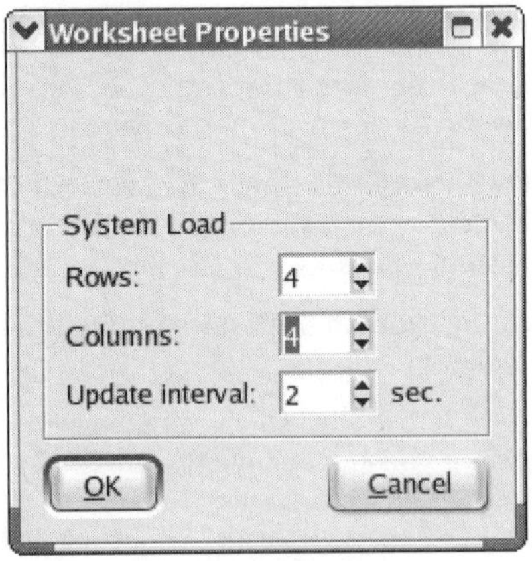

• **Figure 41-18: Add sensors to new fields.**

4. Expand the tree control in the Sensor Browser panel on the left to see the list of available sensors.

5. To add a sensor, drag the sensor name from the tree and drop it on a Drop Sensor Here label (in the worksheet).

A pop-up menu appears showing the sensor display options, as shown in Figure 41-19.

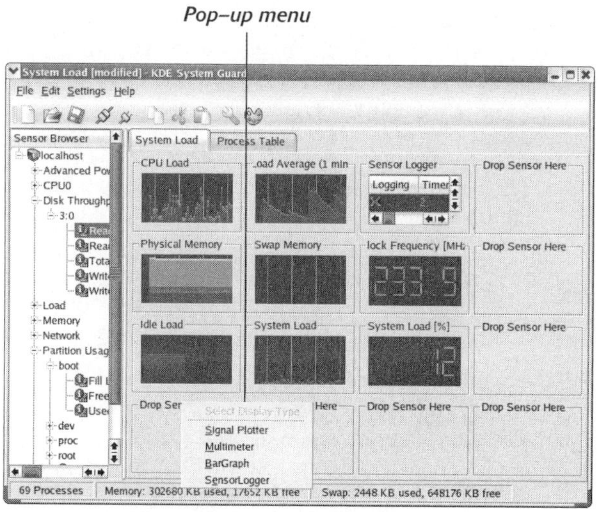

• **Figure 41-19:** Sensor display options.

The sensor types are as follows:

▶ **Signal Plotter:** This is the default display type for the System Load window.

▶ **Multimeter:** This is a large digital display.

▶ **BarGraph:** Drag multiple sensors into one window to show value comparisons.

▶ **SensorLogger:** Create custom logs for your system resources.

6. Choose a sensor type from the pop-up menu.

The new sensor is added to the display grid.

7. To change the properties of a sensor, right-click on the sensor and choose Properties from the pop-up menu.

The Settings window appears, as shown in Figure 41-20. The Settings window varies with the sensor type. A quick look through the tabs will help you decide on the customizations you'd like for your display.

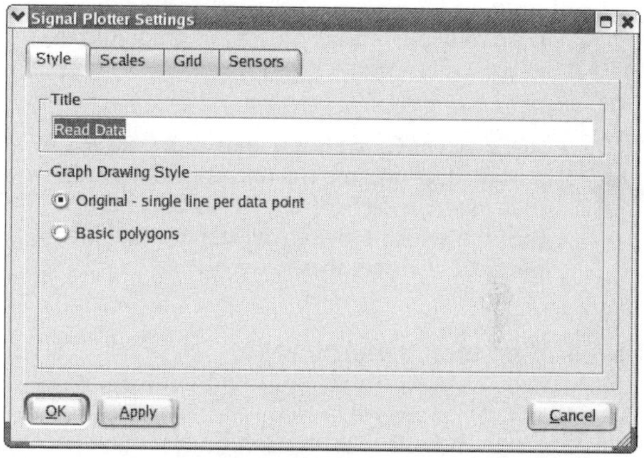

• **Figure 41-20:** The Settings window for a Signal Plotter sensor type.

A few sensors can display the status of multiple objects in table form. For example, the Partition Usage⇨Table Sensor displays the free space available on all disk partitions. That's a handy way to view a group of resources quickly.

After you set up the sensors and preferences you need, you can monitor your system for performance or resource bottlenecks.

Creating a new worksheet

If you'd like to create a new worksheet instead of revamping the System Load page, or if you want to create multiple worksheets to display the various system attributes, it's easy to do with KDE System Guard. Here's how:

1. Click the New icon on the toolbar.

The Worksheet Properties dialog opens.

2. **Enter the number of rows and columns you want in the new worksheet and then click OK.**

Your new worksheet is created, ready for new sensors.

 Drag multiple sensors onto a bar graph display to compare sensor values.

 KDE System Guard has a few resizing issues. If a worksheet gets too full (or contains too many sensors), it likes to delete titles and/or hide the sensor browser selector. It's nothing personal — it does that to everyone.

Creating system resource logs

You can use KDE System Guard to create system resource logs to your custom specifications. If the system seems slow at 1:00 p.m., when your users come back from lunch, you can create a custom resource log to help confirm your suspicions and track down the bottlenecks.

To create a custom resource log, follow these steps:

1. **Click the New icon on the toolbar to create a new worksheet.**

The Worksheet Properties dialog opens.

2. **Enter a title for the worksheet and click OK.**

A blank worksheet appears, ready for the new sensors.

3. **Drag sensors onto the worksheet.**

Here are some sensors you may want to include in a system usage log:

▶ Free Physical Memory

▶ Free Swap Memory

▶ CPU Load

▶ Disk Throughput

Throughout the day, watch the sensors that we mention and see how they change as your system load changes throughout the day. Watching how the sensors vary will help you identify resource bottlenecks. For example, if Disk Throughput is very high but CPU Load is low, you know that your computer is spending a lot of time waiting for the disk drive (and you may want to invest in some more drives to share the load).

As you add each sensor, here's how to spot the bottlenecks:

1. **Choose the Sensor Logger type from the pop-up menu.**

The Sensor Logger dialog opens, as shown in Figure 41-21.

• **Figure 41-21: The Sensor Logger dialog.**

2. **Complete the Sensor Logger dialog for each sensor:**

▶ Enter the name of the file that you want to contain the sensor log.

▶ If you'd like the log to alert you to extreme drops in resources, check the Enable Alarm box in the Alarm for Minimum Value frame and enter a Lower Limit value in the activated field.

▶ If you want the log to alert you to extreme spikes in resource usage, check the Enable Alarm box in the Alarm for Maximum Value frame, and enter an Upper Limit value in the activated field.

3. When you suspect a system slowdown, right-click on each sensor and choose Start Logging to start the log files.

Keep an eye on your sensor logs. They can get really huge really fast (and eat up the resources you're trying to preserve)!

4. When you suspect the system is returning to normal, right-click on the sensor and choose Stop Logging to stop the logs.

Most log files are written to the /var/log directory, but if you haven't started KDE System Guard with superuser privileges, be sure to write the logs to a file you have the privileges to create.

If you've told System Guard to alert you when extreme values are reached, the worksheet changes the sensor name to red and notifies you based upon the settings in your Control Center. To customize your notification settings for KDE System Guard, follow these steps:

1. Open the Main Menu and choose Control Center.

2. Expand the Sound and Multimedia entry in the Index tree control.

3. Click System Notifications.

4. From the drop-down list at the top of the screen, choose KDE System Guard.

The System Notifications window opens, as shown in Figure 41-22. Use this dialog to customize system notifications for KDE System Guard and other tools on your system. Several options for alert customization are available. Experiment to find a combination that will help you get your work done, but not drive you nuts with whistles, klaxons, and pop-ups.

5. After you finish changing the System Notifications, click Apply and then close the Control Center.

• **Figure 41-22:** The System Notifications window.

Displaying network resources

One really cool feature of KDE System Guard is its ability to monitor resources on *other* computers. System Guard supports a number of methods for establishing a remote connection, but the quickest (and most foolproof) is to use SSH.

Follow these steps to add sensors for another computer:

1. Click the Connect Host icon on the toolbar (the icon looks like a plug and socket, plugged together).

The Connect Host dialog opens, as shown in Figure 41-23.

• **Figure 41-23:** The Connect Host dialog.

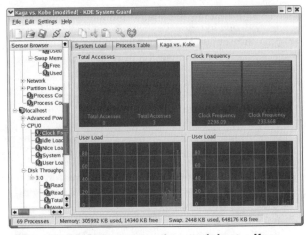

• **Figure 41-24:** System comparison worksheet — Kaga versus Kobe.

2. Enter a host name in the Host field, or choose a host from the drop-down list.

3. The ssh option button is chosen by default. If you don't have an ssh connection to the other machine, click the Help button for information about other connection types.

> Better yet, see Technique 33 for help setting up an SSH connection. `ssh` is easy to use and your best bet.

4. Click OK.

If you've configured public-key authentication for the remote host (see Technique 33), the computer name appears in the sensor list. If not, you have to enter a user name and password before the remote computer appears. Now you can create comparison worksheets showing computer against computer, as shown in Figure 41-24.

This is a great way to monitor network load and disk space. Set up signal-plotter graphs for each resource or use bar graphs to compare resources.

> Create a bar graph by dragging the same resources from each machine on a network into a single sensor frame to compare resource usage on the fly. It's easy to spot at a glance which system has resources to spare and which system needs help.

Taking the time to explore KDE System Guard can really add to your productivity levels. It's a great timesaving tool that gives you the information in just about any configuration you could want.

Part VIII

Serving Up the Internet and More

The 5th Wave   By Rich Tennant

"Someone want to look at this manuscript I received on e-mail called, 'The Embedded Virus That Destroyed the Publisher's Servers When the Manuscript was Rejected.'?"

42 Technique

Keeping an Apache Server in Top Form

Save Time By

- ✔ Using Synaptic or your distribution's installer to resolve Apache's dependencies
- ✔ Using OpenOffice.org Writer to set up a quick Web page
- ✔ Using dynamic DNS to keep your server at home, but make your data available to the world
- ✔ Using the HTTP Configuration tool to make easy changes to your Apache server

The Apache Web server is without a doubt the most popular Web server today. It's easy to use, and it's powerful. You can use Apache to serve up data to users on your own network or to locations across the Web.

If your company is already bogged down with e-mail, using a Web server can be a great way to publish information to users on your network. You can create company newsletters and change important information quickly and easily with a WYSIWIG editor like OpenOffice.org. Users can easily browse to the company's local site to find out what's going on without your making the information available for the whole world to see.

If you *do* want to take your site public, you may or may not want to rent space on someone else's host machine. Keeping a server up and running on your local network is a great idea if your site requires a lot of monitoring and upkeep. With dynamic DNS, you keep just a name and IP address registered on someone else's server — your data stays home where you can take good care of it. Your IP address may change, but your host name never will. If your IP address changes, you update the new address to the name server. When customers or associates search for you by name across the Internet, the name server relays the current IP address to them to complete the search. You save the high cost of machine rental on someone else's servers, and because your system is local, maintenance is quick and easy.

In this technique, we show you how to get your Apache server running at full speed in no time. We also show you a few quick tools you can use to populate and distribute your Web site and to keep it running in good condition. Serving up data is simple and quick with Apache.

Setting Up Apache — Quick!

The Apache Web server is easy to install, but it has quite a few dependencies (53!) that can really slow you down. The easiest (and quickest) way to install Apache is from disc (with your distribution's installer) or by downloading and installing it with Synaptic.

You can set up Apache by installing individual RPM packages with the rpm command, but the process goes a lot faster with a tool like Synaptic or the Fedora Package Manager. Resolving the dependencies manually can seem to take forever.

Using Synaptic to download and install Apache

Manually satisfying all the dependencies of a program like Apache can be a real pain and time-consuming. You have to round up and install each RPM package before the next will allow you to continue. Using a tool like Synaptic can save you a ton of time when you need to install a complex program with many dependencies.

Synaptic is the right tool for downloading or updating any of the software on your system. Technique 19 is all about using Synaptic to keep your software current. Check it out for details about downloading and installing Synaptic. It's a definite timesaver.

If you've installed Synaptic on your system, a pain-free installation of Apache is just a few clicks away. To download and install Apache, follow these steps:

1. **Open a terminal window and enter the following command:**

```
# synaptic
```

You're prompted to enter the root password.

2. **Enter the root password and click OK.**

Synaptic opens.

3. **Click the Update button (on the toolbar).**

Synaptic connects to each repository and updates the local index that tells Synaptic which programs are available (see Figure 42-1).

4. **Enter httpd in the Find field in the upper-right corner of the window.**

Synaptic finds the first package whose name starts with httpd.

Status	Size	URI
Done	1174	http://ayo.freshrpms.net redhat/8.0/i386 release
Done	1278 kB	http://ayo.freshrpms.net redhat/8.0/i386/os pkglist
Done	144	http://ayo.freshrpms.net redhat/8.0/i386/os release
100%	478 kB	http://ayo.freshrpms.net redhat/8.0/i386/updates pkglist
Done	157	http://ayo.freshrpms.net redhat/8.0/i386/updates release
Done	125 kB	http://ayo.freshrpms.net redhat/8.0/i386/freshrpms pkglist
Done	161	http://ayo.freshrpms.net redhat/8.0/i386/freshrpms release

6 /7 files   23.9 kB B/s ETA   0s
[Receiving...] [Processing...]

• **Figure 42-1: Updating the Synaptic packages.**

5. **Click the Find Next arrow (the right arrow just to the right of the Find field) to move through the matches that Synaptic finds and then click the Install Latest Version button when you find the following packages:**

```
httpd-manual
httpd
```

If you already have either of these packages installed on your system, the Install Latest Version button will be labeled Update instead. Update your versions of Apache as long as you're here. It only takes a minute.

6. **Click the Execute button (on the toolbar).**

A Summary dialog opens, as shown in Figure 42-2.

7. **Click Proceed to start the download.**

A dialog opens, showing the progress as Synaptic retrieves the package files. When the download completes, the installation begins.

When Synaptic is finished with the installation, another dialog signals that the installation is complete (see Figure 42-3).

8. **Close the dialog and Synaptic.**

Your installation of Apache and its dependencies is complete!

Summary

86 packages were kept back and not upgraded;
4 new packages will be installed;

12.1MB will be used after finished.

2121kB need to be downloaded.

Package changes

▶ To be installed
▷ To be kept back

☐ Perform package download only.

| Show Details | Cancel | Proceed |

• **Figure 42-2:** Synaptic, waiting to install new packages.

Package Manager output

Extra output was generated during Package Manager operation

While installing package httpd-devel-2.0.48-1.2:

Done.

✕ Close

• **Figure 42-3:** The installation is complete.

Installing Apache from disc

If you have a set of installation discs for your Linux
distribution, you can use the installer program (the

Fedora Package Manager, YAST, or Rpmdrake) to
install Apache instead of downloading Apache from
the Web. In this section, we show you how to install
Apache using the Fedora Package Manager.

If you're running SuSE Linux, the procedure is
similar — use System⇨YAST⇨Install and Remove
Software; choose the Selections filter and click
Simple Webserver. Mandrake users can install
Apache using Rpmdrake (Main Menu⇨System⇨
Configuration⇨Packaging⇨Install Software).

If you happen to have a copy of *Red Hat
Linux Fedora For Dummies,* by Jon 'maddog'
Hall and Paul G. Sery (published by Wiley),
you already have the Fedora distribution on
DVD; you can install Apache from that DVD.
Just insert the disc, enter the root password
when prompted, and follow along.

To install Apache from the Fedora install discs, follow these steps:

1. **Open the Main Menu and choose System
Settings⇨Add/Remove Applications.**

A dialog opens, prompting you for the root
password.

2. **Enter the root password and click OK.**

A dialog opens and confirms that Fedora is
checking the system package status. The
Package Management window opens.

3. **Scroll down to the Servers section and check
the Web Server box (see Figure 42-4).**

If you plan on incorporating other programs
(like PHP or PostgreSQL) into your Web
server, you can save time by adding them
now. Click the Details button to the right of
the Web Server entry to view the package
contents. Check the boxes next to any additional packages you'd like to add. When you're
finished, click the Close button to return to the
Package Management window.

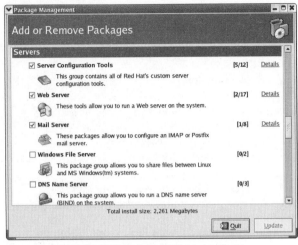

• **Figure 42-4: The Package Management window.**

4. **Click Update.**

A dialog opens confirming that the system preparation is completed.

5. **Click the Continue button.**

A dialog opens, confirming that your system is being updated.

6. **Click Continue, and when prompted, insert the Fedora disc and click OK.**

 The last few steps may vary a bit depending on which disc images you're using. Just follow along and click — the Package Manager is easy to get along with.

When the system updates are complete, a window opens confirming the successful installation. Now, you need to start the service, which we explain in detail in the next section.

Starting the Apache Service

The Apache Web server is a daemon — it lurks in the background, waiting for inquiries from browsers that just happen to come looking for you on TCP port 80.

To start the Apache Web server on a Fedora system, you need to start the httpd service. To start the service, follow these steps:

1. **Open the Main Menu and choose System Settings➪Server Settings➪Services.**

A dialog opens, prompting you for the root password.

2. **Enter the password and click OK.**

The Service Configuration window opens, as shown in Figure 42-5.

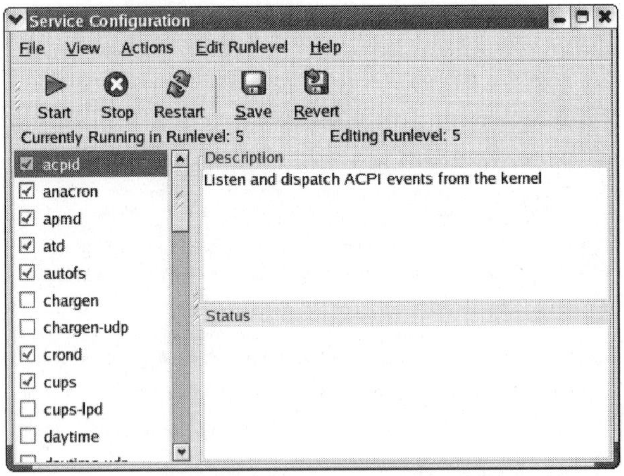

• **Figure 42-5: The Service Configuration window.**

3. **Use the scroll bar to scroll down through the list of services, and check the box next to httpd when you find it.**

The Status frame shows that the httpd service is stopped.

4. **Click the Start button on the toolbar.**

An Information pop-up informs you that httpd started successfully (see Figure 42-6).

5. **Click OK to close the pop-up.**

6. **Click the Save button in the Service Configuration window and then close the window.**

Your Apache Web server is up and running!

• **Figure 42-6:** The `httpd` service is Apache.

If you're running SuSE, you can use YaST to start the Apache Web server by following these steps:

1. **Open the Main Menu and choose System➪YaST.**

2. **If you're not logged in as the superuser, SuSE prompts you for the root password. Type in the `root` password and click OK.**

3. **Click Network Services, and then click HTTP Server.**

4. **When the HTTP Server Configuration window appears, click Enabled and then Finish.**

   After a short delay, your Apache Web server is ready to serve browser requests.

If you're a Mandrake user, follow these steps to start the Apache Web server using the Mandrake Control Center:

1. **Open the Main Menu and choose System➪ Configuration➪Configure Your Computer.**

2. **If you're not logged in as the superuser, Mandrake prompts you for the `root` password. Type in the root password and click OK.**

3. **Choose System➪Services.**

4. **Use the scroll bar to scroll down through the list of services, and select the On Boot check box next to httpd.**

5. **Click the Start button (next to httpd).**

   The Apache Web servers starts.

6. **Click OK, and then close the Mandrake Control center.**

   The Apache Web server is up and running and will automatically start each time you reboot your Mandrake computer.

To check the installation and service status of your new Apache Web server, open a Web browser and surf to `http://127.0.0.1`. Your browser displays the Apache Server Test Page, shown in Figure 42-7.

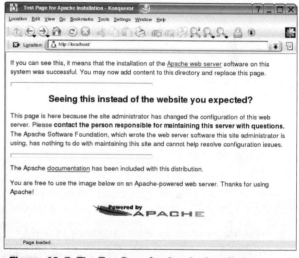

• **Figure 42-7:** The Test Page for Apache Installation.

At this point, you're ready to serve up Web content to machines on your local network. Apache is a quick way to distribute a company newsletter or share other in-house information. In the next section, we show you how to create simple Web content with OpenOffice.

 To make your server accessible to your company or network, but not vulnerable to the outside world, allow traffic from port 80 at your local interface, but disallow traffic on port 80 from the outside world. See Technique 34 for helpful ideas about using Webmin to set up a functional firewall.

If you want to serve up data to the rest of the world, you need an IP address and domain name — more about that later.

Building a Quick Web Page with OpenOffice.org

After you have a server up and running, you need to provide some content for your users. A quick and easy way to set up and maintain an internal newsletter is with OpenOffice.org. One of the great features of OpenOffice.org Writer is a WYSIWIG editor that lets you create and save HTML documents in no time. It's also very affordable.

 If you haven't already installed OpenOffice, you need to install it before you proceed with the steps in this section. See Technique 17 if you need help installing software on your system.

To create a simple Web page with OpenOffice.org Writer, follow these steps:

1. Open a terminal window and give yourself superuser privileges with the su command.

2. Enter the following command and press Enter:

```
# oowriter
```

OpenOffice.org Writer opens to a blank document, waiting for you to add content to your new Web page.

3. Add content to the Web page — text, pictures, and any graphics you want to distribute.

 If you add graphics, don't forget to copy them into place within the directory structure of your Web page so that Apache can find them. If you copy pictures into an OpenOffice.org document that you later save to an HTML file, the pictures are added as links. The links are replaced with images when the document is viewed in a browser.

4. When you're finished creating your opening Web page, choose File⇨Save As from the menu bar.

If you're running Fedora or Mandrake Linux, save your file as

```
/var/www/html/index.html
```

If you're running SuSE, save your file as

```
/srv/www/htdocs/index.html
```

5. Use the scroll bar next to the File Type field to highlight the HTML Document (OpenOffice,org Writer)(.html;htm) option in the drop-down list.

6. Click the Save button.

Your new Web page is saved where your Apache server can find it.

To check out your new network Web site, open your browser and surf to http://127.0.0.1.

Your new page is displayed; it should appear nearly identical to the document you created in Writer (see Figure 42-8).

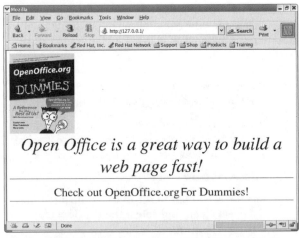

• **Figure 42-8:** Start your site quick with OpenOffice.org.

 For a top-notch tour of OpenOffice.org and a complete rundown of its capabilities, look for *OpenOffice.org For Dummies,* by Gurdy Leete, Ellen Finkelstein, and Marty Leete (Wiley) at your favorite online or local bookstore.

To edit and update your page with the current news of the day, just fire up OpenOffice.org Writer and open your document. Make your changes and save the file, and your local network site is automatically updated.

Taking Your Site Public with Dynamic DNS

You can make your Web site public by renting server space from an ISP or by obtaining your own domain name and hosting the site from your Apache server. When you rent machine space from an ISP, you pay not only for the room your data takes up, but also for the Web traffic to your site. If you have a small and simple site with little traffic, that's not a problem. If you have a large or complex site with a lot of traffic, renting server space can get costly.

 You can save time and money by running high-maintenance Web sites on local machines. If you use PHP to build your site or have live database access from the site, keeping the data where it can be updated easily is a real timesaver.

In order for others to find your Web site, you have to have a host name, and the host name must be fully qualified — that is, your host name must include a domain name (something like `www.example.com`). If your ISP is willing to assign you a fully qualified host name, you're good to go. If not, don't despair — you can *borrow* someone's domain name by using dynamic DNS.

Understanding how dynamic DNS works

When a user surfs to your spanking new Web site, he types a name (say `www.example.com`). His Web browser asks a name server to convert the site name into an IP address. His local name server defers the request to a well-known name server somewhere on the Internet. Eventually, the name server chain locates a server that's responsible for the `example.com` domain. That name server returns the IP address for host `www` (that is, host `www` within the `example.com` domain).

A normal name server maintains a database that converts host names into IP addresses for the hosts on the name server's local network. A *dynamic* DNS server provides the same service (host name to IP address translation), but it lets *you* change the database. To use a dynamic DNS server, you send your IP address and desired host name to the server, and it agrees to give out your IP address whenever someone asks for your fully qualified host name. Of course, the domain name that you get to use is owned by the dynamic DNS provider, but it gives you a permanent, fully qualified name that you can hand out to friends and business partners (without purchasing a domain name for yourself).

What happens if your Internet service provider changes your IP address? Simple — just update the dynamic DNS database.

Setting up dynamic DNS

To use dynamic DNS, you first contact a company (often an ISP) that will register your site name. You can find quite a few free (and paid) dynamic DNS providers online.

 Each service provider has its own how-to's for setting up a dynamic DNS service. The basics are pretty much the same, but read the FAQs for each service online before registering an account with that service.

One dynamic DNS service worthy of mention is DynDNS.org. Follow the simple how-to page at `www.dyndns.org/services/dyndns/howto.html` to set up your dynamic DNS account in no time. Follow the links to do the following:

1. **Register for an account.**

   You'll receive an e-mail confirming the account registration.

2. **Confirm the account registration to activate the account.**

3. **Add host information for your computer:**

> ▶ Choose a host name and an extension. Our personal favorite has to be is-a-geek.com.

> ▶ The DynDNS service automatically detects and fills in the IP Address field.

 Select the Wildcard check box if you want your name to be accessible from both www.sitename.dyndns.com and sitename.dyndns.com.

4. **Click the Add Host button, and you're done.**

If your Apache server is running and your firewall is allowing access through port 80, your Web site should be exposed to the Web.

 The exposure you get through the Web is also a liability. Build a good, sturdy firewall to protect the rest of your system — see Technique 34 for more information about firewalls.

 Better yet, keep your site in a UML jail. Visit Technique 58 for information about installing Apache in a UML jail with ADIOS.

Updating your IP address

Different ISPs have different policies about changing the IP address of your local network. If you're connected to the Internet using a dial-up account, your IP address changes each time you connect. Other connection types may assign you a semi-permanent IP address or change your address every few days. If your ISP changes your IP address only when you log out, you need to update the dynamic DNS host information only when you've logged out and back in again. If your IP address changes more often, you'll probably want to use a client program to monitor the changes and update the host information for you.

You can also update the host information manually by visiting your account information at DynDNS. Choose your host from the list of hosts that you manage, and its server will detect your address. If your address has changed, click the Modify Host button to update the information.

 Be sensitive to the fact that updating your IP address when it hasn't changed will invoke the ire of the good people at DynDNS. Compare IP addresses and update your account only if the IP address has changed. Otherwise, your service will be interrupted for abusing your privileges.

 Technique 45 is all about creating a self-signed SSL certificate for your Apache Web site. Check it out!

Keeping Your Apache Server Up-to-Date the Easy Way

If you run an Apache server for any length of time, you'll probably find it needs a bit of tweaking. You may want to enable new features or add virtual hosts (whole new Web sites) to your servers. You can make those changes directly with a text editor and the Apache configuration file, but you can save time by configuring your server with a good graphical tool.

Fedora Linux comes with a very friendly configuration tool that makes it easy to manage your Apache server: It's called the HTTP Configuration tool, and we show you how to install and use it in this section. If you're using a distribution other than Fedora (say, Mandrake or SuSE), we recommend that you get familiar with Webmin's Apache configuration module — it's not as friendly as Fedora's tool, but it's better than editing configuration files by hand. See Technique 17 for more information about Webmin.

Fedora's HTTP Configuration tool is an easy-to-use, graphical interface that allows you to access many of the Apache configuration options with just a few mouse clicks. For simple configuration changes, or complex virtual host setups, it's great.

Installing the Fedora HTTP Configuration tool

The Fedora HTTP Configuration tool is not installed by default with a standard Fedora installation, but it is included on the Fedora distribution media. So you can have it up and running in no time.

To install the HTTP Configuration tool, follow these steps:

1. Open the terminal window and give yourself superuser privileges with the su command.

2. Mount your Fedora media and move into the directory containing the RPM packages.

3. Enter the following command:

```
# rpm -Uhv redhat-config-httpd-
    1.1.0-5.noarch.rpm
```

With a few whirrs and clicks, the package installs.

Putting the HTTP Configuration tool to work

After you install the HTTP Configuration tool, it's ready to use. Follow these steps to open the HTTP Configuration tool:

1. Open the Main Menu and choose System Settings⇨Server Settings⇨HTTP.

A dialog opens, prompting you for the root password.

2. Enter the password and click OK.

The HTTP Configuration tool opens, as shown in Figure 42-9.

• **Figure 42-9: The HTTP Configuration tool.**

The tool features four tabs, each controlling a different aspect of the Apache service:

✔ **Main:** The Main tab controls the basic setup of the server. Use this tab to specify the server name and the Webmaster's e-mail address, and to add or change the IP address(es) that Apache listens to. Click the Edit button to edit the IP address and port information (see Figure 42-10).

• **Figure 42-10: Edit the address for your Apache server.**

 If you have multiple network interface cards on your system, each card has a unique IP address (and, probably, a unique host name). Specify which card Apache should service by selecting the Address radio button and entering the address of the preferred card.

✔ **Virtual Hosts:** Choose the Virtual Hosts tab to add or edit information about virtual hosts residing on your Apache server. Your Apache server can host multiple Web sites. Each virtual Web site has its own set of properties defining its name, where its root directory resides, and security information for that site.

Click Edit to open the Properties window for existing hosts, or click Add to create additional hosts.

▶ Click the General Options entry in the left frame to open the Basic Setup menu. Use the Basic Setup menu to enter information about the name and location of the Web site files, as well as the Webmaster's e-mail address.

▶ Use the Site Configuration menu to edit the directory name list and error pages that display for the virtual host.

▶ Click the SSL entry in the left frame of the Virtual Host Properties window to edit the SSL certificate information for the virtual host. If you choose to enable SSL certification, enter the location of the certificates on this menu.

▶ Use the Logging menu to control the transfer logs and error logs for the virtual host.

 Adding a reverse DNS lookup to the error log shows you who generates errors, but it also slows down your server. Gain a bit of speed by changing the drop-down list to read No Reverse Lookup.

▶ Use the Environment Variables and Directories menus for advanced management of scripts and directories.

✔ **Server:** Choose the Server tab on the HTTP Configuration tool to edit user and group ownership information and set the file locations for the process ID, lock file, and core dump directory.

✔ **Performance Tuning:** Choose the Performance Tuning tab to set the number of connections allowed to the Apache server, and the connection timeout information.

The HTTP Configuration tool manipulates variables in the Apache configuration file. You can edit the configuration file directly with your favorite editor, but if you're trying to keep life simple, the HTTP Configuration tool is about as quick as it can get.

 The configuration file for your Apache server is located at `/etc/httpd/conf/httpd.conf`. You need superuser privileges to make changes to this file.

 We recommend that you make a copy of the configuration file before making any changes to the original. It's always good to have something to fall back on.

43 Technique

Keeping an Eye on Your Servers

Save Time By

✔ Using apachetop to monitor your Apache server

✔ Using the MySQL Control Center to monitor and maintain your MySQL server

✔ Using mtop to audit your MySQL statistics at the command line

When you expose a server to others, you need to be able to monitor the server traffic and statistics. With good monitoring tools, you can find the slowdowns and tailor the server's responses to your users' needs.

apachetop is a handy, open-source monitoring tool designed specifically to return information about an Apache Web server. It's similar in nature to top, running at the command line, and it displays statistics about your server and the users who are visiting it. apachetop is easy to install and use, and although it doesn't go all out with bells and whistles, it returns a good amount of information. You can use apachetop to monitor not only the visitors to your server, but also your server speed as it serves up the resources in its repertoire.

The MySQL database server is a great tool by itself, but it's even better with good monitoring and management tools. The MySQL Control Center (MySQLCC) is a graphical tool that lets you monitor, test, and repair the tables in your MySQL databases. You can also use the handy features of the Control Center to manage database users and supervise the database processes.

If you're working with MySQL in a nongraphical environment, mtop is a handy tool that gathers and displays information about the traffic on your MySQL server. It's similar to top (and apachetop), and it's a breeze to use. Installation is a bit of a chore, but don't worry — we help you through that.

This technique is all about using the tools to monitor and improve your servers. Whether it's an Apache server or a MySQL server, keeping track of the vital statistics about its operation will let you make decisions that make your servers run faster and keep your users happy.

Watching Your Web Server Traffic with apachetop

apachetop is a real-time monitor for the Apache Web server. It's an open-source project, readily available on the Web. Installation is quick, and it's an easy program to use.

With apachetop, you can see the host machine that your visitors are using, determine whether they came by way of a search engine, and find out what pages they visited while they were there.

 You can also use apachetop to see if your visitors are repeatedly asking for documents that don't exist. You may want to rename your Web pages if the same page name is mistyped over and over.

Installing apachetop

To download and install apachetop, follow these steps:

1. **Open a browser window and surf to**

clueful.shagged.org/apachetop

2. **Click the link to download the latest stable release. As of this writing, it's**

apachetop-0.11.tar.gz

3. **When the Download Manager opens, save the download to your home directory.**

4. **Open a terminal window and give yourself superuser privileges with the** su **command.**

5. **Unpack the tarball with this command:**

tar -zxvf apachetop-0.11.tar.gz

6. **Move to the** apachetop **directory:**

cd apachetop-0.11

7. **Configure the package with the following command:**

./configure --with-logfile=/etc/
  httpd/logs/access_log

This command tells apachetop where to find the Apache log file. (The Apache server distributed with Fedora writes log files in an unusual location, so you have to tell apachetop how to find them.)

configure checks out your system, looking for the compilers and libraries it needs to properly build a working program.

8. **Compile the program with the following command:**

make

9. **Then copy the file into a useful place with this command:**

make install

With apachetop installed, you're ready to run the program and start putting it to use. See the following sections for details.

Running and exiting apachetop

To run apachetop, move to the /usr/local/sbin directory and enter the following command:

./apachetop

apachetop opens, displaying a status window that shows your server activity (see Figure 43-1).

```
susan@localhost:/usr/local/sbin - Shell - Konsole

Session  Edit  View  Bookmarks  Settings  Help

last hit: 21:40:59        atop runtime:  0 days, 00:03:40          21:41:04
All:            18 reqs (   0.1/sec)        15.0K (   0.1K/sec) (   0.8K/req)
2xx:        0 ( 0.0%) 3xx:        2 (11.1%) 4xx:   16 (88.9%) 5xx:   0 ( 0.0%)
R ( 30s):        6 reqs (   0.2/sec)         5.2K (   0.2K/sec) (   0.9K/req)
2xx:        0 ( 0.0%) 3xx:        0 ( 0.0%) 4xx:    6 (100.0%) 5xx:   0 ( 0.0%)

REQS REQ/S    KB  KB/S URL
   1  0.05   0.3   0.0*/garbanzo
   1  0.06   0.3   0.0 /kidney
   1  0.07   0.3   0.0 /pinto
   1  0.08   0.3   0.0 /adzuki
   1  0.12   0.3   0.0 /lima
   1  0.20   3.8   0.8 /
```

• **Figure 43-1:** apachetop **in action.**

When you're done using apachetop, just type q to quit, and apachetop returns you to the command line.

Navigating apachetop

The top portion of the `apachetop` display (refer to Figure 43-1) shows the statistics for the server. The lower portion of the display lists information about specific HTTP requests. Here are some navigation tricks that help you find your way around `apachetop`:

✔ Use the up- and down-arrow keys to move the selection asterisk through the list of specific requests.

✔ For more information about a specific request, move the cursor to the request line and press the right-arrow key. The request screen now includes the host and referrer IP addresses for the visitor, as shown in Figure 43-2.

```
susan@localhost:/usr/local/sbin - Shell - Konsole          _ □ ×
Session Edit View Bookmarks Settings Help

last hit: 21:44:21      atop runtime:  0 days, 00:07:01         21:44:25
All:            27 reqs (   0.1/sec)        20.9K (   0.1K/sec) (    0.8K/req)
2xx:          0 ( 0.0%) 3xx:       2 ( 7.4%) 4xx:    25 (92.6%) 5xx:    0 ( 0.0%)
R ( 30s):       5 reqs (   0.2/sec)         4.9K (   0.2K/sec) (    1.0K/req)
2xx:          0 ( 0.0%) 3xx:       0 ( 0.0%) 4xx:     5 (100.0%) 5xx:    0 ( 0.0%)

REQS REQ/S    KB   KB/S
  1  0.06   0.3   0.0  /garbanzo
                       HOST
  1  0.06   0.3   0.0  127.0.0.1

                       REFERRER
  1  0.06   0.3   0.0  -█
```

• **Figure 43-2: Extended information about who's visiting your server.**

✔ To customize the information displayed about a specific request from a user visiting your Apache server, type t to view the Toggle Subdisplay menu. From here, type

  ▶ u to exclude URL information

  ▶ r to exclude or include referrer information

  ▶ h to exclude or include host information

When you're finished looking at detailed information about a specific request, use the left-arrow key to return to the request list.

✔ You can sort the information in the request list by typing s to access the Sort By menu. From this menu, you can choose from

▶ r to sort by the number of requests made

▶ R to sort by the number of requests per second

▶ b to sort by the size of the request in bytes

▶ B to sort by the number of bytes per second transferred

Enter #`apachetop -h` **at the command line (or type** ? **while** `apachetop` **is running) to see online help.**

Switching among the log files (or watching several at once)

By default, Apache records activity in five different log files, which you can find in the `/etc/httpd/logs` directory:

✔ `access_log`

✔ `error_log`

✔ `ssl_access_log`

✔ `ssl_error_log`

✔ `ssl_request_log`

At configuration time, we told `apachetop` to watch the `access_log`. To view entries in one of the other log files, use the following command:

```
# apachetop -f /etc/httpd/logs/filename
```

You can watch many log files at the same time by appending multiple `-f logfile` options to the end of the command line:

```
# apachetop -f /etc/httpd/logs/access_log
  \
        -f /etc/httpd/logs/error_log \
        -f /etc/httpd/logs/ssl_access_log
  \
        -f /etc/httpd/logs/ssl_error_log
```

Changing the display time of apachetop statistics

By default, `apachetop` displays statistics for only the previous 30 seconds. Unless you have a lot of traffic at your server, you may want to extend the display time to hold the information longer.

 You can customize the `apachetop` display to retain statistics about your server for a longer or shorter length of time, depending on your needs. If you have a lot of server traffic, shortening the display time leaves you with easier-to-read reports. If your server traffic is low, a longer display time allows you to gather information over the course of hours for the sake of comparison and easy monitoring.

Use the following command to extend the display time to an hour (3600 seconds):

```
# apachetop -T 3600
```

The default refresh rate for the display is 5 seconds. If you have a lot of traffic and want the screen to refresh more often, use the following command:

```
# apachetop -r 2
```

Now, the screen refreshes every 2 seconds. Of course, you can combine display options on the command line:

```
# apachetop -r 2 -T 3600
```

This command refreshes the statistics every 2 seconds and displays the request activities for the previous hour.

Monitoring MySQL Server with the MySQL Control Center

One cool tool for monitoring and maintaining your MySQL databases in a graphical environment is the MySQL Control Center (MySQLCC). The MySQL Control Center is available from the official MySQL

Web site (`www.mysql.com`). The Control Center (like MySQL) is dual-licensed — see the MySQL Web site for licensing specifics.

Downloading and installing the MySQL Control Center

To download and install the MySQL Control Center, follow these steps:

1. **Open a browser and surf to**

`www.mysql.com/downloads/mysqlcc.html`

2. **Click the Pick a Mirror link for the Linux (x86, glibc 2.3) download.**

It's the second link in the Linux Downloads portion of the page.

3. **When the Select a Mirror page opens, click an HTTP link from a mirror close to your location.**

4. **When the Download Manager opens, save the tarball to your home directory.**

We're telling you to download and install MySQLCC in your home directory for the sake of having a consistent point of reference for this technique. You may want to save it elsewhere on your system. To make it easy to run (no matter where you install it), include the directory in your search path so you can run it without issuing the complete pathname every time. See Technique 7 to find out how.

5. **Open a terminal window, give yourself superuser privileges with the `su` command, and unpack the tarball with the following command:**

```
# tar -xzvf \
  mysqlcc-0.9.4-linux-glibc23.tar.gz
```

6. **Move into the `mysqlcc-0.9.4-linux-glibc23` directory:**

```
# cd mysql-0.9.4-linux-glibc23
```

That's it! MySQLCC doesn't come with any fancy installers; you just load the program onto your computer and run it as we describe in the next section.

Accessing MySQL Control Center features

After you install the MySQL Control Center, you're ready to take advantage of its handy tools. Here's how to get to them:

1. **Start the Control Center with the following command:**

```
#./mysqlcc
```

The MySQLCC window and the Register Server dialog both open (see Figure 43-3).

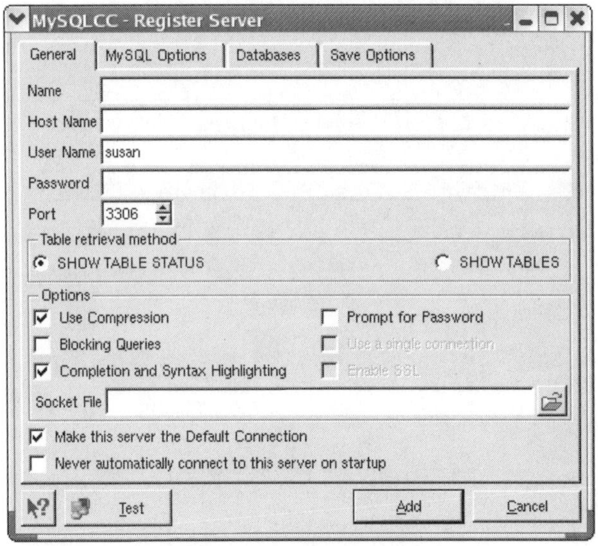

• **Figure 43-3: MySQLCC's opening view.**

2. **On the General tab of the Register Server dialog, enter the name of the computer in the Host Name field.**

If you have multiple MySQL servers running (scattered around your network), you may want to enter a server name that's meaningful to you in the Name field to make the different servers easy to distinguish.

3. **Click Add to display the session properties neatly in the Console Manager (see Figure 43-4).**

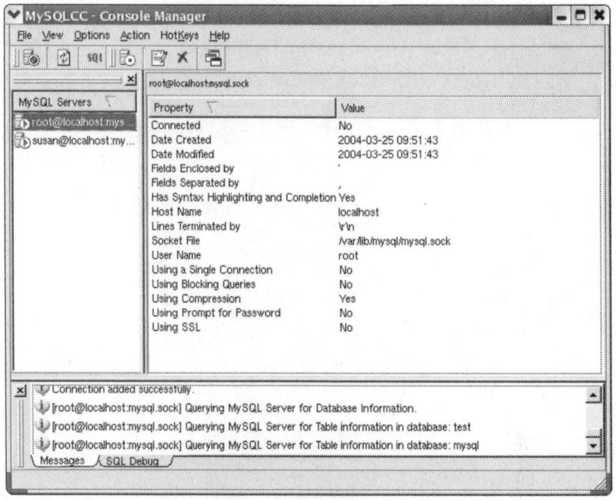

• **Figure 43-4: The Console Manager.**

4. **Double-click a server name in the MySQL Servers frame to expand the tree control and display the controls for Databases, Server Administration, and User Administration.**

5. **Highlight any entry in the Server tree control (Databases, Server Administration, or User Administration) to display status information about that aspect of the MySQL server.**

The following sections have more details on each of these controls.

Viewing, managing, and repairing a database with the Databases controls

The Databases controls enable you to view your database, and you also have tools for managing data and fixing problems as well.

MySQLCC is a complete MySQL client application. You can use MySQLCC to execute SQL commands and queries, but it's really designed to give you a quick overview of the state of your database. To view the statistics for databases, follow these steps:

1. Follow the steps in the section, "Accessing MySQL Control Center features," earlier in this technique, to access the controls.

2. Highlight the Databases entry, as shown in Figure 43-5.

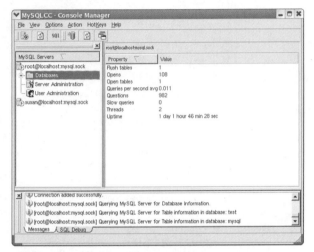

• **Figure 43-5: The Databases statistics.**

3. Click the tree control next to the Databases folder to display the databases on the server.

4. Click the tree control next to the Tables entry to view the tables in the database.

5. Highlight a table name to view the fields within that table (see Figure 43-6).

6. Double-click the table name to see the data within that table.

The table data is displayed, as shown in Figure 43-7.

 You can adjust the number of rows displayed, but by default, MySQLCC displays the first 1,000 rows. To adjust the default row limit, highlight the server (in the left-most pane), click the Edit button (in the toolbar), then choose MySQL Options and type a row count into the limit field.

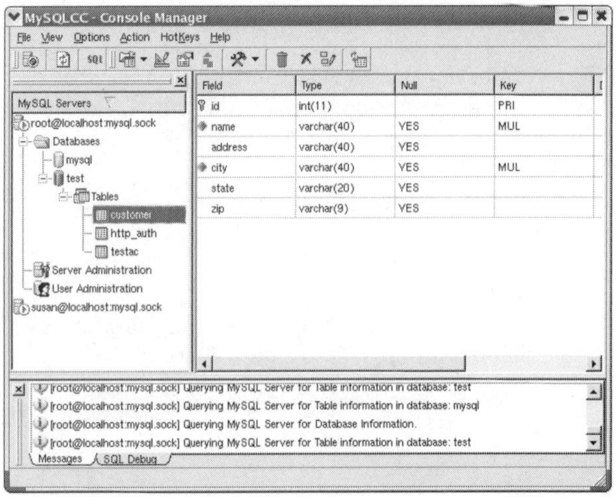

• **Figure 43-6: A quick view of the fields within a table.**

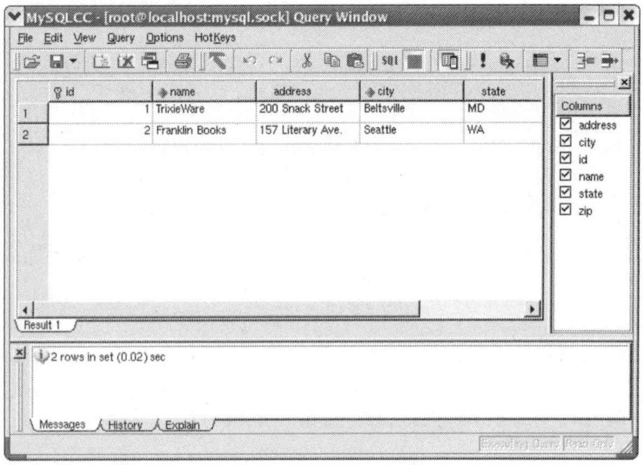

• **Figure 43-7: Table data displayed with the Control Center.**

The Databases controls include some handy tools to help you manage and repair your MySQL database:

1. Highlight Tables in the tree control and then choose Action➪Tools to open the drop-down menu (see Figure 43-8).

2. Choose an option from the Tools menu. Here are your choices:

▶ **Analyze Table:** This tool updates the data statistics used by the MySQL optimizer. Run this when you've made significant changes to the data in your tables.

▶ **Check Table:** This tool checks the table for errors. If you get an error message that you don't understand, run Check Table to look for possible problems.

▶ **Repair Table:** This tool repairs the table. Choose this tool if Check Table reports any errors.

▶ **Optimize Table:** This tool reclaims free space and rebuilds indexes to increase performance.

▶ **Show Create:** This tool displays the Create Table and Create Index statements that created the table.

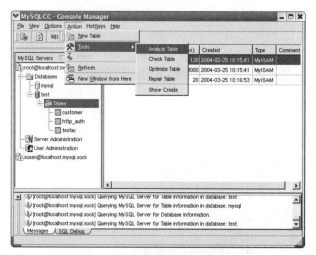

• **Figure 43-8: The tools included with MySQLCC.**

After you select the tool that you want to run, a pop-up window opens, displaying the tables in your database (see Figure 43-9).

3. **Choose the table you want the tool to act on and then click the Action button (for the Analyze Table tool, it's labeled Analyze, for the Check Table tool, it's labeled Check, and so on).**

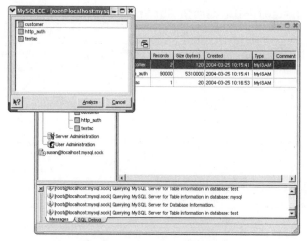

• **Figure 43-9: Choose a table from the list.**

It's a good idea to analyze, check, and optimize your MySQL tables on a regular basis to keep them in top form (database performance tends to degrade over time and the analyze and optimize tools can give you a quick speed boost). If the Check Table tool reports any errors, use the Repair Table tool to correct the problem.

Putting the Server Administration controls to work

Follow these steps to begin working with the Server Administration controls:

1. **Follow the steps in the section, "Accessing MySQL Control Center features," earlier in this technique, to find the Server Administration controls.**

2. **Double-click the Server Administration entry on the tree control to open the Administration Panel.**

   The panel has three tab controls. Table 43-1 gives you a quick look at what each tab has to offer.

TABLE 43-1: USING THE MYSQL CONTROL CENTER SERVER ADMINISTRATION TOOLS

Tab	What It Does	Timesaving Bonus Info
Process List	Displays a list of the MySQL client sessions	Click the clock icon at the right end of the toolbar to turn the auto-refresh option on and off. With auto-refresh on, the Process List tab displays the on-going activities on your server (see Figure 43-10). If a process in the Process List is running slow, you can use the MySQL Control Center to kill it off. Check the box in the ID column to the left of the session and choose Action⇨Kill Process.
Status	Displays statistical information about the server	The values shown in the Status tab give you a detailed look at how your MySQL server is being used. You can see the number of client connections, number of queries executed, as well as a count of how many times each MySQL command has been executed since your server booted.
Variables	Displays configuration information for the server	The Variables tab shows you each MySQL configuration parameter and its information for the servercurrent value.

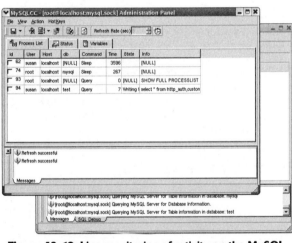

• **Figure 43-10:** Live monitoring of activity on the MySQL server.

Adding a new user

Here's how to add a new user with the MySQL Control Center:

1. **Follow the steps in the section, "Accessing MySQL Control Center features," earlier in this technique, to get to the User Administration controls.**

2. **Right-click User Administration and choose New User from the pop-up menu.**

The Add User dialog opens, as shown in Figure 43-11.

• **Figure 43-11:** The Add User dialog.

3. **Fill in the dialog and then click the Add button to add your new user.**

If you use MySQL, the MySQL Control Center is a handy tool to add to your collection. Check it out!

Watching Your MySQL Traffic with mtop

MySQLCC is a great monitoring tool if you're running in a graphical environment, but if you keep your servers and data in a non-GUI environment, use `mtop`. `mtop` is a handy command line tool that lets you watch your database traffic and transactions. You can also use `mtop` to help find and debug slow queries.

 Graphical tools are available everywhere nowadays, but you can save money and improve performance by keeping your MySQL servers in a nongraphical environment.

Gathering all the packages that mtop needs

You need a number of prerequisite packages to run `mtop`. Obviously, you need to be running MySQL. You also need the `mysql-devel` RPM package that goes with the MySQL version you're running. Both are included on the Fedora and SuSE distributions and can be added with either the Package Manager or as RPM packages from a distribution disc. If you're a Mandrake user, you'll have to find the `mysql-devel` package on the Web.

You need to download and install a few Perl modules before you can install `mtop`. The easiest way to install Perl modules is to use the CPAN (Comprehensive Perl Archive Network) interface. CPAN retrieves Perl modules and installs them on your system automatically.

 You need to have Internet access for the machine you're using CPAN with.

To install Perl modules with CPAN, follow these steps:

1. **Open a terminal window, give yourself superuser privileges with the** `su` **command, and enter the following command:**

    # perl -MCPAN -e 'install DBI'

2. **When you're asked if you're ready for manual configuration, type** `no` **and press Enter.**

CPAN continues to work, retrieving the Perl DBI modules. Depending on your system and connection speed, this could take a few minutes.

3. **Enter the following command:**

    # perl -MCPAN -e 'install DBD::mysql'

If you have trouble installing the `DBD::mysql` module, be sure you've installed the `mysql-devel` **RPM package.** `DBD::mysql` **won't install without it.**

4. **Enter the following command:**

    $ perl -MCPAN -e 'install Getopt::Long'

5. **Enter this command:**

    $ perl -MCPAN -e 'install Net::Domain'

The last Perl module that you need is Curses. At the time we're writing this, the Curses module available from CPAN fails to install on Fedora (and possibly other distributions as well). To install Curses, follow these steps:

1. **Open a Web browser and surf to**

    bastille-linux.org/perl-rpm-chart.html

2. **Click the most recent link to download** `perl-Curses (Text/Console)`.

Currently, that version is for Red Hat 9; it works fine with Fedora.

3. **Save the RPM package to your home directory.**

4. **Open a terminal window and give yourself superuser privileges with the** `su` **command.**

5. **Move to your home directory.**

6. **Install the** `perl-Curses` **RPM package with the following command:**

    # rpm -Uhv perl-Curses-1.06-219.i586.rpm

Now that the program dependencies are in place, you're ready to download and install `mtop`, as described in the next section.

Installing mtop

To install `mtop`, follow these steps:

1. **Open your favorite Web browser and navigate to**

`sourceforge.net/projects/mtop/`

2. **Scroll down and click the download link for the most recent `mtop` release.**

3. **When the download page opens, click the link to download the most recent tarball.**

4. **On the mirror page, click the link for the download site nearest you.**

5. **Save the file to your home directory.**

6. **Open a terminal window and give yourself superuser privileges with the `su` command.**

7. **Extract the contents of the tarball with the following command:**

`# tar -xzvf mtop-0.6.4.tar.gz`

8. **Move into the `mtop` directory:**

`# cd mtop-0.6.4`

9. **Now you're ready to compile `mtop`. Enter these commands:**

```
# perl Makefile.PL
# make
# make install
```

`mtop` is now installed in `/usr/local/bin` and is ready to use!

Monitoring traffic

`mtop` is a MySQL client application so you must provide a MySQL user name when you run `mtop`. To start `mtop`, use the following command:

`$ ./mtop --dbuser=root`

 You can substitute any reasonably privileged user for `root` in our example.

When you press Enter, the `mtop` display opens, showing the activity on your MySQL server (see Figure 43-12).

• **Figure 43-12:** `mtop` **monitoring a MySQL Server.**

Across the top of the display, you see the vital statistics on your MySQL server and its activity. The load average, the length of time that the server has been running, and performance indicators are all included in the statistical information.

Type ? while `mtop` is running to display a list of command options. Here are some of the more useful options:

- ✔ z: Type z and enter a process ID from the process list to zoom in on a process.

- ✔ e: Type e and enter a process ID from the process list to display the optimizer plan for the query that is executing.

- ✔ s: Type s and enter the number of seconds between screen refreshing.

- ✔ u: Type u and enter a user name to display only the server transactions for the named user.

- ✔ q: Type q to quit.

If a given query runs for a while, the color progresses from white to purple, yellow, and red to indicate the length of time the query has run. You can use the k option to kill off unwanted or runaway processes. Type k, type the process ID, and press Enter to terminate the process (see Figure 43-13).

 If you're running MySQL servers in a nongraphical environment, mtop is a definite timesaver. Getting acquainted with its features can help you monitor and manage your server with just a few keystrokes.

 Enter $ ./mtop --help at the command line to display a list of command line options to use at startup.

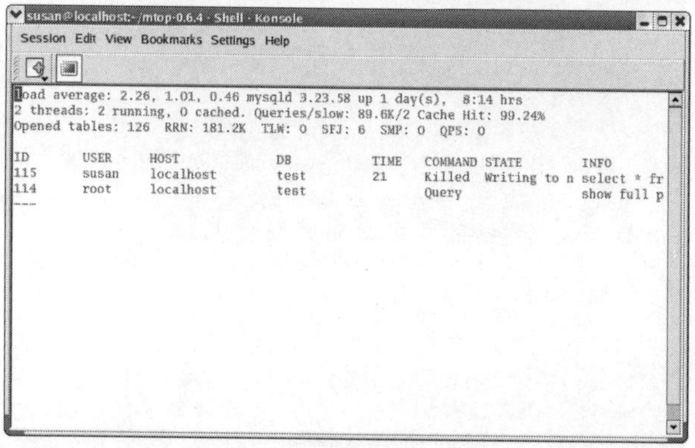

• **Figure 43-13:** mtop **killing off an unwanted process.**

Technique 44

Making a MySQL Server Your SQL Server

MySQL is a fast, powerful, reliable, low-cost database that's distributed with most Linux systems. You can use MySQL to store business records, baseball scores, user account information, network configurations, and just about anything.

MySQL is very flexible. One of the hallmarks of MySQL is that when it comes to performance, you don't pay for features that you don't need. When you store data in a MySQL database, you can choose from a variety of storage engines. If you don't need the extra reliability offered by secure transactions, you gain extra performance (and reduce multiuser contention) by using nontransactional tables. If the data that you're storing just *has to be* right (maybe you're storing payroll information or customers' credit card numbers), use InnoDB tables. They offer ACID (that is, *safe*) transactions in exchange for a bit of performance.

We don't have enough room to give you a complete overview of MySQL (we recommend Paul Dubois's wonderful book, *MySQL* [New Riders/ Sams Publishing]), so we give you a few tips that can make MySQL your database. In this technique, we cover these topics:

- **Installing MySQL the *easy* way.** The MySQL team has turned a complex procedure into a simple two-step process.

- **Pushing your data to remote offices (or just spreading a heavy user load across multiple servers) with MySQL's replication features.**

- **Keeping your data safe by archiving it with MySQL-specific tools or file system backup tools.**

- **Using the up-and-coming tool MySQL Administrator.** MySQL Administrator is an enterprise-level control center written by the MySQL team. It's designed for MySQL version 4 (and above), but many features work with older servers.

The MySQL software is distributed under a dual licensing scheme. If you're not redistributing MySQL as part of a closed-source package, you can use MySQL under the terms of the GNU General Public License. If you are redistributing MySQL as part of a proprietary software package, or you want warranty support from MySQL AB, you have to purchase a license. We're not attorneys, so please see the MySQL Web site (www.mysql.com) for the official license policies.

Building a MySQL Server

If you've slogged through the installation instructions at the MySQL Web site, you'll be happy to know that creating a MySQL server on Linux is surprisingly easy. The MySQL team has followed all the instructions on your behalf and wrapped everything up in a tidy RPM package that does all the dirty work for you.

Installing the necessary packages

To create a MySQL server on your computer, use your distribution's installer to install the MySQL server, MySQL client, and all necessary dependencies.

If you're a Mandrake user, use Rpmdrake and select Server⇨Database⇨Other⇨MySQL. Rpmdrake automatically installs the MySQL client and a whole slew of dependencies for you.

If you're a Fedora user, use Add/Remove Packages and scroll down to the Servers section. Click the Details link next to SQL Database Server and choose MySQL-server. Fedora automatically resolves all dependencies and installs the MySQL client software for you.

SuSE fans should use YaST2 to install MySQL. You'll find MySQL in Productivity⇨Databases⇨Servers. Like the Fedora and Mandrake installers, YaST2 will install the MySQL client software and any dependencies.

Starting the MySQL server

Before you can use MySQL, you need to start the MySQL server:

1. **Open the Main Menu and choose System⇨ Services (or, if you're using GNOME, choose System Settings⇨Server Settings⇨Services).**

2. **Enter the root password if prompted.**

3. **Scroll through the list of services (in the leftmost column) and find the service named mysqld.**

4. **Check the box to the left of mysqld and then click Save (on the toolbar).**

5. **Click Start (also on the toolbar).**

   A message appears confirming that the mysqld service started successfully.

6. **Click OK and close the Service Configuration window.**

You must hold superuser privileges to start the MySQL server. Open a terminal window and give yourself the required privileges with the su - command.

To start the MySQL server on a Mandrake system, type in the following command:

```
# /etc/init.d/mysql start
```

On a SuSE computer, use this command:

```
# /usr/sbin/rcmysql start
```

If you're running Fedora, use the following command:

```
# /etc/init.d/mysqld start
```

MySQL is up and running. The first time you start the MySQL server, it creates the server environment and an empty database named test.

 The data files for your MySQL database are stored in the /var/lib/mysql directory. For convenience, we refer to that directory as $MYSQL.

If you plan to use MySQL in your daily work, it's a good idea to configure your system to start the MySQL server each time you boot your computer: See Technique 20 for the details. Just remember, the MySQL service is named `mysql` on SuSE and Mandrake systems, and `mysqld` if you're running Fedora.

After you start the server for the first time, create a MySQL password for the `root` user:

1. **Open a terminal window and give yourself superuser privileges:**

```
$ su -
Password:
```

2. **Type in the following command (substituting your desired password for** *new-password***):**

```
# mysqladmin -u root password new-
    password
```

Now you're ready to use your MySQL server. If you're already comfortable with MySQL, we give you a few more timesaving tips in the rest of this chapter. If not, it's time to hit the books. You can find a wide variety of books on MySQL in your local book store (or at a bookseller online), but we happen to think that *MySQL* [New Riders/Sams Publishing] by Paul Dubois is one of the best.

Replicating MySQL Data

MySQL supports data replication. When you configure replication, MySQL automatically forwards data modifications (INSERTs, UPDATEs, and DELETEs) from one MySQL server to another. If you have a geographically distributed organization, MySQL can automatically *push* data from your central database out to your branch offices. Changes that you make to the master database appear almost instantly in each of the remote servers.

Replication offers three important benefits:

✔ **It improves the overall reliability of your database.** If the master database becomes unavailable for some reason (hardware problems, a system crash, or normal maintenance), a slave database can take over.

✔ **It improves the overall performance of your database.** Create a replication slave on a separate computer, and you've spread the user load onto two systems. MySQL's replication architecture makes it easy to configure as many slave servers as you need.

✔ **It improves availability while you're backing up your data.** Because the slave servers contain the same data as the master, you can take a slave offline and archive the data from there instead of from the master server.

Configuring replication: The three topologies

Different database vendors offer different replication *topologies* (the topology of a replication system describes which servers push data to other servers). MySQL supports three basic topologies:

✔ Single-master/single-slave

✔ Single-master/multiple-slave

✔ Single-master/chained-slaves

The single-master/single-slave topology is easiest to understand. One server acts as the replication master. When you change a table in the master, the modification is pushed to another server, called the replication slave.

A single replication master can push data to multiple slave servers. That's a single-master/multiple-slave topology.

A replication slave can push changes (which it receives from the replication master) to another slave, resulting in a single-master/chained-slaves topology.

Replication data always flows in one direction: from the master to the slave. The replication master records all data modifications to a binary (that is, not human-readable) log file. When a replication slave connects to the master, it reads the log file and applies all the changes to its own copy of the data.

That means that you should never change the data on a replication slave. If you *do* change data on a slave, the master and slave servers get out of synch, and you may lose data. When you create a slave, you start with a copy of the data as it exists on the master.

MySQL lets you choose which tables you want to replicate (you don't have to replicate all the tables in a database). That means that a single server can act as both a master and a slave, as long as it's a master for some tables and a slave for others.

Setting up replication for a single slave and master

Creating a single-slave/single-master topology is easy, but you have to do a bit of work on both the master and slave servers, as outlined in the following steps:

1. **Log in to your MySQL server on the replication master:**

   ```
   # mysql
   Welcome to the MySQL monitor. Command
       end with ; or \g.
   Your MySQL connection id is 5 to server
       version 3.23.58

   Type 'help;' or '\h' for help.
   Type '\c' to clear the buffer.

   mysql>
   ```

2. **Create a new MySQL user account — the replication slave will log into the replication master using this account:**

   ```
   mysql> GRANT FILE ON *.* TO 'repl_slave'
       IDENTIFIED BY 'repl_pass';
   Query OK, 0 rows affected (0.13 sec)
   ```

3. **Exit MySQL and shut down the server:**

   ```
   mysql> quit
   # service mysqld stop
   ```

4. **Create a backup of all the databases that you want to replicate:**

   ```
   # cd /var/lib/mysql
   # ls
   ```

   ```
   mysql prod devel
   # tar -zcvf data.tgz prod devel
   prod/
   prod/cust.frm
   prod/cust.MYI
   prod/cust.MYD
   ...
   ```

5. **Copy the archive (`data.tgz`) to the replication slave:**

   ```
   # scp data.tgz slave:/tmp/data.tgz
   test.tgz        100%   108.0KB/s 00:05
   ```

6. **Edit the `/etc/my.cnf` file and find the section that starts with**

   ```
   [mysqld]
   datadir=/var/lib/mysql
   socket=/var/lib/mysql/mysql.sock
   ```

7. **Add the following lines to the end of that section:**

   ```
   log-bin
   server-id = 1
   ```

8. **Restart the master server:**

   ```
   # service mysqld start
   ```

On the replication slave(s), follow these steps:

1. **Shut down the MySQL server:**

   ```
   # service mysqld stop
   ```

2. **Edit the `/etc/my.cnf` file and find the section that starts with**

   ```
   [mysqld]
   datadir=/var/lib/mysql
   socket=/var/lib/mysql/mysql.sock
   ```

3. **Add the following text to the end of that section:**

   ```
   master-host     = master-hostname
   master-user     = repl_slave
   master-password = repl_pass
   server-id       = 2
   ```

4. **Unpack the archive you made on the server:**

   ```
   # cd /var/lib/mysql
   ```

Choosing a Method to Back Up MySQL Data

Archiving (or backing up) the data in a MySQL database can be a bit tricky. The archive method that you choose is primarily influenced by three factors:

- Database availability (hot-backup or shutdown)
- Table type (MyISAM, InnoDB, and so on)
- Archive size

If your database must be online 24/7, you must use a hot-backup technique. If you can afford to take your MySQL server down for a while, you can use a file-system backup technique.

If you can take your server offline, you can use normal filesystem backup tools (like `tar`). If you need to use a hot-backup technique, you can use `mysqlhotcopy` or `mysqldump`. Or, for the ultimate in availability, use replication to archive your data. We explain how each of these backup tools works in the sections that follow.

Backing Up and Restoring with mysqldump

To back up a table using `mysqldump`, follow these steps:

1. **Open a terminal window.**

2. **Execute the following command:**

   `$ mysqldump database > backup.sql`

   Replace *database* with the name of the database that you want to archive.

3. **Copy the resulting file (`backup.sql`) to CD (or tape) or move it to a different host to safeguard the data.**

The `mysqldump` program creates an archive in the form of a series of SQL commands that will re-create the data should you restore from the archive. As `mysqldump` processes each table, it writes a `CREATE TABLE` command to re-create the table and all indexes defined for that table. Then it writes an `INSERT` command for each row in the table.

Listing 44-1 shows a snippet from a typical `mysqldump` archive.

LISTING 44-1: MYSQLDUMP ARCHIVE

```
          . . .
--
-- Table structure for table `customer`
--
CREATE TABLE customer (
  id      int(11)      NOT NULL default '0',
  name    varchar(40) default NULL,
  address varchar(40) default NULL,
  city    varchar(40) default NULL,
  state   varchar(20) default NULL,
  zip     varchar(9)  default NULL,

  PRIMARY KEY  (id),
  KEY cc_name (name),
  KEY cc_city_state (city,state)
) TYPE=MyISAM;

--
-- Dumping data for table `customer`
--
INSERT INTO customer VALUES (1,'TrixieWare',
  '200 Snack Street',
  'Beltsville','MD','25525');
INSERT INTO customer VALUES (2,'Franklin
  Books','157 Literary Ave.','Seattle',
  'WA','97745');
          . . .
```

mysqldump backup options

The `mysqldump` command supports a variety of command line options, many of which affect the format of the data in the archive itself. One particularly handy option is `--add-drop-table`. This option tells `mysqldump` to include a `DROP TABLE` command before each `CREATE TABLE` command. If you don't use `--add-drop-table`, the resulting script will fail if `tablename` already exists when you run the script (which is usually the case).

You should also consider using the `--all` option. `--all` writes all the table options (character set, comment, row format, and so on) used when each table was originally created. If you don't use `--all`, you'll lose all those table options if you restore from an archive script. Table 44-1 lists the `mysqldump` options that affect the format of the resulting archive.

 It's a good idea to use the `--opt` option in most scenarios. `--opt` produces an archive that saves all data (even the extra table options normally saved with the `--all` flag) in a form that's optimized for quick restores.

The `--complete-insert` option is useful when you suspect that you may restructure a table between the time you create the archive and the time you restore from that archive.

Backing up multiple databases

To archive all databases, add the `--all-databases` option to your command line when you create the archive. Or you can archive a set of databases like this:

```
$ mysqldump --databases db1 db2 db3
```

Compressing the archive

 The archive produced by `mysqldump` can get very big very fast. Instead of storing the raw archive on disc, you can compress the script that `mysqldump` produces by using `gzip` or `bzip2`.

Because `mysqldump` writes the script to its standard output stream, you can easily pipe the script into the standard input stream of a compression tool, like this:

```
$ mysqldump database | gzip > backup.sql.gz
```

This command archives the given `database`, pipes the resulting script to `gzip`, and saves the compressed script to `backup.sql.gz`.

TABLE 44-1: MYSQLDUMP ARCHIVE OPTIONS

Option	Description
`--all`	Force `mysqldump` to archive all table options (`TYPE`, `COMMENT`, and so on).
`--complete-insert`	Include column names in every `INSERT` command.
`--extended-insert`	Insert multiple rows with a single `INSERT` command.
`--add-drop-table`	Insert a `DROP TABLE` command before each `CREATE TABLE`.
`--add-locks`	Lock each table for `WRITE` access before inserting new rows.
`--disable-keys`	Update indexes after all data has been inserted.
`--no-autocommit`	Restore each table in a single transaction.
`--no-create-db`	Don't write `CREATE DATABASE` commands to the script.
`--quote-names`	Quote all column and table names in the script. Use this option only if you've created a table (or column) whose name conflicts with a reserved keyword.
`--xml`	Produce the archive in the form of an XML document rather than an SQL script.
`--where=`*where-clause*	Only archive rows that satisfy the *where-clause*.
`--opt`	Optimize the archive for best restore performance.

Restoring a mysqldump archive

After you've created an archive with `mysqldump`, it's easy to restore your data if something goes wrong. Because `mysqldump` created an SQL script for you, all you have to do to recover lost data is to run the script.

For example, if you've created an archive named `backup.sql`, simply feed that script back into the `mysql` client, like this:

```
$ mysql database < backup.sql
```

Note that you must provide a *database* name if you archived a single database.

If you back up multiple databases in the same archive file with the `--all-databases` option or the `--databases` option, you don't have to specify a database when you restore (the database names are stored in the archive).

To restore from a compressed archive, use the `zcat` program to decompress the script and pipe the result into `mysql`:

```
$ zcat backup.sql.gz | mysql database
```

 If you normally back up your data to CD or DVD, see Technique 50 for a handy way to stream your MySQL archive directly onto a set of one or more discs.

Backing Up with File System Tools

If you can afford to take your MySQL server offline occasionally, you can use normal Linux backup tools, such as `tar` and `gzip`. (See Technique 50 for information about using file system backup tools to archive your data.)

MySQL tables are stored in normal file system data files. If you have a MyISAM table named `customer` (in a database named `acctg`), you see three customer-related files in `/var/lib/mysql/acctg`:

- ✔ `customer.frm`: Contains the metadata for the `customer` table (that is, the table, column, and index definitions)

- ✔ `customer.MYD`: Contains the rows in the `customer` table

- ✔ `customer.MYI`: Contains the indexes defined for the `customer` table (if any)

You can back up an entire database by archiving the files in the database directory. For example, use the following command to create a file system backup of the `acctg` database:

```
$ tar -zcvf acctg.tgz /var/lib/mysql/acctg
```

Remember to be safe and shut down your MySQL server before you copy the table files.

If you *can't* shut down your MySQL server on a regular basis, you can still use file system archive tools, but you have to ensure that the tables that you're backing up are not being modified at the time you archive them.

Making a mysqlhotcopy of Your Database

The `mysqlhotcopy` program creates a copy of MyISAM table files from a running server. When `mysqlhotcopy` archives a table, it acquires a READ lock on the table, creates a copy of the table's data files, and then releases the READ lock. The READ lock prevents updates but allows other users to read the table at the same time.

To back up the `acctg` database using `mysqlhotcopy`, use the following command:

```
$ mysqlhotcopy acctg
```

The table files are copied to a directory named `/var/lib/mysql/acct_copy`. You can use a file system archive tool to back up the copy.

The `mysqlhotcopy` utility copies only MyISAM tables, not InnoDB or BDB tables. Using `mysqlhotcopy` is less intrusive than taking your database offline, but it can slow things down if you're backing up a busy database. (`mysqlhotcopy` has to wait for the `READ` lock on *all* tables before it proceeds and blocks all table modifications until it finishes.)

Archiving a Replication Slave

Another very useful alternative to `mysqlhotcopy` is replication. When you replicate a database (or a table within a database), the replication slave maintains an exact copy of the data stored in the replication master.

To back up your data, simply shut down the slave and use a file system backup tool to archive the slave database. While your slave database is offline, users can still read and modify the master. Then when the slave comes back online, the replication mechanism automatically applies any changes to the slave database. When you back up a replication slave, you must archive the `$MYSQL/master.info` and `$MYSQL/relay-log.info` files, too.

Taking Care of Business with MySQL Administrator

MySQL Administrator is a graphical interface that helps you manage your MySQL server. It's a very young tool (in fact, it's still in alpha-release land), complete with all the bugs you would expect from a program at this stage of maturity. It does show a ton of promise though, and it's worth getting familiar with. We think it has a great future as it grows and develops.

 The official voices at MySQL say that this tool will not work well with the release-3 servers — but only a few of the features don't work. Fedora is currently distributed with release-3 servers but should be stepping up to release-4 servers any day now. SuSE and Mandrake ship with MySQL release 4.

You can run release-4 MySQL servers on Fedora, but they're not standard issue. However, they should become standard equipment soon.

 This is alpha-release software. It seems pretty stable, but it shouldn't be used in a production environment yet (that is, with really, really important data). It's a good product to get familiar with though — just keep lots of backups of any data dear to your heart or business.

Installing MySQL Administrator

To install MySQL Administrator, follow these steps:

1. **Open a browser window and surf to**
   `www.mysql.com/downloads/`

2. **Scroll down the page to the Graphical Clients section and click the MySQL Administrator link.**

3. **Scroll down the MySQL Administrator page and click the Pick a Mirror link next to the Linux download labeled** `Linux (x86, glibc 2.3, stripped)`.

   The nonstripped version contains debug information and other stuff you most likely don't need, and it will just slow down the download.

4. **Scroll through the mirror sites to find a download location geographically near you. Click the HTTP link to start the download.**

5. **Save the download to your home directory (or** `/tmp` **— you won't need the tarball after you've installed it).**

6. **Close the download manager and the browser.**

7. **Open a terminal window and give yourself superuser privileges with the** `su` **command.**

8. **Unpack the tarball with the following command:**

```
# tar -C / -zxvf mysql-administrator-
  1.0.2b-alpha-linux-stripped.tar.gz
```

The installation instructions on the MySQL Administrator Web page are wrong at the time we're writing this. If you've downloaded version 1.0.2b-alpha, use the preceding command to install the program in the correct location.

Starting MySQL Administrator

After you install MySQL Administrator, you're ready to start the program and begin using its tools. To start the program, follow these steps:

1. **Move to the directory containing the program:**

```
# cd /opt/mysql-administrator/bin
```

2. **Start the program with the following command:**

```
# ./mysql-administrator
```

 Add /opt/mysql-administrator/bin **to your shell's search** $PATH, **and you'll be able to start the program from anywhere on your system with just the program name. See Technique 7 for details about updating** $PATH.

The MySQL Administrator connection dialog opens, as shown in Figure 44-1.

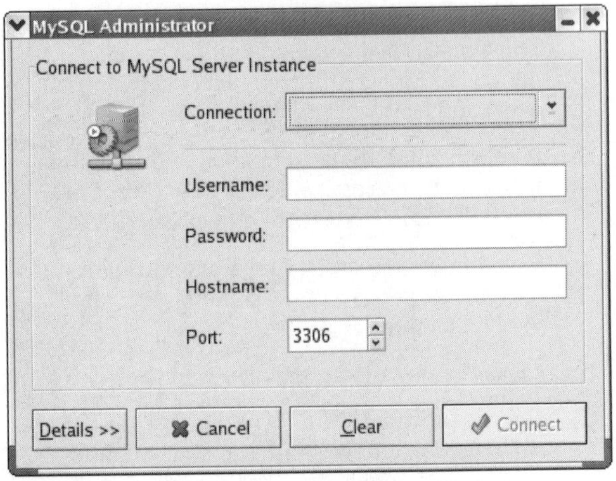

• **Figure 44-1: The MySQL Administrator connection dialog.**

3. **Enter the connection information for your MySQL server — a user name, password, and host name — and then click the Connect button.**

The MySQL Administrator window opens to the Server Information page, displaying information about the connection, the server version, and the client (see Figure 44-2).

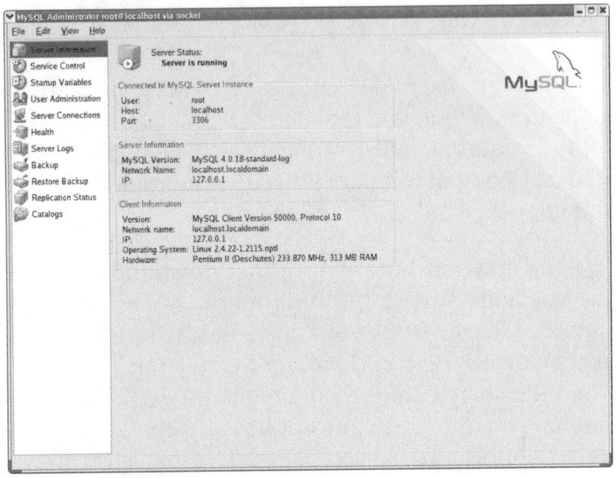

• **Figure 44-2: The MySQL Administrator opening window.**

Exploring MySQL Administrator's tools

The panel on the left side of the MySQL Administrator window contains menu names for the different features that MySQL Administrator can help control. Highlight a menu name to view (and change) a set of features. Here's an overview of the tools you'll find:

✔ **Service Control:** Click Service Control in the menu panel to open the Service Control menu. From this menu, you can monitor the startup log messages. You can also start and stop the server by clicking the Stop the Server (or Start the Server) button.

✔ **Startup Variables:** Click Startup Variables to change the configuration parameters for your

MySQL server. The Startup Variables menu has a series of tab controls that group the configuration parameters into manageable chunks, as shown in Figure 44-3.

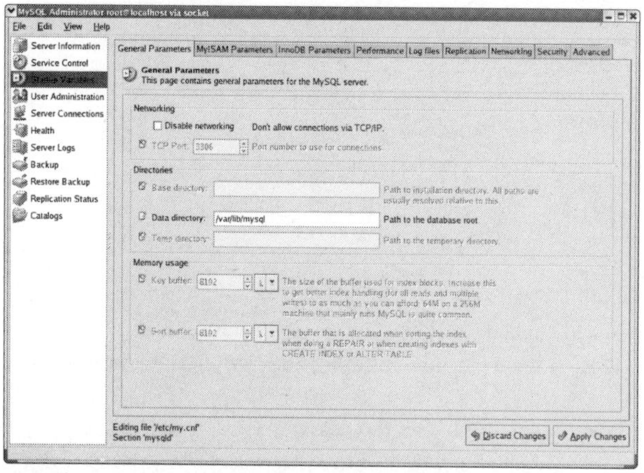

• **Figure 44-3: The Startup Variables menu.**

With the tabs on this menu, you can adjust many configuration parameters, including the following:

▶ **General Parameters:** On this tab, check the Disable Networking box to restrict access to your MySQL server to those clients on the same machine as the server.

▶ **Log Files:** On this tab, click the Slow Queries Log box to generate a log file that displays "slow" queries. If you find that performance is lagging, this tells you which queries are consuming the most resources.

▶ **Security:** On this tab, check the Make All Tables Read-Only box for your replication slave servers. You shouldn't modify replicated tables from slave servers.

Check out all the tabs and the options they include to find new ways to customize and optimize your MySQL server.

✔ **User Administration:** Click User Administration in the menu listing to open the User Administration menu. MySQL user accounts are listed in the lower-left frame of the window, as shown in Figure 44-4.

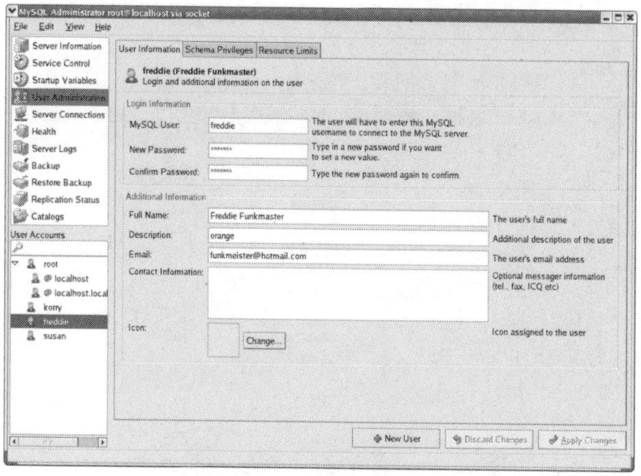

• **Figure 44-4: The User Administration menu.**

To create a new MySQL user account, click the New User button. Complete the user information and then click Apply Changes. Use the Schema Privileges and Resource Limits tabs to view (or modify) user privileges.

> If you're running a version of MySQL younger than version 4.0, you'll get an error message when you modify user information. Ignore the message and consider upgrading to a more recent version of MySQL.

✔ **Server Connections:** Click Server Connections to view all active connections and see what users are up to. The User Connections tab displays a detailed list of user sessions. Highlight a user name to display the active threads for that user, as shown in Figure 44-5.

> If you have runaway (or really slow) queries, you can kill them off on the User Connections tab with the Kill Thread button, or terminate all threads for a single user with the Kill User button. Just highlight the thread or user name and click the appropriate button.

✔ **Health:** Click Health in the left panel to access graphs of performance and server statistics for your MySQL server. The Health menu opens, displaying a trio of Connection Health graphs, as shown in Figure 44-6.

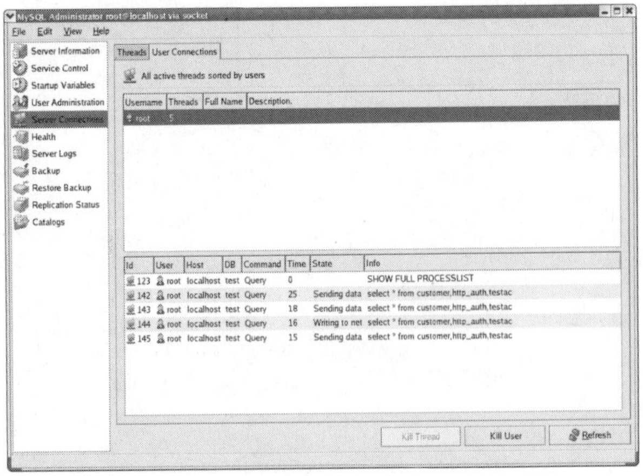

• **Figure 44-5: User and thread information on the User Connections tab.**

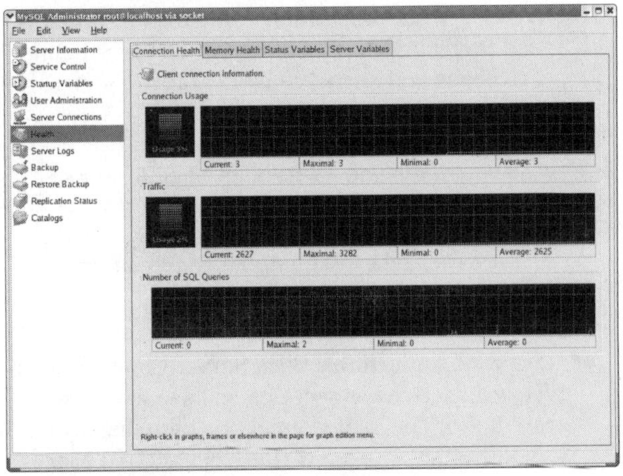

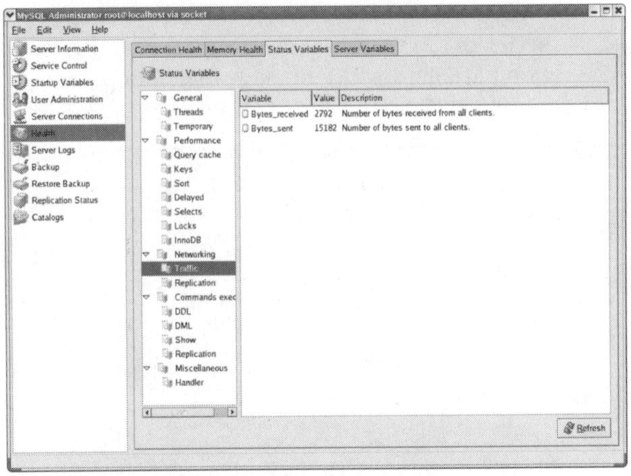

• **Figure 44-7: Status variables for a MySQL server.**

Server Logs: Click Server Logs in the menu panel to open the log viewer (the log viewer does not appear to work with a version-3 MySQL server). This feature needs a bit of help right now, but we're sure the problems will be worked out.

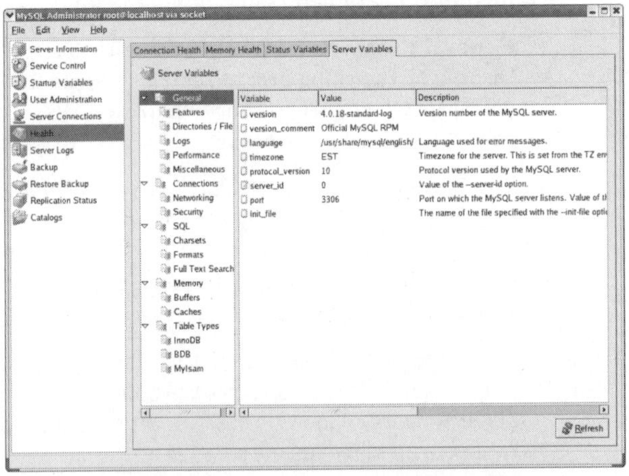

• **Figure 44-6: Server Health graphs.**

Every MySQL server maintains a set of *status variables* that track performance and usage statistics. Click the Status Variables tab to see the server status variables. Highlight a group in the Status Variables column to view the variables within that group, as shown in Figure 44-7.

Click the Server Variables tab to view the configuration parameters for your server. Highlight a group in the Server Variables column to see the configuration parameters in that group, as shown in Figure 44-8.

• **Figure 44-8: Configuration parameters for the MySQL server.**

Backup: The Backup menu lets you create (and execute) backup *profiles*. With this menu, you can define jobs that archive all or part of your server data. Click the New Profile button and enter a name for the backup profile in the Project Name field. Highlight a database name in the

Databases column and click the right-arrow button to include that database in the Backup Content pane. Expand the database into a tree control form by clicking the arrow next to the database name. Check the boxes next to each table name to include (or uncheck the boxes to exclude) the tables in the backup (see Figure 44-9).

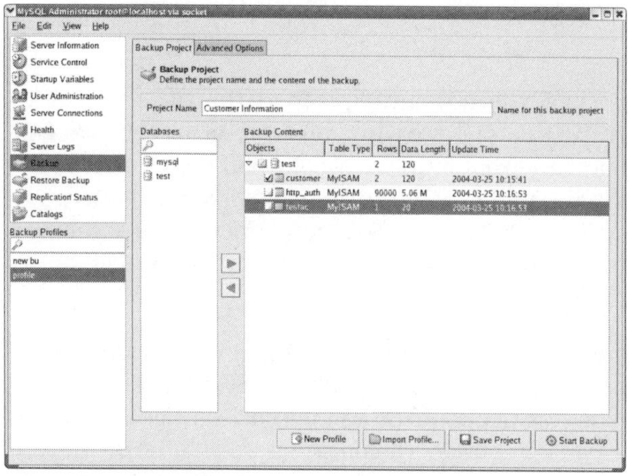

• **Figure 44-9:** Creating a new backup profile.

When your profile is complete, click the Save Project button. To run the backup, click the Start Backup button.

In this technique, we've given you other, dependable ways to back up. They're not graphical, but dependability counts when you're making backups. Until this product matures a bit, we recommend sticking to tried and true backups for data you treasure.

✔ **Restore Backup:** The Restore Backup menu selection opens a dialog designed to restore from archives created with the Backup menu. For now, we recommend that you use more dependable methods to back up and restore.

✔ **Replication Status:** The Replication Status menu selection opens a dialog displaying information about the state of your replication topology. (We cover MySQL replication features earlier in this technique.)

✔ **Catalogs:** The Catalogs menu selection displays information about the databases and tables defined on your MySQL server.

The creators of MySQL Administrator are a bit loose with their labels. The Catalogs and Schemata labels both refer to what are normally called databases.

Highlight a database name in the Schemata frame to see the tables stored in that database. Highlight a table name in the top panel to display the columns within that table, as shown in Figure 44-10.

Use the tab controls in the lower panel to view information about the Columns, Indices, Table Status, and Row Status.

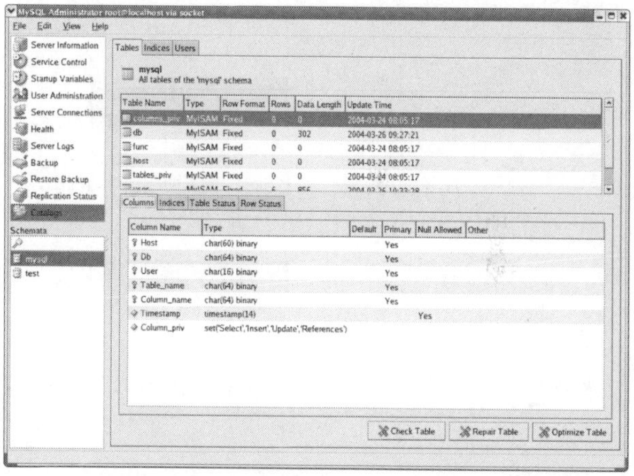

• **Figure 44-10:** Table information displayed with MySQL Administrator.

MySQL Administrator should grow up to be a nifty timesaving tool. If you're just starting to use MySQL, you may want to avoid the frustration (and slowdowns) caused by the bugs and skip the installation of the version distributed with Fedora (3.x). You can download the RPM packages that you need to install MySQL version 4.0 or better from `www.mysql.com/downloads`.

Technique 45

Safeguarding Your Apache Server with SSL Certificates

Save Time By

- ✔ Generating your own SSL certificate
- ✔ Signing your own SSL certificates for private use
- ✔ Viewing the CAs that your browser currently trusts

SSL (Secure Sockets Layer) is a security protocol that assures users visiting your Web site that you are who you say you are. OpenSSL is a Linux software package that implements the SSL protocol. If you're running a Web server that handles financial transactions or sensitive documents, an SSL certificate tells your customers or colleagues that their information is really in *your* hands, and not in the hands of some troll who has intercepted the transaction.

To use SSL security at your Web site, you need a signed SSL certificate. Your Web server (typically Apache) sends your certificate whenever a browser requests a secure connection. You can purchase a signature from a trusted authority, or you can obtain a signature from an intermediate authority to generate a certificate that's part of a chain of trust. In a chain of trust, a high-level certification authority entrusts an intermediary who in turn signs your certificate, guaranteeing that you're reputable.

You can also sign your own certificates by becoming your own certificate authority without a chain of trust. Your certificate may not convey enough trust for consumers to send in their credit card numbers, but within a circle of colleagues, having an active certificate is an assurance that their transactions are being handled with respect.

In this technique, we explain the trust levels associated with each type of certificate. We also show you how to request a signed certificate from a trusted certificate authority, how to create a self-signed certificate that you can use to test your Web server configuration, and how to create your *own* certificate authority. You'll save time and assure your colleagues and customers that they really are in contact with your computer and not an interceptor.

Understanding the Basics of How Certificates Work

In geek-speak, a *certificate* is a document that proves your identity. Certificates are like passports in that they contain information about your identity. A passport contains your name, birth date, and birthplace. An SSL certificate contains your name, location (country, state/province, and city), organization name, and e-mail address.

Passports (and SSL certificates) also provide some method for ensuring that your identity is correct. Your passport contains a photograph that someone can compare with your face. An SSL certificate contains the public half of a public/private key pair.

A passport also contains safeguards against forgery: Every passport contains a watermark, and many governments will soon issue passports that contain holograms (which are very difficult to forge). Likewise, an SSL certificate is digitally signed with the issuer's private key, and any tampering makes the digital signature invalid.

Passports and SSL certificates share another important characteristic: They're both issued by trusted third parties. A border authority isn't likely to trust a passport that you've issued to yourself. Instead, a passport office (the U.S. State Department, for example) verifies your identity and issues a passport. Foreign governments trust that the passport office has done a thorough job investigating your identity. SSL certificates work the same way.

Choosing an SSL Certificate

To obtain an SSL certificate, you send a request (called a certificate signing request, or CSR), along with proof of your identity, to a trusted authority. The trusted authority (also known as a certification authority, or CA) compares your request to the proof of identity that you provide, and if it's satisfied that you are who you claim to be, it issues you a certificate. The certificate that you receive is signed with the issuer's private key — you can verify the signature by using the issuer's public key.

You can get three different types of SSL certificate, and each provides a different level of trust:

- ✔ A self-signed certificate is untrustworthy (but useful for testing).

- ✔ A certificate signed by a local CA (a CA that you create and manage yourself) can be trusted by your peers.

- ✔ A certificate signed by a well-known CA can be trusted by outside parties (that is, customers).

Obtaining a signed certificate costs money. The CA assumes the work of verifying your identity and maintaining a database of valid certificates. A number of companies are in the certification business, and two of the best known are VeriSign (`www.verisign.com`) and thawte (`www.thawte.com`). If you decide to go this route, see the following section, "Creating a Certificate Signing Request," for details on how to get the certificate from a CA.

If you want to test out your Web site *before* you shell out a few bucks to a CA, you can create a self-signed certificate. A self-signed certificate looks and acts like a normal certificate except for one very important difference: You should never *trust* a self-signed certificate. Trusting a self-signed certificate is like trusting a self-issued passport. Anyone can create a self-signed certificate, and more importantly, anyone can forge a self-signed certificate. We explain how this is done in the "Creating a Self-Signed Certificate" section, later in this technique.

In some cases, you may want to act as a CA yourself. For instance, if you head up the IT department at a large company, you can issue certificates to in-house Web servers without having to pay a third-party CA for each one. You might use your in-house CA to distribute trusted software or deliver confidential content such as payroll information.

Creating a Certificate Signing Request

To request a signed certificate from a CA, you must first create a *certificate signing request* (or CSR). The

CSR contains two important pieces of information: your identity and your public key.

In an SSL certificate, the identity is called the subject (and the CA is called the issuer). Every subject (and every issuer) is identified by the following information:

- ✔ Location (country, state/province, city)
- ✔ Organization (organization name and organizational unit)
- ✔ Common name (the name of your Web server, as seen by the outside world)
- ✔ E-mail address

If you're a Fedora user, you can use the tools installed with Apache to generate a CSR (we show you how in a moment). If you're not using Fedora, you have a bit more work to do: We suggest using Webmin and Webmin's Certificate and Key Management module to generate a CSR. Technique 17 shows you how to install and use Webmin (the Certificate and Key Management module is an add-on that you'll have to download separately from the `www.webmin.com` Web site).

Fedora makes it easy to create a CSR (and the public/private key pair that you need in order to sign the CSR):

1. **Open a terminal window and give yourself superuser privileges with the** `su` **command.**

2. **Move to the directory** `/etc/httpd/conf`:

   `# cd /etc/httpd/conf`

3. **Type** `make certreq` **and press Enter.**

4. **If you have an existing server key (it's stored in** `/etc/httpd/conf/ssl.key/server.key`**), you're prompted for the passphrase for that key. If you don't have an existing server key, OpenSSL creates a new server key for you and asks for a passphrase that will protect your private server key from unauthorized use. In either case, type in the passphrase and press Enter.**

The OpenSSL program now asks you a series of questions regarding your identity.

5. **Enter the two-letter code for your country.**

   For example, type `US` for United States or `CA` for Canada.

6. **Enter the full name (not the abbreviation) for your state or province.**

7. **Enter the name of your organization (a company name, for example).**

8. **Enter the name of your department within the organization. Or, if you're requesting a certificate for your entire organization, just press Enter.**

9. **Enter the name of your Web server (for example,** `www.example.com`**). If you have (or plan to have) multiple Web servers at your site, use a** `*` **in place of the host name, like this:** `*.example.com` **(you still need to include your domain name).**

   It's very important that you enter your *real* Web server name here. When the CA issues a certificate, it belongs to a specific Web site. If you try to use that certificate on a Web server with a different name, visitors to your Web site will be greeted with a scary message warning of certificate forgery.

10. **Enter your e-mail address.**

11. **Next, you're prompted for two extra pieces of information: a challenge password and an optional company name. Just press Enter twice to ignore those questions.**

    OpenSSL saves the resulting CSR (certificate signing request) in `/etc/httpd/conf/ssl.csr/server.csr`.

If you'd like to see what's inside the CSR in human-readable form, use the following command:

```
$ openssl req -text -in
  ssl.csr/server.csr.
```

You see a result similar to that shown in Listing 45-1.

LISTING 45-1: EXAMINING A CERTIFICATE SIGNING REQUEST

```
Certificate Request:
    Data:
        Version: 0 (0x0)
        Subject: C=US, ST=Virginia, L=Anytown, O=TrixieWare, OU=Cosmology,
    CN=www.trixieware.com/emailAddress=newdoo@trixieware.com
        Subject Public Key Info:
            Public Key Algorithm: rsaEncryption
            RSA Public Key: (1024 bit)
                Modulus (1024 bit):
                    00:ac:fd:51:b4:b0:42:80:eb:cf:7f:53:54:64:1b:
                    8a:13:fe:45:81:9c:7b:d5:a4:58:23:68:3a:d1:84:
                    0e:51:77:57:21:27:b6:3a:5b:e1:50:ca:81:2e:5e:
                    e2:65:36:9e:64:ed:63:88:a7:d0:55:2f:58:a9:19:
                    39:2b:85:0a:c2:a2:3b:a6:ce:3e:a1:57:a8:99:72:
                    32:6d:40:70:32:86:10:a6:f0:09:ac:f9:66:e9:64:
                    c1:a0:d3:ca:7a:61:01:4a:b0:3f:5b:0d:15:1d:58:
                    6a:01:b9:ca:e2:c8:dd:ac:49:03:4e:e4:3e:1d:fb:
                    c3:ef:ca:30:c0:1e:6f:a9:39
                Exponent: 65537 (0x10001)
        Attributes:
            a0:00
    Signature Algorithm: md5WithRSAEncryption
        04:61:e0:3d:4b:69:2b:92:27:fb:e7:f1:a1:e2:2a:21:3d:89:
        7f:ba:67:9a:34:9c:9e:73:00:f4:79:6c:0a:bf:57:99:6d:08:
        0e:ad:4d:a8:0c:5a:f3:fc:43:a2:4a:fc:5a:24:c7:4b:02:55:
        1d:be:d8:2a:12:49:91:d0:f1:c3:61:62:d8:73:95:62:c9:f8:
        ca:6a:c2:34:f7:67:02:34:5d:dc:b6:36:59:46:c7:9d:36:7a:
        29:8a:4d:de:5e:f6:b9:52:26:33:e5:8d:f2:fd:cf:da:4b:65:
        f6:4f:fa:12:cf:10:13:d7:bb:1b:f7:22:60:b9:9a:4d:20:49:
        81:80
-----BEGIN CERTIFICATE REQUEST-----
MIIB3DCCAUUCAQAwgZsxCzAJBgNVBAYTAlVTMQswCQYDVQQIEwJWYTETMBEGA1UE
BxMKRnJvZyBMZXZlbDETMBEGA1UEChMKVHJpeGllV2FyZTESMBAGA1UECxMJQ29z
bW9sb2d5MRswGQYDVQQDExJ3d3cudHJpeGlld2FyZS5jb20xJDAiBgkqhkiG9w0B
CQEWFW51d2Rvb0BOcml4aWV3YXJlLmNvbTCBnzANBgkqhkiG9w0BAQEFAAOBjQAw
gYkCgYEArP1RtLBCgOvPf1NUZBuKE/5FgZx71aRYI2g6OYQOUXdXISe2O1vhUMqB
L17iZTaeZO1jiKfQVS9YqRk5K4UKwqI7ps4+oVeomXIybUBwMoYQpvAJrPlm6WTB
oNPKemEBSrA/WwOVHVhqAbnK4sjdrEkDTuQ+HfvD78owwB5vqTkCAwEAAaAAMAOG
CSqGSIb3DQEBBAUAA4GBAARh4D1LaSuSJ/vn8aHiKiE9iX+6Z5o0nJ5zAPR5bAq/
V51tCA6tTagMWvP8Q6JK/FokxOsCVR2+2CoSSZHQ8cNhYthzlWLJ+MpqwjT3ZwIO
Xdy2N1lGx5O2eimKTd5e9rlSJjPljfL9z9pLZfZP+hLPEBPXuxv3ImC5mkOgSYGA
-----END CERTIFICATE REQUEST-----
```

You can see that the certificate contains all the information that you entered. The CSR is digitally signed with your private key; the CA verifies the signature by using the public key included in the CSR.

Send the CSR (`/etc/httpd/conf/ssl.csr/server.csr`) to the certification authority that you've selected, along with the proof-of-identity documents that it requires.

When you receive the final certificate, simply copy it to `/etc/httpd/conf/ssl.crt/server.crt` and restart your Apache server.

Creating a Self-Signed Certificate

Creating a self-signed certificate with Fedora is just as easy as creating a CSR, but you end up with a test certificate rather than a request that you send to a CA. Again, if you're not using Fedora, we recommend that you generate SSL certificates with the help of Webmin's Certificate and Key Management module (see Technique 17 for more details).

Here are the steps you need to follow to create a self-signed certificate with Fedora:

1. **Open a terminal window and give yourself superuser privileges with the** su **command.**

2. **Move to the directory** `/etc/httpd/conf`:

   ```
   # cd /etc/httpd/conf
   ```

3. **Type** `make testcert` **and press Enter.**

4. **You're prompted for the password that protects your private server key. Type in the password and press Enter.**

5. **OpenSSL prompts you for the same information that you provide when creating a CSR (location, organization, e-mail address, and so on). Answer each question in turn.**

   After you've answered the last question (your e-mail address), OpenSSL creates a self-signed certificate and saves it in `/etc/httpd/conf/ssl.crt/server.crt`.

To view the certificate at the command line, use the following command:

```
# openssl x509 -in ssl.crt/server.crt -text
```

You'll see that the issuer and subject are identical — that's a self-signed certificate.

Fedora automatically saves the self-signed certificate where Apache expects to find it. To see your certificate in action, restart your Apache server:

```
# /sbin/service httpd restart
Stopping httpd:    [OK]
Starting httpd:
Apache/2.0.47 mod_ssl/2.0.47
  (Pass Phrase Dialog)
Some of your private key files are
encrypted for security reasons.

In order to read them you have to provide
us with the pass phrases.

Server localhost.localdomain:443 (RSA)
Enter pass phrase:

Ok: Pass Phrase Dialog successful.
```

Notice that Apache now asks for the passphrase that protects your server's private key.

Now, open a Web browser and connect to

```
https://127.0.0.1
```

 Notice the preceding URL starts with `https` rather than `http`. That means it's connecting to a secure server.

You've just created a self-signed certificate and installed it on your own Apache server.

Because your users may receive a warning when they encounter this certificate, it's a good idea to give them a little forewarning about what's going on. See the sidebar, "When Mozilla encounters a self-signed certificate," for details on how this works.

> ## When Mozilla encounters a self-signed certificate
>
> Self-signed certificates are not very trustworthy. When you visit a site with a self-signed certificate, you should receive a warning screen from Mozilla asking if you know this joker and if his certificate is good enough for you (see the following figure). From here, follow these steps to examine the certificate:

Creating a Signing Authority with openssl

Use openssl to create a certificate authority (CA) yourself if you want to sign certificates for use within your organization. Running your own CA can be useful if you want to hand out trusted software to other people in your organization. A CA is also useful if you want to serve secure content (payroll benefits and in-house sales, for example).

A CA has three responsibilities:

- ✔ Verifying identity
- ✔ Signing requests
- ✔ Maintaining a database of signed certificates

openssl comes with a program that can handle the last two responsibilities for you. You still have to verify identities yourself using whatever method is appropriate for your site: If you are creating a CA for your company, a photo ID card may be sufficient.

Creating a certificate authority

To create a CA, follow these steps:

1. **Open a terminal window and give yourself superuser privileges with the** su - **command:**

```
$ su -
Password:
#
```

2. **If you're using Fedora or SuSE, move to the directory that contains the CA shell script:**

```
# cd /usr/share/ssl/misc
```

If you're using Mandrake:

```
# cd /usr/lib/ssl/misc
```

3. **Create the CA infrastructure with the following command:**

```
# ./CA -newca
```

---

1. **Click the Examine Certificate button to see the details of the certificate (see the following figure).**

2. **Click the Details tab, and then highlight the Issuer line in the Certificate Field frame.**

In the Field Value frame, you'll see the name and e-mail address of the certificate issuer. You can decide for yourself if this person is trustworthy.

On Mandrake and SuSE systems, use this command instead:

```
# ./CA.sh -newca
```

The CA script now asks you a series of questions, most of which will be familiar by now. The first step in creating the CA infrastructure is to create a new, self-signed certificate. You're prompted for an existing CA certificate:

```
CA certificate filename
(or enter to create)
```

4. **Just press Enter to create a new certificate.**

5. **Enter a passphrase that will protect your CA's private key:**

```
Making CA certificate ...
Generating a 1024 bit RSA private key
................++++++
writing new private key to
   './demoCA/private/./cakey.pem'
Enter PEM pass phrase:
Verifying - Enter PEM pass phrase:
```

6. **The CA script prompts you for the same bits of information that you provide when creating a self-signed certificate or a certificate signing request. Answer each question in turn.**

After you've answered the last question, the CA script creates a self-signed certificate in ./demoCA/cacert.pem.

Take a peek at this certificate with the following command:

```
# openssl x509 -in demoCA/cacert.pem -text
```

Notice that the issuer and the subject are identical — that tells you that this is a self-signed certificate.

Signing a CSR

When you have a CA up and running, you can start to sign CSRs (converting them from requests into actual certificates).

To sign a CSR, follow these steps:

1. **Open a terminal window and give yourself superuser privileges with the su - command:**

```
$ su -
Password:
#
```

2. **Move to the directory that contains the CA shell script:**

```
# cd /usr/share/ssl/misc
```

3. **Type in the following command:**

```
# openssl ca -policy policy_anything \
    -in filename.csr \
    -out filename.crt
```

Substitute the CSR name where you see *filename*.csr and the desired certificate name where you see *filename*.crt. For example, if you want to sign the CSR for your own Apache Web server, you would type this:

```
# openssl ca -policy policy_anything \
  -in /etc/httpd/conf/ssl.csr/server.
   csr\
  -out /etc/httpd/conf/ssl.crt/server.
   crt
```

Next, the openssl program asks for the passphrase that protects your CA's private key:

```
Enter passphrase for ./dem...
   /cakey.pem:
```

4. **Type in the password that you assigned when you created the CA and press Enter.**

openssl displays the content of the CSR (in human-readable form) and asks if you want to sign the certificate.

5. **Look over the content, and if the information looks correct, press Y and then Enter to sign it.**

6. openssl **asks if you want to commit your changes to the CA database: Press Y and then Enter to finish.**

That's it! The new, signed certificate is saved in the file that you specified. If you signed the certificate for another user, e-mail the certificate to the recipient. If you signed a certificate that you want to use in your Web server (and you followed our example), the certificate is already in place in `/etc/httpd/conf/ssl.crt/server.crt`; all you have to do now is restart `httpd` (the Apache server):

```
# service httpd restart
Stopping httpd:    [OK]
Starting httpd:
Apache/2.0.47 mod_ssl/2.0.47
  (Pass Phrase Dialog)
Some of your private key files are
encrypted for security reasons.

In order to read them you have to provide
us with the pass phrases.

Server localhost.localdomain:443 (RSA)
Enter pass phrase:

Ok: Pass Phrase Dialog successful.
```

Trusting in Trusted Certification Authorities

When customers visit a Web site with the intent to make a purchase, they want a serious guarantee that their personal information — name, address, and credit card number — isn't being distributed across the Internet for just anyone to use.

When you connect to a Web site secured with an SSL certificate, a little gold padlock appears in the browser tray. Hover your mouse over the lock icon to see a short description of the CA that signed the certificate. To see more information about the certificate (and the signer), click the lock icon. In the Page Info window that appears, click View to see all the gory details.

Exploring Your Certificate Collection with Mozilla

As you browse the World Wide Web, you're bound to encounter certificates from various sites. How does

your Web browser know which certificates to trust? Each browser (Mozilla, Internet Explorer, Netscape, and so on) comes with a set of predefined trusted authorities.

To explore the certificates and authorities trusted by your Mozilla browser, follow these steps (the procedure is similar if you're using a browser other than Mozilla):

1. **Open the Main Menu and choose Internet⇨Mozilla Web Browser.**

   The Mozilla Web browser opens.

2. **To view the certificate authorities that are currently trusted by your Mozilla browser, choose Edit⇨Preferences.**

   The Preferences dialog opens.

3. **Expand the Privacy & Security portion of the tree control in the Category column and then click Certificates.**

   The Certificates dialog opens, as shown in Figure 45-1.

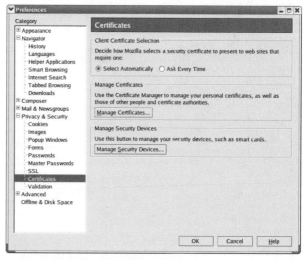

• **Figure 45-1: The Certificates dialog.**

4. **Click the Manage Certificates button to open the Certificate Manager.**

5. Click the Authorities tab to see the signing authorities trusted by your browser (see Figure 45-2).

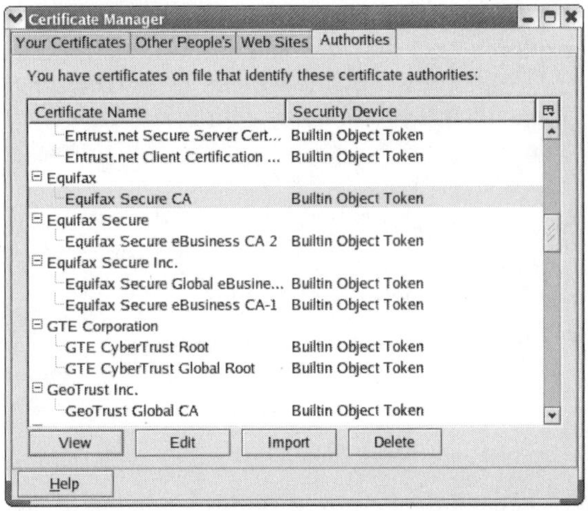

• **Figure 45-2: The authorities trusted by our browser.**

6. Highlight a certificate name and click the View button (located in the lower left-hand corner of the Certificate Manager window).

The Certificate Viewer dialog opens with information about the certificate, as shown in Figure 45-3.

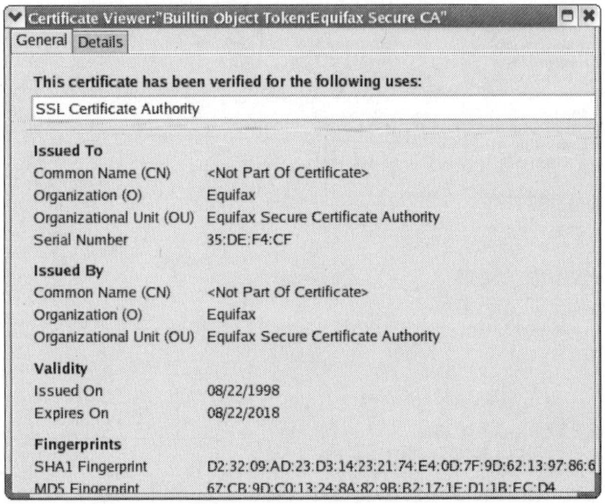

• **Figure 45-3: Information about a specific CA.**

You can remove certificates that are currently accepted by Mozilla with a click of the mouse in the Certificate Manager. If you want to remove a certificate, highlight the certificate and click the Delete button. You'll be asked to verify that you want to delete the certificate — click OK, and it's history.

7. You can view additional certificate details by clicking the Details tab on the Certificate Viewer (see Figure 45-4).

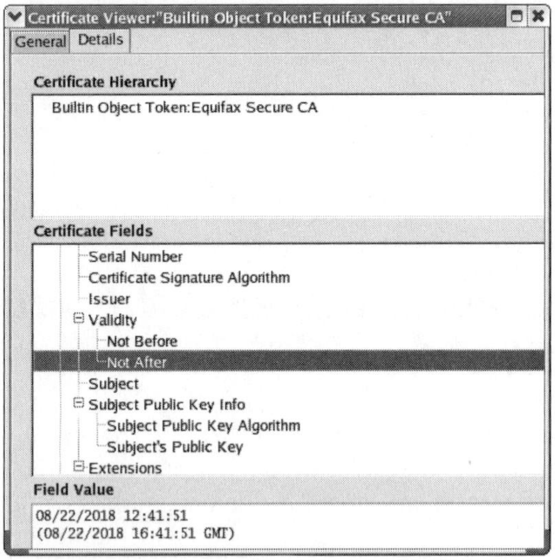

• **Figure 45-4: Detailed certificate information.**

8. Highlight the fields in the tree control in the center pane to view the specific details of the certificate in the Field Value pane.

46

Technique

Retrieving HTTPMail Using hotway and Evolution

Most e-mail service providers use three standardized protocols to send and retrieve e-mail. SMTP is used to send e-mail, and POP and IMAP are used to retrieve e-mail. Some of the larger Web portals — such as Microsoft's Hotmail, MSN, and Lycos — have developed their own e-mail protocols based on HTTP, which is the underlying transport mechanism used by Web browsers.

E-mail accounts from portals using HTTPMail servers often come with a catch: Because of the strange protocol, you must access their services with a Web browser, logging in to their servers and stopping to view all the advertisements along the way. You can use an open-source tool called hotway to retrieve your e-mail with an e-mail client, avoiding the hassles and slowdowns of ads, pop-ups, and online logins.

 Check with your e-mail provider and make sure that its user service agreement doesn't include any legalese that requires you to use a browser to view your e-mail.

In this technique, we introduce you to an open-source project called hotway. hotway can retrieve your mail from an HTTPMail server and deliver it your to e-mail client. hotway can also forward e-mail that you send from a mail client to an HTTPMail server. We also take you on a quick tour of Ximian Evolution — a great tool to use in combination with hotway. You'll save time by accessing your HTTPMail accounts without stopping to view the ads along the way, and get to know a great e-mail client in the process.

Introducing hotway

The hotway (hotmail gateway) project at hotwayd.sourceforge.net provides an open-source gateway that retrieves e-mail from an HTTPMail server and delivers it to your Linux mailbox. You can also send e-mail from your Linux client (Ximian Evolution, KMail, Mozilla mail, and so on) to an HTTPMail server.

`hotway` works with the following accounts:

- ✔ Accounts at `hotmail.com`
- ✔ Accounts at `msn.com`
- ✔ Lycos accounts with the suffixes `.co.uk`, `.ch`, `.de`, `.es`, `.it`, or `.at`
- ✔ Accounts at `spray.se`

Getting Started with hotway

You typically interact with an HTTPMail server by pointing your Web browser to the portal, typing in your user name and password, and navigating through tons of advertisements before you can read your e-mail. If you're using Windows, you can avoid the portal Web site by reading your e-mail with Microsoft Outlook (or Outlook Express) mail clients. If you're using Linux, you haven't been so lucky — until now.

 Read your e-mail provider's end-user agreement to be sure that dodging its advertising is okay.

`hotway` is quick and easy to set up, and after it's in place, you'll never even know it's there. When you install `hotway`, you're running a daemon (background process) named `hotwayd` that listens for e-mail requests. `hotwayd` is controlled by `xinetd` — `xinetd` lurks in the background, waiting for activity on TCP port 2500. When an e-mail request comes in, it fires up `hotway` to handle the request.

To install `hotway` on your Linux machine, follow these steps:

1. **Open a Web browser and surf to**

   `hotwayd.sourceforge.net`

2. **Click the Download link.**

3. **Click the link for**

   `hotwayd-0.8-1.i386.rpm`

You're directed to a download page listing available mirrors.

4. **Click a download link to a mirror site near you.**

5. **Save the RPM package to your home directory.**

6. **Close the browser window and the Download Manager. Open a terminal window and give yourself superuser privileges with the su command.**

7. **Install the RPM package with the following command:**

   `# rpm -Uhv hotwayd-0.8-1.i386.rpm`

That's all there is to it — you're ready to use `hotway`.

 `xinetd` **automatically starts the** `hotway` **daemon when it's needed — no extra work is required.**

Setting Up Evolution to Read HTTPMail Accounts with hotway

`hotway` works with any e-mail client, but we're particularly fond of Ximian Evolution. Evolution is a quick, slick e-mail client bundled with most Linux distributions. If you've already installed Evolution (it should appear in the Internet menu or Internet⇨ Mail menu), you're ready to go. If not, install Evolution before proceeding.

To set up an e-mail account using Evolution and `hotway`, follow these steps:

1. **Open the Main Menu and choose Internet⇨Evolution E-Mail.**

   The first time you use the Evolution e-mail client, it greets you with the Evolution Setup Assistant.

2. **Click the Forward button to continue with setup.**

3. Enter your full name and e-mail address in the appropriate fields. You can also choose to complete the Optional Information portion of the window to redirect any e-mail responses to another e-mail account (see Figure 46-1).

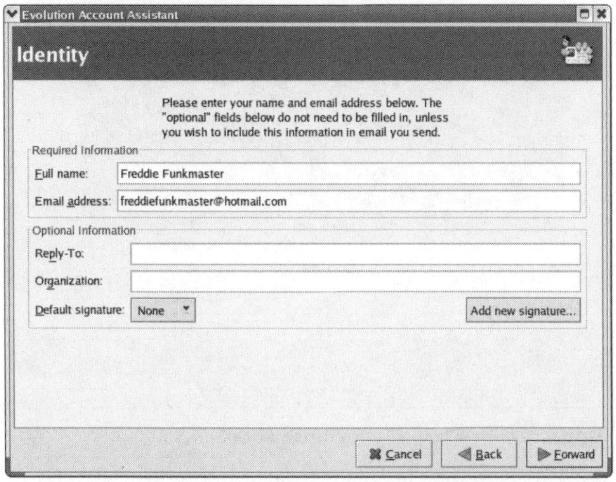

• **Figure 46-1:** Enter your Identity information.

If you want all e-mail responses to be sent to a single account, enter the e-mail address that you want to use in the Reply-To field. In most cases, you can leave the Reply-To and Organization fields blank.

4. Click the Forward button to continue.

The Receiving Email window opens.

5. From the Server Type drop-down list box, choose either the IMAP or POP server type to display a more complete Receiving Email form, as shown in Figure 46-2.

Unless there is a compelling reason to use IMAP, we usually use POP. It's just a bit more reliable than IMAP.

6. Click the Check for Supported Types button and Evolution will connect to the server to ask it what Authentication Types it supports. The results are copied into the Authentication Type list box. Alternatively, use the list box to choose the authentication type you prefer.

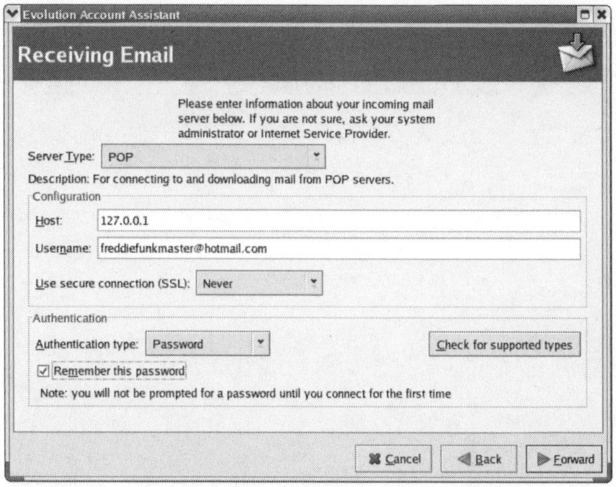

• **Figure 46-2:** The complete Receiving Email form for a POP server.

7. Enter 127.0.0.1 in the Host field and then click the Forward button.

The Receiving Mail Options window opens.

8. Check the Automatically Check for New Mail Every box, and customize the time options to determine how often Evolution checks your e-mail account.

9. Use the options listed in Message Storage to control whether the messages are deleted after download. Be sure to disable support for POP3 extensions when you're creating an account serviced by hotway. Click the Forward button to continue.

The Sending Mail window opens, as shown in Figure 46-3.

10. Enter 127.0.0.1:2500 in the Host field, check the Server Requires Authentication box, and make sure that the Username field contains a complete e-mail address. Click Forward to continue.

The Account Management window opens, as shown in Figure 46-4.

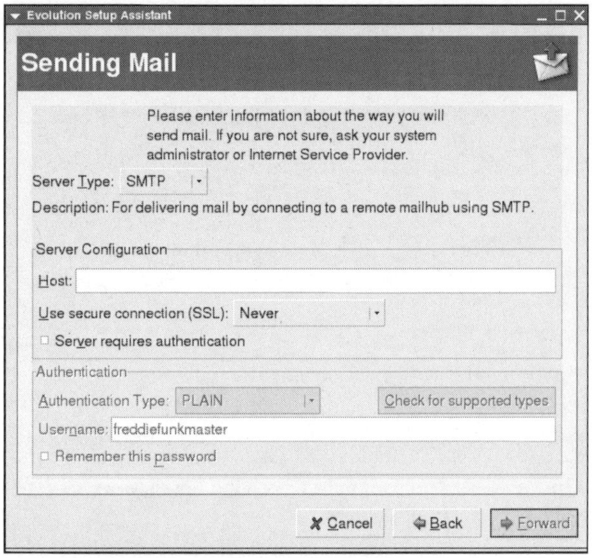

• **Figure 46-3:** The Sending Mail window.

11. Enter a user-friendly name in the Name field and click the Forward button. Click Forward to continue.

The Timezone window opens, as shown in Figure 46-5.

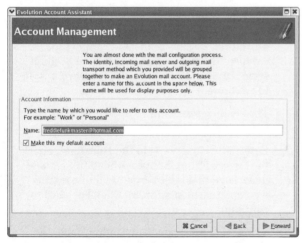

• **Figure 46-4:** The Account Management window.

• **Figure 46-5:** Choose your time zone.

12. Click the map to choose your time zone and then click Forward to continue.

A window opens, indicating you've successfully entered the information needed.

13. Click Apply to continue.

Evolution opens, ready to retrieve your e-mail.

14. Click the Inbox button in the Shortcuts panel on the left, and then click the Send/Receive mail button on the toolbar.

The Send & Receive Mail and Enter Password dialogs open, as shown in Figure 46-6.

15. Enter your password and click OK.

Your e-mail should arrive in the inbox any second now!

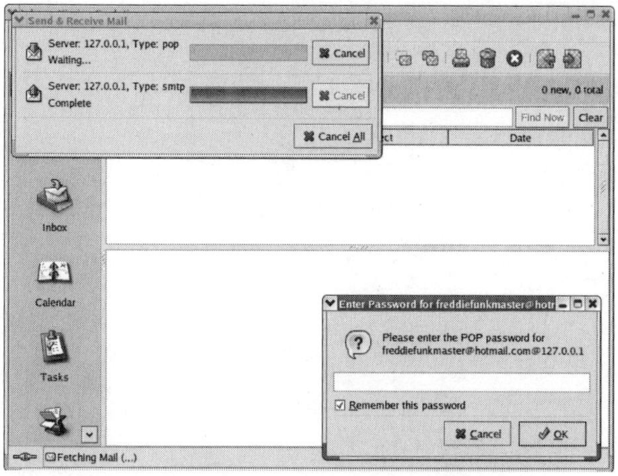

• **Figure 46-6:** Getting ready to retrieve e-mail.

Ringing the Bells and Blowing the Whistles: Your Evolution Summary Page

When you open Ximian Evolution, you're treated to a feast of information, all displayed in a tidy summary page. What's the best thing about the summary page? You can customize it in a snap!

> When you customize your summary page to include information, news, and appointments, you're also creating browsable links from your e-mail client to information that is important to you.

Follow these steps to customize your summary in Evolution:

1. **Choose Tools⇨Settings.**

The Evolution Settings dialog opens, as shown in Figure 46-7.

You can use the Evolution Settings dialog to customize the features shown in the left panel. The tabs in the right panel change to reflect the features that you can customize.

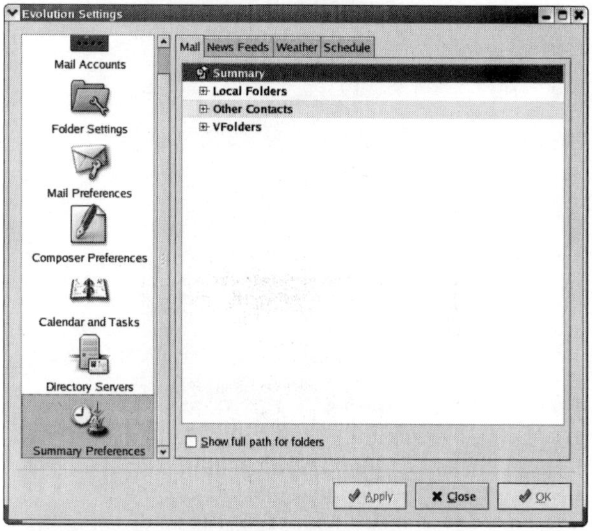

• **Figure 46-7:** The Evolution Settings dialog.

2. **Use the scroll bar to scroll down and choose the Summary Preferences button in the left panel.**

The tab dialogs are now labeled as follows (refer to Figure 46-7):

▶ Mail

▶ News Feeds

▶ Weather

▶ Schedule

3. **Click the Mail tab, and then expand the Local Folders tree control to view the folders you can include on your summary page, as shown in Figure 46-8.**

4. **Check the boxes next to the folders you want to include on the summary page and then click Apply.**

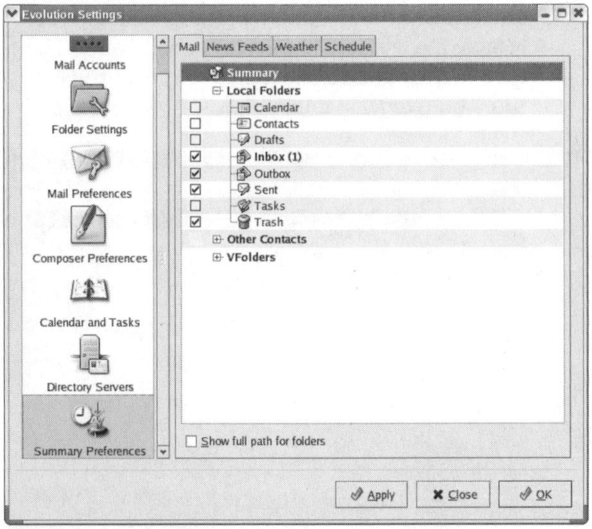

• **Figure 46-8:** Customizing the folders on your summary page.

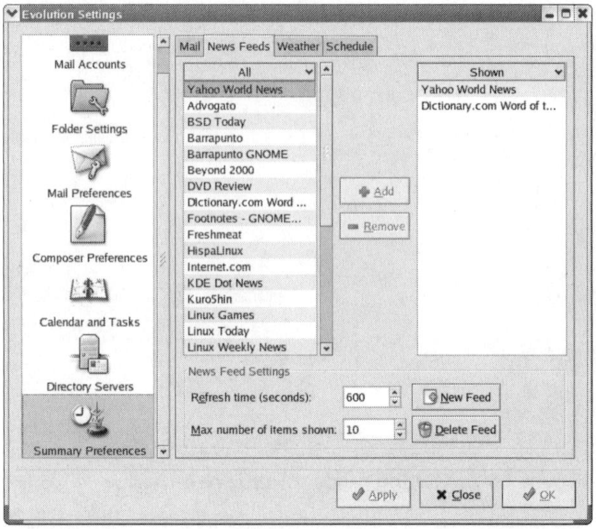

• **Figure 46-9:** Customize the RSS news feeds displayed on your summary page.

Select the mailboxes you need to access most often. You'll have fast access to them with a single click on your summary page.

5. Click the News Feeds tab to add RSS feeds to your summary page.

RSS (Really Simple Syndication) feeds are little snippets of headline-making news that you can customize to suit your interests (see Figure 46-9).

6. To add an RSS news feed to your summary page, highlight the name of the feed in the list in the All panel and then click the Add button. When you're finished adding feeds, click the Apply button.

When you click Add, the feed name is copied to the Shown panel.

You can also find and add new RSS feeds from the Web. Click New Feed to open the New News Feed dialog. Fill in the Name and URL fields and click OK to add it to the list of feeds.

Yahoo! offers a few RSS feeds that you might be interested in:

▶ Yahoo! World News at `rss.news.yahoo.com/rss/world`

▶ Yahoo! Tech News at `rss.news.yahoo.com/rss/tech`

▶ Yahoo! Science News at `rss.news.yahoo.com/rss/science`

Do a Web search for *RSS news feeds* to find feeds about interesting topics that you can add to your summary page.

To remove a news feed from the summary page, highlight it in the Shown panel and click the Remove button. Click the Apply button to make the changes take effect — it's quick and easy!

7. Click the Weather tab to customize the weather reports displayed on your summary page. Expand the tree control in the All panel, find the city whose weather you want to monitor, and click the Add button.

The name is added to the list in the Shown panel, as shown in Figure 46-10. You can monitor the weather for multiple locations.

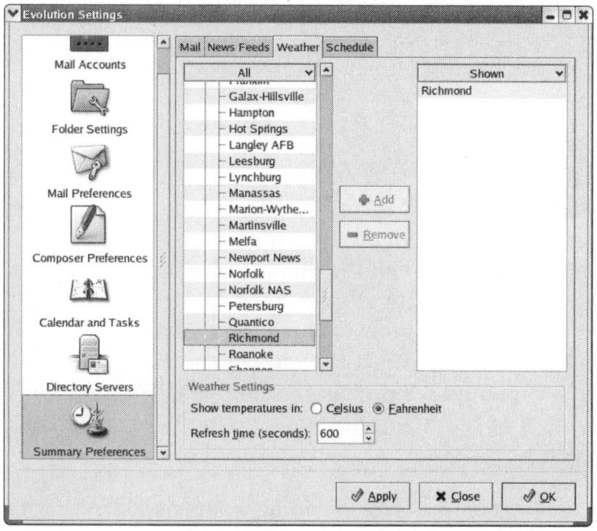

• **Figure 46-10:** Add custom weather information to your summary page.

8. You can also choose to display the temperatures in Celsius or Fahrenheit, and set the refresh time with the controls found on the Weather tab. Click the Apply button to save your changes.

9. Click the Schedule tab (shown in Figure 46-11) to customize the calendar and task information displayed on your summary page.

10. In the Calendar area, specify the number of days you want to display in the calendar. In the Tasks area, decide whether to display all pending tasks or just those tasks scheduled for today. Then click the Apply button to save your choices.

11. When you've finished customizing your summary page, click the Close button to return to your newly updated summary.

    Custom weather, news, and appointments are all waiting for you, along with one-click access to your most frequently used mail folders (see Figure 46-12).

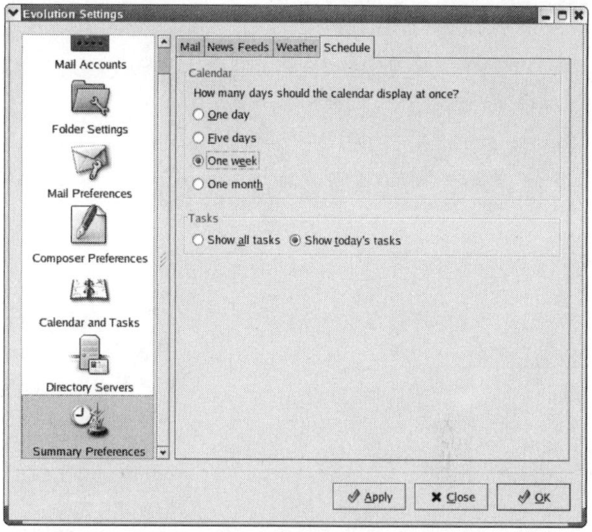

• **Figure 46-11:** Customize your calendar display for the summary page.

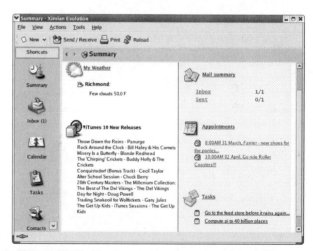

• **Figure 46-12:** Create a custom summary of the info you need for the day.

Creating a custom summary page can save you time because the information you need is right at your fingertips. Evolution keeps you up-to-date on appointments, weather, news, and e-mail.

Stopping Spam with SpamAssassin

Spam is a major waste of time and resources. The kind of spam we're talking about isn't the pink stuff in a can — it's junk e-mail. (We wanted to include a technique about the edible Spam, but our editors said no: See www.spam.com for your daily dose of pink meat.) Unsolicited commercial e-mail not only takes up your valuable time reading and weeding through it, but also ties up your CPU and consumes valuable storage space on your server. And it's downright annoying. Fortunately, you can reduce the amount of spam you receive with the help of a great tool called SpamAssassin.

SpamAssassin has several mechanisms for deciding what is and isn't spam:

- ✔ **Rule set that computes a *spam threshold:*** A numerical score identifies an e-mail message as spam or ham (ham is the opposite of spam — we're not making this up).

- ✔ **Bayesian filtering:** Bayesian filtering figures out what spam looks like as it reads your e-mail. It learns and evolves to keep up with spammers' tactics.

- ✔ **Character-set and language sensitivity:** You can specify languages and character sets that should be considered spam. (For example, unless you're conversing in Russian, e-mail composed entirely of Cyrillic characters is likely to be spam.)

In this technique, we introduce you to your new e-mail assistant, SpamAssassin. With the added tool, RulesDuJour, updating your rule sets is a breeze. With up-to-date rule sets, SpamAssassin learns and grows to keep up with the ever-changing antics adopted by spammers, and saves you time and frustration by letting you read the ham without having to wade through the spam.

Installing SpamAssassin

SpamAssassin is an open-source project that screens incoming e-mail for unwanted or commercial e-mail. It's a smart tool, with ever-evolving rule sets that can keep pace with even the slickest of spammers.

You can install SpamAssassin from the Fedora or SuSE distribution media or by downloading the latest RPM packages from www.spamassassin.org, the official Web site of SpamAssassin.

Installing from the distribution media

If you're a Fedora user, the quickest and easiest way to install SpamAssassin is with the Fedora Add or Remove Packages program and the Fedora distribution media. The procedure is similar on SuSE systems except that you use YAST2 (SpamAssassin is well-hidden in Productivity⇨Networking⇨Email⇨ Utilities).

 Check out Technique 56 for details about downloading and burning your own set of distribution discs.

To install SpamAssassin from the Linux distribution media, follow these steps:

1. Open the Main Menu and choose System Settings⇨Add or Remove Packages. Click the Forward button.

A scan for currently installed packages begins.

2. When the Add or Remove Packages window opens (see Figure 47-1), scroll down and check the Mail Server box.

3. Click the Details link to the right of the Mail Server entry to open the Mail Server Package Details window.

4. Check the Spamassassin box to include the package in the installation, as shown in Figure 47-2.

5. Click the Close button, and then in the Add or Remove Packages window, click the Forward button.

The system update is prepared, and a Package Installation Overview window appears, displaying SpamAssassin and any dependencies (see Figure 47-3).

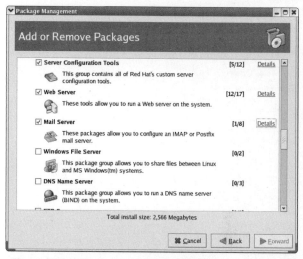

• **Figure 47-1:** Check the Mail Servers box.

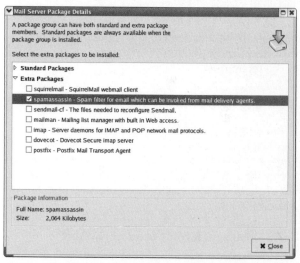

• **Figure 47-2:** Check the box next to Spamassassin.

6. Click the Forward button.

The system update begins. When installation is complete, the Package Installation Complete window is displayed.

7. Click the Finish button.

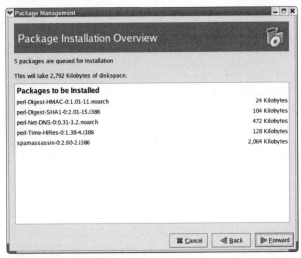

• **Figure 47-3: These are the packages that will be installed.**

That's it. Fedora (or SuSE) takes care of resolving the dependencies as it installs the spamassassin RPM package. Now, you need to start SpamAssassin, as described in the section, "Starting the service," later in the technique.

Installing from RPM downloads

If you don't have the Fedora or SuSE distribution media and don't want to take the time right now to make a set, you can get SpamAssassin up and running with a quick visit to the SpamAssassin Web site. Follow these steps to download and install SpamAssassin:

1. Open your favorite browser and surf to

www.spamassassin.org/released/RPMs

2. Click the download links to retrieve the following RPMs:

perl-Mail-SpamAssassin-*version*.i386.rpm
spamassassin-*version*.i386.rpm

Be sure to choose the most recent version and save the files to your Desktop.

3. Close the browser and open a terminal window. Give yourself superuser privileges with the su command.

4. Move to your Desktop directory and install the packages with the following commands:

```
# cd ~/Desktop
# rpm -Uhv perl-Mail-SpamAssassin-
  2.63-1.i386.rpm
# rpm -Uhv spamassassin-2.63-1.i386.rpm
```

That's it — the perl-Mail-SpamAssassin package satisfies the dependencies of the spamassassin RPM package. You're ready to start the service! See the next section for details.

Starting the service

You'll get the best performance from SpamAssassin by running it as a client/server installation. Keeping the spamd daemon alert and on its toes saves startup time every time you get an e-mail message.

To start the SpamAssassin service, open a terminal window and give yourself superuser privileges with the su - command. Then enter the following command:

```
# service spamassassin start
```

The terminal echoes this message:

```
Starting spamd:  [OK]
```

That's it. You're ready to configure SpamAssassin.

Fine-Tuning SpamAssassin to Separate the Ham from the Spam

You can fine-tune SpamAssassin to screen your e-mail more aggressively or less aggressively. If you screen more aggressively, you run the risk of missing a message that might be trapped by mistake; if you don't screen aggressively enough, you'll be greeted by spam in your e-mail client. It's important to note that your e-mail client decides what to do with mail classified as spam, not SpamAssassin — SpamAssassin classifies each piece of e-mail; your e-mail client can throw out spam messages or route it to a specific mailbox (we show you how to configure your e-mail client in the section, "Adding a New Filter to Evolution").

The easy way to configure SpamAssassin is with the help of the SpamAssassin Configuration Generator. Open your favorite browser and surf to

```
www.yrex.com/spam/spamconfig.php
```

You're taken to the SpamAssassin Configuration Generator, shown in Figure 47-4. The next two sections explain how to customize SpamAssassin and then save your configuration file.

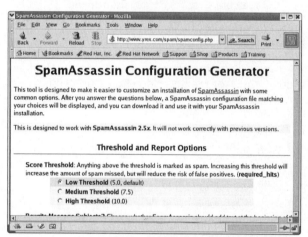

• **Figure 47-4: The SpamAssassin Configuration Generator.**

 If you're using Webmin for administrative tasks, be sure to check out the Webmin interface for configuring the SpamAssassin Mail Filter. You find it in the Servers menu of your Webmin client. The SpamAssassin Configuration Generator at yrex.com is quick and easy, but Webmin gives you finer control over SpamAssassin. See Technique 17 for more information about Webmin.

Customizing settings

The Configuration Generator lists a series of settings that you can customize. Check the radio button next to the desired setting to add that value to the custom configuration file. The settings are described in the following list:

- ✔ **Score Threshold:** The first setting in the Configuration Generator is for the Score Threshold. Each e-mail is assigned a score based on its content. The higher the score, the more likely the e-mail is spam.

  For example, if your threshold is set to 5, an e-mail with a spam score of 7 is considered spam, and an e-mail with a score of 3 is considered ham.

   If you start out at 5, you'll probably want to eventually lower the threshold. We've noticed that even at 3, we still get spam. Our suggestion is to start at 5, and watch what's getting through before you set the threshold too low.

- ✔ **Rewrite Message Subjects:** If you check the Rewrite Subjects box, the text string shown is written into the subject line before the e-mail is added to your inbox. This feature doesn't work with the Evolution e-mail reader. If you're using an e-mail client other than Evolution, a string such as "POSSIBLE SPAM - " is a good choice that will make it easy to spot spam in your mailbox.

- ✔ **Encapsulate Spam in Attachments:** If you accept the default, SpamAssassin encapsulates any message that scores above the spam threshold into a new message as a MIME attachment. This can help prevent accidental virus infection. For even more protection, select the Use Text-Only Attachments radio button. This feature doesn't work with the Evolution e-mail client either.

- ✔ **Use Terse Reports:** If enabled, SpamAssassin issues a shorter version of the spam report. If you get a lot of spam, you may want to go with a shorter report. This feature also does not work with Evolution (don't worry; you don't need it).

When used with Evolution, SpamAssassin acts as a filter. SpamAssassin classifies the e-mail as spam or ham, but it doesn't make modifications to the e-mail. It does, however, put the e-mail into a separate folder so you can speed cruise it later.

✔ **Bayes Options:** By enabling the Bayes Options, you allow SpamAssassin to learn what spam looks like from e-mails that score highly on the spam threshold. As each message arrives, SpamAssassin Bayesian filter searches it for words and phrases that appear often in spam messages. If a message contains many words and phrases that are commonly found in spam, SpamAssassin assumes that the new message is likely to be spam as well. SpamAssassin *learns* what spam looks like if you enable Bayes filtering.

Rather than shipping a set of rules to every user in the world, a custom set of rules is built for each user. For example, if a doctor actually *wants* all that e-mail about Viagra, he or she can tell the filter that.

▶ **Use Bayes System:** Accept the default setting to use Bayesian analysis to identify spam.

▶ **Use Auto Learning:** Accept the default setting to allow SpamAssassin to automatically train its Bayes database based on non-Bayesian classification rules.

✔ **Network Test Options:** The Network Test Options uses information gleaned from the Internet to separate the spam from the ham.

The Network Test Options will slow down your e-mail traffic. The more e-mail you get, the slower your e-mail arrives because each piece needs to be verified against an Internet resource.

▶ **Enable RBL Checks:** If you accept the default and enable RBL (Realtime Black List) checks, your incoming e-mail is compared to a blacklist. If the sender of the e-mail is on that list, the e-mail is considered spam.

▶ **Use Network Checksum Tests:** Computed checksums on known spam are kept in several distributed databases. If you select this option and install the appropriate client software, your incoming e-mail messages are screened against the checksums maintained in the databases. Any matches are considered spam and are treated as such.

✔ **Language Options:** You can set SpamAssassin filters to watch for the character sets or recognized language patterns in the body of the e-mail message. By default, all languages are accepted — check the boxes next to any languages you would consider to be spam.

Check the Use Language Testing box to read the body text of a message looking for recognized languages that can't be distinguished by the character set alone. Hungarian and English use the same character set, so check this box to screen out excessive Hungarian spam.

Saving your settings

After you've customized your settings in the Configuration Generator (as described in the preceding section), follow these steps to save your configuration file:

1. **Click the Generate the Configuration File button.**

You're taken to a new Web page, displaying the new configuration file (see Figure 47-5).

2. **Click the Download This File button and save the file to disk.**

You can either save the file in place or copy it into place later.

To save the configuration file into place for a single user, enter the following code in the File Name field of the Download Manager:

```
~/.spamassassin/user_prefs
```

To save the file into place for the entire system, copy the local.cf file into

```
# /etc/mail/spamassassin/local.cf
```

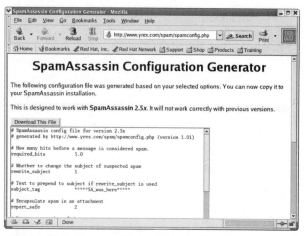

• **Figure 47-5:** Your new SpamAssassin Configuration File.

 You may need to create the `.spamassassin` subdirectory in your home directory.

3. Click Save, and your configuration file is copied into place.

Need to tighten your configuration? Just revisit the Configuration Generator and copy the new configuration file into place over the old one. Easy!

Adding a New Filter to Evolution

After you've created an awesome spam filter by configuring SpamAssassin, you'll want to apply it to your e-mail client. If you're using Evolution, the process is simple:

1. Open your Evolution e-mail client.

2. Open your Inbox, and choose Tools⇨Filters from the menu bar.

The Filters dialog opens, as shown in Figure 47-6.

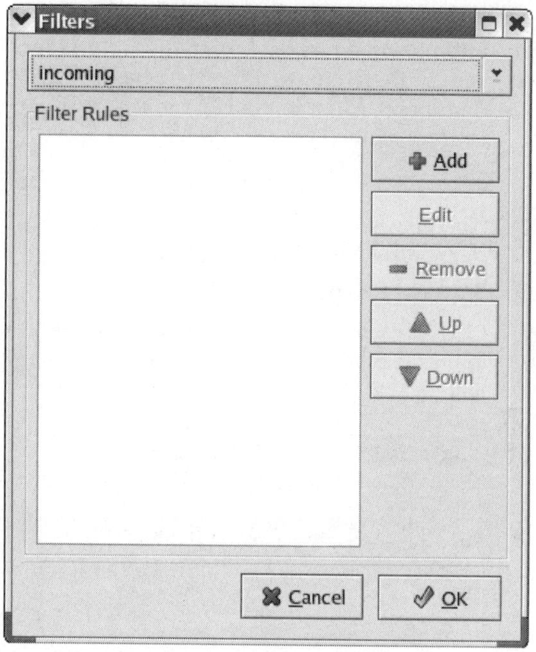

• **Figure 47-6:** The Evolution Filters dialog.

3. Click the Add button.

The Add Rule dialog opens, as shown in Figure 47-7.

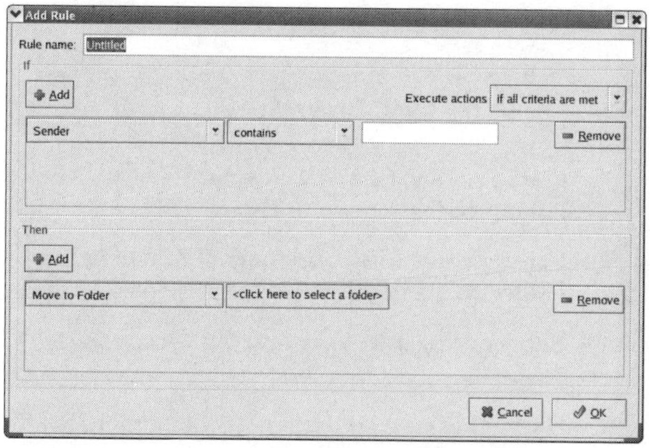

• **Figure 47-7:** Add a new rule for SpamAssassin.

4. **Enter a new name in the Rule Name field. In the drop-down list box to the right of the Sender field, choose Pipe Message to Shell Command. Then to the right of that drop-down list box, enter:**

```
spamc -c > /dev/null
```

5. **Use the arrow to the right of the Returns field to open the drop-down list box and change the field to Returns Greater Than.**

6. **Click the Click Here to Select a Folder field to open the Select Folder dialog, shown in Figure 47-8.**

• **Figure 47-8: The Select Folder dialog.**

7. **Click the New button to open the Create New Folder dialog, shown in Figure 47-9.**

8. **Enter a name for your junkmail folder in the Folder Name field.**

   Harry or Roger would work, but we call ours junkmail.

9. **Highlight Local Folders in the Summary list, and click OK.**

10. **Select your new junkmail folder from the list in the Select Folder dialog. Then click OK.**

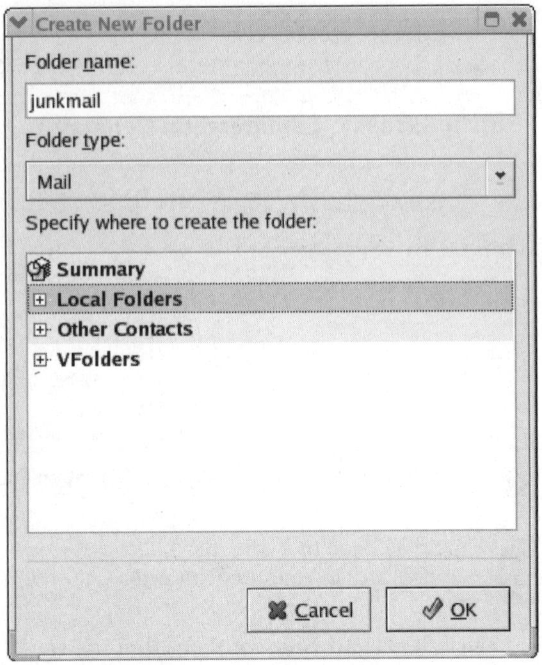

• **Figure 47-9: Create a new junkmail folder.**

The completed rule is displayed, as shown in Figure 47-10.

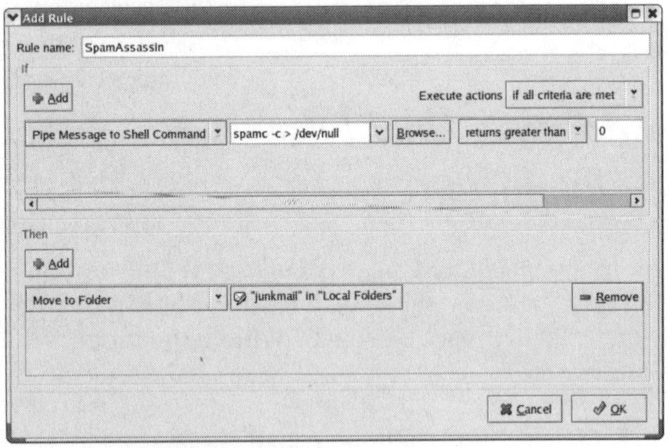

• **Figure 47-10: The completed rule.**

The new rule is now included in the Filters list.

11. Click OK to close the dialog.

SpamAssassin is now actively protecting you and your Evolution account from spam.

Serving Up a Big Bowl of the RulesDuJour

RulesDuJour is a neat script that downloads new SpamAssassin rule sets. Spammers are becoming more sophisticated (well, more persistent anyway) on an almost daily basis. Keeping your rule set up-to-date helps SpamAssassin screen the spam more efficiently.

To install RulesDuJour, follow these steps:

1. Open your Web browser and surf to

```
www.exit0.us/index.php/RulesDuJour
```

2. Scroll down the page and click the download link for `rules du jour.` When the download manager opens, save the files to your home directory.

3. Open a terminal window and edit the `rules_du_jour` file:

```
$ kedit rules_du_jour
```

4. Scroll down and change the entry in line 40 to this:

```
["${SA_DIR}"] || SA_DIR="/etc/mail/
spamassassin";
```

5. Change the entry in line 44 to this:

```
["${MAIL_ADDRESS}"] || MAIL_ADDRESS=
"example@e-mail.com";
```

6. Save the file and close the editor.

7. Make the script executable with the following command:

```
$ chmod u+x rules_du_jour
```

8. To run the script, give yourself superuser privileges with the `su` command and then enter the following command:

```
./rules_du_jour
```

Rules Du Jour goes to work and retrieves the most recent rule set for SpamAssassin.

 This task is a natural for automating. Check out Technique 20 for information about using Task Scheduler to schedule RulesDuJour to run nightly, while network usage is low.

Technique 48: Using Webmin to Simplify Sendmail Configuration

The Internet e-mail system consists of three components:

- **MUA (mail user agent):** Evolution and Mozilla mail are both popular mail user agents (also known as e-mail clients).
- **MDA (mail delivery agent):** The MDA moves the e-mail from Sendmail into your local mailbox. Procmail is a popular Linux MDA.
- **MTA (mail transfer agent):** The MTA moves e-mail from one machine to another across the Internet. Sendmail is an MTA.

Most users' interaction with e-mail stops with their mail agent, when they press the Send button. However, if you're running the mail service for a domain (rather than having an ISP provide the mail service), you need to interact with the mail transfer agent.

Sendmail is easy to use, but also incredibly flexible and powerful. In this technique, we introduce you to Sendmail, and the easy-to-use configuration interface provided by Webmin. If you need to manage configuration files, Webmin is a definite timesaver.

Registering Your Address

Before you can send or receive e-mail with Sendmail, you need a registered domain name. You can purchase a name with a permanent address from an ISP or a name registry, or use a free Dynamic DNS service for sites that change addresses from time to time. Technique 42 has good information about using Dynamic DNS services — check it out.

Taming a Sendmail Server

Setting up an e-mail server with Sendmail is simple. The `sendmail` RPM packages are included in most Linux distributions, and come with a pretty fair configuration file to get you started. The installation and initial setup is super-fast!

To install Sendmail, follow these steps:

1. **Open a terminal window and give yourself superuser privileges with the** su - **command.**

2. **Insert and mount your distribution media. Use the** cd **command to move into the directory containing the** sendmail **RPM packages.**

3. **Install** sendmail **with the following command:**

```
# rpm -Uhv sendmail-version.i386.rpm
```

4. **Install the** sendmail **configuration file with the following command:**

```
#rpm -Uhv sendmail-cf-version.i386.rpm
```

Be sure to choose the *version* that you see on your distribution media.

That's it — Sendmail is installed.

To start Sendmail on a Fedora computer, use the following command:

```
# service sendmail start
```

If you're a SuSE user, type in this command:

```
# rcsendmail start
```

Or, if you're running Mandrake Linux, use this command:

```
# /etc/init.d/sendmail start
```

The configuration can still use some tweaking, but Webmin can help with that, as described in the next section.

Tweaking Your Configuration Files with Webmin

In Technique 17, we walk you through an installation of the top-notch tool, Webmin. If you haven't

installed it already, check out Technique 17 for instructions.

 Webmin is a browser-based administration tool that provides an easy-to-use interface for servers, security issues, and other administrative tasks. It's definitely worth getting to know.

After installing Webmin, follow these steps to access the Sendmail Configuration menu:

1. **Open your favorite Web browser and surf to**

```
localhost:10000/
```

Webmin opens to the login screen.

2. **Enter your user name and password and click the Login button.**

The Webmin main menu appears, as shown in Figure 48-1.

• **Figure 48-1:** The Webmin main menu.

3. **Click the Servers button at the top of the page.**

The Servers page opens.

4. **Click the Sendmail Configuration button, near the bottom of the page.**

The Sendmail Configuration menu opens, as shown in Figure 48-2.

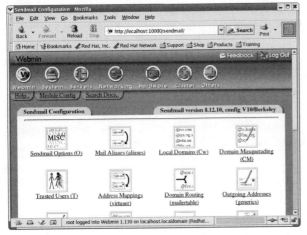

• **Figure 48-2:** The Sendmail Configuration menu.

One quick glance tells you that Sendmail is a complex but powerful program. Fortunately, most of the default configuration options are okay, and the customizations are simple with Webmin. The following sections detail how to customize settings from the Sendmail Configuration menu.

Serving up mail for multiple domains

You can use Sendmail to retrieve e-mail from multiple DNS servers if you have multiple registered names that point to the same server address. To serve up e-mail for multiple domains, you need two things:

✔ Multiple DNS records that list your server and its current address

✔ Multiple listings in the Local Domains list for your Sendmail configuration file

From the Sendmail Configuration menu, follow these steps to add the listings to the Local Domains list:

1. **Click the Local Domains (Cw) button near the top of the Sendmail Configuration menu.**

The Local Domains page opens, as shown in Figure 48-3.

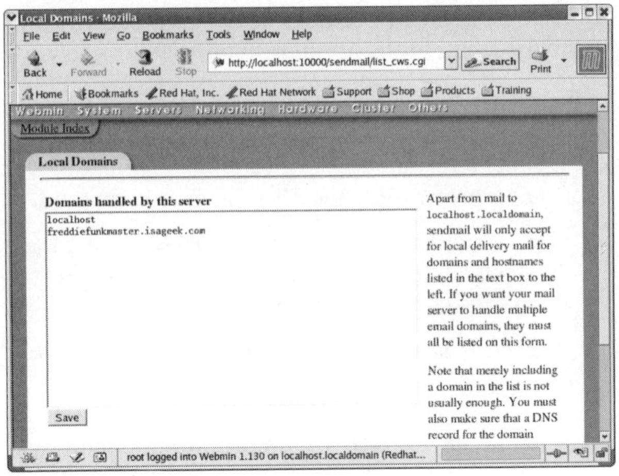

• **Figure 48-3:** The Local Domains list.

2. **Add your domain names to the list and then click the Save button.**

You can send and receive e-mails only from registered names that point to your current e-mail address.

Relaying e-mail

If you need to allow remote employees to send e-mail through your local network, take advantage of the Spam Control (Access) feature of Sendmail. With message relaying, the end user sees your employee's e-mail as coming from your local network even if the employee is accessing your mail server from a distance.

This feature is really intended to keep nasty people out of your system. Spammers with ill intentions often hack systems to route e-mail through unsuspecting Sendmail hosts. Be cautious about setting up relays for friends or employees with loose security habits.

From the Sendmail Configuration menu (refer to Figure 48-2), follow these steps to set up message relaying:

1. Click the Spam Control (Access) button to open the Spam Control menu, shown in Figure 48-4.

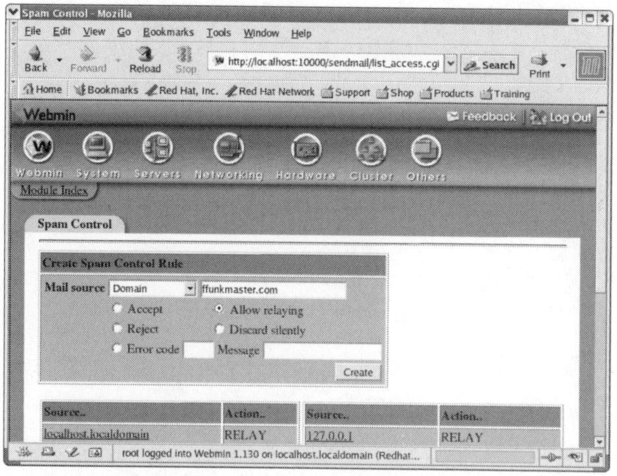

You may want to use the Alias feature to distribute sales inquiries to your entire sales force, technical inquiries to an entire support department, or a humorous mailing to everyone.

2. Enter the address in the Alias Address field.

The address should not include a domain or an extension.

3. If you want the alias to take effect immediately, check the Enabled radio box.

4. In the Alias To drop-down list box, select Addresses in File, and to the right of the list box, enter the file name, as shown in Figure 48-5.

5. Click Create to add the new alias.

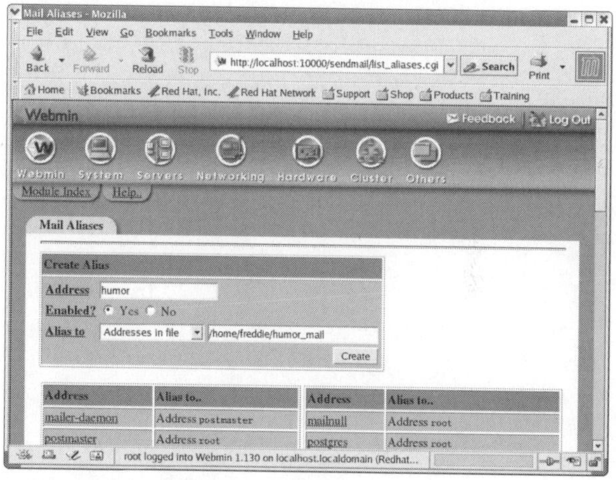

• **Figure 48-4:** The Spam Control menu.

2. Choose Domain from the Mail Source drop-down list, and to the right of this list, enter the domain address of your remote employee. Then select the Allow Relaying radio button and click Create.

The new relay is added to the list of sources.

3. Click the Return to sendmail configuration link (at the bottom of the page) to go back to the Sendmail Configuration menu.

4. Click the Stop Sendmail button at the bottom of the page. When the button name changes to Start Sendmail, click it again to make the changes to your configuration file take effect.

• **Figure 48-5:** Creating a mail alias.

The new alias is created and added to the list. Now, when an e-mail is sent to the address in the alias, Sendmail redistributes it to all the e-mail addresses in the file.

You can create e-mail address files quickly with your favorite text editor. Enter one address per line and save the file somewhere safe but memorable.

Using aliases to simplify mail handling

You can redirect e-mail on your system with Sendmail's Alias feature. If you have an incoming address that you want distributed to multiple individuals, follow these steps:

1. Click the Mail Aliases (Aliases) button on the Sendmail Configuration menu.

The Mail Aliases menu appears.

Any server is a potential security risk. With an e-mail server, you run multiple risks from hackers that want to exploit the free use of your server (and address) to create potential system vulnerabilities. A UML jail might be a good place to keep a mail server — see Technique 58 for details.

Part IX

Backing Up Means Never Having to Say You're Sorry

The 5th Wave   By Rich Tennant

"You ever get the feeling this project could just up and die at any moment?"

Technique 49

Getting Ready to Back Up Your Data

Save Time By

✔ Choosing the right backup media

✔ Choosing the right backup scheme

✔ Choosing the right archive type

Archiving important data is vital — no question about that. Setting up an archiving scheme that's easy to use (and easy to restore from) is important. Unless you make the process quick and easy, and enforce your routine with discipline, you'll find it too easy to slack off and forget to back up an irreplaceable piece of work. We know — we've had to learn the hard way.

For the small system or single computer, the consequences of data loss might not affect other people, but losing your own work is still losing time. Having a dependable backup system is just as important to single users as it is to administrators of large networks.

Choosing the right backup media can make the difference between painful and tedious backup jobs, and backup jobs that are simple and unobtrusive. If you're the administrator of a large network, it's especially important that you choose your media well — other people's work is in your hands. Choosing dependable media (preferably stored off-site) helps ensure a safe recovery if you do need to restore from backup.

In addition to choosing the type of media you'll be using to back up your system, you need to consider whether incremental, differential, or full backups are best for your system. Differential backups are great if resources (such as money for media) are limited and you don't need to restore often. Incremental backups are quicker to restore, but they consume more media than a differential backup. If you need to restore from backup often but have the resources to do full backups, automating full backups saves restoration time in the long run.

Selecting a good archive tool is important, too, and you have a large number of options. Commercial backup tools are typically easy to use and well suited for both commercial and home use. A *ton* of free archive tools are also available, a few of which are already loaded on your computer.

In this technique, we give you some food for thought about choosing a backup scheme for your system. Whether your system is large or small, if you've got important information on it, backing up is important. We give you some factors to consider to help you choose the right media, archiving scheme, and archive type.

Deciding What to Archive

When you consider putting together a backup plan, your first instinct might be to back up *everything*. That way, if anything goes wrong you can get your data back quickly. But consider how much media you would need to archive your entire system. These days, it's not uncommon to find notebook computers with 60GB hard drives. Given that a CD holds only 660MB (or 0.66GB), you would need 100 discs to back up the whole drive. (Actually, you would need fewer than that if you use compression.) You wouldn't want to back up your system very often at that rate.

Instead, back up only data that you can't easily reproduce. You know that you can reinstall Linux on your computer without too much hassle. You can reinstall all the RPM packages and other software that you've loaded. And you certainly don't need old log files and temporary files. That narrows your backup requirements considerably.

So what *should* you archive? Basically, anything that you've created or modified, including the following:

- ✔ Configuration files
- ✔ User home directories
- ✔ E-mail (if you store e-mail on your computer rather than at your ISP)
- ✔ Software (or other projects) that you've developed

Choosing Archive Media

Choosing an archive media type is a matter of finding a balance among the following factors: the cost of the backup device and media, the speed and ease of use,

and how much data the media can hold. The value of your data should definitely impact your choice as well. Here are several media types to consider:

- ✔ Tape drives
- ✔ Removable disks (SCSI drives or external hard drives)
- ✔ Removable non-optical media (Jaz and Zip drives)
- ✔ Removable optical media (CDs and DVDs)
- ✔ Online storage services

The size and configuration of your system influences the requirements of your backup scheme. Good backup media for one system isn't necessarily a good choice for another.

Making the trade

When putting together a backup plan, a major trade-off to consider is recovery time versus the amount of media you need. If you're a small network or single computer user, you can choose to back up only the things you can't replace — e-mail files, data files, high score files for your favorite games, and so on. On the other hand, if you archive data *and* programs, you won't have to reinstall (and reconfigure) all of the programs you already have on your system.

Tape drives

A tape drive is a good choice for backing up large systems. In fact, a tape drive is often the *only* practical choice if you have a lot of data to archive. Many consumer and business tape drives are available with a wide range of prices and capacities. Tape drives can be either internal or external, and they come in a variety of formats. You can choose from dozens of drive manufacturers.

The biggest advantage of a tape backup scheme is the storage capacity. Depending on the tape drive, the contents of a complete system can easily be archived onto a single tape. Tape media is also very affordable, so keeping archived backups generally isn't a problem. The biggest investment is in the tape drive itself.

 Tape drives can range in price from hundreds to thousands of dollars, depending on the backup capacity. Although the drive might be expensive, the media is affordable, making it feasible to archive backups.

One disadvantage of using tape backup is the relatively high failure rate compared to other media types. Tape drives also tend to be slower than other backup types. For a large system, they can be a good choice, but for a small system, you might want to consider other options.

Removable and external disk drives

If you're backing up a single machine, removable or external hard disks are good options to consider. They're fast and dependable, and the prices are dropping almost daily. With an external FireWire drive, you can back up an entire computer in minutes.

 FireWire is a *very* fast hardware protocol. If your system supports FireWire, look for FireWire-enabled devices to save time.

Removable hard drives are drives that fit into a slot on your computer. Plug one in, and you've got an extra drive that you can use to hold archived data. Unplug it and store it someplace safe so you'll have a backup if you need it.

Removable hard drives are too expensive for most people to use for archiving backups; buying a bunch of hard drives to store would add up fast. They are also more fragile than other media — jostling a removable drive in and out of the slot doesn't help its longevity. Still, for backing up a small system, removable hard drives can be a good choice.

External drives are a better choice for many people than removable hard drives. They're sturdier, and because the connection is made with a cable instead of a slot, the chance of damaging the drive in the

process of connecting it is minimal. External drives hold a good amount of data and are very affordable. With a FireWire interface, they're also fast. Many external drives offer both FireWire and USB connections for more flexibility.

 Depending on your system, you can also use a FireWire external drive as an alternate boot disk.

Flash drives, SD memory cards, CompactFlash, and other removable media types also deserve mention. They're little, but they're really handy if you just need to back up a small amount of data.

 Use a flash drive as a backup container for your passwords. Make copies of your `~/.gnupg` **directory** and `~/.ssh` **directories**, as well as encrypted text files containing other passwords you need often. Now, you can easily take your passwords and keys with you when you travel.

Be sure to encrypt cleartext password files and your private keys in case you lose the flash drive.

Removable media

A Zip drive is like a floppy drive on steroids. It can hold a good amount of data, it's easy to store off-site, and it's portable and network friendly.

A Zip drive can be either internal or external (Iomega even has an external FireWire available), and the media itself is rugged and portable. The largest Zip drive currently holds 750MB — that's a little bit more than a CD.

Zip disks are more expensive than blank CDs or DVDs, and most systems now come with a CD or DVD writer. On the upside, Zip drives have two main advantages: Writing data to a Zip drive is *much* faster than writing to a CD or DVD, and a Zip drive is inherently rewritable (it's just a disk drive). Zip disks are about as durable as CDs.

Optical media (CDs and DVDs)

CDs and DVDs might be the best backup media for the small network or single system user. They're dirt-cheap, durable, easy to use, and fast. They store forever (well, a long time anyway) and move easily from one machine to another. Most new computers come with a CD or DVD recorder, and if it's not included, it's easy to add at a fair price.

What's the downside? A CD doesn't hold very much data — 660MB or so. A DVD can hold 4.7GB. Is that a problem? Probably not if you're backing up a single computer or a small network. Each disc holds enough data that you can most likely back up an entire system with just a handful of discs.

 DVD recorders are just starting to show up in consumer-level computers, but you can easily add an external DVD writer, and the once-high price tags are dropping fast. A DVD holds considerably more data than a CD, so the time you can save in backing up makes the investment in a DVD recorder worth considering.

CDs or DVDs may not be the perfect storage answer for a large system, but for a single machine or small network, they're great.

Online storage

Online storage services abound — just run a Google search, and you'll find hundreds of them. The services range in price from free (for 5GB or so of backup space) to reasonable, and if you have a good (fast) network connection, online backup is a good choice. Online storage has the added advantage that your data is being stored at a different physical location from your home or business. If your building burns down, you know your backups are safely stored somewhere else. Of course, if you use an online storage service, you're trusting them with your data — and it may be difficult to recover your data should the provider go out of business.

Online backup services offer the single user or small network administrator a user-friendly and secure interface for quick updates to archive files. The administrator of a larger system will find convenience in scheduling whole-system backups for times when network usage is lowest. In either case, online services are friendly (usually), easy to use, and safe.

Choose a dependable service (preferably one that's been in business for a while, with good references), with an interface that works for you. With a fast (and secure) connection, online storage might be the best choice for you.

Choosing an Archive Scheme

You can choose from three basic backup schemes: full, differential, and incremental. They each have advantages — some save restoration time, and some save media.

Cost, convenience, and time are the primary considerations when choosing an archiving scheme. For example, if you need to shuffle a lot of discs to do a full backup, run a full backup once a week, and schedule unattended incremental backups on the days in between. Or, if you use a tape changer (or an online service), you can schedule a full backup every night.

Full backups

A *full* backup is just that — an archive that contains all the data that you want to save. You can create a full backup without archiving *every* program and data file on your computer; you can pick and choose only the files that you can't conveniently re-create. What makes a full backup different from the other schemes is that you archive all the selected data every time you back up.

Differential backups

A *differential* backup saves only the data that changes from one day to the next. To build a differential backup set, you start each cycle with a full backup on the first day. Each backup after that is a snapshot of the changes made since the previous backup. Keep the initial backup and all the snapshots in a safe place in case you need to restore data. Every so often, start the cycle over again. The cycle always starts with a full backup.

 You need at least two full sets of backup media to use incremental media safely so you don't write over a backup that you may need to restore from.

To restore from a differential backup, apply the entire chain of archives, starting with the most recent complete backup and appending each snapshot in sequence. If the last full backup was a month ago and you back up daily, you'll have 31 tapes in your archive to restore.

Incremental backups

To use an *incremental* backup scheme, take a full backup on the first day and then a differential backup on the second day. The second day's backup includes only those files that have changed since the last full backup. The third day of an incremental backup scheme captures all file changes that have taken place since the last *full* backup.

Incremental versus differential backups

You may be thinking that an incremental scheme sounds suspiciously similar to a differential scheme. They are in fact very similar — each scheme archives only the data that's changed. The difference is that a differential scheme archives the changes since the previous *differential* backup; an incremental backup archives the changes since the previous *full* backup.

Here's an example:

1. You start with a full backup Sunday night.
2. On Monday, you create a new file named `/home/freddie/spybusiness.html`. Monday

night, you create a differential archive that contains only the new file (`spybusiness.html`).

3. Tuesday morning, you create another new file named `/home/freddie/gadgets.html`. Here's where the difference appears:

   ▶ If you create a differential backup, Tuesday's archive will only contain `gadgets.html`. (A differential backup archives the data that's changed since the previous differential backup.)

   ▶ If you create an incremental backup, Tuesday's archive contains both files: `spybusiness.html` *and* `gadgets.html` (an incremental backup archives the data that's changed since the last *full* backup).

You can see that an incremental backup scheme takes more media than a differential scheme. The big advantage of an incremental backup scheme (compared to a differential scheme) shows up at recovery time. If you need to recover from a hardware failure (or from a nasty typo), you only restore the latest full backup and the last incremental backup.

Having a backup plan

Formalize your backup plans and make them part of a routine instead of just performing a backup when you think you've accomplished something really monumental. Sometimes, truly monumental or important things go unnoticed until disaster strikes; unless you have a backup, you'll lose a great piece of work. Make a plan and stick with it.

It's not good enough to just have a backup plan. You also need to make sure that you can restore a backup if you need to. Don't wait until the last minute to find out that your tapes are unreadable or that an online service is flaky. Test your media whether it's on-site or off.

How often you back up is a decision only you can make, but consider how long it will take to reproduce the work lost if your backup routine is sporadic. Backing up is easy and painless, but losing a month's work hurts.

Choosing an Archive Program

Many archiving programs are available for backing up Linux computers. Here are a few that you should consider:

✔ **AMANDA (Advanced Maryland Automatic Network Disk Archiver):** This suite of tools is designed to archive entire networks. With AMANDA, you create a single "backup server," and from there, you can archive any computer that you can reach over the network. You can even use AMANDA to back up Windows-based computers. You can find AMANDA at `www.amanda.org`.

✔ **Arkeia Light:** Arkeia is another network-enabled backup tool. You can find it at `www.arkeia.org`. The free version is missing a few features that are included in the commercial program, but Arkeia Light is still a very useable tool with a nice-looking user interface. One of the big advantages to Arkeia (the commercial version) is that you can talk to a support person if something goes wrong (a service you *don't* get with open-source tools).

✔ **Bacula:** A relatively recent addition to the open-source archive arena, Bacula has some heavy-duty features that you may need in a large organization. Bacula keeps a complete history of all archive operations in a relational database (SQLLite, PostgreSQL, or MySQL), which makes it quick and easy for you to find the archive volume that contains the data that you're interested in. And, because the history is stored in a database, you can create custom tools and custom reports from the archive history tables.

Bacula lives at `www.bacula.org`. Its motto is "It comes by night and sucks the vital essence from your computers" — how could you resist a tool like that?

✔ **Mondo:** Mondo is not really an archive program as such — it's a rescue tool. After you build a bootable Mondo rescue disk, you can restore your entire operating system without reinstalling everything from scratch. Combine Mondo with a complete backup plan, and you'll recover from hardware failures much faster. You can find more information about Mondo at `www.microwerks.net/~hugo`.

✔ `tar`: Short for *tape archiver,* `tar` is the long-running standard for backup. It's versatile, flexible, and reasonably easy to use. It's also available on every Linux (or UNIX) computer you're likely to encounter (it's even available on many Windows systems). In the next technique, we show you how to use `tar` (together with a helper tool named `cdbackup`) to create multidisc backup sets on CDs or DVDs.

50 Technique

Backing Up Your Data

Save Time By

- Estimating how much media you'll need for your backup
- Taking interim backups of the directories that are most likely to be lost
- Using incremental or differential backup schemes
- Using tar and cdbackup to make backup CDs

Backing up data may mean backing up a single file, a directory tree, or an entire system. You may choose to do incremental backups, differential backups, or full backups depending on the amount of data you need to store and the value of that data (see Technique 49 for details on the different backup types). One way or the other, you'll be using an archiving program.

tar is a simple but flexible tool that creates sturdy, portable archives. You can use tar to create archives quickly and easily, and you can write those archives straight onto your hard drive or onto other devices. You can use tar to bundle files into archives, and move them easily and quickly to CDs or thumb drives or across your network.

Performing interim backups of important directories that might be lost through user error (such as home directories and e-mail files) can save you from restoring from a system backup just to extract a single file.

tar won't write straight to CD without a helper application — it's great with tape drives, but it's not so hot with CDs. We've found a great helper tool called cdbackup that we show you how to use in this technique. cdbackup works *with* tar to create archives that can span multiple CDs (or DVDs).

In this technique, we show you some useful variations on the tar command and give you a step-by-step introduction to differential and incremental backup schemes. Remember, backing up means never having to say you're sorry.

Estimating Your Media Needs

It's nice to know how much media you'll need before you start a backup. You don't want to get halfway through and find out that you need to run to Office Depot to pick up more tapes. It's also nice to know your archive size if you're planning on carrying it with you on a thumb drive or other removable media.

The easiest way to find out how much media you'll need to hold an archive is to make a dry run first. If you're using `tar` to create the archive, use the same options that you plan to use when you create the real backup, but pipe the results to `wc -c` instead of writing it to media:

```
# tar -cvplf - backupcontents | wc -c
```

The `-f -` option tells `tar` to write the archive to its standard output stream. When `tar` completes, `wc` displays the total number of bytes required to hold the archive. If you plan to create a compressed archive, be sure to include the compression option when you compute the archive size; otherwise, you'll overestimate the amount of media that you need. For example, if you use bzip2 compression to create an archive, calculate the archive size like this:

```
# tar -jcvplf - backupcontents | wc -c
```

The `-j` flag tells `tar` to use bzip2 compression; use `-z` if you want to use gzip compression instead.

 You need superuser privileges to back up files that aren't your own.

Creating Data Archives with tar

`tar` is an archive tool that you can use to create backups. It's been around for a long time, it's stable, and it's relatively easy to use. Much of the data and programs out on the Web are distributed as compressed `tar` archives (affectionately known as tarballs). `tar` runs just about everywhere — Linux, UNIX, Windows, and Mac — so the archives that you create are portable. It's included in even the most basic of Linux installations, so you don't need to spend any time installing it.

 `tar` also has the advantage of knowing how to manage incremental and differential backups. That's a huge bonus if you're an administrator on a tight media budget. Of course, you can compress archives as you create them, saving even more time and money.

Backing up files and directories

 Before you start a backup, use the `lsof` command to be sure files aren't in use. The command `lsof | grep directoryname` will tell you if any files are open in the *directoryname* directory tree. If the fourth column has any *u*'s or *w*'s in it, someone has a file open in update or write mode. See Technique 36 for more information about using `lsof`.

To archive a single file or directory with `tar`, enter the following command:

```
# tar -cvzf archivename filename
```

Here's a breakdown of this command:

- ✔ The `-c` flag tells `tar` to create an archive.
- ✔ The `-v` flag tells `tar` to run in verbose mode (listing the archive content as it's created).
- ✔ The `-z` flag compresses the archive using gzip compression.
- ✔ The `-f archivename` option tells `tar` where to write the archive. *archivename* can name a data file, a device name, or `-` (standard output stream).

You can follow the first *filename* with more file and directory names to write multiple files to the same archive.

 `tar` can write archives to files, to devices, or to `-` (standard output). Use the `-` to pipe the archive to other commands.

In our examples, we use `/dev/rmt0` as the device name — a pretty common name for a tape drive.

Backing up account information and passwords

Use the following command to back up user account information and passwords:

```
# tar -cvzf /dev/rmt0 \
  /etc/passwd /etc/shadow
```

This command tells `tar` to create a gzip-compressed archive containing the `/etc/passwd` file and the `/etc/shadow` directory and write the archive to a tape drive (`/dev/rmt0`).

 Any user can read the user account information stored in `/etc/password`, **but you must be the superuser to read the** `/etc/shadow` **file** (where the passwords are really stored).

Targeting bite-sized backups for speedier restores

Keeping individual backups of the data that you're most likely to need is a good idea — especially if you use differential backups on a long backup cycle. Instead of doing a complete restore cycle just to recover the lost home directory of one sad user, you can unpack the lost data from a small archive.

Here are a few directories that you may want to archive separately to avoid a lengthy restore cycle:

- ✔ `/home`: The `/home` directory contains the home directories of all the system users.

- ✔ `/etc`: The `/etc` directory contains most system configuration files.

- ✔ `/spool`: The `/spool` directory contains mailboxes and print files.

To back up the `/home` directory and the `/home/user` directories of all users, use the following command:

```
# tar -cvzf /dev/rmt0 /home
```

The `tar` command automatically recurses into subdirectories, which means all files and subdirectories underneath the parent are included in the new archive.

Rolling whole file systems into a tarball

Use the `tar` command to back up an entire file system by adding the `-l` flag to the command:

```
# tar -cvlzf /dev/rmt0 filesystem
```

The `-l` (lowercase L) option tells `tar` to stay within the given `filesystem`. That's important if you think that `filesystem` might contain mount points for other file systems.

To back up multiple file systems, append a list of the file system names to the end of the command. To find a complete list of the file systems on your system, use the `mount` command with superuser privileges:

```
# mount
```

The `mount` command returns a list of file systems that looks similar to the list shown in Figure 50-1.

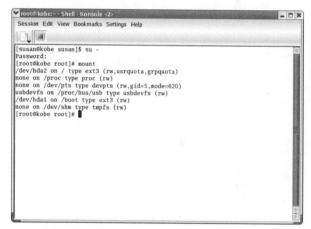

• **Figure 50-1: The file system listing.**

Use the listing to find the mounted file systems you want to include in the backup.

If you need to create a multitape archive, add the `-M` flag to the command:

```
# tar -cvlzfM /dev/rmt0 filesystemname
```

The `-M` flag won't help if you're using CDs or DVDs to hold your archives, but we show you how to create multidisc backup sets in the section, "Backing Up to CD (Or DVD) with cdbackup," later in this chapter.

Starting a Differential Backup Cycle

You can use the `tar` command to create incremental or differential backups. We explain the subtle differences between incremental and differential backups in Technique 49. You may want to check out that technique before deciding on the type that's right for you.

Each time you create a backup in a differential or incremental cycle, you include an extra command line option:

```
-g snapshotFileName
```

The snapshot file keeps track of which files and directories you've written to an archive. The next time you create an archive using the same snapshot file, `tar` saves only those files that have changed since the previous backup. (It knows which files to save by comparing the current state of your disk with the information saved in the snapshot.)

 It's a good idea to store `tar` snapshot files in a directory that you aren't likely to clean out on a regular basis. Don't put the log files in the `/tmp` or `/var/log` directories. Instead, create a separate directory to hold snapshot files. In our examples, we assume that you want to store snapshot files in `/backups`.

For a differential (or incremental) backup scheme, you start each cycle by creating a full backup. `tar` creates a snapshot file that records the fact that the archive contains a complete copy of everything that you want to save.

To employ a differential backup cycle, follow these steps:

1. On the first day of the backup cycle (assume it's Monday for this example), start by removing the log file:

```
# rm /backups/etc.snap
```

2. Next, create a full backup with the following command:

```
# tar -cvlfz /dev/rmt0 \
    -g /backups/etc.snap
    /etc
```

Substitute your tape drive name for `/dev/rmt0`.

This command backs up the `/etc` directory and everything underneath it. If you want to back up more file systems, just append the names to the end of the command line (and choose a more meaningful name for the snapshot file).

Store the backup tape somewhere safe, like in a fireproof safe or an off-site location.

3. On the second day of the cycle (Tuesday), use the same command:

```
# tar -cvlfz /dev/rmt0 \
    -g /backups/etc.snap
    /etc
```

This time, `tar` compares `/backups/etc.snap` to the current state of the `/etc` directory tree and saves only those files that have changed (or new files).

`tar` also updates the snapshot file to reflect the new state of your archive collection.

Store this backup in a safe place.

4. On the third day (Wednesday), use the same command:

```
# tar -cvlfz /dev/rmt0 \
    -g /backups/etc.snap
    /etc
```

Again, `tar` compares the snapshot to the current state of the `/etc` directory tree. But this time, the snapshot records the archive cycle as of the end of the day on Tuesday. So, the archive you create on Wednesday contains only the files that have changed since Tuesday. When it's finished, `tar` updates the snapshot file to reflect the state of your archive collection.

Wednesday's archive stores only the changes made between Tuesday and Wednesday. The changes made between Monday and Tuesday are in the first differential archive.

Store Wednesday's tape with Monday's and Tuesday's tapes. If you need to restore from backup, you need all the tapes to capture an accurate picture of all the changes made to the /etc directory tree.

You can see the pattern start to form. This cycle goes on and on until you start over again with a full backup. Each time you start the cycle, delete the snapshot file first so that the first archive is a complete backup.

 Keep at least two cycles of media to be sure that you have a backup to restore from in case of emergency.

On the upside, although it takes a lot of media to create a differential backup, it takes less time because each backup represents only one day's worth of changes.

On the downside, if you need to restore data, you have to restore all the days in the backup cycle.

Starting an Incremental Backup Cycle

Incremental backups are a bit confusing at first, but the concept is simple when you understand it. An incremental backup works very much like a differential backup, except you have to manage the snapshot file more carefully.

A differential backup saves only the files that have changed since the most recent backup. An incremental backup saves only the files that have changed since the most recent *complete* backup. In other

words, an incremental backup contains everything that's changed since the start of the cycle.

tar uses a snapshot file to decide which files it needs to save. tar only saves files changed since the snapshot was last updated.

So how do you get tar to save *all* files changed since the beginning of the cycle? Simple — throw out the update snapshot file after each incremental backup. If you start an incremental cycle every Monday, you want tar to use Monday's snapshot file on Tuesday, Wednesday, Thursday, and Friday. (With a *differential* scheme, you use Monday's snapshot on Tuesday, Tuesday's snapshot on Wednesday, Wednesday's snapshot on Thursday, and so on.) Shuffling snapshot files might seem like an odd way to get a good backup, but it does work.

 The advantage to an incremental backup scheme is when you have to restore lost data. You restore the first archive in the cycle and the last archive — you don't have to apply all the intermediate archives like you would in a differential scheme. That might not sound like a big timesaver, but if your backup cycle is 30 days long instead of 7, you get to go home for the weekend instead of shuffling tapes.

Follow these steps to start an incremental backup cycle:

1. **On the first day of the backup cycle (assume it's Monday for this example), start by removing the log file:**

```
# rm /backups/etc.snap
```

2. **Create a full backup with the following command:**

```
# tar -cvlfz /dev/rmt0 \
    -g /backups/etc.snap
    /etc
```

Store the backup tape somewhere safe.

3. **On the second day of the cycle (Tuesday), make a temporary copy of Monday's snapshot file:**

```
# cp /backups/etc.snap \
     /backups/etc.tmp
```

4. **Now invoke** `tar`, **but this time tell it to read from (and update) the temporary snapshot file rather than the master copy:**

```
# tar -cvlfz /dev/rmt0 \
     -g /backups/etc.tmp
     /etc
```

`tar` compares `/backups/etc.tmp` to the current state of the `/etc` directory tree and saves only those files that have changed since the *first* archive in the cycle.

`tar` also updates the snapshot file (`/backups/etc.tmp`), but you'll overwrite that file on the next day anyway.

Store this backup in a safe place.

5. **On every other day in the cycle, repeat Steps 3 and 4.**

In an incremental backup, each backup after the initial backup contains all the changes that have occurred between the first full backup and the current state of the system.

On the downside, incremental backups take longer to create, and they consume more media.

On the upside, if you need to restore data, you only need to use two tapes to do it: the initial (full) backup and the most recent incremental.

Restoring from Backup with tar

Restoring from backup with `tar` is as easy as backing up with `tar`. Instead of creating archives, you use `tar`'s extract command to extract the data that you need.

To restore an entire directory tree, move to the root directory and use the following command:

```
# tar -xzvf /dev/rmt0 /directoryname
```

To restore a single file, use this command:

```
# tar -xzvf /dev/rmt0 /directory/filename
```

You can restore many files (or directories) at once by listing the names at the end of the command line. Be sure to use the same compression options that you used when you created the archive.

If you've used an incremental backup scheme, extract the files that you want from the full backup tape first, and then extract the same files from the most recent incremental backup. (If the files that you want to extract haven't changed since the full backup, they won't appear in the incremental archive, but that's okay. You should still try to restore from the incremental archive just in case.)

If you're keeping incremental backups, you'll restore two backups: the first backup and then the most recent incremental backup.

Restoring from a differential backup is the same basic procedure, but it takes more time because you have more tapes to go through.

Hopefully you've kept simple interim backups of the files you're most likely to need to restore (see the section, "Targeting bite-sized backups for speedier restores," earlier in this technique), and you'll have to restore from a differential backup only in the case of an extreme disaster — we'll all hope that doesn't happen.

If your system is damaged to the point where you can't boot into Linux, don't panic. Just reinstall Linux and then restore your data from backup. See — aren't you glad you have a good backup plan?

Backing Up to CD (Or DVD) with cdbackup

Without a little help, `tar` cannot write archives directly to CD or DVD media. You could write an archive to your hard drive and then copy the archive to a CD (or DVD) with a tool like `k3b` or `nautilus`, but that's a hassle. You'd need enough free space on your hard drive to hold the intermediate copy, and you'd have to figure out how to split a *big* archive onto multiple discs — definitely *not* a timesaving technique.

Fortunately, the open-source community comes to the rescue again. The `cdbackup` and `cdrestore` commands are helper programs that you can use *with* `tar` to write archives onto a CD or DVD. `cdbackup` writes straight onto a CD or DVD without laying down a file system first. That saves you some space and time, but you won't be able to read the discs with other programs. `cdbackup` can write a large archive to multiple discs (something that `tar` can't do by itself). Because `cdbackup` cooperates so well with `tar`, you can use the combination to create complete backups, incremental backups, and differential backups that span multiple discs.

You can find the CDBackup package at the author's Web site: `www.muempf.de/index.html`.

Creating the backup

Creating a multidisc backup with `tar` and `cdbackup` is easy:

1. Type in the `tar` command that archives the data that you want to save and then tell `tar` to write the archive to its standard output stream, like this (but don't press Enter yet):

   ```
   # tar -zcvf - /home /etc
   ```

2. Then pipe the archive to `cdbackup`:

   ```
   # tar -zcvf - /home /etc | cdbackup -m
     -r 0,0,0 -a "My Backup"
   ```

   If you're burning a DVD instead of a CD, be sure to include `-l 4600` in your command line so `cdbackup` knows that it can write up 4.6GB per disc (`-l 4700` might be safe too, but leave yourself a little wiggle room).

   `tar` starts building the archive, and when it has enough data, `cdbackup` starts writing it to CD (or DVD).

3. Press Enter, and your backup begins.

4. When `cdbackup` **fills the first disc, it prompts you to insert a new one. After you do so, press Enter to continue.**

Under the hood, `cdbackup` uses the `cdrecord` package to do the tough work. In fact, you can pass command line options to the underlying `cdrecord` command when you invoke `cdbackup`. Table 50-1 lists some of the more useful `cdbackup` options.

TABLE 50-1: HANDY CDBACKUP OPTIONS

Option	What It Does
`-m`	Enables multidisc recording
`-r device`	Specifies which CD/DVD drive to record to
`-s speed`	Specifies the write speed (the default write speed is 4, or 4 times the normal write speed)
`-a label`	Adds a descriptive name (*label*) to the archive set
`-l size`	Tells `cdbackup` how many megabytes can fit on one disc (the default is 650 — about the size of a blank CD)
`-- options`	Passes command line *options* to the `cdrecord` command

"No, I don't want a moment to reflect on my backup."

By default, cdrecord (and therefore cdbackup) pauses for ten seconds before it starts burning a CD, giving you a chance to change your mind and cancel the burn. That pause can get a bit annoying after a while. You can shorten the delay by including a cdrecord option at the end of the command line:

```
# tar -zcvf - /home /etc | cdbackup -m -r
    0,0,0 -a "My Backup" -- gracetime=2
```

The -- flags tells cdbackup to pass the rest of the command line options to cdrecord. In this case, gracetime=2 shortens the preburn delay to 2 seconds (the minimum allowed by cdrecord).

If you don't know the full name of your CD/DVD recorder, run the following command:

```
# cdrecord -scanbus
```

You should see a result similar to this:

```
scsibus1:
  1,0,0 100) 'TEAC' 'DW-224E ' 'F.0A' CDRW
  1,1,0 101) *
  1,2,0 102) *
  1,3,0 103) *
  1,4,0 104) *
  1,5,0 105) *
  1,6,0 106) *
  1,7,0 107) *
```

Find your recorder in the list: The first three numbers on that line make up the device number. If you see more than one device in the list, choose your drive by its model name. In our case, we would tell cdbackup to record on device 1,0,0.

Restoring from a CD or DVD backup

To restore a file (or set of files), you use cdrestore and tar. For example, to restore the /etc/passwd file from a backup set, place the first disc in the drive and then type this command:

```
# cdrestore /dev/cdrom -t 1 | \
    tar -zxvf - /etc/passwd
```

If the file you're looking for is not on the first disc, cdrestore prompts you to insert the next disc; press Enter to continue. In fact, cdrestore asks you to insert the next disc even if it does find /etc/passwd on the first disc. cdrestore can't tell when tar has finished its work, so when you're sure you have the files that you need, you can just press Ctrl-C to kill the job. Be careful though, because the file that you're looking for may be split across multiple discs.

When you run cdrestore, you can use the normal /dev/cdrom device name instead of -r 1,0,0. The -t 1 option tells cdrestore to read from the first track on the disc (yes, cdbackup can *write* multiple tracks so cdrestore can read them). Pipe the output from cdrestore to tar and tell tar to extract the files that you want. Notice that you can use compression (either the -z gzip variety or the -j bzip2 variety). You have to specify the compression type when you create the archive and when you restore from the archive.

To see a listing of the archive content, use the following command:

```
# cdrestore /dev/cdrom -t 1 | tar -ztvf -
```

The cdrestore part of the command is the same, but you use the -t flag to list the content instead of -x to extract it. You can also use the -q flag to view information about the disc that you have in the drive:

```
# cdrestore -q /dev/cdrom
Tracks: 1
Disk size:   666000 kB ( 333000 blocks)
Space used:    1872 kB (    936 blocks)
Space avail: 641328 kB ( 320664 blocks)
Track 01: 1 MB: Part 2: My Backup
```

Restoring from a disc containing multiple archives

One of nicest cdrecord features is that you can write multiple archives to the same disc. For example, if you use an incremental or differential backup plan, you might do a complete backup on Sunday and an incremental (or differential) backup every weekday. The weekday backups are likely to be small enough to fit on a single disc without filling it up. With cdrecord, just put Monday's disc in the drive when you create Tuesday's archive because cdbackup is smart enough to append the new archive to the end of the disc. If you have multiple tracks on the same disc, cdrestore -q shows you all of them:

```
# cdrestore -q /dev/cdrom
Tracks: 3
Disk size:   666000 kB ( 333000 blocks)
Space used:   64442 kB (  32221 blocks)
Space avail: 587758 kB ( 293879 blocks)
Track 01:10 MB: Part 1: Monday's backup
Track 02:20 MB: Part 1: Tuesday's backup
Track 03:10 MB: Part 1: Wednesday's backup
```

When you restore from a multitrack disc set, just tell cdrestore which track you want to start with, as in the following example:

```
# cdrestore /dev/cdrom -t 2 | \
    tar -zxvf - /etc/passwd
```

The -t 2 flag tells cdrestore to read from track 2 (Tuesday's backup).

Technique 51

Quick Backup to Remote Storage

Save Time By

- ✔ Creating and moving archives with `tar` and `ssh`
- ✔ Backing up to tape drives on remote hosts
- ✔ Using `rdist` with `ssh` for simple remote backups
- ✔ Creating simple remote backup commands that you can automate

The price of a well-outfitted computer has dropped to the point where it's feasible to use a second computer as a backup device. Keeping a backup computer system on your own network or at another office accessible from the Web is a viable option for many companies. You don't need fancy backup software to mirror your data on a remote computer; Linux already includes the tools to do the job.

In Technique 50, we show you how to use the `tar` program to create archives of your data. In this technique, we show you how to combine `tar` and `ssh` (the secure shell) to create archives on a remote computer. When you use `ssh` to back up your data, the data stream is encrypted, so you're guaranteed that your important files won't be read by the world. You can use `ssh` across your local network or across the Web with equal ease. Backing up with `ssh` is easier and quicker than mounting a network drive — you don't even need superuser privileges.

Piping compressed archives created by the `tar` command to the `ssh` command makes it easy and quick to back up to remote hosts. You can create an archive containing your important files and move it to a remote host with just one command. It doesn't get much quicker than that.

You can also use the `tar` command in combination with `ssh` to write to tape drives on remote machines. It's a quick way to share resources on your network without a lot of hardware investment or software conflicts.

We also introduce you to the `rdist` command. With `rdist`, you can create a mirror image of your working system on a remote machine. A complete copy of your important information is not only safe, but also ready to use in an instant. Use the `rdist` command with `ssh` to make the remote connection simple, fast, and secure. By using Task Scheduler with `rdist` and `ssh`, you can even automate your nightly backups.

In this technique, we show you some shortcuts that work with some old favorites to make backing up to remote systems quick and easy.

Combining the Power of tar with ssh for Quick Remote Backups

`tar` is an archiving tool that can create new archives, display the contents of an existing archive, or extract data from an archive. An archive is just a simple file that contains other files within it. Archives are handy because they let you work with (e-mail, copy, or back up, for example) a whole collection of files with ease. When you use `tar` to create an archive, `tar` copies the contents of each file into the archive, along with some bookkeeping information such as the file owner, file permissions, and modification date. The Linux version of `tar` (actually, the GNU version included with Linux) can compress an archive on the fly, and the compressed archive is usually smaller than the sum of its parts.

`tar` by itself is a useful command, but add the power of `ssh`, and you've got a great combination that makes it easy to back up your data to a remote system. You can also use `tar` and `ssh` to access tape drives mounted on remote machines.

Testing the ssh connection to the remote host

`tar` and `ssh` are installed with most Linux distributions by default — you already have a working copy of each program on your system. Before you try to use `tar` and `ssh` together, test the `ssh` connection to the remote host:

```
$ ssh remotehost
```

If the `ssh` connection is good, you're prompted for your password.

 It's unlikely that you'll get connection errors, but if you do, you need to resolve them before you can continue.

Creating a tar archive over the ssh connection

After you've tested the `ssh` connection, you're ready to go. To create a `tar` archive over an `ssh` connection, use the following command:

```
$ tar -zcv -f - /source | ssh remotehost
  "cat > targetfile.tgz"
```

Replace the source and destination names with your own. Then press Enter to start the backup.

Here's a closer look at the preceding command:

- ✔ `tar -zcv -f -`: Creates a `tar` archive, using the following options:
  - ▶ `z`: Create the archive in compressed gzip format.
  - ▶ `c`: Create a `tar` archive.
  - ▶ `v`: Use verbose mode. Display progress on the screen.
  - ▶ `-f -`: The `-f` *archive* option tells `tar` where to write the archive. In this case, you want `tar` to write the archive to the standard output stream (which you'll connect to the standard input stream of the `ssh` command with the pipe character `|`).

- ✔ `/source`: Specifies the files and/or directories that should be added to the `tar` archive. You can add multiple files or directories to the archive by listing each filename (or directory name), separated by a space:

```
$ tar zcvf - /home /usr | ssh remotehost
  "cat > targetfile.tgz"
```

  The preceding command creates an archive (on the machine *remotehost*) containing the contents of the `/home` directory and the contents of the `/usr` directory.

- ✔ `|`: Pipes the standard output from the first command into the standard input for the second command.

- ✔ `ssh` *remotehost*: Opens an encrypted connection to the remote computer.

- ✔ `cat > targetfile.tgz`: Receives the data coming through the standard input of the `ssh` command and directs it, byte-by-byte, to the file named *targetfile.tgz*. This creates a duplicate of the archive on the remote host, in the filename specified.

Whenever the remote command contains spaces, you need to enclose the command in quotes.

That simple `tar` and `ssh` command makes creating `tar` archives on a remote machine about as quick and easy as it gets.

Check out Technique 13 for more information about using archives and `tar`. The `tar` man page also details tons of options you can add to the `tar` command to tailor this technique to your system.

When you execute the command, you're prompted for your password on the other machine. Adding public key authentication to the SSH connection allows you to skip password authentication.

Setting up a key ring for authentication takes only a few minutes and can save you a lot of time in the long run. See Technique 33 for the lowdown on setting up `ssh` to accept public keys.

Backing up to tape drives on remote machines

One other quick trick you can do with `tar` and `ssh` is to back up to remote tape drives. Just replace the destination filename with the device name, and `ssh` delivers your archive to the tape drive. For example, if the tape drive on your remote host is named `/dev/rmt0`, use the following command:

```
$ tar zcvf - /source | ssh remotehost "cat
  > /dev/rmt0"
```

With just a few variations, the `tar` command provides a powerful backup tool. Use it with Task Scheduler to automate nightly backups, and you'll really save time! (See Technique 20 for more information about scheduling automated tasks).

Backing Up to a Remote Computer with rdist and ssh

`rdist` is a command line tool that helps you maintain identical copies of files or directories over multiple hosts. You can use `rdist` with `ssh` to distribute sales reports, inventory lists, or other files to remote offices that need access to shared data. `tar` and `ssh` make it easy to create an archive on a single remote computer, but `rdist` can push complete directory trees to *any number* of remote systems.

You can easily back up a single system to multiple remote hosts with `rdist`.

You can also use `rdist` to back up important system and data files to a remote host. With the cost of well-outfitted computers at an all-time low, keeping a mirror image of important files is financially feasible. Using `rdist` to create a mirror image of treasured files makes backing up quick and easy.

An `rdist` backup isn't a perfect mirror image of your complete working system. The boot sectors of your local machine and any files being used at the time of backup will be different on the remote host.

Testing the ssh connection to the remote host

Before you can use `rdist`, you need to have a clean `ssh` connection with each of your targets. Test the `ssh` connection at the command line with a trial connection:

```
$ ssh remotehostname
```

If you've lived a good clean life, you should be able to make an `ssh` connection to the remote host. If the connection succeeds, you're prompted for a password and allowed to log in to the remote system.

Save time by setting up `ssh` to handle public-key authentication for you so you don't need to enter a password. Check out Technique 33 for details.

Creating the distfile

After you've tested the `ssh` connection to the remote machine, you must create a file (called `distfile`) that contains the information that `rdist` needs to run — such as the remote host name, the files you want to transfer, and any exceptions to the default rules.

To create a `distfile`, follow these steps:

1. **Open a terminal window to your home directory and enter the following command:**

```
$ kedit distfile
```

`kedit` opens into a fresh file, waiting for your `distfile` code.

2. **Enter the following code (substituting your *username* and *remotehost* name):**

```
HOSTS  = ( username@remotehost )
FILES  = ( ~/ )
EXCEPT = ( ~/Desktop/Trash )

${FILES} -> ${HOSTS}
  install -oyounger,whole target ;
  except ${EXCEPT} ;
```

3. **Click the Save icon on the toolbar and close the editor.**

You've just created a basic `distfile`. The first three lines of the `distfile` define a few variables that make it easy to write the rest of the file:

✔ HOSTS: This variable holds a list of one or more host names. (If you want to distribute data to more than one host, list each host name between the parentheses, separated by spaces.) If you're using `ssh` to establish the connection to a remote machine, you can prefix the host name with a user name followed by an @ character, like this:

```
HOSTS = ( freddie@bastille freddie@
  louvre )
```

✔ FILES: This variable contains a space-separated list of the files or directories that you want to copy to the remote host. In our example, we want to copy the `$HOME` directory.

✔ EXCEPT: This variable names the files that you *don't* want to send to the remote host(s). You usually don't need a duplicate of the Trash bin.

The second half of the `distfile` contains the commands for `rdist`:

✔ The first line tells `rdist` to move the files (as defined by the `FILE` variable at the top of the `distfile`) to the hosts named by the `HOSTS` variable (also defined at the top of the `distfile`).

✔ The `install` command follows with the options that `rdist` should use for the backup. In our example, the option `-oyounger` tells `rdist` to check the timestamp on the file and update only those files that have been changed since the last backup. The `target` names the directory on the remote host that receives the backup. If you leave it blank, `rdist` creates a duplicate of the local directory tree on the host and copies the files into the mirror image.

 The `-o` needs to be right next to the `install` option; otherwise, `rdist` copies the files into a directory named whatever `install` option you try to use (for example, if you typed in "`-o younger`" instead of the correct "`-oyounger`", rdist would create a directory named `younger`). To use multiple `install` options, chain them together with commas, like this: `-oyounger,quiet,remove`.

✔ The `except` command tells `rdist` to skip the files that are named in the `EXCEPT` variable.

Table 51-1 lists some of the more useful `install` options.

TABLE 51-1: USEFUL INSTALL OPTIONS

Option	What It Does
younger	This option compares the datestamp of the files on the remote machine to the local machine, and updates only the files that have been changed since the last backup. This is a great option if your systems are time-synced.
compare	This option compares the *contents* of the files and updates the remote version if the files are different. Use the compare option if your computers aren't time-synced; otherwise, you may transfer more data than you need to, or you may miss important changes.
savetargets	This option makes a backup of each file *on the target* before it overwrites the content. The backup file is named *filename*.OLD.
whole	This option preserves the whole pathname when making the backup copy on the remote host.
quiet	This option silences the feedback from rdist as it creates the backup.
remove	Use this option carefully because it removes all the files on the remote host before copying in the new backups of your files.

 Make sure that you want to remove files from the backup before you use the remove option. In the process of testing these commands, we accidentally wiped out the CVS repository for this book and the results of a (fortunately completed) consulting project on one of our systems. remove really does remove everything. It's a good thing we had backups!

 For more options to use with rdist, visit the rdist manual page: $ man rdist.

Backing up

After you've tested your ssh connection and created the distfile, you're ready to back up. Open a terminal window and enter the following command:

```
$ rdist -P /usr/bin/ssh
```

rdist takes it from there, consulting the distfile for the information it needs to complete the backup. It doesn't get much quicker than that!

 The last argument in the command must be the complete pathname to the ssh program. It would be nice if you could specify the transfer program (ssh) in the distfile, but you can't.

 As a real timesaver, set up a cron job to transfer your files every night. See Technique 20 for help using Task Scheduler to set up an automatic backup in a snap!

Technique 52

Archiving Changes with CVS

Save Time By

- ✔ Using CVS to archive projects
- ✔ Using cervisia to manage your repository
- ✔ Reverting to a previous project stage in an emergency
- ✔ Creating project branches and development lines

CVS (Concurrent Versions System) enables multiple developers to work on the same project without the risk of losing work. CVS tracks changes to the files that make up the project. For example, while writing this book, we stored each technique in a separate file in a CVS repository. When we wanted to make a change to a technique, we *checked out* the file, made our changes, and *committed* the changes back to the repository. We both used the same CVS repository (in fact, Susan was writing with a Macintosh, and Korry was making typos on a Linux computer). Sometimes, the same technique was checked in and out several times before it was done. With CVS, there's no risk of data loss. If we would have both gotten the same technique accidentally, the merge feature would have resolved the differences in the versions (not that it would ever have happened). We also had a complete history of all the changes that we ever made.

When using a CVS repository, it's a good idea to commit your changes frequently. In addition to ensuring that your coworkers have access to the latest version of your work, if something happens to your CVS client, the CVS server will always have a copy of your latest work. This technique shows you how to use a CVS system to keep your work safe with minimal time and effort.

CVS can be used with any type of file (though it's not particularly powerful for binary files). System administration files, sales lists, artwork, and programming projects are all good candidates for a CVS repository. If a project goes awry, and you need to revert to a previous stage in your development, CVS can reconstruct a working version from a previous point in the project. We show you how in this technique.

CVS is a great timesaver — saving you time by avoiding the potential problems that come from lost data and crossed development paths. With CVS, you can secure your files and keep creativity flowing at a pace that suits everyone.

Getting Started with CVS

A CVS repository contains all the files that are relevant to a developing project. Each developer (or administrator, or author, or artist) checks out a *copy* of a project file to make changes to it. The revised file is then committed back to the repository, along with comments (for easy review later). The master copies always live in the repository; each developer checks out a *sandbox* to play, er, work in.

CVS client software is available for most platforms, so having many developers on a mixed-machine network is easy. You can work in the environment of your choice without causing any conflicts with the overall project.

Checking whether CVS is installed

If you installed the Development Tools package when you set up your Linux system, you probably already have CVS installed. To check, type `cvs` at the command line and press Enter. If CVS is installed, Linux displays a list of command options.

If CVS isn't installed on your system, you can find the RPM package on your Linux CD (or DVD), or just search and download an RPM file from the Web. Visit Technique 17 if you need help installing the RPM.

RCS versus CVS

RCS (Revision Control System) is the old versioning software that is included with Linux. Unlike CVS, RCS works only on a local machine, so its usefulness is limited to small projects. CVS is constructed as a wrapper around RCS. The storage mechanisms are the same, but CVS offers more advanced functionality for managing complex projects.

Discovering what to use CVS for

CVS is good for all sorts of projects. It was developed primarily to track changes to software development projects, but it's great for the following uses as well:

- ✔ Keeping system configuration changes
- ✔ Tracking Web site versions
- ✔ Keeping manuscript backups
- ✔ Tracking sales lists, inventories, art work, and so on — basically any project that evolves over time

CVS ensures that you won't lose work. Whatever project you're working on, you occasionally need to back up, change direction, or just figure out what changed. CVS can do all that in a snap, for anything you can keep in a file.

Creating a CVS Repository

After CVS is installed on your system, you're just a few quick steps away from having a working CVS repository.

Be sure you have plenty of disk space available on your CVS repository system. Remember that it's keeping not only the current project, but also the project history. Repositories can be huge, and not having to move them later is a big timesaver.

In this example, you create a CVS repository to track the changes in configuration files. You have to play a few games with permissions because configuration files can be modified only by someone with superuser privileges. Most of the Linux configuration files reside in the /etc directory (or a subdirectory of /etc). You'll be creating a repository to hold the master copies (and revision histories) of each configuration file. The /etc directory becomes a sandbox; that is, you can check a working copy out of the repository and into the /etc directory tree.

Follow these steps to create a `cvs` group (only members of this group can interact with the repository) and a CVS repository:

1. **Open a command line and give yourself superuser privileges:**

```
$ su
```

2. When prompted, enter the superuser password.

3. Create the `cvs` group:

```
# groupadd cvsusers
```

If you see a message stating that group `cvs` already exists, just ignore it.

4. Move to the root directory:

```
# cd /
```

5. Create a new directory for `cvs`:

```
# mkdir cvs
```

> Keeping our repository directly under the `root` directory is just a matter of preference. It can reside anywhere you like.

6. Change the group ownership of the CVS repository:

```
# chgrp cvsusers /cvs
```

7. Set the permissions for the `cvs` directory:

```
# chmod g+srwx /cvs
```

These permissions allow any member of the `cvs` group to view or modify the files in the repository. The `g+s` part ensures that all the files that you store *within* the repository are also owned by the `cvs` group.

8. Initialize the repository by typing the following command and pressing Enter:

```
# cvs -d /cvs init
```

If you look in your new directory, you'll find a subdirectory called `CVSROOT`. The `CVSROOT` directory contains administrative files for use by CVS.

Don't forget to add the appropriate users to the `cvs` group (at least add yourself).

> A fast way to add a user to your new group is with the command `/usr/bin/gpasswd -a username groupname`. To use this command, you must hold superuser privileges.

Populating Your Repository with Files

After you've created a CVS repository, you need to populate it. For now, just add a few files; you can always add more later.

To add files to your repository, follow these steps:

1. Move to the directory that you'll be archiving:

```
# cd /etc
```

2. Check out the top-level CVS directory:

```
# cvs -d /cvs checkout .
```

Don't forget the . (dot) at the end.

The `checkout` command creates a sandbox. At this point, the repository holds only CVS bookkeeping information, but later, a sandbox will contain a working copy of each file in the repository.

3. The `cvs add` command inserts a new file into the repository, so add the `hosts` file as follows:

```
# cvs add hosts
```

4. You can also add subdirectories. This command creates a new subdirectory within the repository:

```
# cvs add xinetd.d/
```

5. Now move into the `/etc/xinet.d` directory:

```
# cd xinetd.d/
```

6. Add all the files in `/etc/xinet.d`:

```
# cvs add *
```

7. After the files and directories are added to the repository, move back to `/etc`:

```
# cd ..
```

8. At this point, you've scheduled a few files to be added to the repository, but you haven't committed your changes. To make your changes permanent, use the `cvs commit` command:

```
# cvs commit -m "Adding initial files"
```

The -m flag tells CVS that you want to include in the revision history the text that follows. If you don't include the -m flag (and a comment), CVS prompts you for a comment.

 The primary Web site for CVS is www.cvshome.org. **This is a handy address to have if you need downloads or more information.**

The CVS repository now contains a *history* file for each file you added. You can't use these files directly; you have to create a sandbox and grab a working copy. From this point forward, you never change the masters.

If you look into each of the directories that you've added files from, you'll also notice that a CVS directory has been added to each directory. These directories hold the internal bookkeeping information that CVS needs to do its thing.

Checking Files In and Out (Or Playing in Your Sandbox)

When you want to change a configuration file, check out a copy of the file you need from the CVS repository and place it into your personal sandbox. When you're finished modifying your local copy, you then commit your changes to the repository. Here's how to do all that:

1. **At the command line, type the following command and then press Enter:**

```
$ mkdir ~/work
```

This command creates a directory to hold your sandbox.

2. **Move into the sandbox directory you just created:**

```
$ cd ~/work
```

3. **Check out a work copy of the hosts file:**

```
$ cvs -d /cvs checkout hosts
```

Now, you've got a copy of the hosts file (in your sandbox) that you can modify. Fire up your favorite editor and czhange the file as you see fit.

4. **Modify your local copy and then commit your changes with the following command:**

```
$ cvs commit -m "your comment here"
   hosts
```

Use the -m flag to include your comment in your commit statement. It's not only faster, but also saves you a trip into vi (or vim). vi can be a cold, dark place.

When CVS is finished, it displays a message like this:

```
Checking in hosts;
/cvs/hosts,v  <-- hosts
new revision: 1.2; previous revision:
   1.1
done
```

Neat and fast! Your changes are now stored in the CVS repository. CVS keeps enough information to reconstruct *any* version of the file. Note that you haven't modified the hosts file in the /etc directory, just the version that's stored in the repository. You still have to update the /etc sandbox by following these steps:

1. **Move into the /etc directory:**

```
$ cd /etc
```

2. **Give yourself superuser privileges with the su command (nonprivileged users can't change the files in /etc):**

```
$ su
Password:
#
```

3. **Update the hosts file from the CVS repository:**

```
# cvs update hosts
U hosts
```

That's it. You've made a change to an important Linux configuration file, but you've saved the original version (in the CVS repository) and a useful comment to tickle your memory later.

Simplifying CVS with cervisia

Life at the command line is great, if you're used to living there. But sometimes a great tool can help speed up the process and, at the same time, be friendly and easy to use. Numerous graphical interfaces for CVS are available, but one that works great with KDE is included in most Linux distributions. It's called cervisia.

Use the command line to create your initial repository. You can use cervisia to check out files or add files to an existing repository quickly, but it's not the right tool for creating repositories.

cervisia is a CVS client that works with local or remote repositories and provides a user friendly and intuitive work atmosphere, as shown in Figure 52-1.

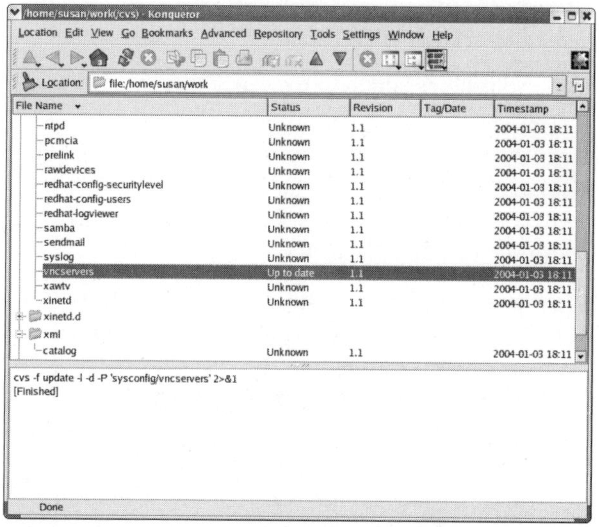

• **Figure 52-1:** cervisia **in action.**

For more information about using cervisia across the Web, you can find the full documentation at cervisia.sourceforge.net/documentation/index.html.

Installing cervisia

cervisia is installed with KDE if you chose to include the KDE Software Development package when you first installed Linux.

If cervisia isn't installed and you want to add it, use your distribution's installer to install the KDE Software Development package (sometimes known as kdesdk).

Putting files in your sandbox

To start cervisia, click the Start Here icon on your desktop to open Konqueror. Navigate to your work directory (your sandbox), and click the brick wall icon at the far right of your toolbar.

Or, to create a new sandbox with cervisia, follow these steps:

1. **Open the Konqueror browser and navigate to your work directory.**

2. **Choose Repository⇨Checkout from the menu bar.**

The CVS Checkout dialog opens, as shown in Figure 52-2.

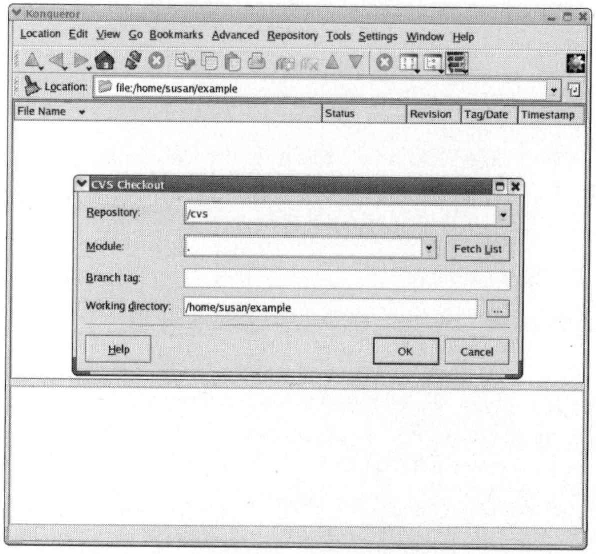

• **Figure 52-2: The** cervisia **CVS Checkout dialog.**

3. In the Repository field, enter the location of your repository (`/cvs` if you've been following along from the beginning of this technique).

4. Enter a . (dot) in the Module field.

5. Enter the pathname of your working directory in the Working Directory field.

6. Click OK.

`cervisia` checks out the contents of your CVS repository into your work directory.

 This is either a bug or an undocumented feature, but we need to exit `cervisia` and restart it before the files show up in the browser window. These things happen.

The contents of your sandbox are displayed in your browser window and organized in the following columns:

- ✔ File Name
- ✔ Status
- ✔ Revision Number
- ✔ Tag/Date
- ✔ Timestamp

To edit a file, double-click it, and the file opens in your favorite editor, ready to edit.

 See Technique 3 to set up the MIME mappings for your editor. Between `cervisia` and MIME, you can edit and update your files in no time!

Adding more files to your repository

Often, you have to add files to your CVS repository — especially if you're using it for tracking your system configuration files. To add a new file to your repository, follow these steps:

1. Enter the file location in the Location line of your browser.

2. Right-click the file you want to add, and from the pop-up menu that appears, choose Add to Repository.

 `cervisia`'s View menu contains an option to Hide Non-CVS Files. If you can't see a file that you know is there, make sure that you don't have that option checked.

3. When the CVS Add dialog opens, verify that the file you've selected is listed and then click OK.

At this point, the file you've chosen has been earmarked for inclusion, but it isn't actually in the repository.

4. Commit your addition by right-clicking the filename and choosing Commit.

5. Enter a log message (the more meaningful, the better) and click OK.

Your file is added to the repository.

 Go work on the file in your sandbox!

Committing your changes

When you've finished editing a file, follow these steps to commit your changes to the CVS repository:

1. Right-click the filename and choose Commit.

A CVS Commit dialog opens (see Figure 52-3). It shows the name of the file (or files) you're committing and supplies a field in which you can enter a log message.

2. Enter a log message and click OK.

`cervisia` checks in your changes.

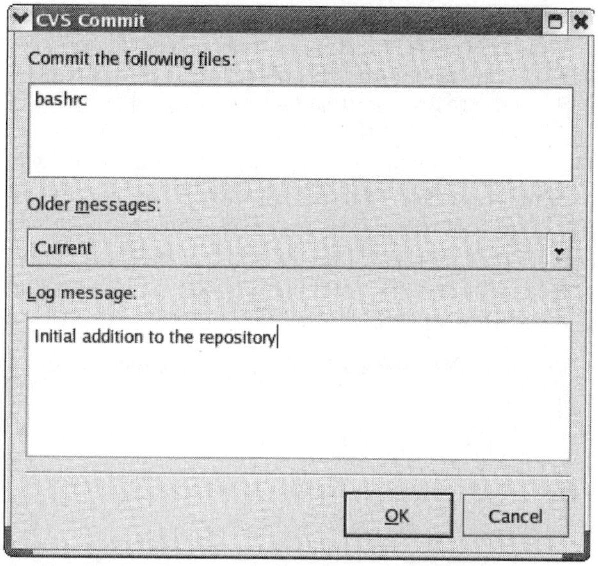

• **Figure 52-3:** The cervisia **CVS Commit dialog.**

The next time you (or another user) check out the file, you get a fresh copy that includes your most recent updates.

Diplomacy 101 — resolving conflicts

At some point in time, despite the best efforts of system administrators, two users will edit the same file, and a conflict will arise. If Freddie and Georgette both check out a file, both change it, and then both check it in, CVS will catch the problem and try to resolve it.

If Freddie and Georgette changed different parts of the same file, CVS graciously merges the changes. If they both change the same part of the file, human intervention is called for.

If Freddie checks in his changes and then Georgette tries to check in hers, Georgette sees an error message stating that her copy of the file is not current. If Georgette then updates her files, the files' status is changed to Conflict (assuming that CVS could not resolve the differences by itself).

cervisia has a handy problem solver built-in: the CVS Resolve feature. If a file is highlighted in red and the status is listed as Conflict, right-click the filename and choose Resolve from the pop-up menu. The CVS Resolve dialog opens (see Figure 52-4).

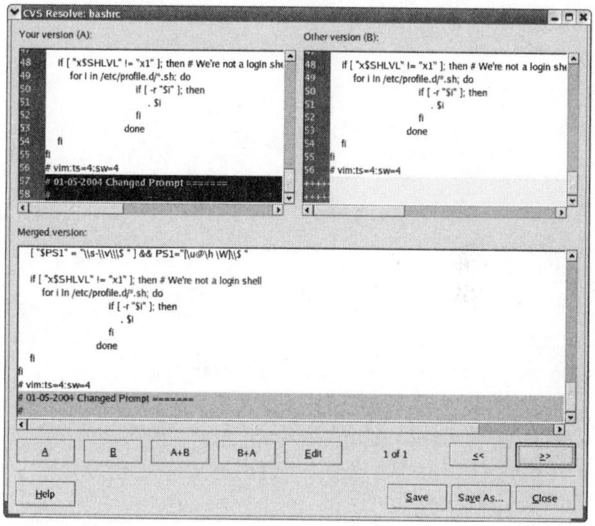

• **Figure 52-4:** The CVS Resolve dialog.

The merged version in the lower half of the screen presents four possible merge options (A, B, A+B, and B+A) and the option to edit the merged results. Click the >> button to highlight the next conflict, and then click the button for the merge option that is the best solution to the conflict. If the combinations offered aren't correct, click the Edit button to edit the text.

Browsing your log files

cervisia includes a nice log file display tool that shows graphical representations of all the changes in a development tree. The browser enables you to quickly determine where your project is and has been recently.

To use the log browser, right-click the filename, and choose Browse Log. The CVS Log dialog opens (see Figure 52-5).

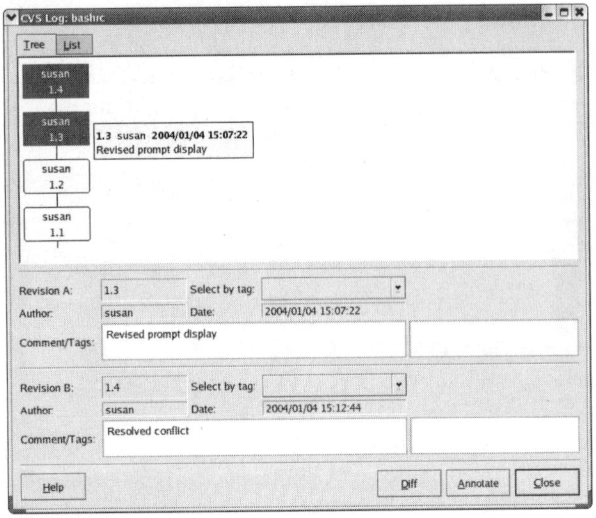

• **Figure 52-5: The** cervisia **CVS Log dialog.**

Choose a revision from the tree, and the information is transferred to the bottom half of the screen and shown in Revision A.

Now, if you middle-mouse click another revision, the information is transferred into Revision B. (Left-click selects a revision into the Revision A fields; middle-click selects a revision into the Revision B field.)

> If you don't have a middle mouse button, move to the List view, and use the arrow keys and Ctrl-A and Ctrl-B to select your revisions.

From the CVS Log dialog, you can use the Diff button to display the differences between revisions, as shown in Figure 52-6.

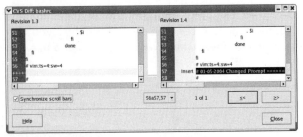

• **Figure 52-6: The** cervisia **CVS Diff dialog.**

> The Diff view can be your best friend in times of trouble. If things get really off course, you can use Diff to help you quickly find the point in the revisions that took you off course.

The Annotate button shows you a line-by-line view of the changes made to reach revision A (we call the Annotate tool the blame button because you can see *who* made a given modification). Hovering over the screen entries shows revision information about that line, as shown in Figure 52-7.

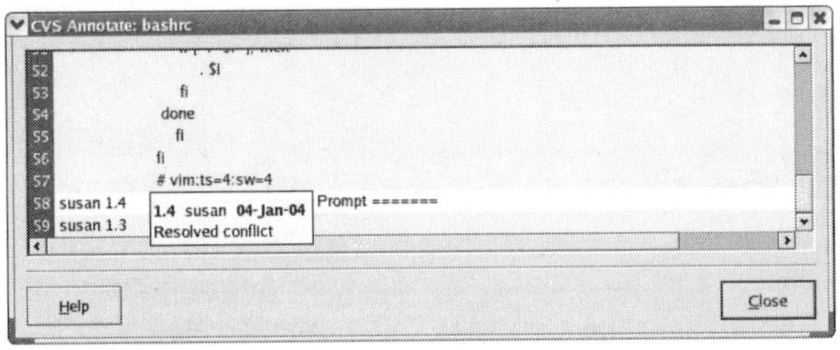

• **Figure 52-7: The** cervisia **CVS Annotate dialog.**

Marking milestones with tags

The typical CVS repository holds many (sometimes thousands) of files. It's unlikely that you'll modify every file in the repository whenever you change one file in the repository. Instead, troublesome files are modified frequently, and stable files tend to remain unchanged. That means that at any point in time, you'll have some files at revision number 1.5, some files at revision 1.200, and a few at revision 4.2. At certain points, you'll want to tag all the files in the repository so that you can get back to that point in time without having to look up all the revision numbers yourself. A *tag* marks a point in time. The tag (usually) includes all the files in the repository as of a given date and time.

It's a good idea to tag the repository whenever you reach a point where the collective revisions make up a release or a working version of whatever it is that you're tracking.

Simple tagging is quick and easy with cervisia. To tag a version, follow these steps:

1. **Highlight the top level directory (your sandbox pathname) and choose Advanced⇨Tag/Branch.**

2. **Enter a tag name and click the OK button.**

That was fast, eh?

Here are a few points to keep in mind when choosing tag names:

- ✔ A common naming convention is the project name followed by a version number.

- ✔ Tag names can't include blanks or punctuation marks.

- ✔ Tags are most helpful when you've chosen meaningful names.

 Names like WorkingConfiguration or JustPriorToMessingUpMyConfigurationFiles aren't a bad idea. They can make it easy for you to find a place to revert to.

To revert to a tagged revision of your project, choose Advanced⇨Update to Tag/Date. You have the option to change your sandbox copy to a branch, a tag, or a previous date.

 Didn't tag, but need to revert? No problem; just select the Update to Date option button, enter your date, and click OK. You'll have a new old sandbox in no time.

Branching off with cervisia

When your project *branches,* it usually means that one part of your project maintains the current development path, while another part heads in a new direction. Software developers create branches all the time. While one release is maintained and stable, another branch is growing with radical changes. If the changes don't work out along the way, the original, stable branch is still there and available for users, or you can revert to it if needed. By branching off, your project can remain on one development line while evolving into another.

 Use a branch or a tag at any point in development where your project will take a radical turn. That way, you have a safe place to go back to!

Branching with `cervisia` is similar to tagging:

1. **Highlight the top level directory in your sandbox and choose Advanced⇨Tag/Branch.**

The Tag/Branch dialog appears.

2. **Enter the branch name, check the Create Branch with This Tag box, and click OK.**

You've branched out!

 Create your branches in your sandbox, and commit them just like any other change.

Part X

Programming Tricks

53 Technique

Using Open-Source APIs to Save Time

Save Time By

✔ Using the libcurl library to Web-enable your programs

✔ Creating Flash movies with Ming

If you're a programmer, you know that the best way to save development time is to build programs using components developed by others. In fact, every time you build a program that runs on a Linux computer, you're using open-source components. The C runtime library, the Linux runtime library, and even the kernel functions are open-source APIs (API stands for *application program interface*). Imagine how difficult your job would be if every time you wrote a new program, you had to write a disk driver, a windowing system, or even a complete operating system.

Using open-source APIs saves development time *and* debugging time. If you start with trusted, well-written components, you can concentrate your debugging efforts on the code that you're writing (and, because you're using prebuilt components, that's a lot less code).

Open-source libraries can also make your programs compatible with standards and protocols used by other applications. In fact, in this technique, we show you how to write simple Web-enabled programs by using two open-source APIs.

In this technique, we also show you the power behind curl, which is a command line program that can upload and download files from FTP and HTTP servers. By adding the curl library (libcurl) to your programs, you can easily interact with FTP, secure FTP, HTTP, secure HTTP, GOPHER, telnet, dict, and LDAP servers. Your programs can handle cookies, use network proxies, and even resume interrupted transfers with just a few lines of code. Imagine how long it would take to write all that code by hand.

We also show you a fun library named Ming. Ming creates Flash movies (Ming, Flash Gordon, get it?). Flash movies are typically played in a Web browser, but you can also download a stand-alone player. If you're not familiar with Flash, surf to the Macromedia Web site (www.macromedia.com) and watch a few of its Flash showcases. You can use Ming to produce static (unchanging) movies that show bar graphs and pie charts (or just about any other type of graph). You can also create interactive movies that you can control with a mouse and your keyboard.

Using the libcurl Library (C Programming)

curl is a command line tool that can upload and download files from HTTP and FTP servers. Actually, that's a gross oversimplification; curl knows how to deal with HTTP, FTP, secure HTTP and FTP servers, gopher servers, telnet servers, local files, and many more protocols.

Downloading a file with curl is easy. For example, to download a file named news.html from the example.com Web site (and save it to a file named mylocalfile), execute the following command:

```
$ curl -o mylocalfile http://example.com/
  news.html
```

curl is very similar to the more familiar wget, except that wget can only download data; curl can move data in both directions.

You can harness the power of curl in your own C programs by making calls to the libcurl API. The libcurl library comes in two flavors that you can mix and match. The *easy* API defines only six functions (and you can write useful, network-enabled programs using only four of those functions). The *multi* interface is more complex. When you call a function in the easy API, your program pauses until the function completes. The multi interface, on the other hand, performs transfers in the background, returning control to your program as soon as you initiate a transfer. In other words, the easy API is synchronous, and the multi interface is asynchronous.

 You can find the curl (and libcurl) Web site at curl.haxx.se. You'll find complete (and easy-to-follow) documentation about both the easy and the multi interface.

The Fedora, SuSE, and Mandrake distributions all include the curl command line program in an RPM package named curl. To write libcurl-enabled programs, install the curl package *and* the curl-devel package.

The multi API is built with functions defined by the easy API. That means that you can mix functions from both interfaces.

 Everything that you know about the easy interface is applicable when you build a more sophisticated program based on the multi interface.

Uploading a File with a Simple Program Using libcurl

Every libcurl program starts with a call to an initialization function (typically curl_easy_init()) and ends with a call to a cleanup function (typically curl_easy_cleanup()). In between these calls, you use the curl_easy_setopt() and curl_easy_perform() functions to create and execute transfer jobs. Listing 53-1 shows a simple program (named curlupload) that uses libcurl's easy API to upload a file.

When you run curlupload (we show you how to compile it in a moment), include two command line parameters:

- ✔ The name of the file you want to upload
- ✔ The upload destination, specified in the form of a URL

For example, to upload a file named photo.jpg to an FTP server, use this command:

```
$ curlupload ./photo.jpg ftp://ftp.
  example.com/pub/upload/
```

 When you use this example in your own code, be sure to add some error checking. Check the command line arguments and be sure the files are valid files. See the libcurl documentation to find out how errors are reported to your program.

The following sections take a closer look at some lines in the curlupload program.

LISTING 53-1: CURLUPLOAD.C

```
 1 /* File: curlupload.c
 2 **      usage: curlupload <filename> <URL>
 3 */
 4
 5 #include <stdlib.h>
 6 #include <string.h>
 7 #include <curl/curl.h>
 8
 9 int main( int argc, char * argv[] )
10 {
11     CURL       * curl;
12     FILE       * srcFile = fopen( argv[1], "rb" );
13
14     if(( curl = curl_easy_init()) != NULL )
15     {
16         char errorMsg[CURL_ERROR_SIZE];
17
18         curl_easy_setopt( curl, CURLOPT_ERRORBUFFER, errorMsg );
19         curl_easy_setopt( curl, CURLOPT_UPLOAD, TRUE );
20         curl_easy_setopt( curl, CURLOPT_URL, argv[2] );
21         curl_easy_setopt( curl, CURLOPT_READDATA, srcFile );
22
23         if( curl_easy_perform( curl ) != 0 )
24             fprintf( stderr, "%s\n", errorMsg );
25
26         curl_easy_cleanup( curl );
27     }
28
29     return( EXIT_SUCCESS );
30 }
```

Line 7: Defining functions and data types

The libcurl C functions and data types are defined in the curl/curl.h header file, so libcurl-enabled programs should #include that file (see line 7).

Line 14: Calling the initialization function

Line 14 shows the call to the libcurl initialization function, curl_easy_init(). curl_easy_init(). This call returns a *handle*.

A handle is a small piece of data that a library uses to keep track of the *state* of something. In the case of libcurl, the handle holds the state of a transfer job. In libcurl programs, a handle takes the form of a CURL pointer (see line 11).

So what does a CURL pointer point to? Who knows? That's the whole point of a handle — the API's author puts anything that he needs into the structure *behind* the handle, but the author of a client application (that's you) can't see the data. The API creates the handle, and the client application just gives it back to the API whenever it's needed.

Lines 18–21: Defining the transfer

To create a transfer job, use curl_easy_setopt() to define the characteristics of the transfer. Each time you call curl_easy_setopt(), you pass three parameters:

✔ The CURL handle returned by curl_easy_init()

✔ The symbolic name of the option you want to change

✔ The new value for the option

To upload a file, you must set four transfer options, as shown on Lines 18–21.

Line 18: Routing libcurl error messages

Line 18 sets the CURLOPT_ERRORBUFFER option. This option tells libcurl where to store any error messages in case something whacks out. When you set the CURLOPT_ERRORBUFFER option, the third argument specifies the buffer where libcurl will store the error messages. The documentation tells you that the error message buffer should be at least CURL_ERROR_SIZE bytes long (see line 16).

 Speaking of documentation, when you install the curl RPM package, the documentation for libcurl is installed as well. See info curl_easy_setopt (or man curl_easy_setopt if you prefer) for a complete list of transfer options and values.

Line 19: Telling libcurl you want to upload a file

At line 19, you define the CURLOPT_UPLOAD option to let libcurl know that you want to upload a file (by default, libcurl assumes that you want to download data).

You may have noticed that the data type for the third argument to curl_easy_setopt() varies. In some cases, the third argument is a char *; in others, it's a numeric value; and a few options expect a Boolean value. Unfortunately, you have to infer the proper data type from the online documentation.

Line 20: Telling libcurl where to send data

To tell libcurl where you want the data sent, set the CURLOPT_URL option (line 20). The destination is

specified in the form of a URL, and curlupload simply passes along the second command line argument (argv[2]). CURLOPT_URL is arguably the most important and most powerful transfer option.

libcurl supports full URL syntax, so you can include a host name, user name, password, directory, and file name when you run curlupload. Here are a few examples:

✔ ftp://example.com

A simple URL specifies a protocol (ftp) and a host name (example.com). libcurl can upload data by using http or ftp. You can't upload to a URL this simple because you have to specify a target filename (but you can download from a simple URL).

✔ ftp://freddie@example.com

If you don't specify a user name, libcurl assumes that you want to log in to an FTP server as user anonymous. If you want to connect using a different user name, just insert the user name, followed by @ in front of the host name.

✔ ftp://freddie:password@example.com

You can also include a password in a URL by inserting a colon (:) and the password following the user name.

✔ ftp://example.com/pub/

A URL that ends with a / specifies a directory name. You can't upload to a URL that ends with /, but you can download from such a URL.

✔ ftp://example.com/pub/drinks.txt

Because this URL does not end in a /, libcurl assumes that drinks.txt is the name of the destination file.

Line 21: Telling libcurl where the data resides

The last option (line 21) tells libcurl where to find the data that you want to upload. You can give upload data to libcurl two ways:

✔ If the data resides in a file, just `fopen()` the file (see line 12) and give the resulting `FILE` pointer to `libcurl` by using the `CURLOPT_READDATA` option.

✔ If the data does not reside in a file (maybe you're computing the data on the fly), you can write a custom function that `libcurl` calls whenever it needs more data. See the description of the `CURLOPT_READFUNCTION` option in `man curl_easy_setopt` for more information.

Line 23: Starting the transfer

After you've primed the `CURL` handle with all the options that you need, start the transfer with the `curl_easy_perform()` function (see line 23). `curl_easy_perform()` carries out the transfer operation that you defined with the series of calls to `curl_easy_setopt()`. In fact, you can use the same `CURL` handle in a whole series of transfer operations just by changing the options in between each transfer. (Typically, you'll change the `CURLOPT_URL` and `CURLOPT_READDATA` before you start the next transfer.)

If the transfer succeeds, `curl_easy_perform()` returns 0. If an error occurs, `curl_easy_perform()` stores an error message in `errorMsg[ ]`, and `curlupload` displays the text of the message at line 24.

Line 26: Finishing the upload

When you're finished with the `CURL` handle, you should call the `curl_easy_cleanup()` function (see line 26). This function discards all the data structures hidden behind the handle and frees any resources that might still be in use.

Installing the Ming Library

If you've crawled around on the Web, you've seen Flash-based Web pages. Flash is an *interactive movie* technology created by Macromedia (`www.macromedia.com`). Flash movies typically play within a Web browser, and you can often interact with the movies by using the mouse and keyboard. Most Flash movies are created with the help of expensive graphical editors, but you can also produce movies from a simple C program.

Ming is a small software library that lets you create Flash movies from several programming languages (C, C++, Perl, Python, and Java). When you run a Ming program, you aren't viewing the movie; you're only creating it. You still need a Flash player (or a Flash play plug-in for your Web browser) to watch the movies that you create.

Ming is easy to install, but it doesn't follow the typical `download`, `configure`, `make` tango. Ming comes in source form, so you have to compile it after downloading. Before you build Ming, make sure you have the `libpng` and `libungif` packages installed on your computer (these two libraries should be included in your distribution media). Use the command:

```
$ rpm -q libpng libungif
```

If `rpm` complains that either package is not currently installed, be sure to install it before you continue (see Technique 17 for help installing RPM packages).

Follow these steps to install and compile Ming:

1. **You can find the latest version of Ming at** `ming.sourceforge.net`. **Just download the version you want and unpack it.**

   The Ming Web site currently hosts gzip, bzip2, and zip versions.

2. **Move into the directory created when you unpacked the tarball and type** `make` **to start the compile process (note, you may see a few warnings but it's safe to ignore them).**

3. **When the compile step finishes, give yourself superuser privileges and type** `make install`.

   That's it — the Ming shared library is copied to `/usr/lib/libming.so`, and the Ming header file is copied to `/usr/include/ming.h`.

Building a Simple Flash Movie with Ming

Listing 53-2 shows a simple Ming program that slowly rotates the colors in a given photo.

Examining the program

The following sections take a closer look at the colors program, shown in Listing 53-2.

Line 6: Defining the functions and data types

Every Ming program must include the ming.h header file (line 6). ming.h defines the data types and function prototype for the Ming library.

Line 19: Creating an empty movie

To create a new Flash movie, start with a call to the newSWFMovie() function (see line 19). newSWFMovie() creates a new, empty movie and returns a handle that you can use later when you call other Ming functions.

LISTING 53-2: COLORS.C

```
 1 /* File: colors.c
 2 **
 3 **    Rotate colors within a photo
 4 */
 5
 6 #include <ming.h>
 7 #include <stdio.h>
 8 #include <stdlib.h>
 9
10 static SWFDisplayItem load_photo( SWFMovie movie, const char * name );
11
12 int main( int argc, char * argv[] )
13 {
14     SWFMovie       movie;
15     SWFDisplayItem item;
16     int            frames = 40;
17     float          count;
18
19     movie = newSWFMovie();
20     item  = load_photo( movie, argv[1] );
21
22     for( count = 0; count < frames; ++count )
23     {
24         SWFDisplayItem_multColor( item, 1.0, 1.0, 1.0 - count/frames, 1.0 );
25         SWFDisplayItem_addColor( item, 255 * count/frames, 0, 0, 1.0 );
26
27         SWFMovie_nextFrame( movie );
28     }
29
30     for( count = frames; count > 0; --count )
31     {
32         SWFDisplayItem_multColor( item, 1.0, 1.0, 1.0 - count/frames, 1.0 );
33         SWFDisplayItem_addColor( item, 255 * count/frames, 0, 0, 1.0 );
34
35         SWFMovie_nextFrame( movie );
36     }
```

```
37
38      SWFMovie_save( movie, "colors.swf", -1 );
39
40      exit( EXIT_SUCCESS );
41  }
42
43  static SWFDisplayItem load_photo( SWFMovie movie, const char * name )
44  {
45      SWFBitmap       bitmap;
46      SWFInput        photo_file;
47      FILE        * photo;
48      int             height;
49      int             width;
50
51      if(( photo = fopen( name, "rb" )) == NULL )
52      {
53          fprintf( stderr, "can't open photo\n" );
54          exit( EXIT_FAILURE );
55      }
56      else
57      {
58          photo_file = newSWFInput_file( photo );
59      }
60
61      bitmap = newSWFBitmap_fromInput( photo_file );
62
63      width  = SWFBitmap_getWidth( bitmap );
64      height = SWFBitmap_getHeight( bitmap );
65
66      SWFMovie_setDimension( movie, width, height );
67
68      return( SWFMovie_add( movie, (SWFBlock) bitmap ));
69
70  }
```

Line 20: Adding a photo to the movie

At line 20, you see a call to the `load_photo()` function. `load_photo()` is not a Ming function (we show it to you in a moment in the section, "Line 43: Telling Ming how to read the photo file"). `load_photo()` returns a handle to a bitmap that's been added to the new movie.

Lines 22–28 and 30–36: Making the photo move through frames

Lines 22–28 create a number of *frames* (a movie is made up of one or more frames), each with a slightly modified version of the photo.

Line 24 adjusts each pixel in the photo. In a Flash movie, every pixel has four values: a red value, a green value, a blue value, and an opaqueness value. The color values range from zero (no color) to 255 (full color). The opaqueness value (also known as the *alpha* value) determines how much of the background shows through. An opaqueness value of zero means the pixel is invisible, and a value of 255 means the pixel is completely opaque (none of the background shows through).

Each time through the loop (lines 22–28), `SWDisplayItem_multColor()` multiplies each color value in each pixel. The first argument identifies the display item you want to adjust. The second item specifies a multiplier for the red value of each pixel (multiplying by 1.0 means the red value is unchanged). The third, fourth, and fifth arguments specify the multipliers applied to the green, blue, and opaqueness values for each pixel.

Line 24 decreases the blue value by a fraction each time through the loop but leaves the other values unchanged. The net effect is that the blueness of your photo slowly fades away with each frame. Line 25 adds a dash of red to each pixel in the frame (again, leaving the other color components unchanged).

Lines 30–36 do essentially the same thing as lines 22–28, but rotate through colors in the opposite direction — subtracting some red and adding back the blue in each frame.

Line 38: Saving the completed movie

After the movie is complete, call `SWFMovie_save()` to write it to disk (in this case, to a file named `colors.swf`).

Line 43: Telling Ming how to read the photo file

Now take a look at the `load_photo()` function (starting at line 43). `load_photo()` starts by opening the file whose name was passed as the second argument. The Ming library can't really do much with a `FILE` handle.

To read the content of the photo, you have to convert the `FILE` handle into an `SWFInput`. Whenever the Ming library needs to read information from some source, it uses an `SWFInput` handle. Ming can create `SWFInput` handles from a number of different source types. For example, the `newSWFInput_buffer()` function will create an `SWFInput` that can read data from an area of memory. Because you already have a `FILE` handle, you can use `newSWFInput_file()` to convert it into an `SWFInput` (see line 58).

Line 61 and 63–66: Showing Ming how to work with the photo

Line 61 reads the photo bits and creates a new structure called an `SWFBitmap` by calling `newSWFBitmap_fromInput()`.

Lines 63 and 64 interrogate the bitmap to find the width and height (in pixels), and line 66 changes the size of the movie to match the bitmap. Finally, `load_photo()` *adds* the bitmap to the current frame of the movie and returns a handle to the caller.

Compiling the program

Before you can run `colors`, you have to compile it, and the following steps show you how to do that using `make`:

1. **Open your favorite editor and enter the following text:**

   ```
   LDFLAGS += -lming -lz
   LDFLAGS += -lungif -lpng12 -lm
   colors:   colors.c
   ```

2. **Save your changes in a file named `Makefile` and close the editor.**

3. **Type `make` and press Enter.**

   The compiler starts running.

If everything goes well, you have a new program in your current directory named `colors`. If you see any error messages, go back and correct the errors before proceeding.

Running the program

To run `colors`, find a photo (JPEGs work well) that you like and then run the following command:

```
$ ./colors /path-to-photo
```

Substitute the name of your photo for *path-to-photo*. When `colors` is finished, you'll have a new Flash movie in your current directory named `colors.swf`.

You can watch the movie with any Flash player. If you have a Flash plug-in installed in your Web browser, simply open the `colors.swf` file in the browser, and the movie appears. You'll see most of the blue fade out of the photo that you chose and then slowly fade back in. With the right photo, the effect is stunning.

Building Interactive Movies with Ming

You can also build *interactive* Flash movies with Ming. When you view an interactive movie, you can manipulate on-screen objects with the mouse and keyboard. Listing 53-3 shows a short Ming program that produces a movie that contains ActionScript. The movie draws a small blue circle that you can drag around with the mouse.

Examining the program

The following sections take a closer look at the `dragme` program.

Lines 4–18: Defining the script

Lines 4–18 define a string of Flash ActionScript. In this case, you're defining three anonymous functions related to an object named `circle` (you create `circle` in just a moment):

- ✔ The first function is fired when you click the mouse while the cursor is over the circle. It simply calls the circle's `startDrag()` method.

- ✔ The second and third functions fire when you release the mouse button (after you've started a drag operation). Both functions call the circle's `stopDrag()` method.

You can include almost any ActionScript verb or function that Macromedia defines (see the Ming Web site `ming.sourceforge.net` for restrictions).

Line 20: Declaring local variables

Now look through the `main()` function. Unlike the first Ming program in this technique, `dragme` produces a movie that can be viewed only by a Flash player newer than version 5 (ActionScript is a recent addition to Flash).

LISTING 53-3: DRAGME.C

```
 1 #include <ming.h>
 2 #include <stdlib.h>
 3
 4 const char * action_script =
 5     "circle.onPress = function()"
 6     "{"
 7     "    this.startDrag('');"
 8     "};"
 9
10     "circle.onRelease = function()"
11     "{"
12     "    stopDrag();"
13     "};"
14
15     "circle.onReleaseOutside = function()"
16     "{"
17     "    stopDrag();"
18     "};";
```

(continued)

LISTING 53-3 *(continued)*

```
19
20  int main( int argc, char * argv[] )
21  {
22      SWFMovie        movie;
23      SWFShape        circle;
24      SWFFill         fill;
25      SWFMovieClip    sprite;
26      SWFDisplayItem f1;
27
28      Ming_useSWFVersion( 6 );
29
30      movie = newSWFMovie();
31      SWFMovie_setDimension( movie, 550, 400 );
32      SWFMovie_setBackground(movie, 200, 200, 200 );
33
34      circle = newSWFShape();
35      fill   = SWFShape_addSolidFill( circle, 0, 0, 128, 255 );
36      SWFShape_setRightFill( circle, fill );
37      SWFShape_drawCircle( circle, 40 );
38
39      sprite = newSWFMovieClip();
40      SWFMovieClip_add( sprite, (SWFBlock)circle );
41      SWFMovieClip_nextFrame( sprite );
42
43      f1 = SWFMovie_add( movie, (SWFBlock)sprite );
44      SWFDisplayItem_setName( f1, "circle" );
45      SWFDisplayItem_moveTo( f1, 100, 100 );
46
47      SWFMovie_add( movie, (SWFBlock)compileSWFActionCode( action_script ));
48      SWFMovie_save( movie, "dragme.swf", -1 );
49
50      exit( EXIT_SUCCESS );
51  }
```

Line 28 and 30–35: Creating the new movie

Use the `Ming_useSWFVersion()` function to tell Ming that you want to create a Flash version 6 movie (see line 28).

At lines 30–33, `dragme` creates a new movie, defines the width and height of the movie, and sets the background color to a light gray.

Next, `dragme` creates a `circle` of radius 40 (line 34) and fills it with an opaque shade of blue (line 35).

Lines 39–45: Adding movement

At line 39, you create a *sprite* — a sprite is something that can move around on the screen. Line 40 adds the shape (the `circle` created at line 34) to the sprite with `SWFMovieClip_add()`. Line 41 creates a new frame for the sprite. Line 43 adds the sprite to the movie by calling `SWFMovie_add()`, which returns a handle to the sprite display item.

Look back at the ActionScript that starts at line 4 — each function refers to an object named `circle`. Line

44 assigns a name (`circle`) to the display item added at line 43; after you've assigned a name to an object, you can manipulate that object in ActionScript code.

Lines 47–48: Compiling and saving the code

Line 47 compiles the `action_script` code (defined starting at line 4) into a more compact (and efficient) form and adds the result to the movie. Finally, the movie is saved to a file named `dragme.swf` (see line 48).

Compiling the program

To compile the `dragme` program, follow these steps:

1. **If you've already created a Makefile (as we described earlier in the section titled "Compiling the program"), open the `Makefile` in your favorite editor, and add the following line to the end:**

   ```
   dragme:   dragme.c
   ```

   If you're creating a Makefile from scratch, the result should look like this:

   ```
   LDFLAGS += -lming -lz
   LDFLAGS += -lungif -lpng12 -lm

   colors:   colors.c
   dragme:   dragme.c
   ```

2. **Save your work and close the editor.**

3. **Type `make` and press Enter.**

   The compiler starts running.

If you see any error messages, correct the problems before proceeding.

Running the program

After you've compiled the program, run `./dragme` to produce a movie file named `dragme.swf`. You can open the `dragme.swf` movie in any Flash player that supports Flash version 6.0 or later. When the movie appears, click the blue circle and drag it around with your mouse.

 You can find more information about the Flash movie format on the Web (just do a Google search for *SWF*). You can also find a number of books that cover Flash and ActionScript — we recommend *Flash ActionScript For Dummies* by Doug Sahlin (published by Wiley).

Technique 54

Timesaving PHP Tricks

Save Time By

✔ Using `curl` with PHP to retrieve data from the Internet

✔ Using XML data in PHP programs

✔ Using the XML parser to manage XML data

✔ Generating e-mail with PHP when something goes wrong

When you write a program in PHP, chances are the program will run within a Web server (most often, Apache). Although PHP is a powerful, general-purpose programming language, most people use PHP to generate dynamic HTML Web pages.

In this technique, we show you how to leverage the power of PHP interfaces to reach from one Web server to another. Using PHP's `curl` interface, your PHP programs can retrieve information from remote servers (Web servers, FTP servers, and so on). After you have the information you need, you can reformat it, pick out only the pieces that you're interested in, and combine it with information from other sources for display on your own Web site.

We also show you how to use PHP's XML parser to find your way through an XML data stream. If you haven't run into XML before, think of it as self-identifying data. For example, the different pieces of a weather report (dew point, wind speed, and humidity) might be represented by the following XML snippet:

```
. . .
<DewPoint>72ûF</DewPoint>
<Wind>From the West at 23 mph</Wind>
<Humidity>98%</Humidity>
. . .
```

You can see that each element is surrounded by a pair of tags that describes the data within. XML data can get pretty complex, but PHP's XML parser makes it easy to deal with.

We show you how to combine PHP, `curl`, and XML to quickly incorporate weather reports (or just about any other type of dynamic data) in your own Web pages. You also find out how to save a ton of development and debugging time by making your PHP programs send you an e-mail when something goes wrong. Imagine a program that notifies you whenever it runs into something it's not prepared to deal with. That's a whole lot easier (and faster) than wading through debug logs. You'll never have to ask your users for a complete error message again.

Doing the curl E-shuffle with PHP

If you read Technique 53, you already know quite a bit about `curl`. `curl` is a command line tool that makes it quick and easy to upload and download data from other computers. `curl` can interact with Web or FTP servers, secure servers, and even directory servers. The `curl` project developers have created an easy-to-use library, named `libcurl`, that you can use to build your own `curl`-enabled programs. `libcurl` programs can be written in a number of languages. In the previous technique, you find out how to use `libcurl` from a C program; in this technique, we show you how to use `libcurl` from a PHP script.

Combining PHP with curl and XML: An overview

PHP scripts usually run within a Web server (not within a Web browser). It might seem a bit strange for a Web server to connect to *another* server to retrieve information, but that's actually a very useful thing to do. You may want to relay information (like news headlines) from a remote server to the Web browser. Or, you may want to translate information

you obtain from another server into a more friendly and useful format. Using `libcurl` from a PHP script makes it easy to retrieve remote information.

Thousands of Web sites publish information in XML format (eXtensible Markup Language). We mention earlier that XML data is somewhat self-identifying; each piece of data is surrounded by a pair of tags that describe the data contained within. For example, suppose you see the following text inside an XML stream:

```
<Forecast>Sunny</Forecast>
```

You could reasonably assume that Sunny is a forecast (probably part of a weather forecast). XML was designed to make it easier for programs to make sense of a piece of data. PHP knows how to parse through an XML data stream and pick out the pieces that you're interested in.

In this section, we show you how to use PHP, `curl`, and XML to display weather conditions on your Web site.

Checking out the XML file

The Web site `www.ejse.com` publishes XML weather conditions for your zip code. A typical weather report from EJSE might look like Listing 54-1.

LISTING 54-1: WEATHER REPORT FOR MICROSOFT

```
<WeatherInfo>
  <Location>Redmond, WA</Location>
  <IconIndex>26</IconIndex>
  <Temprature>47ûF</Temprature>
  <FeelsLike>44ûF</FeelsLike>
  <Forecast>Cloudy</Forecast>
  <Visibility>Unlimited </Visibility>
  <Pressure>29.43 inches and rising</Pressure>
  <DewPoint>40ûF</DewPoint>
  <UVIndex>0 Minimal</UVIndex>
  <Humidity>77%</Humidity>
  <Wind>From the Northwest at 6 mph</Wind>
  <ReportedAt>Renton, WA</ReportedAt>
  <LastUpdated>
    Thursday, February 26, 2004, at 9:53 AM Pacific Standard Time (Thursday, 12:53 PM EST).
  </LastUpdated>
</WeatherInfo>
```

(That's not a typo; the XML stream misspells temperature.)

Notice that each piece of data is surrounded by a pair of tags that describes the data within. For example, the forecast (Cloudy) is surrounded by the tags <Forecast> and </Forecast> — that's the essence of XML.

Downloading and displaying the XML file with a PHP script (and curl)

Listing 54-2 shows a reasonably short PHP script that downloads the current weather conditions for a given zip code (currently hard-coded to 98052) and parses through the XML.

LISTING 54-2: FINDING WEATHER CONDITIONS WITH PHP

```php
1  <?php
2
3    $weather = array();
4
5    $xmlData = loadWeather();
6    parseWeather( $weather, $xmlData );
7    displayWeather( $weather );
8
9    function loadWeather()
10   {
11     $url =
  "http://www.ejse.com/WeatherService/Service.asmx/GetWeatherInfo?zipCode=98052";
12     $curl = curl_init();
13
14     curl_setopt( $curl, CURLOPT_URL, $url );
15     curl_setopt( $curl, CURLOPT_RETURNTRANSFER, 1 );
16
17     $xmlData = curl_exec( $curl );
18
19     curl_close( $curl );
20
21     return( $xmlData );
22   }
23
24   function parseWeather( $weather, $data )
25   {
26     $parser = xml_parser_create();
27
28     xml_set_element_handler( $parser, "startTag", "endTag" );
29     xml_set_character_data_handler( $parser, "dataHandler" );
30
31     xml_parse( $parser, $data );
32
33     xml_parser_free( $parser );
34   }
35
36   function startTag( $parser, $tagName, $tagAttributes )
37   {
38     global $tag;
39
```

```
40      $tag = $tagName;
41    }
42
43    function endTag( $parser, $tagName )
44    {
45      global $tag;
46
47      $tag = "";
48    }
49
50    function dataHandler( $parser, $data )
51    {
52      global $weather, $tag;
53
54      $weather[ $tag ] = $data;
55    }
56
57    function displayWeather( $weather )
58    {
59      echo( "<html>\n" );
60      echo(  "<head>\n" );
61      echo(  " <title>" );
62      echo(    "Current Conditions At " . $weather["LOCATION"] . "</title>\n" );
63      echo(  "</head>\n" );
64
65      echo(  "<body>\n" );
66      echo(  "<h4>\n" );
67      echo(    "Current Weather for: " . $weather["LOCATION"] . "<br>" );
68      echo(  "</h4>\n" );
69
70      echo(  '<TABLE CELLPADDING="2" CELLSPACING="0" BORDER=1>' );
71      echo(    "<TR><TD>Forecast</TD> <TD>"     . $weather["FORECAST"]    . "</TD></TR>"
  );
72      echo(    "<TR><TD>Temperature</TD> <TD>" . $weather["TEMPRATURE"] . "</TD></TR>"
  );
73      echo(    "<TR><TD>Wind</TD>         <TD>" . $weather["WIND"]        . "</TD></TR>"
  );
74      echo(    "<TR><TD>Wind Chill</TD>  <TD>" . $weather["FEELSLIKE"]   . "</TD></TR>"
  );
75      echo(    "<TR><TD>Dewpoint</TD>     <TD>" . $weather["DEWPOINT"]    . "</TD></TR>"
  );
76      echo(    "<TR><TD>Pressure</TD>     <TD>" . $weather["PRESSURE"]    . "</TD></TR>"
  );
77      echo(    "<TR><TD>UV Index</TD>     <TD>" . $weather["UVINDEX"]     . "</TD></TR>"
  );
78      echo(    "</TABLE>" );
79      echo(  "</body>\n" );
80      echo( "</html>\n" );
81    }
82
83 ?>
```

This script is very simple:

Line 5: The script calls `loadWeather()` to retrieve the current conditions and store them in `$xmlData`.

Line 6: `parseWeather()` parses the XML stream and stores the result in `$weather`.

Line 7: `displayWeather()` picks apart the `$weather` array and creates an HTML table that's sent to the Web browser.

Line 9: The `loadWeather()` function (starting at line 9) downloads an XML stream from the URL shown on line 11. (Change the zip code at the end of the URL to match the location that you're interested in.)

Line 12: Before you can start a transfer using `libcurl`, you initialize the library and save a copy of the handle returned by `curl_init()`.

Lines 14 and 15: Next, you see two calls to `curl_setopt()`. The first call (line 14) gives the URL to `libcurl`, and the second call (line 15) tells `libcurl` that you want to download data and store it in a variable (as opposed to storing the data in a file).

Line 17: `curl_exec()` starts the download, waits for it to complete, and stores the result in `$xmlData`. When `curl_exec()` finishes, `$xmlData` contains the current weather conditions, in XML form, as shown in Listing 54-1.

Line 19–21: Finally, `loadWeather()` closes its connection to `libcurl` (see line 19) and returns the XML data to the caller (line 21).

Line 24: `parseWeather()` (lines 24–34) expects two parameters: the destination array (`$weather`) and the raw XML data (`$data`). `parseWeather()` doesn't do any of the hard work itself; instead, it calls on PHP's XML library to pick apart the XML data.

Line 26: You see a call to the `xml_parser_create()` function. `xml_parser_create()` creates a new XML parser and returns a handle. An XML parser doesn't do much by itself; it just identifies the various pieces of an XML stream. To make use of an XML parser, you have to provide *callback* functions. When an XML parser recognizes a chunk of data that you're interested in, it calls the callback function that you provide.

Line 28: The call to `xml_set_element_handler()` tells the parser that you're interested in *elements* (or, as we call them, *tags*). When the parser finds the beginning of an element, it calls the `startTag` function. When the parser finds the end of an element, it calls `endTag` (you see `startTag` and `endTag` in a moment).

Here's a typical XML element:

```
<Location>Redmond, WA</Location>
```

When the parser sees `<Location>`, it calls `startTag()`; when it sees `</Location>`, it calls `endTag()`. The stuff in between the tags is called character data — we can trap that, too (see the call to `xml_set_character_data_handler()` at line 29).

Line 31: `parseWeather()` starts the XML parser with a call to `xml_parse()`, passing the raw XML data that you want to parse.

Line 32: When `xml_parse()` completes, the call to `xml_parser_free()` shuts down the parser and frees up any lingering resources.

Lines 36–42: `startTag()` and `endTag()` are simple. When the parser calls `startTag()`, it sends along the tag name, which you store in a global variable named `$tag`. The `tagAttributes` parameter contains XML element attributes (if there are any); the weather information that you're looking at won't contain attributes, so you can safely ignore this argument.

Lines 43–48: The `endTag()` function (lines 43–48) is called whenever the parser sees an end tag. In this function, you simply set the global variable `$tag` to an empty string.

Lines 50–56: In between calls to `startTag()` and `endTag()`, the XML parser calls `dataHandler()` to handle the data within the tags. `dataHandler()` simply stores the data that it's given (a string contained between a pair of tags) in the `$weather` associative array.

The process is clear when you follow a typical element through the parser. Say that the parser runs into the following text:

```
<Location>Redmond, WA</Location>
```

When the parser sees the start tag, it calls `startTag()`. `startTag()` stores the tag name (`Location`) in the `$tag` global variable. (Actually, the parser converts all tag names to uppercase, so `$tag` is set to `LOCATION`.) Next, the parser calls

`dataHandler()` with the chunk of text (`Redmond, WA`) between the start tag and the end tag. `dataHandler()` stores the data in an element of the `$weather` array using the tag name as in index into the array. In other words: `$weather["LOCATION"] = "Redmond, WA"`. Finally, `endTag()` wipes out the global `$tag` name (that's not strictly necessary, but it makes your code a bit more obvious).

When the parser finishes its work, `$weather` looks like this:

```
$weather["LOCATION"]   = "Redmond, WA"
$weather["ICONINDEX"]  = "26"
$weather["TEMPRATURE"] = "47ûF"
$weather["FEELSLIKE"]  = "44ûF"
$weather["FORECAST"]   = "Cloudy"
$weather["VISIBILITY"] = "Unlimited"
...                      ...
```

Lines 57–81: The `displayWeather()` function builds an HTML page that it sends to the Web browser. The result looks similar to Listing 54-3.

LISTING 54-3: WEATHER CONDITIONS IN HTML

```
<html>
 <head>
  <title>Current Conditions At Redmond, WA</title>
 </head>
 <body>
  <h4>Current Weather for: Redmond, WA<br></h4>

  <TABLE CELLPADDING="2" CELLSPACING="0" BORDER=1>
    <TR><TD>Forecast</TD>     <TD>Cloudy</TD></TR>
    <TR><TD>Temperature</TD>  <TD>48ûF</TD></TR>
    <TR><TD>Wind</TD>         <TD>From the South at 6 mph</TD></TR>
    <TR><TD>Wind Chill</TD>   <TD>45ûF</TD></TR>
    <TR><TD>Dewpoint</TD>     <TD>42ûF</TD></TR>
    <TR><TD>Pressure</TD>     <TD>30.22 inches and rising</TD></TR>
    <TR><TD>UV Index</TD>     <TD>0 Minimal</TD></TR>
  </TABLE>
 </body>
</html>
```

Sending E-Mail from PHP When Problems Occur

The PHP script described in the previous section works well when conditions are perfect. We omitted error-checking code that you would normally include in a real-world application. Quite a few things can go wrong while checking for weather conditions: The server (`ejse.com`) could be down, the zip code you've entered may be incorrect, or the XML stream may contain invalid data. Checking for errors is important if you want your Web site to be robust and well-behaved.

If you don't do anything special to intercept error messages, they are displayed in the Web *browser*. That's not a very nice way to treat your users because PHP error messages are often detailed, a bit abrasive, and of little use to the user.

Given that PHP programs usually run within a Web *server,* you don't have too many options when something goes wrong. You're not sitting in front of a PHP debugger, so you can't step through the program, checking return codes and variables as the script runs. The most obvious way to find out what's gone wrong is to send error messages to the browser, but that's not very friendly (and the chances of a Web user writing down all the details that you need are slim). You could write messages to a debug log, but then you'd have to remember to look through those logs occasionally to check for problems.

 What you really want is a PHP program that actively *notifies* you by e-mail when something goes wrong.

Listing 54-4 shows a short PHP function that will intercept errors, warnings, and informational messages and send an e-mail describing the problem to the recipient of your choice.

`my_err_handler()` doesn't do anything without a little help. To enable `my_err_handler()`, call PHP's `set_error_handler()` function, giving it the name of the function that you want to run whenever an error (or warning) occurs, like this:

```
set_error_handler( "my_err_handler" );
```

All PHP error handler functions are called with the same five arguments:

- ✔ The first argument indicates the severity of the problem encountered. `$severity` will be one of the following values:

  - ▶ E_USER_ERROR
  - ▶ E_USER_WARNING
  - ▶ E_USER_NOTICE
  - ▶ E_WARNING
  - ▶ E_NOTICE

- ✔ The second argument (`$errmsg`) contains the text of the error message.

- ✔ The third and fourth arguments (`$filename` and `$lineno`) indicate the point at which the error occurred.

- ✔ The last argument is an array that contains the variable values and variable names in the function in which the error occurred.

You can often resolve a problem given only the argument values provided to the error handler function, but on occasion, you need more details. The `my_err_handler()` function in Listing 54-4 e-mails you the error message, filename, and line number, but Listing 54-5 shows a new version of `my_err_handler()` that gives much more detail. Use the new version while you're debugging your PHP code and the original version when things seem to be humming along tickety boo (that's a technical term).

LISTING 54-4: MAILING ERROR MESSAGES FROM PHP

```
function my_err_handler( $severity, $errmsg, $filename, $lineno, $context )
{
    $err_text  = "At " . date("Y-m-d H:I:s (T)");
    $err_text .= " an error occurred at line " . $lineno;
    $err_text .= " of file " . $filename . "\n\n";
    $err_text .= "The text of the error message is:\n";
    $err_text .= $errmsg . "\n";

    mail( "my-email@example.com", "PHP Script Error", $err_txt );
```

LISTING 54-5: MAILING DETAILED ERROR MESSAGES FROM PHP

```
function my_err_handler( $severity, $errmsg, $filename, $lineno, $context )
{
    $err_text  = "At " . date("Y-m-d H:I:s (T)");
    $err_text .= " an error occurred at line " . $lineno;
    $err_text .= " of file " . $filename . "\n\n";
    $err_text .= "The text of the error message is:\n";
    $err_text .= $errmsg . "\n";

    ob_start();                       // Redirect output to the temporary buffer

    print_r( debug_backtrace());     // Generate (and format) a stack trace

    $err_text .= "Stack Trace follows:\n";
    $err_text .= ob_get_contents(); // Add the stack trace to the body of the e-mail message

    ob_end_clean();              // And clean out the temporary buffer

    mail( "my-email@example.com", "PHP Script Error", $err_txt );
}
```

Technique 55

Using the DDD Graphical Debugger with Perl

Save Time By

- ✔ Using DDD to debug Perl programs
- ✔ Using the data window to track variable values
- ✔ Watching your code with breakpoints
- ✔ Using the Backtrace dialog to view the contents of your stack

Perl is often referred to as the duct tape of the Internet. If you need to write a utility or script, Perl is a standard that you can count on. How can you save time when you use Perl? With a good debugger! Unless your code works perfectly the first time through, you'll be spending some time behind the window of a debugger, working the kinks out of your script.

Linux offers a great open-source debugger called DDD (data display debugger). DDD is a graphical front end for several different command line debuggers and saves you time by clarifying and simplifying the process of debugging programs. DDD can debug not only Perl code, but also C, C++, Java, and other programming languages.

You can use the source window in DDD to review your source code at a glance; you can even define and delete breakpoints and see cute little stop signs where your program will stop. DDD also provides an easy button interface to step through your program, stepping into subroutines to view the complete code or bypassing subroutines.

With DDD, you can create a graphical display of the variables in your program and watch their values change as you step through the program. DDD dialogs help you in your debugging tasks by providing easy-to-read information about the status of your program. An easy-to-access help menu makes certain you have not only technical information, but also advice about debugging your program (in case you get stuck).

A lot of good books about the Perl programming language are available. The best timesaver we could think of was a quick introduction to an open-source debugger that will save you time and make your life a lot easier. In this technique, we introduce you to DDD, which is a huge improvement over the command line debuggers of the past.

Debugging Perl Code with DDD

If you've written many Perl programs, you're probably familiar with Perl's source-level debugger. To run a program under the control of the Perl debugger, use the -d option, like this:

```
$ perl -d program.pl
```

After a bit of clicking and whirring, the debugger appears, waiting for commands. If you type h and press Enter, you're greeted with a helpful page of intimidation, as shown in Listing 55-1.

Don't panic; there's an easier way to debug Perl. Even if you're a hardened Perl veteran (and you have the mental scars to prove it), you'll love DDD, the data display debugger. DDD is a graphical front end for a number of different debuggers (GDB, DBX, the Perl debugger, and even the Python debugger).

Installing and starting DDD

DDD is included on most distribution media, so getting it up and running is simple. To install and start the DDD debugger, follow these steps:

1. Open a terminal window and give yourself superuser privileges with the su - command.

2. Insert and mount the distribution media.

3. Move to the directory containing the RPM packages and enter the following command:

```
# rpm -Uhv ddd-version.rpm
```

4. To run a Perl program under the control of the DDD debugger, use this command:

```
$ ddd --perl /usr/bin/xql.pl
```

DDD opens, displaying a Tip of the Day and an information window in front of the main window.

 If the DDD RPM package isn't included on your distribution media, you can download a copy of the RPM package from www.gnu.org/software/ddd.

Examining the main window

DDD divides the main window into three panes, stacked vertically, as shown in Figure 55-1:

- ✔ The top pane, named the *data window,* displays variable values. (The data window is empty at first, but we show you how to put stuff there in a moment.)

- ✔ The middle pane, named the *source window,* shows the code that you're executing. A big green arrow points to the line of code that's about to execute.

- ✔ The bottom pane, the *Perl console,* is where you type in debugger commands.

Source window

Data window

Perl console

• **Figure 55-1: The DDD main window.**

LISTING 55-1: PERL DEBUGGER COMMANDS

```
List/search source lines:            Control script execution:
  l [ln|sub]  List source code        T              Stack trace
  - or .      List previous/current line s [expr]    Single step [in expr]
  v [line]    View around line        n [expr]       Next, steps over subs
  f filename  View source in file      <CR/Enter>    Repeat last n or s
  /pattern/ ?patt?   Search forw/backw  r             Return from subroutine
  M           Show module versions     c [ln|sub]    Continue until position
Debugger controls:                     L              List break/watch/actions
  o [...]     Set debugger options     t [expr]       Toggle trace [trace expr]
  <[<]|{[{]}|>[>] [cmd] Do pre/post-prompt b [ln|event|sub] [cnd] Set breakpoint
  ! [N|pat]   Redo a previous command  B ln|*         Delete a/all breakpoints
  H [-num]    Display last num commands a [ln] cmd    Do cmd before line
  = [a val]   Define/list an alias     A ln|*         Delete a/all actions
  h [db_cmd]  Get help on command      w expr         Add a watch expression
  h h         Complete help page       W expr|*       Delete a/all watch exprs
  |[|]db_cmd  Send output to pager     ![!] syscmd    Run cmd in a subprocess
  q or ^D     Quit                     R              Attempt a restart
Data Examination:     expr     Execute perl code, also see: s,n,t expr
  x|m expr       Evals expr in list context, dumps the result or lists methods.
  p expr         Print expression (uses script's current package).
  S [[!]pat]     List subroutine names [not] matching pattern
  V [Pk [Vars]]  List Variables in Package.  Vars can be ~pattern or !pattern.
  X [Vars]       Same as "V current_package [Vars]".
  y [n [Vars]]   List lexicals in higher scope <n>.  Vars same as V.
For more help, type h cmd_letter, or run man perldebug for all docs.
```

Reviewing and stepping through source code

If displaying your code was all that DDD could do, it would be marginally useful, but not much of a time-saver. But find a Perl program that you want to dance through, and we'll show a few of DDD's more useful features.

In the following example, we use a script that comes with the kdeaddons RPM package, but you can use DDD to debug any Perl program.

First, fire up the debugger:

```
$ cd /usr/share/apps/knewsticker/scripts
$ ddd --perl bbc.pl
```

The DDD debugger window opens, displaying bbc.pl (see Figure 55-2).

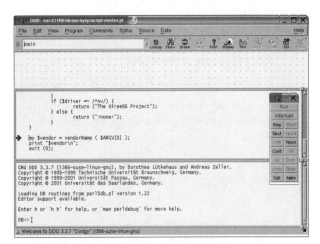

• **Figure 55-2:** bbc.pl, **as viewed from DDD.**

The source window shows you the source code for `bbc.pl`, and a big green arrow points to the first executable line of code in the program. The green arrow always points to the line of code that's *about to* execute.

To step through the source code one line at a time, press F5 (or click the Step button on the pop-up menu). DDD then executes a single line of code in your Perl program and moves the green arrow to the next executable line of code.

Making Stop Signs: Using Breakpoints to Watch Code

When you debug your program, you can use breakpoints to stop the execution of the code at a given moment during the programs execution for a closer examination of the state of the program. This is, of course, assuming your program executes for long enough to reach the breakpoint.

Setting a breakpoint

In the source window, find some code that you want to watch and right-click in the blank area to the left of the code (in other words, right-click in the left margin). A pop-up menu appears showing the following options:

- ✔ **Set Breakpoint:** Sets a permanent breakpoint at that line. The debugger will stop when your program reaches that statement.

- ✔ **Set Temporary Breakpoint:** Sets a temporary breakpoint at that line. The debugger will stop when your program reaches that statement and then will delete the breakpoint.

- ✔ **Continue Until Here:** Sets a temporary breakpoint and then immediately continues the program.

- ✔ **Set Execution Position:** Moves the point of execution (that is, the big green arrow) to the line you're pointing at.

 That last option (Set Execution Position) doesn't work with Perl programs — sorry.

When you set a breakpoint, a little red stop sign appears to the left of the code.

Modifying a breakpoint

In the process of debugging your program, you may find you want to temporarily disable or completely remove a breakpoint. To modify a breakpoint, right-click on a stop sign and choose Properties. The Properties: Breakpoint dialog opens (see Figure 55-3).

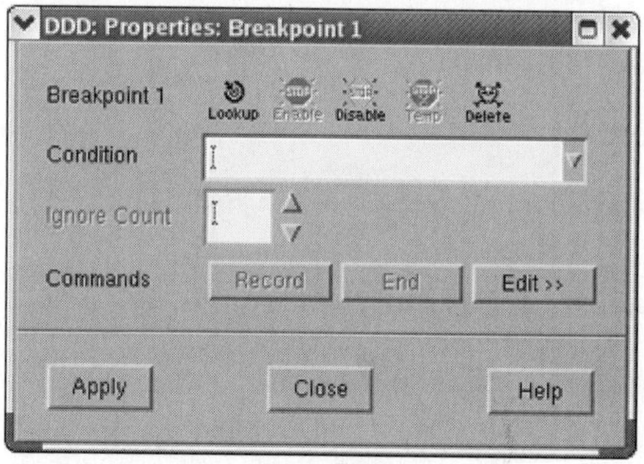

• **Figure 55-3: The Properties: Breakpoint dialog.**

From the Properties: Breakpoint dialog, you can enable, disable, or delete the breakpoint by clicking the appropriate button. You can also assign a condition to the breakpoint or associate commands with the breakpoint, as described next.

Assigning a condition to a breakpoint

You can assign a *condition* to the breakpoint to streamline its functionality. For example, if you want to break only when `$headline` is undefined, type the following command into the Condition field and then click Apply:

```
!defined( $headline )
```

You can build complex breakpoint conditions with the usual Perl *and*, *or*, and *not* operators.

Associating debugger commands with a breakpoint

You can associate debugger commands with a breakpoint to display variable values or display a stacktrace. Click the Edit button and then enter a list of commands for DDD to execute each time the breakpoint fires. When you assign a command to a breakpoint, you have to use commands supported by the Perl debugger (refer to Listing 55-1) and surround them with double quotes. For example, to print the value of the $headline variable when a breakpoint is hit, click Edit and type the following command into the box provided:

```
"x $headline"
```

Then click Apply or Close when you're finished.

Tracking Variable Values in the Data Window

The next example shows the functionality and time-saving values in DDD. This example takes a couple of steps to set up, but it's worth the time.

The Perl script ./stock.pl is a stock value tracker. You need to install a few extra Perl programs before you can run stock.pl, but the MCPAN shell can handle that for you easily:

1. **Open a terminal window and give yourself superuser privileges with the su - command. Enter the following command:**

    ```
    #perl -MCPAN -e "install
       Finance::Quote"
    ```

2. **When the installation program asks if you would like it to satisfy the program dependencies, press Enter to answer yes.**

MCPAN takes a few moments to download and install the stock.pl prerequisites.

To start the DDD debugger and step through the stock.pl script, enter the following command:

```
# ddd --perl ./stock.pl
```

The DDD debugger opens, displaying the source code for stock.pl, as shown in Figure 55-4.

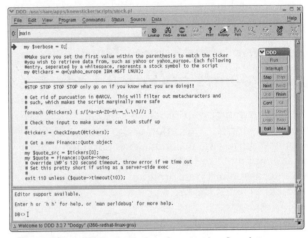

• **Figure 55-4: DDD displaying the** stock.pl **script.**

Opening the data window

To open the data window, choose View⇨ Data Window. The data window opens at the top of the display.

 The data window makes quick work of keeping an eye on the value of variables as you step through a Perl script.

Adding a variable to the data window

To add a variable to the data window, right-click on the variable and choose Display Variable from the pop-up menu. The variable is added to the data window, with the current value displayed beneath the header.

You can also add variable displays to the data window by entering commands in the Perl console. To add the fields to the data window as shown in Figure 55-5, use the following three commands:

```
graph display @tickers
graph display %quotes
graph display $quote->{"TIMEOUT"}
```

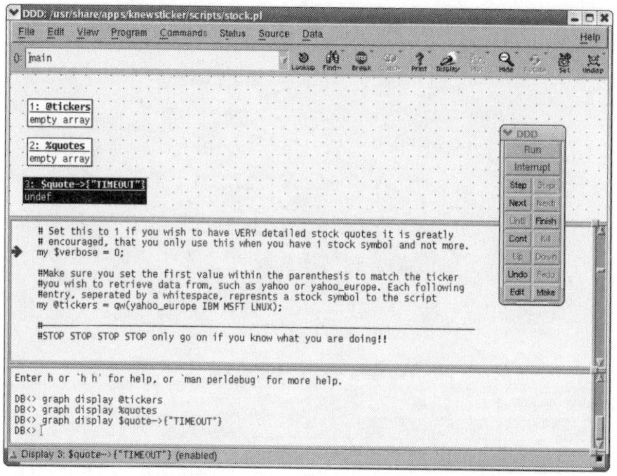

• **Figure 55-5:** Variables and their values in the data window.

As you step through the code, the values of the variables change in the data window (see Figure 55-6).

Use the Step button to step into functions and subroutines. The Next button steps over the function (executing the function) but doesn't display the activities within the function line-by-line.

When the code executes, the TIMEOUT variable is assigned a value, as shown in Figure 55-7.

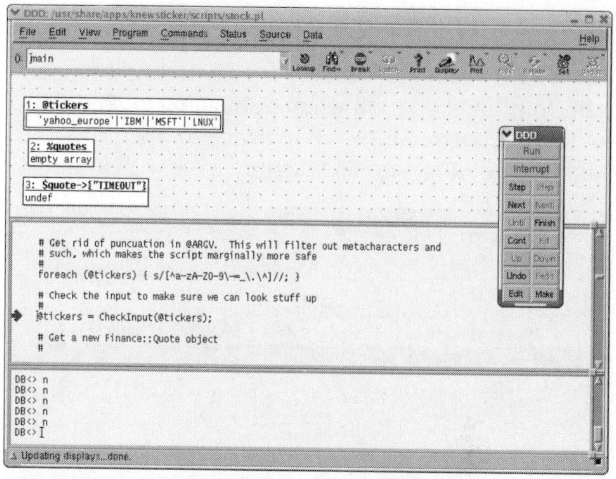

• **Figure 55-6:** Timeout is currently undefined.

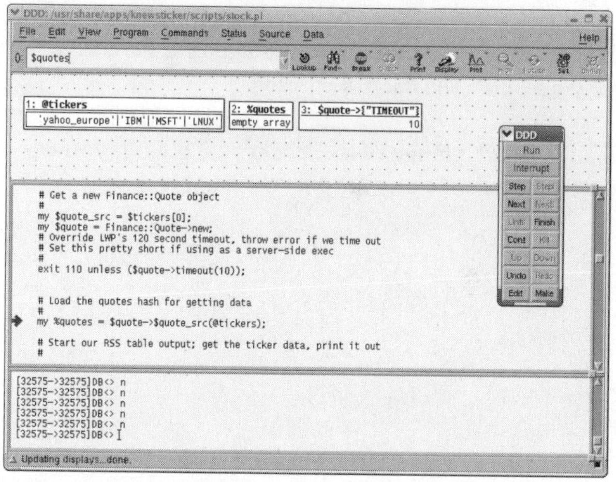

• **Figure 55-7:** Timeout now has a value of 10.

Changing the display to a table

If the data displayed is hard to read in a row format, you can change the display to a table. Right-click on the header for the data display and choose Rotate from the pop-up menu to change the orientation of the data display.

Using the Backtrace feature

The Backtrace feature makes it easy to find the current point of execution when debugging nested subroutines. Choose Status⊅Backtrace to open the Backtrace dialog, shown in Figure 55-8.

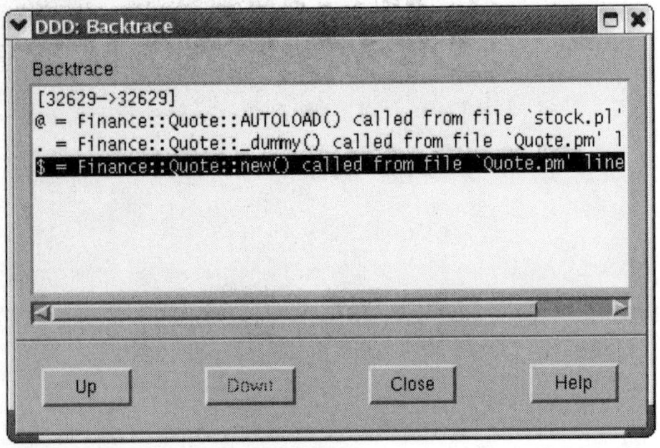

• **Figure 55-8: The Backtrace dialog.**

With a quick glance of the Backtrace dialog, you can see the contents of your current call stack.

Using the Help menu

Click the Help button in the upper-right corner to open a drop-down menu of help options. One noteworthy option on the Help menu is What Now. Click the What Now option to open a handy dialog with suggestions of how you might want to proceed, as shown in Figure 55-9.

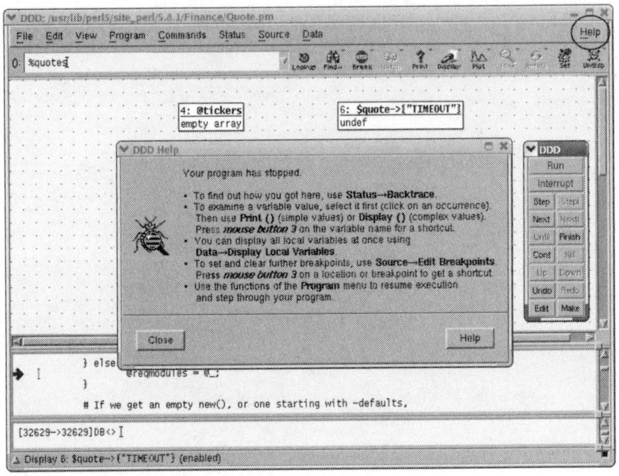

• **Figure 55-9: What Now?**

The DDD Reference menu choice on the Help menu opens the DDD documentation. This is a quick way to get up to speed on using the DDD debugger with Perl.

Part XI

The Scary (Or Fun!) Stuff

The 5th Wave By Rich Tennant

"It's called Linux Poker. Everyone gets to see everyone else's cards, everything's wild, you can play off your opponents' hands, and everyone wins except Bill Gates, whose face appears on the jokers."

Technique 56

Burning CD-Rs without Getting Burned

Save Time By

- ✔ Making your own distribution CDs
- ✔ Writing CDs or DVDs without creating ISO images first
- ✔ Creating ISO-formatted images when you need to

This technique is all about writing CDs and DVDs. Burning your own CDs is a quick and easy way to keep the information you use over and over again at your fingertips. Keep backups of your public/private key pairs, downloaded RPM packages, and data files on CD to save time and money. CDs are small, inexpensive, portable, and easy to create, and with a little care, they last practically forever.

Burning a DVD is just like burning a CD, except that DVDs hold a lot more data and you need a DVD burner to do it. In this technique, if you see a reference to burning a CD, you can safely assume that the technique also works for a DVD.

As we mention throughout this book, one timesaving set of CDs you'll want to make is a copy of your distribution discs. In this technique, we walk you through making a set of Fedora distribution media from downloaded disc images by using `cdrecord` at the command line. The same technique applies to any version of Linux distributed with ISO images — just burn each ISO image to a separate CD.

You can find a ton of open-source software on the Web, free for downloading. If you find a package you like, keep an installable copy of the RPM package on CD because open-source projects are known to come and go. Even if worldwide enthusiasm for the software you like disappears, you'll still have a copy on CD.

You can save time by writing backup files to CD without making an ISO disc image first, but if you want to write CDs to save RPMs for later use, saving them in ISO image format is much more convenient. You can mount an ISO-formatted disc and explore the contents without using custom software. The ISO file system is an industry standard, so if you want to share programs with a friend, save them on an ISO-formatted disc, which your friend's machine will have a better chance of understanding. In this technique, we show you how to create discs with or without ISO formatting.

Making Fedora Distribution CDs

Sure you can download RPM packages off the Web whenever you need them, but it's a whole lot easier (and quicker) to have your own set of distribution CDs, handy and ready for use. You no longer have to search Web sites for the packages (hundreds of them exist) that are included with your distribution — just pop in the CD and unpack.

In this example, we walk you through downloading and burning a set of distribution media for Fedora Linux. The process is the same for SuSE or Mandrake — just download and substitute the ISO images from the distribution of your choice.

Downloading the ISO images

To download the ISO images to make your own set of Fedora discs, follow these steps:

1. **Open your browser window and browse to**

fedora.redhat.com/download/

2. **Click the Download the Files You Need link.**

3. **Click the link to the ISO images.**

An ISO image is like a snapshot of the data on a disc. The image contains not only the files on the disc, but the structure of the file system as well.

On the download page, you see links for SRPMS disc images (source RPMs) and i386 disc images. The ready-to-run RPM packages are on the i386 disc images.

4. **Click the link to download**

yarrow-i386-disc1.iso

A pop-up window appears asking if you want to open the file or save it to disk (see Figure 56-1).

• **Figure 56-1: The Question dialog.**

5. **Click the Save As button.**

6. **When the Save As window opens, as shown in Figure 56-2, click the Save button.**

• **Figure 56-2: The Save As window.**

The download begins. Even with a fast connection, the download takes a while.

7. **When the download for the first disc completes, repeat the download process for disc 2, and disc 3, collecting the three ISO images.**

yarrow-i386-disc2.iso
yarrow-i386-disc3.iso

After you've downloaded the three ISO images, you need to verify the checksums to make sure you have a clean download. The next section explains how to do this.

Verifying the checksums

Verifying a file's checksum is like comparing finger-prints. If the fingerprints match, it's likely that the download was successful. To verify the checksums of the ISO images you've downloaded, follow these steps:

1. **Click the Back button on your browser to return to the first Fedora download page. Below the link to the ISO images, look for the names of the discs you've downloaded.**

   Each name is followed by an md5 checksum:

   ```
   yarrow-i386-disc1.iso (md5sum:
      76ef22495d186580e47efd8d7a65fe6b)
   ```

2. **Write down the three checksums; you'll need them to compare to your computed results.**

3. **Open a terminal window and** cd **to the directory containing the downloaded ISO images.**

4. **Use the following command to calculate the checksum for the first disc image:**

   ```
   $ md5sum yarrow-i386-disc1.iso
   ```

5. **Compare the result to the checksum from the Fedora Web site.**

   The checksums should match. If they don't, download the file again.

6. **Repeat the process for the other disc files.**

   When you have three ISO files with good check-sums, you're ready to burn the Fedora CDs! See the next section for details.

Burning an ISO File to Disc at the Command Line

If you have access to a graphical environment, you'll find easy-to-use tools that help you make CDs or DVDs with a few clicks of the mouse. But the easiest way to burn an ISO image onto a disc is to hit the command line.

Before you burn an ISO image, you need to find the identity of your CD or DVD drive and then run a test burn. When those steps are complete, you're ready to burn the discs.

 The cdrecord **package is included in the standard Fedora distribution. It is part of the Sound and Video package and included in most installations by default.**

Finding the identity of your drive

Before you can burn the ISO file to disc, you need to find the identity of your CD drive:

1. **Open a terminal window and enter the following command:**

   ```
   $ cdrecord --scanbus
   ```

   The results look something like this:

   ```
   scsibus1:
     1,0,0 100) 'TEAC' 'DW-224E ' 'F.0A'
       CDR
     1,1,0 101) *
     1,2,0 102) *
     1,3,0 103) *
     1,4,0 104) *
     1,5,0 105) *
     1,6,0 106) *
     1,7,0 107) *
   ```

2. **Find your drive in the list. If you see more than one device in the list, choose your drive by its model name. The first three comma-separated numbers make up the drive identifier. Write down the drive ID because you'll need it in a moment.**

Running a test burn

A test burn does everything but turn the laser on. It tests the system speed and determines whether the image will fit on a disc. Basically, it prevents you from making a shiny coaster.

To run a test burn, move to the directory containing the ISO disc images and enter the following command:

```
$ cdrecord --dummy dev=1,0,0 yarrow-i386-
   disc1.iso
```

Use the device identifier that you discovered in the previous section to identify the drive in the command. The test results print to screen, displaying statistics and errors about the burn.

The most common error you're likely to encounter is a buffer underrun. A *buffer underrun* means your computer wasn't able to feed data to the burner quickly enough to keep up with the drive. Your computer may be too busy or too slow to burn a CD at the maximum rate supported by your recorder. If you get a buffer underrun error, run another test record, but set the speed to half of the speed listed in the statistics of the test burn:

```
$ cdrecord --dummy dev=1,0,0 speed=8
   yarrow-i386-disc1.iso
```

 If you still have buffer underrun errors, halve the speed and try again. Don't forget to stop any unnecessary programs running on your system.

Burning the distribution discs

When you get a successful result set from the test burn, take `--dummy` out of the command line and let the burning begin:

```
$ cdrecord -eject dev=1,0,0 yarrow-i386-
   disc1.iso
```

 Add the `-eject` flag to eject the disc when the write is complete.

cdrecord displays a nine-second countdown before turning on the laser. When the drive is finished writing, the disc ejects. Repeat the steps to make discs 2 and 3 of the Fedora distribution, and your set is complete!

Creating an ISO Image at the Command Line

You can put data on a CD or DVD two ways: You can just burn the bytes that make up the data straight onto the disc, or you can create a file system to hold the data and then burn the file system onto the disc.

Here's an example to clarify what you get with each option. Say you want to store your e-mail inbox on CD. Typically, a mailbox is made up of two files: The mail messages are stored in one file (`inbox.mbox`), and the index is stored in a separate file (`inbox.idx`). You *could* simply stream both files onto the CD, one right after the other, but you'll find this method has a few disadvantages down the road:

✔ **You'll lose useful information.** First, you would lose the filenames — the filename is part of the file system, not part of the file content. In fact, you would lose the boundary between the two files. If you stream two files to a CD, you can't tell where one file ends and the other begins. You would also lose the creation and modification dates for the file, the owner and group IDs, and the file permissions — that information is stored in the file system, not in the file.

✔ **You can't mount a raw data disc later on.** You'll have to stream the data back off the disc instead and re-create the two data files yourself.

✔ **You can't really tell what's on the disc if you forget to label it properly.** This is one of the biggest disadvantages to writing raw data.

 By creating an ISO image so that the file system travels with the data, you'll reap all sorts of timesaving benefits. The alternative is to create a mini–file system that holds the two files and then burn the file system to disc. The filenames are preserved, the owner and group IDs are preserved, the permissions are preserved, and the boundary between the two files is managed by the file system. You can mount a CD that contains a file system.

There are still a few legitimate reasons to create a raw-data CD (in fact, we show you how to do that in the next section), but in most cases, you should create a file system first.

Although you can write just about any type of file system to a CD (ext2, resierfs, xfs), most computers expect to find an ISO 9660 (or ISO for short) file system when you put a CD in the drive.

To make an ISO file system that holds the two mailbox files, open a terminal window and enter the following command:

```
$ mkisofs -o mailbox.iso inbox.mbox
    inbox.idx
```

The `-o mailbox.iso` option tells `mkisofs` to write the resulting file system to a file named `mailbox.iso`. (You typically create the ISO image on your hard drive and then transfer it to a CD.)

 Use the `isovfy` command to verify that the ISO file is in good shape: `$ isovfy imagename.iso`.

To write the ISO file to disc, use `cdrecord` just like we describe in the section, "Burning an ISO File to Disc at the Command Line," earlier in this technique. For our example, we added the inbox ISO files to the command:

```
# cdrecord -eject dev=1,0,0 mailbox.iso
```

Of course, you have to use the device ID that you found in the section, "Finding the identity of your drive," earlier in this technique.

 If you haven't tested your recorder's burn performance, be sure to do a `--dummy` burn first to find the correct write speed. You can also find details on speed in "Running a test burn," earlier in this technique.

You can also mount an ISO file system *without* first burning it to disc. When you mount an ISO image (using Linux's loopback adapter), you're sort of

treating the file system like an archive: It's a collection of files and directories just like a `tar` archive. *Any* program can look inside a mounted file system and get to the files inside; you can't do that with a `tar` archive.

To directly mount an ISO image, follow these steps:

1. **Give yourself superuser privileges.**

2. **Create a mount point:**

    ```
    # mkdir /mnt/myiso
    ```

3. **Mount the image to the mount point:**

    ```
    # mount -o loop ./mailbox.iso
        /mnt/myiso
    ```

4. **Check out a listing of the ISO image with the `ls` command:**

    ```
    # ls /mnt/myiso
    ```

The mounted ISO image acts just like a drive. Look inside it and be sure it's just right before you write it to disc.

Burning CDs without Making an ISO First

If an ISO 9660 file system is so great, why would you ever want to burn a disc without one? To save time, of course (and disc space, too).

 Sometimes, burning a raw data disc is the best way to save time and space. If you're creating a backup CD or DVD, the archive tool that you're using already builds a wrapper around all the files in the archive. Why wrap a file system around an archive when the archive already contains all the information that you need (filenames, permissions, owner IDs, and such)? Also, it takes *time* to create an ISO image. An ISO image takes up space on your hard drive until you've burned it to disc. If all you need is the data an ISO has to offer, then don't waste time creating the ISO.

You can pipe the output of a command directly into the standard input of cdrecord without creating an ISO image. For this to work, the recorder must support RAW-mode writing. Not all recorders support RAW mode. If you have a drive that doesn't, you get an error message when you try to burn a CD.

To burn a CD (or DVD) with a backup of the /etc directory (the /etc directory is full of your config files — a good thing to back up), enter the following command:

```
# tar -czvf - /etc | cdrecord -eject
  dev=1,0,0 -
```

The -f - in the -czvf portion of the command tells tar to write the archive that it creates to its standard output stream. The | directs the output from the tar command to the cdrecord command. The - at the end of the cdrecord command tells cdrecord to read a data stream from its standard input (cdrecord burns whatever data you send to its standard input stream when you include a - at the end of the command line).

 cdrecord doesn't know how to split the data stream if the stream contains more data than the disc can hold. Use the cdbackup program that we cover in Technique 50 to split the stream across multiple discs.

You can't mount a CD or DVD that's been created this way because it doesn't have a file system. Instead, you have to use a program that understands the raw data. To read a CD that you've created with raw tar data, use tar:

```
# tar -xzvf /dev/cdrom
```

This isn't too difficult, and you've skipped all the intermediate disc image files, too.

 Don't forget that you can use the Nautilus browser with the burn:// protocol to make CDs. Check out Technique 1 for all the details!

Technique 57

Search and Destroy setuid and setgid Programs

Save Time By

- ✔ Understanding the true powers of a user's identity
- ✔ Using kfind to identify the setuid programs on your system
- ✔ Carefully choosing which setuid bits to disable

There are valid reasons for having setuid and setgid programs on your system. Programs that allow other users to log in to your system are often setuid or setgid programs, and they have the power to grant elevated privileges to otherwise unprivileged users.

Hackers are always looking for security loopholes that allow them to exploit even the slightest of vulnerabilities. Fortunately, popular programs like ssh are pretty tight, but other programs might not be so trustworthy. Security is ssh's business — simple user applications that allow access to your system through a server might not be so careful to prevent program breakouts through a shell escape.

Keeping a vigilant eye on programs with setuid and setgid privileges is the quickest way to protect yourself from an intruder posing as an innocuous user. Closing the back door to hackers that would exploit that security lapse can save you a lot of time repairing damage to the system caused by an intruder. In this technique, we introduce you to setuid and setgid, and show you how to add another line of security to your system that will stop intruders in their tracks.

Exploring How setuid and setgid Can Be Dangerous

Every user in a Linux system has a unique numeric user ID (called a UID). Every group has a unique numeric group ID (called a GID). If you log in twice (from two different workstations or from a remote computer), you still have the same UID. The UID is associated with the user, not with the login session.

Each time you run a program, Linux creates a new process for the program to run within. If you run two Solitaire games at the same time, you have two processes (but only one program). Each process has four attributes that determine what that process is allowed to do: a real UID, an *effective* UID (EUID), a real GID, and an *effective* GID (EGID).

When Linux creates a process on your behalf, the effective and real UIDs are set to *your* user ID. The effective and real GIDs are set to your primary group ID (you can belong to many groups, but at any one time, you have a single primary group ID).

The effective UID and effective GID are used to determine whether the process can access a given file. When you try to access a file, Linux classifies your effective user ID (and group) into one of three categories:

- ✔ **File Owner:** If the effective user ID of the process matches the numeric UID of the file, you're the file's owner.

- ✔ **Group Member:** If the effective GID of the process matches the numeric GID of the file, you're a member of the file's group.

- ✔ **Other:** Your process is classified as an "other" if the effective UID doesn't match and the effective GID doesn't match.

After your identity has been classified, Linux checks the file permissions assigned to your category to be sure you have the privileges required to access that file.

When you run a program that has the setuid bit turned on, the effective user ID of the process is changed from your UID to the file's UID. In other words, if you're logged in as user `freddie` and you run a normal (*non*-setuid) program, the effective and real UID of the process is `freddie`. If `freddie` runs a

setuid program (owned by, say, user `franklin`), the effective UID of the process is changed from `freddie` to `franklin` (the real user ID remains `freddie`). Just by running a setuid program, `freddie` gains the privileges and permissions assigned to user `franklin`.

That isn't a problem if `franklin` has limited privileges, but what if `freddie` runs a setuid program owned by `root`? The system would be at `freddie`'s mercy if he could start a terminal window from the program he's running.

 Anyone who runs a setuid program owned by `root` is automatically granted superuser privileges.

Remember, the superuser can

- ✔ Kill off any process
- ✔ Override file privileges
- ✔ Grant program privileges
- ✔ Lock users out
- ✔ Change file ownerships

You can see from the list of privileges why you would want to limit the number of setuid and setgid programs on your system!

When you turn on the setuid and/or setgid bits for a program, the file's owner and group IDs are *very* important. That's because the privileges assigned to the owner (or group) are now assigned to anyone who runs the program. If you run a setuid program that's owned by user `root`, you become the superuser while that program is running. Any processes spawned by the program run with superuser privileges, too. Imagine what would happen if you turned on the setuid bit for the `bash` shell (which is typically owned by user `root`) — anyone who ran the shell would suddenly become a superuser. Nasty business.

Just turning on the setuid or setgid bit for a program isn't enough to let intruders sneak into your system. They still need to have execute privileges, either from their own logins or someone else's.

Identifying the Potential Troublemakers — Fast

Search your system with the `find` command, and you'll be surprised at how many setuid and setgid programs you have. Most of these programs are benign, but a real troublemaker needs only one good opportunity to get in. Changing the setuid or setgid bit can close a door before a hacker finds it open.

The first step in checking your system for back doors through setuid and setgid is to figure out which programs have setuid and setgid turned on. You have two ways of doing this: By using an easy-to-use program called `kfind` or by working from the command line. The following sections have all the details.

Finding setuid quickly and easily with kfind

The KDE Desktop includes a great tool called `kfind` that can help you find the setuid programs on your system in no time. `kfind` has a friendly graphical interface that leads you to the setuid programs on your system with just a few mouse clicks.

To use the `kfind` File Finder to locate the setuid programs on your system, follow these steps:

1. **Open the Main Menu and choose Run Command.**

2. **Enter** `kfind` **in the Command field and then click Run.**

The `kfind` Find Files dialog opens, as shown in Figure 57-1.

`kfind` can find all sorts of files for you. It's a handy tool worth getting to know.

If you're running KDE, you can also start `kfind` by opening the Main Menu and clicking Find Files.

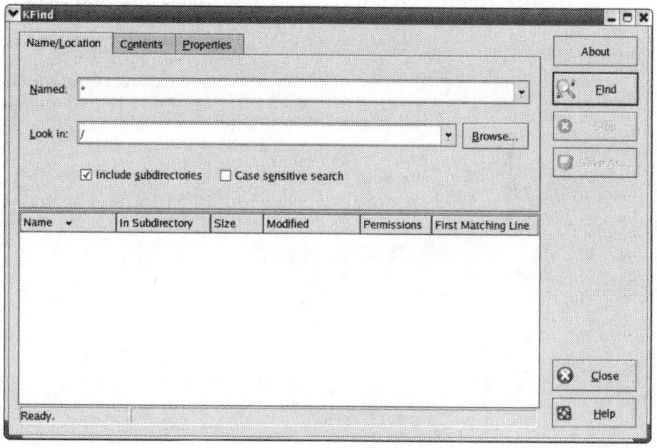

• **Figure 57-1:** The kfind Find Files dialog.

3. **On the Name/Location tab, use the * default entry in the Named field.**

This suits our purposes well — we want to find all the files that have the setuid bit set.

4. **Enter the directory you want to search in the Look In field.**

For a thorough system search, start with a search of the `root` directory. Just enter a / in the Look In field.

5. **Choose the Contents tab and choose SUID Executable Files from the File Type drop-down list.**

6. **Click the Find button in the upper-right corner of the screen.**

The search begins. Depending on how much of your system you're searching, the process can take a while. Now's a good time to go get a cup of coffee.

When the search is complete, a list of the files with the setuid bits turned on displays in the results frame, as shown in Figure 57-2.

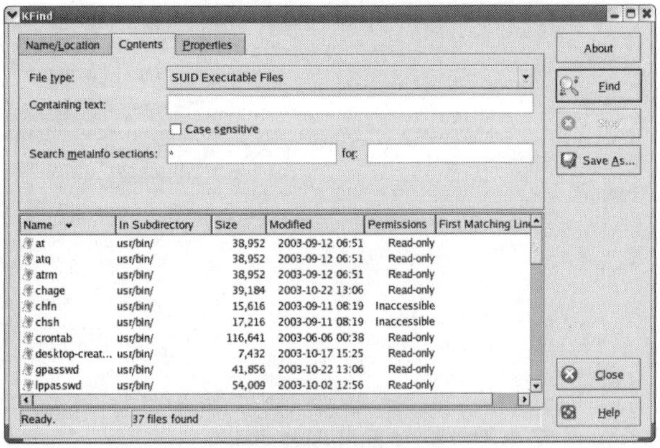

• **Figure 57-2:** Search results for setuid programs.

7. **Cruising through the list of names in the result set, you should recognize most of the programs as commands you use. If a program is unfamiliar, check it out (see "Deciding to Turn Off setuid or setgid" later in this technique for details).**

The File Finder searches only for setuid programs. For a list of the setgid programs on your system, you use the command line. The next section has all the details.

> Searching out setuid and setgid programs at the command line can also save you time by showing you a complete list of ownership and privileges at the same time. Use the File Finder for a quick glance, but review any questionable programs in a terminal window.

Finding setuid and setgid programs at the command line

If you don't have a desktop environment or need more information about a questionable program you found with the KDE File Finder, the command line can give you a more complete rundown on the ownership and privileges of a setuid or setgid program.

To use the command line to generate a complete list of the setuid programs on your system, open the terminal window, give yourself superuser privileges with the su command, and enter the following command:

```
# find / -perm +u+s -type f -ls
```

The results look something like Figure 57-3.

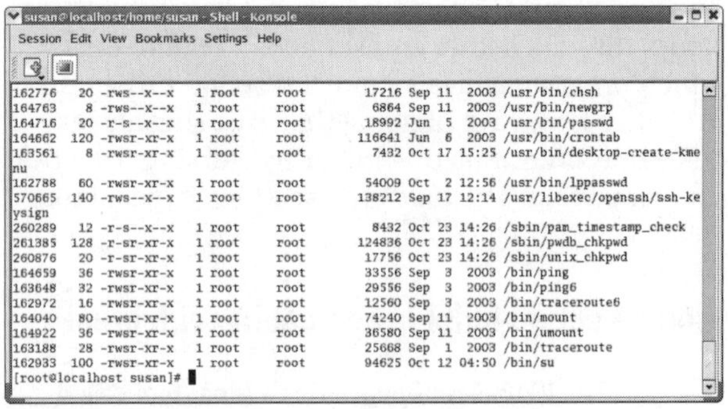

• **Figure 57-3:** The programs in the root directory with the setuid bit turned on.

To locate setgid programs on your system, you use a slight variation on the find command:

```
# find / -perm +g+s -type f -ls
```

To use the find command to locate all the setuid and setgid programs on your system, use the following command:

```
find / -perm +ug+s -type f -ls
```

Deciding to Turn Off setuid or setgid

The big secret to creating a more secure system is to figure out what programs don't *need* the setuid bit turned on and then turn the bit off for those programs. If you see a setuid or setgid program that you don't recognize, Google for it on the Web. If in doubt, turn off the setuid or setgid bit (see the next section for details) and see if anything breaks.

 Turning off the wrong setuid bit or setgid bit can lock you out of your system. Know your programs and permissions, and keep a terminal window open with superuser privileges until you've tested the program with your regular login.

 Use `sudo` to distribute extra privileges to the users that need them. It's a lot safer than handing out unlimited access to everyone. See Technique 31 for some great ideas about using `sudo`.

Changing the setuid or setgid Bit

You may want to disable the setuid or setgid bits on some of the programs that aren't used often or anything that you can't really identify.

 Try to find out what a program is before you disable its setuid or setgid bit. If the program looks questionable and leaves a door open, it may be a security risk.

You can tell that a program has the setuid (or setgid) bit turned on by looking at the output from an `ls -l` command. If you see an s in the fourth (from the left)

permission column, you're looking at a setuid program. If you see an s in the seventh permission column, you're looking at a setgid program.

If you look at a normal Linux program (that is, a program that is *not* setuid or setgid), you won't see any s:

```
-rwxrwxr--    1 fred  fred         1001
Dec 13 18:50 myprogram
```

To turn on the setuid bit, use the following command:

```
$ chmod u+s myprogram
```

`ls -l` then shows this:

```
-rwsrwxr--    1 fred  fred        1001 Dec
13 18:50 myprogram
```

 You have to be the file's owner (or have superuser privileges) to change the setuid or setgid bits.

To turn on the setgid bit, use the following command:

```
$ chmod g+s myprogram
```

`ls -l` then shows this:

```
-rwsrwsr--    1 fred  fred        1001 Dec
13 18:50 myprogram
```

 A program that has the setgid bit turned on assigns the file's group ID to the process.

To turn the bits back off again, use these commands:

```
$ chmod u-s myprogram
$ chmod g-s myprogram
```

If you see an uppercase S instead of a lower-case s, the setuid (or setgid) bit is turned on, but the execute bit is turned off. That's usually a nonsensical combination.

A directory with setuid or setgid privileges turned on forces all the files and subdirectories within them to be owned by the directory owner or group instead of the user creating the file. A setuid (or setgid) directory is not a security risk in the same way that a setuid/setgid *program* is. You don't have to disable setuid/setgid directories to make your system more secure.

Quarantining Suspicious Programs with UML

Technique 58

You can put the most secure server behind a firewall, allow only secured logins, and limit administrative access, but somebody's gonna find a way to break in. You can only do so much to keep people out of your server and still keep it functional. The only truly secure system is one that's completely isolated from the outside world, which makes it pretty hard to offer network services (like e-mail and Web pages). Instead of taking your servers completely offline, create a *sacrificial* server that you can afford to lose if someone does manage to break in. Of course, most of us can't afford to throw out a compromised system and replace it with new hardware. Instead, you can use UML (User Mode Linux) to create a virtual server.

Running a server from within a UML virtual machine isolates the server from the rest of your system. As far as your server knows, the rest of your Linux machine doesn't exist, so to the eyes of an invading hacker, your *real* computer doesn't exist either.

The open-source software movement has a lot to offer, but even high-quality programs sometimes harbor unintentional vulnerabilities. Even if you get your software from long-established and trusted sources, software often contains back doors and Trojan horses. Confining those programs can protect the rest of your system from any viruses, Trojan horses, or other security breaches that they might include.

In Technique 15, we show you how to install User Mode Linux; be sure to review that technique before you go much further. In this technique, we show you how to use UML to create a defensive boundary of protection between vulnerable software and your system. UML can save you from having to repair damage to your system, whether accidental or intentional.

If you've searched around on the Web for information about creating jails, you've probably seen references to chroot jails. chroot jails are notoriously difficult to create and offer limited protection. In this technique, we show you how to build a whole penitentiary with UML instead. UML jails are easier to build and manage, and provide a stronger line of defense than chroot jails.

Who Belongs in Jail?

In the real world, troublemakers belong in jail. In the world of computer software, potentially bad or vulnerable programs belong in jail. The programs and data you're trying to protect remain outside the jail, beyond the reach of intruders. A UML jail acts as a security barrier protecting the sensitive data and programs on your system from hackers, Trojan horses, and viruses that might come in by way of a back door — through servers or through software that might be a bit suspicious.

Good candidates for confinement in a UML jail include the following:

- ✔ All kinds of servers, including mail, data, FTP, and Web servers

- ✔ Downloaded but potentially vulnerable software

 Technique 18 shows you how to check the signature key on downloaded software with `rpm -V`. Checking the signature ensures that the software came from a reliable source (or at least from the same person who claims to have built the software). Check it out — protecting your system is worth the time.

The files that belong *outside* the jail are the files that need protecting:

- ✔ Password files
- ✔ Configuration files
- ✔ Data files
- ✔ Anything *really* important

By putting these files outside the jail, you protect them from the jailed programs and from anyone who might break into the programs in the jail. With a UML jail, you create a defensive barrier to protect the files outside the jail from both the programs in the jail, and the users with access to those programs.

In the sections that follow, we explain how to set up a UML jail and install a simple Apache server in the jail. It's a great way to use a UML jail, and you can have a secure server up and running in no time.

Using UML to Jail Programs

UML is a jail in and of itself — an isolated environment where you can run programs without the programs having easy access to the rest of your system files. ADIOS installs four different UML configurations in your KDE menu: LIDS Off, LIDS On, SELinux Permissive, and SELinux Enforcing. LIDS and SELinux are hardening tools that further clamp down on vulnerabilities in a Linux system (in this case, a UML VM).

Check out Technique 15 for quick installation instructions for UML.

We tell you more about LIDS in Technique 61, but for now, here's a quick summary: LIDS takes away the superhuman powers of the superuser. When you're running in LIDS On mode, LIDS doles out superuser privileges to specific programs (hopefully programs that you trust) rather than give every possible privilege to someone who knows (or absconds with) your `root` password. The big advantage to LIDS is that it protects your system (or your jail) against a hacker who somehow manages to impersonate user `root`.

With a few easy steps, you can isolate your host system, protecting it from adventurous hackers, while still offering network services to the outside world. If anyone *does* manage to compromise your server, that person has access only to the files and programs that you've installed in the jail. If you keep a trusted backup of your UML jail, recovering from an intrusion is trivial.

To create a UML jail, follow these steps:

1. Open the main KDE menu and choose User Mode Linux⇨LIDS On.

2. When the happy penguin appears, log in as user `root` (the password is `12qwaszx`) (see Figure 58-1).

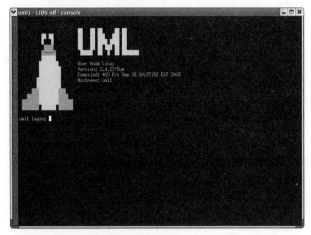

• **Figure 58-1: The UML login screen.**

When you're inside a UML VM, you have complete access to the *host* file system through the directory `/mnt/host`. If you peek at `/mnt/host`, you'll see subdirectories like `/mnt/host/bin`, `/mnt/host/etc`, `/mnt/host/usr`, and `/mnt/host/home`. Those directories correspond to the `/bin`, `/etc`, `/usr`, and `/home` directories on the host computer.

That's not a good arrangement when you're trying to block off access to those files.

3. To close that security hole, find a directory that you *do* want to expose to the jail (or better yet, just create an empty directory) and grant the VM access to that directory instead.

For example, create a staging area like this:

```
# mkdir /tmp/uml/jail
```

Run that command in the host, not in the UML VM.

 Be sure that the `/tmp/uml/jail` directory contains no symbolic links to the rest of the host system. Use the `ls -l` command to list the directory contents; if any of the permissions begin with an `l`, they're symbolic links and should be deleted.

Any files that you put into `/tmp/uml/jail` will appear inside the VM in the directory `/mnt/host`.

After you create the jail and add files to it, adjust the script that boots your VM:

1. Open the file `/usr/bin/uml` with your favorite editor.

2. Find the line (near the top of the file) that says

```
LIDS_KERNEL=uml_linux_lids
```

3. Change the line to read

```
LIDS_KERNEL="uml_linux_lids
    hostfs=/tmp/uml/jail"
```

 Don't forget the quotes, or your UML VM won't boot.

4. Find the line that says

```
SELINUX_KERNEL=uml_linux_selinux
```

This line should be just below the line in Step 2.

5. Change the line to read

```
SELINUX_KERNEL="uml_linux_selinux
    hostfs=/tmp/uml/jail"
```

6. Save your work and close the editor.

Now you can easily copy files between the host and the VM to populate your UML jail. You can copy files into (or out of) `/tmp/uml/jail` from your host system. Inside the VM, copy files into (or out of) `/mnt/host`. It doesn't get any quicker or easier than that.

Actually, it *does* get a bit quicker. Open a terminal window and grant yourself superuser privileges. Start two Konqueror (or Nautilus) sessions by typing in konqueror (or nautilus) at the command line. With one browser window open to /tmp/uml/jail, and the other browsing for the programs or files you want to add, you can populate your UML jail in no time!

When you need to add software to your new UML jail, you can copy program files in at the command line, or use your browser. Either way, you'll find it a snap to populate the Apache server you set up later in this technique.

Changing the Default Password to the Jail

The UML VM comes with a simple and easy-to-remember default password that works as both the root login and the LIDS password. That might be handy at first, but you should change it quick: It's easy for *everyone* to remember, even the bad guys.

To change the LIDS password, follow these steps:

1. **Open the main KDE menu and choose User Mode Linux⇨LIDS Off.**

2. **Log in using the default password.**

 The default password is 12qwaszx.

3. **Enter the following command:**
```
# lidsconf -P
```

4. **When prompted, enter a new password and then reenter the new password.**

5. **Stop the UML VM with the** halt **command.**

6. **Start UML again with LIDS on. Open the main KDE menu and choose User Mode Linux⇨ LIDS On.**

That's all there is to it.

 To change the root password, log in to the UML VM as root, and use the passwd command, just like you normally would.

Installing New Software and Resolving Conflicts

After you set up the jail and change the default password, your new UML jail is ready for software. Remember, any software you need to run (and manage) inside your new jail must be installed in the jail. You can't reach into the outside world to borrow utilities anymore.

One thing you might want to install into your UML jail is Apache (or, more precisely, the Apache httpd Web server). The Apache RPM package is included in most Linux distributions.

The following steps explain how to install the Apache RPM in the UML jail, but you can modify these steps for any program:

1. **From your host machine, copy the RPM package from the distribution CD to the UML VM:**
```
# cp httpd-2.0.47-10.i386.rpm
  /tmp/uml/jail
```

2. **Move into the UML jail and make your session a LIDS off session with the following command:**
```
# lidsadm -S -- -LIDS
```

This loosens restrictions on the superuser account while you do system maintenance.

3. **Move to the directory containing the RPM package:**

```
# cd /mnt/host
```

4. **Install the RPM package with the following command:**

```
# rpm -Uvh httpd-2.0.47-10.i386.rpm
```

5. **Start the httpd daemon by entering this command:**

```
# service httpd start
```

> When you start the httpd daemon, you may get a series of LIDS violation reports. You need to resolve any conflicts with the LIDS security issues before your server can run.

You are likely to encounter the following errors:

```
Violated CAP_NET_BIND_SERVICE
Trying to bind port 443
Attempt to unlink /etc/httpd/logs
```

To resolve these errors, follow these steps:

1. **Give yourself a LIDS off session with the following command:**

```
# lidsadm -S -- -LIDS
```

2. **Resolve the first two error messages with these commands:**

```
# lidsconf -A -s /usr/sbin/httpd -o
   CAP_NET_BIND_SERVICE 80-80 -j GRANT
# lidsconf -A -s /usr/sbin/httpd -o
   CAP_NET_BIND_SERVICE 443-443 -j GRANT
```

You've just granted httpd the right to service ports 80 and 443.

3. **Resolve the third error message with the following command:**

```
# lidsconf -A -s /usr/sbin/httpd -o
   /etc/httpd/logs -j WRITE
```

You've just given Apache the right to modify its own logs.

4. **Reload the LIDS configuration database:**

```
# lidsadm -S -- +RELOAD_CONF
```

5. **Restart the Web server daemon:**

```
# service httpd start
```

When httpd starts, it tells you the IP address of the Apache session. Make a note of this IP address because you'll need it in a moment.

6. **Return to a LIDS on session with the following command:**

```
# lidsadm -S -- +LIDS
```

7. **Enter the LIDS password, and you're running the Apache server in a secure environment.**

8. **To verify that Apache is running, open a browser on the host machine and enter the IP address of the service in the Location field:**

```
http://192.168.202.1
```

The Apache test screen opens, confirming the server is running. The service isn't configured yet — you find out how to do that in Technique 42. The service is secure though.

> Use the same technique to install other RPM packages. You may have different LIDS conflicts to resolve — see Technique 61 for more information about LIDS.

> To make a quick backup of your UML VM, just back up the cow file in /tmp/uml. See Technique 15 for more information about cow files.

Technique 59

Troubleshooting Persnickety Programs

Save Time By

- ✔ Using lsof to find open files
- ✔ Using strace to track down trouble spots
- ✔ Watching your programs with ltrace
- ✔ Recording memory usage errors with valgrind

Linux is a fairly mature operating system. In the early days of Linux development, users found problems everywhere they turned. That's not to say that Linux is any different from other operating systems; it takes time to iron out the wrinkles in any program. In fact, the "super-buggy" stage of Linux development was remarkably short, and you can now run a Linux system for months at a time without encountering a bug. Often, the problems that you run into aren't really bugs — they're configuration problems.

Tracking down the cause of a problem in a program (whether it's a bug or a configuration issue) can be tricky, but Linux has a number of tools that can help.

The lsof command shows you information about open files, open devices, and open network connections. Ever tried to unmount a CD and found that some process has a file open on the CD drive? lsof is the answer. Need to create a clean backup of a complex database? Use lsof to make sure that your database is not in use.

We also introduce you to two related tools:

- ✔ strace reaches inside a program and shows you a complete list of all the *system calls* (calls into the Linux kernel) made by that program. You can browse through the log produced by strace to find which files are opened by the program causing problems. Configuration problems often appear because a file is missing or protected too strongly. If you have a program that's reading configuration information from a mysterious location, use strace to find the hidden files.

- ✔ ltrace is similar to strace. While strace logs all system calls, ltrace displays calls made to shared libraries. To a programmer, Linux is more than just a kernel. It's also a huge collection of code libraries, written by others, but designed to share among many different programs. Shared libraries take care of operations like memory allocation, encryption, compression, GUI interaction — just about everything that *doesn't* happen in the kernel. Watching the library calls made by a program can help pin down a configuration error whether the problem trips up the kernel (strace) or a shared library (ltrace).

Finally, we show you a tool that can help *somebody else* track down a bug. `valgrind` watches running programs for memory usage errors and produces a report that can show a developer *exactly* where a program gets whacked. If you're a developer, `valgrind` makes it easy to track down intermittent problems. If not, run `valgrind` and send the report to the developer of the program that you're trying to use.

In this technique, we introduce you to a few diagnostic tools that you should keep in your troubleshooting toolbox. Each tool exposes different information, so each one is useful in tracking down a particular type of problem. Using these tools together, you can make quick work of troubleshooting difficult programs.

Using lsof to Find Out Which Files Are Open

Linux is pretty forgiving when it comes to file sharing. In most cases, two (or more) users can work on the same file at the same time (don't try that with a text editor though). You can share devices, too. For example, mount a CD, and anyone with the proper privileges can access the content, even if you're using the CD at the same time. Sometimes, however, a device (or a file) can't be shared.

Say that you're in the middle of burning a multisession CD using a program like `k3b`. You've just finished burning the first track, you've selected the files you want to burn to the second session, you click the Burn button, and you're rewarded with the following error messages:

```
Could not retrieve multisession
   information from disk
The disk is either empty or not appendable
```

Now, you know that the CD is not empty, and you're pretty sure that you selected Start Multisession when you burned the first track. Just to make sure the disc really has something already on it, you try to mount the CD at the command line:

```
# mount /dev/cdrom /mnt/cdrom
mount: /dev/cdrom already mounted
```

That looks pretty fishy — Linux thinks that someone has already mounted the CD. Try to unmount the CD:

```
# umount /dev/cdrom
umount: /mnt/cdrom: device is busy
```

That explains the original error message (well, sort of — that's not a very helpful error message). How do you find the culprit? Use the `lsof` command. `lsof` provides information about open files. The `lsof` command operates in three modes:

- If you run `lsof` without any arguments, you're greeted with a (very long) list of all the open files, devices, and network connections on your system.

- Give `lsof` the name of a file, directory, or device, and you see a list of all the processes currently using that file.

- Finally, if you give `lsof` a process ID, it shows you all the files being used by that process.

Use the second form to find out who's using your CD drive:

```
# /usr/sbin/lsof /dev/cdrom
COMMAND  PID  USER    FD    NAME
bash     1406 freddie cwd   /mnt/cdrom
```

Aha! `freddie` has managed to mount the CD just after you finished burning the first session. The `cwd` (in the column labeled `FD`) tells you that the current working directory of `freddie`'s `bash` session is `/mnt/cdrom`.

 Check out Technique 36 for the complete lowdown on `lsof`.

Now that you know who's using your CD drive, you can ask him to unmount the drive and let you continue. Drop an e-mail to the developers suggesting a more meaningful error message while you're burning the next track.

Debugging Your Environment with strace

Software problems can be subtle. Every once in a while, you run into a program that worked yesterday but refuses to work today. When that happens, start out by assuming that the program didn't suddenly break just because it happens to be Friday the 13th. Find out what's changed in your environment.

In the preceding section, you saw that the `lsof` command can tell you which files are *currently* opened by a process, but it has one drawback: It won't tell you about files that the process tried to open, but failed. Fortunately, Linux has another tool that can tell you much more about a process: `strace`.

The `strace` command reaches into a running program and exposes all the interaction between the program and the operating system. You can find out a lot from `strace`, but you can also get lost in the mass of data. Here's how we recently used `strace` (and its cousin `ltrace`) to track down a problem. We wanted to download an RPM package using `wget` (see Technique 14) and found that `wget` was getting stuck somewhere: It simply refused to connect to the remote server.

Here's the command that we used:

```
$ wget http://www.example.com/package.rpm
```

This command *should* connect to the `www.example.com` Web server and download the file named `package.rpm`. To use `strace` to track down the problem, simply run the command that you want to watch, but put the word `strace` at the start of the command line, like this:

```
$ strace wget http://www.example.com/
  package.rpm
```

`strace` runs the program (`wget`) for us and starts tracing all the *system* calls (calls to the kernel). Because we know that `wget` is hanging (just stopping) after a while, we let `strace` messages scroll by and hope that the display pauses after a while.

Eventually (after a few seconds), we notice that `wget` seems to get stuck in a loop, repeating the system calls shown in Listing 59-1.

We *could* read up on all the functions shown in Listing 59-1, trying to figure out what `wget` is doing, but we noticed that two functions seem to be delaying the loop. Because we're looking for something that causes a delay, it makes sense to focus on those functions first: `nanosleep()` and `connect()`. The man page for `nanosleep` tells us that `nanosleep` "pauses execution for a specified time." That doesn't sound like a bug — `wget` would not include a call to `nanosleep()` unless it was required. The second function, `connect()`, looks more promising.

It's difficult to tell from the `strace` output, but `wget` calls `connect()` with three arguments: 3, an IP address (`192.168.0.22`), and 16. A quick glance at the manual confirms that `connect()` does in fact expect three parameters: a socket (3), a server address (`192.168.0.22`), and the length of the server address (16). If you look closely at the end of Listing 59-1, you'll see that `connect()` returns an error: `EHOSTUNREACH` (`No route to host`).

Next, we ping `www.example.com` and notice two interesting points (see Listing 59-2):

- ✔ We *can* connect to `www.example.com` (that is, `ping` is not reporting an `EHOSTUNREACH` error like `wget` did).

- ✔ The IP address of `www.example.com` is `192.0.34.166`, but wget is trying to connect to a different host (`192.168.0.22`). Why?

To paraphrase Lewis Carroll, fishier and fishier. Time for a new tool: `ltrace`.

LISTING 59-1: STRACE DISPLAYS WGET SYSTEM CALLS

```
...
time(NULL)                                = 1079184678
rt_sigprocmask(SIG_BLOCK, [CHLD], [], 8)  = 0
rt_sigaction(SIGCHLD, NULL, {SIG_DFL}, 8) = 0
rt_sigprocmask(SIG_SETMASK, [], NULL, 8)  = 0
nanosleep({2, 0}, {2, 0})                 = 0
time(NULL)                                = 1079184680
access("-", F_OK)                         = -1 ENOENT (No such file or directory)
socket(PF_INET, SOCK_STREAM, IPPROTO_IP)  = 3
connect(3, {sa_family=AF_INET, sin_port=htons(9877), \
        sin_addr=inet_addr("192.168.0.22")}, 16) = -1 EHOSTUNREACH (No route to host)
close(3)
    ...
```

LISTING 59-2: PINGING WWW.EXAMPLE.COM

```
$ ping www.example.com
PING www.example.com (192.0.34.166) 56(84) bytes of data.
64 bytes from www.example.com (192.0.34.166): icmp_seq=0 ttl=54 time=736 ms
64 bytes from www.example.com (192.0.34.166): icmp_seq=1 ttl=54 time=802 ms
64 bytes from www.example.com (192.0.34.166): icmp_seq=2 ttl=54 time=756 ms
    ...
```

Investigating Programs with ltrace

strace shows you the system calls that a program makes — calls into the Linux kernel. ltrace is another program that lets you peek under the hood of a running program. ltrace displays a running log of the shared-library calls made by a program. A shared library is a collection of functions that provide common functionality to many programs. The C runtime library is a shared library. The KDE graphical toolkit is a shared library (so is the GNOME library, GTK).

To run ltrace, use the same technique that you use to run strace. Just prefix the command that you want to watch with the word ltrace:

```
$ ltrace wget \
  http://www.example.com/package.rpm
```

The output from ltrace is usually more voluminous than strace, but it's often more interesting. If you run ltrace, you'll probably notice that the display is whizzing by too fast to read. Press Ctrl-C to stop the program and then change the command line to this:

```
$ ltrace -o /tmp/wget.trc wget \
  http://www.example.com/package.rpm
```

The -o *filename* option redirects ltrace output to the named file (in this case, /tmp/wget.trc). A nice side effect of the -o *filename* option is that normal output from wget is clearly displayed rather than buried in ltrace output.

After letting wget (and ltrace) run for a few moments, we cancel the program by pressing Ctrl-C and then start browsing through the log.

Before going much further, here's a quick reminder of how we got here:

✔ We're trying to download a package from www.example.com, and the wget command is hanging.

✔ strace shows that wget is spending a lot of time trying to reach host 192.168.0.22.

✔ The call to connect (192.168.0.22) is failing with a "no route to host" error.

✔ ping reveals that wget is trying to connect to the wrong host.

Because we're interested in finding out why wget is trying to connect to the wrong host, we search for 192.168.0.22 in the ltrace log and find a section that looks like this:

```
...
memcpy(0x0866c985, "", 0)  = 0x0866c985
getenv("http_proxy") = "192.168.0.22:9877"
strlen("192.168.0.22:9877")= 17
malloc(25)              = 0x0866c990?
...
```

The first reference tells us that the getenv() function returned 192.168.0.22:9877. The man page for getenv() states that getenv() returns the value of an environment variable; in this case, the environment variable is named http_proxy. Now we're getting somewhere. A quick check shows that we do in fact have an environment variable named http_proxy and its value is indeed 192.168.0.22:9877:

```
$ echo $http_proxy
192.168.0.22:9877
```

The documentation for wget explains that the http_proxy environment variable specifies a *proxy server* (a server that carries out network requests on behalf of another computer). Now we know where wget is getting the mystery IP address. The solution to this problem is simply to remove the environment variable and try again, as shown in the following example:

```
$ unset http_proxy
$ wget http://www.example.com/package.rpm
--10:48:38--  http://www.example.com/
   package.rpm
           => `package.rpm'
Resolving www.example.com... done.
Connecting to
   www.example.com[192.0.34.166]:80...
   connected.
HTTP request sent, awaiting response...
...
```

Problem solved — the host 192.168.0.22 is a computer on our local network that we were using to test out proxy server software.

Handy strace and ltrace Options

strace and ltrace are both powerful tools, but they can generate a ton of output. Table 59-1 lists a few command line options that make strace easier to use.

TABLE 59-1: HANDY STRACE OPTIONS

Option	What It Does
-o *filename*	Redirects the strace log to *filename*. You can browse through the strace log after the program completes, or you can follow along by opening a second terminal window and running the command tail -f *filename*.
-f	Forces strace to trace child (and grandchild, great grandchild, and so on) processes spawned by the program you're tracing.
-v	Tells strace to print complete structure content rather than an abbreviated (space-saving) version.
-s *size*	This option tells strace to print, at most, *size* characters when displaying string arguments. (The default value is 32, and that may be too short for some programs.)

Option	What It Does
-e trace=file	Forces strace to trace functions that expect a filename argument (this includes functions like open, unlink, and so on). Use this option to see which files a program uses.
-e trace=network	Displays all network-related system calls.
-p process-ID	Attaches strace to a running process, identified by process-ID. (You must have the proper privileges to use this option.)

ltrace has similar options, listed in Table 59-2.

TABLE 59-2: HANDY LTRACE OPTIONS

Option	What It Does
-f	Forces ltrace to trace child (and grandchild, great grandchild, and so on) processes spawned by the program you're tracing.
-S	Displays system calls (similar to strace) as well as calls to functions defined in shared libraries.
-C	*Demangles* the name of each C++ function. (C++ function names are *mangled* by the C++ compiler, making them difficult to read without special treatment.)
-s size	This option tells ltrace to print, at most, size characters when displaying string arguments. (The default value is 32, and that may be too short for some programs.)
-n indent	Indents nested function calls by indent spaces. (This option makes it easier to read complex logs.)
-e function1, function2,...	Traces only calls to the named functions.
-e !function1, function2,...	Forces ltrace to ignore calls to function1, function2, and so on.
-l library	Traces calls to functions defined in the given library. (For example, to see calls to the libz compression library, use the option -l /usr/lib/libz.so.1.)

 That last option (-l *library*) is bit tricky because you have to know the complete pathname of the library that you're interested in. Use ldd to find out which shared libraries are used by a particular program. For example, to find the shared libraries required by wget, use the following command:

```
$ ldd $(which wget)
libssl.so.4 => /lib/libssl.so.4
libcrypto.so.4 => /lib/libcrypto.so.4
libgssapi_krb5.so.2 => /usr/lib/
    libgssapi_krb5.so.2
libkrb5.so.3 => /usr/lib/libkrb5.so.3
libcom_err.so.2 => /lib/libcom_err.so.2
libk5crypto.so.3 =>
    /usr/lib/libk5crypto.so.3
libresolv.so.2 => /lib/libresolv.so.2
libdl.so.2 => /lib/libdl.so.2
libz.so.1 => /usr/lib/libz.so.1
libc.so.6 => /lib/tls/libc.so.6
/lib/ld-linux.so.2 => /lib/ld-
    linux.so.2
```

Recording Program Errors with valgrind

Sometimes, buggy code is just, well, buggy. You can't get a program to run properly, and you've done everything you can to ensure that the configuration and environment are correct. Time for another tool.

Unless you're willing to read through the source code, compile your own copy, and get down and dirty with a debugger, the best thing you can do is to gather information for the developers.

valgrind is a programmer's dream tool. valgrind runs your program and watches for programming errors such as the use of uninitialized memory, use of invalid memory regions, and memory leaks.

The valgrind package is *not* included with most distributions, but you can easily find valgrind RPM packages on the Web. (We found one at dag.wieers. com/packages/valgrind.)

After you've installed `valgrind`, it's easy to use. Just run your program as usual, but put `valgrind` at the beginning of the command line, like this:

```
$ valgrind xmms
```

When you `valgrind` a program, `valgrind` messages are sent to the standard error stream (which is usually connected to your terminal window), so they can get lost in the output from the program that you're watching. You can redirect `valgrind` messages to a file with the `--logfile=`*filename* option:

```
$ valgrind --logfile=/tmp/xmms.vg xmms
```

`valgrind` works by running your program on a synthetic, software-only CPU and watching all memory references. If your program uses an invalid hunk of memory, `valgrind` complains.

 Your program will run *many, many* times slower on the synthetic CPU than it does on the real CPU.

Listing 59-3 shows a few sample error messages that `valgrind` produced when we ran the `xmms` media player.

Each message starts with a one-line description of the error encountered and then a stack dump that shows what the program was doing at the time the error occurred. (The `==10247==` at the beginning of each line is the process ID of the program that you're watching.)

Now that you have a collection of `valgrind` messages, what do you do with them?

- ✔ **If you're a programmer and you're interested in helping out the developers,** read through the documentation at the `valgrind` Web site (`valgrind.kde.org`). You'll find out how to connect `valgrind` to a source-code debugger like `gdb`.

- ✔ **If you're not a programmer,** find the Web site that deals with your program and search around for a mailing list or some other mechanism for reporting bugs. When you send in a bug report, include the `valgrind` log and as much information as possible about your environment (especially the version number of the program you're using). You'll be doing the developers a big favor by telling them exactly *where* the bug was encountered.

LISTING 59-3: VALGRIND'ING XMMS

```
==10247== Syscall param write(buf) contains uninitialised or unaddressable byte(s)
==10247==    at 0x57FC48: __GI___libc_write (in /lib/libc-2.3.2.so)
==10247==    by 0xAEC7DF: (within /usr/X11R6/lib/libICE.so.6.3)
==10247==    by 0xAED58E: _IceTransWrite (in /usr/X11R6/lib/libICE.so.6.3)
==10247==    by 0xAE430A: _IceWrite (in /usr/X11R6/lib/libICE.so.6.3)
==10247==    Address 0x21CA45C is 12 bytes inside a block of size 1024 alloc'd
==10247==    at 0x992B00: calloc (vg_replace_malloc.c:284)
==10247==    by 0xAE141F: IceOpenConnection (in /usr/X11R6/lib/libICE.so.6.3)
==10247==    by 0xAD52B8: SmcOpenConnection (in /usr/X11R6/lib/libSM.so.6.0)
==10247==    by 0x80A156D: sm_init (in /usr/bin/xmms)

==10247==
==10247== Conditional jump or move depends on uninitialised value(s)
==10247==    at 0x1BA72E: (within /usr/lib/libgtk-1.2.so.0.9.1)
==10247==    by 0x1C28F6: (within /usr/lib/libgtk-1.2.so.0.9.1)
==10247==    by 0x1C3895: gtk_marshal_BOOL__POINTER (in /usr/lib/libgtk-1.2.so.0.9.1)
==10247==    by 0x18E0F9: (within /usr/lib/libgtk-1.2.so.0.9.1)
```

Technique 60

Securing the Fort with Bastille

Save Time By

- ✔ Using Bastille to build a strong line of defense
- ✔ Using the Bastille firewall to create robust customized security
- ✔ Setting up psad to keep an eye on your ports
- ✔ Keeping an eye on the official computer security experts

Faith-based security isn't too dependable when it comes to computer systems. Building a strong line of defense is your system's best protection from hackers. The open-source project, Bastille, is a real asset to have in your repertoire of security programs.

Bastille uses a question-and-answer session to choose a series of configuration changes for your system. Bastille implements these changes after the questions end. You could make all the changes manually, one file at a time, but the process is much quicker (and easier) with Bastille leading the way.

In addition to making some basic security changes to take away unneeded privileges from non-root users and tightening account security, Bastille can create a very tight firewall and an optional port scan detector to tell you if intruders are probing your system for vulnerabilities. You can use Bastille to harden your entire security system in a fraction of the time it would take you to find all the individual files and tools to create the same level of security. You can also go back and modify the changes that Bastille has implemented on your system if you find security to be too tight for your users. With Bastille, you have flexibility.

In this technique, we walk you through the question-and-answer session to set up Bastille on your system. The defaults recommended by Bastille are usually pretty good, but we point out a few things that you might want to change to tighten up your system even more.

Hardening Your Hat with Bastille

The open-source movement has spawned a lot of admirable projects, among them is the security implementation tool Bastille. Bastille is a security wizard, guiding you through a series of questions and deciding on a course of action that will create a secure but usable system for you and your users.

Bastille is a tremendous timesaver. It takes a while to thoughtfully answer all of its questions, but if you had to track down each security issue that Bastille handles, it would take you days!

Downloading and installing Bastille and its dependencies

 Use Synaptic to download and install Bastille in one easy step. Start Synaptic and then enter `bastille` in the Find box. Install the `bastille-linux` package, and you're ready to go! Technique 19 is all about installing and using Synaptic — check it out!

To download and install the Bastille RPM package without Synaptic, follow these steps:

1. **Open your browser and surf to the official Bastille Web site:**

    www.bastille-linux.org/

2. **Scroll down the page, and click the Download link labeled** `Bastille RPM`.

You're escorted to the download page for the Bastille RPM package at SourceForge.net.

3. **Click the download link nearest to your geographical location to download the following package:**

    Bastille-2.1.1-1.0.i386.rpm

4. **When the download manager opens, save the package to your home directory.**

To run Bastille with a graphical interface, you also need to install the Perl toolkit. To download the Perl toolkit RPM package, follow these steps:

1. **Return to the Download/Install Bastille 2.x page.**

You can use your browser's Back button if you just followed the preceding steps.

2. **Click the Consulting This Table link. Then click the link for the most recent** `perl-Tk` **(Graphical) package for your Linux distribution.**

3. **Save the package to your home directory.**

Now you're done downloading the packages you need and can begin installing them.

To install the packages, open a terminal window and give yourself superuser privileges with the `su -` command. Return to your home directory and install the packages you've just downloaded with the command:

    # rpm -Uhv packagenames

 Use command completion (described in Technique 5) to make quick work of typing in complex commands. Enter the `rpm -Uhv` portion of the command, then a space, and then the first few letters of the package name. Then press the Tab key to complete the name.

Welcome to the Bastille

To run Bastille, open a terminal window and give yourself superuser privileges with the `su -` command. Enter `bastille` and press Enter.

 The first time you run Bastille, you'll see a Copyright and Disclaimer notice. Read the document quickly (you have just five minutes to respond), type `accept` at the `>` prompt, and press Enter.

The Bastille window opens, as shown in Figure 60-1.

The Title Screen contains a simple explanation of the navigational rules for Bastille. Check them out and then click OK.

You'll find the configuration questions in the Question frame, which is the top frame of the window. The Explanation frame displays a brief explanation of the question to help guide your choices.

Enter your answers to questions in the Answer frame, which is located below the explanation. The Modules frame on the left side of the window shows your progress as you move through the series of analysis questions. As you complete the questions in each module, Bastille places a check mark next to the module name to show your progress.

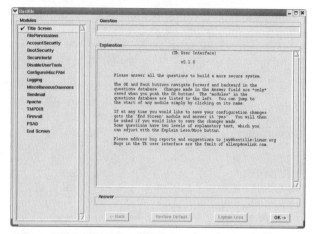

• **Figure 60-1:** Welcome to Bastille.

Brace yourself — we're moving on to the questions.

Addressing file permission issues

Would you like to set more restrictive permissions on the administration utilities? (see Figure 60-2).

If you live on a good-sized system (or a small system with crafty users), it's a good idea to select the Yes radio button in the Answer frame of the window. You can hand out the privileges that your users need individually with sudo (see Techniques 31 and 32).

Click the OK button to continue.

Clamping down on SUID privileges

The next series of questions guides Bastille through disabling SUID permissions for some programs so that only user root can run those programs. Click OK to move on.

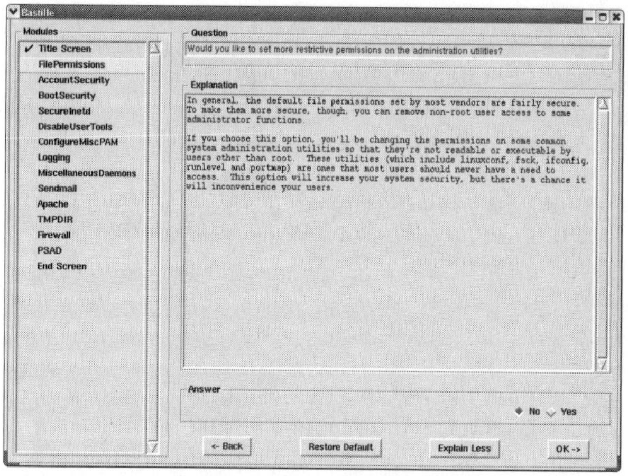

• **Figure 60-2:** Moving on to the questions.

Would you like to disable SUID status for mount/umount?

If you choose to disable SUID status, only user root can mount or unmount drives (including floppies, CDs, and tape drives). If your users don't need access to removable media in their daily work, it's generally a good idea to accept the default of Yes and click OK. This ensures that you won't have any surprise software loaded onto your system (or have media mysteriously vanish from the drives).

Would you like to disable SUID status for ping?

If ping is working properly, it's not a dangerous program. However, if some hacker finds a vulnerability in ping, you don't want ping granting superuser privileges to someone who exploits the security hole. Unless your users really need to check out the status of the network, accept the default response of Yes and click OK. You can still ping as long as you give yourself superuser privileges first.

Would you like to disable SUID status for at?

This is generally a good idea. Hackers can easily exploit at (a program that schedules jobs for later execution), and you can use Task Scheduler to do the scheduling work much quicker. Accept the default of Yes and click OK.

Technique 20 is all about setting up automatic services with Task Scheduler. You don't need at when you have a tool like Task Scheduler.

Would you like to disable the r-tools?

The r-tools make remote connections that are often less than secure. The r-tools are as follows:

- ✔ rsh

- ✔ remsh

- ✔ rcp

- ✔ rlogin

- ✔ rdist

Disable the SUID status for the tools — user root can still use them if need be. Insist that the non-root users on your system use ssh or distribute individual privileges to the r-tools as they're needed.

Would you like to disable SUID status for usernetctl?

usernetcl allows users to change network interfaces. Really, only the system administrator needs to control network interfaces. It's a good idea to accept the default answer of Yes and click OK.

Would you like to disable SUID status for traceroute?

Like ping, traceroute is a safe program — until someone finds a vulnerability. Unless your users are debugging your network, accept the default answer of Yes and click OK. The fewer SUID programs you leave lying around the better.

Would you like to disable SUID status for Xfree86?

If you're sure that a nonprivileged user will *never* log in to the console of your workstation, you can disable SUID for the Xfree86 server. We recommend answering No to this question.

Moving on to account security

Should Bastille disable clear-text r-protocols that use IP-based authentication?

The r-protocols use an authentication method that sends unencrypted passwords across your network where they can be intercepted and used by hackers to gain access to your network. The r-protocols also use IP-based authentication (an authentication protocol based on the address of the client). IP addresses are easily faked by crafty hackers.

If the r-protocols are enabled, your users can accidentally help a hacker access your system. We recommend that you disable the r-protocol tools altogether: Click Yes and then click OK.

Would you like to enforce password aging?

If a nefarious user manages to get a copy of your system password file, that person can attack your passwords with a *cracker* program that cycles through random (or not so random) combinations, trying to find a cleartext password that matches one of your encrypted passwords.

Programs that try to crack encrypted passwords can take *weeks* to run. If you use password aging, passwords are likely to expire before an intruder can crack them. It's a good idea to accept the default answer of Yes and click OK. If you enable password aging, you (and your users) will be prompted to change your password shortly before the password expires (or after it expires, if you haven't logged in for a while).

Would you like to restrict the use of cron to administrative accounts?

You should probably accept the default answer of Yes and click OK. The power of cron can be abused, and it's likely that most of your users won't need it.

Do you want to set the default umask?

The umask for every process is inherited from the user account that starts the process. The umask controls the permissions for a file; the permissions are assigned when the file is created. If the umask lets everyone read and write everything, your system isn't very secure. Accept the default answer of Yes and click OK.

What umask would you like to set for users on the system?

The umask setting affects file permissions. The default answer, 077, is the most secure setting. With a umask of 077, new files are protected so that only the file's owner is allowed read, write, or execute access. You may want to relax this setting a bit, depending on your work environment. If you're a tight-knit, trustworthy group that knows better than to keep any sensitive information in unencrypted files, you'll be safe enough with a lower umask setting. Technique 27 contains helpful information about interpreting and setting file permissions. Enter your umask level and click OK.

 Check out Technique 28 for some helpful ideas about encrypting documents.

Should we disallow root login on tty's 1-6?

This question is phrased a little strangely. If you answer Yes to this question (which we recommend), you must have physical access to your computer to log in as user root. That's a good idea because if intruders manage to steal your root password, they'll need to be seated at the console before they can use it (or, they'll have to steal a second, nonprivileged password as well).

Disabling root login on tty lines does not prevent you from gaining superuser privileges when you're logging in remotely; you'll just have to log in with a nonprivileged account first and then use su to give yourself superuser privileges.

We think this one's a good idea, so check the Yes box and click OK.

Making the boot process more secure

Would you like to password protect the GRUB prompt?

This is a touchy one. If you enable it, you've got a really secure system. But if you forget the boot password, you're out of luck; you pretty much need to reload the operating system at that point. We suggest choosing No, for safety's sake. While this may seem like you're leaving your boot process unprotected, you're really ensuring that you can get back in without completely reinstalling Linux from scratch if you accidentally forget your boot password. Click OK when you've made your choice.

 If you do choose to not password protect your boot prompt, be sure that you control physical access to your workstation. Anyone with physical access to your machine will be able to boot it if there is no GRUB password.

Would you like to disable CTRL-ALT-DELETE rebooting?

Many of these questions have to do with the physical security of your system. If your system is behind a locked door, you may want to leave some of these loopholes open for your use. We usually accept the default answer of No for the sake of convenience. That way, anyone with physical access to the workstation keyboard can reboot your computer.

Would you like to password protect single-user mode?

It's a good idea to protect single-user mode, especially if you've left Ctrl-Alt-Delete rebooting active. If single-user mode is unprotected, anyone with physical access to your computer can reboot your system, lock out all users (including you), and change the root password. If you do choose to password protect single-user mode, anyone choosing to boot into single-user mode will be prompted for a password at boot time. Accept the default answer of Yes and click OK.

Securing connection broker

The securelnetd server (`xinetd`) acts as a connection broker for a number of network services. `xinetd` listens for client requests coming in on specific ports and starts the associated server when a request arrives.

Would you like to set a default-deny on TCP Wrappers and xinetd?

If your computer has multiple network interfaces, you can define a default policy that determines whether your services are offered only to your local network, or provided to the world. It's a good idea to follow Bastille's recommendation and choose No. Click OK to continue.

Should Bastille ensure the telnet service does not run on this system?

Yes, please. `telnet` is *very* insecure and can give a hacker an easy way to break into your computer. You and your users will benefit from using `ssh` instead. Accept the default answer (Yes) and click OK.

Should Bastille ensure inetd's FTP service does not run on this system?

Unless you really need an FTP server, it's a good idea to accept the default answer of Yes. You can use the `scp` program to copy files securely instead (see Technique 33). Click OK.

Would you like to display "Authorized Use" messages at log-in time?

This isn't a bad idea. If you catch a cracker in your system, a "legaleeze" banner may help if you choose to prosecute. Accept the default answer of Yes and click OK.

The banner is placed in `/etc/issue`. Add specific information about your site to the banner. If you're running a corporate site, it's a good idea to seek legal advice about the banner verbiage.

Click OK to continue.

Who is responsible for granting authorization to use this machine?

Enter contact information in the Answer field and click OK.

Limiting compiler access

Would you like to disable the gcc compiler?

If you choose to disable the `gcc` compiler, hackers who do get into your system won't be able to compile troublemaking software without the `root` password. However, if your users regularly compile programs, they'll need access to `gcc`. Check the box next to the answer that best suits your company's scenario and then click OK.

Limiting access to hackers

Would you like to put limits on system resource usage?

A denial of service attack shuts down your system by tying up system resources. Limiting system resource usage can make most denial of service attacks somewhat ineffective. If you're on a machine shared by many users, it's a good idea to limit system resources. On your own personal machine, you may want to accept the default of No. Check the appropriate box and click OK.

Should we restrict console access to a small group of user accounts?

On some systems, if you log in at a console (as opposed to logging in across the Net), you gain special privileges (such as the ability to mount drives). Accept the default of No and click OK to continue.

Logging extra information

Would you like to add additional logging?

If you choose Yes, this setting enables additional logging. Kernel messages are sent to `/var/log/kernel`, and system errors and warnings are sent to

`/var/log/syslog`. You can also view the optional logs by pressing Ctrl-Alt-F7 and Ctrl-Alt-F8. These files won't interfere with the regular log files. Accept the default answer of Yes and click OK. Then click OK to continue.

`Do you have remote host logging?`

If you've configured your computer to write system log files to a remote host, click Yes. If not, click No and click OK to continue.

`What is the IP address of the machine you want to log to?`

If you answered Yes to the last question, enter the IP address of the remote machine and click OK.

Keeping the daemons in check

Bastille uses the answers to your questions in this module to decide if it's safe to disable daemons (background server processes) running on your system that might leave an open door for a hacker.

`Would you like to disable apmd?`

This daemon monitors battery power on notebook computers. If you frequently work *off the grid,* you may want to leave `apmd` turned on; otherwise, click OK to accept the default answer of Yes.

`Would you like to disable GPM?`

GPM is a daemon that makes the mouse work when you're running in console mode (that is, when you're not using X Windows). If you're planning on working in console mode, but want to retain your mouse functionality, click No; otherwise, choose Yes and click OK.

Securing sendmail

`Do you want to stop sendmail from running in daemon mode?`

You really only need to have `sendmail` running in daemon mode if you're running a mail server. If you're not running a mail server, accept the default answer of Yes and click OK.

`Would you like to run sendmail via cron to process the queue?`

If an outbound message doesn't make it through to its destination on the first try, choosing Yes schedules a `cron` job telling the mail queue to try again in 15 minutes. Accept the default answer of Yes and click OK.

`Would you like to bind the web server to listen only to the localhost?`

If you choose this option, only your machine can access your Apache Web server. It's kind of pointless unless you do a lot of Web development and need to preview your pages in a live server. Accept the default answer of No and click OK.

`Would you like to bind the web server to a particular interface?`

If you have two network cards, choose Yes to tell Apache to listen to only one card. This is particularly useful if you're hosting a Web server for in-house data distribution. Make your choice and click OK.

If you chose Yes, enter your card's IP address and click OK.

Closing the gaps in Apache

If you have an Apache server running on your system, you'll be prompted to answer a series of questions designed to better tailor the security surrounding your server.

The next few questions help close specific security gaps in Apache. Click OK to continue.

Would you like to deactivate the following of symbolic links?

Deactivating symbolic links helps prevent visitors from viewing files that are not included in the Web page directories. Accept the default answer of Yes and click OK.

Would you like to deactivate server-side includes?

A server-side include (SSI) is a program that generates or modifies an HTML Web page. If intruders manage to inject a Trojan server-side include program on your system, they can exploit your Web server to their liking. If you disable server-side includes, it's one less security risk. Accept the default answer of Yes and click OK.

Would you like to disable CGI scripts, at least for now?

If you're not using them, shut 'em down. Accept the default answer of Yes and click OK.

Would you like to disable indexes?

If you turn off the indexes, people can't discover the things that you've left lying around on your Web server. To access any page, the visitor needs to start with a specific address and then browse using links that you provide. If you leave automatic indexes enabled, Apache will happily create indexes on the fly, possibly exposing your dirty laundry. As a rule, we think it's a good idea to turn off automatic indexes. Check the box next to Yes and click OK.

Keeping temporary files safe

Would you like to install TMPDIR/TMP scripts?

This creates a safe temporary directory for each user. If you can't all share one temporary directory, you have the option to create individual directories. Based on your system usage, choose your option and click OK.

Building a better firewall

Would you like to run the packet filtering script?

If you choose this option, you're led through a series of questions to build and customize your firewall. Choose Yes and click OK if you want to configure a Bastille firewall. The Bastille firewall is a very robust and highly customized piece of software. We'll try to offer some guidance as you go, but you'll need to keep the requirements of your network in mind as you answer the questions.

Do you need the advanced networking options?

Generally, answer No if you're on a small system, and Yes if you deal with multiple interfaces or provide IP Masquerading services. Enter your choice and click OK.

DNS Servers:

Most Linux distributions use kernel version 2.4 (or later), so you can safely ignore this question. Just accept the default value and click OK.

Public Interfaces:

List the names of all the network interfaces connected to public networks. If you have an Ethernet card in your computer, type eth+. If you have a modem attached to your computer, type ppp+ slip+. If you have both, enter eth0 ppp+ slip+. Click OK to continue.

TCP services to audit:

Bastille wants to know which TCP services you want to log. Bastille logs connection attempts on the following services by default:

```
telnet ftp imap pop3 finger sunrpc exec
    login linuxconf ssh
```

But you can customize it to better suit your needs. Accept the default or customize the answer, and then click OK.

UDP services to audit:

Specify any UDP services that you want to log. The default connection is 31337, a well-known security hole. Add any ports you want to monitor or accept the default and then click OK.

ICMP services to audit:

Specify any ICMP services that you want to audit. This includes logging for connection attempts from services like `ping`. Unless you have a specific security concern that you want to address, accept the default and click OK.

TCP service names or port numbers to allow on public interfaces:

If you're running a Web server and want to allow public access, you need to make port 80 accessible to the public. Another port you may want to leave open is 22 — `ssh` gains access through port 22. Enter the port numbers in the Answer field (separated by a blank space) and click OK.

UDP service names or port numbers to allow on public interfaces:

If you're running caching or DNS servers, you need to allow access to port 53. For most workstations, leave this blank and click OK.

 You've likely just hit a blank window — no questions, no answers. This is a good time to get a cup of coffee and stretch. More questions are coming when you click OK.

Force passive mode?

This option determines how FTP clients on your system access other servers. Forcing passive mode is more secure, but is also somewhat inconvenient for your users. Unless you have a very high-profile network with serious security risks, it's probably a good idea to accept the default of No and click OK.

TCP services to block:

Bastille recommends a series of services you should consider blocking. You can find the names that correspond to the default entries in the file /etc/protocols. As Bastille says, this question is not important for 2.4 (and higher) kernels. Most distributions use a 2.4 (or higher) kernel, so we recommend accepting the default entry.

UDP services to block:

Like the TCP services, Bastille recommends the UDP services you should block. Click OK to accept the default.

ICMP allowed types:

The default recommendations from Bastille are good:

- ✔ `destination-unreachable`: Allows other servers to inform you when a connection fails
- ✔ `echo-reply`: Must be enabled for `ping` to work
- ✔ `time-exceeded`: Must be enabled for `traceroute` to work

Enable source address verification?

Enabling source address verification helps the kernel block traffic with falsified addresses. It's a *very* good idea to accept the default answer of Yes and click OK.

Break time again. Click OK to continue.

Reject method:

The reject method determines how the kernel deals with blocked traffic.

If you choose to reject the traffic, a remote machine feeling around for a connection gets a polite reply stating that the requested service is not available. The disadvantage of this kindness? Now potential intruders know you're out there if they want to launch an attack.

If you choose to deny the traffic, the connection is dropped without a reply to the visiting system. This gives you a bit of camouflage — potential intruders don't know you're there.

As a rule, we recommend accepting the default of DENY. Click OK to continue.

`Interfaces for DHCP queries:`

If you don't assign static IP addresses to your network interfaces (and most people don't), your computer uses DHCP (Dynamic Host Configuration Protocol) to configure the network. Enter the names of the interfaces that require DHCP configuration (you can leave the field blank if you're using a regular PPP modem connection for dial-up service). Click OK to continue.

`NTP servers to query:`

If you're using NTP (Network Time Protocol) to synchronize your network clocks, enter the host name of the NTP server in the Answer field. If not, leave the field blank and click OK to continue.

`ICMP types to disallow outbound:`

Disabling outbound ICMP types can help mask your system from unwanted system probes. Accept the default entries and click OK to continue.

`Should Bastille run the firewall and enable it at boot time?`

If you're not sitting in front of your computer's console, choose No; otherwise, you may lock yourself out of your own network. If you feel that your answers to the firewall configuration questions are accurate (and you're logged in to the console), choose Yes to start the firewall and enable it at boot time. Click OK to continue.

 The configuration file for your firewall is in `/etc/Bastille/bastille-firewall.cfg`. You can modify it later.

Port scanning with Bastille

If you have enabled the Bastille firewall, you can use PSAD (the Port Scan Attack Detector) to find out if someone is scanning your machines. To set up PSAD, check the Yes box and click OK.

`psad check interval:`

This interval (in seconds) is how often `psad` checks for denied packets. Accept the default of 15 seconds and click OK.

`Port range scan threshold:`

This setting determines the sensitivity of the `psad` setup. A setting of 1 allows one port to be scanned without triggering an alert. If a second scan occurs (within the `psad` check interval), an alert is sent. If you want `psad` to be fairly sensitive to scanning, accept the default of 1 and click OK.

`Enable scan persistence?`

If you choose Yes, `psad` keeps a listing of scanned ports in memory: An attacker trying to avoid detection by scanning your ports over a long period of time will trigger an alert. In most cases, accepting the default of No is adequate to catch intruders. Choose the level of security you're comfortable with and click OK to continue.

`Scan timeout:`

This is the length of time (in seconds) that `psad` keeps the data about a port scan. The default is 3600 seconds (or one hour). Enter a new value or accept the default, and then click OK.

`Show all scan signatures?`

When PSAD sends you a scan-alert e-mail, it includes a list of the scan signatures that it found. A *scan signature* is a pattern that PSAD finds in the attack. PSAD is preconfigured to recognize a number of well-known attach patterns.

If you answer Yes to this question, PSAD includes all signature matches in *every* e-mail. If you answer No to this question, PSAD e-mails only the signatures that triggered the scan alert. Make your choice and click OK to continue.

Danger Levels:

If PSAD detects a scan signature, it assigns a *danger level* based on the number of packets received. The higher the danger level, the higher the risk the intruder poses. The default values are reasonable, so we recommend that you just click OK to continue.

Email addresses:

Enter the e-mail address (or addresses) that should be notified if a problem occurs. If you enter more than one recipient, leave a single space between the addresses. Click OK to continue.

Email alert danger level:

By default, PSAD notifies you (via e-mail) when an attack of danger level 1 is detected. You can change the danger level to a higher number if you don't want to know about all the scans that are aimed at your system. Click OK to continue.

Alert on all new packets?

Accept the default of Yes to be informed of any new packets that are sent to your machine during the course of a reported scan. Click OK to continue.

Enable automatic blocking of scanning IP's?

This security feature actually poses some security threats. An intruder can pose as another computer and block your system from accessing that system by tripping the automatic blocking threshold.

If you're configuring a personal workstation, we recommend changing the answer to Yes (the default is No). If you're configuring a computer that provides network access to a number of users, accept the default of No and click OK.

Should Bastille enable psad at boot time?

If you're confident of your answers, click the Yes box before clicking OK.

 To manually start psad, **enter** # /etc/rc.d/init.d/psad start.

To manually stop psad, **enter** # /etc/rc.d/init.d/psad stop.

You're almost done!

When you reach the End Screen module, you're asked to confirm that you're finished making changes to the Bastille configuration (see Figure 60-3).

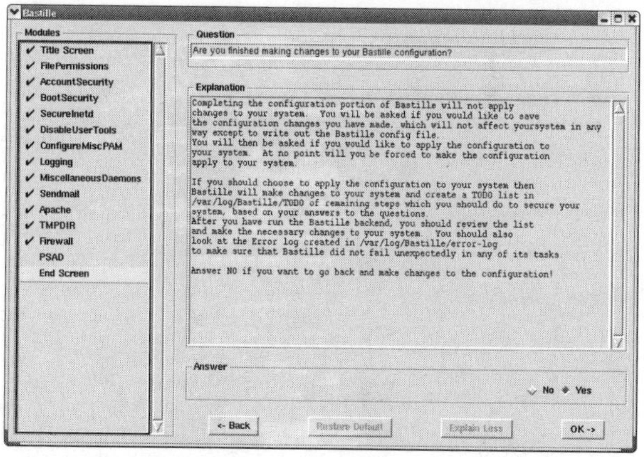

• **Figure 60-3:** You're almost finished.

1. **If you're satisfied with the configuration, check the Yes box and click OK.**

Double-click any of the module names to return to previous sections of the configuration to make changes.

A dialog opens, asking if you'd like to save the configuration changes (see Figure 60-4).

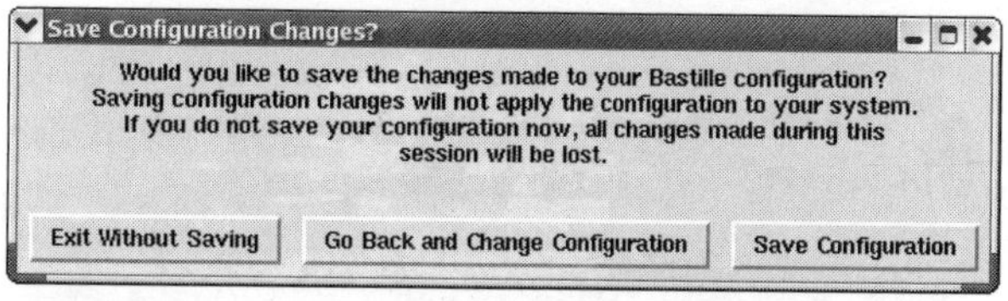

• **Figure 60-4:** Save your configuration changes.

2. **Click the Save Configuration button.**

The Finishing Up dialog opens, as shown in Figure 60-5.

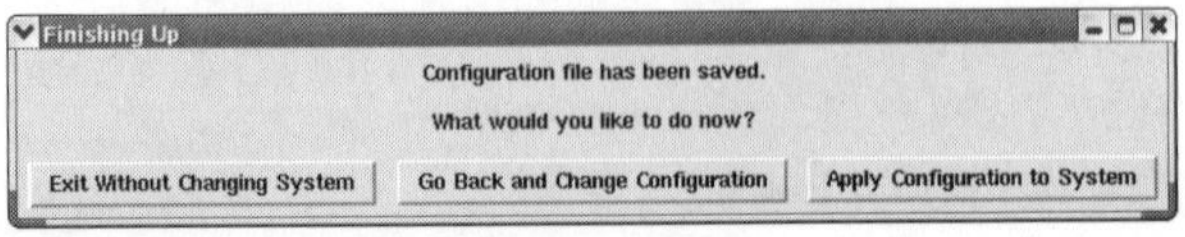

• **Figure 60-5:** The Finishing Up dialog.

3. **Click the Apply Configuration to System button.**

A window opens displaying programmer credits, as shown in Figure 60-6.

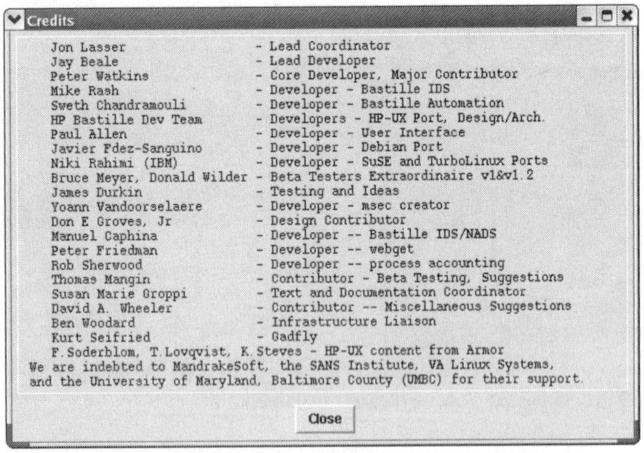

• **Figure 60-6:** These people worked hard to bring you Bastille.

4. **Pause for a moment to appreciate the work done by these dedicated developers and then click the Close button.**

A series of changes are made to your system as Bastille executes the changes to your configuration files.

If errors occur while Bastille applies your configuration choices, they're listed in the file `/var/log/Bastille/error-log`.

5. **Reboot your system to make the changes take effect.**

After rebooting, your system should be sturdier than ever before.

Keeping Abreast of Security Issues

Knowing about security problems before they strike is a great way to protect your system. The sooner you know about the vulnerabilities, the sooner you can take steps to block intruders from exploiting weaknesses.

The news media is pretty good about keeping the public informed of mainstream viruses and Trojan horses that are traveling through the Internet, but a few agencies are at the forefront of security. You can sign up for mailing lists or monitor their Web sites to stay informed of the most recent (and most obscure) security issues. Here are a few sites you may want to visit:

✔ **CERT Coordination Center at Carnegie Mellon University** (www.cert.org): This center created the first computer security incident response team. The advisories page is a great place to find the latest information on security issues affecting computer users.

✔ **U.S. Computer Emergency Readiness Team** (www.us-cert.gov): You can read about or report new vulnerabilities, or sign up to receive security information via e-mail.

✔ **U.S. Department of Energy Computer Incident Advisory Capability (CIAC)** (www.ciac.org/ciac): Watch its security listings for issues that could affect the well-being of your system.

✔ **Red Hat's listing of security alerts and advisories specific to Red Hat Linux** (www.redhat.com/solutions/security/news): Cruise through the lists online, or sign up for e-mail notification of problems that are specific to Red Hat products.

61
Technique

Creating a Second Line of Defense with LIDS

In a standard Linux distribution, either you're a superuser or you're not; there is no middle ground. You have all the privileges, powers, and responsibilities, or you have none of them. That's a pretty dangerous way to run a computer. Your users might need superuser privileges to mount a CD, perform server maintenance, or run a debugger, but you don't want the average Joe taking down your system with the `reboot` command or bypassing file permissions willy-nilly.

The Linux kernel picks apart the superuser's powers into individually named *capabilities*. With a normal Linux kernel, a superuser capability is enabled for all programs, or it's disabled for all programs — again, no middle ground. In this technique, we introduce you to LIDS (the Linux Intrusion Detection System). With LIDS, you can take away the privileges of the superuser, but grant access for individual programs so the power is there when you need it. Granting a capability to a program does *not* grant the capability to all users; you still have to be a superuser to use the capability. LIDS also lets you protect important data files and programs. When you protect a program (or data file) with LIDS, even the superuser can't touch it.

This technique is like carrying around a little piece of Kryptonite; an intruder who somehow gains superuser privileges on your computer magically loses his villainous powers. With LIDS, you can control, privilege-by-privilege what the superuser can do. Good passwords, strong firewalls, and an effective backup strategy are still important, but LIDS provides a second line of defense against intruders who somehow get a password they shouldn't have.

Turning LIDS On and Off

In a standard Linux kernel, you can disable individual capabilities, but any capability that you disable is completely unavailable. There's no way to let some programs use a capability and disable it for others. LIDS gives you the power to pick and choose.

Testing LIDS before Applying It to Your System

You can use LIDS to secure your computer, but it's a good idea to experiment in a UML virtual computer first. Fortunately, LIDS is bundled with the ADIOS UML distribution we talk about in Technique 15.

A quick way to find out just how good your potential system configuration will work for you is to make a practice run inside a UML VM.

Here's an overview of how testing in a UML VM works:

1. **Set up the system in a confined environment (a UML VM).**

   See Technique 15 for details on downloading, installing, and setting up LIDS in a UML VM.

2. **Test the LIDS configuration.**

   You find the details on configuring LIDS in the sections that follow.

3. **If you like the LIDS configuration in the VM, copy the access control list to your system.**

 A LIDS-enabled kernel runs in two distinct modes. In secure mode (called LIDS On mode), all the access control rules that you define are enforced. In nonsecure mode (LIDS Off), you're running a standard Linux kernel; LIDS has no effect in nonsecure mode. The easiest way to manage LIDS is to boot into LIDS Off mode, make the configuration changes that you want, and then boot back into LIDS On mode. Throughout this technique, we assume that you're using the ADIOS UML distribution. To boot in LIDS On mode, just open the KDE Menu and choose User Mode Linux⇨LIDS On; to boot in LIDS Off mode, choose User Mode Linux⇨LIDS Off.

Understanding the LIDS Access Control List

LIDS is controlled by a set of configuration files, typically stored in the /etc/lids directory. When you configure LIDS, you add *access control entries* to an *access control list* (we use the terms ACE and ACL, respectively). An ACE controls access to a file, a directory tree, or a superuser capability. The ADIOS VM is preconfigured with a reasonable set of access rules that you can use as a starting point.

To view your current LIDS configuration (the access control list), type in the command `lidsconf -L`. You see a list that looks something like this (we've modified the following example to fit on the page):

```
Subject    ACCESS  inherit time    Object
----------------------------------------------
           -
Any file   READONLY: 0 0000       /bin
    0
Any file   READONLY: 0 0000       /lib
    0
Any file   READONLY: 0 0000       /sbin
    0
Any file   READONLY: 0 0000     /usr/bin
    0
Any file   READONLY: 0 0000     /usr/sbin
    0
/sbin/insmod GRANT: 0 0000   CAP_SYS_MODULE
    0
...          ...    .  ...
```

Here's how to interpret the configuration info:

- **Subject:** The first (leftmost) column shows the subject. If you see a program name in the subject column, the ACE controls that specific program. If you see `Any file` in the subject column, the ACE controls *all* programs.

- **ACCESS:** The second column shows how the subject can access the object.

✔ **Inherit:** The `inherit` column displays a 1 for ACEs that are inherited by the subject's child processes and a 0 for ACEs that are not inheritable.

✔ **Time:** The `time` column shows the hours during which the ACE will be enforced.

✔ **Object:** The second-to-last column shows the object. The object is the thing that you're securing. In the sample listing, the first ACE controls access to the `/bin` directory (and all files and subdirectories underneath `/bin`). If you see the same object listed more than once, the first ACE generally restricts access for *all* subjects, and the other ACEs grant exceptions for specific programs. An object can be a file or directory, or a capability. When you secure a directory, you secure everything underneath that directory as well.

✔ **Parameters:** The last (rightmost) column lists ACE parameters. ACE parameters are rarely needed. In fact, you can include parameters only when you create a `CAP_BIND_NET_SERVICE` ACE (the parameter specifies a range of port numbers).

Controlling File Access with LIDS

To create a new entry, or ACE, you need to know three things:

✔ The complete pathname of the program that you want to manage (unless you want to restrict all programs).

✔ The complete pathname of the file (or directory) that you want to protect.

✔ The type of access you want to grant (or deny). You can assign four security levels to an object:

   ▶ `WRITE`: This level does not protect the object at all; if users hold superuser privileges, they can do whatever they want with the object.

   ▶ `APPEND`: This level grants read permission, and lets you add to the object but not delete (or otherwise alter) it. This is the protection level you should assign to all log files. If you grant `WRITE` protection to a log object, intruders could edit the object to hide their tracks.

   ▶ `READONLY`: This level grants read permission, but the object cannot be altered (or deleted).

 Use the `READONLY` level for all system configuration files and programs.

   ▶ `DENY`: Objects that are secured at the `DENY` level are hidden from view. Use `DENY` to hide password files and then grant exceptions to only those programs that require access.

After you have those three pieces of information, create an ACE with the `lidsconf -A` command. For example, to protect all files (and subdirectories) in the `/etc` directory from modification, use this command:

```
# lidsconf -A -o /etc -j READONLY
```

In this case, `/etc` is the object, and because you didn't include a subject, this ACE will control the type of access granted for *all* programs. To grant an *exception* to the default rule, use this command:

```
# lidsconf -A -s /usr/bin/passwd \
            -o /etc/passwd \
            -j WRITE
```

The `-s` *subject* parameter defines the subject, and `-o` *object* defines the object.

Delete an ACE with `lidsconf -D`. To delete an ACE, you supply a subject and an object, just like you did when you created the ACE:

```
# lidsconf -D -s /usr/bin/passwd \
            -o /etc/passwd
```

You must protect a program before you can use it in another ACE. For example, if you want to grant write privileges to the `passwd` command, you have to protect `/usr/bin/passwd` first. That makes sense because you don't want to grant privileges for a command that might be modified by an intruder.

 It's a good practice to protect just about *everything* first, and then grant exceptions.

For example, to protect Samba configuration files, start out by denying write access for all programs:

```
# lidsconf -A -o /etc/samba -j READONLY
# lidsconf -A -o /var/samba -j READONLY
```

Next, grant write access to the Samba daemons (`smbd` and `nmbd`). Don't forget to protect the daemons against modification:

```
# lidsconf -A -o /usr/sbin -j READONLY
```

Now you can grant write access to the two Samba executables:

```
# lidsconf -A -s /usr/sbin/smbd \
            -o /var/samba \
            -j WRITE

# lidsconf -A -s /usr/sbin/nmbd \
            -o /var/samba \
            -j WRITE
```

If you forget to protect a program before you grant privileges for that program, you'll see an error message such as `lidsconf: subject file is not protected`.

Hiding Processes with LIDS

Another nifty feature of LIDS is the `CAP_HIDDEN` capability. `CAP_HIDDEN` is a pseudo-capability. It's not really part of a normal Linux kernel but a feature added by LIDS itself. Why would you want to hide a process? So intruders don't know that you're watching them. Protect network sniffers, log file analyzers, and security monitors with `CAP_HIDDEN`, and intruders will think they're all alone on your computer.

When you hide a process, you don't actually hide the program itself (use `DENY` to do that); instead, you're hiding the process from the process list. In other words, you can still see the program if you browse through a directory listing, but if you run the program and then search through the output from a `ps` command, you won't find it.

If you're accustomed to using `top` to watch what your system is doing, here's how you can hide the `top` process from intruders (or anyone else for that matter):

1. **Open the file** `/etc/lids/lids.cap` **in your favorite text editor.**

2. **Find the line that says**

    `+29:CAP_HIDDEN`

3. **Change that line to read**

    `-29:CAP_HIDDEN`

    Basically, you change the + sign to a – sign.

4. **Save your work and close the editor.**

    This change disables the `CAP_HIDDEN` capability. (You have to *disable* a capability before you can grant it to a specific program.)

5. **At the command line, disable LIDS for your login session:**

    ```
    # lidsadm -S -- -LIDS
    SWITCH
    enter password:
    ```

6. **Enter your LIDS password when prompted.**

    The default LIDS password for the ADIOS UML VMs is `12qwaszx`.

    When you disable LIDS for a login session, LIDS continues to enforce the security policies for all other uses, but you can bypass LIDS in your login session in order to change the LIDS access control list.

7. **Find the program that you want to hide (in this case,** top**):**

```
# which top
/usr/bin/top
```

8. **Grant the** CAP_HIDDEN **capability to** top**:**

```
# lidsconf -A -s /usr/bin/top \
            -o CAP_HIDDEN \
            -j GRANT
```

9. **Tell LIDS to reload its configuration file:**

```
# lidsadm -S -- +RELOAD_CONF
```

10. **And finally, enable LIDS for your login session:**

```
# lidsadm -S -- +LIDS
```

Now when you run top, it doesn't appear in the list of processes. You can't see it with the ps command. You can't find it by looking through the /proc directory. You can't even see it in top! Now you can spy on other users, er, intruders, without anyone knowing.

Running Down the Privilege List

Table 61-1 lists the superuser capabilities that you can enable and disable with LIDS. If you're testing a prototype configuration in a UML, start by disabling most of the superuser capabilities and then adding back the privileges you find you need. Copy the access control list (stored in /etc/lids/*) to your main system when you're happy with the results.

TABLE 61-1: LIDS CAPABILITIES

Name	Description
CAP_CHOWN	If disabled, the program cannot change the owner or group owner of any file.
CAP_DAC_OVERRIDE	If disabled, the program cannot ignore file access permissions even with superuser privileges.
CAP_DAC_READ_SEARCH	Disable this capability, and the program cannot ignore file access permissions when reading a file or searching a directory. (This is a little less restrictive than CAP_DAC_OVERRIDE.)
CAP_FOWNER	Most of the actions that you can perform on a file (such as updating the modification time or changing the permissions) are prohibited unless you're the file's owner or the superuser. If you disable CAP_FOWNER, the superuser can change the attributes of a file only if he or she owns the file.
CAP_FSETID	Normally, a superuser can turn on the setuid and setgid attributes for any program. (If the setuid bit is turned on for a program, any user who runs that program gains the privileges of the program's owner.) If you disable CAP_FSETID, a superuser can turn on the setuid or setgid bits only for programs owned by the superuser.
CAP_KILL	If disabled, a superuser can kill processes only if he or she owns them. (Technically speaking, this capability controls whether or not a superuser can send a signal to another process.)
CAP_SETGID	If disabled, a superuser cannot add himself or herself to a group that he or she is not a member of (using the newgrp command, for example).
CAP_SETUID	If disabled, a superuser cannot impersonate other users with the su command. This is a good capability to disable, but you have to reenable CAP_SETUID for selected programs that *must* change user IDs (the sshd daemon for example).
CAP_SETPCAP	If disabled, a superuser cannot grant capabilities to other programs.

(continued)

TABLE 61-1 (continued)

Name	Description
CAP_LINUX_IMMUTABLE	Some file system types (like ext2 and ext3) support *immutable* files — files that cannot be changed by anyone. Disable CAP_LINUX_IMMUTABLE, and the superuser cannot make files immutable.
CAP_NET_BIND_SERVICE	TCP port numbers 1–1024 are privileged — only the superuser can create a service that listens for clients on a privileged port. That's handy because a client knows that if it's connecting to a privileged port, it's probably not connecting to a joker that's set up a private service to impersonate a legitimate service. If you disable CAP_NET_BIND_SERVICE, the superuser cannot create services on privileged ports; you can grant CAP_NET_BIND_SERVICE to selected programs such as the sshd daemon.
CAP_NET_BROADCAST	Disable this capability, and the superuser can't broadcast network messages (he or she has to send messages to each computer, one at a time).
CAP_NET_ADMIN	If this capability is disabled, the superuser can't manage network interfaces. By default, LIDS disables this capability and then grants it to selected programs.
CAP_NET_RAW	If a program can access a network interface in *raw* mode, it can fabricate network packets in order to fool other computers. Disable CAP_NET_RAW, and the superuser is denied raw access to network devices. By default, LIDS disables this capability and then grants it to selected programs.
CAP_IPC_LOCK	If this capability is disabled, the superuser is not allowed to lock shared-memory segments that he or she doesn't own. This is a rather obscure capability that you can probably ignore without serious consequence.
CAP_IPC_OWNER	Normally, a superuser can access any shared memory segment, semaphore, or message queue. If you disable CAP_IPC_OWNER, the superuser can only access interprocess communication objects that he or she owns.
CAP_SYS_MODULE	Disable CAP_SYS_MODULE, and the superuser can't load or unload kernel modules. This is a good capability to disable because if a superuser can load good kernel modules, he or she can also insert pesky modules that can really mess up your system.
CAP_SYS_RAWIO	If you disable this capability, the superuser doesn't have raw access to disk drives and can't poke around in kernel memory. If the superuser has raw access to a disk drive, he or she can easily bypass file system permissions and can even corrupt your data.
CAP_SYS_CHROOT	Disable CAP_SYS_CHROOT, and the superuser can't create chroot jails — he or she can't break out of chroot jails either. By default, LIDS disables CAP_SYS_CHROOT. You have to grant CAP_SYS_CHROOT to the sshd daemon if you want to run an ssh server.
CAP_SYS_PTRACE	The CAP_SYS_PTRACE capability is typically granted to debuggers. It's a good idea to disable CAP_SYS_PTRACE and then grant it when needed.
CAP_SYS_PACCT	Turn off this capability, and the superuser can't manipulate the process accounting package on your computer (see Technique 21 for more information).
CAP_SYS_ADMIN	This capability is something of a catch-all for all system administration actions. If you disable this service, the superuser can't perform administrative tasks like changing the host name, configuring disk quotas, mounting new file systems, or shutting down your computer. By default, LIDS disables this capability and grants it to selected programs (such as mount and halt).

Name	Description
CAP_SYS_BOOT	Disable this capability, and a superuser is not allowed to reboot your computer.
CAP_SYS_NICE	The superuser can normally raise or lower the runtime priority of any process. Disable this capability, and the superuser can't change priorities.
CAP_SYS_RESOURCE	Disable this capability, and the superuser can't ignore resource quotas (such as the amount of disk space he or she is allowed to consume).
CAP_SYS_TIME	If you disable CAP_SYS_TIME, the superuser cannot change the clock on your computer.
CAP_SYS_TTY_CONFIG	This capability allows a superuser to manage serial ports — which isn't very exciting; just use the default value that LIDS has chosen for you.

Technique 62

Getting Graphical with Shell Scripts

When you think of writing a shell script, you think about the command line. If you need to ask the user a question, you probably echo a string to the terminal window (standard output stream) and read the reply from the keyboard (the standard input stream). If you want to give feedback to the user, you echo a string to the terminal window. That works, but it's not very flashy.

Linux offers several graphical toolkits that you can use from within a shell script to display information dialogs. By using the toolkits with your shell scripts, you can graphically

✔ Query your users for passwords with a pop-up dialog.

✔ Use calendars to retrieve important dates from your users.

✔ Display text boxes showing file contents to your users.

✔ Display completion gauges (for file uploads or downloads).

✔ Use checklists and forms to retrieve user information.

Because your users are (probably) used to working in a graphical environment, the dialogs will be friendlier and easier to use. You'll also have better control of the result set returned to your program — your users can choose their input from the buttons you give them instead of improvising at the command line.

In this technique, we introduce you to using graphical toolkits to share information with your users. Use these kits to make work easier and more attractive for you and your users. The little time it takes to build them into shell scripts is worth the effort.

Getting Graphical at the Command Line

Linux works with several graphical toolkits, but three are worth special mention. Depending on which desktop environment you like to work in, you'll find one or more of the toolkits installed.

Getting graphical in GNOME

The zenity command displays GTK dialogs (GTK, or the GIMP Toolkit, is part of GNOME) and can return information to the shell script.

If you work in a GNOME desktop environment, you'll likely find the zenity toolkit installed on your system. If it's not installed on your system, you can add it in a snap by installing the gnome-utils package from your distribution disc.

You can also find information about zenity through the Help Browser in GNOME utilities. Find the listing for zenity (see Figure 62-1).

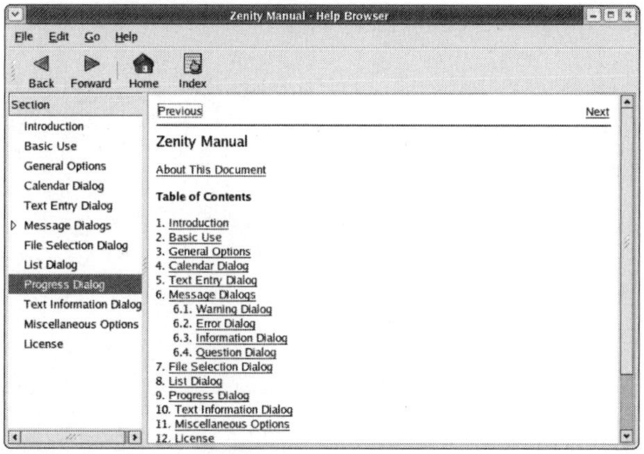

• **Figure 62-1: The Zenity Manual.**

zenity can display

✔ Calendar widgets

✔ Text entry widgets

✔ Error, info, and warning dialogs

✔ File selection dialogs

✔ List boxes

✔ Progress indicators

✔ Question dialogs (prompting for user input)

zenity is fairly easy to use. For example, to display a calendar widget that looks like Figure 62-2, you would execute the following command:

```
$ choice=$(zenity --calendar)
```

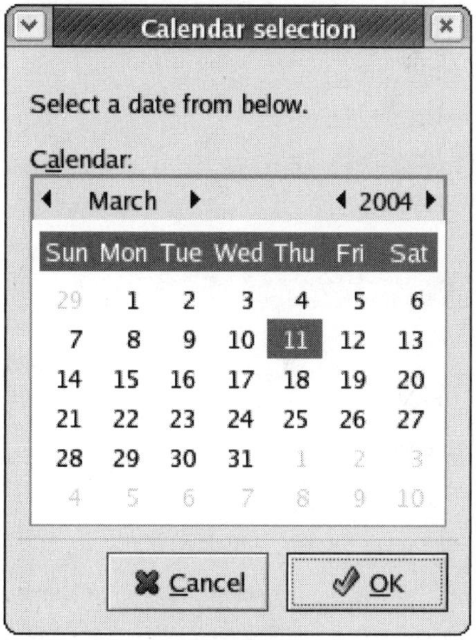

• **Figure 62-2: The** zenity **calendar.**

After the user selects a date, the $choice variable contains a value, such as 03/11/2004. (You can control the format of the date with a simple command line option.)

You can incorporate zenity into shell scripts to gather information from a user or to report progress. Listing 62-1 shows a simple shell script that uses zenity to burn a CD.

LISTING 62-1: BURNING A CD WITH ZENITY

```
1 #!/bin/bash
2
3 mkdir /tmp/$$ || (echo "can't create working dir /tmp/$$" ; exit )
4 echo "Created staging area in /tmp/$$"
5 echo "Select the files you want to burn, press Cancel when complete"
6
7 while $(true)
8 do
9  src=$(zenity --title "Select Files" --file-selection)
10
11  if [ "x$src" = "x" ]
12  then
13   break;
14  fi
15
16  echo "Selected: $src"
17
18  ln -s $src /tmp/$$/
19
20  srcs=$srcs:$src
21
22 done
23
24 if [ "x$srcs" = "x" ]
25 then
26   echo "No files selected"
27   exit
28 fi
29
30 mkisofs -f -R -r -l -J -o /tmp/$$.iso /tmp/$$ || (echo "mkisofs failed" ; exit)
31 rm -rf /tmp/$$
32
33 MESSAGE="$(du -sh /tmp/$$.iso|cut -f 1) selected Burn CD now?"
34
35 zenity --title "File selections complete" --question --text $MESSAGE || exit
36
37 echo "Burning CD"
38
39 cdrecord speed=8 dev=0,0,0 /tmp/$$.iso
40 rm /tmp/$$.iso
```

Here are a couple of highlights from Listing 62-1 that show how to use zenity in a shell script:

✔ **File selection dialog:** The command at line 9 displays a file selection dialog (see Figure 62-3). zenity stores the user's choices in the variable $src. If the user clicks Cancel instead of OK, $src is empty.

✔ **Question dialog:** The command at line 35 displays a question dialog (see Figure 62-4). zenity waits for the user to click Cancel or OK. If the user clicks Cancel, the zenity command returns 0 (or *false*); otherwise, zenity returns 1 (or *true*).

Select Files

New Folder	Delete File	Rename File

/home/susan ▼

Folders

./
../
Desktop/
scans/

Files

5717372201.png
5717372202.png
5717372203.png
5717372204.png
5717372205.png
5717372206.png

Selection: /home/susan

✖ Cancel   ✔ OK

• **Figure 62-3:** The zenity **file selection dialog.**

File selections complete

(?) 20 meg selected Burn CD now?

✖ Cancel   ✔ OK

• **Figure 62-4:** The zenity **question dialog.**

You can find more information about zenity at the man page: $ man zenity.

See Technique 10 for more information about the rest of the script in Listing 62-1. It's not a perfect example, but it gets the job done.

Getting graphical with KDE

If you prefer to work in the KDE desktop environment, you can install and use zenity, or use the KDE-flavored graphical toolkit, kdialog.

If you're already running KDE, kdialog is most likely installed on your system. If it's not, install the kdebase RPM package from your distribution discs to add kdialog to your installation. kdialog is included in the kdebase RPM package.

The kdialog command is similar to zenity, but it has even more options. kdialog offers the following forms:

✔ Yes/no dialog

✔ Yes/no/cancel dialog

✔ Warning yes/no dialog

✔ Warning continue/cancel dialog

✔ Warning yes/no/cancel dialog

✔ "Sorry" error message dialog

✔ "Error" error message dialog

✔ Message box dialog

✔ Input box dialog (prompting user for information)

✔ Password dialog

✔ Text box dialog

✔ Combo box (similar to a list box)

✔ Menu

✔ Checklist

✔ Radio list

✔ Get open filename (file selection box labeled Open)

✔ Get save filename (file selection box labeled Save To)

✔ Get directory name

✔ Open a URL

✔ Save to URL

Use `kdialog` in your scripts the same way that you would use `zenity`.

One drawback to choosing `kdialog` is the lack of documentation. You can find *some* help by opening a terminal window and entering the following command:

```
$ kdialog --help-all | more
```

The command line options for `kdialog` are displayed, along with a brief explanation. If you want more in-depth help, we can recommend visiting the KDE Developers Corner and checking out the tutorial at

```
developer.kde.org/documentation/tutorials/
    kdialog/t1.html
```

Staying desktop neutral

One other optional toolkit worthy of mention is `dialog`. `dialog` is included with the Fedora and SuSE Linux distributions, and you can install it from the distribution media with the following command:

```
#  rpm -Uhv dialog-version.i386.rpm
```

`dialog` offers the following forms for use in your shell scripts:

- ✔ Calendar
- ✔ Checklist
- ✔ Form
- ✔ File selector
- ✔ Gauge
- ✔ Information box
- ✔ Input box
- ✔ Input menu
- ✔ Message box
- ✔ Password input box
- ✔ Radio list
- ✔ Text box
- ✔ Time box
- ✔ Yes/No box

After it's installed, `dialog` functions very much like either `zenity` or `kdialog`. The `man` page, found at `$ man dialog`, has a good listing of the various options and forms that work with `dialog`.

Index

Symbols

A